Michigan Biographies

INCLUDING MEMBERS OF CONGRESS, ELECTIVE STATE OFFICERS,
JUSTICES OF THE SUPREME COURT, MEMBERS OF THE
MICHIGAN LEGISLATURE, BOARD OF REGENTS OF
THE UNIVERSITY OF MICHIGAN, STATE
BOARD OF AGRICULTURE AND
STATE BOARD OF
EDUCATION

VOL. II. L-Z

Published by
The Michigan Historical Commission
Lansing, 1924

PREFACE.

THE sketches in this second volume, as in Volume I, end with the date of the last appearance of their respective subjects as public officers in Michigan. Since the material in the previous and present volumes is inaccessible except in the largest libraries, it is believed that the immediate publication of the material at hand in an edition large enough to supply all libraries in the state, will be appreciated by the general public and will take care of their immediate needs. Material is being gathered for a supplementary work' which will bring the sketches forward. The gathering of this material is a considerable task and involves research in newspaper files, public records, and the carrying on of voluminous correspondence. To assist in gathering material for the supplementary work that will bring the sketches as near up-to-date as possible, the Commission has appointed a "Council of Research," consisting of about one hundred public spirited citizens in various parts of the state to serve without pay in assisting in the work. This method necessarily involves delay, but we hope the results will be satisfactory.

MICHIGAN BIOGRAPHIES

EDWARD S. LACEY

Member of Congress, 1881-3 and 1883-5. Was born in Chili, N. Y., Nov. 26, 1835. In 1842 he removed to Union City, Mich.; in 1843 to Kalamo, and in 1857 to Charlotte. His education was received in the common schools and Olivet College. He was elected Register of Deeds of Eaton County in 1860, and re-elected in 1862; began the banking business in 1862, and assisted in organizing the first National Bank of Charlotte in 1871, of which he was a director and cashier. He was Mayor of the city of Charlotte; a delegate to the Republican National Convention at Cincinnati in 1876, a trustee of the Michigan asylum for the insane from 1874 to 1880. He was a Representative in Congress as a Republican. Mr. Lacey was elected chairman of the Republican State Committee in 1882, which position he held for two years. He was president of the National Bank at Charlotte, and was a leading Republican candidate for United States Senator in 1887. In 1889 he was appointed Commissioner of Currency by President Harrison. He died at Evanston, Ill., Oct. 2, 1916.

ELIJAH LACEY

Delegate from the Fourteenth District, to the Constitutional Convention of 1835; and Representative from Berrien County, 1838; and Senator from the Seventh District, 1840-1, and from the Eighteenth District, 1861-2. Was born in London County, Va., Mar. 28, 1795. He received a limited education. At the age of ten became a resident of Ohio. He settled at Richmond, Ind., in 1820, and was for five years an editor. He settled at Niles, Mich., in 1829, where then only two log houses had been erected. He laid out the village and built a saw and flouring mill. In 1845 he built the mill race and mills near the railroad bridge, in which he retained an interest until his death. He was President of the village and Mayor of the city of Niles. He died before the expiration of his term as Senator.

OBED P. LACEY

Representative from Berrien County, 1843. Was born in Ohio in 1810, and came to Niles, Mich., in 1828. He gave the name of Niles to that place in honor of the editor of the Niles *Weekly Register*, a noted New England paper of that time. He established a trading house with the Indians, had a Postoffice established, and was the first Postmaster, and the first Clerk of the town of Niles. He built the first bridge over St. Joseph River, and owned two additions to Niles and West Niles. In politics, he was a Democrat. He died May 13, 1844.

SAMUEL S. LACEY

Commissioner of the State Land Office, 1861-5. Was born in Bennington, Vt., May 28, 1815. His father was a Captain in the War of 1812, and both his grandfathers served in the Revolution. His father removed to western New York in 1818, and the son received an academical education, and graduated at Hamilton College. He resided in Arkansas four years, and was Judge of Hot Springs County. He settled at Homer, Mich., in 1846, and was ten years a farmer. He removed to Marshall, where he resided in 1855. He was Clerk of Calhoun County four years; was agent to select lands for the agricultural college; was commandant of camp with authority to raise the 28th Mich. Infantry; Collector of Internal Revenue; Postmaster of Marshall in 1867, and was in that position in 1887; ten years member of City Board of Education, and for some time editor of the Marshall *Expounder*. He was a Whig until 1854, a Republican until 1872, and a Democrat after that time.

EMMOR O. LADD

Representative from Grand Traverse County, 1919-20, 1921-2, and 1923—. Was born Jan. 5, 1853, at Old Mission, Mich., of American parents, who were among the earliest settlers of the Grand Traverse region. He received his education in the public schools of Old Mission and the Michigan Agricultural College, working his way through school by teaching. He graduated from the latter institution in 1878. After again teaching school two years, he entered the employ of D. M. Ferry & Company, of Detroit, but returned four years later to the old homestead at Old Mission, where he has since resided. Mr. Ladd is married and has one son and two daughters. He has been an active member of the Grange and has also devoted considerable time to the work of farmers' institutes, being for many years one of the state lecturers. For the past ten years he has been a member of the executive board of the Western Michigan Development Bureau. He has also been active in public affairs and has held nearly every township office. He served four years as Register of Deeds, and for the past fourteen years has been a member of the County Board of School Examiners. In politics he is a Republican.

NATHANIEL LADD

Senator from the Third District, 1855-6. Was a native of Vermont, born Dec. 20, 1805. He enjoyed a New England common school education, was a farmer by occupation, and settled in Dearborn in 1836. In politics he was a Republican.

STALLHAM W. LADU

Representative from Montcalm County, 1881-2 and 1883-4. Was born in Duchess County, N. Y., Feb. 28, 1823. His education was mainly received at Red Creek Union Academy, N. Y. After teaching he entered the ministry of the M. E. Church in Canada. While acting in this capacity he became one of the originators and founders of Albert University, located at Belleville, Ont., removal to Michigan in the fall of 1867. Owing to loss of health he was obliged to forego his ministerial duties, and in 1874 located in Montcalm County, where his time was principally occupied in farming. Originally a Democrat, he embraced abolitionism during the time he was pursuing his academic studies, and from that graduated into the Republican party. He was a State Oil Inspector, 1885-7.

FRANK LADNER

Representative from the Third District of Kent County, 1903-4 and 1905-6. Was born at Newlyn, Cornwall County, England, Feb. 25, 1845. In March, four years later, he together with his parents removed to this country, settling on a farm in Cannon Township, Kent County. He received his education in the district school of Kent County. In politics he was a Republican. He held the offices of Justice of the Peace, Treasurer, and was for many years Supervisor. He was engaged in the lumbering business for eighteen years, and then resided on his farm.

CHARLES H. LAFLAMBOY

Representative from Montcalm County, 1899-1900 and 1901-2; and Senator, 1903-4, from the Eighteenth District, comprising the counties of Montcalm and Ionia. Was born in LeRoy, Lake County, O., May 12, 1856. When nine years of age he came with his parents to Oakland County, Mich., where he attended the district school until he was eleven years old, when he began life for himself. He went to McBride in 1878 and secured employment with Wood & Thayer, with whom he remained seven years, when he formed a partnership with a Mr. Lewis and started a small general store. At the close of the first year he bought out his partner and conducted the business, enlarging it and building a feed mill. He also acquired control of the only hotel in McBride and refitted it.

WARREN BRAINERD LAFLER

Representative from the Second District of Monroe County, 1901-2. Was born in Willoughby, Lake County, O., Feb. 12, 1845. When about seven years of age he removed with his parents to Michigan where he obtained his education in the district school at Dundee. In 1861 he enlisted in the 7th Mich. Infantry, taking part in all the principal battles in the Army of the Potomac and was present at the surrender of General Robert E. Lee. He was wounded twice at the Battle of Spotsylvania Court House. Married. In politics he was a Democrat. He held various offices in his township.

ALBERT LaHUIS

Representative from the Second District of Ottawa County, 1907-8 and 1909-10. Was born and reared on a farm in Zeeland Township, Ottawa County, Mich., May 19, 1858, of Holland parentage. He received his early education in the district schools, attended Hope College and the Michigan State Normal College, graduating from the latter in 1879. Mr. LaHuis was married to Miss Christine

DenHerder in 1883. He served as Superintendent of the Zeeland village schools five years. He then engaged in the mercantile business with his father-in-law under the firm name of Herder and LaHuis. In 1890 the large store building and contents, owned by the firm, was destroyed by fire, and immediately after Mr. LaHuis, individually, re-established and continued the business. He was a stockholder and director of the Zeeland State Bank and Holland Sugar Company, president and director of the Colonial Manufacturing Company and president and treasurer of the A. LaHuis Co. In politics he was a Republican.

WILLIAM P. LAING

Representative from Shiawassee County, 1865-6. Was born in Milton, N. Y., June 26, 1813, and came to Ann Arbor in 1833. He removed to Shiawassee County in 1836, and helped build the second log house in Owosso. In 1837 he settled in Sciota, where he held the offices of Supervisor and Justice of the Peace. In 1850 he moved to Perry Center, Shiawassee County, secured a mail route from Lansing to Byron through Perry, and was appointed Postmaster. In 1856 he was elected Sheriff of Shiawassee County, and was re-elected in 1858. By occupation he was a farmer, and a Republican in politics.

WILLIAM S. LAING

Senator from the Thirty-first District, 1887-8. Was born in Scotland in 1845, and came to Canada with his parents in 1849. He removed to Michigan in 1865, where he was engaged to work in the lumber woods and at farming until 1878, when he removed to Iron Mountain, and engaged in the butcher business. He was interested in a large wholesale and retail meat market at Iron Mountain, and at Marinette, Wis., and a saw mill and general store at Wilson. He was elected to the Senate as a Republican.

ALBERT L. LAKEY

Representative from Kalamazoo County, 1887-8. Was born at Uxbridge, Mass., Mar. 25, 1846. He resided in New York and Pennsylvania until 1861, when he enlisted at the age of fifteen and served until May, 1865. He located at Kalamazoo in 1867, and engaged in the manufacture of paints and roofing. He was a member of the Common Council. He died Aug. 14, 1916, at Kalamazoo.

JACOB C. LAMB

Representative from Lapeer County, 1871-2 and 1873-4. Was born in Springfield, N. J., Apr. 10, 1828. In 1852 he came to Michigan and settled in Dryden, Lapeer County, as a farmer. He was for several years a member of the Republican State Committee. He was a prominent business man at Imlay City.

JOHN M. LAMB

Representative from Lapeer County, 1841-3; Senator from the Twenty-seventh District, 1857-8, and from the Twenty-sixth District, 1863-4; and Delegate from Lapeer County to the Constitutional Convention of 1867. Was born in Springfield, N. J., Aug. 11, 1808. He came to Michigan in 1834, and in 1836 settled in Dryden, Lapeer County, improved a large farm, and was also in mercantile business from 1841 to 1869. He was first a Whig and then a Republican. He died Nov. 3, 1871.

GEORGE A. LAMBERT

Representative from the Second District of Berrien County, 1891-2. Was born in Niles, that county, in September, 1856. Married and a lawyer by profession. He held the office of Circuit Court Commissioner two terms, 1882 and 1884, and was elected Supervisor five times in succession, from 1882 to 1887, and was elected City Recorder in 1887, representing Berrien County before the State Board of Equalization in 1886, and was chairman of the Democratic County Committee from 1888 to 1890. He was elected to the House of 1891-2 on the Democratic ticket.

ROBERT D. LAMOND

Representative from Genesee County, 1844. Was a graduate of the Vermont Medical College at Castleton, and Fairfield Medical College, N. Y. He settled in Flint about 1838, coming there from Pontiac where he was in practice prior to 1833. He was a member of the Oakland County Medical Society and was its secretary in 1835. He was one of the original members of the Genesee County Medical Society, and became the leading physician of Genesee County. He died at Flint in 1871.

ALLAN L. LAMPHERE

Representative from the Second District of Wayne County, 1915-16 and 1917-18. Was born at Vassar, Mich., May 25, 1877. He was educated in the Vassar High School and the Detroit College of Law, graduating from the latter in 1909. He was appointed Assistant Prosecuting Attorney of Wayne County in 1909 and reappointed in 1911. He also served four terms as Trustee of Redford village. Married. A member of the F. & A. M., R. A. M., K. T., Shrine, O. E. S., B. P. O. E., and the Social Order of Moose. In politics he was a Republican.

COLUMBIA LANCASTER

Representative from St. Joseph County, 1838; and Delegate from St. Joseph County to the First Convention of the Assent, 1836. Was born in New Milford, Conn., Aug. 26, 1803. By profession he was a lawyer, in politics a Democrat. He came to White Pigeon, Mich., in 1830, where he remained until the county seat was removed to Centreville, when he erected the first residence there. In 1838 he left Michigan with his wife and daughter and with an ox team traveled to Oregon Territory, where he arrived in September of the same year. At the crossing of the Missouri River he was elected to the command of emigrating company, consisting of 84 wagons, the command terminating at Ash Hollow, beyond the hostile tribes of Indians. He found a provisional government established in Oregon. In 1847 he was appointed Supreme Judge of Oregon, which he held until Congress organized the territory and appointed judges. He was afterwards delegate to Congress from Oregon. He resided at Vancouver, Washington Territory, in 1887.

JOHN LANDON

Representative from Jackson County, 1865-6 and 1871. Was born in 1833, in Cayuga County, N. Y. He came with his father's family to Springport, Mich., in 1835, his father building the first house in that township. The son received a fair education, and was elected Supervisor when quite young, holding that position several terms. He was a farmer; a Republican in politics. He died Mar. 13, 1871, before the expiration of his second term, and his funeral was attended by eight representatives as pall bearers, and by the speaker and clerk of the House. He was succeeded by Hiram C. Hodge.

REYNOLDS LANDON

Representative, 1891-2, from the Charlevoix District, comprising the counties of Charlevoix, Antrim and Manitou. Was born in Grand Isle County, Vt., 1818. He was not in any business in 1891, but for the preceding seventeen years was with the Dexter and Noble, millers. He was Treasurer of Jackson County for six years and Judge of Probate of Antrim County for four years. He was elected to the House of 1891-2 on the Democratic ticket.

RUFUS W. LANDON

Senator from the Eighteenth District, 1863-4. Was born in Falls Village, Litchfield County, Conn., May 3, 1815. He received a common school education and came to Niles, Berrien County, May 9, 1832, at the age of seventeen, in the midst of the excitement caused by the breaking out of the Black Hawk War. He was one of the first settlers in Berrien County, and always lived at Niles. In politics he was a Democrat, and by occupation a dealer in real estate. He was Postmaster of Niles from 1837 to 1841, and Treasurer of Berrien County for ten years, from Jan. 1, 1843, to Dec. 31, 1852. He was a gentleman highly respected in the city and county, which was his home for more than fifty years. He died at Niles, Dec. 26, 1886.

JOHN LANE

Representative from the First District of Berrien County, 1901-2 and 1903-4. Was born in Livingston County, Ky., Apr. 12, 1843. His education was obtained by home study. He came to Michigan in 1856, and on May 16, 1861, enlisted in Co. G, 6th Wisconsin Infantry, and was severely wounded at the Battle of Antietam, on account of which he was discharged from service Jan. 27, 1863. He re-enlisted in Co. B, 6th Mich. Heavy Artillery, in January, 1864, and served as color bearer until the close of the war, when he went to Benton Harbor, where he remained fourteen years and then purchased the farm in St. Joseph Township. Married. In politics he was a Republican.

MINOT T. LANE

Member of the Board of Regents of the University of Michigan, 1845-9. Was born at Marlborough, N. H., Mar. 12, 1807. He came to Michigan in 1831 and settled at Romeo. He was a Representative in 1838 and 1848. In politics he was a Democrat. He removed to Detroit in 1848. He held several municipal offices in Detroit, including that of Police Justice from 1866 to 1870. He died at Detroit Feb. 23, 1875.

ORVILLE B. LANE

Representative from Hillsdale County, 1903-4 and 1905-6. Was born at Geneva, O., Oct. 13, 1850. He received his education in the public schools of Ohio and Michigan. He married and resided on his farm in Hillsdale County. He represented his township as Supervisor and served as chairman of the board for a number of years; president and treasurer of the Hillsdale County Farmers' Mutual Fire Insurance Company. In politics a Republican.

PETER LANE

Representative from Saginaw County, 1869-70. Was born Apr. 23, 1823, in Aurelius, N. Y., came to Flint, Mich., in 1844. He moved to Saginaw in 1850, where he resided. He was Town Clerk in 1851, and Treasurer in 1852. He went to California in 1853 on horseback. He was Alderman and Supervisor in Saginaw, and for three years chairman of the County Board of Supervisors. He was a millwright, and sawmill engineer, and for eight years was in the lumbering business. He was retired in 1887. He was a Republican in politics.

THOMAS D. LANE

Representative from Washtenaw County, 1859-60; and Senator from the Seventh District, 1861-2. Was born in Victor, N. Y., June 26, 1820. He came with his parents to Salem, Mich., in 1836. His father served in the war of 1812. The son was reared on a farm, and most of his education was obtained nights, by the aid of burning tamarack knots. He was Inspector of Schools fifteen years and Supervisor four years. He taught school seventeen years.

NATHANIEL LANGDON

Senator from the Ninth District, 1865-6. Was born in the State of New York, June 18, 1810. By occupation he was a farmer, in politics a Democrat. He came to Ida, Monroe County, 1847. He was Supervisor of that town for over twenty years. He died Aug. 1, 1889.

LEANDER LAPHAM

Representative from Barry County, 1865-6. Was born in Erie County, N. Y., Oct. 8, 1819. He came to Michigan in 1830, lived in Wayne County seven years, and in 1837 settled upon a farm in the town of Maple Grove, Barry County, where he resided in 1887. He was fifteen terms Supervisor. In politics he was a Republican.

SMITH LAPHAM

Representative from the Second District of Kent County, 1855-6; and Senator from the Twenty-ninth District, 1857-8. His postoffice address was Laphamville. (Further data not obtainable).

CHARLES LARNED

Attorney General of Michigan Territory, 1831-4. Was born in Pittsfield, Mass. He graduated at Williams College in 1806, and studied law in Kentucky with Henry Clay. While a student there he enlisted in Colonel Owen's regiment, which marched to the relief of General Harrison at Fort Wayne. He rapidly rose to the rank of Major, and was in the battle of the Thames and other engagements. At the close of the war he engaged in law practice in Detroit, and became distinguished in the profession. As Attorney General of the Territory, he conducted the difficult negotiations that grew out of the Black Hawk War. He died Aug. 13, 1834.

JAMES B. LARUE

Representative from Berrien County, 1840 and 1841. Was born in Franklin, N. J., Feb. 6, 1800. He ran a paper mill in New Prospect, N. J. He came to Michigan in 1838, and took up large tracts of land in Berrien County, near St. Joseph. He built a double saw mill and improved a farm seven miles up the St. Joseph River. He had 1,000,000 feet of the best whitewood lumber piled up which all went to waste during the great depression, because it would not pay for shipping to Chicago. He was Representative as a Whig. He went to California in 1849 with ox teams, working at gold digging a year or two, then negotiated with a Spaniard for two hundred acres of land near Oakland, opened a store and boarding house, laid out the town of San Antonio, now a part of Oakland, was elected to the California Legislature, organized a steam ferry company, and ran two steamers across the bay from San Francisco to Oakland and San Antonio for several years. He died in 1872, leaving a valuable property.

HENRY B. LATHROP

Representative from Jackson County, 1840; and Senator from the Second District, 1847. Was born in Hanover, N. H., in 1808. In 1815 he went to Buffalo, N. Y., and remained in that vicinity until 1834, then came to Detroit, where he followed the occupation of mason and contractor. In 1838 he was an Alderman. In 1838 he removed to Jackson, where the State Prison had been located on twenty acres of his farm. He donated the stone for the west half of the prison buildings. In 1849 he became a government agent, and traveled extensively through the states and Canada. In 1852 he went to California with a drove of horses, cattle and sheep, and engaged in mining. He was the first man who made a success of carrying water by a wrought iron pipe thirty inches in diameter, crossing Feather River by a truss bridge, 1,081 feet below the head or inlet, thence rising 900 feet in a half mile so as to command the mines. Against the predictions of engineers it carried 36,000,000 gallons of water per day for sixteen years. Hundreds of miles of pipe were used for the same purpose. In politics he was first a Whig, then in 1854 a Republican. He removed to Ionia where he died Aug. 20, 1890.

HORACE N. LATHROP

Representatives from Lapeer County, 1853-4. Was born at Norwich, Conn., Mar. 9, 1805. He settled in Oregon, Lapeer County, Mich., in 1836, was the first Supervisor of the town, and held that position several terms, also other local offices. By occupation he was a farmer and miller, in politics a Democrat. He died in May, 1871.

W. IRVING LATIMER

Auditor General, 1879-81 and 1881-3; Representative from Mecosta County, 1895-6; and Senator, 1897-8 and 1899-1900, from the Twenty-fifth District, comprising the counties of Isabella, Mecosta, Newaygo and Osceola. Was born in Duchess County, N. Y., in 1836. He acquired a common school education, and in 1859 came to Michigan. He held the offices of City Treasurer of Big Rapids and Mayor of said city; was County Treasurer of Mecosta County three terms; was Auditor General of the State, 1879-81, 1881-3; was a member of the Republican State Central Committee in 1876; was a member of the House of 1895-6, and elected to the Senate of 1897-8, and was re-elected to the Senate of 1899-1900. He removed to Oregon. He died at Portland, Oregon, Apr. 19, 1922.

DAVID L. LATOURETTE

Senator from the Twenty-second District, 1867-8. Was born in Senaca County, N. Y., Aug. 26, 1823. He came to Michigan in 1835, and was engaged in the manufacture of linseed oil and woolen goods, later became a banker and established a national bank at Fenton, of which he was president. He held various positions of trust and responsibility. He was Senator as a Republican. He died at Prescott, Ark., Sept 22, 1885.

BENJAMIN LAUBACH

Representative from Ottawa County, 1877-8 and 1879-80. Was born in Fishing Creek, Pa., Oct. 8, 1823, and, with his parents, removed to Seneca County, O., in 1836. He received a common school education. In 1853 he removed to Michigan and purchased and cleared a farm four miles north of Berlin, Ottawa County, upon which he continued to reside. He held the office of Justice for fifteen years and Supervisor for four years, and was largely engaged in the settlement of estates of deceased persons. In politics he was a Republican.

EDWIN LAWRENCE

Representative from Washtenaw County, 1848; and Justice of the Supreme Court, 1857. His postoffice address was Ann Arbor. This is undoubtedly the same Edwin Lawrence who was selected in May, 1857, as Justice of the Supreme Court in the place of David Johnson who had resigned. (Further data not obtainable).

PETER E. LAWRENCE

Representative from Jackson County, 1843. Was born in Marcellus, N. Y., in 1807. He came to Michigan in 1837 and went into business as a merchant at Leoni. In politics he was a Democrat. He was Postmaster of Leoni in 1838. He died in California in 1854.

SAMUEL J. LAWRENCE

Senator, 1897-8, from the Fourth District, comprising the twelfth, fourteenth and sixteenth wards of the city of Detroit, the city of Wyandotte and the townships of Brownstown, Canton, Dearborn, Ecorse, Huron, Monguagon, Nankin, Romulus, Springwells, Sumpter, Taylor and Van Buren. Was born on the Island of Guernsey, English Channel, Aug. 15, 1848. He came to America with his parents in 1852 and located in Wayne County, Mich., where he acquired a common school education. At the age of sixteen years he enlisted in the 4th Mich. Vol. Infantry, Co. D., where he served for twenty-two months; six months of said time he served as mounted orderly on Gen. Stanley's staff. At the close of the war he went West; spending some time in nearly every western State and Territory, returning to Michigan in 1872, when he was appointed lighthouse keeper by the Hon. Zachariah Chandler, which position he held for five years. In 1872 he moved to the city of Wyandotte. In politics he was a Republican. He served his city as Alderman two terms; was chosen president *pro tem.* of the Council and Supervisor. He died in 1919.

SOLOMON L. LAWRENCE

Representative from Branch County, 1851. Was born in Weybridge County, Vt., Mar. 1, 1811. By occupation he was a farmer. He came to Coldwater, Mich., in 1836, removed to Iowa in 1856, and resided in Wilton, Muscatine County, in 1887. He was a Democrat until 1861, then a Republican. In Iowa he was Justice twelve years, Mayor two years, and held other positions. He was for fifteen years chairman of the Board of School Inspectors in Girard, Mich.

WOLCOTT LAWRENCE

Member of the Legislative Council from Monroe County, 1824-5 to 1830-1. (Further data not obtainable).

CHARLES DE WIT LAWTON

Member of the Board of Regents of the University of Michigan, 1898-1906. Was born at Rome, Oneida County, N. Y., Nov. 4, 1835, son of Nathan and Esther (Wiggins) Lawton. Both parents were of English ancestry. He received his early education in the district schools, and later was prepared for college education in the LeRay and Auburn academies in New York State. He was graduated Bachelor of Arts at Union College in 1858, received the degree of Civil Engineer the following year, and the Master's degree, in course, in 1861. He married Lucy Lovina Latham, July 31, 1861. His first professional work was as principal of the Academy at Auburn, N. Y., from 1859 to 1863. At the end of this period he devoted himself to engineering work. From 1862 to 1865 he was City Engineer of Auburn. In 1865 he removed to Lawton, Mich., a town which had been laid out by his father on land acquired from the government and on which the Michigan Central Railroad Company located a depot. His first interest on coming to Michigan was in fruit raising, in which he was a pioneer in that quarter of the State. Later he became interested in the mineral resources of the State through his connection with the Michigan Central Iron Company, a concern which built a blast furnace at Lawton for the reduction of Lake Superior iron ore. He was engaged with this company until 1870, when he was appointed Assistant Professor of Engineering at the State University. In 1871 he resigned this position and in 1872 he was appointed Assistant to Major Brooks in the work of the State Geological Survey of the Marquette iron district of Lake Superior. He assisted in writing the valuable report of this survey. Thenceforth for several years he was engaged in mining and topographical surveying in the Lake Superior region, doing also a considerable amount of railroad engineering. From 1879 to 1882 he was Acting Commissioner of Mineral Statistics for Michigan, and from 1884 to 1890 held the office of Commissioner. In these offices he wrote the reports to the State from 1879. In April, 1897, he was elected Regent of the University of Michigan for the full term of eight years.

EZRA D. LAY

Representative from Washtenaw County, 1875-6. Was born Dec. 6, 1807, at Saybrook, Conn., and was educated at district and select schools. He removed to Michigan in 1833, settling on a farm in Ypsilanti. He was Supervisor of Ypsilanti seven terms. By occupation he was a farmer, and was president of the Eastern Michigan Agricultural Society. At one time he was vice president of the Michigan Pioneer Society. In politics he was a Republican. He died at Ypsilanti, Apr. 29, 1890.

DEWITT C. LEACH

Representative from Genesee County, 1850; Delegate from Genesee County to the Constitutional Convention of 1850; member of Congress, 1857-9 and 1859-60; and Delegate from Grand Traverse and other counties to the Constitutional Convention of 1867. Was born in Clarence, N. Y., Nov. 23, 1832; received a public school education; came when young to Genesee County, Mich. He was private secretary to Gov. Bingham, and was appointed Indian Agent by President Lincoln; was State Librarian in 1855 and 1856, removing to Lansing in 1855; was editor of the Lansing *Republican* some years. He removed to

Traverse City after 1861, and purchased and edited the Grand Traverse *Herald* for many years, and later went to Springfield, Mo., where he edited and published a paper. He was early a strong anti-slavery man, and a Republican after 1854. He died Dec. 21, 1909.

PAYNE K. LEACH, JR.

Representative from Macomb County, 1846. Was born in West Bloomfield, N. Y., Jan. 31, 1809. He received a common school education and worked on his father's farm until 1830. He then came to Utica, Mich., and engaged in milling until 1836, when he moved upon a farm in the same town. He was a Whig until the dissolution of that party; then a Republican. He held the office of Supervisor several times. He was one of the veterans of the Toledo War. He died March, 1901.

TRAVIS LEACH

Representative from the Second District of Tuscola County, 1891-2. Was born in Steuben County, N. Y., Mar. 25, 1838, and in 1854, removed to Elkland Township, Tuscola County, Mich., where he worked at lumbering winters and clearing land summers until the spring of 1864, when he enlisted in the Union Army and served in the 23rd and 28th Regiments, Mich. Vol. Infantry, until 1866. After his discharge he engaged in scaling logs, lumbering, clearing land, farming and surveying. In 1877, he went west to Colorado, New Mexico and Texas, and for eight years gave his attention to surveying and cattle ranching. Returning to Tuscola County in 1885, he bought a farm in Ellington Township. He was elected County Surveyor of Tuscola County, served as Supervisor of Elkland Township and as Supervisor of Ellington Township; was the Industrial candidate for Representative and was elected to the House of 1891-2.

CHARLES WIRT LEAVITT

Representative from Oceana County, 1893. Was born in Ashtabula County, O., Feb. 24, 1851. He moved with his parents to Jackson County, Mich., in 1857, and five years later to Oceana County. He acquired a common school education, read law two years but never practiced that profession. By occupation he was engaged in lumbering and farming, his farm of seven hundred acres being located near Stetson. In politics a Republican. He died at Eagle Hotel, Grand Rapids, Mar. 11, 1893.

ROSWELL LEAVITT

Senator, 1889-90, from the Twenty-ninth District, comprising the counties of Antrim, Charlevoix, Grand Traverse, Leelanau and Manitou. Was born at Turner, Androscoggin County, Me., Dec. 2, 1843. Was born and reared on a farm, and in former years was a teacher. He later practiced law. During the war he was a member of the 17th Maine Infantry. He held various town and school offices, and was Representative in the Maine Legislature in 1868. He was Prosecuting Attorney of Antrim County, Mich., from 1877 to 1885, and Circuit Court Commissioner from 1877 to 1881.

SIRRELL C. LEBARRON

Representative from Lenawee County, 1840. Was born in Woodstock, Vt., Jan. 25, 1807. He was educated at Woodstock, and removed to Harrisburg, Pa., in 1825. He was delegate to the Clay Convention at Washington, in 1832. He removed to Tecumseh, Mich., in 1832. He was the second Clerk of Lenawee County in 1834, and held the office until Michigan became a State, and was the first County Clerk under the state organization. He was a merchant for some years at Tecumseh. He opened the first grammar school in the county in 1832 and kept it until 1836.

HUBERT LECROIX

Member of the Legislative Council from Monroe County, 1824-5 and 1826-7. (Further data not obtainable).

HENRY LEDYARD

Senator from the Third District, 1857-8. Was born in New York City, Mar. 3, 1812, and his early life was passed there. He was a graduate of Columbia College and was admitted to practice as an attorney. His first official position was as secretary of legation at the French court under the ministry of Gen. Cass, and from this position sprang an intimacy with the Cass family which resulted in his marriage in 1839 to Matilda C., a daughter of Gen. Cass. On the return of the latter from Europe in 1844 he came to Detroit and assumed the management of the large property interests of his father-in-law. He was Alderman of his ward, 1849-50, was one of the first members of the Board of Water Commissioners of the city, organized in 1853, and was Mayor of the city in 1855. He also served as a member of the School Board, 1846-7, and his name appears in various business and philanthropic enterprises. He removed to Washington and resided there during Gen. Cass' service as Secretary of State, and for a short time discharged the duties of Assistant Secretary of State. He removed to Newport, R. I., in 1861. He was a Democrat in politics. He died in London, England, in 1880.

BENN H. LEE

Representative from the First District of Kent County, 1913-14. Was born in Thornapple Township, Barry County, Mich., Nov. 25, 1867. He was educated in the Hastings High School, and graduated from the dental department of the University of Michigan. Married. He engaged in the dentistry business and was also interested in farming and fruit growing. A member of Grand River Lodge No. 34, F. & A. M., Grand Rapids Chapter No. 7, De Molai Commandery K. T. No. 5, and Saladin Temple Mystic Shrine. In politics a Democrat.

DANIEL S. LEE

Representative from Oakland County, 1843; and Delegate from Livingston County to the Constitutional Convention of 1850. Was born in Yates County, N. Y., in 1808. He settled as a merchant in Farmington, Mich., in 1836, and in 1839 purchased a farm in Novi and removed his business there. In 1844 he became a merchant and farmer at Brighton. He was largely interested in lands. With Bush & Thomas he owned large property interests in Lansing. They built the Benton, later Everett House, in 1850. He died Sept. 26, 1857.

HENRY LEE

Representative from the County of Lapeer, 1895-6 and 1897-8. Was born at Metamora, in Lapeer County, Nov. 17, 1840. He was educated at the public schools, commenced teaching at the age of sixteen years, which occupation he continued winters for twenty-two terms, always taking a great interest in all questions pertaining to education and advancement. He was a farmer by occupation. In politics he was a republican, a strong advocate of the principles of protection. He filled a number of official positions, including School Inspector, Supervisor and County Treasurer; was elected Representative to the House of 1895-6, and re-elected to that of 1897-8. He died before the close of his term and was succeeded by Edmund Brownell.

JAMES HENDERSON LEE

Senator, 1911-12, from the Fourth District of Wayne County. Was born at New York City, Mar. 27, 1887, and was educated in the Detroit public and high schools, later taking a law course at the Detroit College of Law from which he graduated in 1909. A member of the law firm of Chawke & Lee, Detroit. In politics a Democrat.

JAMES LEE

Representative from Leelanau and Benzie Counties, 1875-6. Was born in Yorkshire, England, Mar. 10, 1816, and received a common school education. In 1832 he emigrated to Michigan, settling in Hamtramck, and engaging in farming and brickmaking. In 1858 he removed to Bingham, Leelanau County. He held several township offices, including that of Supervisor for five years, and pursued the business of farming.

JAMES B. LEE

Representative from Livingston County, 1869-70. Was born in Milo Centre, N. Y., Apr. 14, 1819. By occupation he was a merchant, in politics a Democrat. He came to Michigan at the age of fifteen and was a clerk in the store of Thomas & Lee at Farmington. He removed to Brighton in 1842, where he was a merchant until 1877. He married Samantha B. Chadwick in 1843. He was for sixteen years Postmaster at Brighton, and held all responsible offices in the village corporation. He died at Brighton, Sept 5, 1886.

JOSIAH LEE

Representative from Macomb County, 1841. Was born in the State of Connecticut, June 24, 1781. He came to this State in 1832, where he worked two years and brought his family in 1834, settling as a farmer in Ray, Mich. He was an early Supervisor of that town, also Justice of the Peace. He was a Democrat. He died Sept. 5, 1855.

THOMAS LEE

Representative from Livingston and Washtenaw Counties, 1837. His postoffice address was Dexter. He resigned before the adjourned session of 1837 and was succeeded by Emanual Case. (Further data not obtainable).

WILLIAM O. LEE

Representative from the First District of St. Clair County, 1921-2, and 1923—. Was born Nov. 7, 1844, in Arbela Township, Tuscola County, of English, Scotch and Holland descent. He was the third white child born in Tuscola County and is now its oldest pioneer. He was educated in the district schools, Vassar High School and Eastman's Business College. He has served as Justice of the Peace and Supervisor of the city of Port Huron. Mr. Lee is a veteran of the Civil War, being a member of 7th Mich. Cavalry. He has been president of the Regimental Association and Custer's Michigan Cavalry Association, Commander of G. A. R. Post and Department Commander, G. A. R., Department of Michigan. He is a member of the board of managers of Michigan Soldiers' Home. He is a Republican.

GURDON C. LEECH

Member of the Board of Regents of the University of Michigan, 1838-40; and Representative from Macomb County, 1841. Was born at West Bloomfield, N. Y., Feb. 8, 1811. He received a common school education, and turned his energies to mercantile pursuits. He started in business at Palmyra, N. Y., but after a few years emigrated to the west. In 1830 he settled at Utica, Mich., where he engaged in the milling and dry goods business. He became a prominent citizen of the place and was Regent of the University in place of Michael Hoffman, resigned, and served out the remainder of the term, retiring in 1840. He died at Utica, May 10, 1841.

DAVID WARREN LEEDY

Representative from Mason County, 1921-2, and 1923—. Was born in Montgomery County, O., Mar. 16, 1856, of Holland, Swiss and English parentage. He received his education in the common schools, and in the fall of 1880 attended a select school at Woodland, Mich., and that winter taught his first school. In 1883-4 he was principal of Woodland school. He completed a commercial course at Valparaiso, Ind., and engaged as a traveling salesman. He is now engaged in farming. Mr. Leedy is married. In politics he is a Republican.

ANDREW J. LEETCH

Representative from Wayne County, 1861-2. Was born in the State of New York, in 1830. In 1835 he removed with his parents to Canton, Wayne County, Mich. He was brought up on a farm and received a common school education. He became a carpenter and joiner by trade and followed it for years. He was a grocer at Ypsilanti in 1865, and in 1866 built a malt house and brewery. He was Supervisor and owned a large farm in the town of Superior.

JOHN LEIDLEIN

Senator, 1899-1900, and 1911-12, from the Twenty-second District, comprising the County of Saginaw. Was born at Buena Vista, Saginaw County, Mich., Sept. 3, 1864, of German parents, and was educated in the public schools. His parents came to Saginaw County from Bavaria. He was twice elected Township Clerk of Buena Vista, the first time when he was but twenty-one years of age, and at the age of twenty-two was elected secretary of the Farmers' Mutual Fire Insurance Company of Saginaw County, holding this position for five years and declining a re-election. He was Supervisor, chairman of the board, five years—being chosen unanimously the last four times; was School Director, a member of the State Senate of 1899-1900, and 1911-12, and later was president of the Farmers' Mutual Fire Insurance Company; president of the State Association of Supervisors and of the State Association of Mutual Fire Insurance Companies. For many years he was manager of the Buena Vista Cheese Company besides conducting a farm. Married. In politics a Democrat.

WILLIAM LEIGHTON

Representative, 1917-18, and 1919, from the Schoolcraft District, comprising the counties of Alger, Luce, Mackinac and Schoolcraft. Was born in the city of New York, of English parents, in 1852. He was educated in the public schools of Bay City and was a resident of the Saginaw Valley during the early years of his life. He moved to Grand Marais, Alger County, in 1894. He served for several years on the Board of Education, and for eleven years was a member of the Board of Supervisors, having served at one time as chairman of the board. He was a member of the County Road Commission. He was married and had one son. In politics he was a Republican. He died Oct. 7, 1919.

JOHN LEITCH

Representative from Sanilac County, 1883-4. Was born in Scotland, Nov. 10, 1832. He moved with his parents to Canada in 1841, and settled in Elgin County. There he passed his boyhood and early manhood. He moved to Sanilac County, Mich., in April, 1856, and settled on the farm, where he continued to reside. He was a farmer by occupation, but held township and school offices the greater part of the time. Politically he was a Democrat.

ELIJAH LELAND

Representative from Branch County, 1857-8. Was born in Mendon, N. Y., in July, 1804. He came to Quincy, Mich., in 1834, bought a farm of 320 acres, and lived there during the remainder of his life. He sent three sons to defend the union.

FRANK BRUCE LELAND

Member of the Board of Regents of the University of Michigan, 1908-23. Was born in Rose Township, Oakland County, Mich., in 1859. He secured his higher education in the Fenton High School and the University of Michigan, receiving the degree of B. L. from the latter institution. After graduating from the University he practiced law ten years when he became general manager of the National Loan and Investment Company, of Detroit, which position he held seven years. For the past eighteen years he has been president of the United Savings Bank of Detroit, of which he was the organizer. He was elected a member of the Board of Regents of the University in April, 1907, and was re-elected in 1915.

GEORGE LELAND

Representative from the Second District of Allegan County, 1915-16, 1917-18, and 1919-20; and Senator from the Eighth District, 1923—. Was born at Painesville, O., June 11, 1858, of English parents. He was educated in the district schools of Allegan County. In 1896 he removed to the village of Fennville, and, in addition to farming, engaged in the fruit and produce business and the selling of fruit packages. He has held the offices of Assessor, Councilman and President of the village, and Treasurer and Supervisor of Manlius Township. He is married. In politics he is a Republican.

JOSHUA G. LELAND

Representative from Washtenaw County, 1844 and 1846. Was born in Madison County, N. Y., July 18, 1805. He came to Michigan in 1831, and settled in Washtenaw County. He was president of the Washtenaw County Agricultural Society, of the Farmers' Insurance Company, and of the County Pioneer Society. He was a successful farmer and business man. He died Apr. 27, 1876.

WILLIAM A. LEMIRE

Representative from Delta County, 1917-18; and Senator, 1919-20, and 1921-2, from the Thirtieth District, comprising the counties of Chippewa, Delta, Luce, Mackinac, Menominee and Schoolcraft. Was born in Nicolet, Canada, Apr. 23, 1877, and came to Michigan with his parents when he was three months old. He was educated in the Houghton County public schools, St. Viator's College, at Kankakee, Ill., and the College of Physicians and Surgeons, at St. Louis, Mo. After receiving his degree of M. D. he located at Garden, Delta County, Mich., to practice medicine and surgery, but removed to Escanaba three years later, where he has since resided. He was County Physician for seven years, and is at present surgeon at St. Francis hospital at Escanaba. He has served three years as secretary, and two years as president of the Board of Education. He was elected Mayor in 1912 and served one term but refused the nomination for a second term. Mr. Lemire is married and has three sons and five daughters. In politics a Republican.

PETER B. LENNON

Representative from the First District of Genesee County, 1919-20, and 1921-2. Is a native of the county in which he now resides, having been born in Clayton Township, Aug. 7, 1878, of American parentage. His education was acquired in the Flint High School, Notre Dame University, at South Bend, Ind., and the law department of the University of Michigan. In 1909 he engaged in the practice of law in Detroit, but five years later removed to Lennon and took up his residence on a farm near that place. Mr. Lennon is married, and has three daughters. In politics he is a Republican.

JOSEPH C. LEONARD

Senator from the Sixteenth District, 1853-4. Was born at Smyrna, N. Y., Aug. 11, 1817. He was educated at Cazenovia, and Hamilton College, and settled at Union City, Mich., in 1842. He was Postmaster there in 1846 and again in 1858, for twenty years Trustee of village schools, and director of the Michigan Air Line Railroad Company. In politics he was a Democrat. At first he was a boot and shoe dealer, but for many years a farmer, also engaged in surveying and conveyancing.

ORVICE R. LEONARD

Representative from the First District of Wayne County, 1911-12 and 1913-14. Was born at Keene, N. H., Sept 24, 1865, and was educated in the public schools of New Hampshire and Vermont. In 1898 he served on the U. S. S. Yosemite; was afterwards employed four years in the Register of Deeds office, Detroit, and later became general agent of the National Surety Company, of New York; later general agent of this company for the Southern Peninsula of Michigan. In 1906 he was appointed by President Roosevelt the first Marshal of the United States Court for China and was located at Shanghai for several months. In 1910 he was appointed by President Taft Supervisor of Census for the First District of Michigan. In politics a Republican. He died at Detroit, Sept 13, 1915.

DANIEL LEROY

Member of the Legislative Council from Oakland County, 1830-1; and Attorney General, 1836-7. Was born in Nova Scotia, May 17, 1775, and was educated there and at Binghamton, N. Y. He studied law and was admitted to practice at the age of twenty-five. He came to Pontiac, Mich., and was the first lawyer admitted to practice at the Oakland County bar, July 17, 1820. He was Prosecuting Attorney of the county for several years and was Chief Justice of the county court from 1829 to 1833. He was a Presidential Elector in 1836. By appointment of Gov. Mason he was the first Attorney General under a State government. Politically he was a Democrat. He was a lawyer of ability and ranked high in the bar of the State. Late in life he retired from business, and died at Fenton, Feb. 11, 1858.

JOHN P. LEROY

Senator from the Third District, 1840-1, and from the Sixth District, 1851. Was born in Johnstown, N. Y., Sept. 22, 1804. He settled in Pontiac, Mich., in 1827; was for many years a Justice, and served as County Treasurer. He was a Whig and assisted in forming that party in Oakland County, and was a delegate to the convention that organized the Republican party. He died Aug. 23, 1867.

DAVID A. L'ESPERANCE, JR.

Representative from the First District of Wayne County, 1907-8. Was born in New York City, Oct. 2, 1874, of French and Scotch-Irish descent. He obtained his education in the public schools of New York City, Barnard Military School, New York City, Princeton University, and New York University Law School, receiving the degree of LL.B. in 1896. Mr. L'Esperance practiced law in New York City from 1896-1902. At Peekskill, N. Y., Nov. 7, 1900, he married Elise Depew Strang, a niece of Chauncey M. Depew, and came to Detroit, Mar. 1, 1902, to practice law. He was Assistant Attorney for the Wabash Railroad Co. from 1902 to Jan. 1, 1905, resigning this position to accept the appointment of Deputy County Clerk of Wayne County. He resigned as Deputy County Clerk, Sept. 1, 1906, and formed the law partnership of Altland and L'Esperance, with offices in the Penobscot building. In politics a Republican.

GEORGE H. LESTER

Representative from the First District of Montcalm County, 1891-2. Was born on the Hudson at Schuylersville, Saratoga County, N. Y., Nov. 5, 1842; came to Michigan with his parents in April, 1858, and located at Newaygo; moved to Ionia County four years later and engaged in farming in the township of Ronald; moved to Crystal in 1867, and engaged in general farming. He held the offices of Township Clerk, Township Treasurer, School Inspector and Highway Commissioner, and held the office of Supervisor at the time of his election as Representative. He was nominated by the Patrons of Industry and indorsed by the Democrats and Prohibitionists. He was thoroughly identified with the grange movement, and represented his county in the State Grange four different session. He was the only candidate on the ticket that received a majority of the votes in Montcalm County.

GEORGE S. LESTER

Representative from Sanilac County, 1850. Was born in Washington County, N. Y., Mar. 4, 1812. He came to Michigan in 1840, and resided at Pontiac, Lexington, Port Huron, and at Alpena. He was a lumberman, and built three steam saw mills, Collector of Customs, merchant and real estate dealer, and in 1887 was Judge of Probate in Alpena County. In politics he was a Republican.

HENRY A. LEVAKE

Representative from Chippewa County, 1835-6, to 1839. His postoffice address was Sault Ste. Marie. He did not take his seat in the adjourned session of 1836. (Further data not obtainable).

DAVID J. LEVEQUE

Representative from the Second District of Houghton County, 1917-18. Was born in Lake Linden, May 22, 1882, of French descent. He was educated in the Lake Linden schools and Ferris Institute at Big Rapids. He was manager of his fruit farm at Lake Linden in 1917, and devoted to his banking and mining interests. Fraternally he was a member of the K. of C., Elks and Grange; secretary and treasurer of Houghton County Pomona Grange, also director of Houghton County Farm Bureau. In politics a Republican.

AMOS LEWIS

Representative from Oceana County, 1879-80. Was born Mar. 6, 1821, at Highland County, O. He moved to Laporte County, Ind., in 1836, and to Oceana County, Mich., in 1866, where he was a farmer. His politics were National.

CHARLES F. LEWIS

Of Pentwater, Representative from Oceana County, 1923——. Was born at Lyons, Ionia County, November 11, 1856, of American parents, and was educated in the Lyons high school. He is married and has one son and two daughters. For a time he was employed by the Pentwater Lumber Co., but for the past thirty-three years has been the proprietor of a retail hardware store in Pentwater. Always a staunch Republican. Mr. Lewis served as Village Trustee six years, as Superintendent of the Poor twenty-one years, nine years as a member of the School Board and six years as Postmaster.

GEORGE LEWIS

Representative from Bay County, 1873-4. Was born in Monroe, N. Y., Nov. 8, 1827. He received his early education in common schools. In 1849, he emigrated to Michigan, and settled in Saginaw. In 1858, he removed to Bay City. He was Supervisor and held minor positions of trust in Bay County. His occupation was that of a banker and lumberman.

JOHN D. LEWIS

Representative from Tuscola County, 1865-6; and Senator from the Twenty-fourth District, 1874. Was born in Ellisburgh, N. Y., Sept. 2, 1834. He was educated at Union College, and graduated from the Albany Law School in 1861. He settled in practice at Vassar, Mich. From 1861 to 1868, he was principal of the Vassar Union School. He held many local positions, including Supervisor, Circuit Court Commissioner and County Superintendent of Schools. He removed to Portsmouth, now part of Bay City, and was two years principal of schools there, later a merchant. He was Alderman, member of Board of Education, and in 1874 was Senator, vice H. H. Wheeler, resigned. He died in Florida, May 27, 1887; buried in Bay City.

LYNN J. LEWIS

Representative from Van Buren County, 1915-16, 1917-18, and 1919-20. Was born at Bangor, Mich., June 3, 1876, of Welsh-Irish parents. He was educated in the district school, Bangor High School, Benton Harbor College, and the University of Michigan. At the age of eighteen he was granted a teacher's certificate and taught school for seven years in his home county. In 1899 he entered the law department of the University of Michigan, and in June, 1901, was admitted to the bar. He immediately began the practice of law at Bangor. Married. In politics a Republican. At the opening of the 1917 session of the Legislature, Mr. Lewis was unanimously chosen speaker *pro tem.*

NATHANIEL W. LEWIS

Senator from the Fourteenth District, 1879-80. Was born in Washington County, Vt., Sept. 11, 1832. He received a common school education. In 1858 he removed to Calhoun County, Mich. He enlisted as private in an independent regiment known as "Merrill's Horse," in 1862; was promoted through the grades to Lieutenant; and was mustered out in the fall of 1865. He soon after removed to Ganges, Allegan County. His occupation was farmer and fruit-grower. He held the offices of Commissioner, Clerk and Supervisor. In politics he was a National.

ROLLIE L. LEWIS

Representative from Charlevoix County, 1921-2, and 1923—. Was born Aug. 2, 1884, at Charlevoix, Mich., of Scotch-Irish parentage. He was educated in the public school in Charlevoix and the University of Michigan. He has served as City Clerk, Prosecuting Attorney and member of Charter Commission of city of Charlevoix. Mr. Lewis is married. In politics he is a Republican.

THOMAS LEWIS

Representative from Wayne County, 1842 and 1846. Was born in Sandwich, Canada, in 1807, settling in Detroit in 1819. His general pursuits were those of merchant and farmer. In 1836, in company with Richard Godfroy, he made a business venture at Grand Rapids, which was mercantile, milling and buying furs. The firm built a steamer, the Gov. Mason, the loss of which, with a cargo of furs, proved so disastrous that he returned to Detroit and located on Grosse Isle, where he owned and managed a farm, and was also interested in the fisheries thereabout. He was for many years a leading citizen, and served his township as Supervisor and Justice. He was a Democrat in politics. He died Oct. 19, 1887.

WILLIAM LEWIS

Representative from Barry County, 1846. Was born at Weatherfield, N. Y., in
1802. He came to Yankee Springs, Mich., in 1836, located a large farm, and
built a hotel which became famous as "Yankee Lewis House." Few people of
olden days failed to partake of the hospitalities of "Yankee Lewis." He was
an enterprising, active, ever busy pioneer, and did his full share in reclaiming
the wilderness. Politically he was a Democrat. He died Sept. 15, 1853.

WILLIAM F. LEWIS

Representative from Oceana County, 1891-2. Was born in Fredonia, Chautauqua County, N. Y., Dec. 12, 1829. A widower, his wife having died Mar. 3, 1882.
His occupation is that of a farmer. He held the office of Supervisor; also president of the County Association of the Patrons of Industry. He was elected to
the House of 1891-2, on the Democratic ticket, indorsed by the Patrons of Industry.

RALPH W. LIDDY

Representative from the First District of Wayne County, 1919-20, and 1921-2.
Was born May 8, 1886, at Detroit, Mich., of Irish parents. He was educated
in the public schools and the Detroit College of Law, receiving his degree from
the latter institution in 1907. He was a teacher in the high schools for a time
and later was Supervisor of Schools in the Philippine Islands for two years.
He served in the 31st Mich. Infantry and was honorably discharged as Lieutenant in 1916. Mr. Liddy is unmarried. In politics he is a Republican.

COLON C. LILLIE

Delegate in the Constitutional Convention of 1907-8 from the Twenty-third
District, Muskegon and Ottawa Counties. Was born on a farm in Tallmadge
Township, Ottawa County, in 1860, of English and Danish descent. He spent
all of his boyhood on a farm, attended the district school and graduated from
the Michigan Agricultural College in the class of '84. He received an appointment as cadet at West Point while in college, but resigned and finished his
course at M. A. C. After leaving college Mr. Lillie taught school, became secretary of the Board of School Examiners and County Commissioner of Schools.
He managed a farm, made a special study of practical agriculture and dairy
farming, and was correspondent of the Michigan Farmer, for many years; later
a traveling salesman. He served as Supervisor, Village Trustee, and member of
the Board of Education; president of Coopersville State Bank, Coopersville
Creamery Company and Michigan Dairymen's Association, and also Deputy State
Dairy and Food Commissioner. In 1890 he married Miss Julia A. Lawton.

LANSING E. LINCOLN

Representative from Huron County, 1885-6, and 1887-8. Was born at Groton,
N. Y., in 1842. He enlisted in 1861, and after his term of enlistment expired

was sutler of the 148th N. Y. Vol. At the close of the war he went into business at Richmond, Va., and in 1867 in New York City. In 1871 he came to Mason, Mich., and was first in the boot and shoe business, then engaged in shipping live stock. After 1881 he was a resident of Huron County, farming and in the live stock business. He was wounded at Ball's Cross Roads, Va. He was elected as a Fusionist.

ALBERT T. LINDERMAN

Representative from the Second District of Muskegon County, 1893-4, and 1895-6. Was born on a farm near Beloit, Wis., July 3, 1847; acquired his early education at the common schools and State Normal of Pennsylvania; removed to Grand Rapids, Mich., in 1867, where he was principal of Coldbrook Union School and member of Board of Education. In the early seventies he inaugurated the movement which resulted in the organization of the State Horticultural Society. In 1876, he located at Whitehall, engaged in mercantile and lumber business; put out 100 acres of apple and cherry trees on the pine barrens, as an experiment, using clay in the setting, which he calls "clay culture." In politics a Republican.

PETER LINDERMAN

Representative from Ingham County, 1857-8. Was born at Wallkill, N. Y., Oct. 5, 1795, and settled at Mason in 1836. A Whig until 1854, he then became a Republican. By occupation he was a farmer. He was the first Supervisor of Vevay, Postmaster of Mason, for many years a Justice, and Judge of Probate for Ingham County. He died Mar. 4, 1865.

FREDERICK LINDOW

Representative from the First District of St. Clair County, 1889. He was a resident of Marine City. His seat was contested by Frank McElroy and vacated Mar. 27, 1889.

FRANCIS O. LINDQUIST

Member of Congress, 1913-15. Was born at Marinette, Wis., Sept. 27, 1869, of Swedish parentage. He embarked in the bazaar business nine years ago, and later started a mail order business in connection. He afterwards began the manufacture of clothing, selling his products by mail. Married. President of the Canada Mills Co., of New York, etc. He was nominated at the primary Aug. 27, 1912, and was elected Nov. 5, 1912.

EDWARD B. LINSLEY

Senator, 1905-6, and 1907-8, from the Sixth District, comprising the counties of Branch, Hillsdale and St. Joseph. Was born in Henrietta, Monroe County, N. Y., July 27, 1847, and removed with his parents to Kalamazoo, Mich., in 1857, where he received his education in the public schools. He engaged in the drug business at Three Rivers, which he carried on successfully for ten years, and in 1881, began the manufacture of small railway cars; this business later became incorporated as the Sheffield Car Co., with Mr. Linsley as secretary and treasurer, and later manager. He served in the Michigan State Troops, much of the time as a commissioned officer. He was instrumental in establishing the Three Rivers Building and Loan Association. Through his efforts the Three Rivers Free Public Library was established. In politics a Republican. He held the offices of member of the School Board and Mayor of Three Rivers city. Deceased.

WILLIAM SEELYE LINTON

Representative from the Second District of Saginaw County, 1887-8; and a member of Congress, 1893-5, and 1895-7. Was born at St. Clair, Mich., Feb. 4, 1856. He moved with his parents to Saginaw, Mich.; was educated in the public schools. He commenced clerking at Farwell, Mich.; a member of Bay County Board of Supervisors; again moved to Saginaw in 1879; and engaged in the lumber and salt business. In politics a Republican. He was elected a member of the East Saginaw Common Council, in 1883, serving two terms; elected Representative to the Michigan Legislature of 1887-8; president of the People's Building and Loan Association of Saginaw County; president of the Michigan State League of Building and Loan Associations during 1891; candidate for Lieutenant Governor on the Republican State ticket in 1890; president of the Saginaw Water Board; Mayor of Saginaw, 1892-4; elected to the Fifty-third Congress and re-elected to the Fifty-fourth Congress; was appointed Postmaster at Saginaw, Mich., by President McKinley.

WILLIAM E. LITTELL

Representative from Oakland County, 1879-80, and 1881-2. Was born May 16, 1838, at Cayuga, N. Y. He was educated in a district school and an academy. Having come to Michigan in 1851, he settled at Orion. He served fifteen months in the 7th Regiment of Mich. Vol., during the war. He taught school and held all the various offices in his township except that of Treasurer; was Postmaster at Maryland. He was Justice fifteen years, member and chairman of the Board of Supervisors of Allegan County for thirteen years, and two years President of the village of Allegan.

CHARLES D. LITTLE

Representative from Saginaw County, 1871-2, 1875-6 and 1877-8. Was born in Livingston, N. Y., in 1823, and received a classical education. He came to Michigan in 1837, but in 1839 went to Canandaigua, N. Y., and studied law. In 1842 he became a law partner of E. H. Thomson, at Flint, and was Judge of Probate for Genesee County. He removed to Saginaw in 1850, practiced law until 1861, then went into the army as Quartermaster of the 23d Mich. Infantry, was appointed Assistant Adjutant General on the staff of Gen. Granger, and held it until 1863, resigning from sickness. He was chairman of the Saginaw Board of Supervisors six years, and held other local offices. In politics he was a Democrat.

LLOYD S. LITTLE

Representative from the Iosco District, 1923——. Was born at Argyle, Sanilac County, February 29, 1892, of Irish parentage. His education was acquired in the public schools and in Ferris Institute. For a time he was employed as telegrapher operator on various railroads, and then he went west to engage in the buying and selling of stock. In 1916 he returned and took a position as traffic manager with a manufacturing concern. At the outbreak of the war he entered the traffic section of the aircraft department. Since his discharge from service he has been the northeastern Michigan district manager for the Ohio State Life Insurance Company. Mr. Little is a Republican and was elected to the Legislature November 7, 1922, without opposition.

NORMAN LITTLE

Representative from Saginaw County, 1839, and 1842. His postoffice address was Saginaw City. (Further data not obtainable).

DAVID LITTLEJOHN

Representative from the First District of Berrien County, 1917-18. Was born in Glasgow, Scotland, in 1876. His mother, Elizabeth Walker Scott, was a lineal descendant of Sir Walter Scott. He was educated in the national public schools of Ireland, the Scientific Academy of Garvaugh, Ireland, and in the College of Science, Kensington, England; attended the medical department of the University of Glasgow, Scotland; a graduate of philosophy from Amity College, Iowa; a Fellow of the Society of Science, London, England, and also a graduate in medicine. He practiced medicine and was also engaged in medical teaching in several of the medical colleges in Chicago, Ill., for some time. He was married to Sadie Kremer of Coloma, in 1913. In politics a Republican.

FLAVIUS J. LITTLEJOHN

Representative from Allegan County, 1842, 1843, 1848 and 1855-6; and Senator from the Fifth District, 1845-6. Was born in Herkimer County, N. Y., in July, 1804. He graduated from Hamilton College in 1827, and delivered the valedictory address. He was admitted to the bar in 1830, and practiced in Little Falls, N. Y., until 1836, when on account of ill health, he removed to Allegan, Mich., and for several years was engaged as surevyor, engineer and geologist. From 1848 to 1858 he was engaged in the practice of law. He was elected Judge of the Ninth Circuit in 1858, which then comprised twenty counties on the western shore, extending from Van Buren to Emmet, and served until 1865. In 1849 he was the Whig and Free Soil candidate for Governor against John S. Barry. He was at one time Circuit Court Commissioner of Allegan County. He took great interest in education and temperance. He was an eloquent and logical speaker, and able lecturer, bore a spotless reputation, and wrote a volume of interesting Indian legends. He died Apr. 28, 1880.

PHILETUS O. LITTLEJOHN

Representative from Allegan County, 1863-4. Was born in Litchfield, N. Y., Dec. 24, 1814. In politics he was a Democrat. He extensively engaged in farming. As a young man he was a railroad contractor in Virginia and Orion six years; Justice of the Peace sixteen years; Supervisor fourteen years, and chairman of the Board of Supervisors of Oakland County.

FIDUS LIVERMORE

Representative from Jackson County, 1843 and 1844. Was born at Waterville, N. Y., July 21, 1811. He learned the trade of tailor and followed that business at Dresden, N. Y., until 1836, then studied law three years and settled in practice at Jackson, Mich., in 1839. He held the offices of Justice, and Prosecuting Attorney two terms. He was a delegate to the Democratic National Conventions of 1860 and 1872, was a Democratic candidate for Elector in 1868, and the candidate for that party for Congress in 1874 and 1876. From 1846 to 1867 he was senior partner of the law firm of Livermore & Wood. He was nine years president of the School Board, and was commandant of camp in the organization of the 20th and 26th Mich. Infantry. Politically he was a Democrat. He died May 22, 1880.

JOHN S. LIVERMORE

Delegate from Oakland County to the Second Convention of Assent; 1836; and Representative from Oakland County, 1839 and 1842. Was born in Sangerfield, N. Y., Jan. 12, 1801. By occupation he was a physician, in politics a Democrat. He was a volunteer in the War of 1812. He located at Rochester, Mich., in 1830. He left there in 1848, and died at Ft. Wilkins, on Lake Superior, Oct. 4, 1861.

WILLIAM LIVINGSTON, JR.

Representative from Wayne County, 1875-6. Was born in Dundas, Ont., Jan. 21, 1842. He removed to Detroit in 1849, and received an academical education and learned the trade of a machinist. In 1861 he became connected with the shipping interest, and from year to year increased his investments in that direction until he was the owner of a number of steam vessels. He was also largely interested in the lumber business. Mr. Livingston was president of Detroit street railroads. In politics he was a Republican. He was appointed Collector of Customs at Detroit by President Arthur, which he held for several years. He also published the Detroit *Journal*.

JOSEPH A. LOCHER

Representative from the Second District of Ionia County, 1899-1900. Was born in Freiburg, Grand Duchy of Baden, Germany, Nov. 18, 1844, and came to this country with his parents in 1849, locating in Norwalk, Huron County, O. He attended school in that city until the Civil War broke out, when he enlisted in the summer of 1861, in Co. F, 3d O. V. C.. Upon the expiration of his term he re-enlisted in Co. F, 2d O. V. C., served until September, 1865, and was discharged. He returned to Norwalk, worked in the railroad shop for three years, and then moved to Michigan, locating in Berlin, Ionia County, on a piece of wild land. In politics a Republican.

DAVID G. LOCKE

Representative from Gratiot County, 1921-2. Was born in North Shade Township, Gratiot County, on the form on which he now resides, Nov. 27, 1860, of New England parents, descendants from the Plymouth Colony. He was educated in the district schools and the Ionia High School. Mr Locke is married and has four children. He has held the office of School Inspector, Justice of the Peace, Clerk and Supervisor of his township. In politics he is a Republican.

CHARLES LOCKE

Representative from Shiawassee County, 1867-8. Was born in Madison County, N. Y., May 11, 1811. He attended common schools and obtained a fair education. From eighteen until twenty-one he worked at building bridges and locks on the Schuylkill River. He then moved to Oneida County, N. Y., and worked a small farm. He came to Michigan in 1836, and finally settled in Antrim, Shiawassee County. After nine years he removed to Perry Center. He was licensed to preach in 1858. He was Justice thirteen years. In politics he was a Republican. He died in 1881.

WILLIAM H. LOCKERBY

Senator, 1901-2 and 1903-4, from the Sixth District, comprising the counties of Branch, Hillsdale and St. Joseph. Was born in West Vienna, Oneida County, N. Y., Feb. 24, 1859. He came to Michigan with his parents in 1869, locating on a farm in Branch County. He attended district schools winters and worked on the farm summers until twenty-three years of age, when he entered the law office of Hon. Milo D. Campbell, at Quincy, where he studied law until 1884, when he was admitted to the bar and practiced law in Quincy. Married. He held various township offices. In 1895 he was appointed by Gov. Rich a member of the Railroad and Street Crossing Board, and held the office of secretary four years; was Circuit Court Commissioner and member of the Board of School Examiners for Branch County. An active member in the Masonic and Grange societies. In politics a Republican.

JAMES K. LOCKWOOD

Representative from Alpena and other counties, 1867-8 and 1873-4. Was born in Ottawa, O., July 31, 1822. His education was that of common schools. In 1848 he settled in Port Huron, Mich., and in 1860 removed to Alpena. He held various local offices. In politics he was a Republican, by occupation a lumber merchant.

MAJOR F. LOCKWOOD

Representative from Oakland County, 1849. Was born Jan. 2, 1810, in Sand Lake, N. Y. He removed to Parma, N. Y., in 1824, and became a farmer. He settled in Novi, Mich., at an early day; for eight years was a merchant, then became a farmer. In politics he was a Democrat.

THOMAS W. LOCKWOOD

Representative from Wayne County, 1861-2 and 1863-4. Was a native of Glastenbury, Conn., born in 1817. His early education, which was partly academical, was acquired at Albany, N. Y., where he was admitted to the bar soon after attaining his majority. He located in Detroit in 1839, and to the time of his death in April, 1866, enjoyed not only a lucrative practice but the public confidence in a marked degree. He served a term as president of the Detroit Young Men's Society, and his name is associated with various business, public and benevolent enterprises. He was a Republican in politics. He was prominently connected with the Westminster (Presbyterian) Church of Detroit.

JOHN C. LODGE

Representative from the First District of Wayne County, 1909-10. Was born at Detroit, Mich., of American and English parentage. He was engaged for a time in newspaper work, later in the real estate and insurance business. In politics a Republican.

HUGO CHARLES LOESER

Senator, 1901-2, from the Tenth District, comprising the counties of Jackson and Washtenaw. Was born in Detroit, Mich., Oct. 20, 1858, where he acquired his education in the German American Seminary and Mayhew Business College. He moved to Jackson in 1876 and clerked in various stores until 1885, when he entered the restaurant business, which he conducted until 1892, after which time he was identified with the hardware business. Mr. Loeser was married in 1885, and held various offices in the city, having been Alderman four years, Supervisor, Fire Commissioner and Police Commissioner. In politics an active Republican.

JOHN LOMISON

Representative from St. Joseph County, 1855-6. Was born in Turbet, Pa., Nov. 14, 1807. He worked at farming until the age of nineteen, when he learned the trade of a tanner and currier, and worked at it eleven years. In 1836 he settled as a farmer in Park, St. Joseph County. He was several times Supervisor, Town Clerk and Justice, and was Representative as a Republican.

CHARLES DEAN LONG

Justice of the Supreme Court, 1888-1902. Was born at Grand Blanc, Genesee County, Mich., June 14, 1841. His early education was acquired at the district school and the Flint city schools. He taught for four years preparatory to a course at the University. The outbreak of the Civil War caused him to substitute the battlefield for his university course, and in August, 1861, he enlisted in Co. A, 8th Mich. Infantry. In the Battle of Wilmington Island, Ga., Apr. 16, 1862, he lost his left arm and received a ball in his left hip. He returned home, and later in the summer entered the law office of Oscar Adams, of Flint. In the fall of 1864 he was elected the County Clerk (Genesee County), which office he held for four successive terms. He was Prosecuting Attorney of his county from 1875 to 1880 inclusive, and was one of Michigan's four Supervisors of the Census for 1880. In 1885 he was Commander of the Department of Michigan, G. A. R. He resided at Flint until September, 1890, when he moved to Detroit and later to Lansing. In politics a Republican. He was elected Justice of the Supreme Court of the State of Michigan, Apr. 4, 1887. In 1891 Judge Long was elected president of the Detroit College of Law. At the national encampment of the G. A. R., held in Pittsburgh, Pa., Sept. 11, 1894, his friends insisted upon his standing for the office of Commander-in-Chief. With an election quite evident, he withdrew his name in the interest of harmony. On Apr. 5, 1897, he was re-elected Justice of the Supreme Court for the full term of ten years. He died June 27, 1902.

GEORGE MARSH LONG

Representative from Gratiot County, 1923—. Was born in Pompeii, in 1863, of Scotch parentage, his father, William Long, being one of Gratiot county's pioneers. He has engaged in farming and the mercantile business and for the past ten years has been dealing in live stock. Mr. Long was married in 1890. He has always been a Democrat and has held several offices of trust in his county.

JEREMIAH D. LONG

Representative from Wayne County, 1885-6. Was born in County of Cork, Ireland, in 1840, came to this country in 1853, and learned the trade of shoemaker, then worked in the grocery business for two years, and in a cotton mill. In 1861 he enlisted in the 3d battalion rifles, and after the war resumed his trade. He was elected as a Labor candidate by a fusion with the Democrats.

JOHN W. LONGYEAR

Delegate from Ingham County to the Constitutional Convention of 1867; and member of Congress, 1863-5 and 1865-7. Was born in Shandaken, N. Y., Oct. 22, 1820. He received an academical education and taught school for several years, at the same time pursuing the study of the law. In 1844 the came to Ingham County, completing his studies at Mason, at the same time teaching select school. He was admitted to the bar in 1846, and removed to Lansing, in 1847, engaging in a successful practice of the law, in partnership with his brother—Ephraim Longyear. He was one of the ablest lawyers at the bar in central Michigan. He was a delegate to the Philadelphia Convention in 1866. In May, 1870, he was appointed Judge of the United States District Court at Detroit, and took high rank as a jurist. In politics he was first a Whig, then a Republican. In 1849 he married Harriet M. Monroe, of Eagle, and left two sons and a daughter. He died at Detroit, Mar. 11, 1875.

PHILO MINER LONSBURY

Representative, 1895-6, from the Osceola District, comprising the counties of Lake and Osceola. Was born in Rochester, N. Y., Mar. 3, 1835; came to Michigan in 1837, with his parents, settled on a farm in Cambridge, Lenawee County, where he spent his early life, attending district school winters; at the age of seventeen he entered Michigan Union College, where he spent two years, and afterwards moved with his parents to Allegan, and taught school. In the spring of 1862, while at the State Normal, he enlisted in the Normal Company, which was assigned to the 17th Mich. Infantry, the "Stonewall regiment." May 12, 1864, he was taken prisoner at Spottsylvania Court House, and remained such at Andersonville, Ga., and Florence, S. C., until Feb. 22, 1865, when he escaped and joined the Union Army at Wilmington, N. C., and served until mustered out in June. Until 1874 he was engaged in teaching school, serving the last year as principal of Reed City Union School; from that date until about 1893, he was engaged in the drug business in Reed City. In politics a Republican. He held the offices of Township Treasurer, and School Trustee of Reed City schools.

DEXTER G. LOOK

Representative from the Second District of Kent County, 1923—. Was born in Lapeer County, March 3, 1863, of English and French ancestry. He attended the country school until he was fourteen years of age when he removed with his parents to Lowell, where he attended high school, graduating in 1880. He started learning the drug business immediately upon finishing school and has followed that line for forty-two years. Besides conducting a drug store in Lowell, he has an interest in one at Alma; is director and vice-president of the City State Bank, of Lowell, and treasurer of the Lowell Specialty Co. He is a trustee of the Congregational church; a member of several Masonic orders, having held various offices, and also a member of the Odd Fellows and Moose. Mr. Look is married and has one daughter. He is a Republican; was a member of the Village Council sixteen years, being president six years and a member of the school board fourteen years.

HENRY M. LOOK

Representative from Oakland County, 1865-6. Was born at Hadley, Mich., Oct. 27, 1837. His ancestors from Scotland, settled at Martha's Vineyard, in 1756. He received a thorough education, studied law, and was admitted to the bar in 1859. He was Prosecuting Attorney of Oakland County in 1871-2; City Attorney of Pontiac, and member of Board of Education, 1864-8; delegate to the Democratic Convention in 1872; chairman of the Democratic State Convention in 1872; chairman of the Democratic County Committee 1870 and 1875. In politics he was a Democrat. He wrote a work on "The law and practice of Masonic trials," and from 1869 to 1876 was the grand lecturer for the Masonic fraternity of Michigan. He was in practice in Utah in 1887.

CHARLES A. LOOMIS

Senator from the First District, 1848-9. His postoffice address was St. Clair. (Further data not obtainable).

PETER B. LOOMIS

Representative from Jackson County, 1859-60. Was born at Amsterdam, N. Y., Apr. 14, 1820. With a fair education he was a dry goods merchant at Rochester, N. Y., at the age of eighteen. He settled at Jackson, Mich., in 1843, and from that year until 1850 was a member of the dry goods firm of Loomis & Dwight. He then bought and operated the Kennedy mill for four years. In 1856 he established the banking firm of Loomis & Whitall, now P. B. Loomis & Co. He was president of the Jackson Gas Company; president and treasurer of the Jackson and Ft. Wayne Railroad Company; chief of the Fire Department, and Alderman. He gave efficient aid in the building of railroads. In politics he was a Republican. He died at Jackson, Dec. 30, 1905.

ROBERT B. LOOMIS

Senator, 1897-8, 1899-1900 and 1901-2, from the Sixteenth District, comprising the city of Grand Rapids (excepting the tenth and eleventh wards). Was born at Newcastle, Lincoln County, Me., Sept. 25, 1832. His parents moved to Boston in 1838, and the subject of this sketch grew up in the public schools of that city. Mr. Loomis subsequently removed to Washington, D. C., and was engaged in mercantile business in that city from 1862 to 1866, when he removed to Grand Rapids, Mich., and engaged in the boot and shoe business. In 1881 he established the firm of R. B. Loomis & Co., fire insurance. In politics a Republican. He served his city and county in several important positions. He was elected Supervisor from the second ward of the city of Grand Rapids in 1877, and served in that office until 1896; was chairman of the County Board two terms; was several times a member of the State Board of Equalization from Kent, and was chairman of the building committee having the erection of the county court house in charge. In 1896 Mr. Loomis was elected to the State Senate, and re-elected in 1898, and again in 1900.

THOMAS N. LOOMIS

Representative from Oakland County, 1847. Was born at Hamilton, N. Y., July 3, 1807. He located on a farm in Brandon, Oakland County, in 1836, where he lived until 1867, passing the remainder of his life in the village of Oakwood. He was eight years Supervisor. By occupation he was a farmer, in politics a Republican. He died Feb. 20, 1879.

GEORGE LORD

Representative from the First District of Wayne County, 1905-6, 1907-8, 1911-12 and 1921-2. Was born in England, Jan. 7, 1865. He is practically self-educated and in early life was thrown upon his own resources. He was interested in mining for several years. In 1893 he was appointed to the clerkship in the Department of State, organizing the building and loan division of the Department, acting as chief of the division for several years. He was Deputy Secretary of State under Hon. Fred M. Warner; secretary of State Tax Commission; Tax Commissioner of Wayne County, member and secretary of State Budget Commission of Inquiry. Mr. Lord is married. In politics he is an active Republican.

HENRY W. LORD

Member of Congress, 1881-3. Was born in Northampton, Mass., in 1821. He received an academical education at Andover, Mass., and removed to Detroit in 1839. In 1842 he went to Pontiac and resided there until 1876, engaged in farming and mercantile business, except from 1861 to 1867, when he was Consul at Manchester, England. He was a Presidential Elector in 1876; a member of the Board of State Charities from 1871 to 1882, and its secretary for five years; and for several years Register of the U. S. Land Office at Devil's Lake, Dakota. He was a resident of Detroit, while in Congress. In politics he was a Republican. He died at Butte, Mont., Jan. 25, 1891.

EDWIN H. LOTHROP

Representative from Kalamazoo County, 1835-7, 1842-4, and 1848. Was born in Easton, Mass., Mar. 22, 1806. He was of Pilgrim ancestory who settled in the Colonies in 1656. He settted on Prairie Ronde, in the township of Schoolcraft, Mich., in 1830, and was a leading farmer, and a prominent Democrat. He reached Kalamazoo when there was only one house. He was largely engaged in raising sheep, sending out the first fleece on the boats. He wished a very modest tombstone, requesting that the money necessary for a monument be used to relieve the suffering. He was speaker *pro tem.* in 1842 and 1843, and speaker in 1844, and was also Commissioner of Railroads. He held the local office of Supervisor. In 1857 he removed to Three Rivers, where he held the office of Justice most of the time until his death, Feb. 17, 1874. He was an older brother of Hon. G. V. N. Lothrop, minister to Russia.

GEORGE VAN NESS LOTHROP

Attorney General, 1848-51; and Delegate from Wayne County to the Constitutional Convention of 1867. Was born at Easton, Mass., Aug. 8, 1817, and spent his early life on a farm. He graduated from Brown University in 1838. In 1839 he came to Michigan for his health, and for three years was with his brother, Edwin H. Lothrop, on Prairie Ronde. In 1843 he resumed the study of law with Joy & Porter, in Detroit. In 1844 he became a partner of D. Bethune Duffield, the firm of Lothrop & Duffield continuing until 1857. He was several times a candidate for Congress, and repeatedly received the votes of the Democratic members of the Legislature for United States Senator. In 1885 he was appointed United States Minister to Russia. He was a fine orator, and long stood among the leading lawyers of the State. He died July 12, 1897.

GEORGE ALVIN LOUD

Member of Congress, 1903-5 to 1911-13 and 1915-17. Was born at Bracebridge, O., June 18, 1852, descending from early Puritan stock, being the tenth generation from Elder William Brewster; later ancestors, Austin Loud and Alvin Kile; grandfathers were respected pioneer settlers of northern Ohio. When Mr. Loud was four years of age, the family removed to Massachusetts, and in his fifteenth year they again changed residence to Au Sable, Mich. He was educated in the English High School (military) Boston; Professor Patterson's school, Detroit, and Ann Arbor High School. On leaving school he became associated with his father and brothers, Henry Nelson and Edward F. Loud, in the lumber business on the Au Sable River. He married Elizabeth Glennie, only daughter of John W. Glennie, a well known lumberman and banker. He served four years on Governor Pingree's staff and during the Spanish War was sent by the Governor to Montauk Point to represent him in caring for sick and disabled soldiers sent from Cuba; later sent in charge of hospital train through southern camps and hospitals to bring home sick soldiers of Michigan regiments, was on board the U. S. revenue cutter "McCulloch," serving as paymaster, at the Battle of Manila. He was elected Representative to the 62nd Congress for the fifth consecutive term and elected to the 64th Congress Nov. 3, 1914.

MEDOR E. LOUISELL

Delegate in the Constitutional Convention of 1907-8 from the Twenty-seventh District, Benzie County. Was born in Fond du Lac. Wis., in 1870, of French descent. When he was seven years of age his father, Joseph Louisell, moved with his family to Dakota, then Dakota Territory, and took up a homestead near Sioux Falls. They resided there until 1883. In that year the family moved to Manistee County, Mich. He attended the district school in the winter and worked in a shingle mill in the summer for five years. Being desirous of getting an education he abandoned the mill and entered the preparatory department of the University of Notre Dame, where he worked for his board and tuition. After remaining three years at Notre Dame University he entered the Manistee High School and graduated with the class of 1891. In the fall of 1891 he matriculated in the literary department of the University of Michigan, and in June, 1896, he graduated from the law and literary departments, completing both courses in five years. During vacations he reported on newspapers and did other work to enable him to get means to complete his course. After graduation he practiced law. He served as Prosecuting Attorney of Benzie County and also as Assistant Prosecuting Attorney of Houghton County for two years. He was married in 1903 to Miss Mary Tallon, of Calumet, Mich.

CYRUS LOVELL

Representative from Ionia County, 1849 and 1855; and Delegate from Ionia County to the Constitutional Convention in 1850. Was born in Grafton, Vt., Sept. 9, 1804. He received an academical education, studied law, emigrated to Michigan in 1829, and settled at Ann Arbor. In 1831 he married Louise Fargo, and in 1832 built the first dwelling at Kalamazoo. He enlisted for a short time in the Black Hawk War. At Kalamazoo he was Justice, Supervisor, and Prosecuting Attorney. In 1836 he removed to Ionia and was the first Supervisor in 1837. In 1855 was elected speaker of the House, the first Republican who held that position. He was a Whig until 1854, then a Republican until 1860, and then supported Stephen A. Douglas, and remained a Democrat. "Uncle Cy," as he used to be known, was a fine scholar, and an able but eccentric man. He lived at Ionia in 1887.

ENOS T. LOVELL

Representative from Kalamazoo County, 1867-8 and 1869-70; and Senator from the Eleventh District, 1881-2. Was born in Grafton, Vt., Jan. 22, 1821; received a common school education, and removed with his parents to Climax, Mich., in 1835, where he resided. By occupation he was a farmer. He was eleven times Supervisor of his township; and twice County Treasurer. In politics he was a Republican. He died at Climax, Nov. 20, 1904.

GEORGE W. LOVELL

Representative from Kalamazoo County, 1853-4 and 1855-6. Was born in Grafton, Vt., Dec. 9, 1818. He came to Climax, Mich., in 1835, where he lived until 1856, when he moved to Iowa, where he resided in 1887. He held the office of Supervisor. After his removal to Iowa he was elected to the Senate of that state. He was originally a Whig, then a Republican, but after 1875 was a Democrat. His education was received in common schools. By occupation he was a farmer and interested in banking.

LAFAYETTE W. LOVELL

Senator from the Twentieth District, 1857-8. Was born at Grafton, Vt., May 27, 1823, and settled in Climax, Mich., in 1835, where he resided in 1887. He was educated at the Kalamazoo branch of the University, graduated at Rush Medical College in 1847, practiced medicine fifteen years, and became a farmer. He was a Supervisor, and Town Clerk and Inspector of the State Prison. In politics he was a Republican.

NATHAN V. LOVELL

Representative from the Second District of Berrien County, 1903-4 and 1905-6. Was born in Livingston County, N. Y., in 1844. His parents were of Scotch and Dutch descent. He was educated in the district schools and attended school one year at Kalamazoo. He enlisted June 12, 1861, in Co. B, 9th Mich. Infantry, and served with his regiment until July 13, 1862, when he was taken prisoner at Murfreesboro, Tenn. On being exchanged he was transferred to the 7th Mich. Cavalry, and was promoted to Sergeant. He was mustered out Aug. 25, 1865. After prospecting in the Northwest part of the country he settled in Berrien County where he engaged in farming and manufacturing. In politics a Republican.

JAMES L. LOWDEN

Representative from the Second District of Washtenaw County, 1889-90 and 1891-2. Was born July 30, 1840, on the farm upon which he later resided, in Ypsilanti, Washtenaw County. By occupation a farmer, but in former years taught school a few terms. He received his education at the common schools and the State Normal. In 1868 he married Miss S. J. Sherwood. In politics a Democrat.

BERRY J. LOWREY

Representative from the Second District of Montcalm County, 1901-2. Was born in Auburn, Ind., Feb. 26, 1859, and received his education in the common schools of that city, after which he was apprenticed to learn the printers' trade in the office of the *De Kalb County Republican*. He was compositor, foreman, assistant editor, business manager and finally editor of that paper until 1881, after which he did more or less work on the Toledo, O., dailies. In 1884 he came to Michigan and became foreman of the Charlotte *Republican*, finally purchasing the Howard City *Record*. Married. In politics a staunch Republican. He was Postmaster under the Harrison administration and Deputy Collector of Internal Revenue for the western district of Michigan from 1898 to 1900. Mr Lowrey received the unanimous nomination as candidate for Representative to the Legislature of 1901-2 and was elected.

JOHN LOWRY, SR.

Representative from Washtenaw County, 1839. Was born in Schoharie County, N. Y., Feb. 14, 1793. He was a Whig until 1854, then a Republican. He located a farm in Lodi in 1825, and moved upon it in 1826. He added to the eighty acres first taken until he had a splendid farm of 700 acres, with a fine house and outbuildings. He worked persistently for the abolition of slavery until it was accomplished. He held town and county offices with acceptance many years. He died Apr. 23, 1872.

ANTHONY LUCAS

Representative from the First District of Houghton County, 1911-12. Was born in Severin, Croatia, Jan. 2, 1880, and came to Calumet, Mich., with his parents when about four years of age. He was educated in the public schools of Calumet. At the age of fifteen he left the public school and went to work as a clerk in his father's store where he remained four years. In February, 1901, he entered the Valparaiso University, and in August, 1903, graduated from there and had

conferred upon him the Bachelor of Science degree. In the fall of 1903 he
entered the University of Michigan and graduated from the law department in
June, 1906. Mr. Lucas was married September, 1905, to Miss Mae A. Frink,
daughter of Mr. and Mrs. F. H. Frink, of Naples, N. Y. His wife died in August,
1909, leaving a daughter. After his graduation from the University he actively
engaged in the practice of law at Calumet. He was appointed Village Attorney
of Red Jacket for two terms; was elected Circuit Court Commissioner of Houghton County, Nov. 3, 1908, and resigned that office in the spring of 1910 to seek
the nomination of Representative at the primary. In politics a Republican.

CHARLES D. LUCE

Representative from Hillsdale County, 1873-4. Was born in Arcada, N. Y., Apr.
6, 1820. He was educated in a common school. In 1846 he emigrated to Michigan and settled in the township of Jefferson, Hillsdale County. His occupation
was that of a farmer. He died in the fall of 1887.

CYRUS GRAY LUCE

Representative from the Second District of Branch County, 1885-6; Senator
from Branch County, 1865-6 and 1867-8; member of the Constitutional Convention of 1867; member of the State Board of Agriculture, 1885-7; and Governor
of Michigan, 1887-9 and 1889-91. Was born in Windsor, Ashtabula County, O.,
July 2, 1824. When twelve years of age he, with his parents, moved to Steuben
County, Ind. His schooling, except three terms at the Collegiate Institute, Ontario, Ind., was obtained winters in the log schoolhouse of the period. From the
age of 17 to 24 he worked at carding wool and dressing cloth. In 1848, he was
nominated by the Whigs for the Indiana Legislature. His representative district, composed of DeKalb and Steuben counties, was heavily democratic, but
he came within eleven votes of being elected. In 1849 he moved to this State
and settled on a farm in Gilead, in Branch County. For eleven years he was
Supervisor of his township. In 1854 he represented his district in the Lower
House of the Legislature, and from 1864 to 1868 was State Senator. During his
six legislative years he was present at every roll call, and voted upon the final
passage of every bill. From 1858 to 1862 he was Treasurer of Branch County.
He was a member of the Constitutional Convention of 1867, and as shown by
the published debates, was one of the best informed and among the most valuable of that body. In 1879 he was appointed State Oil Inspector by Gov. Croswell, and was re-appointed by Gov. Jerome. For several years he was Master
of the Michigan State Grange. Jan. 15, 1885, he was appointed a member of the
State Board of Agriculture. In 1886 he became the unanimous nominee of the
Republican party of the State for Governor, and was elected to the office. In
1888 he was unanimously re-nominated by the Republicans for the same office
and was elected. When elected Governor, contrary to custom, he took up his
residence at Lansing, where he lived and devoted his whole time and energies
to the duties of his office. The rural life led by Gov. Luce, his wide official experience, the evenings of many years at his farm home spent in valuable reading,
his familiarity with the State, its institutions, needs and requirements were of
great service to him as well as to the people, in the discharge of his duties. He
died at Coldwater, Mar. 18, 1905.

ALFRED LUCKING

Member of Congress from the First District of Michigan, 1903-5. Was born of English and Scotch parentage, at Ingersoll, Ont., Dec. 18, 1856. While an infant his parents removed to Ypsilanti, Mich., where he was reared. He received his education at the Ypsilanti High School, Michigan State Normal College, and graduated from the Law Department of the University of Michigan in 1878. He began the practice of law May 1, 1878, in the office of John D. Conely, Jackson, Mich., and on Jan. 1, 1880, was admitted to partnership under the firm name of Conely & Lucking. He was married Feb. 23, 1881, to Vie Loree Rose. He removed to Detroit, Mich., May 1, 1880. On May 1, 1882, William C. Maybury became a member of the firm under the firm name of Conely, Maybury & Lucking, which continued under this name until July 1, 1892, when Mr. Conely retired. The firm was then Maybury & Lucking. A Democrat in politics. He was temporary chairman of the Democratic State Convention in 1900, and was both temporary and permanent chairman of the State Convention of 1902. He received the nomination of the Democratic Congressional Convention Oct. 17, 1902, and was elected.

JEREMIAH LUDINGTON, JR.

Representative from Huron County, 1875-6 and 1879-80. Was born in Middlebury, Vt., May 5, 1828. He received a common school education and removed to Huron County, Mich., in 1850. For seven years Postmaster of Verona Mills. He was Township Treasurer, County Surveyor, and local State Swamp Land Road Commissioner. Up to the time of the great fires of 1871, he was engaged in lumbering, but having lost two saw mills and a grist mill, he followed the occupation of a farmer and a merchant. In politics he was a Republican.

LUTHER H. LUDLOW

Representative from Jackson County, 1877-8. Was born July 10, 1814, at Ludlowville, N. Y. He was educated in the common schools, and removed to Springport, Jackson County, in 1839. He served as Justice four terms; Supervisor from 1853 to 1861; in 1861-2 Register of Deeds; in 1869-70 County Treasurer, and in 1873-4 County Clerk of Jackson County. In politics he was a Republican. He died at Parma Village, Dec. 30, 1888.

SAMUEL LUDLOW

Representative from Wayne County, 1857-8. Was born in Ireland in 1815, and became a resident of Springwells in early life. He held the office of Justice of the Peace for many years, was a farmer by occupation, a Democrat in politics. He died Apr. 1, 1885.

LUKE LUGERS

Representative from the First District of Ottawa County, 1899-1900 and 1901-2, and Senator, 1906-7, from the Twenty-third District, comprising the counties of Muskegon and Ottawa. Was born in Laketown Township, Allegan County,

Mich., Feb. 2, 1853, of Holland parentage. His early education was acquired in
the public schools which he attended winters, and worked on a farm summers.
He subsequently attended the Otsego and Wayland Normals, and taught school
seventeen years. He served as Supervisor of Laketown and of Holland Township, Ottawa County; also held the offices of Township Clerk, School Inspector
and Justice of the Peace. He was bookkeeper for five years and afterwards
bought an interest in the lumber business known as the Scott-Lugers Lumber
Company of which he was either secretary or manager. Married and an elder
in the Reformed Church. In politics an active Republican.

GEORGE L. LUSK

Representative from the Second District of Bay (West Bay City), 1897-8 and
1899-1900. Was born in Oswego, N. Y., Nov. 18, 1866, and moved to West
Bay City five years later. His education was acquired in the public schools of
that city, supplemented by a year at Albion College. He began active life when
thirteen years of age, as a newsboy, two years later took up the study of pharmacy in a local drug store, and remained almost continuously in the drug business for twelve years, three years of this time as the proprietor of a pharmacy
at Owosso. In 1891 he was united in marriage to Miss Alta M. Ludington of
West Bay City, and in 1893, having disposed of the drug business he had established in his home city, he entered the journalistic field, assuming the management of the West Bay City *Tribune*. He continued in the newspaper work until
elected City Recorder in April, 1894, and was re-elected to the same office in
1896. Mr. Lusk is a prominent worker in the fraternal field, being a member
of several orders. In politics he is a Republican. He was appointed Deputy
Secretary of State by Coleman C. Vaughan; resigned December, 1918, to become
secretary of the Public Domain Commission in place of A. C. Carton, resigned.

JOHN J. LUSK

Representative from the First District of Kalamazoo County, 1889-90 and
1891-2. Was born in the township of Hunter, Greene County, State of New
York, Oct. 30, 1828. He moved with his parents at the age of six years to
Albany County, removing to Niagara County two years later, where, on a farm,
he grew up to manhood, receiving such an education as the common schools
at that time afforded. He moved to Michigan in 1854, working on the farm
and teaching school winters, until June, 1857, when he went to California and
Oregon, remaining about two years, returning to Michigan in the spring of 1859,
settling in the township of Oshtemo, Kalamazoo County, on a farm. He was
formerly a Whig in politics, voted with the Republican party at its first election
after organization, and continued to vote the Republican ticket. He was elected
to and filled most of the township offices, holding the office of Supervisor for
ten terms, the last six in succession.

GEORGE LUTHER

Representative from Ottawa County, 1863-4 and 1865. Was born in Bristol,
R. I., May 3, 1823. By occupation he was a merchant, in politics a Republican.
He came to Grand Rapids, Mich., in 1841. He removed to Lamont, Ottawa
County. He resigned as Representative Feb. 25, 1865. He died Dec. 23, 1884.

FRANK A. LYON

Senator, 1899-1900, from the Sixth District, comprising the counties of St. Joseph, Branch and Hillsdale. Was born at Walworth, Wayne County, N. Y., Jan. 4, 1855. His father, Newton T. Lyon, removed to Michigan a year later, and the family settled on a farm in the township of Quincy, Branch County. The subject of this sketch was educated in the country schools of Quincy and Butler townships, Branch County, until 18 years of age, when he attended the Quincy and Coldwater high schools, and graduated from the Northern Indiana Normal School at Valparaiso, Ind. He worked at farming and carpenter work in the meantime, taught school winters until 1877, and then taught one year in a graded school. He was married in 1878, and subsequently studied law with Hon. Charles Upson of Coldwater; was admitted to the bar in February, 1880, and received an appointment as clerk at the Winnebago Indian agency, Nebraska, in March of that year, which he held until August. He then returned to Michigan and commenced the practice of law in Montcalm County in November, 1880. His wife died in December, 1881. He remained at Stanton until February, 1886, and then returned to the old home at Quincy on account of ill health, remaining until July 14, 1891, when he removed to Hillsdale, succeeded A. B. St. John in the practice of law. He was married a second time, in August, 1885, to Emma Fink of Ionia. While in Stanton he served on the County Board of School Examiners about three years; in Branch County was elected Circuit Court Commissioner one term, and declined re-election; and was Village Attorney of Quincy one year, declining re-election. September, 1898, Mr. Lyon engaged in the mercantile business in Hillsdale. He was nominated for the Senate of 1899-1900 against his protest, and was elected. He died at Hillsdale Oct. 14, 1891.

FRANK B. LYON

Representative of the First District of Houghton County, 1893-4. Was born in Newman, Ill., in 1859. He engaged in the hardware business at Calumet; Colonel of the 5th Infantry Michigan State Troops. In politics a Republican.

LUCIUS LYON

Territorial Delegate in Congress, 1833-5; United States Senator, 1836-40; Member of the Board of Regents of the University of Michigan, 1837-9; and Member of Congress, 1843-5. Was born at Shelburne Falls, Vt., Feb. 26, 1800. He received a common school education and studied engineering and surveying. He came to Detroit in 1822, and was appointed by the Surveyor General, Deputy in the territory northwest of the Ohio. He held the position until elected to Congress in 1832. In 1840, after his senatorial term, he removed to Grand Rapids, where he had large land interests. In 1845, he was appointed Surveyor General of Ohio, Michigan and Indiana, and removed to Detroit, holding the position until his death. In politics he was a Democrat, in religion a Swedenborgian. He never married. He died at Detroit, Sept. 24, 1851.

TRUMAN H. LYON

Senator from the Twenty-fourth District, 1853-4. Was born at Shelburne, Vt., Feb. 24, 1801. He had the advantages of common schools, learned the business of a cloth dresser, and carried on that business at Hopkinton, N. Y. He was early a Justice of the Peace. In 1836 he came to Lyons, Mich., where he kept hotel, was Justice, Side Judge, and held other local offices. He was also in United States employ and was superintendent of light-houses on Lake Michigan and let the contracts for their construction. He moved to Grand Rapids in 1840, where he kept hotel and was a merchant, and for many years Postmaster. He was a leading business man, and prominent Mason. He died Sept. 14, 1872.

GEORGE C. McALLISTER

Representative from Barry County, 1879-80. Was born in Norfolk, N. Y., June 12, 1833. He received a common school education; came to Hickory Corners, Mich., in 1856. In 1860 he went to Sonora, Calif., and worked in the mines four years. He returned to Michigan in 1864. He removed to Ft. Wayne, Ind., and engaged in insurance business, first as Deputy secretary, afterwards as director and general agent of the Fort Wayne Insurance Company. Returning to Prairieville, Mich., in 1866, he engaged in farming. In politics a National.

AARON VANCE McALVAY

Justice of the Supreme Court, 1905-15. Was born at Ann Arbor, Washtenaw County, Mich., July 19, 1847. His early years when not in school, were spent on his father's farm. Mr. McAlvay received his early education in the public schools of Ann Arbor, being graduated in 1864. He was graduated from the literary department of the University of Michigan in 1868, with the degree of A.B., and in 1869 from the law department with the degree of LL.B. He taught school for one year before graduation, located at Manistee in 1871, and began the practice of law, continuing his practice until 1878, when he was appointed judge of the Nineteenth Judicial Circuit to fill vacancy caused by the resignation of Hon H. H. Wheeler. At the expiration of the term he returned to practice and continued the same until June, 1901, when he was appointed judge of the same circuit, and was elected November, 1902, without opposition. He was appointed a non-resident lecturer in the law department of the University of Michigan in 1897 and filled that position until his resignation in October, 1903. In 1910 the University of Michigan conferred upon him the degree of LL. D. Mr. McAlvay was united in marriage with Miss Barbara Bassler of Ann Arbor in 1872. He was elected Justice of the Supreme Court for the three year term, Nov. 8, 1904, and re-elected for the full term April 1, 1907. He died at Lansing, July 9, 1915.

GEORGE ELMER McARTHUR

Representative from Eaton County, 1917-18; and Senator, 1921-2, from the Fifteenth District, comprising the counties of Barry, Clinton and Eaton. Was born at Irving, Barry County, Mich., Sept. 25, 1877, of Scotch-German descent. He acquired his preliminary educational training in the public schools of Grand Rapids, Albion and Eaton Rapids. He left high school and enlisted as a volunteer in Co. B, 32nd Michigan, in the Spanish-American War, and after the close of the war worked as salesman and prospected in Wyoming until 1901, when he entered the law department of the University of Michigan and graduated in 1905, with the degree of LL.B., and at once began the practice of law at Eaton Rapids. During the World War he served with the 16th Co., C. O. T. S. Mr. McArthur is married. In politics a Republican, and has served as City Attorney of Eaton Rapids.

WILLIAM McARTHUR

Representative from Cheboygan and other counties, 1877-8. Was born in Steuben County, N. Y., April 13, 1825. He received an academical education, and was a resident of Rochester, N. Y., 1860-70, and of Chicago, Ill., 1870-3. He settled at Cheboygan, Mich., in 1873. After 1850 he was largely engaged as a contractor on railroads, canals, etc. After 1866 he was the head of a large lumber firm at Cheboygan. In politics he was a Democrat.

JAMES H. McAULEY

Representative from the First District of Wayne County, 1905-6. Was born in Macomb County, Mich., July 1, 1855, of Irish parentage. He received his education in the public schools of Detroit. Mr. McAuley practiced dentistry for several years. Married. In politics a Republican.

CHARLES HAMILTON McBRIDE

Representative from the First District of Ottawa County, 1911-12 and 1913-14. Was born at Lansing, Mich., Aug. 30, 1874, of American parentage. He was educated in the Holland High School, Hope and Olivet Colleges, graduating from the latter in 1894. In 1896, he graduated from the law department of the University of Michigan. He was married Aug. 16, 1899, to Emily L. Lowing. Mr. McBride began to practice law on July 5, 1896. In politics a Republican.

CHARLES R. McCABE

Representative from the First District of Marquette County, 1909-10. Was born at Rockland, Ontonagon County, Mich., Apr. 3, 1867, of Irish descent. He acquired his education in the Marquette schools. Married. Occupation, a bookkeeper. In politics a Republican. He held the office of Supervisor.

JAMES McCABE

Senator from the Sixth District, 1848-9. His postoffice address was Pontiac. (Further data not obtainable).

ARTHUR McCAIN

Representative from the First District of Jackson County, 1905-6. Was born in Summit Township, Jackson County, Mich., June 17, 1865, of Scotch and Irish descent. He entered the public school of Jackson in 1879, and graduated in 1885. He then attended the University of Michigan until 1887, when he engaged in farming for twelve years, and in 1899 moved to the city of Jackson and took up the real estate business. In 1904 he was appointed secretary of the Jackson Business Men's Association. In politics a Republican. He was Supervisor of Summit Township in 1898.

LYMAN H. McCALL

Representative from the Second District of Eaton County, 1899-1900 and 1901-2. Was born in Delaware County, N. Y., Aug. 31, 1860, and received his early education in the schools of that county. He removed to Michigan in 1877 and located in Eaton County, graduating from Olivet College. He subsequently entered the law office of Judge Edward A. Foote of Charlotte and was admitted to practice by the Circuit Court of Charlotte in 1883, after which time he was in the active practice of law, residing in that city. He was elected and served as Prosecuting Attorney of Eaton County for the years 1893-4. In politics a Republican.

THOMAS W. McCALL

Representative from the Second District of St. Clair County, 1905-6 and 1907-8. Was born Nov. 17, 1849, of Scotch and Irish descent. He acquired his education in the district schools at Columbus. He was engaged in farming for a period of thirty years, and in later years interested in grain and elevator business. In politics an active Republican. He held the offices of Treasurer for two years, Supervisor of Riley Township for seven years, and was chairman of the Board of Supervisors for two years.

GEORGE PERCY McCALLUM

Representative, 1899-1900 and 1901-2, from the Delta District, comprising the counties of Alger, Schoolcraft and Delta. Was born at Lapeer, Mich., Mar. 27, 1871. His childhood and youth were spent at his birthplace and in Ogemaw and Delta counties, graduating at the West Branch High School in June, 1890, and entering Albion College in the fall of the same year to prepare for the University. In the fall of 1895 he entered the law department of the University of Michigan, graduating in June, 1898, with the degree of L.B. In the intervals of his studies he was engaged in various capacities by the Delta Lumber Co., of which his father, John H. McCallum, was superintendent, and to help out his cash account he worked in the pineries as a scaler. While at Ann Arbor Mr. McCallum was president of the U. of M. Republican Club. He was also chairman of the executive committee of the National League of College Republican Clubs and a member of the advisory council of the Republican State League of Michigan; a member of the County Board of School Examiners of his county; greatly interested in fraternal societies, being a Freemason, a Pythian, and a Maccabee.

JOHN H. McCALLUM

Representative, 1907-8, from the Schoolcraft District, comprising the counties of Alger, Luce, Mackinac and Schoolcraft. Was born at Mumford, Monroe County, N. Y., Oct. 10, 1846, of Scotch, Dutch and English descent. He attended the common schools of Avon, N. Y., and of Ont., Canada. He removed with his parents to Arnprior, Ont., in 1858. At the age of seventeen he went into the lumber woods and engaged in the lumber business in various capacities from teamster to manager of logging and manufacturing concerns for thirty-seven years. Married. He came to Michigan in 1868, settling in Flint, moved to Lapeer in 1870, to Ogemaw County in 1881, and to Schoolcraft County in 1892, where he resided in 1907. He was manager of the Delta Lumber Co. at Thompson until 1898, and in 1899 removed to Manistique. He engaged in real estate and newspaper business for several years; a member of the Board of Supervisors in the counties of Ogemaw and Schoolcraft, School Director, Township Treasurer, Justice of the Peace and U. S. Commissioner. In politics a Republican.

SANDS McCAMLEY

Representative from Calhoun County, 1837 and 1843; and Senator from the Sixth District, 1839-40. Was born in Orleans County, N. Y., and came to Nottawa Prairie, Mich., in 1831, then went to Marshall, and in 1834 bought land forming part of the site of Battle Creek, Gen. Convis being his partner. He dug the long race, built a saw mill and made other improvements. He was Representative in place of Ezra Convis resigned in 1837. He was County Associate Judge, 1883-6. He was a man of intellect, sagacity, sound judgment and resolute will. He died Apr. 30, 1864.

JOHN J. McCARTHY

Representative, 1903-4, 1905-6 and 1907-8, from the Iosco District, composed of the counties of Iosco, Alcona, Arenac and Ogemaw. Was born in the Township of Pine River, Gratiot County, Mich., Jan. 7, 1858, his parents being among the first settlers of that county. He was educated in the common schools of the township and the St. Louis High School. He studied law in an office in St. Louis, Mich., and was admitted to the bar in 1884. He was elected Circuit Court Commissioner for Gratiot County for the term of 1885-6. He moved to Mio, Oscoda County, in 1887, and was elected Prosecuting Attorney for the terms of 1889-90 and 1891-2. He located in Standish, Arenac County, in 1896, and was elected Prosecuting Attorney for the term of 1899-1900. He was united in marriage to Miss Gertrude E. Barden, in 1886. In politics a Republican.

THOMAS McCARTY

Representative from Saginaw County, 1850. Was born in Boston, Mass., Sept. 10, 1810. He came with his father to Saginaw County in 1835, and settled as a farmer in the township of Tittabawassee. He was several terms a Supervisor. In politics he was a Democrat. He died Sept. 22, 1855.

WILLIAM McCAULEY

Senator from the Twenty-seventh District, 1853-4. His postoffice address was Brighton. (Further data not obtainable).

HUGH McCLELEND

Representative from Wayne County, 1885-6. Was born in Toronto, Ont., Oct. 27, 1851; received a common school education; learned the trade of cigar making, and removed to Detroit in 1871. In 1872 he took a trip east, working in several towns in New York State; returned to Detroit in 1875, where he remained working at his trade. In politics Labor-Republican.

ROBERT McCLELLAND

Delegate from Monroe County to the Constitutional Conventions of 1835 and 1850, and from Wayne County to the Constitutional Convention of 1867; member of the Board of Regents of the University of Michigan, 1837 and 1850-2; Representative from Monroe County, 1838, 1840 and 1843; member of Congress, 1843-5 to 1847-9; and Governor of Michigan, 1851-3. Was born at Greencastle, Pa., Aug. 2, 1807. As a teacher he acquired means to take the course at Dickinson College, Carlisle, Pa., from which he graduated in 1829, and in 1831 was admitted to the bar at Chambersburg, Pa., coming to Monroe, Mich., in 1833. He there entered upon practice. He was speaker *pro tem.* of the House in 1839, and speaker in 1843. He was appointed member of the Board of Regents of the University in 1837, but resigned the same year; was re-appointed in 1850 for a two-year term. In 1851, he was elected Governor of the State for the short term of one year, and in 1852 re-elected for the term of two years; 1853, appointed Mar. 4, Secretary of the Interior by President Pierce, serving the full term of four years, having of necessity resigned the office of Governor, the term extending to Dec. 31, 1854, being filled by Lieutenant Governor Parsons. During his congressional term Gov. McClelland was a member and then chairman of the committee on commerce, and favored and procured in some degree legislation for the improvement of lake harbors. Gov. McClelland supported John Quincy Adams in his demand for the right of petition, and voted to receive a bill offered by Mr. Giddings for the abolition of slavery in the District of Columbia, also supported the "Wilmot Proviso," designed to prohibit slavery in newly acquired territory. As Secretary of the Interior, Gov. McClelland introduced many reforms, and his administration of the department was above reproach. He was a delegate to the National Conventions in 1848 and 1852. At the close of his term as Secretary of the Interior he settled in Detroit, doing some office practice, though mainly giving his attention to private business. He made a European tour in 1870, and died at his home in Detroit, Aug. 30, 1880.

JAMES McCLOY

Representative from the Fourth District of Wayne County, 1891-2. Was born in Buffalo, N. Y., Mar. 5, 1853. He formerly worked in the rolling mills. He was elected to the House of 1891-2 on the Democratic ticket. He was a widower in 1891.

JAY ROBERT McCOLL

Member of the State Board of Agriculture, 1922—. Was born on a farm in Webster Township, Washtenaw County, Michigan, March 24, 1867, of Scotch parentage. He received his early education in the district school at Webster, and high school at Ann Arbor. He graduated from the mechanical engineering department at M. A. C. in 1890. Later he took up a post graduate course at Cornell University. For a number of years he was head of the mechanical engineering department of the University of Tennessee, going from there to Purdue University, Indiana, where he became head of the steam engineering department. In 1905 he came to Detroit as chief engineer of the American Blower Company, which position he held until 1910, when he became consulting engineer for the city of Detroit and still acts in that capacity. He is a member of various clubs and societies. Mr. McColl is married and has one daughter. April 4, 1922, he was appointed by Governor Groesbeck to fill the unexpired term of John A. Doelle, resigned.

AUGUSTIN C. McCORMICK

Senator, 1891-2, from the Fourth District, comprising Washtenaw and Monroe counties. Was born on Mar. 3, 1862. He attended the district school winters and worked upon the farm in the summer season until the age of nineteen, when he applied for and received a certificate to teach in the public schools of Monroe County; taught three winters, when he entered the Normal School at Ypsilanti to better improve himself as a teacher, which he intended to make a life work; but was called home by the failing health of his father to take charge of the farm upon which he resided, and taught winters. He was elected to the Senate of 1891-2, on the Democratic ticket.

HENRY F. McCORMICK

Representative from Kent County, 1879-80. Was born July 18, 1844, at Alcott, N. Y. He removed with his father's family to Grand Rapids, in 1856. He was in the army during the war. He was Supervisor of Grand Rapids five terms. He received an academical education. Occupation, farming. Politics Greenback.

JAMES W. McCORMICK

Representative from the First District of Allegan County, 1885-6 and 1887-8; and Senator, 1889-90, from the Tenth District, comprising the counties of Allegan and Van Buren. Was born in Allegan County, Mich., Feb. 22, 1838. He was a lawyer and subsequently a farmer and fruit grower. He held the offices of Supervisor, Justice of the Peace, and was president of the Fennville Mining Company, which was incorporated under the laws of this State.

HENRY McCOWEN

Representative from the First District of Hillsdale County, 1869-70. His post-office address was Moscow. (Further data not obtainable).

DANIEL McCOY

State Treasurer, 1901-3 and 1903-5. Was born in Philadelphia, Pa., July 17, 1845, and received his education in the public schools of that city. In 1867 he came to Michigan, locating at Romeo, Macomb County, where he engaged in the grain business and the furnishing of supplies to the lumber regions. He sold out the business in 1872, and began lumbering on the south branch of the Manistee River. In 1873 he settled in Clam Lake—now Cadillac—and continued in the lumbering business for ten years, holding in the meantime the office of President of the village of Clam Lake, and later that of Mayor of Cadillac. In 1883 he removed to Grand Rapids, where he organized the Edison Light Company in 1886, and the State Bank of Michigan in 1892, and was interested in other enterprises. Mr. McCoy was married in 1879. A Republican in politics.

HARRY N. McCRACKEN

Representative from the First District, Oakland County, 1905-6 and 1907-8. Was born on a farm in the township of Farmington, Oakland County, Mich., July 14, 1865. His early life was spent on the farm on which he was born, working summers and attending district school in the winter until he received sufficient education to qualify him as a teacher. He taught district school for seven years and attended the State Normal School at Ypsilanti, and Cleary's Business College of the same place. He was Superintendent of the Farmington High School for seven years, and resigned to become editor and proprietor of the Farmington *Enterprise*, which paper he conducted for two years. He then returned to the farm and followed that occupation. In August, 1902, he was married to Isabella F. McKenzie of Pictou, Nova Scotia. He held the offices of Village Trustee, member of the School Board, a member of the Board of County Examiners. In politics a Republican.

WILLIAM B. McCREERY

State Treasurer, 1875-7 and 1877-9; and member of the State Board of Agriculture, 1887-90. Was born at Mt. Morris, N. Y., Aug. 27, 1826. He came with his father to Genesee County, Mich., in 1838, and received a common school and academical education. He worked in his father's saw-mill until 1852, then was chief clerk to his father, as County Treasurer, six years. He studied law, was admitted in 1860, and began practice at Flint. He went into service as a private in 1861 in the 2d Mich. Infantry. He was gradually promoted to Lieutenant Colonel, was transferred to the 21st Michigan, and became Colonel. He was three times wounded, and confined in Libby Prison, from which he made his escape. He resigned from ill health in 1864, the acceptance by Gen. Thomas being the most noteworthy received by a Michigan soldier. After the war he engaged in lumbering and in the mercantile and banking business. In politics a Republican. He was Mayor of Flint, 1865-6, and in 1871-4 Internal Revenue Collector; was appointed member of the State Board of Agriculture Jan. 12, 1887, and resigned Apr. 10, 1890.

HUGH McCURDY

Senator from the Twenty-third District, 1865-6. Was born in Hamilton, Scotland, in 1829. He came with his parents to Birmingham, Mich., in 1837. He learned the trade of cooper, and worked at it for years. He attended select school, was a freight agent, and from 1847 taught several years. He attended Romeo Academy, studied law, was admitted in 1854, settled in practice at Corunna. He was Prosecuting Attorney, Judge of Probate, many years Supervisor, and from 1865-73, president of the national bank at Corunna. In politics he was a Democrat. A prominent Mason, he held all the high offices in that order, and was grand generalissimo of the grand encampment of the United States. He laid the corner stone of the state capitol as grand master in 1872.

WARREN McCUTCHEON

Representative from Hillsdale County, 1867-8. Was born at Epsom, N. H., Sept. 17, 1815. By occupation he was a farmer; in politics, a Whig until 1854, then a Republican. He emigrated to Ohio where he held local offices, and settled at Ransom, Hillsdale County. He was ten years Supervisor. He died May 10, 1876.

JOHN McDERMID

Senator from the Fourteenth District, 1861-2. Was born in Ballston, N. Y., in 1808. He was a farmer and miller, and a Republican in politics. He came from Livingston County, N. Y., in 1835, and settled in Cambria, Hillsdale County. The village of Cambria Mills takes its name from the mills built by him. When he settled there were no traces of civilization. He died May 16, 1868.

JOHN McDERMOTT

Representative from Wayne County, 1859-60. Was born in Enniskillen, Ireland, in 1826, and came to Detroit in 1844. He was a ship-builder by occupation and was connected with vessel interests until 1861, when he raised a company which was mustered into the service as Company "A" of the 23d Ill. Infantry, and formed part of the famous "Mulligan brigade," in the war of the rebellion. He was taken prisoner at the siege of Lexington, Mo., resigned his captaincy in November, 1861, and in January, 1862, was appointed Lieutenant Colonel of the 15th Mich. Infantry, serving until Sept. 18, 1863, when he was mustered out at his own request. In 1864 Col. McDermott removed to Bay City, and was Deputy Collector of Customs at that port from 1866 to 1883. He was later engaged in the insurance business at Bay City. He was a Democrat prior to and during his legislative term, but a Republican during and since the war. He died at Bay City, July 9, 1910.

JAMES McDONALD

Representative from Lenawee County, 1840 and 1846. Was born Aug. 11, 1796. He was a farmer; in politics a Whig. He settled in Lenawee County, Mich., in 1837. He died Aug. 19, 1848.

JOHN SAMUEL McDONALD

Justice of the Supreme Court, 1922—. Was born in the province of Ontario, Canada, February 8, 1865, of Scotch parentage. He received his education in Victoria University, Ontario, and the University of Michigan. He served as Prosecuting Attorney of Kent county for two terms, and as Circuit Judge of the seventeenth judicial circuit for fourteen years, when he was appointed to fill the vacancy on the supreme bench caused by the death of John W. Stone. At the general election, November 7, 1922, he was elected to fill the unexpired term. Mr. McDonald is married and has one son.

JOHN McDONELL

Member of the Legislative Council from Wayne County, 1826-7 to 1834-5; Delegate from the First District to the Constitutional Convention of 1835; Delegate from Wayne County to the First Convention of Assent, 1836; and Senator from the First District, 1835-6 and 1837-8. Was a native of Scotland, born in 1779. The time of his coming to Michigan is not known, but he was in business in Detroit during the War of 1812, and thoroughly Americanized. His name appears with those of other residents signed to a protest against an order of the British commandant, Proctor (after Hull's surrender), requiring a number of leading citizens to leave the country. He also rendered much benevolent service in ransoming American captives from the Indians during the British occupation. He was appointed an Associate Justice of the County Territorial Court in 1817, and Collector of the port of Detroit, 1839-41. He was president of the fifth and sixth Territorial Legislatures. He resigned as Senator on Mar. 23, 1838. He held besides, the local offices of Alderman, Justice, etc. Politically he was in sympathy with the National administration during the period of his public life. He died Oct. 1, 1846.

MALCOMB McDOUGALL

Representative from Washtenaw County, 1853-4. Was born in the State of New York, in May, 1813. He was a farmer; in politics a Democrat. He came to Bridgewater in 1838, where he resided in 1887. He was a Justice in that town for thirty-six years.

ARCHIBALD McEACHERN

Representative, 1911-12, from the Schoolcraft District, comprising the counties of Alger, Luce, Mackinac and Schoolcraft. Was born in Argyleshire, Scotland, Jan. 10, 1844, of Highland Scotch parentage. He came to America with his parents in 1852, and was educated in the common schools of Middlesex County, Ont. In 1873 he was married to Miss Mary Lowe, of Elgin, Ont. Mrs. McEachern died in 1906. He held the offices of County Treasurer and was County Clerk. In politics a Republican.

FRED F. McEACHRON

Representative from the Second District of Ottawa County, 1923—. Was born in Jamestown Township, Ottawa County, September 1, 1875, of Scotch-English parentage. He acquired his education in the public schools of Ottawa County and the high school of Lansing. He served for ten years as Deputy County Clerk of Ottawa County, after which he was elected and served two terms as Clerk. He has also held the offices of Alderman of the city of Grand Haven, Justice of the Peace, member of the Township Board, treasurer of the Board of Education and has served as Under-sheriff. In 1911 he organized the Hudsonville State Bank and has been its cashier from that time until the present. Mr. McEachron is an active member of the Congregational church and is a thirty-second degree Mason. In 1900 he was married to Jennie Pellegrom, of Grand Haven, and they have one daughter.

CROCKETT McELROY

Senator from the Twenty-first District, 1877-8 and 1879-80. Was born Dec. 31, 1835, near Dundas, Ont. He received a common school education; came to Michigan in 1848; lived about five years in Detroit; ten years in St. Clair County; ten years in Macomb County, then in St. Clair City. He was Supervisor, Justice, School Inspector and Commissioner of Highways, Village Trustee, a Postmaster, and Mayor of St. Clair City. He was clerk, teacher, merchant and manufacturer. For many years he was extensively engaged in the manufacture of cut staves and circled heading, and president and general manager of the Marine City Stave Company. He published a volume of poems, history, on Great Lakes and some novels. In politics he was a Republican. He died at home of his daughter, Mrs. E. H. Recor, Baltimore, Md., Dec. 6, 1919; buried at St. Clair, Mich.

FRANK McELROY

Representative from the First District of St. Clair County, 1889-90. Was born in the township of Ira, St. Clair County, Mich., Nov. 13, 1854, lived in New Baltimore, Macomb County, ten years. He attended public schools and graduated from Goldsmith, Bryant & Stratton's Business University at Detroit in 1873; went to Marine City in 1874. He was secretary of the Marine City Stave Company eight years, and engaged in the hardware business in 1885; identified with business since sixteen years of age. He held the offices of School Inspector, Village Treasurer, Township Treasurer, and Village Trustee, and was induced to accept the Presidency of Marine City in 1886, being re-elected in 1887. In recognition of his services he was elected Marine City's first Mayor, July 11, 1887. He married Miss Susie Robertson, Mar. 12, 1885. In politics a Republican. At the opening of the session of the Legislature of 1889-90, Mr. McElroy filed a protest against the administration of the oath of office to Frederick Lindow on the ground of fraud, illegal voting and irregularities in the election which gave Mr. Lindow the certificate of election. The House of Representatives, after investigation by the Committee on Elections, on Mar. 27, 1889, by a vote of 56 to 30 declared Mr. McElroy to have been legally elected, and on the same day he was sworn in as a member.

WILLIAM H. McFADZEN

Representative from Manistee County, 1909-10. Was born at Chatham, Canada, Feb. 14, 1862, of Scotch parentage. When four years of age he came with his parents to Michigan and settled in Filer Township, Manistee County. He acquired his education in the public schools of Filer Township, which he attended until the age of fifteen. He then began work in the shingle mills, which work he followed as packer and jointer until 1889, when he engaged in the general merchandise business at Oak Hill, Filer Township. In politics a Republican. He was elected Supervisor of Filer Township in 1903, and was elected chairman of the board in 1907 and again in 1908.

DUNCAN McFARLANE

Representative from the First District of Wayne County, 1901-2. Was born in Harrisville, Alcona County, Mich., Mar. 16, 1869. His education was obtained in the public school at Au Sable, supplemented by one year at the State Normal. After leaving school he entered a grocery store, where he remained ten years and since then in the employ of the Street Railway Company. Unmarried. In politics a strong Republican. He was elected to the Legislature of 1901-2 on the general legislative ticket.

JAMES McFARLAN

Representative from Wayne County, 1847. Was a native of Scotland, born May 10, 1810. He came to the United States at the age of eighteen, residing for brief periods at Paterson, N. J., Hudson, N. Y., and Peru, Ill., and in 1839 settled in Greenfield, Mich. He was Supervisor ten years. He was a Democrat in politics, although voting for Fremont in 1856 and Lincoln in 1860. His occupation was that of a farmer. He died Mar. 30, 1880.

NEAL McGAFFEY

Representative from St. Joseph County, 1837. Settled at White Pigeon in 1829, and was the first lawyer in St. Joseph County, having been admitted to practice Aug. 17, 1830. He was one of the four who owned and recorded the plat of the village of White Pigeon in 1830. He taught the first school at White Pigeon in 1831. He built a house in 1830 and planted the first apple tree. He was Town Clerk in 1830-1, Justice of the Peace from 1829 to 1835, and was Public Prosecutor in 1839, and President of the village in 1837. After practicing over a quarter of a century he removed to Texas.

CHARLES WILLIAM McGILL

Representative from the First District of Kent County (Grand Rapids), 1897-8. Was born in Troy, Rensselaer County, N. Y., July 14, 1865, and is a lineal descendant from some of the most noted families of Scotland. In the spring of 1867 his parents came to Michigan and located on a farm in St. Joseph County. In 1885 he graduated from the White Pigeon Union School and immediately took up the study of law under private tutorage; came to Grand Rapids in the fall of 1886 and was admitted to practice Sept. 18, 1888, and engaged in the practice of his profession. In politics a Republican. He was elected Circuit Court Commissioner in 1892 and re-elected in 1894. His office expired Jan. 1, 1897. He was elected to the House of 1897-8 on the general legislative ticket of Grand Rapids.

WILL McGILLIVRAY

Representative 1917-18 and 1919-20, from the Iosco District, comprising the counties of Alcona, Arenac, Iosco and Ogemaw. Was born at Thornbury, Ont., Apr. 12, 1877, of Scotch-Irish parents, who removed to Oscoda, Mich., while he was an infant. At the age of fifteen he entered the office of the *Press*, the local Republican paper, of which he was the publisher for many years. He was Postmaster at Oscoda under three administrations. Married.

CHARLES H. McGINLEY

Senator, 1893-4, from the Twentieth District, comprising the counties of Sanilac and Huron. Was born in Kingston, N. Y., May 22, 1856. His early days were spent on a farm in the Adirondack Mountains, also working in the woods, log cutting and bark hauling; in the winters he attended school. He was married before his majority to Miss Effie E. Harrison, of Hague, N. Y., and soon afterwards came to Michigan, locating at Forestville, where he began work as photographer; he soon added to his business the retail of drugs, which he continued for three years, in the meantime privately engaged in the study of law. Persistency and hard labor admitted him to the bar of the State Court in 1878, and later to the United States Circuit. He soon acquired an extensive practice in his own and other counties of the State, and in 1888 moved his business to Minden City. Mr. McGinley made criminal law a specialty and was counsel and attorney in some of the largest murder and other criminal cases of the State. He held the office of Circuit Court Commissioner of Sanilac County, and was elected to the Senate of 1893-4 on the Republican ticket.

PATRICK McGINNIS

Representative from Wayne County, 1877-8. Was born in 1820, at the village of Aranghantareghan, Ireland. In 1834 he emigrated to the United States and settled at Mt. Clemens, Mich. He afterward removed to Detroit and went to work in the printing office of the old *Morning Post* in 1836. He subsequently went into the mercantile business, afterwards selling out and removing to Laingsburg, Mich., where he kept a general store and traded with the Indians. He returned to Detroit and went into the real estate auctioneering business. He was Deputy City Marshal and City Marshal, and for three years an Alderman. In politics he was a Democrat. Deceased.

JAMES McGONEGAL

Representative from Wayne County, 1871-2. Was a native of Ireland, born in 1821. He came to Detroit when a young man and engaged in active business, being for many years a wood dealer, receiving supplies by the cargo by means of the river boats. He was an Alderman, 1863-7. In politics he was a Democrat, although affiliating with the Greenbackers, 1876 to 1880. In business at Kansas City, Mo., in 1887.

DANIEL McGOVERN

Representative 1891-2, from the Osceola District, comprising the counties of Osceola and Missaukee. Was born in Ireland, Feb. 3, 1833, and came to America with his parents the next year. His mother died when he was nine years old and two years later he commenced the battle of life for himself. His early life was spent on a farm. He served in the Union Army during the War of the Rebellion as a private in the 3d N. Y. Light Artillery, and at the close of the war moved to Michigan and settled in Osceola County in 1868. He engaged in farming and in various other occupations. He was the Democratic candidate for Sheriff of Osceola County in 1876 and for Judge of Probate in 1884, in both instances suffering defeat with his party. He held the offices of Supervisor, Township Clerk and School Inspector, and Justice of the Peace. He was elected to the House of 1891-2 as a Democrat.

JONAS H. McGOWAN

Member of the Board of Regents of the University of Michigan, 1870-7; Senator from the Tenth District, 1873-4; and member of Congress, 1877-9 and 1879-81. Was born in Mahoning County, O., Apr. 2, 1837. He graduated at the Michigan University in 1861, became principal of the high school at Coldwater, in 1862 enlisted as a private in the 5th Mich. Cavalry, was Captain in the 9th Cavalry, and served until 1864. He studied law and was admitted to practice in 1867, graduating from Ann Arbor law school in 1868. He practiced at Coldwater, was Prosecuting Attorney four years, and Regent of the University from Jan. 1, 1870, until his resignation, Jan. 2, 1877. Politically he was a Republican. After two terms in Congress he took up his law practice in Washington, D. C., and was living in 1902.

JOHN W. McGRATH

Justice of the Supreme Court, 1891-5. Was born in Philadelphia, of Irish-Scotch extraction. In 1843 he removed to Detroit with his parents, where he resided for the next eleven years, putting in most of his spare time in storing up knowledge in the public schools. In 1854 his father bought 160 acres of wild land in Warren, Macomb County, whither John moved and spent the next seven years in clearing up 50 acres of the heaviest timber land in the State, and in splitting rails and cutting saw logs. He attended school one year after leaving Detroit, and in the winter of 1861 taught school at Warren for the munificent sum of $18 per month and boarded himself. In the spring of 1862 he entered Albion College, paying his tuition by work in the hay-fields at harvest time and by teaching winters at Parma, Jackson County, and Homer, Calhoun County. He entered the law department of the Michigan University in the fall of 1864, but the following March went to Detroit, and under General Flanigan obtained two months' employment in the Provost Marshal's office, and during this time attended a night course in a commercial college. Subsequent to the fall of 1867 he spent two years in commercial pursuits in the oil regions of Pennsylvania, giving up this, however, to complete his law course at Ann Arbor, and was a full-fledged lawyer in December, 1868. Until 1878 Mr. McGrath was a Republican. An active friend of the working man; under Gov. Begole's administration he organized the famous labor bureau, and was by the governor appointed

Labor Commissioner in June, 1883, serving until March, 1885, during which time he issued two annual reports. In 1882 he was made chairman of the Democratic County Convention, 1884, of the Congressional Committee, and in June, 1887, was appointed City Counselor by Mayor Chamberlain, which office he held until Dec. 15, 1890. While a Republican, Mr. McGrath was a member of the School Board from 1872 until 1877, and during his term of office worked much reform. A strong advocate of individual rights and personal liberty, he had implicit confidence in the people. He was nominated by the Democratic convention to fill the vacancy caused by the death of Judge Campbell, and elected.

HOMER McGRAW

Representative from the First District of Wayne County, 1915. Was born at New Baltimore, Mich., Jan. 26, 1856. He came to Detroit in 1850 and four years later married Miss Anna Anthony. Mr. McGraw was engaged in the insurance business and caring for the large McGraw estate; he also served as one of the City Estimators. He was very prominent in Masonic circles. He died at his home in Detroit, Jan. 27, 1915.

THOMAS McGRAW

Representative from Oakland County, 1847. Was born in County Armagh, Ireland, Mar. 1, 1783, where he learned the trade of linen weaving. Being dissatisfied with the union of Ireland and England, which took place early in 1801, he left Ireland that year and came to Orange County, N. Y., married and lived there, weaving and farming until 1830, when he removed to Bloomfield, Mich., settling on a farm where he died, April 19, 1858. He was a Democrat in politics.

WILLIAM T. McGRAW

Senator, 1899-1900, from the Fourth District, comprising the twelfth, fourteenth, and sixteenth wards of the city of Detroit, the city of Wyandotte, and the townships of Brownstown, Canton, Dearborn, Ecorse, Huron, Monguagon, Nankin, Romulus, Springwells, Sumpter, Taylor and Van Buren. Was born in Livonia Township, Wayne County, May 12, 1868. He was educated in the public schools of Plymouth, graduating from the high school of that village, and subsequently took a course in Detroit Business University. He served two years in the First National Bank of Plymouth, and then accepted a position as traveling salesman for the Globe Tobacco Company, subsequently organizing the Detroit Tobacco Company. He engaged in the tobacco business and was also chairman of the Globe Cash Register Company, of which invention he was the patentee. He served in the City Council of Detroit as a representative of the twelfth ward.

JAMES E. McGREGOR

Senator, 1913-14, from the Twelfth District, comprising the counties of Oakland and Washtenaw. Was born at Landreth, Ont., Aug. 12, 1858, of Scotch parents. He was educated in the grammar schools and at business college. Married. He engaged in the retail dry goods business in Ypsilanti. He held various offices as follows: City Clerk, member Board of Public Works, member of Park Commission, chairman Board of County Auditors and Probate Register. In politics a Democrat.

JOHN A. McGREGOR

Representative from the Fourth District of Saginaw County, 1885-6, 1887-8 and 1889-90. Was born in the township of Tittabawassee, in that county, Sept. 7, 1839. His father and two uncles were the first settlers in what now comprises the township of Tittabawassee, they having removed from Scotland in 1833 and settled in Michigan while it was still a Territory. His father was accidentally killed by a falling tree while clearing his farm, leaving a widow with six children, four of whom were younger than the subject of this sketch, who was not then ten years old. Mr. McGregor received a common school education. His principal occupation was farming. In politics a Republican. He held the offices of Township Treasurer, Supervisor, member of the House of Representatives in 1885-6, and again in 1887-8, and was re-elected for 1889-90.

JAMES R. McGURK

Representative from St. Clair County, 1879-80; and Senator from the Twenty-first District, 1881-2. Was born in Belfast, Ireland, Mar. 16, 1843. He came with his parents to Hamilton, Canada, in 1848. He received a good education and studied medicine in Canada, Ann Arbor and Detroit. He was a teacher six years. He graduated at the Detroit Medical College and in 1870 commenced practice at Capac, Mich. He was many years Town Superintendent of Schools. In politics he was a Republican.

DONALD McINTYRE

Representative from Washtenaw County, 1855-6; and member of the Board of Regents of the University of Michigan, 1858-64. Was born in Johnstown, N. Y., June 5, 1807. He received a common school and academical education, studied law, was admitted in 1826, and commenced practice. He was the first Judge of the new county of Fulton. He opened a banking office at Ann Arbor, Mich., in 1845, and continued in that business until 1872, then returned to Johnstown, N. Y., and was president of the Johnstown bank. In politics he was a Republican. He died at Ann Arbor, Dec. 21, 1891.

DUGALD McINTYRE

Representative from Sanilac County, 1881-2. Was born in Argyleshire, Scotland, July 15, 1840. He received a common school education; came to Michigan in the fall of 1860, and engaged in lumbering. He later engaged in farming. He was elected Supervisor of the township of Argyle in 1878, which office he held several years. He was chairman of the Board of Supervisors. Politically a Republican.

GEORGE R. McKAY

Representative from Calhoun County, 1865-6. Was born in 1817, and came to Michigan in 1852. He purchased and lived upon a farm in Marengo, Calhoun County. He was Supervisor, master of the Grange. He moved to Kansas but returned to Marengo in 1888. He died in Marengo, Mar. 21, 1890.

JOHN McKAY

Representative from Macomb County, 1909-10 and 1911-12. Was born in Bruce Township, Macomb County, Aug. 16, 1843. His father, Robert McKay, was a native of Scotland, descendant of a long line of Scottish ancestry. Mr. McKay received his education in the common schools. On Feb. 21, 1866, he was married to Miss Lucinda E. Day. In the spring of 1866, Mr. McKay moved to a farm of his own in the township of Armadia, and the next year commenced the breeding of shorthorn cattle, of which he made a specialty for thirty years. In 1900 Mr. McKay located at Romeo. Always interested in matters pertaining to agriculture, he was a member of the Armadia Agricultural Society for a number of years, and was its president for four years; also a member of the executive committee of the State Agricultural Society. Other offices of honor and trust held by him—President of the Macomb County Farmers' Mutual Fire Insurance Company; first vice president of the Romeo Savings Bank, and member of the State Live Stock Sanitary Commission. In politics he was a Republican. He died Feb. 21, 1916.

WILLIAM McKAY

Representative from Tuscola County, 1889-90, 1899-1900, 1901-2 and 1905-6; and Senator, 1907-8, from the Twenty-first District, comprising the counties of Lapeer and Tuscola. Was born in Ayrshire, Scotland, Sept. 9, 1840, his education being acquired in the schools at Kilmarnock, Scotland. In April, 1854, he immigrated to the United States, coming direct to Almont, Lapeer County. Jan. 1, 1863, he was married to Mary A. Mackie, at Romeo, Mich. In 1876 he removed to Dayton Township, Tuscola County, where he followed farming. He was elected Supervisor in 1877 and held that office six consecutive years. He was elected Sheriff in 1882 and held that office two terms. In politics a Republican.

ROBERT G. McKEE

Representative from Clinton and other counties, 1839. Was born in Arlington, Vt., Jan. 10, 1813. He received an academical education and attended Rensselaer Institute, at Troy, N. Y. He came to Michigan in 1836, and followed his profession, surveying roads and farms in the central part of the State. While a resident of DeWitt, he was nominated by the Democrats, being the youngest member of that body, his district comprising Genesee, Shiawassee and Clinton counties. In 1852 he went overland to California, where he remained until 1856. Of late years he followed farming, and lived in the village of Laingsburg.

SILAS D. McKEEN*

Representative from Lapeer County, 1837. Came to Lapeer County from New Hampshire and began practice. He had ability and would have risen to wealth and high station except for his habits. He died prior to 1887.

JAMES E. McKEON

Representative from the Second District of Bay County, 1919-20 and 1921-2. Was born in Essex County, Ont., in 1881, of Irish and French parents. He came to Michigan with his parents in 1893 and located on a farm near Pinconning, where he now resides. His education was obtained in the public schools of Bay County. Mr. McKeon is married. He has held township offices several years and is at present Clerk of Fraser Township. He is a member of the Pomona Grange. In politics he is a Republican.

JOHN Q. McKERNAN

Representative from Houghton and Keweenaw counties, 1863-4 to 1869-70; and Delegate from Houghton County to the Constitutional Convention of 1867. Was born in Little Britain, N. Y., Jan 10, 1823. He came to Washtenaw County in 1832, lived in White Oak from 1837 to 1848, then removed to Houghton County, lived in several towns there, and was Postmaster at L'Anse. In politics he was a Democrat. He was four years Sheriff of Houghton County, was Supervisor, Justice, Village President, Superintendent of the Poor, and held many other offices. By trade he was a carpenter, but was a lumberman, surface agent of copper mines, etc.

ANTHONY McKEY

Senator from the Second District, 1837-8. Was born in Delhi, N. Y., Jan. 3, 1800. When nine years old his father removed to Chemung County, N. Y., where he worked until eighteen, when he commenced teaching school. He came to Michigan in 1826, taught school for a time at Monroe, and in 1828 settled on a farm in Deerfield (then Blissfield). In 1828 he was appointed Postmaster at Kedzie's Grove (now Deerfield), and held that position until his death, Jan. 28, 1849. He was a surveyor and prominent contractor on the Lake Shore Road, located and surveyed several state roads, and was seven years a Supervisor. In politics he was a Democrat, and an intimate friend of Cass, Barry and McClelland.

JAMES L. McKIE

Representative from Berrien County, 1885-7. Was born in Neshoba County, Miss., Feb. 10, 1837. He lived in Illinois from 1844 to 1854, then at Three Oaks, Mich., except two years a clerk at Niles. He was Supervisor five terms, and held many village and town offices. In politics he was a Democrat.

JOHN F. McKINLAY

Representative from the First District of Wayne County, 1893-4. Was born in Brunswick, Medina County, O., Sept. 7, 1859. His father was of Scotch descent and Canadian nativity, his mother being a native of Ohio. When he was about two years of age the family removed to Ridgetown, Ont., where in the common and high schools he acquired his education. For some time thereafter he assisted in the work and management of his father's farm. In 1882 he came to Detroit and read law in the office of the Hon. D. C. Holbrook, now deceased, was admitted to the bar and engaged in the practice of his profession in that city. In politics a Republican. He was elected to the Legislature of 1891-2 under the cumulative voting law, but the Supreme Court declaring the law unconstitutional, he did not take his seat.

PETER McKINLEY

Representative from Manitou County, 1857-8. His postoffice address was St. James. (Further data not obtainable).

JOHN McKINNEY

Representative from Van Buren County, 1848; Senator from the Fourth District, 1849-50; Secretary of State, 1855-9; and State Treasurer in 1859-60. Was born in Pennsylvania in 1803. He came to Michigan in 1837, settled in Van Buren County. In politics he was first a Democrat, a Republican after 1854. He died July 10, 1870.

WILLIAM H. McKINSTRY

Representative from the First District of Muskegon County, 1889-90 and 1893-4. Was born in Ypsilanti, Mich., July 1, 1852. When quite young he moved with his parents to Battle Creek, Mich., where he received a common school education. He early learned the trade of cigarmaker and resided in various places in the State, working at his trade. In 1885 he located at Muskegon. In politics a Democrat.

SHELDON McKNIGHT

Representative from Wayne County, 1857-8. Was born in Herkimer County, N. Y., in 1810. He came to Detroit in 1820, learned the trade of a printer, in 1827, took an interest in the Detroit *Gazette*, which was merged in the *Free Press* in 1830, and edited by him until 1836. He was Postmaster of Detroit, 1836 to 1841. In 1845, he was appointed by President Polk, agent to examine the mineral resources of the Upper Peninsula, took up his residence at the Sault, established a line of vessels, and was the chief factor in building a railroad around the rapids, which was the means of transit until the canal was built. Politically he was a Democrat. He was efficient in the establishment of the insane asylum at Kalamazoo, and was one of its first board of trustees. He died at Washington, July 21, 1860.

WILLIAM J. McKONE

Member of the State Board of Education, 1905-15. Was born at Montezuma, N. Y., Aug. 23, 1866. He obtained a common school education in his native village and afterwards attended the Port Byron Free School and Academy. Mr. McKone came to Michigan in 1884 and spent the three following years in the State Normal School at Ypsilanti, from which he was graduated in 1887. He at once began teaching school, having been Superintendent of the Morrice schools, Almont, and the Albion schools. He was prominently identified with National, State and local educational interests; conducted teachers' institutes in nearly one-half the counties of Michigan; took an active interest in church and social affairs and held many offices of trust and honor in different societies and fraternities. Married. He was in demand as a lecturer, a frequent contributor to educational journals, and is the author of a popular text-book, "Michigan, State and Local Government." Mr. McKone was the unanimous choice of the Grand Rapids Republican Convention, Feb. 14, to succeed Patrick H. Kelley, resigned, and was elected Apr. 3, 1905, and re-elected Nov. 3, 1908. The constitution of 1909 provided for the election of one member at the April election in 1909 and on Apr. 5, 1909, Mr. McKone was elected.

DONALD P. McLACHLAN

Representative from the Second District of Washtenaw County, 1913-14. Was born in New Brunswick, Canada, Sept. 15, 1848, of Scotch parentage. He was educated in the common schools and Provincial Training School of New Brunswick. Married. He came to Michigan in 1873, having practiced medicine since 1876. In politics a Democrat.

DYCKES McLACHLIN

Representative from Monroe County, 1875-6. Was born in the town of Ayr, Scotland, June 26, 1814. He came to Whitehall, N. Y., in 1822, and in 1850 he removed to Summerfield, Mich., where he was engaged in farming, lumbering and selling goods. He was a Justice, Notary Public, and Supervisor. In politics he was a Republican. He died at Petersburg, Monroe County, June 30, 1882.

JAMES C. McLAUGHLIN

Member of Congress, 1907—. Was born in Illinois in 1858. He received his education in the Muskegon high school and the literary and law departments of the University of Michigan. He is a practicing attorney, is president of the Muskegon Abstract Company, and has resided in Michigan since 1864. Mr. McLaughlin has been Prosecuting Attorney of Muskegon County, and in 1901 was appointed a member of the Board of Tax Commissioners, serving until November, 1905, when the board was reorganized by the Legislature of 1905. He was elected to the 60th Congress in 1906, and has served in each succeeding congress. He was re-elected November 7, 1922.

JOSEPH R. McLAUGHLIN

Senator, 1893-4 and 1895-6, from the Third District, composed of the fourth, sixth, eight and tenth wards of the city of Detroit. Was born in Detroit, June 5, 1851; moved to Oakland County; worked on a farm during the summer months and attended the Birmingham High School during winters; entered the University of Michigan, graduating from the literary department in 1877 and the law department in 1879; went to Detroit and engaged in the practice of law. In 1882 he organized the Edison Electric Light Company; was for two years its secretary and manager; engaged in real estate, dealing in Detroit. In politics a Republican.

JOSEPH McLEAN

Representative from the First District of Bay County, 1899-1900. Was born in Ireland, Dec. 25, 1849. His parents emigrated to Canada. He was educated in the common schools of that province, and followed the profession of contractor and builder. In 1871 he removed to Michigan, and for many years a resident of Bay City. He served as School Trustee for one term.

CLARENCE JOHN McLEOD

Member of Congress, 1923——. Was born in Detroit, July 3, 1895, of Scotch and French parentage. He was educated in the public schools, the University of Detroit and the Detroit College of Law. Mr. McLeod is married and has two children. During the late World War he served in the Intelligence Division. November 7, 1922, he was elected to the 68th Congress.

MALCOLM J. McLEOD

Representative from the First District of Detroit, 1899-1900. Was born in Huron County, Ont., Jan. 22, 1868, of Scotch parentage, and removed with his parents to Attica, Lapeer County, Mich., the same year. From thence they moved to Sarnia. Ont., in 1880. Mr. McLeod's early education was obtained in the common schools of Attica and Sarnia, and in 1882 he went to work in a grocery. In 1889 he was employed in the St. Clair tunnel at Port Huron; removed to Detroit in 1891, taking a position as street car conductor for the Citizens' Street Railway Company; December, 1897, he was elected traveling delegate for the Street Railway Employees' Association, and re-elected in December, 1898. In politics a Republican.

WILLIAM NORMAN McLEOD

Representative from Mackinac County, 1843 to 1845. His postoffice address was Mackinac. (Further data not obtainable).

JAMES McMAHON

Representative from Washtenaw County, 1857-8 and 1859-60. Was born in County Clare, Ireland, Apr. 4, 1819. He received his education there, leaving college before graduating. He settled in Ann Arbor in 1837, and worked as a blacksmith, a trade learned by him when a boy. He was a Whig, but became a Republican at the organization of that party. He studied law and served fourteen years as Justice, with over 5,000 cases on his docket. He was Supervisor and chairman of the County Board for several years; Circuit Court Commissioner two years; during the war Provost Marshal two years. He was an able and influential member. He died July 10, 1885.

JOEL W. McMAHON

Senator from the Eighteenth District, 1883-4. Was born in Sanilac County, June 29, 1848, and never had a residence outside of that county. He was admitted to the bar in 1873, after which time he resided at Marlette, engaged in the practice of his profession. He served as Prosecuting Attorney one term. In politics a Republican.

DANIEL D. McMARTIN

Representative from Allegan County, 1863-4. Was born in Amsterdam, N. Y., Feb. 8, 1808. By occupation he was a farmer, in politics a Republican. He came to Michigan in 1838, and settled in an unorganized town in Allegan County, since called Martin, a part of his name. Afterwards he removed to Gunplain, where he lived until 1865. He resided at Kalamazoo in 1887. He was Justice four terms, and six times a Supervisor.

HERMAN I. McMILLAN

Representative from Charlevoix County, 1913-14 and 1915-16. Was born at Oak Grove, Livingston County, Mich., Jan. 19, 1868, of Scotch and English descent. He was educated in the district schools. Married. He engaged in the flour milling business. He served on the councils at Charlevoix and at East Jordan, and was Mayor of the last named city. Fraternally, a member of the F. & A. M., being past master of his lodge. In politics a Republican.

JAMES McMILLAN

United States Senator, 1889-1902. Was born at Hamilton, Ont., May 12, 1838; was prepared for college, but in 1855 removed to Detroit, where he entered upon a business life. In 1860 Mr. McMillan married Miss Wetmore, of Detroit. In 1863, he, with others, established the Michigan Car Company, of which enterprise, with its various branches, he was the president. In 1876 he was a member of the Republican State Central Committee, and on the death of Zachariah Chandler was made chairman. Again, in 1886 and in 1890, he was elected chairman of the committee. For three years he was president of the Detroit Board of Park Commissioners, and for four years was a member of the

Detroit Board of Estimates. He was a Republican Presidential Elector in 1884. He received the unanimous nomination of the Republican members of the Legislature and was elected to the U. S. Senate to succeed Thomas Witherell Palmer, and took his seat Mar. 3, 1889; re-elected in 1895 and 1901, serving until his death, Aug. 10, 1902.

NEAL McMILLAN

Representative from the Third District of Kent County, 1887-8 and 1889-90. Was born at Godmanchester, Province of Quebec, Dec. 25, 1845. He was formerly farmer and teacher, then a druggist. He held the offices of Supervisor of his Township, County Superintendent of Schools, Village Recorder, Treasurer and Alderman, and was elected Representative for 1887-8 as a Republican, and re-elected to the House of 1889-90. He died at Rockford, Kent County, Dec. 11, 1920.

HENRY McMORRAN

Member of Congress, 1903-5 to 1911-13. Was born in Port Huron, July 11, 1844. He was educated in the district schools. A business man carrying on many successful enterprises. In politics a Republican. In 1866 he was married to Miss Emma C. Williams. He was elected Representative to the 58th, 59th, 60th and 61st Congresses; was renominated at the primaries Sept 6, 1910, and elected Nov. 8, 1910.

DANIEL P. McMULLEN

Senator, 1899-1900 and 1901-2, from the Twenty-ninth District, comprising the counties of Emmet, Cheboygan, Presque Isle, Otsego, Montmorency and Alpena. Was born in Kent County, Canada, Sept. 8, 1852, was educated in the common schools of that county, and entered a printing office at the age of fourteen years. Two years later he came to Michigan, where he continued in the printing and publishing business, starting in Wenona (now West Bay City) *Herald*, and conducting it successfully for several years, and subsequently engaging in job printing at Bay City. In 1880 he purchased the Alpena *Reporter* and conducted it for two years. In 1882 he settled at Cheboygan, first connecting himself with the *Democrat*, but a year later he accepted a position with the *Tribune*. In politics an active Republican. He was elected Mayor of Cheboygan and re-elected in 1892. In April, 1898, he was nominated for the third time, and elected over his democratic competitor by 252 votes—the largest majority ever given any candidate in the city. He was past grand chancellor of Michigan K. P., filled all the prominent positions in the fraternal orders of A. O. U. W. and Woodmen of the World, and an active member of the Maccabees and National Union.

JOHN W. McNABB

Representative from Newaygo County, 1879-80 and 1885-6. Was born in Wyandotte County, O., Jan. 20, 1846. His parents moved to Indiana in 1851, where he attended the common schools and academy until seventeen, when he entered Fort Wayne College. After one year in that institution he entered Wabash College, and remained two years; taught school one year; studied medicine three years at Rochester, Ind., then entered the medical department of the University of Michigan. He returned to Indiana and practiced medicine one year, after which he removed to Newaygo County, Mich., where he engaged in his profession. Dr. McNabb held the office of Justice, Township Clerk, and Superintendent of Schools; was elected to the Legislature in 1878 on the National Greenback ticket.

WILLIAM McNAIR

Representative from Lenawee County, 1849. Was born in Bucks County, Pa., Jan. 1, 1800. He emigrated to Michigan in 1826 and became a merchant at Tecumseh, and afterwards a farmer. In politics he was a Democrat.

B. FRANK McNALL

Representative from the County of Gratiot, 1895-6. Was born in Royalton, Niagara County, N. Y., July 23, 1849. He attended the public schools, and remained on his father's farm until 1881, when he came to Michigan, locating on the farm in Lafayette Township, Gratiot County. In October, 1876, he was married to Mary C. Bissell, of Lockport, N. Y., who died in 1893. In politics a Republican. He held the township offices of Treasurer and Supervisor.

MOSES A. McNAUGHTON

Senator from the Twelfth District, 1853-4. Was born in Argyle, N. Y., Jan 3, 1813. He received an academical education, and was two years in Union College; read medicine and graduated at Fairfield, N. Y., in 1840. He settled at Jackson, Mich., in 1841, and practiced medicine successfully for ten years, when he turned his attention to real estate, in which he was successful. He also was interested in the building of railroads, among them the Jackson branch of the Michigan Southern, and the Grand River Valley, of which he was treasurer. He was elected Senator on the Free Soil ticket. He was Mayor of Jackson in 1866-7.

JOHN L. McNEIL

Representative from Genesee County, 1849. Was born at Charlotte, Vt., Oct. 9, 1813. He received a common school education and worked on his father's farm until twenty-one, and then took charge of his father's hotel in Charlotte. In 1836 he emigrated to Michigan and settled in Atlas, Genesee County, upon a farm. He filled various local offices, and as a Democrat was a Representative.

HENRY CLAY McNITT

Representative, 1911-12 and 1913-14, from the Wexford District, comprising the counties of Lake and Wexford. Was born in Sparta Township, Kent County, Mich., Mar. 19, 1849, and was educated in the union schools of Grand Rapids.

At the age of twenty-four he embarked in the mercantile business at various places, mostly at and near Cadillac. He continued this business until the age of forty-four, then engaged in cattle-raising and dairy farming. He served several terms as Supervisor in Wexford County. Married. In politics a Republican.

JACOB L. McPEEK

Senator from the Fifteenth District, 1879-80. Was born in Oxford, O., May 4, 1848, and removed to Michigan with his parents in 1852, settling on a farm near Grand Ledge. In 1867 he moved into the village. He received a good education and opened a real estate and collection office in Grand Ledge. In 1875 he was admitted to the bar, and since was in the practice of the law. In politics a Republican.

MELVILLE B. McPHERSON

Member of the State Board of Agriculture, 1922——. Was born in Vergennes Township, Kent County, Dec. 11, 1876, and is of Scotch descent. He was educated in the public schools of Lowell and the Grand Rapids Business College. After teaching school for two years he took up farming, in which occupation he has since been engaged. He held office as member of the School Board, Township Treasurer and Supervisor; was elected member of State Board of Agriculture, Apr. 4, 1921.

FRANK McPHILLIPS

Representative from the First District of Saginaw County, 1913-14; and Senator from the Twenty-second District, 1915-16. Was born at Chili, Monroe County, N. Y., May 8, 1848, of Irish parentage, and was educated in the district schools. At the age of fifteen years he enlisted in the Union Army and served two years or until the close of the war, celebrating his sixteenth year in the Battle of the Wilderness. He was also in the battles at Spottsylvania Court House, Cold Harbor and the siege of Petersburg. For thirty-five years he worked in the lumber woods, farmed for six years, and was in the cigar and tobacco business for six years. Politically a Democrat.

DUNCAN McRAE

Senator, 1917-18, 1919-20 and 1921-2, from the Twenty-eighth District, comprising the counties of Alcona, Arenac, Clare, Crawford, Gladwin, Iosco, Ogemaw, Osceola, Oscoda and Roscommon. Was born in AuSable, Mich., Feb. 16, 1869, of Scotch-Irish parentage. He received his education in the public schools of AuSable and Greenbush. Mr. McRae served in the Spanish-American War with Company E, 35th Mich Vol. Infantry. For six years he engaged in the mercantile business, and later entered the lumbering business, in which he is still engaged. He has served as School Director, Township Treasurer and Supervisor, and for ten years was Postmaster of Greenbush. Mr. McRae is married and has two children, Mary Jean, born at Lansing, Mar. 21, during the legislative session of 1917, and Duncan Jr., born at Lansing, Mar 24, during the legislative session of 1919. In politics a Republican.

ANDREW T. McREYNOLDS

Representative from Wayne County, 1840; and Senator from the First District, 1847. Was born at Dungannon, Ireland, Dec. 25, 1808, came to Pittsburg, Pa., in 1840, and was a member of the "Duquesne Greys," the first military company west of the Alleghanies, after the war of 1812. He removed to Detroit in 1833, in 1834 became a Major on the staff of Gen. A. S. Williams, then commanding the State militia. In 1834-5 he organized the Brady Guards. He studied law and was admitted in 1840. He was eleven years Lieutenant Colonel or Colonel of the 1st Mich. Regiment; was Captain of the Montgomery Guards; in 1847 was Captain of dragoons, U. S. army, and served in the Mexican War; his company and that of Phil Kearney, forming Scott's body guard; for his bravery in the charge of the gates of Mexico received the thanks of the President and Senate, having been disabled for life; returned to Detroit and practiced law until 1861; in 1861 was commissioned Colonel of the "Lincoln Cavalry," the first regiment in that arm of the service; was in command of a brigade two years, and of a division six months. He was an Alderman of Detroit two years; Indian agent three years; member and first president of the Detroit Board of Education; U. S. District Attorney of Western Michigan under Johnson; Democratic candidate for Congress in 1872; Prosecuting Attorney of Muskegon County in 1874. He was first a Whig, and was a delegate to the National Convention of 1840 that nominated Harrison, but of later years a Democrat. He resided at Grand Rapids in 1887, and was long president of the State association of veterans of the Mexican War.

DAVID McWHORTER

Representative from the First District of Jackson County, 1853-4. His post-office address was Grass Lake. (Further data not obtainable).

JOSEPH P. MAAS

Representative from the First District of Wayne County, 1913-14. Was born at Detroit, Mich., Feb. 8, 1856, of German parents. His education was acquired in St. Anthony's Catholic school of Detroit. At the age of seventeen he entered the employ of B. Youngblood and Brother, and after seven years in their employ, engaged in the retail grocery business on his own account. He married Catherine Kettel. In politics a Republican.

JAMES H. MACDONALD

Lieutenant Governor, 1887-9 and 1889. Was born in Northwest Iverness-shire, Scotland, in May, 1832, and was a resident of the State of Michigan for over twenty years, his home being at Escanaba, Delta County. He was roadmaster of the C. & N. W. R'y Co., P. Division, but retired and received an income from royalty on iron ore land. He held the office of Justice of the Peace, and was elected to the office of Lieutenant Governor for 1887-9, and re-elected to that office for 1889-91. He was killed in a railroad accident which occurred Jan. 19, 1889, near Elmwood station, Gogebic County, Mich.

ROBERT BRUCE MacDONALD

Representative from the First District of Houghton County, 1921-2 and 1923—. Was born Sept. 16, 1889, at Calumet, Mich., of Scotch parentage. He was educated in the public schools of Calumet, graduating from the high school in 1909. He received the degree of B. L. from the Detroit College of Law in 1917, and immediately took up the practice of law at Laurium. He is a member of Calumet Lodge No. 271, F. & A. M., Calumet Mich.; Peninsula Chapter No. 16, R. A. M., Detroit, Mich.; Montrose Commandery, No. 38, K. T., Calumet, Mich.; Francis M. Moore Consistory, Marquette, Mich. Mr. MacDonald is married. In politics he is a Republican.

ALMON MACK

Representative from Oakland County, 1848. Was born in Tunbridge, Vt., in 1806. He joined his father at Pontiac in 1822, and was his agent. He was offered and declined the position of secretary of the First Territorial Council in 1824, but furnished the eighteen names from which the president selected the first council of nine. He was a merchant at Rochester, Mich., from 1830 to 1853, and held many positions of trust and honor. In politics he was a Democrat.

ANDREW MACK

Representative from Wayne County, 1839. Was born in New London, Conn. He became a Captain in the ocean merchant service and made three voyages around the world. In 1804 he drove some merino sheep, purchased in Spain, over the Cumberland mountains to Cincinnati, and built a woolen factory there, and was a member of the Ohio Legislature. He was a Colonel in the War of 1812. He came to Detroit as Collector of the port in 1829, which he held until 1839. He opened and kept the Mansion hotel in 1830, and was Mayor of Detroit in 1834, during the cholera visitation, and did much to relieve the sick, and as a health officer. In politics he was a Democrat. He died in 1875, and was buried on his farm near St. Clair.

STEPHEN MACK

Member of the Legislative Council from Oakland County, 1824-5. Was born in Lyme, Conn., in 1764. He married Temperance Bond, and settled in Tunbridge, Vt., when a young man and engaged in mercantile business. He built a hotel, and became Colonel of the State militia. In 1810 he came to Detroit and engaged in mercantile business with Thomas Emerson, and they were in trade when Gen. Hull surrendered Detroit. He again, after the War of 1812, was one of the firm of Mack & Conant until 1818. He was one of the first four settlers of Pontiac, in 1818, and was a member and agent of the "Pontiac Company." As one of the firm of Mack, Conant & Sibley, they built the first dam, and the first saw and flouring mill at Pontiac. He also built a grist mill at Rochester. He was a member of the First Territorial Council of Michigan, which met at Detroit, in 1824. He died at Pontiac, Nov. 11, 1826.

JOHN DONALD M. MacKAY

Senator from the Third District of Wayne County, 1905-6, 1907-8 and 1909-10. Was born of Highland Scotch parentage in Atlantic, Cass County, Ia., Aug. 13, 1871. He received his education in the public schools of Iowa and South Dakota, graduated from Olivet College in 1894, and from the Detroit College of Law in 1895. A member of the firm of Stellwagen & MacKay, formerly Cutcheon, Stellwagen & MacKay, one of the best known law firms in the State, and member of the board of trustees of Olivet College. He lived for a time on his father's ranch in South Dakota, associated in mining interests in Montana, and engaged in the practice of law at Detroit. In politics he was a Republican. He died July 23, 1923.

ARTHUR CUSTER MacKINNON

Representative from the First District of Bay County, 1923—. Was born in Cleveland, Ohio, Aug 3, 1870, of Scotch ancestry. His parents removed to Bay City when he was an infant and his early education was acquired in the schools of that city. He left school when sixteen years of age to learn the machinist's trade and worked at it for five years, after which he entered the engineering department of the Michigan Agricultural College. He engaged in the manufacturing business for twenty years, being associated with his father until his retirement, and then with his brother. For the past four years he has been retired from active business. He was married in 1899 and has three children. Mr. MacKinnon is a Republican and has served his city as Alderman and Commissioner. He was elected to the Legislature November 7, 1922.

THOMAS H. MacNAUGHTON

Representative from the Second District of Kent County, 1909-10 and 1911-12; and Senator, 1913-14, 1919, from the Seventeenth District, comprising the west side of the city of Grand Rapids and all territory outside of the city limits. Was born May 1, 1861, on a farm in the township of Ada, Kent County, Mich., of Scotch parents. His education was acquired in the public schools of that township. He has been a farmer all his life and is at present master of the Kent Pomona Grange, this being his eighteenth year as head of that organization. He was a member of the executive committee of the Michigan State Grange for ten years, and for a time served as president of the Kent County Farmers' Institute. He was a member of the legislative committee of the State Grange for three years and for nine years was a member of the Board of Education of the Ada High School. Mr. MacNaughton is married. In politics he is a Republican.

JOSHUA B. MADILL

Representative from Huron County, 1895-6 and 1897-8. Was born in the Province of Ontario, Nov. 24, 1850; acquired a common school education, and spent his boyhood days on his father's farm. In 1873 he was married, pursued the vocation of farming for two years, and came to Lexington, Sanilac County, Mich., where he became interested in carriage building and farming. In 1877 he moved to a farm in Marion Township, where he was engaged in farming until the forest fires of 1881; two years following was engaged in lumbering in Huron County. In 1883 he moved to Ubly and erected a flour mill, where he became interested in milling, grain dealing and general store. In politics a Republican.

ISAAC MAGOON

Representative from Washtenaw County, 1842 and 1845. His postoffice address was Silver Lake. (Further data not obtainable).

ALEXANDER MAITLAND

Senator from the Thirty-first District, 1897-8 and 1899-1900; and Lieutenant Governor, 1903-5 and 1905-7. Was born in Scotland, June 20, 1844, and came to the United States in 1864, making his home at Negaunee, Mich. His education was obtained in the common schools of Scotland and in an academy at Troon, Ayrshire. On his arrival at Negaunee he secured a position as rodman with a surveying party which was running lines for the Mineral branch of the Chicago & Northwestern Railroad. Soon after this he entered the employment of the Iron Cliffs Company, rising by grade of service until he became its general manager. He was also appointed to the supervision of the Cambria and Lillie mines; also general manager of the mining department of the Republic Iron & Steel Company, and interested in four national banks. In politics a Republican. He held the office of County Surveyor, Mayor of Negaunee and State Senator from his district. He was married June 10, 1874, to Miss Carrie V. Sterling. He was elected Lieutenant Governor of Michigan in 1902 and re-elected Nov. 8, 1904.

JOHN MAKELIM

Representative from Sanilac County, 1885-6 and 1887-8. Was born at Nassaga-weya, Ontario, June 30, 1847. In 1864 he went to Illinois, and was a railroad employe. He returned, secured an acamemical education, and in 1867 was a teacher at Brockway, Mich., and taught for some years. He moved to Maple Valley, Mich., in 1875, where he resided, in 1887. He was a merchant and station agent for the P. H. & N. W. R. R.; was Supervisor, Justice, and held other offices. In politics he was a Republican.

PETER D. MAKLEY

Representative from Oakland County, 1847. Was born in Columbia County, N. Y., in 1796. He came to Michigan in 1836, and settled on a farm in Oxford, and was the first Supervisor in 1837. He removed to Pontiac in 1852, where he kept hotel until his death, Aug. 11, 1856. Politically he was a Democrat.

ROBERT W. MALCOLM

Representative from Oakland County, 1885-6. Was born in West Bloomfield, Mich., Feb. 18, 1844, and received his education in the common schools. He enlisted in Co. A, 22d Mich. Vol. Infantry, Aug. 11, 1862. He was wounded and captured at the Battle of Chickamauga, Sept. 20, 1863; was held a prisoner fifteen months; was discharged at the close of the war in 1865, and engaged in farming. He held the office of Township Clerk and Supervisor several terms. He was elected as a Republican.

CHARLES F. MALLARY

Representative from Macomb County, 1863-4 and 1865-6. Was born at Albany, N. Y., Jan. 11, 1811. He came to Romeo at an early day and followed successfully the business of a merchant, from which he retired in 1879. He was a Democrat until 1856, then a Republican until 1874, since a Greenbacker and Fusionist. He held the positions of Postmaster, President, Clerk and Trustee of the village, and Township Clerk; was also Justice, and in 1878 was the Greenback nominee for Congress, but was defeated.

CHARLES G. MALLETT

Representative from Monroe County, 1867-8. Was born in Connecticut, Oct. 16, 1829. By occupation he was a lumberman, in politics a Republican. He settled in Monroe County in 1858, and was six years director of the Farmers' Insurance Company, and eleven years School Director at Lambertville. He moved to Toledo in 1871, and to Chicago in 1880, where he resided in 1887.

GEORGE L. MALTZ

Member of the Board of Regents of the University of Michigan, 1878-80; and State Treasurer, 1887-9 and 1889-91. Was born in Brooklyn, N. Y., in 1842. He removed with his parents to Detroit in 1846, and was educated in the public schools of Detroit. At the age of 18 years he enlisted as a private in the 4th Mich. Infantry, was wounded in the seven-days fight before Richmond, taken prisoner and confined at the "Old Libby"; was exchanged and returned to his regiment. At the Battle of Fredericksburg he was promoted to a Lieutenancy. He commanded Co. E (of Hillsdale), at the Battle of Gettysburg. Here he was made Adjutant of his regiment, which position he held until the expiration of his service. In 1866 he was married at Detroit, to Miss Elvira E. Whiting. By profession he was a banker and lumberman. In Detroit he was made cashier of the Internal Revenue Office. In 1872 he removed to Alpena and founded the banking house of Geo. L. Maltz & Co., which in 1883 was organized as the Alpena National Bank; also treasurer for the Minor Lumber Company. He held honorable positions in his city, three times made Mayor, and filled very acceptably the position of Regent of the University.

WILLIAM CHARLES MANCHESTER

Delegate in the Constitutional Convention of 1907-8, from the Fourth District, Wayne County. Was born on a farm near Canfield, O., Dec. 25, 1873, of English, Irish, Welsh and Scotch descent. He attended the district schools, later entering the public schools of Canfield. Afterwards he spent six years in the Northeastern Ohio Normal College of Canfield, completing the six-year classical course in 1894, taking the degree of A. B. He entered the law department of the University of Michigan in 1894, and took the degree of LL B. in 1896. The following summer he spent in travel through the western part of the United States and Canada. After returning from the West he entered the law office of Hine & Clark, of Youngstown, O. In January, 1897, he came to Detroit, and actively engaged in the practice of law. He was married to Miss Margaret Katherine McGregor, of Bay City, in 1898, who graduated from the literary department of the University of Michigan in 1896, with the degree of Ph. B.

JAMES W. MANDIGO

Representative from St. Joseph County, 1869-70. Was born in the State of New York, Nov. 30, 1819. He was a physician and druggist; in politics a Republican. He came to White Pigeon in 1843, where he resided in 1887. He studied medicine with Dr. W. N. Elliott; was Supervisor of White Pigeon many years, several times President of the village, and Trustee of the union school.

CHARLES H. MANLY

Representative from Washtenaw County, 1887-8. Was born in Livingston County, Sept. 16, 1843, and was a resident of Michigan his lifetime. He was formerly a farmer but in 1887 was an abstractor of real estate titles. During the war he served in Co. A, 1st Regiment, Mich, Infantry, and participated in the various battles fought by his regiment; was twice wounded and lost his left arm at the Battle of Gettysburg, July 2, 1863. He was City Collector, City Recorder, Justice of the Peace, and Register of Deeds three times. In politics he was a Democrat.

EMANUEL MANN

Senator from the Sixth District, 1871-2. Was born in Stuttgart, Germany, June 4, 1814. His parents came to Pennsylvania in 1826, and to Ann Arbor, May 20, 1830, being the first German family in that city. By occupation he was a druggist, in politics a Republican. He retired from business but resided at Ann Arbor.

RANDOLPH MANNING

Delegate from Oakland County to the Constitutional Convention of 1835; Senator from the Fifth District, 1837; Secretary of State, 1838-40; member of the Board of Regents of the University of Michigan, 1842; member of the State Board of Education; 1849-50; and Justice of the Supreme Court, 1858-64. Was born in Plainfield, N. J., May 19, 1804. He studied law in New York City, came to Michigan in 1832, and settled at Pontiac in the practice of the law. In the Constitutional Convention of 1835, he was a member of the committee on judiciary, and, as such, was associated with Judge Ross Wilkins, William Trowbridge, Isaac E. Crary, Robert McClelland and others. He was elected Senator in 1837 to fill the vacancy caused by the resignation of Charles C. Hascall. In 1836 a court of chancery was established, and in 1842 he was chancellor as the successor of Chancellor Farnsworth. This office he held for about three years, and filled it in a manner that reflected the highest credit upon him both for integrity and professional ability. At the organization of an independent Supreme Court in 1858, he was elected Associate Justice, and re-elected on the expiration of his term in 1861, and died in 1864 while holding that position. He was a man of spotless integrity, sound discriminating judgment, and of a capacity that enabled him to fill every office with honor to himself and advantage to the State. He was appointed Regent of the State University in 1842 but resigned the same year. In politics he was a Democrat, until 1854, after that a Republican. He died at Pontiac, Aug. 31, 1864.

EDWARD B. MANWARING

Representative from the First District of Washtenaw County, 1921—. Was born at Windsor, N. Y., Mar. 26, 1851, of English parents. He received his education at Windsor Academy and the University of Wisconsin, graduating from the law department of the latter institution in 1875. He practiced law at Menominee, and Superior, Wis., until 1903, when he retired and moved to Ann Arbor, Mich. He is married and has a family of nine children. In politics he' is a Republican. He has served on the Board of Education, as Alderman of his city for ten years, and as Supervisor.

JOSEPH MANWARING

Representative from Lapeer County, 1885-6. Was born in Burlington County, N. J., in 1829. He removed with his parents to Avon, Oakland County, Mich., in 1836. He received a common school and academical education at Rochester, Mich. In 1852 he went to Dryden, where he entered into the mercantile business. He was elected Supervisor several years. He served as Township Clerk at various times for five years. He was Postmaster in 1861, and held that office until November, 1884. He was a Republican after 1854. He died at Dryden, Lapeer County, Feb. 6, 1905.

JOSHUA MANWARING

Senator from the Sixteenth District, 1883-4 and 1885-6. Was born in Burlington County, N. J., Oct. 2, 1824. He removed to Avon, Mich., in 1836, and received a common school education. In 1845 he went to the present site of Greenville and engaged two years in sawing and rafting lumber. In 1847 he became a merchant at Dryden, Mich., and in 1850 built the Manwaring mill at Attica, and erected buildings at Dryden and Imlay City, carrying on a lumber business. He resided in Lapeer in 1887. He was Supervisor. In politics he was a Democrat. He was vice-president of the Michigan Pioneer Society and his death was reported but no date given.

CHARLES MANZELMANN

Representative from the First District, Wayne County, 1905-6. Was born in Stralzund, Germany, Nov. 11, 1861, and came to Detroit, Mich., about 1878. He received his education in the St. Paul and Trinity Evangelical Lutheran schools of Detroit. Married. Mr. Manzelmann worked as an apprentice at broom-making. He engaged in the manufacture of brooms with Peter Farley, Jan. 1, 1881, and continued the partnership until the death of Mr. Farley, Aug. 6, 1891, when he assumed entire control of the business, making the institution the largest establishment of this kind in the State. He was an ardent worker in the Evangelical Lutheran Church, and served as elder for seven years in the St. Mark's English Evangelical Lutheran Church; also served as director in the Evangelical Lutheran Deaf and Dumb Institute at North Detroit. In politics a Republican.

CARL E. MAPES

Representative from the First District of Kent County, 1905-6; Senator from the Sixteenth District, 1909-10 and 1911-12; and member of Congress, 1913. Was born on a farm in Eaton County, Mich., Dec. 26, 1874. He graduated from Olivet College in 1896 and from the law department of the University of Michigan in 1899, and has practiced law in Grand Rapids since that time. He served one term in the Michigan House of Representatives and two terms in the Senate. He is married and has three children. He was elected to Congress in 1912, served in the 63d, 64th, 65th, 66th and 67th Congresses, and was re-elected Nov. 7, 1922, to the 68th Congress.

PATRICK MARANTETTE

Representative from St. Joseph County, 1847. Was born at Sandwich, Canada, Mar. 11, 1807. At the age of sixteen he superintended the Indian trading post for Peter and James Godfrey. In 1833 he became superintendent of the trading post at Nottawa, Mich., and was of great service to the government in the removal of the Indians from that reservation in 1840. He purchased a large farm in Mendon. He left an estate valued at $100,000. He died at Mendon, Mich., May 23, 1878.

ADOLPH N. MARION

Representative from the First District, Detroit, of Wayne County, 1891-2. Was born in Detroit, Oct. 4, 1859. Married. In 1891 he was a dealer in real estate and loans; was formerly connected with the purchasing department of the Detroit Stove Works. He was elected to the House of 1891-2 on the Democratic ticket.

DANIEL P. MARKEY

Representative from the counties of Crawford, Oscoda, Roscommon and Ogemaw, 1885-6 and 1887-8. Was born in the township of Bunker Hill, Mich., June 27, 1857. Most of his early life was spent in Pinckney, Livingston County, where he pursued his studies, graduating at the school in that village and afterwards engaged in teaching for several years. In 1879 he removed to Ann Arbor, obtaining a position as book-keeper for a manufacturing company. He at the same time entered upon the study of law, and was admitted to the bar in April 1881, in September of which year he removed to West Branch, Ogemaw County, where he resided in 1887, and began the practice of his profession as an attorney. In 1881 he was appointed Circuit Court Commissioner, and elected in 1882. In 1883 he was Judge of Probate. In politics a Republican.

MATTHEW MARKEY

Representative from Wayne County, 1873-4; and Senator from the Third District 1877-8. Was born Sept. 13, 1820, in the county of Cavan, Ireland. He was educated in a common school. In 1838 he settled in Haverstraw, N. Y. In 1848 he removed to Springwells, Mich., where he resided until 1873, when he removed to Nankin. He held several township offices. He engaged in the manufacture of brick and in farming.

GILES B. MARKHAM

Representative from St. Joseph County, 1877-8 and 1881-2. Was born in Sandisfield, Mass., Mar. 2, 1828. He came with his parents to White Pigeon, Mich., in 1838, and received his education at a branch of the State University at that place. By occupation he was a farmer. He spent five years in California. He was twice elected Supervisor of White Pigeon town. In politics he was a Republican.

HERMAN MARKS

Representative from the First District of Wayne County, 1901-2. Was born in Detroit, Mich., June 3, 1873, and acquired his education in the public schools of his native city. At the age of eight years he began his career as a newsboy and continued in the business until fifteen years of age, during which time he assisted in organizing the famous Detroit Newsboys' Association, and was appointed from their ranks as page in the State Senate of 1893, after which he served as furrier's apprentice, and later as salesman for Walter Buhl and Co., of Detroit, until 1898; then identified with Wm. Jackman's Sons, Furriers, of New York City, and Cleveland, O. Unmarried. In politics a strong Republican. He was elected to the Legislature of 1901-2 on the general legislative ticket.

THOMAS MARS

Senator from the Thirteenth District, 1881-2. Was born in Giles County, Va., May 4, 1829. In the same year the family moved to Berrien Township, Mich. He was raised on a farm, working in the summer and attending district school in the winter. At the age of twenty he served a year's apprenticeship at the carpenter and joiner's trade, at which he worked ten years, securing quite a competence. In 1857 he went to Kansas, spending two summers there, and then went to Missouri, where he purchased an interest in a sawmill. When the war broke out the Confederates burnt his mill and his debtors all went into the

Southern army, leaving him nearly financially ruined. Having returned to Berrien County in 1861, he purchased 120 acres of land and a steam sawmill located thereon. He filled various offices of trust and honor. He was president of the Berrien County Agricultural Society two terms, president of the Berrien County Pioneer Society, and chairman of the executive committee of the State Grange. In politics he was a Republican. He was vice-president of the "Under the Oaks" Convention. He died at Berrien Springs, Jan. 11, 1907.

HOLLISTER FESTUS MARSH

Member of the State Board of Agriculture, 1899-1903. Was born in the city of New York, in 1837, son of Hollister F. Marsh of Massachusetts and Jane (Morehouse) Marsh of New York City. He married Maria E. Regan in Chicago, Ill., who was born in New York State and educated in the girls' seminary in Illinois. Mr. Hollister attended Rockville Seminary, Conn., not graduating. Member of the Congregational Church. In politics a Republican. He was a bookkeeper in New York City, 1854-5; in the lumber business in Chicago, 1856; opened an office for loans and investments in Allegan, Mich., 1870; was City Clerk in Chicago, 1859-60; member of the State Board of Agriculture, 1899-1903.

LESTER M. MARSH

Representative from Branch County, 1895-6. Was born in Gilead, Branch County, Mich., Oct. 6, 1845; attended school at Albion and Coldwater, Mich., and Orland, Ind., and graduated from Bryant and Stratton's Business College at Cleveland, O.; married in 1870 and moved to the farm. In politics a Republican. He held the office of Supervisor and Justice of the Peace.

WILLIAM D. MARSH

Representative, 1891-2, from the Midland District, comprising the counties of Clare, Gladwin and Midland. Was born in Novi, Oakland County, Nov. 9, 1847. His early boyhood was spent in Oakland and Genesee Counties, except five years among the coal mines of the Cumberland Mountains in Lawrence County, Ky., his father being physician for the coal company. Returning to Michigan with his parents, he attended school at Fenton for ten years and then obtained a position in the bank of that village and was soon given charge of a new bank established at Holly. He then engaged in the banking business at Bay City and Midland, being a stockholder and cashier of the bank of M. Anderson & Co., in the latter city. In politics a Democrat.

ISAAC MARSILJE

Representative from the First District of Ottawa County, 1895-6 and 1897-8. Was born in the town of Groede, Province of Zeeland, Netherlands, Nov. 17, 1846. Four years later came with his parents to the United States; the family first settling in Rochester, N. Y., and in 1853 they came to Kalamazoo, Mich., where he acquired his rudimentary education. He early removed to Holland Township, Ottawa County, where he was engaged in farming from 1862 to 1884, also being somewhat extensively engaged in fruit growing; then in real estate, loans, insurance and banking, in the city of Holland; in 1897, assistant cashier of the First State Bank of Holland. In politics a Republican. He held the offices of Township Clerk and Justice of the Peace; secretary and treasurer of the Farmers' Mutual Insurance Company of Ottawa and Allegan Counties.

ISAAC MARSTON

Representative from Bay County, 1872; Attorney General, 1874; Justice of the Supreme Court, 1875-83. Was born at Poyntzpass, County Armagh, Ireland, Jan. 2, 1839. His father, Thomas Marston, was a small landed proprietor, of English descent. His mother maintained and educated her children after their father's death. She apprenticed Isaac, at the age of thirteen, to a grocer, with whom he remained three years. In 1856 he emigrated to the United States, and went to work upon a farm in Southfield, Oakland County, Mich., attending school about two months. In 1859 he entered the law department of the University of Michigan, and graduated in 1861. He practiced law for six months at Alma, Gratiot County, where he lost his office and library by fire. He then practiced for a little while at Ithaca, and in 1862 removed to Bay City where he resided. While there he was elected Justice of the Peace, Prosecuting Attorney, and City Attorney. In 1872 he was elected Representative for the extra session of that year to fill vacancy caused by the resignation of W. R. Bates. In 1874 he was appointed Attorney General by Governor Bagley, to fill the vacancy caused by the resignation of Byron D. Ball. He held the office nine months, and dispatched more business than had ever before been done in that office in an equal length of time. In April, 1875, he was elected Justice of the Supreme Court, to fill the vacancy caused by the election of Judge Christiancy to the United States Senate. He was re-elected Justice in 1881, but resigned in 1883, and engaged in a lucrative law practice in Detroit. He was baptized into the Church of England, but attended the Presbyterian Church. In politics he was a Republican. He removed to Bay City on account of impaired health where he died of pneumonia, Nov. 1, 1891.

THOMAS FRANK MARSTON

Member of the State Board of Agriculture, 1897-1903 and 1905-8. He was born in Bay City, Mich., Mar. 15, 1869. He married Frances Sheldon, of Rutland, Vt. He was well educated, though not a graduate of any college. He attended grammar school in Bay City; Detroit High School; during the summer of 1888 he attended the Michigan Agricultural College; some time in the University of Michigan; and Agricultural School of the University of Wisconsin; and was a member of the Presbyterian Church. In politics a Republican. In succession the following indicates his occupations: Farming and breeding Jersey cattle; County Commissioner for building stone roads; member of the State Board of Agriculture, 1897-1903, 1905-8; president of the same; member of the State Live Stock Commission.

CHESTER W. MARTIN

Senator, 1895-6, from the Nineteenth District, composed of Clinton and Gratiot Counties. Was born in Batavia Township, Branch County, Mich., Aug. 11, 1853; attended common schools and remained on the farm until 1874, when he engaged in the oak stave business at St. Louis; continued in that occupation ten years, also bought a farm near St. Louis which he improved. In the spring of 1886 he was elected President of the village of St. Louis and in the fall of the same year was elected Register of Deeds of Gratiot County, which position he held four years, and then engaged in real estate and abstract business in Ithaca; also held the offices of Supervisor and Village Assessor. In politics a Republican.

E. BROOX MARTIN

Representative from Osceola County, 1881-2 and 1883-4. Was born in Oakland County, Mich., Aug. 12, 1841. He received a collegiate education, and in 1862, engaged in the milling business. After a few years he became a resident of Battle Creek, then of Detroit, and in 1877 of Reed City. He was still in the milling business in 1887. Politically he was a Republican.

GEORGE MARTIN

Representative from Wayne County, 1851. Was born in the State of New York, July 9, 1819. He came to Michigan with his father's family in 1824. He held the position of Deputy Collector of Customs, and the offices of Supervisor and Justice. He was by occupation a farmer. He was a Democrat in politics; and resided in Grosse Pointe in 1887.

GEORGE MARTIN

Justice of the Supreme Court, 1857-67. Was born in Middlebury, Vt., in 1815. He graduated at Middlebury College, studied law, and was admitted in 1836, and the same year commenced practice at Grand Rapids, Mich., and soon took high rank in the profession. He was appointed Judge of the 6th Circuit to fill vacancy caused by the death of Judge Mundy, and in 1852 elected to that position for six years. In 1857 he was elected Chief Justice of the Supreme Court. In the allotment of terms he drew the shortest, of two years, and was again Chief Justice for eight years in 1859, holding the position until his death, Dec. 15, 1867. He was a Republican, and helped give the Supreme Court its high standing with the bar of this, and the courts of other states.

JOHN MARTIN

Representative from Wayne County, 1837. Was a native of the State of New York, born 1785. He came to Michigan in 1824, residing thereafter, with slight exceptions, either in Hamtramck or Grosse Pointe, until the time of his death, May 1, 1848. He was Captain of a company of New York militia, and was engaged at the sortie of Fort Erie in 1814, receiving wounds by reason of which he drew a government pension. He was the first keeper of the Windmill Point lighthouse at the foot of Lake St. Clair. He was the father of fourteen children, was a farmer by occupation, and a Democrat in politics.

JOHN Y. MARTIN

Representative from Shiawassee County, 1915-16, 1917-18 and 1919-20. Was born in Caledonia Township, Shiawassee County, Mich., June 8, 1863, and was educated in the district schools and the Corunna High School. He served three terms as Treasurer of Caledonia Township, eight years as Supervisor, eight years as County Clerk and four years as Postmaster at Corunna. Married. In politics a Republican.

MORGAN LEWIS MARTIN

Member of the Legislative Council from the Seventh District (Chippewa and other counties), 1832-3 and 1834-5. (Further data not obtainable).

MORTIMER B. MARTIN

Representative from Shiawassee County, 1848 and 1850. Was born in Johnstown, N. Y., Oct., 18, 1806. He received something more than an ordinary education, and became a clerk at the age of fourteen and at sixteen took entire charge of the business. At the age of twenty-one he became a merchant. He sold out in 1834, and was made the agent of a New York syndicate to purchase lands in the West. He spent two years in Illinois, but came to Michigan in 1836. In 1837 he bought lands in Antrim, Shiawassee County, where he resided until his death, Sept. 26, 1884. He was a Supervisor for sixteen years, and in politics a Democrat. He had a beautiful home, and entertained many men of distinction. The roses and flowers set out by him were the first ever planted in Shiawassee County.

STEPHEN MARTIN

Representative from Wayne County, 1877-8. Was born at High Park, Ireland, Dec. 26, 1821. He received a liberal education, pursued the study of architecture, and adopted the trade of a mason and builder. At the age of seventeen he emigrated to America, residing first in Brooklyn, N. Y., for eleven years. In 1849 he removed to Detroit and followed his avocation of a builder. He was a member of the Detroit Board of Education; Alderman for two terms; Justice of the Peace and Director of the Poor for the city of Detroit. He enlisted a company of volunteers and joined the 16th Mich. Infantry as Captain, participating in all the battles of the regiment until April, 1863, when, having become disabled, he resigned. In July, 1863, he received an appointment as Captain in the veteran reserve corps, serving therein until he resigned in November, 1865. In politics he was a Democrat. He died at Detroit, Apr. 4, 1890.

VINCENT A. MARTIN

Senator, 1917-18, from the Twenty-third District, comprising the counties of Muskegon and Ottawa. Was born in Dane County, Wis., Feb. 17, 1870, of American parentage. He was educated in the common schools of Muskegon and Van Buren counties. When he was two-and one-half years old his parents removed to Van Buren County, later settling in Muskegon County, and he has resided in that vicinity for thirty-six years. Mr. Martin was married in 1895 to Sarah E. Smith. After 1904 he engaged in electric railway work in various capacities. In politics a Republican.

WELLS R. MARTIN

Representative from Eaton County, 1848. Was born at Hoosack Falls, N. Y., Mar. 18, 1811. He was brought up a farmer, and came to Vermontville, Mich., in 1838. He filled many local offices. He engaged in farming, mercantile business and lumbering. He secured a competence and always exerted a strong moral influence in the community. In politics he was a Democrat.

FREDERICK C. MARTINDALE

Representative from the Second District of Wayne County, 1901-2; Senator from the First District, 1905-6 and 1907-8; and Secretary of State, 1909-11, 1911-13 and 1913-15. Was born in the Province of Ontario, Dec. 18, 1865. He came to Michigan with his parents in 1867, settled on a farm in Greenfield Township. He obtained his education in the Detroit grammar school, and Detroit High School, after which he taught for six years, and for three years had charge of the Delray public schools. Owing to loss of health he spent three years in the southern states, then took up the study of law at the Detroit College of Law and was admitted to practice in 1897. Mr. Martindale immediately formed a partnership with Edwin Henderson under the firm name of Henderson and Martindale. He was married to Miss Mary Tireman, Feb. 23, 1899, whose grandfather settled on a farm near Detroit in the early part of the last century. In politics he is a Republican. He was Representative from the Second District of Wayne County in the Legislature of 1901-2 and was elected to the Senate from the First District of Wayne County for the terms of 1905-6 and 1907-8. The Secretary of State is by statute a member of the Public Domain Commission and at the annual meeting in May, 1911, Mr. Martindale was chosen president of the Commission. Mr. Martindale was the unanimous choice of the State Convention, held at Detroit, Sept. 29, 1908, for Secretary of State, and was elected Nov. 3, 1908. He was renominated without opposition at the State Convention held at Detroit, Oct. 6, 1910, and elected Nov. 8, 1910. At the Republican State Convention held at Detroit on Sept. 24, 1912, he was again nominated for the office of Secretary of State and elected Nov. 5, 1912.

WILLIAM H. MARTZ

Representative from the First District of Wayne County, 1911-12 to 1917-18. Was born at Detroit, Mich., Apr. 21, 1877, of German parents. The public and

German schools of Detroit were his alma mater. He was elected Justice of the
Peace of Macomb County upon attaining his majority, and later served six years
as Deputy Sheriff of Wayne County through changing administrations. He was
married July 23, 1896, to Lotta Blackwell. In politics a Republican.

DIGHTON R. MARVIN

Representative from Osceola County, 1905-6. Was born in the township of
Elbridge, Onondaga County, N. Y., June 2, 1852, of English and Irish descent.
His boyhood was spent on a farm in New York and he acquired his education in
the common schools of Onondaga County. In the fall of 1872 he removed with
his parents to the State of Virginia, where he resided until the spring of 1873,
when he left the parental roof and came to Lansing, Mich. In 1874 he was married to Carrie A. Bailey, left Lansing and settled on land in Sherman Township,
Osceola County. He held many of the township offices, including Supervisor for
eight years; and chairman of the Board of Supervisors; was elected Register of
Deeds at the general election in 1900 and held that office for two terms.

JARVIS E. MARVIN

Representative from Washtenaw County, 1851. His postoffice address was Ypsilanti. (Further data not obtainable).

ANTHONY L. MASON

Representative from Kalamazoo County, 1867-8. Was born in Medina, N. Y., in
1826, and came to Galesburg, Mich., in 1848. His early education was that of
common schools. He went into the dry goods trade at Galesburg, in which he
continued until 1867. He removed to Kansas City in 1869, with a capital of
$200,000, since increased to half a million. At one time while in trade he
stocked three flouring mills, selling the flour east at a good profit. In politics a
Republican. He was Supervisor of Galesburg in 1857.

EDWARD M. MASON

Representative from the Second District of Genesee County, 1869-70. His postoffice address was Flint. (Further data not obtainable).

GEORGE T. MASON

Representative from Shiawassee County, 1899-1900 and 1901-2. Was born in
Owosso Township, Feb. 2, 1842. His Father, Ezra L. Mason, of Rochester,
N. Y., settled in Owosso Township, Shiawassee County, Mich., in 1839, upon the
farm on which Mr. Mason was born. It was then an almost unbroken wilderness.
He remained on the farm until twenty-one years old, receiving his education in
the district school, and in 1863 enlisted for the Civil War in the Eleventh Mich.

Cavalry, remaining with his regiment until the close of the war, and returning with it Sept. 26, 1865. Upon reaching his old home in Owosso Township, Mr. Mason purchased a farm adjoining the homestead. On Nov. 25, 1869, he was married to Miss Hannah A. Shepard, who was born in Owosso Township Mar. 11, 1845, her parents being also pioneers of Owosso Township, having come from Lockport, N. Y., and settled on a farm in 1841. Mr Mason held the various offices of Township Clerk, Treasurer, Highway Commissioner, Drain Commissioner (both township and county), and all the various official positions in the school district. In politics he was a Republican; was an Odd Fellow, and also a member of Quackenbush Post No. 205 G. A. R. He died in the state of Oregon, Jan. 9, 1918.

HENRY MASON

Representative from Monroe County, 1845. Was born in Washington County, N. Y., Aug. 10, 1791. By occupation he was a farmer, in politics a Democrat. He came to Monroe County in 1834, settled upon a farm, upon which he lived until his death in June, 1878.

HENRY M. MASON

Representative from the Counties of Delta, Chippewa, Mackinac and Schoolcraft, 1885-6. Was born in the State of New York in 1841. He removed to Michigan in 1844; enlisted in 1861 in the 8th Mich. Infantry, and served until the close of the war. Then he engaged in the drug business at Flint. Politically a Republican.

JOHN THOMSON MASON

Secretary and Acting Governor of the Territory of Michigan, 1830-1. Was born at "Raspberry Plain," Loudon County, Va., Jan. 8, 1787, and educated at Charlotte Hall Academy, Md., and William and Mary College, Va. He removed in 1812 to Lexington, Ky., and was appointed by President Monroe United States Marshal of the District of Kentucky, 1817. In 1830 he was appointed by President Jackson Secretary of the Territory of Michigan and Superintendent of Indian Affairs, offices of which he soon after resigned in favor of his son, Stevens Thomson Mason, "Boy Governor" of Michigan. Afterwards he resided principally in New York City and Washington, D. C. He died at Galveston, Texas, in 1850, after an association with that State of twenty years' duration as agent for a land company and in connection with other land enterprises; and at the two critical periods, 1833 and 1836, as the friend and promoter of Texan liberties.

LORENZO M. MASON

Senator from the First District, 1844-5, and from the Second District, 1869-70; Delegate from St. Clair County to the Constitutional Convention of 1850; and Representative from Wayne County, 1863-4. Was born in Castleton, Vt., in 1810, was educated at Castleton Academy, studied law, and was admitted to practice in his native state. He came to Michigan in 1836, locating at Port Huron, and served a term of two years as Prosecuting Attorney of St. Clair

County. He located in Detroit in 1851. He served as Police Commissioner in Detroit, 1865-9, and as inspector of the House of Correction, 1862-72. Mr. Mason did little or no law practice in Detroit, his tastes running more to active business, mainly lumbering and banking. He was a clear thinker, of cheerful and even temperament, of kindly heart and firm principles. His politics were Democratic. He died in 1872.

RICHARD MASON

Senator, 1895-6 and 1897-8 from the Thirtieth District, composed of the counties of Chippewa, Delta, Luce, Mackinac, Menominee and Schoolcraft. Was born in Spring Lake, Ottawa County, 1842; moved to Chicago in 1848; to Masonville, Delta County, in 1852; returned to Chicago in 1859, where he worked in his father's lumber yard until 1869. The following year he returned to Masonville and took charge of a saw-mill; suspended business in 1873; resumed in 1880; and became managing partner of the lumber manufacturing firm of Davis & Mason at Gladstone. He read law in 1874-5, but never applied for admission to the bar. In politics he was a Republican. He held the office of Supervisor of Masonville Township and Mayor of the city of Gladstone. He died at Escanaba, Sept. 18, 1918.

STEVENS THOMSON MASON

Secretary and Acting Governor of the Territory of Michigan, 1831-5; and Governor of the State of Michigan, 1835-40. Was born in Virginia in 1812. His father emigrated to Kentucky, where the son received his education. His father was Secretary of the Territory, and Acting Governor for a short time in 1830-1, and through his influence, the son was appointed Secretary of the Territory of Michigan by President Jackson, although but nineteen years of age. As secretary he was *ex-officio* Governor, during the absence of that officer, and much feeling was manifested, indignation meetings were held, and a deputation was sent to him to demand his commission to be returned to its source. To this demand he replied: "General Jackson appointed me with his eyes open, go home and mind your own business." The boy in years proved to be a man in thought and action, and repeatedly was Acting Governor, before the death of Gov. Porter, which occurred July 6, 1834. After that time he was *ex-officio* Governor of the Territory, and the people, taking upon themselves the right to organize a State, without asking the advice of Congress, elected him Governor of Michigan, Nov. 3, 1835, although the State was not admitted into the Union until 1837. Governor Mason served two terms, from Nov. 3, 1835, to Jan. 7, 1840. During his administration occurred the great panic of 1837, bringing ruin to many pioneers and closing the banks which had been started without paid-in capital, bringing to a termination the gigantic projects contemplated in canals, railroads and other internal improvements. These disasters were in part attributed to him, and at the close of his second term he was not a candidate, but withdrew from political life, removing to the city of New York, where he was engaged in the practice of law until his death, Jan. 4, 1843.

SHERIDAN F. MASTER

Representative from the First District of Kalamazoo County, 1903-4 and 1905-6. Was born in Canada, Mar. 7, 1869. He was educated at Albion College, graduating from that institution in 1888. Married. Lawyer by profession, having practiced law since 1891. Mr. Master was Prosecuting Attorney of Kalamazoo County from 1899 to 1902 inclusive. In politics a Republican. He was elected to the Legislature of 1903-4 and re-elected Nov. 8, 1904. Mr. Master was unanimously chosen speaker of the House of 1905-6.

ALONZO T. MATHER

Representative from Wayne County, 1841. Was born in Moncton, Vt., May 13, 1802. He came to Detroit in 1836 and engaged in mercantile and manufacturing pursuits. He afterwards removed to a farm in Dearborn, and was among the leading and prominent citizens of that township until his death, July 8, 1846. He was for some years a deacon in the Baptist Church in Detroit, and was father of Rev. A. E. Mather, a well known Baptist clergyman. His politics were Whig and Republican.

GEORGE MATHEWS

Representative from Ingham County, 1848. Was born in Watertown, Conn., Apr. 17, 1799. He came to Michigan in 1837, settled in the town of Meridian, Ingham County, and gave the name to the town. He was the first Supervisor and held that position several terms. He built the first schoolhouse, and was County Treasurer four years. He built twenty-three miles of the Lansing and Detroit plank road, was elected its superintendent in 1853, and held the position seventeen years. By occupation he was a clothier; politically Whig, then Republican. He removed to Farmington, where he was President of the village Board at the time of his death, Apr. 20, 1870.

CHARLES W. MATTHEWS

Representative from the First District of Berrien County, 1915-16. Was born in St. Joseph County, Ind., Dec. 6, 1857, of American parentage. He was educated in the district schools. Married and followed the occupation of farmer. He served as Supervisor in Berrien County for twelve successive years and was chairman of the board three years. In politics a Democrat.

JOHN A. MATTHEWS

Representative from the First District of Wayne County (Detroit), 1895-6. Was born in London Township, Ont., Sept. 25, 1866; attended the common school until twelve years, and was on the farm until sixteen years of age; entered a clothing store at London, Ont., as clerk; came to Detroit, Mich., in 1887; clerked for a time, and engaged as stenographer. While engaged as such for the law firm of Walker & Walker, he read law, and in 1891 was admitted to the bar before the Supreme Court, and engaged in the practice of the profession. In politics a Republican. He was elected Representative to the House of 1895-6 on the general legislative ticket of the city of Detroit.

LEVI C. MATTHEWS

Representative from St. Joseph County, 1849. Was born in Connecticut and removed to Colon, St. Joseph County, Mich., in 1833. By occupation he was a farmer.

RUFUS MATTHEWS

Representative from Washtenaw County, 1835 and 1836. Was born in Connecticut, Oct. 10, 1791, was reared in western New York, acquired a common school education, worked as a carpenter and joiner, came to Michigan about 1831, and settled in Northfield as a farmer, helped organize the township, was for over twenty years Supervisor and Justice, and served a term as County Treasurer. He was a Democrat. He died at Ann Arbor, Nov. 17, 1869.

THOMAS P. MATTHEWS

Representative from Wayne County, 1853-4. Was born in Middlebury, Vt., Dec. 27, 1791. He was a man of liberal education, having graduated from Middlebury College in 1811, and from Fairfield Medical College in 1815. He was a Representative in the Vermont Legislature in 1815. He came to Detroit in 1834, soon after removing to Redford, and establishing a medical practice which he followed successfully for thirty years. His politics were Whig and Republican. He died Nov. 16, 1869.

JOHN O. MAXEY

Representative, 1909-10, from the Iron District, comprising the counties of Baraga, Iron, Keweenaw and Ontonagon. Was born in Stockbridge, Calumet County, Wis., Sept. 4, 1871, of Irish parentage. His father served in the Civil War, in the 24th Wis. Regiment. Mr. Maxey attended the common school until fifteen years of age, when he went north to the lumber woods, working in the woods during the winter and in the mills during the summer. He became a millwright and followed this occupation for some time. In 1890 he entered the railway train service and continued in this until 1899, when he resigned to study law in the University of Wisconsin, completing the course in 1902. He was appointed to a position in the Bureau of Labor and Industrial Statistics, and later appointed State Factory Inspector, which position he resigned in 1904. He then removed to Marquette, Mich., and engaged in the real estate business. Two years later he moved to L'Anse, Mich., where he had extensive lumbering interests. In politics he was a Republican. He died at Detroit, Jan. 8, 1920.

ANDREW C. MAXWELL

Representative from Bay County, 1865-6. Was born at Pompey Hill, N. Y., July 11, 1831. In 1844 his father settled on a farm at White Lake, Mich. From 1849 to 1852 he was a student at Oberlin College. He taught school at Lapeer in 1852. He studied law at Pontiac and was admitted in 1853, practiced at

Lapeer and was Prosecuting Attorney in 1854. In 1857 he removed to Bay City and practiced law, also engaged in farming and real estate. He was many years a Supervisor. He was twice candidate for the State Senate, and ran for Congress in 1882. In politics he was a Democrat. He died at Bay City, Feb. 15, 1902.

BENJAMIN MAY

Representative from Wayne County, 1865-6. Was a son of Judge James May, a prominent citizen of Detroit in the early days. He was born in Detroit in 1815. He was a retail trader, and a resident of Springwells. He seemed to have contributed but little to local history. He was a Democrat in politics. He died prior to 1887.

CHARLES S. MAY

Lieutenant Governor, 1863-5. Was born at Sandisfield, Mass., Mar. 22, 1830. In 1834 he removed with his father's family to Richland, Mich., and worked on the farm until fifteen, and then became a student of the Kalamazoo branch of the State University. He studied law and was admitted to the bar in 1854. He was in 1855-6 associate political editor of the Detroit *Tribune*, and later its Washington correspondent. He commenced practice at Battle Creek, but soon removed to Kalamazoo, and was elected Prosecuting Attorney in 1860. In 1861 he resigned, raised a company for the 2d Mich. Infantry, went into the field, but on account of ill health was compelled to resign after taking part in several battles. As Lieutenant Governor he was an able presiding officer. From 1856 to 1870 he was a leading Republican speaker on the stump. In 1872 he supported Greeley for President, and acted with and spoke for the Democratic party, but later was a political Prohibitionist. He practiced law for a time in Detroit, but moved to Kalamazoo, where he died, Mar. 25, 1901.

DWIGHT MAY

Lieutenant Governor, 1867-9; and Attorney General, 1869-73. Was born in Sandisfield, Mass., Sept. 8, 1822, and removed with his father to Richland, Mich., in 1834. He graduated at the University in 1849, and was admitted to the bar in 1850. He removed to Kalamazoo in 1852, and from 1855 to 1862 was Prosecuting Attorney. He was also School Inspector, Village Trustee and President. In 1861 he enlisted as a private, and was elected Captain of Co. I, 2d Mich. Infantry. He resigned in December, 1861, and in October, 1862, was commissioned Lieutenant Colonel of the 12th Mich. Infantry, became Colonel and was brevetted Brigadier General. He married Amelia S. Kellogg in 1849. He was a Republican. He died at Kalamazoo, Jan. 28, 1880.

HENRY F. MAY

Representative from Grand Traverse and Wexford counties, 1879-80. Was born at Plymouth, Mich., Feb. 14, 1842, where he received a common school education. In 1872 he removed to Clam Lake (now Cadillac) and engaged in the mercantile business.   He was Village Treasurer, Trustee, County Superintendent of the Poor, and a member of the Cadillac City Board of Education.   In politics he was a Republican.   He died at Grand Rapids in 1899.

WILLIAM C. MAYBURY

Member of Congress, 1883-5 and 1885-7.   Was born in Detroit, Nov. 20, 1849. He was educated at the University of Michigan, which gave him the degree of Master of Arts; studied law; was admitted to the bar, and practiced.   He was City Attorney of Detroit, 1875-80; lecturer on medical jurisprudence in Michigan College of Medicine; and elected to the Forty-eighth and Forty-ninth Congresses as a Democrat.   After his retirement from Congress he resumed the practice of law; in 1897 was elected Mayor of Detroit, and twice re-elected.   He died May 5, 1909.

SAMUEL W. MAYER

Representative from the First District of Ingham County, 1897-8.   Was born in Sandusky, O., May 13, 1858.   He acquired a common school education and followed the occupation of stone cutter three years, but owing to poor health he gave it up.   He went to Saginaw in 1878 and was engaged in a store two and one-half years; secured a position as traveling salesman for a wholesale house in Saginaw, which occupation he followed two and one-half years.   In 1883 he moved to Holt and engaged in general merchandise, grain, produce and farming business.   In politics he was a Republican.   He was a member of M. S. T. of Saginaw and held a commission of Second Lieutenant of Co. E, 3d Regiment; was Postmaster four years under Harrison's administration, and elected Representative to the House of 1897-8.   He moved to Lansing where he died, July 19, 1918.

DAVID P. MAYHEW

Member of the State Board of Education, 1874-5.   His home was at Ypsilanti and Detroit.   He was principal of the Monroe branch of the University; principal of Albion Seminary and professor and principal at State Normal School at Ypsilanti.   He was appointed member State Board of Education, Jan. 3, 1874, in the place of Daniel E. Brown, deceased.   He died at Detroit.

IRA MAYHEW

State Superintendent of Public Instruction, 1845-9 and 1855-9.   Was born in Ellisburg, N. Y., in 1814.   He received an academical education, and taught school from 1832 to 1836.   He was principal of the Adams Academy, 1837 to 1841, then Superintendent of Schools in Jefferson County, N. Y.   He came to Michigan in 1843 and was principal of the Monroe branch of the University. By appointment he became Superintendent of Public Instruction, and held it from Apr. 17, 1845, to Mar. 28, 1849.   He was active and efficient in his duties, and in 1849 published a book entitled, "Means and ends of universal education." In 1851 he published a treatise on bookkeeping.   In 1852 he was principal of

Albion Seminary, and in 1854 was elected Superintendent of Public Instruction, and again elected in 1856, and in all holding that position eight years. He then established the Albion Commercial College, which was removed to Detroit and successfully managed by him for many years. He was collector of Internal Revenue for the Third District, 1862-5. He was a Democrat until 1854, then a Republican.

FRED AUGUSTUS MAYNARD

Attorney General, 1895-7. Was born in Ann Arbor, Jan. 20, 1852; was educated in the public schools of that place and the University of Michigan, graduating from the literary department in 1874 and law department in 1876; located at Grand Rapids, where he engaged in the practice of law. In politics a Republican. He was nominated for Judge of Superior Court of Grand Rapids in 1887, being defeated by 105 votes; was presented to President Harrison by unanimous vote of Michigan Senators and Representatives in Congress for the office of Governor of Alaska, but the appointment went to Vermont; was Prosecuting Attorney of Kent County for term of 1881-2, was elected Representative to the State Legislature in 1890 under cumulative voting law, which law was afterwards declared unconstitutional, hence did not take his seat; was elected Attorney General of the State of Michigan for the term of 1895-7.

LOREN MAYNARD

Senator from the Fourth District, 1846, and from the Fifth District, 1847. Was born in Madison, N. Y., Dec. 22, 1801. By occupation he was a farmer, politically a Democrat. He settled in Marengo, Mich., in 1833, erected a log house and opened a tavern. The first ball in the town was given there in 1834. He built a better hotel in 1836, which he kept until 1844. He was Sheriff of Calhoun County from 1839 to 1842. He held the offices of Postmaster and Supervisor. He died Dec. 5, 1855.

PERRY MAYO

Senator from the Seventh District, 1887-8. Was born in Hancock, N. Y., June 14, 1829. He settled on a farm with his father in 1850 at Convis, Mich., had a fair education, and was a teacher for some years. He served three years as a private in the 2d Mich. Infantry, and was twice wounded. He was Town Superintendent of Schools, and lecturer and general deputy for the Michigan State Grange. He was a Republican in politics. He died in Grand Rapids, Jan. 5, 1921; buried at Marshall, Mich.

GEORGE MEACHAM

Representative from Cass and Van Buren counties, 1839; and Senator from the Seventeenth District, 1859-60. Was born in Oneida County, N. Y., June 18, 1799. He came to Ann Arbor in 1826, but soon became a farmer in Cass County, and was the first Sheriff of that county. He was Supervisor many terms. He was first a Whig, then a Republican. Deceased.

DARIUS MEAD

Representative from Lenawee County, 1835. Was born in Lanesboro, Mass., in 1800. He was a farmer and a Democrat. He settled in Michigan in 1833, and was Justice and Associate County Judge of Lenawee County. He died at Blissfield, in 1859.

ELISHA F. MEAD

Representative from Macomb County, 1867-8 and 1869-70. Was born in Hinesburg, Vt., in 1826. He was a Republican in politics, a lawyer by profession. He came to Michigan with A. B. Maynard, in 1854, opened an office in Romeo, and practiced law until his mind failed. He returned to Vermont in 1871. He served one term as Prosecuting Attorney of Macomb County.

FRANK DAY MEAD

Delegate in the Constitutional Convention of 1907-8, from the Thirteenth District, Delta County. Was born in Ann Arbor in 1856, graduated from the University of Michigan in 1879, and then moved to Upper Peninsula, where he studied law in the office of Chandler & Grant, of Houghton. He was admitted to the bar in 1881, and began the practice of law in Escanaba in 1882. In 1884 he was married to Sara F. Myrick. He held the offices of Prosecuting Attorney of Delta County, City Attorney of Escanaba, and member of the Board of Education of Escanaba.

HENRY S. MEAD

Representative from Hillsdale County, 1850; and Senator from the Third District, 1851. Was the first lawyer in Hillsdale, Mich., and settled in that place about 1840. He was an able and popular man. He practiced law for twelve years, and died at Hillsdale in 1852.

STEPHEN MEAD

Representative from Washtenaw County, 1839. His postoffice address was Paint Creek. He was the first Supervisor of York Township, in 1836. (Further data not obtainable).

CHARLES MEARS

Senator from the Thirty-first District, 1863-4. Was born in North Billerica, Mass., in 1814. He received an academical education and was for a time a general merchant in Lowell, Mass., but in 1836 opened, with his brothers, a store at Paw Paw, Mich. Later he removed to White Lake, and then to the present site of Ludington. He built the fine harbors of Duck Lake, White Lake, Pentwater, Ludington and Pere Marquette, and was a lumberman and owner of pine lands. Later he became a leading business man in Chicago.

WILLIAM J. MEARS

Senator from the Twenty-seventh District, 1893-4. Was born in Norwich, Canada, in 1844. He came to Michigan at the age of twelve and located in Kalamazoo County, where he attended the public schools and the Kalamazoo Union School. During the war he enlisted in the 25th Mich. Infantry and remained in the service until the close of the war, when he returned to Kalamazoo County and engaged in lumbering. Dec. 6, following, he was married to Celestia I. Tyler, of Wakeshma, Kalamazoo County. Three years later he moved to Newaygo, and in 1870 to Sherman, Wexford County, continuing the lumber business. He remained at Sherman until 1881, when he moved to Boyne Falls, Charlevoix County, where in connection with lumbering he engaged in the mercantile business. In politics a Republican. He held the office of Supervisor, Justice of the Peace, and Judge of Probate.

THOMAS D. MEGGISON

Representative from Antrim County, 1921. Was born in Ontario, Feb. 24, 1875, of English-Irish parentage. He was educated in the district schools, Ferris Institute at Big Rapids and University of Michigan. He taught school for a number of years, acquiring a life certificate and was principal of schools at Onekama and Central Lake. While teaching he studied law, attending summer school at the University of Michigan, and being admitted to the practice of law, located at Central Lake, Mich. Mr. Meggison is married and has four children. In 1910 he was elected Prosecuting Attorney of Antrim County and has continued in that position. In politics he is a Republican.

HARVEY MELLEN

Representative from the Second District of Macomb County, 1889-90 and 1891-2; and Senator, 1893-4, from the Twelfth District, comprising the counties of Oakland and Macomb. Was born in Middlebury, Genesee County, N. Y., Apr. 3, 1822; came to Michigan in 1837. In 1840 he entered the employment of the government as surveyor in the Upper Peninsula, working with and under the late Judge Wm. A. Burt, for seven years, and until the township lines were there established. In 1848 he was appointed United States Surveyor, and after completing the surveys in the Upper Peninsula, worked three years on resurveys of the Lower Peninsula, and afterwards in Minnesota and Wisconsin. In 1848 he settled in Macomb County, where he made his home, being principally engaged in lumbering. Mr. Mellen, as a Democrat, has held the office of Supervisor four years. He died at Romeo, Aug. 8, 1893.

JOHN N. MELLEN

Senator from the Twenty-first District, 1873-4 and 1875-6. Was born Sept. 30, 1831, at Garry, N. Y. He received a common school education. He emigrated to Washington, Mich., in 1837. In 1841 he removed to Lenox, and in 1869 to Romeo. From 1849 to 1864 he was engaged in the United States topographical survey of California, Oregon and Washington Territory. He was one of the discoverers of iron ore in the Upper Peninsula. He was also employed by the government in establishing the subdivisions of counties and towns in Dakota Territory, Minnesota, Wisconsin and Michigan. His occupation in 1887 was that of a grain and lumber merchant. Politically he was a Democrat.

MARTIN MENEREY

Representative from Isabella County, 1921-2. Was born in Brockway Township, St. Clair County, Mar. 26, 1869, of Irish-Scotch parentage. He received his education in the common schools. He held the elective offices of Justice of Peace, Township Clerk, Supervisor and Register of Deeds. He was engaged in farming and the insurance business. Mr Menerey was married. In politics he was a Republican. He died Aug. 30, 1922.

DAVID MENZIE

Representative from Jackson County, 1845. Was born about 1815 in Johnstown, N. Y. He received a common school education, and his medical diploma at Hartford, Conn. He came to Concord, Mich, about 1837, and served as Supervisor several years. He died in 1854.

JAMES MERCER

Representative from Keweenaw and other counties, 1881-2; and Senator from the Thirty-second District, 1883-4. Was born in London, England, in September, 1830. His parents emigrated in 1833, and were residents of Michigan when it became a State. He received his education at common schools and from private tutors. He acquired his early business education in Detroit. In 1850 he removed to Lake Superior, where he remained, being closely identified with the general development of that section of the State.

WILLIAM MERCER

Representative from Ionia County, 1875-6. Was born in Saratoga County, N. Y., Oct. 12, 1824. He completed his education at the Pontiac District School. He removed to Michigan in 1831, and was the first Supervisor elected in Campbell, Ionia County. He was Town Treasurer and Deputy Sheriff, a merchant and grain dealer, and extensively engaged in manufacturing boat oars. In politics he was a Democrat.

JOSEPH MERRELL

Delegate in the Constitutional Convention of 1907-8, from the Third District, Wayne County. Was born on a farm near Belleville, Mich., in 1859. He was educated in the public schools of Detroit. At the age of twenty-one years he engaged in the grocery business. He has been very successful and owned a large amount of real estate in Detroit. He served as Alderman of the tenth ward for four years.

ELIAS W. MERRILL

Representative from Ottawa County, 1857-8; and Senator from the Thirtieth District, 1865-6. Was born in Falmouth, Me., Oct. 2, 1812, and was educated at the common schools and Maine Wesleyan Seminary. He came to Grand Rapids in 1837, removed to Muskegon in 1844, and there engaged in the lumbering business. He held various offices in town and county. In 1869 he was appointed Postmaster of Muskegon, and held the office until 1875. He was a prominent business man of Muskegon. In politics he was a Republican.

GEORGE W. MERRIMAN

Senator, 1895-6 and 1897-8, from the Eighth District, composed of the counties of Allegan and Van Buren. Was born on a farm in Savannah, Wayne County, N. Y., Feb. 4, 1851; attended district school and high school; taught in the union school at South Butler, N. Y.; came to Michigan in 1872, and took a position in the bank at Plainwell, Allegan County, where he remained ten years. In 1882 he graduated from the law department of the Michigan University; was admitted to practice, and located at Hartford, and engaged in banking and practice of law. In politics a Republican. He was a delegate to the National Convention at Minneapolis, in 1892.

JOEL C. MERRIMAN

Representative from Sanilac County, 1917-18 and 1919-20. Was born at South Butler, Wayne County, N. Y., in 1852. He was educated in the district schools in South Lowell, Mich. In 1882 he removed to Sanilac County, after which time he engaged in general farming. Married. In politics a Republican.

ADOLPHUS MERRITT

Representative from the First District, Wayne County, 1905-6. Was born at Detroit, Mich., Dec. 3, 1846, of French parentage. He was left an orphan at the age of twelve, and worked on a farm for his board and education, attending the Barstow Public School of Detroit. He spent one year in the U. S. Survey Service, and at the age of sixteen tried to enlist in a Michigan regiment in the fall of 1863, but was rejected on account of age and height. He went to New York State and was accepted in the 9th N. Y. Cavalry at Rochester, and joined his regiment in the Shenandoah Valley. He was with Sheridan during the Shenandoah Campaign, participating in all battles through the valley until the end of the campaign at Appomattox Court House. He was mustered out of service at Cloud's Mill, Va. He returned to Detroit and served one enlistment in the Michigan National Guard and Detroit Scott Guard. Married. He worked at his trade of painter and decorator for many years. In politics a Republican. He served one term on the Board of Estimates.

WILLIAM SMITH MESICK

Member of Congress, 1897-9 and 1899-1901. Was born Aug. 26, 1856, at
Newark, Wayne County, N. Y.; educated in the common schools and at Kalamazoo (Mich.) Business College, and the University of Michigan. He was admitted
to the bar in 1881. In politics a Republican. He held the office of Prosecuting
Attorney of Antrim County for one term; elected to the 55th and 56th Congresses.

ABRAHAM T. METCALF

Representative from Kalamazoo County, 1875-6. Was born Feb. 26, 1831, in
Whitestown, N. Y. He received an academical education, and graduated at the
New Orleans Dental College. In 1848 he went to Battle Creek, but shortly
afterwards returned to New York State. In 1854 he again came to Michigan,
and in February, 1855, commenced the practice of his profession in Kalamazoo.
He was chairman of the Democratic County Committee from 1860 to 1865;
Trustee of the village of Kalamazoo in 1869, and a member of the Board of Edu-
cation. In 1855 he took an active part in the organization of the Michigan State
Dental Association. In politics he was a Democrat.

ALFRED R. METCALF

Representative from St. Joseph County, 1841. Was born in Otsego County,
N. Y., Oct. 3, 1802. He came to Michigan in 1834. He was a farmer, and
politically, first Republican, then Prohibitionist. He lived for forty-five years
on his farm in Michigan, but moved to Blandinsville, Ill., in 1879, where he
resided in 1887.

HENRY MEYER

Representative from St. Clair County, 1883-4. Was born Jan. 1, 1828, at Vorie,
Germany. He received a common school education. He learned the carpenter's
trade in Hanover. In 1851 he came to Detroit, where he worked twelve years
for James Shearer, builder. In 1863 he moved to Fair Haven, St. Clair County,
and built in 1875, the Swan Creek steam grist mill; his occupation was farming and milling. In politics he was a Republican. He held the office of Town
Treasurer and Supervisor, each eight years.

LOUIS MEYER

Representative from Livingston County, 1875-6. Was born in Hanover, Germany, in 1838. He was educated in German and English, and removed from
Germany to Michigan in 1852. By occupation he was a farmer. In politics he
was a Democrat. He resided in Lansing and was connected with the Lansing
Wagon Works in 1887.

EARL C. MICHENER

Member of Congress, 1919. Was born in Seneca County, near Attica, O., Nov.
30, 1876, and removed with his parents to Adrian, Lenawee County, Mich., in

1889. He was educated in the public schools of Adrian, the law departments of the University of Michigan and the Columbian University, of Washington, D. C., graduating from the latter institution in 1903. In the same year he was admitted to practice law in Michigan and the District of Columbia, and has been engaged in that profession since that time. In politics a Republican. He served four years as Assistant Prosecuting Attorney and four years as Prosecuting Attorney of Lenawee County. During the Spanish-American War he served with Co. B, 31st Mich. Vol. Infantry. Mr. Michener is married and has two children.

JOHN MICK

Representative from the Second District of Ionia County, 1901-2. Was born in Wurtemberg, Germany, Aug. 26, 1841, in which country his early education was obtained. He came to America in 1860, and worked on a farm until Dec. 29, 1862, when he enlisted as private in the Eighth Mich. Cavalry, and served during the Civil War under the flag of his adopted country, being honorably discharged at Louisville, Ky., Dec. 20, 1865. He came to Michigan in 1866. After following the occupation of brick moulder for a number of years, he finally purchased a farm, and married, settling down to the occupation of farmer. He held various offices in his township, having been Drain Commissioner and Supervisor, and in 1892 was appointed Under Sheriff. In January, 1899, he was appointed Deputy County Treasurer. In politics a strong Republican.

JOHN MICKLE

Representative from Hillsdale County, 1842. Came from Oswego, N. Y., to Michigan in 1831. He was the first settler in Reading, Hillsdale County. He was a Whig. He served as Associate Judge of the County. The home he built of black walnut logs in 1838, was still standing in 1887. By occupation he was a farmer.

CHAS. E. MICKLEY

Representative from Lenawee County, 1865-6 and 1867-8; and Senator from the Sixth District, 1873-4. Was born Aug. 26, 1818, in Bucks County, Pa. He emigrated to Michigan in 1833, and settled in Fairfield, Lenawee County. He was the first to move in the matter of admitting women to the State University. He was also a member of the State Public School Board, and president of Lenawee County Agricultural Society. He was a farmer by occupation.

EMERY T. MIDDLETON

Representative from the Second District of Genesee County, 1913-14. Was born in Leeds County, Ontario, Feb. 20, 1870, of American parents, and was educated in the Owosso public schools and at Albion College. He was for ten years foreman in furniture and carriage factories, traveling salesman for three years and then owner and occupant of an eighty-acre farm three miles from Flint. He was married. He served as a member of the School Board three terms, held most of the offices in subordinate grange, served two years as Treasurer of Genesee County, Pomona Grange, comprising the eighteen granges of the county, and two years as master of the same organization; was also a sixth degree member of the Michigan State Grange and deputy state organizer for the same. When the National Progressive Party was organized he joined that party, at its first county meeting held in the city of Flint, at which time he was made a member of the committee on resolutions and elected a delegate to the first State Convention held at Jackson. He was the unanimous choice of the party for Representative from the Second District of Genesee County. He was a very active public spirited citizen and president of the Genesee County Crop Improvement Association. He was killed, Aug. 27, 1915, by an automobile.

ABRAHAM MIDDLESWORTH

Representative from the Second District of Genesee County, 1855-6. His post-office address was Argentine. (Further data not obtainable).

AARON W. MILES

Representative from Mecosta County, 1919. Was born at Watsontown, Pa., Dec. 6, 1874, of German-Irish parents. He came to Michigan with his parents in 1879 and located at Big Rapids, where he received his education in the public schools. He is engaged in the cigar manufacturing business. Mr. Miles is married and has one son. In politics he is a Republican. He has served as chairman of the Board of Supervisors and also as City Commissioner.

CYRUS MILES

Representative from St. Clair County, 1865-6 and 1869-70. Was born in Fowler, N. Y., Apr. 13, 1828. By occupation he was a lawyer and banker, politically a Democrat. He came to Port Huron in 1852, and went into the banking business in 1856. He was Mayor of Port Huron in 1864 and 1865. He died Mar. 2, 1877.

FABIUS MILES

Representative from Van Buren County, 1859-60. Was born in Watertown, N. Y., Dec. 31, 1814. He received an academical education, and became a teacher. In 1838 he established the Watertown Normal School, and continued it with great success until 1844. In 1844 he located at Hartford, Mich., built a saw mill and engaged in lumbering from 1847 to 1860. He was the owner of several hundred acres of land. Originally a Democrat, he became a Free Soiler in 1848, and helped organize the Republican party in 1854. He supported Greeley in 1872, and Peter Cooper in 1876.

GEORGE MILES

Justice of the Supreme Court, 1846-50. Was born at Amsterdam, N. Y., Apr. 5, 1789. He was of New England descent and was self educated. He studied law and was admitted in 1822.   He attained distinction and was District Attorney of Alleghany County, N. Y.   In 1837 he removed to Ann Arbor, and engaged in the practice of his profession.   On the resignation of Judge Goodwin from the Supreme Court in 1846, he was appointed to fill the vacancy, and held it until his death in 1850.   He was a man of commanding personal appearance, presided with diginity, and his opinions upon legal questions were concise and able.   He died at Ann Arbor, Aug. 25, 1850.

MARCUS H. MILES

Representative from St. Clair County, 1867-8; and Delegate from St. Clair County to the Constitutional Convention of 1867.   Was born in the State of New York in 1813.   He emigrated to Michigan about 1836, and settled at Port Huron. In 1837 he went to Newport, now Marine City, and engaged in mercantile business.   He was Postmaster there and a Whig in politics.   In 1838 he was elected Clerk of St. Clair County and removed to St. Clair.   He was re-elected in 1840, serving from 1839 to 1843.   In 1848 and 1850 he was elected County Clerk, serving in that office eight years.   In 1852 he was admitted to the bar and began practice; in 1854 was elected Circuit Court Commissioner; in 1856 was elected Judge of Probate, serving until 1861.   In 1863 he enlisted in the 11th Mich. Cavalry as a Lieutenant, and during nearly all the time of his service acted as Judge Advocate at headquarters in the department at Kentucky.   In 1870 he was appointed Inspector of Customs at Toronto, Canada, held the position until 1875.   He died Dec. 13, 1877, at St. Clair.   He was first a Whig in politics, a Republican after 1854.

WINFIELD S. MILLARD

Representative from Berrien County, 1881-2.   Was born at Three Rivers. Mich., Jan. 22, 1846.   He was educated at high school and State Agricultural College. In 1861 he enlisted in the 11th Mich. Infantry, and served through the war. For three years he was in the wholesale grocery trade at Laramie City, Dakota; general freight and ticket agent for C., W. & M. R. R. Co. nearly three years; moved to Niles in 1872, and was secretary and treasurer of the Michigan Wool Pulp Co., the Three Rivers Pulp Co., and Niles Water Power Co.   He was a Major of State Militia.

GEORGE W. MILLEN

Senator, 1919-20, from the Twelfth District, comprising the counties of Washtenaw and Oakland.   Was born at Ann Arbor, Mich., Oct. 17, 1863, of American parents.   He was educated in the public schools of Ann Arbor, and after leaving high school wes employed as dry goods clerk in that city until 1888, when he entered the employ of the New York Life Insurance Company.   He remained with this company twenty-three years, the latter part of the time acting as inspector of agencies.   In 1911 he resigned this position to look after various business enterprises in Ann Arbor and elsewhere in which he was interested. Vice-president of the Farmers' and Mechanics' Bank, of Ann Arbor, and also vice-president of the Dixie Portland Cement Company of Chattanooga, Tenn., which latter concern he helped to organize.   Married.   A life member of Detroit Commandery, No. 1, the Fellowcraft Club of Detroit, the Shrine and Consistory, besides numerous social and athletic clubs.   He was chairman of the Washtenaw County War Board.   In politics a Republican.

ALBERT MILLER

Representative from Saginaw County, 1847. Was born in Hartland, Vt., May 10, 1810. With a common school education he settled at Grand Blanc, Mich., in 1831, and taught school. He removed to a farm near Saginaw City in 1833; taught the first school in the Saginaw Valley in 1834-5; was Inspector of Elections, 1833 to 1848; Judge of Probate, 1835 to 1844; Justice thirteen years. He laid out Portsmouth, now part of Bay City. In 1836-7 built the second saw mill on the Saginaw River. He was Postmaster, director in banks and manufacturing companies. In politics he was first a Democrat, then a Republican. In the winter of 1887-8 he celebrated his golden wedding. He was a charter member of the Michigan Pioneer and Historical Society which records his death at Bay City, Sept. 19, 1893.

CHAS. L. MILLER

Representative from the First District of St. Joseph County, 1853-4 and 1855-6. His postoffice address was Colon. (Further data not obtainable).

CHESTER A. MILLER

Representative from the Second District of Montcalm County, 1897-8 and 1899-1900. Was born in Orion, Oakland County, Mich., Apr. 30, 1846. When eight years of age he moved with his parents to Fairplains, Montcalm County. His education was acquired in the district and Greenville schools. His life occupation that of a farmer. In politics a Republican. He was Township Treasurer five years.

ELI R. MILLER

Representative from Kalamazoo County, 1871-2 and 1873-4. Was born in Winsted, Conn., Oct 12, 1818. He received an academical education, emigrated to Michigan in 1834, and settled as a farmer at Richland, Kalamazoo County. He was active in securing appropriations for fish propagation, and for several years was one of the State Fish Commissioners. In politics he was a Republican.

FRANK C. MILLER

Representative from Ionia County, 1909-10. Was born Nov. 24, 1860, of American and German descent. His early years were spent on a farm, attending district school until the age of fourteen, when he began working by the month, receiving seven dollars per month for the first six months. He continued working upon the farm several years, in the winter attending the district school, later attending the Ionia High School. He taught school three years, during which time he began the study of law, his Saturdays and vacation days being spent in the law office of Morse, Wilson & Trowbridge. He was admitted to practice in 1886. In February, 1887, he was married to Miss Sarah J. Reid. About 1906 he became interested in real estate and timber, which business he carried on in connection with his law practice. He held the offices of Alderman, City Treasurer and Mayor of Ionia City. In politics a Republican.

GEORGE H. MILLER

Representative from the Second District of Kent County, 1919-20 and 1921-2. Was born Jan. 27, 1866, at Grand Rapids, and has always lived in that city. He received his education in the public schools and at a local business college. After leaving school he obtained employment in a boat livery at Reeds Lake, near Grand Rapids. He has been engaged in that line of work every since, and is now proprietor of the business in which he first found employment. Mr Miller is married. In politics he is a Republican.

GEORGE W. MILLER

Representative from Montcalm County, 1915-16 and 1917-18; and Senator, 1919-20, from the Eighteenth District, comprising the counties of Ionia and Montcalm. Was born in Fair Plain Township, Montcalm County, Mich., Feb. 10, 1852. He was educated in the public schools and later taught school two winters. In 1882 he went to South Dakota, where he filed a claim for 480 acres of government land. While in South Dakota he held several township offices and was State Senator one term. He returned to Michigan in 1905 and settled on a farm near Greenville. Two years later he was elected Supervisor of Fair Plain Township. He was re-elected each suceeding year from that time to 1917 and served as chairman twice. In 1911 and 1914 he was chosen to represent the county before the State Board of Equalization. Married. In politics a Republican.

GUY ALONZO MILLER

Representative from the First District of Wayne County, 1907-8 and 1909-10; and Senator from the Third District of Wayne County, 1911-12. Was born at Aurora, Ill., Sept. 11, 1875, of American parentage, and came to Michigan in 1876. He attended the Detroit High School, graduating in 1894, and the University of Michigan; was graduated from the literary department in 1898 and from the law department in 1900. He was married in 1901. After graduation in 1900, Mr. Miller engaged in the active practice of his profession at Detroit. In politics a Republican.

HENRY MILLER

Representative from Oakland County, 1853-4 and 1863-4. Was born in Buffalo, N. Y., in 1816. He came to Michigan in 1821, and was Justice for several terms at Rochester. He was a merchant, in politics a Republican. He removed to Grand Rapids in 1866, and died Apr. 24, 1879.

HIRAM L. MILLER

Representative from Saginaw County, 1841 and 1844; Delegate from Saginaw County to the Constitutional Convention of 1867; and member of the State Board of Education, 1855-7. In 1841 he received a tie vote with Jeremiah Riggs, and elected at special election; seated Feb. 26. His postoffice address was Saginaw City. He was elected member of the State Board of Education under constitution of 1850, vice Isaac E. Crary, Nov. 7, 1854; resigned July 15, 1857.

JOHN MILLER

Representative from St. Clair County, 1857-8 and 1863-4. Was born at Sugar Loaf, Canada, Feb. 1, 1818, his parents settling at Rochester, Mich., when he was young. With a limited education he went to lumbering at St. Clair, and served as clerk, general manager and superintendent of the Black River Steam Mill Company. Then he went into business for himself, was thrice Mayor of Port Huron, and became cashier and manager of the First National Bank at Port Huron. In politics he was a Democrat. He died in 1873.

JOHN C. MILLER

Representative from Berrien County, 1863-4. Was born in Ames, O., Mar. 9, 1822. He came with his parents to Michigan in 1836, but in 1843 removed to New Buffalo, where he resided. He obtained a common school education. By occupation he was a farmer, was a Whig until 1856, a Republican until 1872, after that time a Prohibitionist. He was Supervisor six years, Justice eight years, and held other local offices.

JOSEPH MILLER

Member of the Legislative Council from Macomb County, 1824-5; and Representative from Kalamazoo County, 1840 and 1841. Was born in Farmington, Conn., Oct. 29, 1779. He graduated at Williams College, studied law, married Sarah Sherman in 1808, a descendant of Roger Sherman, and settled at Winsted, Conn., in practice. He was a Justice twenty-five years, and a member of the State Legislature. In 1834 he removed to Richland, Mich., and was Associate Judge. He died in June, 1864.

LEONARD MILLER

Representative from Hillsdale County, 1841-2. Was born in the State of New York, in 1820, and came to Moscow, Mich., in 1839. Later he removed to Jonesville.

LEWIS T. MILLER

Delegate from the Ninth District to the Constitutional Convention of 1835; and Representative from Hillsdale County, 1835 and 1836. Was born in Rensselaer County, N. Y., June 11, 1787. By occupation he was a farmer, in politics a Democrat. He moved to Moscow, Mich., in 1833, and was the first Postmaster. He died Feb. 14, 1856.

LUCIEN B. MILLER

Representative from Monroe County, 1877-8, and 1879-80. Was born in the State of New York, Mar. 6, 1831. His parents removed to LaSalle, Mich., the May following, and he resided there. He received a common school education. He held the offices of Justice, Supervisor, School Director, Assessor and notary public. By occupation a farmer. In politics a Democrat.

NORTON L. MILLER

Representative from Macomb County, 1869-70 and 1871-2. Was born in Berkshire County, Mass., Dec. 2, 1815, his parents removing to Monroe County, N. Y., in 1818, and in 1832 to Macomb County, Mich. He was a miller by occupation. He was Register of Deeds for Macomb County, from 1857 to 1861. He received an academical education, and held various local offices. He was a resident of Ludden, Dakota, in 1887. He died Apr. 18, 1891.

OLE HERMAN MILLER

Representative from Manistee County, 1923——. Was born in the township in which he now resides, May 6, 1883. He was educated in the rural schools and has always followed farming as an occupation. He is a Republican; served as Supervisor of Manistee Township four terms and was elected to the Legislature November 7, 1922.

OLIVER MILLER

Delegate from Lenawee County to the Second Convention of Assent, 1836; and Representative from Lenawee County, 1844. Resided at Ridgeway, and was in politics a Democrat. He was a brother of Dan B. Miller, of Monroe, a prominent business man at an early day.

PHILIP D. MILLER

Representative from the Second District of Kalamazoo County, 1893-4 and 1895-6. Was born in Union County, Pa., Feb. 11, 1838, his parents, Enos and Christiana (Frazier) Miller, being natives of that State. He received his education at the public schools of Danville, Pa., and when about fifteen years old engaged in surveying and civil engineering with John C. Trautwine; then studied telegraphy, and in August, 1856, was placed in charge of the company's office in Philadelphia, which he resigned in 1858 to come with his parents to Michigan, locating on land in Schoolcraft Township, Kalamazoo County, which he assisted in clearing, clerking winters in a drug store. August, 1862, he enlisted as a private in the 5th Mich. Cavalry, was transferred to the 25th Infantry as hospital steward, promoted to Second Lieutenant and Assistant Surgeon. Returning with the regiment in July, 1865, he engaged in the drug business and later in banking. Aug. 23, 1870, he was married to E. Sophronia Fisher. In politics a Republican.

RICHARD C. MILLER

Representative from Montcalm County, 1871-2 and 1873-4. Was born in Hartland, Conn., Apr. 17, 1820, and received a common school education. He settled in Greenfield, Wayne County, in 1830, and removed to Fairplains, Montcalm County, in 1853, where he resided in 1887. By occupation he was a farmer and commission merchant, in politics a Republican.

SAMUEL MILLER

Representative from the First District of Eaton County, 1891-2. Was born on Jan. 28, 1834, and reared on a farm in Niagara County, N. Y., where his parents settled in an early day—having removed there from Perry County, Pa., their birthplace—on a heavily timbered farm, and reared a family of nine children, five older and three younger than the subject of this sketch. He received a common school education, attending school in the winter and working on the farm summers until 21 years of age, when he started out in life, working by the month for two years, when he began farming in 1857 on shares. Dec. 8, 1859, he was married to Miss Mary A. Hohn, daughter of Mr. John Hohn, of Lockport; continued farming until January, 1866, when he moved to Michigan, settling near Eaton Rapids. His political views have been varied, as the good of the country seemed to demand; a born Democrat, afterwards with the Republicans until the licensing of the liquor traffic, which he considered a great wrong, therefore his affiliations were with the Prohibition party until 1890, when he allied himself with the Patrons of Industry and the Industrial parties. He was nominated by the Industrials and supported by the Prohibition and Democratic parties and elected to the House of 1891-2.

WILLIAM MILLER

Senator, 1891-2, from the Eleventh District, comprising the counties of Barry and Eaton. Was born in Genesee County, N. Y., Jan. 6, 1826. His mother was of an Irish family and his father was of Scotch extraction. The early members of the family settled in Connecticut. In 1812, the parents of Senator Miller emigrated to western New York and settled in Genesee County, where the subject of this sketch was born; his early education was received in the historic district school of New York, and later in the practical school of life. When in his twenty-fourth year he came to Michigan and took an active part in the early settlement and progress of the State. He engaged in the agricultural interest of Eaton County, and became a prosperous farmer and stock breeder, and living in the city of Eaton Rapids. The only offices for which he was ever a candidate besides Senator, were Highway Commissioner and Justice, and was elected to both and filled them acceptably.

WILLIAM F. MILLER

Representative from the Third District, Houghton County, 1921-2. Was born at Hancock, Mich., Jan. 1, 1865, of German descent. He was educated in the Calumet public school and Valparaiso University. He was secretary of the

Republican County Committee for fifteen years and was chairman for one year. He has served as Village President, County Treasurer and secretary of the School Board twenty-one years. Mr. Miller is secretary-treasurer of the Arcadian Consolidating Mining Co. He is a member of the Knights of Pythias and I. O. O. F. He is married and has two sons.

JAMES W. MILLIKEN

Senator, 1899-1900, from the Twenty-seventh District, composed of the counties of Antrim, Benzie, Charlevoix, Grand Traverse, Kalkaska, Leelanau, and Wexford. Was born at Denmark, Me., May 30, 1848. What schooling he received was obtained in the common schools of Saco, Me. At the age of sixteen he was obliged to leave school, and engaged as a clerk in a retail dry goods store in Saco, remaining there for three years, when he removed to Traverse City, Mich., arriving in June, 1868. He was employed by Hannah, Lay & Co., for five years, when the firm of Hamilton, Milliken & Co. was organized to do a dry goods and clothing business. Increasing trade made it desirable to separate the two stores, which was done in 1892, Mr. Milliken succeeding to the dry goods store, which he conducted for twenty-five years. He served as an Alderman in Traverse City for a single term, but declined a re-election. He was elected to the Senate of 1899-1900, to fill the vacancy caused by the resignation of George C. Covell.

JAMES H. MILLIKIN

Representative from Tuscola County, 1909-10 and 1911-12. Was born in the Township of Bruce, Macomb County, Mich., Sept. 23, 1855, of Scotch parentage. He received his education in the district schools and the Almont High School. In 1880 he was married to Hattie S. Morton. In politics an active Republican. In 1888 he removed to a farm in Almer Township, Tuscola County. In 1896 he was elected Supervisor and held the office for nine successive years. He resigned in 1904, and was elected County Treasurer, which office he held four years.

ABEL MILLINGTON

Member of the Legislative Council, 1834-5. Was born at Rutland, Vt., Feb. 5, 1787. He became a physician, and removed to Ypsilanti, Mich., in 1826. He was Sheriff of Washtenaw County. He removed to St. Charles, Ill., in 1838, and died there the same year.

CHARLES R. MILLINGTON

Representative from St. Joseph County, 1869-70 and 1873-4. Was born Aug. 5, 1818, at Lebanon, N. Y. The next year removed to Shaftsbury, Vt., where he resided until 1836, when his father's family settled in Bennington, Vt. He received a good academical education, and taught school winters for five years. He studied law and was admitted to the bar in Vermont. He removed to Constantine, Mich., in 1847, where he resided until 1873. After that time he was a resident of Independence, Ia. He was a Whig until 1854, after that time a Republican, and was a delegate to the Convention at Jackson which organized that party.

CHARLES BLUNT MILLS

Representative from Tuscola County, 1877-8; and Senator from the Twenty-seventh District, 1869-70. Was born at Waterborough, York County, Me., May 5, 1823. He received a common and high school education. At an early age he became a minister in the Free Baptist denomination. He was a close student and gave frequent lectures in addition to his regular pastoral work. He removed to Ohio, and from there to Tuscola County, in 1856, where he bought a farm. He was for several years Judge of Probate. He was trustee of Hillsdale College for many years, and was one of the incorporators of the Free Baptist Printing House at Dover, N. H. In late years he was in the employ of Hillsdale College. He died at Mayville, Mich., Mar. 11, 1896.

FRANK E. MILLS

Representative from the First District of Washtenaw County, 1893-4. Was born in Pittsfield, said county, Sept. 13, 1848. His early education was obtained at the district school, the Ann Arbor High School and the business college. He was married in 1875 to Isadore M. Crane of Eaton Rapids. By occupation he was a farmer and dairyman, was for eight years a member of the board of managers of Washtenaw Agricultural Horticultural Society, three years general superintendent and re-elected the second term as secretary of said society; was for twenty-three years a member of the School Board of his district. In politics a Democrat.

JOHN W. MILLS

Representative from Jackson County, 1855-6. Was born in Phelps, N. Y., Apr. 24, 1821. He came to Michigan in 1835, and settled on a farm in Pittsfield, Washtenaw County. He lived at Leoni, Jackson County, from 1853 to 1856, when he moved to Illinois, and was a member of the Legislature of that State. In 1865 he removed to Grinnell, Ia. By occupation he was a farmer, politically a Republican. He died Dec. 15, 1865.

WILLIAM S. MILLS

Senator from the Twenty-seventh District, 1859-60. Was born in the State of Vermont, Oct. 29, 1820. He came to Michigan in 1854, and was Prosecuting Attorney of Sanilac County in 1860-1. He was a printer, editor, lumberman, lawyer, publisher, and later superintendent of a mining company in El Dorado Canon, Lincoln County, Nev. Politically he was a Republican.

WILLIS N. MILLS

Senator, 1905-6 from the Thirtieth District, comprising the counties of Chippewa, Delta, Luce, Menominee and Schoolcraft. Was born at Anamosa, Ia., Oct. 1, 1881, of American parents. He received his education in the Englewood High School, Ill., and at Hamilton College, Hamilton, N. Y., receiving the degree of Bachelor of Arts in 1894, and Master of Arts in 1897. He practiced law; and held the office of Prosecuting Attorney of his county two terms. Married.

HIRAM MILLSPAUGH

Representative from Wayne County, 1850. Was a native of the State of New York. The time of his birth and the date of his coming to Belleville, Mich., are unknown. He was a Democrat in politics, a farmer by occupation, and died Nov. 3, 1883.

ALFRED MILNES

Senator, 1889-90 and 1891-2, from the Seventh District, comprising the counties of Branch and Calhoun; Lieutenant Governor, 1894-5; member of Congress, 1895-7; and Delegate from the Third District in the Constitutional Convention of 1907-8. Was born at Bradford, England, May 28, 1844, and came with his parents to this country in 1854. They came over in a sailing vessel and landed at New Orleans, went up the Mississippi River to St. Louis, thence to Kansas City, Mo., and thence with "ox-team" to Salt Lake City, Utah, where they resided until May, 1859, then moved to Newton, Ia., and in the spring of 1861 to Coldwater, Mich. He enlisted in Co. C, 17th Mich. Infantry, in June, 1862, and served with the regiment, taking part in all its engagements until the close of the war, when he returned to Coldwater, in June, 1865, and engaged with his father in the grocery and produce business until 1871, when he engaged in business on his own account. In politics he was a Republican. He was elected Alderman one term, Mayor of Coldwater two terms, and was elected to the Senate of 1889-90, and re-elected to that of 1891-2; elected Lieutenant Governor in 1894 and served until June 1, 1895, when he resigned, having been elected to the 54th Congress to fill a vacancy caused by the election of J. C. Burrows to the United States Senate; was appointed Postmaster of Coldwater by President McKinley; and was a Delegate to the Constitutional Convention of 1907-8 from the Third District. He died at Coldwater, Jan. 15, 1916.

JOHN MINER

Representative from the First District of Wayne County, comprising the city of Detroit, 1891-2. Was born in the city of New York, Sept. 14, 1849, and removed with his parents to the city of Detroit when very young. He received his education in the public schools of that city, and when young learned and worked with his father at the trade of a tailor. Later he practiced law; and served three successive terms, twelve years, as Police Justice of Detroit. In politics always a Democrat. He was elected to the House of 1891-2 on the Democratic ticket.

FRED R. MING

Representative from Cheboygan County, 1905-6 and 1923—; and Senator from the Twenty-ninth District, 1907-8 and 1909-10. Was born in Rochester, N. Y., but has been a resident of Michigan for forty years. He was educated in the Toronto Veterinary College and Belleville College. Mr. Ming is a Republican and served six years as Sheriff of Cheboygan County; as Representative during the session of 1905, and as State Senator from the Twenty-ninth District in 1907 and 1909, being president *pro tem.* during the latter session. At present he is Supervisor of the fourth ward of the city of Cheboygan and president of the city school board. He was again elected to the Legislature November 7, 1922.

JOSEPH P. MINNE

Representative from St. Clair County, 1851. Was born at Point Aux Trembles, Mich., Apr. 21, 1812. When young he went to St. Louis, Mo., and learned the trade of a tailor. Returning, he located at Monroe. In 1834 he located at Port Huron, and was a merchant tailor. He was Justice for twenty years, amassed a large property, took an important part in all progressive enterprises, and was one of the most favorably known of the early pioneers. He died Mar. 10, 1865.

JOSEPH F. MINNE

Representative from the First District of St. Clair County, 1871-2. His post-office address was St. Clair. (Further data not obtainable).

ADAM MINNIS

Senator from the Third District, 1865-6. His postoffice address was Wayne. (Further data not obtainable).

PRESTON MITCHELL

Representative from Calhoun County, 1871-2 and 1873-4. Was born in Meredith, N. Y., Apr. 24, 1812; received a common school education, and was a teacher at sixteen; afterwards a clerk and merchant at Baldwinsville and Syracuse, N. Y.; came to Marshall, Mich., in 1836, and from 1837 to 1842 was a merchant at Marengo; in 1842 removed to Marshall and was County Treasurer six years; was Alderman and Mayor of Marshall, also Supervisor; Assessor of Internal Revenue, 1862-3; and Presidential Elector in 1876. In politics he was a Democrat, a Republican from 1854. He had landed interests West, and was a real estate abstract business. Deceased.

THOMAS MITCHELL

Representative from St. Joseph County, 1859-60. Was born in Washington County, N. Y., June 25, 1819. He came to St. Joseph County, Mich., in 1843, and engaged in the manufacture of agricultural implements and a general foundry business. In politics he was a Republican. In 1887 he resided at Constantine, retired from business.

WILLIAM H. C. MITCHELL

Representative from Grand Traverse and other counties, 1869-70 and 1871-2; and Senator from the Thirty-first District, 1873-4 and 1875-6. Was born in Perry County, O., May 30, 1825, received a common school education, and went to California in 1849. He returned to Ohio in 1853, and in 1866 settled at East Bay, Grand Traverse County, Mich. He was in the army as sutler, 1862-5. He was a delegate to the Republican National Convention in 1876. He was several years Register of the U. S. Land Office at Reed City, and in 1887 resided in Grand Traverse County. In politics he was a Republican, and by occupation was a tinsmith, sash and furniture manufacturer, lumberman and farmer.

WILLIAM T. MITCHELL

Representative from St. Clair County, 1853-4. Was born at Middlebury, N. Y., May 27, 1817. He received a good education, read law, and was admitted to the bar in 1839. He removed to Lapeer, Mich., and was admitted to the Michigan bar in 1839. In 1840 he edited the Lapeer *Plaindealer*, the same year was appointed Prosecuting Attorney, and in the fall was elected Register of Deeds. In 1842 he removed to Romeo, and became Prosecuting Attorney and master in chancery of Macomb County. He moved to Port Huron in 1847, where he now resides. In 1869 he was elected Circuit Judge, which he resigned after three years from insufficient salary. In politics he was a Democrat. He died at Port Huron, Feb. 7, 1916.

OTTO MOE

Representative from St. Joseph County, 1879-80. Was born Jan. 29, 1845, in Conneaut, O. He received a common school education, and removed in 1836 to Fawn River, Mich. Occupation, farmer. He was Supervisor several years. In politics a National.

ORLANDO MOFFATT

Representative from Calhoun County, 1849. Was born in Otsego County, N. Y., Feb. 20, 1808. By occupation he was a farmer, in politics Whig and Free Soiler. He came to Michigan in 1836, and died Feb. 20, 1868.

ORLANDO C. MOFFATT

Senator, 1903-4 and 1905-6, from the Twenty-seventh District, comprising the counties of Antrim, Grand Traverse, Kalkaska, Leelanau and Wexford. Was born at Lyons, Mich., Aug. 6, 1865. He removed with his parents to Northport, Mich., in 1868, and to Traverse City in 1874. He received his education in the public schools of Traverse City. He left school at the age of eighteen to go into the banking house of Hannah, Lay & Co., and left there to accept a position in the old National Bank of Grand Rapids. He returned to Traverse City in 1888 where he purchased the abstract books of Grand Traverse County, in which business he engaged. Married. He held the offices of Township and Village Treasurer, member of Board of Education and Register of Deeds. In politics a Republican.

SETH C. MOFFATT

Senator from the Thirty-first District, 1871-2; member of the Constitutional Commission of 1873; Representative from Grand Traverse and Wexford counties, 1881-2; and member of Congress, 1885-7. Was born at Battle Creek, Mich., Aug. 1, 1841. He received a common school education, and was two years a teacher at Colon. He graduated from the law department of the University in 1863, began practice at Lyons, Mich., removed to Northport in 1866, and was Prosecuting Attorney of Leelanau County four years. Politically he was a Republican. He was Register of the U. S. Land Office at Traverse City, 1874-8;

Prosecuting Attorney of Grand Traverse County; Delegate to the Republican National Convention at Chicago in 1884; and Representative in Congress from the Eleventh District from Mar. 4, 1885, until his death at Washington, Dec. 22, 1887.

CHRISTOPHER MOHR

Representative from the Second District of Bay County, 1893-4. Was born in Germany, Sept. 2, 1850. At the age of eighteen he came to New York, where he worked at the tannery trade until 1873, when he came to Michigan, locating in West Bay City, where he engaged as a clothing merchant. In politics a Democrat.

JAMES MOL

Representative from the First District of Kent County, 1919-20. Was born in Holland, May 21, 1874. He came to America with his parents in 1878 and settled in Kent County, Mich. He received his education in the public schools of Grand Rapids. After leaving school he was with the Jacob Mol Company of that city, for ten years, and later in the building material business. He served six terms in the Common Council and was president of that body one term. In politics a Republican.

JOHN A. MOLL

Representative from the Second District of Sanilac County, 1893-4. Was born in New Gehlenbeck (now Warden), Madison County, Ill., near the historic farm where Abraham Lincoln split rails. His father, Rev. J. M. Moll, a clergyman of the Lutheran Church, came to America, with his parents, from Bavaria, when fourteen years of age, locating where now is the city of Saginaw. His mother came from Hessia, Germany. He obtained his early education under the tutorship of his father, whose family on account of his ministerial duties was located respectively in Illinois, Wisconsin, Michigan, New York, Maryland and in 1882 returned to Michigan, locating at Forestville, Sanilac County. Supplementary to his father's teaching he attended Concordia College, Fort Wayne, Ind., from which he graduated in 1881. He commanded the English, German, Latin, Greek, Hebrew and Volapuk languages; was interpreter for the Consolidate Coal Company for New York and Maryland, at Eckart Mines, Md., in 1881. The following year he studied medicine which was relinquished on account of ill health. In 1885 he read law; taught school the following year and then engaged in the sale of pianos, organs and musical merchandise. In politics a Republican. He was Township Clerk from 1887-9; and Census Enumerator, 1890.

WALTER MOLSTER

Representative from the First District of Wayne County (Detroit), 1897-8. Was born in Portsmouth, Scioto County, O., June 24, 1864. He acquired his education in the public schools of Portsmouth and engaged as clerk in the office of the Adams Express Company of said city, afterwards learning the trade of shoe cutting; moved to Chillicothe, O., in May, 1883, and three years later he came to Detroit, where he followed his trade. In politics a Republican. He was elected to the House of 1897-8 on the general legislative ticket of Detroit.

GEORGE FRANCIS MONAGHAN

Senator, 1899-1900, from the Third District, comprising the fourth, sixth, eighth and tenth wards of Detroit. Was born in the city of Detroit, Oct. 28, 1875. His early education was obtained in Trinity School of Detroit, and at the age of eleven he began his collegiate studies in Detroit College. After eight years study of science and the classics he graduated from the institution with the degree of A. B., two years later receiving the degree of A. M. He then entered upon his duties as professor of Latin, Greek and mathematics in his Alma Mater, and at the same time served as principal of night schools under the direction of the Detroit Board of Education, He remained at Detroit College as one of its professors only two years, and having meanwhile commenced the study of law at the Detroit College of Law, graduated from the latter in the class of 1895, and engaged in the active practice of his profession. In the year 1898 he became associated with James H. Pound, one of Detroit's leading lawyers. Being a staunch Democrat, he took an active part in the politics of his city and State, even previous to the time of his first vote. The district represented by him had been for many years strongly Republican, and in 1897 the normal Republican majority was named as 2,500, according to Hon. C. W. Moore, the senatorial candidate for that year. In 1899, at the age of 23 years, he was nominated on the Democratic ticket and was elected to the Senate of 1899-1900. He died at Detroit, July, 1920.

ISAAC MONFORE

Representative from Macomb County, 1835 to 1837. Was born in Delaware County, N. Y., in 1803. He was educated at Rochester, N. Y., High School, and taught several seasons. In 1828 he settled on a farm in Ray, Mich., afterwards in Shelby. He studied law, was a Justice, County Clerk, and Supervisor. As a Legislator he was one of four Representatives who opposed the Wildcat banking law. In politics he was a Democrat. He died Apr. 21, 1871.

FRANK R. MONFORT

Delegate in the Constitutional Convention of 1907-8, from the Nineteenth District, Gratiot County. Was born at Utica, Macomb County, Dec. 25, 1876, but lived nearly all his life at Ithaca, Gratiot County. He was a graduate of the Ithaca High School, and also a graduate of the law department of the University of Michigan. He began the practice of law in 1900, and in the same year was elected Circuit Court Commissioner for Gratiot County. He removed to Lake City in 1901, where he remained until 1903, when he was tendered a partnership with Kelly S. Searl, which he accepted, removing to Ithaca. He was married to Miss Anna E. Barber of Ithaca, in 1903. After Judge Searl's promotion to the bench he continued in the practice of law alone.

CHARLES J. MONROE

Senator from Allegan and Van Buren counties, 1883-4, 1885-6 and 1887-8; and member of the State Board of Agriculture, 1894-1907. Was born in Lawrence, Mich., Nov. 20, 1839. He was two and a half years a student in the Agricultural College, taught eight terms, and was engaged in surveying and land agent several years. He settled in 1866 at South Haven, was Supervisor three years, and in real estate, insurance and banking after 1867. He took a law course at Ann Arbor in 1878-9, and in 1879 organized a bank at Bangor of which he was president, and also a director and president of Kalamazoo Savings Bank. In politics he was a Republican. He died at South Haven, Oct. 2, 1919.

DARIUS MONROE

Senator from the Fifteenth District, 1861-2 and 1863-4; and Representative from Branch County, 1865-6. Was born at Williamstown, Mass., Apr. 16, 1797. He removed with his parents to Cayuga County, N. Y., in 1809, and became a tanner, then a printer at Auburn, then a hatter. He was a Justice at Victory, N. Y., twelve years, Supervisor four terms, and a member of the New York Assembly in 1841. In 1852 he settled at Bronson, Mich., and was a Supervisor. In politics he was a Republican. He was appointed a member of the State Railroad Board by Gov. Crapo, and held it until his death in November, 1881.

JAMES MONROE

Representative from Calhoun County, 1857-8 and 1859-60. Was born in the State of New York, in 1816. He settled at Albion, Mich., in 1838. In 1848 he started a furnace and shop for the manufacture of stoves, threshers, and general jobbing, which he continued until 1859. He held the positions of Sheriff of Calhoun County, and of United States Marshal for western Michigan. Politically he was a Republican. He died at Kalamazoo, July 16, 1899.

JAMES H. MONROE

Representative from Grand Traverse County, 1903-4, 1905-6 and 1907-8. Was born in Steuben County, N. Y., Aug. 5, 1847. He was educated in the common schools, and was for a number of years engaged in farming. He was a member of the Board of Supervisors of Grand Traverse County for several years, and served the county as Judge of Probate for eight years. In politics he was a Republican. He died Dec. 8, 1921, at Traverse City, Mich.

JAMES S. MONROE

Representative from Gogebic County, 1901-2 to 1909-10. Was born at Paterson, N. J., Dec. 29, 1855, of Scotch ancestry. His paternal ancestor emigrating from Scotland to this country in 1770. He received his education in the public schools of his native State and the State of New York, and was graduated from Cornell University in 1880. In October of that year he went to Ontonagon and was principal of the Ontonagon Union Schools for five years. Resigning his position, he came to Ironwood in 1886. In 1887 he was admitted to the bar and from that time followed his profession, paying particular attention to real estate matters. He held numerous municipal offices, both elective and appointive. He was elected Speaker *pro tem.* of the House of 1909-10.

DANIEL N. MONTAGUE

Representative from Genesee County, 1855-6. Was born in Hadley, Mass., June 9, 1811. He came to Michigan in 1839, and settled in Vienna, Genesee County, and in 1887 still lived on the farm he carved from the wilderness. Politically he was a Republican.

HENRY MONTAGUE

Representative from Kalamazoo County, 1885-6. Was born in Hadley, Mass., July 30, 1813. He came to Michigan in 1835 and in 1887 resided at Kalamazoo. By occupation he was a farmer, politically a Republican. He was a trustee of the Michigan Asylum from 1857 to 1859, when he was appointed Steward, which position he held until Oct. 1, 1885.

DAVID T. MONTEITH

Representative from the First District of St. Clair County, 1913-14. Was born at Port Huron, May 21, 1882, of Scotch-Irish parents. He was educated in the Martin and Port Huron high schools and Alma College. At the age of five years he went with his parents, Rev. and Mrs. Thomas W. Monteith, to Vassar, Mich., where the family resided for a short time. Leaving Vassar, the family removed to Martin, Mich. In 1899, the family returned to Port Huron, where Rev. Monteith assumed the pastorate of the First Presbyterian Church. Representative Monteith was a lifelong Republican in politics. After his election to the Legislature, he resigned his position as managing editor of the Port Huron *Times Herald* to accept the office of general agent for the Detroit Life Insurance Company.

JOHN MONTGOMERY

Representative from Eaton County, 1850. Was born in Ireland, Mar. 22, 1804, and came to this country with his parents, while young, who settled in Oneida County, N. Y. He received an ordinary education, came to Michigan in 1831, and in 1835 located on a large farm in Hamlin, Eaton County. He was Supervisor, and in 1850 a Brigadier General of State militia. In politics he was a Democrat. Deceased.

MARTIN V. MONTGOMERY

Representative from Eaton County, 1871-2. Was born near Eaton Rapids, Mich., Oct. 20, 1840. He received a fair education, became a teacher, and in 1861 enlisted in the 2d Mich. Cavalry, serving until the summer of 1862, when he resigned from sickness. He studied law and was admitted in 1865. He removed to Jackson, became a successful lawyer, and in 1874 was the Democratic candidate for Attorney General. He settled at Lansing, in 1875, and became a leading member of the Ingham County bar, and had a State reputation as a jury lawyer. He was appointed Commissioner of Patents by Cleveland in 1885, resigned after two years' service, and was appointed and confirmed Associate Judge of the Supreme Court of Columbia. He died at Lansing, Nov. 12, 1898.

ROBERT M. MONTGOMERY

Justice of the Supreme Court, 1892-1911. Was born in Eaton Rapids, Mich., May 12, 1849; attended the Eaton Rapids High School until eighteen years of age, when he entered the law office of F. J. Russell, at Hart, Oceana County, where he remained three years. During the war he enlisted and was mustered in the 7th Mich. Cavalry, but never saw any active service. At the age of twenty-two he was admitted to the bar and began the practice of his profession at Pentwater, continuing until 1877, when he moved to Grand Rapids. While at Pentwater he was Prosecuting Attorney of Oceana County four years, and on moving to Grand Rapids was appointed Assistant United States Attorney, which office he held until October, 1881. At the spring election of 1881 he was elected Judge of the Seventeenth Judicial Circuit, and was re-elected to a second term, which office he held until September, 1888, when he resigned and resumed the practice of his profession at Grand Rapids, continuing as a member of the firm of Montgomery & Bundy until he assumed the duties of Justice of the Supreme Court to which he was elected in 1891 on the Republican ticket. At the April election of 1901 he was re-elected for the term commencing Jan. 1, 1902.

STANLEY D. MONTGOMERY

Representative from the First District of Ingham County, 1907-8. Was born in Grand Rapids, Mich., Feb. 13, 1878. Unmarried, and the son of Hon. Robert M. Montgomery, Justice of the Supreme Court of Michigan. He received his education at the Lansing High School and the University of Michigan. He was admitted to the bar, April, 1902, and engaged in the practice of law at Lansing, being a member of the firm Dunnebacke & Montgomery. In politics a Republican. He was elected to the Legislature Nov. 6, 1906; resigned and was succeeded by Alex. Cohen.

WILLIAM H. MONTGOMERY

Representative from Monroe County, 1838; and Senator from the Eighth District, 1855-6. Was born in Ovid (now Lodi), N. Y., Aug. 8, 1805. He settled on a farm in Dundee on the River Raisin in 1831. In 1833 he was made Postmaster at West Raisinville. He taught school in New York and Michigan for nine years; was School Inspector twelve years; and Justice of the Peace sixteen years. He was County Judge in 1849; Supervisor of Raisinville in 1839 and of Dundee in 1851; president of the Monroe County Agricultural Society; for two years one of the executive committee of the State Agricultural Society; and County Drain Commissioner. He removed to Hudson in 1862 and became a druggist. He went through various grades of military service, was made Briga-dier General by Gov. Barry in 1844, and Major General by Gov. Greenly in 1847. He died at Hudson, Oct. 13, 1884.

_____

WILLIAM R. MONTGOMERY

Representative from Hillsdale County, 1851. Was born at Bath, N. Y., Mar. 12, 1813. He moved with his parents to Rochester, N. Y., in 1816, where he lived until 1844. He received a good education, studied law, and was admitted to the bar in 1835. He moved to Camden, Mich., in 1844, and settled on an un-improved farm of 320 acres. He cleared 150 acres and removed to Hillsdale in 1855, where he still resided in 1887. He held the office of Assessor and Super-visor twenty-one years and was twelve years chairman of the County Board. He was Register of Deeds for Hillsdale County eight years. In politics he was a Whig and Republican until 1878, then an Independent Cleveland man.

_____

SILAS MOODY

Representative from Gratiot County, 1893-4. Was born in Medina County, O., May 30, 1839. He was educated in the high school of Chatham Centre, Medina County, and later taught district school five years. Apr. 6, 1861, he was married and came to Michigan, locating on a farm of four hundred acres in Pine River Township, Gratiot County, near the village of Forest Hill. Later he gave his attention to dealing in grain, wool and stock, also lumbering; his two grown and married sons having charge of the farm. A member of the Christian Church of Forest Hill, he was superintendent of its Sunday School for more than twenty-five years. In politics a Republican. He held several of the township offices.

_____

WILLIAM J. MOODY

Senator from the Fourth District, 1835-6 and 1843-4. Was a lawyer and came to Jackson, Mich., prior to 1838. He was also a speculator and politician. He was also a County Judge, and Justice of the Peace. He removed from Jackson to Racine, Wis., where he died in 1853.

_____

JOHN W. MOON

Senator from Ottawa and Muskegon Counties, 1885-6 and 1887-8; and a mem-ber of Congress, 1893-5. Was born in Wayne County, Mich., Jan. 18, 1836. Until he was 18 years of age he worked on his father's farm, attending school during the winters; moved to the northern part of the State in 1854 and soon connected himself with the lumbering business. In politics he was a Republican. He held the offices of Supervisor, Township Treasurer, and President of village; elected to the State Senate in 1884 and re-elected in 1886; elected to the 53rd Congress. He died Apr. 5, 1898.

ALEXANDER H. MOORE

Representative from St. Joseph County, 1851. Was born near Pittsburg, Pa., Nov. 8, 1817. He came to Michigan in 1844. After serving in the Legislature of 1851 as Representative, he went to LaPorte, Ind., graduating at the Indiana Medical College, and went into practice at Mottville, Mich., where he remained nine years. He resided at Osage, Mitchell County, Ia., in 1887. He was Justice and County Judge.

ANDREW L. MOORE

Delegate in the Constitutional Convention of 1907-8 from the Twelfth District, Oakland County. Was born in West Bloomfield, in 1870, of American descent. He is a direct descendant of Gen. Nathaniel Green of the Revolutionary War. Mr. Moore lived on a farm until he was eighteen years of age. He went to the district school and worked his way through college, graduating in law and elocution at the Northern Indiana Normal, Valparaiso, Ind. After leaving college he went into law practice with Judge A. C. Baldwin, at Pontiac. Mr. Moore married Miss Emma M. Hinkley, who was born in Shiawassee County in 1871. In addition to his law business, Mr. Moore was interested in several manufactories and president and general manager and owner of the controlling interest of the Pontiac Turning Company. A member of the Knights of Phythias, Odd Fellows and Maccabees.

CHARLES FREEMAN MOORE

Representative from St. Clair County, 1877-8; and member of the State Board of Agriculture, 1893-9. Was born at St. Clair, Mich., Aug. 30, 1842. He married Harriet Rice, of Detroit. He finished attending the common school when seventeen years old. He was a Congregationalist. In politics he was a Republican. The following were his leading occupations: Lumbering until 1885; farming, 1866 to 1902; salt business, 1886. He resided in Saginaw, 1869-73, in Detroit, 1873-4; St. Clair the rest of the time. Offices held: Member of the School Board; Alderman and Mayor of St. Clair; Representative, 1877-8; member of the State Board of Agriculture, 1893-9; director of the American Shorthorn Breeders' Association, 1903. He died at the Sanitarium, Battle Creek, March, 1912.

CHARLES W. MOORE

Representative from the First District of Wayne County, 1893-4; and Senator, 1897-8, from the Third District, composed of the fourth, sixth, eighth and tenth wards of the city of Detroit. Was born at Canterbury, N. H., 1845, near the birthplace of the great statesman, Daniel Webster. His early education was obtained in the district schools of his native home. His first business experience was in the dry goods line. In 1865 he engaged in life insurance and devoted his attention to that business. In March, 1880, he came to Detroit as Michigan manager for the New York Life Insurance Company, which he raised from the sixth to the first place in the State in point of premium income. A member of the Michigan Club, a thirty-second degree Mason. When a member of the House of 1893-4, he was honored by being chosen speaker *pro tem.* of that honorable body and received a place upon the most important committees.

EDWARD S. MOORE

Delegate from St. Joseph County to the Constitutional Convention of 1850; member of the Board of Regents of the University of Michigan, 1852-8; and Senator from the Seventeenth District, 1853-4. Was born in Trenton, N. J., June 4, 1805, and removed when young to Mooresburg, Pa., became a tailor and worked several years at the trade. He became a merchant in 1830, and had stores at Danville and Pottsville, Pa. In 1834 he settled at Three Rivers, and with A. C. Prutzman had a store at Prairie Ronde, removed it to Three Rivers, bought a flouring mill, and continued in business until 1859. In 1864 he helped organize and became president of the National Bank at Three Rivers. Politically he was a Democrat. He died at Three Rivers, May 2, 1885.

EPHRAIM W. MOORE

Representative from the Second District of Calhoun County, 1897-8. Was born at Rochester, N. Y., in 1854. He was raised on a farm and acquired a common school education, supplemented by a course in the Rochester public schools and in the De Groffs Military Academy, at Rochester. He began life a merchant in the State of New York, which occupation he followed for a number of years; sold out and came to Battle Creek, Mich., where he made a specialty of journalism in which he was very successful and became one of the publishers of the Battle Creek *Daily Journal;* a member of the Inland Daily Press Association, and the Michigan Republican Press Association, also correspondent to journal published in the interest of newspaper men. In politics a Republican. In the spring of 1896 he was elected Alderman by the largest majority of any Alderman in the city; his nomination for the Legislature was unanimous and he was elected to the House of 1897-8.

FRANKLIN MOORE

Representative from the Second District of St. Clair County, 1899-1900 and 1901-2. Was born in the township of St. Clair, Sept. 6, 1845. Up to his fourteenth year he attended the public school in his district with the exception of about two years, when he attended private schools in the city of St. Clair. After that he was a pupil in Williston Seminary, at Easthampton, Mass., going from there to Yale College, from which institution he graduated in 1868. He then returned to Michigan, where he was engaged in the lumber business in Saginaw until 1875. In that year he bought a farm in his native township of St. Clair, which he conducted for ten years. While engaged in farming, he bought the St. Clair *Republican* and owned and edited that paper for seventeen years. During this time he was twice appointed Postmaster at St. Clair, first under the administration of President Hayes and again under the administration of President Harrison, serving about nine years in all. While still editing the *Republican* he joined with three other citizens in organizing the Diamond Crystal Salt Company, of which he was elected the secretary and treasurer. He was a member of the Board of Education of the St. Clair city schools and Supervisor of the first ward of the city of St. Clair. He died at St. Clair, July 12, 1915.

FRANKLIN MOORE

Representative from the Second District of St. Clair County, 1919-20 and 1921-2. Was born in St. Clair Township, Sept. 6, 1877. He is a son of Franklin Moore, member of the Michigan Legislature in 1899 and 1901. His education was secured in the public schools and the St. Clair High School. He is connected with the Diamond Crystal Salt Company, of St. Clair, acting as traffic manager for ten years, and at present as secretary and treasurer of the company. He has served as Supervisor, Alderman and Mayor. He is married. In politics he is a Republican.

GEORGE W. MOORE

Senator from the Eleventh District, 1899-1900 and 1901-2; and Delegate in the Constitutional Convention of 1907-8, from the Eleventh District, St. Clair County. Was born in St. Clair Township in 1859, and received his education in the district school of his neighborhood. At the age of seventeen he left his native place and secured work in a saw mill at Muskegon, but subsequently engaged in logging, and built and operated a steam logging road in Missaukee County. Returning to St. Clair County, Mr. Moore organized the St. Clair County Savings Bank of Port Huron, in 1890, in which he served as cashier. He served as chairman of the St. Clair County Republican Committee and was a member of the Board of Supervisors of Missaukee County and chairman of the Board. He was appointed Commissioner of Banking in 1905.

GEORGE W. MOORE

Representative from Wayne County, 1847. Was born in Albany, N. Y., July 4, 1812, and came to Michigan in 1833. He was one of two sons (the other J. Wilkie Moore, of Detroit) of Gen. Wm. Moore, of Massachusetts, a distinguished officer in the war of the Revolution. He held the position of Postmaster in Brownstown under three administrations, and was Township Clerk of his township. He was a Democrat, and a merchant by occupation. He died at Council Bluffs, Ia., in 1856.

GEORGE W. MOORE

Representative from the First District of Wayne County (City of Detroit), 1879-80. Was born in Cazenovia, N. Y., June 29, 1846. His earlier training was that afforded by educated parents and the common schools. At twelve years of age he removed to Utica, N. Y., where the public schools and the well known Utica Free Academy continued his education. Some experience at the mercantile counter and desk followed by an appointment in the U. S. mustering volunteer troops. In 1863 he received an appointment in the War Department at Washington, was rapidly promoted, and a little later in the Deserters' Bureau of the Provost Marshal General's office, re-organized the work of returning the then 120,000 reported absentees to their regiments. In 1864 he took the chief clerkship of the Assistant Provist Marshal General's office at Hartford, Conn., which position he filled until after the close of the war. In 1866 he came to Detroit. A severe illness in 1868 required out-of-door life and nearly two years of gold mining, quartz mining, lumbering, hunting and Indian warfare experiences in the Rocky Mountains, Wyoming Territory, succeeded. Returning with renewed health, in 1870 he resumed the study of law begun in 1864, and attended the law department of the U. of M. In 1872 he formed with George W. Moore (a classmate bearing the same name) the law firm of Moore & Moore, at Detroit, and engaged in the active practice of law. In 1874 he became connected with the business of the late Capt. E. B. Ward in his fight for the control of the Burlington & Southwestern Railway, and after his death under the receiver conducted its business for a time. In politics he was a Republican.

HENRY M. MOORE

Representative from Montcalm County, 1851. Was born in Tompkins County, N. Y., about 1803. He came to Oakland County, Mich., in 1836, and settled at Greenville in 1845. He was a merchant, and opened the first store in Montcalm County. He was also a lawyer. Politically he was a Democrat. He was a radical temperance man. He removed to the Pacific Coast in 1852, and was said to be living at Copperopolis, Calif., in 1887.

HIRAM MOORE

Representative from Kalamazoo County, 1850. Was born in New Hampshire, in 1800. He was a farmer and inventor, in politics a Democrat. He was the inventor of Moore's harvester, which cut a swath fourteen feet wide, threshed, cleaned, and put the grain in bags. He also claimed the invention of the first sickle, and that the McCormick improvement was an infringement on his patent, and the case was in the courts for several years. He died at Brandon, Wis., May 5, 1875.

JOHN W. MOORE

Representative from the Third District of Houghton County, 1919-20. Was born at Carthage, Mo., May 21, 1871, of American parents. He removed to Detroit in 1882, and received his elementary education in the public schools of that city. He attended the Detroit College, the Michigan Military Academy, and the Detroit College of Medicine, graduating from the latter institution in 1895. After graduation he located at Atlantic Mine, Houghton County, where he acted as assistant physician and surgeon of the Atlantic Mining Company. Later he accepted the position of surgeon of the Atlantic, Baltic, Winona, Elm River, Wyandotte, and Erie Ontario Mining Companies, resigning this position in 1905 to engage in private practice. Married. He has taken all the degrees of Masonry excepting the thirty-third, and also a member of the I. O. O. F. In politics a Republican.

JOSEPH B. MOORE

Senator from the Twentieth District, 1879-80; and Justice of the Supreme Court, 1896—. Was born at Commerce, Oakland County, Mich., Nov. 3, 1845. His early education was acquired in the common schools, supplemented by parts of three years at Hillsdale College, and one year in the law department of the Michigan University. In June, 1879, Hillsdale College conferred upon him the degree of A. M., and in June, 1903, the degree of LL. D. At the outbreak of the Civil War an elder brother enlisted. The two boys who were left at home also desired to go to the front; the family could spare but one of them, so, on one December morning in 1864, they drew cuts for the privilege of serving their country. The lucky number fell to Joseph B., who went at once to Detroit, where he enlisted. He was in the barracks but ten days when, to his great disappointment, the surgeon in charge refused to accept him and sent him home. He was nineteen years old when he made this attempt. The next day after the surgeon's edict his brother went to Detroit, where he enlisted and served faithfully until the close of the war. Mr. Moore removed to Lapeer in 1868, and engaged in the practice of the legal profession. He was elected Mayor of Lapeer, Prosecuting Attorney of Lapeer County for two terms, and was a prominent member of the State Senate in 1879. He served as Judge of the Sixth Judicial Circuit for eight years. Justice Moore is much interested in the subject of international arbitration, and for several years has been a member of the executive committee of the Lake Mohonk Conference. He is now a member of the executive council of the judicial section of the American Bar Association, and of the general council of the American Bar Association. He was one of the three commissioners who selected the lands for the permanent reservations of the Mission Indians of California. He was elected Justice of the Supreme Court on the Republican ticket for the term of ten years in the spring of 1895 and re-elected, April 3, 1905, for the term of eight years. At the Republican State Convention held at Lansing, Feb. 11, 1913, he was nominated to succeed himself and was elected April 7, 1913. He was Chief Justice during the years 1904, 1905, 1912 and 1920. On Apr. 4, 1921, he was re-elected for a term of eight years.

MILLER G. MOORE

Representative from the First District of Wayne County (Detroit), 1895-6 and 1897-8. Was born in Anthony, N. J., July 20, 1869; attended school at Chester Seminary; at ten years of age he moved to Middle Valley and six years later to Califon, N. J., where he entered the employ of the N. J. C. R. R. Company as telegraph operator. He afterwards moved to Sugar Loaf, N. Y., where he worked for a short time in the same capacity for the Lehigh & Hudson R. R. After closing his services for said last named company he came to Detroit, Mich.; sailed on the lakes two seasons, then was engaged as conductor in the Detroit street car service for three years; was secretary and treasurer of the Street Car Men's Union two years, and Oct. 8, 1894, was elected secretary and treasurer of the National Association, with headquarters at Detroit. In April, 1895, he was engaged as division superintendent of the Detroit railway system. In politics a Republican. He was a member of the House of 1895-6 and elected to that of 1897-8 on the general legislative ticket of Detroit city.

THOMAS F. MOORE

Representative from Lenawee County, 1861-2; and Senator from the Eleventh District, 1863-4. Was born in Peterboro, N. H., Oct. 2, 1819. He received a fair education, and in 1838 went to western New York, working at farming and teaching; in 1839 came to Michigan, and in 1840 settled on a farm in York, Washtenaw County, where he lived until 1854. He then purchased a farm in Madison, Lenawee County. He held the offices of Justice and Supervisor. In 1865 he was appointed Inspector of the State Prison and served four years. In 1869 he was made Superintendent of the Poor in Lenawee County, and served ten years. In 1877 he became a manager of the Ionia House of Correction and served two years.

WILLIAM MOORE

Delegate form Washtenaw County to the Constitutional Convention of 1835; Senator from the Fourth District, 1837-8; and Representative from Washtenaw County, 1843. Was born at Peterboro, N. H., Apr. 9, 1787. At the age of eighteen he emigrated to Phelps, N. Y., where he married Lucy Rice in 1806. During winters he made wheels for spinning flax, farming summers. He was the first Justice there, serving sixteen years, and was Supervisor, removing to York, Mich., in 1831. He served in the war of 1812, as did his father in the Revolution. By occupation he was a farmer, politically a Democrat, in religion a Baptist. He died Dec. 4, 1850.

WILLIAM H. MOORE

Representative from the First District of Lenawee County, 1913-14 and 1915-16. Was born in Cambridge Township, Lenawee County, Jan. 23, 1849, of English and German descent. He resided with his parents until 1864, when they removed to the township of Palmyra. He was educated in the district schools and at Adrian College, graduating from the latter in 1876. His father having died in May of the same year, Mr. Moore returned to the farm where he remained. He was five times elected Supervisor, three times as Prohibitionist and twice as a Democrat. Married. In politics a Democrat.

ASA P. MOORMAN

Representative from Wayne County, 1855-6. Was a native of Ohio, born in 1803. The time of his coming to Detroit is not known. He was a member of the Board of Education of the city in 1861-2, was a carpenter and builder, a Republican in politics, and died in 1879.

CHARLES MORAN

Member of the Legislative Council, 1832-3 and 1834-5; Delegate from Wayne County to the Second Convention of Assent, 1836; and Representative from Wayne County, 1836, 1838 and 1840. Was born in Detroit, Mich., Aug. 3, 1797. He resided there until his death, Oct. 13, 1876. He was a member of the Moran family, prominent in Detroit history. At the age of fifteen he enlisted in the War of 1812, fought side by side with the late Judge Witherell in Captain Jaques Company, was under Hull when he surrendered Detroit, and served through the war. He married Julia Campau. He was Associate Judge of the County Court in 1831, and 1837-41; Justice, and many years Alderman, and held other positions of trust. In 1836 he succeeded Jonathan P. Fay in extra session of the Legislature. In politics he was a Democrat. He had large real estate interests which occupied much of his time.

GEORGE MORAN

Representative from Wayne County, 1846 and 1849. Was born in Detroit in May, 1805. He descended from the early French settlers of that name, became a resident of Grosse Pointe when twenty-one years of age, and reside there until his death in 1881. He was Supervisor of Hamtramck in 1845, and of the township of Grosse Pointe in 1848. He was Paymaster in the service of the Indian Bureau for many years, and carried the mail to Mackinac on a trail through the woods. He was widely known, and was especially influential with the Indians. His occupation was nominally that of a farmer on the farm where he resided, but he was a free operator in real estate in the vicinity. He was Democratic in politics.

ELISHA MORCOM

Representative from Menominee County, 1883-4. Was born in Cornwall, England, May 5, 1835. He emigrated to Michigan in 1854. He resided two years in Keweenaw County, going from there in 1856 to Rockland, Ontonagon County, where he served two terms as Township Clerk and was Supervisor of Carp Lake for four years. He also held important and responsible positions as mining captain and Superintendent in the copper mines. He removed to Quinnesec in 1878. He took charge of the underground works of the Quinnesec iron mine as mining captain. He was appointed superintendent in 1882. He was Supervisor of Breitung four years.

GEORGE MORELL

Justice of the Supreme Court, 1836-45. Was born at Lenox, Mass., Mar. 22, 1786. He was a descendant of the French Huguenots. He was educated at Lenox Academy and Williams College, and received his degree in 1807. He studied law at Troy, N. Y., was admitted to the bar in 1810, and settled at Cooperstown, N. Y., where he remained until 1832. During that time he was Clerk of the court of common pleas of Otsego County; master in chancery; and Judge of the court of common pleas. In 1828 he was a member of the New York Assembly. In 1832 he was appointed a Judge of the United States Court for Michigan, and removed to Detroit. He held that office until 1837, when Michigan was admitted into the Union. In 1836 he was appointed a Judge of the State Supreme Court, and in 1842 Chief Justice, on the resignation of Chief Justice Fletcher. He married Maria, daughter of Gen. Samuel B. Webb. While a resident of the State of New York Judge Morell rose through all the ranks of military service up to Major General. While serving as Chief Justice he died at Detroit, Mar. 8, 1845. His funeral was attended by the State Legislature and the bar of Detroit. As a Judge he presided with great dignity and was distinguished for his legal attainments and untiring industry. In social life he was always a welcome guest. In politics he was a Democrat.

PETER MOREY

Delegate from Lenawee County to the Second Convention of Assent, 1836; and Attorney General, 1837-41. Was born in Cazenovia, N. Y., in 1798, was educated at Hamilton Academy, studied law and was admitted in 1831. He practiced four years in the State of New York, and in 1835 removed to Tecumseh, Mich., In 1837 he removed to Detroit, having been appointed Attorney General of the State, which office he held four years. After the expiration of his term of office he returned to Tecumseh, where he continued in practice for many years, finally going to Marion, O., to live with his daughter, until his death in the fall of 1881. He was a fine scholar, a courteous old school gentleman, an able and energetic lawyer. In politics he was a Democrat.

J. LEE MORFORD

Representative from the Presque Isle District, 1911-12 and 1913-14; and Senator, 1915-16 and 1917-18, from the Twenty-ninth District, comprising the counties of Alpena, Charlevoix, Cheboygan, Emmet, Montmorency, Otsego and Presque Isle. Was born at Unionville, Tuscola County, Mich., June 14, 1873, of Scotch parentage. His early life was spent on a farm, and at the age of fifteen he assumed the sole management of the farm work. His education was acquired in the district schools and the Caro High School, the family having moved to Caro in his eighteenth year. In 1900 he went to Gaylord, purchasing an interest in a furniture and undertaking business with R. H. Russell, and ten months later bought Mr. Russell's interest in the business which had been well established. On June 27, 1904, he was placed in charge of the Otsego County Bank, a position which came unsolicited. He was elected Village President in 1906 and held this office four terms. Upon the reorganization of the Gaylord Motor Car Company, he was elected director. Married. In politics a Republican.

DAVID T. MORGAN

Delegate from the Thirty-first District in the Constitutional Convention of 1907-8; and Representative from the Second District of Marquette County, 1909-10 and 1911-12. Was born at Charleston, Tioga County, Pa., Oct. 2, 1857, and a resident of Michigan since 1879. He received his education at Mt. Union College, O. He entered the employ of the Republic Iron Co., Apr. 1, 1879, and resigned his position Jan. 1, 1907. In politics a Republican. He held the office of Supervisor of Republic Township continuously from 1893 to 1907.

FRANKLIN E. MORGAN

Senator from the Tenth District, 1877-8. Was born in Warsaw, N. Y., June 9, 1836. He was educated at Albion College, Mich. He afterwards pursued select studies at the Michigan University for one year, after which he entered the law school at Ann Arbor, and graduated in 1863. The same year he settled in Coldwater, where he practiced his profession and dealt in real estate. He was a member of the Common Council of Coldwater, and held the office of Circuit Court Commissioner. In politics he was a Republican.

MICHAEL H. MORIARTY

Senator, 1903-4 to 1911-12, from the Thirty-first District, comprising the counties of Alger, Dickinson, Gogebic, Iron and Marquette. Was born at Hudson, Mich., Sept. 27, 1859, of Irish parentage. He was educated in the Hudson High School. He studied law in the office of Thomas J. Hiller, of Hudson, and was admitted to practice in 1887. He had a clerkship in the Legislature of 1889, and at the close of the session opened a law office in Crystal Falls. He held the offices of County Commissioner of Schools, Prosecuting Attorney, County Treasurer of Iron County, and member of the Board of Control of the State House of Correction and Branch Prison at Marquette. In politics a Republican.

JAMES L. MORRICE

Representative from Emmet County, 1903-4 to 1909-10. Was born on a farm in Ionia County, Mich., Mar. 21, 1847. He received his education in the district schools, the common high school, Olivet College, and the Agricultural College, and was graduated from the latter in 1873. He was married to M. Ella Lance, Mar. 31, 1885. He held the offices of County Examiner of Teachers, County Treasurer, Register of Deeds, and for four years represented his township on the Board of Supervisors. In politics he was a Republican. He died May 9, 1920.

WILLIAM MORRIS

Representative from St. Joseph County, 1848. Was born in Surrey, England, Sept. 25, 1804. He came to this country in 1823, and settled with his parents in New York City. In 1834 he removed to Michigan, first settling at Sturgis, but in 1852 removed to a farm in Burr Oak. He was Justice, Postmaster of Sturgis four years, and Supervisor of Burr Oak. In politics he was a Democrat.

ALEXANDER H. MORRISON

Senator from the Eighteenth District, 1857-8; and Representative from Berrien County, 1861-2. Was born at Quebec, Canada, Feb. 22, 1822, of Scotch and American parentage. He was educated at a private academy, at sixteen went to Chicago, and was an employe of a contractor on the Illinois and Michigan canal. At nineteen he became a merchant and contractor on public works in Illinois and Iowa. In 1850 he removed to St. Joseph, Mich., where he resided as a merchant, manufacturer and railroad builder. In connection with James F. Joy, he constructed the Chicago & Michigan Lake Shore Railroad, and managed it for six years. He owned and operated with others, railroads in Dakota. He was formerly a Whig, later a Republican. In 1862 he was Collector of Internal Revenue, and from 1866 to 1869 Assessor. He was six years one of the Republican State Committees, and on the Governor's staff from 1854 to 1861. He died at Chicago, Ill., Sept. 4, 1890.

DAVID F. MORRISON

Representative, 1921—, from the Schoolcraft District, comprising the counties of Alger, Luce, Mackinac, and Schoolcraft. Was born on a farm in Elba Township, Gratiot County, Mich., Nov. 23, 1873, of Scotch parentage. He received his education in the district schools of Clinton County. He engaged in teaching, removing in 1894 to Schoolcraft County to teach. He was married in 1895 and has two daughters, one son, G. Dale Morrison, a member of Co. M., 125th Infantry, having been killed in action in France, July 31, 1918. Mr. Morrison has for twenty years been engaged in the general merchandise business. In 1901 he was appointed Postmaster at Germfask and served as such for fifteen years. He is a member of I. O. O. F. and Grange. In politics he is a Republican. He held the offices of Supervisor, Township Clerk, and secretary of the Board of Education.

DWIGHT S. MORRISON

Representative from Clinton County, 1909-10 and 1911-12. Was born in Orleans County, N. Y., Dec. 4, 1856. He acquired his education in the common schools. He came to Michigan with his parents when he was nine years old, and settled in Gratiot County. In 1882 he was married to Miss Josephine Bryant and removed to Clinton County. By occupation a farmer. In politics a Republican. He held several minor township offices, having been elected Supervisor seven times and County Treasurer two terms.

THOMAS MORRISON

Representative from Wayne County, 1877-8; and Senator from the Third District, 1881-2. Was born in Perth, Scotland, in 1829. He came to Canada with his parents while very young, received a classical education, and afterward studied medicine, graduating at the Buffalo Medical College in 1855. He then settled in Wayne County, Mich., where he resided in 1887, practicing his profession, but engaged principally in the drug trade. In the war he served one year as Acting Assistant Surgeon, U. S. A., and resigned at the close of the war.

WILLIAM M. MORRISON

Delegate from Calhoun County to the Constitutional Convention of 1850. Was born at Lansing, N. Y., Feb. 15, 1805. His ancestors on both sides served in the Revolutionary War. He was brought up on a farm, became a clerk and bookkeeper, and in 1837 removed to Michigan with his parents, who settled on a large farm in Jackson County. He engaged in farming and teaching, removed to Albion in 1844, became interested in milling and carried on that business until 1871. In politics he was a Democrat. For nearly forty years he was a Justice in Albion.

JAMES H. MORROW

Senator from the Fifth District (Lenawee and Monroe counties), 1891-2 and 1893-4. Was born in St. Johns, New Brunswick, Apr. 10, 1845. In 1849 he moved with his parents to Boston, Mass.   In 1852 the family located at Pembroke, where he, at the age of nine years, began work for the Pembroke Iron Works.   In 1857 he began work at the shoemaker's trade, attending school three months of the year.   Sept. 10, 1862, he enlisted in a company of volunteers, was with Gen. Banks at Port Hudson; served until Aug. 31, 1863, when his regiment was mustered out.   In 1864 he engaged as clerk in a boot and shoe store in Boston, and two years later began the business for himself which was his occupation.   In 1876 he came to Michigan, locating at Detroit, where he remained until 1882, when he moved to Adrian, Lenawee County.

ALLEN BURTON MORSE

Senator from the Twenty-seventh District, 1875-6; and Justice of the Supreme Court, 1886-1893.   Was born in Otisco, Ionia County, Mich., Jan. 7, 1839.   He was educated at the common schools with exception of two years (1857-9) at the Agricultural College, at Lansing.   He enlisted as a private in the 16th Michigan Infantry, July 30, 1861.   From July 30, 1861, to Dec. 26, 1862, he served in Co. B, 16th Infantry.   The balance of service to Sept. 16, 1864, when he was mustered out, he was Adjutant of the 21st Mich. Infantry.   He lost his left arm at Mission Ridge, Nov. 25, 1863.   He married Frances Marion Van Allen, Nov. 25, 1874, who died Oct. 29, 1884; and was married a second time, in 1888, to Miss Anna Babcock of Ionia.   He was admitted to the bar Feb. 28, 1865, and practiced his profession in Ionia County twenty years.   In politics he was a Republican until 1872.   He supported Horace Greeley for President and after that acted with the Democratic party.   He was a delegate to the convention that nominated Hancock for President, and was Prosecuting Attorney of Ionia County from 1867 to 1871 (two terms) and State Senator from Ionia and Montcalm counties in 1875.   In 1885 he was elected Justice of the Supreme Court. He died at Ionia, July 1, 1921.

CHARLES H. MORSE

Senator from the Twenty-eighth District, 1877-8; and Representative from Gratiot County, 1873-4 and 1875-6.   Was born in Orangeville, N. Y., Jan. 27, 1838.   With a common school education he settled in Orleans, Mich., in 1855; in 1861 enlisted in the 3d Mich. Cavalry; was made Captain of the 117th colored troops in 1864, Lieutenant Colonel in 1865, and Brevet Colonel in 1866, serving until August, 1867, after that year he resided in Gratiot County and was a farmer.   He was Town Clerk and a Supervisor seven years.   Politically he was a Republican.   Deceased.

JOHN L. MORSE

Representative from Ionia County, 1846.   Was born in Homer, N. Y., May 13, 1815.   He taught school at the age of sixteen.   He came at an early day to Oakland County, Mich., with his father, and married Susan Ann G. Cowles, at Avon, Mich., in 1834.   Lived in Lapeer and Oakland counties until 1838, when he settled in Otisco, Ionia County, where he lived until 1866.   He held various township offices; was County Commissioner; elected Judge of Probate in 1848, and resigned in 1850, going to California.   He returned in 1853, was again elected Judge of Probate in 1856, and in 1860. In 1866 he removed to Belmond, Ia., where he was County Judge in 1868, County Auditor in 1867, holding this office seven years. In 1876 he was a member of the General Assembly of Iowa. He was a Democrat until 1848, then Barnburner, but a Republican after 1854. He still resided at Belmond, Ia., in 1887.

JOSEPH D. MORSE

Representative from the Second District of Ionia, 1893-4 and 1895-6. Was born on a farm in Otisco, Ionia County, Mich., May 17, 1842; son of Hon. John L. Morse, one of the first settlers of that township, and brother of Allen B. Morse, United States Consul to Scotland; was educated in the Union schools in Otisco Township; taught school in the winter of 1862, and in 1863 enlisted in the 1st Mich. Engineers and Mechanics; served until the close of the war; returned home, and bought a farm in Otisco Township, where he resided. In politics a Republican.

RICHARD E. MORSE

Representative from Washtenaw County, 1835 and 1836. Was born in Otsego County, N. Y., in 1809. He came to Ypsilanti, Mich., in 1833, and engaged in practice as a physician. He was a surgeon of the Michigan forces in the "Toledo War;" was Postmaster of Ypsilanti from 1837 to 1841; and United States Consul to Curacao from 1862 to 1865. He was a Democrat until 1861, then a Republican. He died at Curacao in 1865 and was buried there.

EDWARD G. MORTON

Representative from Monroe County, 1849, 1850, 1853-4, 1863-4 and 1865-6; Delegate from Monroe County to the Constitutional Convention of 1867; and Senator from the Seventh District, 1869-70 and 1871-2. Was born at St. Albans, Vt., Dec. 15, 1812. When four years old his parents removed to the State of New York, where he lived until 1834, when they came to Monroe, Mich., where Mr. Morton lived until his death, with the exception of two years at Detroit. He had few educational advantages, and in all attended school less than a year. At the age of fourteen, at his own request, he was apprenticed for six years, to learn the trade of a printer, at $35 a year and board. For more than forty years he was connected with the newspaper press. As a writer he was sharp, incisive and keenly alive to the weak points of the enemy, and politically was always a Democrat. He held various local offices, and was Mayor of Monroe in 1851. His services as a Legislator were not small, but he particularly distinguished himself in securing the establishment of the insane asylum at Kalamazoo, and the asylum for the deaf, dumb and blind at Flint. No man was more efficient in establishing the asylum for the insane than Mr. Morton, and a speech made by him on that subject in March, 1865, was published in the journals of both Houses, was republished in the journal of insanity in New York, and 2,000 copies were printed for free distribution, of which he said it was "the greatest compliment he ever received for public service." He died at Monroe, Dec. 15, 1875.

EUROTAS MORTON

Representative from Wayne County, 1841. Was born in Hatfield, Mass., July 31, 1799, and came to Detroit in 1837. He soon afterwards removed to Rawsonville, and engaged in active business as a merchant. He held the local offices of Postmaster and Justice of the Peace for many years during his residence at Rawsonville. He was a Whig, and subsequently a Republican in politics. His later years were passed at Ypsilanti, as a retired capitalist, where he died Jan. 7, 1876.

FRANK MORTON

Representative from Mecosta County, 1889-90. Was born in Onondaga County, N. Y., Oct. 1, 1835. The following year (1836), his parents removed to Lenawee County, then to Clinton County, thence to Ingham County, settling on a farm. In 1862 he enlisted in the 6th Mich. Cavalry, and served to the close of the war. He was elected County Coroner one term and Supervisor four terms.

HENRY C. MORTON

Representative from Berrien County, 1863-4. Was born in Genesee County, N. Y., in 1817. He received a common school education. He came with his parents to Michigan in 1834, and early became interested in the development of Benton Harbor, with his father, Eleazar Morton. He was prominent in politics and business, and as a Republican, was Representative. He was the first Postmaster of Benton Harbor, and was a leader in building the ship canal which has made the village prosperous.

WILLIAM F. MOSELY

Member of the Legislative Council from Oakland County, 1826-7; and Representative from Saginaw and other counties, 1837. Was a native of Connecticut. He was the second practicing lawyer in Oakland County, and was admitted to the bar in 1825. He was Judge of Probate and Prosecuting Attorney of Oakland County, Prosecuting Attorney in Genesee County, and also in Shiawassee County. He died in 1860.

CHARLES MOSHER

Representative from Hillsdale County, 1863-4, 1877-8 and 1879-80. Was born at Chatham, N. Y., Jan. 2, 1822. He settled in Scipio, Hillsdale County, in 1842. In 1849 and 1850 he and his brothers laid out the village of Mosherville, named in honor of their father. They built a saw and grist mill. He was a practical miller and followed that business for twenty years. Originally a Whig, he became a Republican, but later a Prohibitionist. In 1884 he was the Prohibition candidate for Congress in the Second District, and in 1886 their candidate for Lieutenant Governor.

JABEZ S. MOSHER

Representative from Lenawee County, 1849. Was born in Springport, N. Y., and came from there to Jackson's mills, in Addison, Mich., about 1840. In politics he was a Democrat. He died about 1856.

THOMAS H. MOSHER

Representative from Lenawee County, 1844. Was born at Union Springs, N. Y., Oct. 18, 1815. He received a common school education, and attended the Cayuga Academy one year. He was a clerk in his father's store from 1831 to 1836, when he came to Cambridge, Mich., and with John Hart carried on a general store until 1848, at Springville, where he built a store for himself. With A. S. Berry he built the "Lake Mills" near Springville, which he owned and operated after 1856. He was Supervisor and Town Clerk.

FRANK R. MOSIER

Representative from the First District of Allegan, 1919——. Was born June 26, 1874, at Scott, Ind., of Irish-Dutch parentage. He came to Michigan in 1880, and was educated in the public schools, the Grand Rapids High School, Valparaiso University and the Michigan State Normal College at Ypsilanti. He taught school for a time but is now engaged in farming. He is married. In politics he is a Republican.

JAMES B. MOSHIER

Representative from Genesee County, 1871-2 and 1875-6. Was born July 19, 1829, at Warrensburg, N. Y. He removed to Genesee County, Mich., in 1852. He was Supervisor of Fenton, and held other town offices. By occupation he was a merchant, in politics a Democrat.

WILLIAM MOTTRAM

Representative from St. Joseph County, 1843. Located at Nottawa Prairie in 1834, as a physician, and for many years had an extensive practice in St. Joseph County. In 1851 he removed to Kalamazoo, where he still resided in 1887. He was president of the local medical society, and a delegate to the American Medical Association.

LUTHER V. MOULTON

Representative from Kent County, 1879-80. Was born in Howard, Mich., Sept. 27, 1843. In 1858 he removed to St. Joseph, and in 1863 engaged in photographing at Muskegon. In 1871 he removed to Beaver Dam, Wis., and in 1875 returned to this State and located at Grand Rapids. Politically he was a National. He wrote and published a work on finance. He was admitted to the bar in 1890 and specialized in patent law. He died at Grand Rapids, Sept. 9, 1919.

JULIUS MOVIUS

Representative from Washtenaw County, 1850. Was born in Hanover, Germany, Nov. 11, 1812. He came to this country in 1833, and settled at Ypsilanti, Mich., in 1838, where he remained until 1849, when he removed to Detroit. In 1852 he removed to Buffalo, N. Y., which was his home until his death, Oct. 14, 1871. He was at first a merchant, and then engaged in railroad business. He was general agent of three great railroads of Canada, and afterwards general agent of the Michigan Central. He married Mary L. Vibbard in 1839. He was a man of unusual ability, and well and widely known.

HORACE MOWER

Representative from Kalamazoo County, 1847. Was born in Woodstock, Vt., and was a graduate of Dartmouth College. He was admitted to the bar in Vermont, came to Kalamazoo in 1838, and engaged in practice. He was afterwards a Federal Judge in New Mexico. He was a fine classical scholar, a good lawyer, gentlemanly in his manners, full of wit and humor, and a master of irony and satire. He was one of the ablest Whig leaders in Michigan, and had great influence with his party. He died Dec. 11, 1860, at Kalamazoo.

ZEBINA M. MOWRY

Representative from Oakland County, 1848; and Delegate from Oakland County to the Constitutional Convention of 1850. Was born in Berkshire, Mass., Sept. 20, 1804. By profession he was a physician, a Democrat until 1866, then a Republican. He removed to Michigan from Madison County, N. Y., in 1838, and settled on a farm in the town of Ann Arbor until 1841, thence to Milford, where he commenced the practice of medicine with H. K. Foot. He died Aug. 1, 1874.

GILBERT MOYERS

Senator from the Thirteenth District, 1857-8. Was born in Macomb County, Mich., Sept. 13, 1833. By profession he was a lawyer, practiced his profession in Allegan County and was Prosecuting Attorney. He enlisted in the 3d Mich. Cavalry, was made Captain Sept. 7, 1861; Major, Feb. 27, 1863; Lieutenant Colonel, Aug. 13, 1862; resigned and was honorably discharged Dec. 21, 1864. In 1865 he removed to Memphis, Tenn., where he still resided in 1887, engaged in the practice of his profession.

ELISHA MUDGE

Senator, 1895-6 and 1897-8, from the Nineteenth District, comprising the counties of Clinton and Gratiot. Was born (of New England and New Work ancestry) Apr. 11, 1834. When four years of age, he moved with his parents to Michigan and settled on a farm in Vergennes Township, Kent County, where he acquired a common school education, supplemented by a course in a private high school during a portion of 1853, and at Antioch College, O., in 1856; on returning to Michigan he at once commenced teaching and preaching, and on

Feb. 1, 1857, he was ordained to the ministry of the Christian Church; the same year he came to Maple Rapids, Clinton County, where he engaged as teacher. He was married to Miss Mary L. Webster, Apr. 7, 1864, from which time until 1867 he was engaged in preaching and teaching; served in the army as private during seven months of 1865. He was elected County Superintendent of Schools in 1867 and re-elected in 1869, was appointed to fill a vacancy in said named position in 1871; was Postmaster at Maple Rapids from 1871-8, then he moved to Belding, Ionia County, where he did service as pastor and published a local newspaper. In 1882, he was chosen president of the Union Christian College, located at Merom, Sullivan County, Ind., in which capacity he served five years; resigned and returned to Michigan, and devoted himself almost exclusively to pastoral work.

JULIAN SCOTT MUDGE

Representative from the First District of Eaton County, 1893-4. Was born in Dodge County, Wis., Oct 2, 1849. Shortly afterwards he moved with his parents to Branch County, Mich., where the father died leaving the family in humble circumstances. They moved to Ohio where he acquired a district school education and engaged in business as undertaker. He returned to Michigan, locating at Grand Ledge, where he established a pleasant summer resort, to which he gave his personal attention. In politics a Republican.

ENOCH T. MUGFORD

Senator, 1891-2 and 1893-4, from the Twenty-sixth District, comprising the counties of Manistee, Mason, Lake and Oceana. Was born in Portland, Me., Jan. 14, 1829. In 1852 he moved to Chicago in the interest of Cragan & Co., meat packers. Two years later he came to Oceana County and was for a long time in the employ of Noah Ferry & Co. In the spring of 1856 he was in the employ of L. G. Mason in building his first sawmill at Muskegon. He returned to Hart Township, Oceana County, and in 1858 pre-empted a piece of land on Sec. 30. In 1850 he married Martha J. Nutter of New Hampshire. He held the offices of Highway Commissioner, Assessor of the village of Hart and Supervisor. In politics a Democrat.

JAMES MULHOLLAND

Representative from Monroe County, 1840 and 1848. Was born in Olean, N. Y., in 1803. He came to Michigan in 1806. By occupation he was a farmer, politically a Democrat. He was Deputy Sheriff of Monroe County for several years, and for several years a Supervisor. He died in 1871.

SAMUEL MULHOLLAND

Representative from Monroe County, 1849, 1857-8 and 1859-60; and Senator from the Ninth District, 1861-2. Was born in Monroe County, Mich., Feb. 10, 1811. By occupation he was a farmer. He lived first in Vienna, and afterwards in Erie.

JOHN MULVEY

Representative from Marquette County, 1887-8. Was born in Carrick-on-Shannon, Ireland, Feb. 20, 1833. He received a common school education, and emigrated to America in 1852, settling in Marquette County in 1855, where he resided. Mr. Mulvey held various offices of trust in Negaunee, having been president of the village, a member of the Common Council, City Assessor, School Trustee, and member of the Board of Supervisors for ten years. A contractor by occupation, and owner of improved real estate in Negaunee. He was elected as a Democrat to the Michigan Legislature. In April, 1886, he was unanimously elected Mayor of Negaunee. Mr. Mulvey was a Democrat until 1884.

EDWARD MUNDY

Delegate from Washtenaw County to the Constitutional Convention of 1835; Lieutenant Governor, 1835-40; member of the Board of Regents of the University of Michigan, 1844-8; Attorney General, 1847-8; and Justice of the Supreme Court, 1848-51. Was born in Middlesex County, N. J., Aug. 14, 1794. He graduated at Rutgers College in 1812. He studied law and commenced practice in his native county. In 1819 he emigrated with his family to Illinois and engaged in practice, but after a time returned to New Jersey and became a merchant. In 1831 he removed to Ann Arbor, Mich., where he became a Justice and from 1833 to 1835 was Associate Territorial Judge. He was also Prosecuting Attorney. In 1848 he was appointed by the Governor and Senate Judge of the Sixth Judicial Circuit and Associate Justice of the Supreme Court. By this appointment his residence was changed from Ann Arbor to Grand Rapids. He continued as Judge until his death, Mar. 13, 1851, when he was succeeded by Judge Martin. He was a dignified presiding officer and an able judge. He was a man of fine personal appearance, and well liked both in public and private life. In religion he was an Episcopalian; in politics a Democrat.

ORRIN W. MUNGER

Representative from Clinton County, 1865-6. Was born Nov. 17, 1837, in Huron County, O. He came to St. Johns, Mich., in 1856. By occupation he was a merchant. During the war he was U. S. Assessor for the first division of the Sixth District. He was a Republican until 1872, then a Democrat. He was president of the state bank at St. Johns.

WILLIAM MUNGER

Representative from Wayne County, 1837, 1845 and 1857-8. Was born at Sacketts Harbor, N. Y., Aug. 9, 1810. With his mother he came to what is now the village of Flat Rock in the spring of 1823. His occupation was that of a farmer, politics Democratic. He died at Flat Rock, May 5, 1884.

SILAS H. MUNSELL

Representative from Livingston County, 1903-4. Was born in Iosco Township, Livingston County, Mar. 17, 1860. After obtaining his education in the district schools and the village schools of Fowlerville, he returned to the farm, teaching winters and working on the farm summers. He was married Apr. 2, 1888, to Viola Fields. A member of Fowlerville Lodge F. & A. M., Fowlerville Chapter O. E. S. and member of the A.˙O. O. G. In politics a Republican.

LOUIS W. MUNTHE

Representative, 1891-2, from the Ontonagon District, comprising the counties of Gogebic, Ontonagon, Baraga, Keweenaw and Isle Royal. Was born in Sweden, Oct. 27, 1838. He served in the Swedish Army as a non-commissioned officer from 1854 to 1860; and entered the Danish Army in February, 1864, serving in the same capacity in the war against the Germans. He came to this country the same year and located in Michigan in the 80's. He served the people in the positions of Township Clerk and Justice of the Peace. He was elected to the House on the Democratic ticket.

JOHN J. MURDOCH

Representative from Huron County, 1899-1900 and 1901-2. Was born in Scotland in 1847, received a common school education in that country, and became a miner. He emigrated to this country in 1868, when but twenty-one years of age, and worked in the mines of Pennsylvania, Indiana, Ohio, Illinois and Iowa until 1873. He was married in Ohio in 1871, to Miss Louisa Sollan of Ohio, and in 1873 he came to Michigan and settled on a backwoods farm, now cleared and in a good state of cultivation. He was connected with the Huron County Agricultural Society for many years; Treasurer of the Huron County Farmers' Mutual Fire Insurance Company, also a director. He served as Supervisor of Caseville Township.

JAMES ORIN MURFIN

Senator from the Second District, 1901-2; and member of the Board of Regents of the University of Michigan, 1918——. Was born at Portsmouth, O., Jan 7, 1875, and was educated in the public schools of that city, graduating from the high school in 1891. He immediately entered the University of Michigan, and graduated from the literary department in 1895. The next year he graduated from the law department of the State University and began the practice of law in Detroit. Later he became a member of the firm of Bowen, Douglas, Whiting & Murfin. He was elected State Senator in 1900 from the Second District and served throughout the session of 1901-2. In 1908 he was appointed Circuit Judge of the Third Circuit to fill a vacancy, and the next year was elected to the same office, but resigned in 1911, since which time he has been practicing law in Detroit. He was elected a member of the Board of Regents of the University in April, 1917.

CHRISTOPHER MURPHY

Representative from the First District of Sanilac County, 1899-1900 and 1901-2. Was born in Cumberland County, England, July 26, 1842, and was educated in the English and Canadian common schools as well as at home, his father being a school teacher. The subject of this sketch was next to the youngest in a family of six. At the age of twelve he emigrated with his father's family to London Township, Ont., where Mr. Murphy worked on a farm and attended school until he was twenty years of age. He was married to Eliza Nelin of London, Ont., and in 1866 removed to Michigan, settling in Greenleaf Township, Sanilac County. At that time his nearest railroad station was Saginaw, sixty miles distant. In 1875 he was elected Supervisor of Greenleaf Township, holding the office nine successive years; was elected Treasurer of Sanilac County in 1884, and re-elected in 1886. In 1892 he purchased and removed to a farm near Sanilac Center, where he lived several years, holding the office of Supervisor of Watertown Township four years and twice representing the county of Sanilac on the State Board of Equalization. Later he retired to the village of Sanilac Center. He died at Sanilac Center, May 14, 1922.

HARRY L. MURPHY

Representative from the First District of Berrien County, 1911-12 and 1913-14. Was born at St. Joseph, Mich., May 13, 1881, of Irish parents. He attended the public schools and was graduated from the high school in 1900. In 1901 he entered the employ of the Threshermen's Review and Gas Power Publishing Company and resigned in 1905 to become city clerk, which office he held for four consecutive terms. In 1909 he became City Assessor and his term expired Mar. 1, 1911. He engaged in real estate and insurance business at St. Joseph. In politics a Democrat.

JOHN MURPHY

Representative from Allegan County, 1853-4. Was born in Dutchess County, N. Y., Oct. 19, 1794, and was brought up in Penfield, N. Y. His education was limited, and mostly obtained by reading. He was a farmer at first, but became a contractor on Ohio and Pennsylvania canals. In 1835 he bought a farm in Allegan County. He was the first Supervisor in Gun Plain Township, was also Justice, and was the first Sheriff of Allegan County. In politics he was a Democrat. He died June 19, 1874.

SEBA MURPHY

Member of the Board of Regents of the University of Michigan, 1837-9; and Senator from the Second District, 1840-1. Was born at Scituate, R. I., July 25, 1788. When quite young he was connected with the large mercantile house of De Graff, Walton & Co., of Schenectady, N. Y. He removed to Ovid, Seneca County, N. Y., in 1817, where he held the office of County Clerk for two successive terms, and engaged in the mercantile business. In 1835 he removed to Monroe, Mich., where he held the offices of County Commissioner, Register of Deeds, and County Treasurer, each for the term of two years. He was also cashier of the River Raisin Bank. In politics he was a Democrat. He died at Monroe, Nov. 16, 1856.

WILLIAM W. MURPHY

Representative from Hillsdale County, 1844. Was born at Ernestown, Canada, Apr. 3, 1816, but removed to Ovid, N. Y., at an early age. He came to Monroe, Michigan, in 1835, and was clerk in the government land office, studying law in leisure hours. In 1837 he removed to Jonesville, and in company with William T. Howell, opened the first law office in Hillsdale County, continuing in practice until 1861, the firm, from 1848, being that of Murphy & Baxter. He was a Democrat, then a Free Soiler until 1854, acting with the Republican party thereafter. In 1861 he was appointed Consul General at Frankfort-on-the-Main, which position he held for nine years, after that continuing his residence in Germany as the financial agent of several American railway companies. It is to him very largely that the country is indebted for its credit during the darkest hour of the war of 1861-5. He induced wealthy German capitalists to invest largely in goverment bonds to meet the financial emergency, and from that time the credit of the country stood high. He was a partner of E. O. Grosvenor at Jonesville in the banking business for a time and started the Jonesville *Telegraph*. He became quite as well known in Germany as in Michigan, and lived there until his death at Heidelberg, June 8, 1886.

ANDREW MURRAY

Representative from Berrien County, 1848. Was born at Harrisburg, Pa., in November, 1813. He graduated at Yale College, studied medicine, settled at Berrien, Mich., in 1835, and commenced practice as a physician. He removed to South Bend, Ind., then resided at St. Joseph, Mich., and finally at Niles, where he died Oct. 13, 1854.

ARCHIBALD Y. MURRAY

Delegate from Wayne County to the Second Convention of Assent, 1836; and Representative from Wayne County, 1843-4 and 1845-6. Was born in Wallkill, N. Y., Mar. 12, 1795. He removed to Michigan in 1826, settling in Canton, Wayne County, where he resided during life. He was a Democrat in politics, by occupation a farmer, miller and lumberman. He held various town offices, and was Coroner of Wayne County. He died May 23, 1865.

DENNIS MURRAY

Representative from the First District of Kent County, 1907-8. Was born at Jackson, Mich., Sept 27, 1868, of American parents. He received his education in the Jackson High School and the Kansas City College, Mo. He was left a widower with one daughter. By profession he was a dentist with office at Grand Rapids, and president of the Keeley Institute Company. With the exception of ten years' absence in Colorado, where he served two years as a member of the State Board of Dental Examiners, he resided in Michigan. In politics a Republican.

LYMAN MURRAY

Representative from Kent County, 1867-8 and 1869-70; Delegate from Kent County to the Constitutional Convention of 1867; and Senator from the Twenty-eighth District, 1875-6. Was born in 1820, in New York; received a common school education, removed to Michigan in 1845, and settled in Kent County. He was Supervisor. His occupation farming, politics Republican.

JAMES P. MURTAGH

Representative from the First District, Detroit, of Wayne County, 1889-90. Was born at London, Canada, in 1853. He was identified with organized labor in an official capacity for years, having served as recording secretary of the Council of Trades and Labor Unions three consecutive terms and was for many years a member of the Detroit Typographical Union, of which body he was president. He was elected to the House of 1889-90 on the Democratic ticket. He died July 3, 1915, at Detroit.

JAMES ALFRED MURTHA

Senator from the Second District of Wayne County, 1911-12 to 1917-18. Was born at Flatbush, Long Island, N. Y., Sept. 3, 1870, and was educated in the public schools of Brooklyn, N. Y., and at Larchmere Academy and Columbia University. In 1891 he engaged in the practice of law. Single. He was a Presidential Elector for the Third Congressional District of New York on the Palmer and Buckner Gold Democrat ticket and was also a Democratic candidate for Congress from the above-named district. In politics he was a Democrat. He died in New York, Nov. 2, 1921.

NEWTON N. MUSCOTT

Representative from Ingham County, 1857-8. Came to Leroy, Ingham County, Mich., in 1844, from Madison County, N. Y., and cleared up a large farm, where he lived until his death in 1869. In politics he was a Republican. He was several times Supervisor.

DEXTER MUSSEY

Representative from Macomb County, 1855-6 to 1861-2; and Delegate from Macomb County to the Constitutional Convention of 1867. Was born in Worcester, Mass., July 12, 1811. With a common school education he became a teacher, then a clerk, then in business for himself. He settled at Romeo, Mich., in 1837. He was in business as a merchant, blacksmith, wagon maker, farming, foundry, etc., after 1845 a Justice of the Peace. In politics he was a Republican. He died at Armada, June 29, 1890, from the effects of a fall.

JOSEPH MUSGRAVE

Delegate from Eaton County to the Constitutional Convention of 1867. Was born in Lancaster County, Pa., May 20, 1811. When young he became a resident of Ohio, a teacher, then clerk, then a merchant at Nashville, O. He was a Representative to the Ohio Assembly, 1846-7, and Senator in 1855-6. He removed to Charlotte, Mich., in 1857; and long president of the National Bank of Charlotte. He aided largely in securing railroad communication. He was a Democrat until 1854, then a Republican. He retired from business on account of his health and died in 1880.

FRANKLIN MUZZY

Senator from the Eighteenth District, 1859-60. Was born in Maine, in 1816, and was a graduate of Bowdoin College. He came to St. Joseph, Berrien County, in 1842, and in 1843 removed to Niles, where he resided until his death in 1878. He was admitted to the bar of Maine, and was at one time a law partner of Hon. Hannibal Hamlin. He was admitted to the Michigan bar in 1846, and practiced his profession during life. He was Mayor of Niles in 1873. He lived and died a bachelor. He was a man of many eccentricities, but as a lawyer had great influence with the court and jury. Deceased.

GEORGE C. MYERS

Representative from the Second District of Genesee County, 1911-12. Was born in Otsego County, N. Y., July 10, 1863, of German and English descent. His parents, George L. and Nancy (Somers) Myers, were both natives of New York, the latter dying Nov. 19, 1864. He was about four years old when his father removed to Genesee County, Mich., and settled on a farm. He received his education in the common schools and attended the Flint High School for one year. On Mar. 14, 1884, he married Miss Carrie E. Estes, of Burton Township. He held the offices of Township Treasurer, Justice of the Peace, and Supervisor. In politics a Republican.

THOMAS WILLIAM NADAL

Member of the State Board of Education, 1911-23. Was born on a farm near Milroy, Ind., of English and French parentage. He spent his boyhood on the farm, attended the district school, and later the township high school in the village of Milroy. At the age of sixteen he entered DePauw University and worked his way entirely through college, graduating in 1898. At the age of seventeen he taught school near Milroy. In college he was a member of the University Debating Team and represented Indiana in the Inter-State Oratorical Contest of 1898. On graduating he was elected to membership in the Phi Beta Kappa Society. He spent three years in Harvard, from which institution he received the degrees of A. M. and Ph. D. He has spent considerable time in travel and study abroad. Since 1898 he has been professor of English and Oratory in Olivet College and has been dean of the college since 1905. Mr. Nadal was married June 2, 1909, to Kathryne Wyckoff, of Laingsburg, Mich. He was appointed by Governor Osborn, Feb. 2, 1911, a member of the State Board of Education to fill vacancy caused by the resignation of William A. Cotton. He was nominated at the Republican Convention held at Saginaw on Mar. 3, 1911, and was elected Apr. 3, 1911, and re-elected Apr. 2, 1917.

JOSEPH NAGEL

Senator from the First District of Wayne County, 1889-90. Was born in Germany, Oct. 29, 1845. In 1889 he was a wholesale liquor dealer. He was Alderman of the ninth ward of Detroit in 1882 and 1884, and was appointed member of the Board of Water Commissioners in July, 1887, for the term of five years. He was elected to the Senate on the Democratic ticket.

NATHAN NAGEL

Representative from the First District of Wayne County, 1919-20. Was born Oct. 15, 1892, in Ruzhon, Russia, of Jewish parents. He came to the United States in 1911 and resided in Atlantic City, N. J., for about a year, when he came to Michigan. He was a student at the Detroit Institute of Technology and later worked two years in a box factory in Detroit. He has engaged in the real estate business in that city the past few years. In politics a Republican.

WILLIAM F. NANK

Representative from Macomb County, 1905-6, 1907-8, 1913-14 and 1915-16. Was born in Schoenhousen, Germany, July 21, 1867. He came to America with his parents in 1873 and located in Sterling Township, Macomb County, Mich., attending the public and Lutheran schools of the township until he was thirteen years of age. He worked for a time on a farm and in the brick yards, until the spring of 1890, when he purchased his father's farm in Sterling Township. He was married Dec. 3, 1891, to Anna Oehmke, of Warren Township. He was elected Clerk of Sterling Township, in 1893, then considered a strong Democratic Township, and was re-elected in 1894; was elected Sheriff of Macomb County in 1894 and re-elected in 1896, the first Republican Sheriff since 1880 in that county. After serving his second term as Sheriff he engaged in the livery business at Mt. Clemens. In may, 1908, he was appointed customs agent and resigned Aug. 1, 1912. In politics an active Republican. A director of the Citizens' Savings Bank and ex-member of the Board of Public Works.

EDWARD P. NASH

Representative from the Third District of Kent County, 1899-1900 and 1901-2. Was born in Livingston County, N. Y., Feb. 27, 1846; came to Michigan with his parents in 1857, locating on a farm near Rochester, Oakland County. He obtained his early education in the district schools, supplemented by one year each in the Rochester and Utica union schools. He taught school for fifteen consecutive winters in the district schools of Oakland, Macomb and Kent counties, working on a farm summers, with the exception of two summers in the shingle mills of Lapeer County. In April, 1879, he removed with his parents to Grattan, Kent County, where he operated a farm which he owned. He was married in January, 1883, to Miss Maria Purdy. In politics a Republican. He held the office of School Inspector and member of the Grattan Union School Board for a number of years; was nominated by acclamation, and was elected to the House of 1899-1900, and re-elected to the House of 1901-2.

WILLARD J. NASH

Representative from the Second District of Saginaw County, 1913-14. Was born in Genesee Township, Genesee County, Mich., May 28, 1879. His boyhood was spent on the farms in Oakland and Lapeer counties. In 1888, his father bought a farm near Cass City. Mr. Nash was educated in the district school and in the Cass City High school, graduating from the latter in 1894. In 1900 he entered the Ferris Institute and besides taking the college preparatory course, took courses in stenography and typewriting and a business course. In 1902, he went to Chicago and secured employment as a stenographer. He worked in a law office during the day and attended the John Marshall Law School at night, thus completing the first year of his law course. In the spring of 1903, he was engaged as secretary to Richard D. Harlan, president of Lake Forest College, to which position he returned during vacations, until completing the law course at the University of Michigan, engaging in the practice of law at Saginaw in November, 1905. In June, 1906, he removed to St. Charles and practiced law at that place. He was married June 24, 1908, to Donna B. MacLachlan. In politics a Democrat.

FRANK S. NEAL

Representative from the Third District of Wayne County, 1901-2 and 1903-4. Was born in Seneca County, N. Y., Sept. 21, 1862, and obtained his education in the common schools. He came to Michigan in 1880, and locating at Dundee, entered the employ of the C. S. & L. S. and M. C. R. R., where he remained eight years, as ticket agent and telegraph operator, after which he went to Northville, and engaged in the mercantile business. Married. In 1891 he bought the Northville *Record* and devoted himself entirely to newspaper work; was a director in the Globe Furniture Co., of Northville, a director of the Northville Telephone Co., and chairman of the Second District Congressional Committee of Wayne County. In politics a Republican.

JOHN L. NEAR

Representative from Wayne County, 1839; and Senator from the Fourth District, 1857-8 and 1861-2. Was born at Middlebury, N. Y., Apr. 4, 1808. He received a common school education; at the age of twenty commenced teaching winters, and at the same time studied medicine. He attended medical schools at Albany and at Castleton, Vt., and graduated in 1833. In 1834 he located in the southern part of Wayne County, Mich., where he had an extensive practice. He was Consul for some time at Sarnia, and also at Windsor from 1873 to 1876. In politics he was a Republican. He resided at Flat Rock in 1887.

JAMES M. NEASMITH

Senator from the Nineteenth District, 1871-2, and from the Fifteenth District, 1873-4; and Commissioner of the State Land Office, 1879-83. Was born Sept. 26, 1823, in Manchester, England, and came to the United States with his parents in 1829. Having spent two years in New York City and Philadelphia, they removed to Pembroke, Genesee County, N. Y. While there, in 1850, he was elected Township Clerk, and in 1853 Township Supervisor. Having come to Michigan in 1854, he purchased a farm in Schoolcraft, Kalamazoo County, where he resided in 1887. In 1856 he was elected Supervisor, holding the office for seven successive years. In 1862 he was elected Treasurer of Kalamazoo County, and re-elected in 1864 and 1866. During three years of that period he was Treasurer of Kalamazoo village. Having returned to his farm, he interested himself principally in its development and in the improvement of sheep. His farm was one of the finest in that county of fine farms. In politics he was a Republican.

CADY NEFF

Representative from Wayne County, 1875-6. Was born in Montgomery County, N. Y. He received a common school education, removed to Michigan in 1855, and settled in Wayne County. He was a carriage maker by occupation; in politics a Republican.

LOUIS NELLER

Representative from the First District of Ingham County, 1913-14. Was born at St. Johns, Clinton County, Mich., Sept. 10, 1873, of German descent. His education was acquired in the district schools. He remained on the farm with his father until seventeen years of age after which he worked as carpenter three years and later engaged in the contracting and realty business. Married. In politics a National Progressive.

CHAS. D. NELSON

Senator from the Twenty-ninth District, 1875-6, and from the Twenty-sixth District, 1877-8. Was born at Newbury, Vt., May 12, 1824. He received a common school education and attended college at Boston. He removed to Muskegon in 1857. He was Alderman, Supervisor and chairman of the Board of Supervisors three terms, president of the Board of Education, and City Treasurer of Muskegon. He was extensively engaged in the manufacture and sale of lumber. In politics he was a Republican.

EDWARD D. NELSON

Representative from Marquette County, 1881-2. Was born at Canal Dover, O., Aug. 27, 1846. Most of his youth was spent on a farm. He removed to Ishpeming in 1873, and was for five years cashier of the First National Bank, but engaged in mercantile pursuits. In politics a Republican.

SIGURD G. NELSON

Representative from Gogebic County, 1915-16 and 1917-18. Was born in Ironwood, in 1890. After attending the public schools, he entered the U. of M. and graduated from the law department in 1912, after which time he followed the practice of his profession in his home city. In politics he was a Republican. Deceased.

THEODORE NELSON

State Superintendent of Public Instruction, 1885-7. Was born at Madison, Lenawee County, Feb. 11, 1841. When fourteen years old he removed with his father to Gratiot County, where he attended the common schools and at seventeen he became a teacher. Desiring better advantages he went on foot to Hillsdale College. He enlisted in the Civil War and rose to the rank of Captain. After the war he entered Kalamazoo College but was elected Register of Deeds, after which he graduated frm Kalamazoo College. He was ordained at Ithaca, and was pastor nine years at Saginaw. His health failing he traveled extensively and made a trip to Europe. He was the president of Kalamazoo College, was professor of English at the State Normal at Ypsilanti in 1885. He next became a professor at Alma College, but resigned to become the pastor of a church at Saginaw. His death occurred at Alma, May 1, 1892.

WILBUR NELSON

Representative from Gratiot County, 1881-2. Was born Jan. 15, 1839, in Madison, Lenawee County, Mich., and removed with his parents to Gratiot County, in 1854. He served over four years in the Union army during the rebellion, and held the rank of Captain when mustered out at the close of the war. He then engaged in mercantile pursuits. In politics he was a Republican.

ALFRED M. NEVINS

Representative from Barry County, 1921—. Was born at Richland, Kalamazoo County, Mich., Apr. 5, 1862, of Scotch-Irish parentage. He was educated in district schools and high school of Otsego, Mich. He served as Supervisor of Orangeville Township for ten years and was for four years County Treasurer. Mr. Nevins is engaged in farming. He is married and has one son and one daughter. In politics he is a Republican.

BARTLETT A. NEVINS

Representative from the First District of Allegan County, 1899-1900 and 1901-2. Was born at Richland, Kalamazoo County, Mich., June 1, 1854. He attended the district schools until he was fourteen years old, when he started out for himself, working on a farm for twelve dollars a month. By hard labor and economy he saved enough to enable him to enter Michigan Agricultural College in February, 1872, and graduated in November, in the class of 1875. In the same year he went to Otsego, Allegan County, and remained there four years as principal of schools. In March, 1880, he purchased a half interest in a planing mill at Otsego, forming a partnership under the firm name of Prentiss & Nevins. The manufacturing part of the plant was burned in December, but was rebuilt the following spring, a partner added, and the firm became Prentiss, Nevins & Co. In 1895 the firm became Nevins & Lindsley, and the plant was finally sold to the Otsego Chair Company. In January, 1890, Mr. Nevins was appointed Postmaster of Otsego, but was superseded by a Democrat four years later. He engaged in various kinds of business, including real estate and insurance. He served as Justice of the Peace, member of the School Board several times, Village Councilman, Deputy Sheriff, and Village Treasurer.

JOHN M. NEVINS

Representative from Barry County, 1857-8; and Senator from the Twenty-first District, 1865-6. Was born in Braintree, Vt., Apr. 26, 1826. He removed to Michigan with his father in 1844, who settled in Richland. The son learned the trade of a carpenter, which he followed summers and taught school winters. He removed to Hastings in 1853, and became a merchant. In politics he was a Whig until 1854, then a Republican. He published the Hastings *Banner* from 1857 to 1866. He was a member of the State Republican Committee in 1860-2 and 1870-2, and a member of the County Republican Committee, and most of the time chairman from 1858 to 1876. He was County Superintendent of the Poor eighteen years; twelve years secretary of the County Agricultural Society; and eighteen years a School Trustee. From 1875 to 1883 he was Postmaster at Hastings. Deceased.

FRANK D. NEWBERRY

Representative from Branch County, 1903-4. Was born in Avon Township, Oakland County, Mich., June 23, 1840; received his preparatory education at the Rochester Academy and the Dickinson Institute at Romeo; entered Williams College, Mass., in September, 1859; left college and enlisted in the 5th N. Y. Vol. Infantry (Duryees Zouaves), May 9, 1861; served his full term of enlistment and was in all the battles in eastern Virginia from Big Bethel to Chancellorsville. He graduated from the Medical department of the University of Michigan, in March, 1865. He was married in 1867, and engaged in teaching. He was principal of the schools at Rochester for two years and then removed to Branch County and had charge of the schools at Union City for four years. He was elected Clerk of Branch County, in 1874, and held that office for six years, during which time he studied law and was admitted to the bar; in addition to County Clerk, he held the offices of City Attorney, member of the School Board, Circuit Court Commissioner and Prosecuting Attorney. In 1876, he joined the National Guards as a private in Co. "A," 2d Infantry; was Captain from '78 to '86; Lieutenant Colonel from '86 to '87, and Inspector General from '87 to '91. He re-entered the service in 1896 and enlisted with his company in the 32d Mich. Vol. Infantry for the war with Spain; was mustered out Nov. 5, 1898, and three days later was elected Prosecuting Attorney, resigned his office July 27, 1899, and accepted a Captain's commission in the 30th U. S. Vol. Infantry; served twenty-one months, sixteen of which were passed in the Philippines, and was mustered out Apr. 3, 1901, at San Francisco, Calif.; returned to his home in Coldwater and resumed the practice of law. In politics a Republican.

JOHN S. NEWBERRY

Member of Congress, 1879-81. Was born at Waterville, N. Y., November, 1826, and was a descendant of Thomas Newberry, who emigrated from Devonshire, England, in 1605. He graduated from the Michigan University at the age of eighteen, and engaged in civil engineering for two years. He studied law and was admitted to the Detroit bar in 1853. He was distinguished in admiralty practice, and published a series of admiralty reports. In 1863 he engaged in manufacturing and became president of the Michigan Car Company, and was largely interested in many other corporations. He was one of the corporation that built the Mackinaw & Marquette Railroad. In 1862 he was Provost Marshal of Michigan, appointed by President Lincoln with the rank of Captain. In 1862 and 1863 he gave $650,000 to charities including Newberry Hall, Ann Arbor, and Newberry Chapel at Detroit. He was a member of Congress from the First District, from 1879 to 1881, when he declined to accept a renomination. He was First a Whig, a Republican after 1854. In religion he was a Presbyterian. He died Jan. 2, 1887, at Detroit.

SAMUEL NEWBERRY

Member of the State Board of Education, 1849-50. Was appointed Mar. 30, 1849, for a term of three years. He resigned Mar. 22, 1850. (Further data not obtainable).

SENECA NEWBERRY

Delegate from Oakland County to the Constitutional Conventions of 1835 and 1850; and Senator from the Fourth District, 1853-4. Was born Dec. 23, 1802, at Windsor, Conn. He came to Rochester, Mich., in 1826, went into business as a merchant, and conducted a flourishing business for years. In the convention of 1835 he was an influential and conspicuous member. He died at Rochester, May 13, 1877.

TRUMAN HANDY NEWBERRY

United States Senator, 1919-22. Has been a resident of Michigan since his birth, Nov. 5, 1864. His father, John S. Newberry, had made an enviable record for himself in Michigan's early history as a railroad builder and as a promoter of industrial enterprises, possibly his greatest achievement being the building of a railroad through the Upper Peninsula of Michigan. The son readily followed his father's footsteps, and after graduating from the Sheffield Technical School of Yale University in 1885, he secured employment with the old Detroit, Bay City & Alpena Railroad. His first work was with the engineering force. His advancement was rapid and he was soon appointed general freight and passenger agent of the company. It was at this time that his father died and young Newberry was called home to take charge of his father's estate. For a number of years these interests occupied all his energies. For the last fifteen years he has been president of Grace Hospital, Detroit, and under his leadership, the hospital has more than doubled its capacity. In 1896 Mr. Newberry and a number of his associates organized the Michigan Naval Militia Brigade. Two years later, on the outbreak of the Spanish-American War, the entire organization enlisted in the United States regular navy, Mr. Newberry serving as Lieutenant on the U. S. S. Yosemite. In 1905 he was appointed Assistant Secretary of the Navy by President Roosevelt, and three years later was advanced to Secretary of the Navy. When, in April, 1917, President Wilson declared a state of war existing between the United States and Germany, Mr. Newberry immediately offered his services to his country. Two months later his services were accepted and, in view of his previous experience, he was given the rank of Lieutenant Commander, the highest rank ever conferred by the U. S. Navy Department on a civilian. In July of the same year he was appointed aide to Rear Admiral N. R. Usher, commandant of the third naval district, which in-

cludes the ports of New York and Brooklyn. Mr. Newberry is married and has
three children, a daughter and two sons. He was elected to the United States
Senate Nov. 5, 1918. He resigned in 1922.

ROLAND B. C. NEWCOMB

Representative from Lenawee County, 1865-6; and Senator from the Sixth District, 1877-8. Was born in Williamstown, Vt., Sept. 25, 1882. He lived with
his father until twenty-one, received a good common school education, and in
1843 went to Madison, O., where he taught school. He studied medicine and
graduated as a physician at Starling Medical College of Columbus in 1848,
locating the same year at Palmyra, Mich., where he commenced practice. He
moved to Blissfield in 1851. He served many years as Trustee and Inspector of
schools; was Supervisor.

GEORGE K. NEWCOMBE

Representative from Saginaw County, 1867-8. Was born in Westfield, N. Y.,
Aug. 16, 1833. He came to Michigan in 1848. He studied law and located first
at Owosso, then at East Saginaw, from whence he removed to Minneapolis,
Minn., in 1885, where he was practicing his profession in 1887. He went into
the Civil War as Captain 9th Mich. Cavalry, Dec. 10, 1862. He was wounded in
action at Gettysburg, Va., July 3, 1863. He resigned Oct. 13, 1863, and was
honorably discharged.

JOHN L. NEWELL

Representative from St. Clair County, 1867-8. Was born in England, in 1828.
He came to Port Huron in 1856, and resided in that vicinity. He was a resident of Fort Gratiot in 1887. He was a painter by trade, but later in the service
of the Chicago & Grand Trunk railroad, as silver plater of coach trimmings and
lamps. He was Mayor of Port Huron in 1868; Supervisor in 1867 and 1881;
Treasurer of the town of Port Huron in 1879 and 1880; was a member of the
Board of Education of Port Huron; Justice of the Peace in 1864. Politically he
was a Democrat.

MINOR S. NEWELL

Commissioner of the State Land Office, 1883-7. Was born in Bennington, N. Y.,
in 1823. He resided at Flushing, Mich., where he came in 1842. In 1847 he
served in the 1st Mich. through the Mexican War. In the Civil War he commanded a company in the 16th Mich. Infantry, and rose to the rank of Major.
By occupation he was a farmer. He held various local offices, and served several
terms as Supervisor. Politically he was a Republican.

HENRY WIRT NEWKIRK

Representative from Osceola and Lake counties, 1893-4; and from the First
District of Washtenaw County, 1907-8, 1909-10 and 1917-18. Was born at

Dexter, Washtenaw County, Mich., Aug. 1, 1854, of American parents. He received his education in the Dexter and Ann Arbor high schools, and the University of Michigan, graduating from the law department of the University in 1879. He located at Bay City and was elected Circuit Court Commissioner in 1880. He was married the same year to Miss Eleanor J. Birkett of Dexter. He removed to Kentucky in 1883 and engaged in the newspaper business, returning to Luther, Lake County, in 1888 and edited the Luther *Enterprise*. He was Prosecuting Attorney of Lake County from 1889 to 1892 when he was elected to the Legislature. In 1893 he located at Dexter as cashier of the Dexter Savings Bank, and in 1896 was elected Judge of Probate of Washtenaw County, serving four years, after which time he practiced law. A member of the following fraternal orders: F. & A. M., I. O. O. F., M. W. A., Ann Arbor Commandery K. T., and Moslem Shrine. In politics a Republican.

ALMERON NEWMAN

Representative from Ionia County, 1859-60. Was born at Newfane, N. Y., Feb. 26, 1804. He came to Portland, Mich., in 1836, and built the first woolen mill in that part of the State. At the organization of the town in 1838, he was elected Justice, and held that position thirty-six years. From 1844 to 1848 he was Associate Judge for Ionia County, was also Town Clerk, and held other offices. He was interested in the building of the Ionia & Lansing railroad. By occupation he was a clothier, in politics first a Whig, then a Republican. He died Nov. 13, 1876.

ORLANDO NEWMAN

Representative from Midland, Alpena, Iosco and Isabella counties, 1869-70. His postoffice address was East Tawas. (Further data not obtainable).

FRANK T. NEWTON

Senator, 1909-10 and 1911-12, from the Twelfth District, comprising the counties of Oakland and Washtenaw. Was born in Washtenaw County, Mich., Sept. 30, 1867, of English parentage. He received his education in the district schools. Mr. Newton taught school for nine years, was traveling salesman for four years, and in the manufacturing business ten years. He held the office of Sheriff of Washtenaw County. In politics a Republican.

GEORGE NEWTON

Representative from Cass County, 1859-60. Was born in Preble County, O., Aug. 10, 1810. He was the son of Col. James Newton, who was a member of the Michigan Constitutional Convention of 1835, and of the Legislature prior to 1840. The son came to Volinia, Mich., in 1831, and became a successful farmer. He held many local offices, including that of Supervisor, and as a Republican was Representative.

JAMES NEWTON

Delegate from the Twelfth District to the Constitutional Convention of 1835; and Representative from Cass County, 1839 and 1840. Was born in England in 1777, and came to this country when a boy, first living at Morristown, N. J., then in Pennsylvania, moving to Ohio in 1804. He became a Colonel in the Ohio militia, and was in active service in the War of 1812, serving under Gen. Harrison. He was a Democrat in politics.

CHARLES A. NICHOLS

Member of Congress, 1915-17, 1917-19 and 1919-20. Was born in Charlevoix County, Mich., Aug. 25, 1875. His grandfather, Jonathan Nichols, settled in Hickory Corners, Barry County, soon after Michigan was admitted to statehood. Mr. Nichols began working in a newspaper office when a boy and grew up and was educated in the business. He was a reporter on Detroit newspapers for many years until he was appointed secretary of the Detroit Police Department, which position he held three years. In 1908, he was elected City Clerk of Detroit and served two terms. He died Apr. 26, 1920.

EDWIN C. NICHOLS

Delegate in the Constitutional Convention of 1907-8 from the Ninth District. Was born in Clinton, Lenawee County, and was educated in the public schools. He engaged in the manufacturing business, was president of the Nichols & Shepard Company, Battle Creek, and also of the Old National Bank of the same place, and vice-president of the Commonwealth Power Company and the Duplex Printing Press Company.

GEORGE E. NICHOLS

Senator, 1901-2, from the Eighteenth District, comprising the counties of Ionia and Montcalm. Was born in Oneida Township, Eaton County, Mich., Aug. 8, 1861. He received his education in the common and Grand Ledge High School. At the age of eighteen he began the study of law, and was in active practice of his profession for many years. Married. Twice he held the position of chairman of the Republican County Committee. In politics a strong Republican.

LEWIS A. NICHOLS

Representative from Barry County, 1881-2. Was born in Dutchess County, N. Y., in 1833. He was brought up a farmer in western New York, and with a common school education became a teacher. He came to Battle Creek in 1854, and engaged in staging and the livery business, and then engaged in farming. In 1873 he removed to Orangeville, Barry County, and became a miller. He was Justice and Supervisor. He died at Greenville, Montcalm County, Feb. 17, 1889.

AUGUST NIEDERMEIER

Representative from the Second District of Monroe County, 1897-8 and 1899-1900. Was born at Lippe, Germany, in the kingdom of Prussia, Feb. 8, 1842. He came with his parents to Monroe County in 1852, and settled on a farm in Monroe Township, where he received a district school education. He remained with his parents until he was twenty-six years old; was married Nov. 26, 1867, and moved to a new farm in the township of Berlin. In politics he was a Democrat. He was elected Drain Commissioner in 1876, but resigned on account of an accident to his person, causing an amputation of one of his limbs; was Supervisor seven years; County Treasurer from 1885-89. He died Oct. 20, 1918.

JOHNSON NILES

Representative from Oakland County, 1835 and 1836; and Senator from the Sixth District, 1844-5. Was born May 2, 1794, at Richfield, N. Y. His father was a Revolutionary soldier. He grew to manhood in New York, and was made Paymaster of the State Militia. In 1821 he came to Michigan and settled in Troy, Oakland County, in 1822, as a farmer. In 1823 he was appointed Postmaster and held the position until 1840. He was a Justice in 1823, and held that office long after Michigan became a state. He was a leading Democrat. He died Mar. 23, 1872.

JEROME W. NIMS

Senator, 1901-2, from the Twelfth District comprising the counties of Macomb and Oakland. Was born in Huntington, Vt., Sept. 28, 1839. He came to Michigan with his parents in 1854. His education was acquired in the common schools and Romeo High School. After teaching for a while he began the occupation of farming which business he successfully conducted for many years. Single. In politics a strong Republican. He held various township offices, having been Supervisor of his township, which office he has held twenty-seven years; also represented the county of Macomb on the State Board of Equalization in 1896.

WILLIAM R. NIMS

Senator from the Twenty-sixth District, 1865-6. Was born in Richmond, Vt., June 7, 1829. By occupation he was a merchant, in politics a Republican. He came to Michigan in 1853, and resided at Lexington.

THOMAS NINDE

Delegate from Washtenaw County to the Constitutional Convention of 1867. Was born at Baltimore, Md., Sept 10, 1815. He removed to Lyons, N. Y., in 1823, and in 1847 to Palmyra, N. Y., and was Postmaster of Palmyra from 1849 to 1853. In 1855 he removed to Ypsilanti, Mich., where he engaged in law practice. He was Judge of Probate of Washtenaw County from 1861 to 1865. He was Mayor of Ypsilanti in 1878. By profession he was a lawyer, in politics a Republican.

ROBERT NIXON

Representative from the First District of Eaton County, 1865-6. His postoffice
address was Oneida. (Further data not obtainable).

SAMUEL NIXON

Representative from Eaton County, 1877-8. Was born in Clarkson, Monroe
County, N. Y., Sept 21, 1819. He came to Michigan in October, 1836, and
resided in Eaton County after that time. His education was principally obtained
in the district school of the times. He held the office of Justice for twenty-seven
years in Delta; also Township Treasurer five years, and other offices. He resided
in Delta in 1887. He was a farmer by occupation, and a Republican in politics.

FRANK A. NOAH

Representative from Wayne County, 1879-80. Was born at Rieneck in Baden,
Germany, Dec. 3, 1841. He emigrated to America in 1849, locating in Detroit.
He received a common school education. He was clerk of the police court for
several years. In 1877 he was admitted to the bar. In politics a Republican.

CHARLES NOBLE

Member of the Legislative Council from Wayne County, 1828-30; and Representative from Wayne County, 1855-6. Was born July 4, 1797, at Williamstown,
Mass. He graduated at Williams College in 1815, studied law, and was admitted
to the bar in 1818. He went to Cleveland, O., the same year, and after a short
stay settled at Monroe, Mich., and engaged in practice. He remained a resident
of Monroe until 1867, and during that time was Justice of the Peace, Register
of Probate, District Attorney, County Judge, and Lawyer General of the United
States for the country northwest of the Ohio River. He was one of the company
that purchased the Michigan Southern Railroad from the State, and was the
first president of the company. He was also cashier of the Bank of River Raisin.
In 1867 he removed to Detroit and became one of the firm of George S. Frost
& Co., engaged in the purchase and sale of pine lands, and continued in that
business until his death, Dec. 26, 1874. He was a Whig as long as that party
had an existence, after that an Independent.

DAVID A. NOBLE

Representative from Monroe County, 1846 and 1847; and member of Congress,
1853-5. Was born at Williamstown, Mass., Nov. 9, 1802. He graduated with
honor at Williams College in 1825, studied law, was admitted and opened an
office in New York city for two years, during which time he was associated with
Charles O'Connor. He came to Monroe in 1831. He was active in his profession, and also in political life as a Democrat. He was Recorder of Monroe in
1833, afterwards Alderman and Mayor in 1842. In the Legislative session of

1846 he took a conspicuous part in the sale of the Michigan Central and Southern Railroads. He was a member of the Convention held at Chicago in 1847 in favor of river and harbor improvements, and as one of a committee of five drew up an elaborate report of the commerce of the lakes. In 1852 he was elected to Congress from the Second District of Michigan, defeating Joseph R. Williams. In 1854 he made an exhaustive speech on tonnage duties, which has been regarded as standard authority on that subject. In 1858 he was appointed manager of the Louisville, New Albany & Chicago Railroad, and held that position four years. He was a delegate to the Democratic National Convention of 1864. He was a polished gentleman and a fine scholar. He died at Monroe, Mich., Oct. 13, 1876.

HERMAN C. NOBLE

Representative from Shiawassee County, 1849. His postoffice address was Byron. (Further data not obtainable).

FRANK NOEKER

Representative from Clinton County, 1879-80 and 1883-4. Was born in Germany in 1834. He received a common school education in German and English; resided in Michigan thirty-seven years, twenty-two in Wayne, and fifteen in Westphalia, Clinton County. He was proprietor of a flouring mill; was Justice of the Peace fourteen years, and Supervisor for two years. In politics he was a Democrat.

LAWRENCE NOLAN

Representative from the First District of Wayne County, the city of Detroit, 1891-2. Was born in the town of Coothall, County Roscommon, Ireland, Nov. 3, 1827, and landed in Detroit at the age of 13, in 1840, with nothing but his love for freedom, and found employment in an iron foundry at 30 cents per day, and by faithful work sifting sand, etc., rose to a full-fledged iron molder with a credit of six dollars per day as a reward. His first position worthy of mention was as foreman of Jackson & Wiley's foundry; afterwards he assumed charge of the Detroit Locomotive Works, later known as the Buhl Iron Works, and remained there for 26 years, during the last three years of which he was a partner, under the firm name of O'Connor, Nolan & Fitzgerald, and made the castings for the Chicago rolling mill engines, also made the pumping engines and 42-inch water mains for the Detroit Water Works. He retired from active business,, having enough to live on, and engaged in the real estate business. He was a strong supporter of union principles and paid a higher scale than the union wages to good men; he was one of the charter members of Iron Molders' Union No. 31, and delegate to the trades assembly in 1861. In politics he was an ardent Democrat. He was elected to the House of 1891-2 on the ticket of that party.

JOHN NOLL

Representative from Cheboygan County, 1913-14. Was born at New York City, N. Y., Oct. 12, 1866, of German parentage. His education was acquired in the

Jackson, Mich., public schools. At the age of five years he removed with his parents to Ann Arbor, and later to Jackson. At the age of seventeen he entered into the employ of the E. M. Estey Furniture Company, at Owosso, Mich. When twenty-one years of age he removed to Cheboygan where he engaged in the manufacturing business. He served as Alderman, Mayor, City Treasurer and member of School Board. Married. In politics a Democrat.

JOHN W. NORMAN

Representative from the First District of Sanilac County, 1893-4 and 1895-6. Was born in York County, Ont., July 31, 1844. He acquired a common school education, and spent his early days on his father's farm. He came to Michigan, locating at the village of Lexington, where he engaged in the practice of dentistry; also engaged to some extent in farming and milling. In politics a Republican. He held several local offices of public trust.

JOHN W. NORRINGTON

Representative from the First District of Ottawa County, 1893-4. Was born in Berkeley County, W. Va., July 28, 1848. He acquired a common school education and also attended the high school at Odin, Ill. In the fall of 1863 he enlisted in Co. C, 3d W. Va. Cavalry, serving the last year of the war under Gen. Custer. On Feb. 10, 1869, he was married to Miss Joanna Barlow, of Berkeley County, W. Va., and settled in Howard County (now Chautauqua), Kan. He came to Michigan and settled on the farm in Olive Township. In politics a Republican. While in Kansas he was twice elected Trustee of the township; in Michigan he held the office of Supervisor eight years, and was a candidate for Register of Deeds in 1889.

EZRA B. NORRIS

Representative from Washtenaw County, 1877-8. Was born July 16, 1846, in Manchester, Mich. He was reared as a farmer and received a common school education. In 1861 he enlisted as private in Co. E, 1st Mich. Infantry. In 1862 he was discharged on account of disability at Fortress Monroe. He returned and attended for a season the State Normal and Ypsilanti High School, and in 1868 commenced the study of law and was admitted to the bar in 1872, after which time he continued in the practice of his profession in Manchester. In politics a Democrat.

JASON B. NORRIS

Representative from Hillsdale County, 1871-2. Was born in Canandaigua, N. Y., Nov. 3, 1823, and was brought up on a farm, where he lived until 1845, when he came to Michigan and settled on a farm, eight miles south of Hillsdale. He was several times Supervisor and Collector. He was a Democrat until 1864, a Republican until 1884, then a Prohibitionist.

LYMAN D. NORRIS

Delegate from Washtenaw County to the Constitutional Convention of 1867; Senator from the Sixth District, 1869-70; and member of the Board of Regents of the University of Michigan, 1883. Was born at Covington, N. Y., May 4, 1825. His father removed to Ypsilanti in 1828. The son, after a preparatory education, entered as the first student of the first class of the Michigan University. After nearly three years there he entered Yale College, and graduated in 1845. He read law with A. D. Frazer of Detroit, and was admitted in 1847. In 1848 he removed to St. Louis, Mo., and engaged in practice. He subsequently studied civil law at Heidelberg, Germany. In 1852 he was retained in the mamous Dred Scott case, and effected a reversal of former decisions of the Supreme Court of Missouri. In 1854 he returned to Ypsilanti and practiced there until 1871, and then became a prominent lawyer at Grand Rapids. He was the Democratic candidate for Supreme Judge in 1875. He was appointed Regent of the University of Michigan, Jan. 19, 1883, in the place of Byron M. Cutcheon, and served the remainder of the year to complete the term. He died at Grand Rapids, Jan. 6, 1894.

SETH D. NORTH

Representative from Houghton County, 1877-8 and 1881-2 to 1885-6; and Senator from the Thirty-second District, 1879-80. Was born Apr. 9, 1823, in Middlesex County, Conn. Having received a common school education, he removed to Michigan in 1855. He resided at Hancock, and engaged in mercantile pursuits, and in mining and lumbering. He was also president of the national bank. He 'was interested in property at Mt. Clemens. In politics he was a Republican.

TOWNSEND NORTH

Senator from the Twenty-fourth District, 1875-6. Was born in Marbletown, Ulster County, N. Y., Sept. 24, 1814. He received a common school education, removed to Michigan in 1836, and for six years worked at his trade of carpenter, mostly in Washtenaw County. In 1846 he built a bridge across the Cass River, and was paid in Michigan Internal improvement lands, which he located in Tuscola County, and removed to Vassar in 1850, and continued to reside there. He held the office of Supervisor for many years, and was Register of Deeds. He was Assessor of Internal Revenue, 1862-6. He was re-appointed in 1871, and held the office until it was discontinued. His occupation was miscellaneous, including lumbering, farming, manufacturing, merchandising, and real estate transactions. In politics he was a Republican. For many years he was a trustee of the State Blind Institute. He died June 11, 1889, at Vassar.

DARWIN B. NORTHROP

Representative from Wayne County, 1875-6. Was born Jan. 19, 1834, at Perrington, N. Y. In 1850 he removed to Northville, Mich., and pursued the trade of an iron moulder until 1858, when he went to California. He returned in 1866 to Northville, and formed a partnership with F. R. Beal in the general hardware line, which business he continued. He held various township and village offices. In politics a Democrat.

ELIJAH S. NORTHROP

Senator from the Thirty-second District, 1863. Was born in Stamford, N. Y.,
in 1829. In 1850 he removed to Michigan, settling first at Saline, where he
engaged in mercantile business. He removed to Houghton County in 1861,
where he became an insurance agent, residing at Hancock. He was a Senator
from the Upper Peninsula in 1863, and while serving in that capacity, died at
Lansing, Mar. 2, 1863, of consumption. Politically he was a Democrat.

HENRY HORATIO NOTHROP

Member of the Board of Regents of the University of Michigan, 1854-8. Was
born at Galway, Saratoga County, N. Y., June 13, 1814. He entered Union College at the age of sixteen and was graduated Bachelor of Arts in 1834. He was
ordained to the Presbyterian ministry, removed to Michigan, and was settled as
pastor over the following churches in succession,—Dexter, White Pigeon, Homer,
Monroe, and Flint. In 1854 he was chosen Regent of the University in place
of Andrew Parsons, who had resigned the office about a year before. He thus
served nearly four years and took a prominent part in the proceedings of the
Board. He was Chaplain of the 13th Mich. Infantry from January to December,
1862. In 1873 he resigned the pastorate of the First Presbyterian Church of
Flint and from that time on lived in comparative retirement. He died at Flint,
Feb. 25, 1905.

ALONZO R. NORTHUP

Representative, 1889-90 and 1891-2, from the Delta District, comprising the
counties of Delta and Iron. Was born in Washington County, N. Y., in 1849.
By profession he was a lawyer; in politics a Republican.

JOHN NORTHWOOD

Representative from Saginaw County, 1885-6. Was born in London, England,
July 17, 1838. In 1849 he came to Ohio with his parents, who removed to
Detroit in 1850. He attended school, and was three years a sailor. He settled
on a farm in Maple Grove, Mich., in 1855. In 1861 he enlisted in the 16th Mich.
Infantry, lost a right arm from wounds received at the Battle of Gaines Mills,
and was in Libby Prison for a short time. He was Supervisor, Justice, held
other local offices, and was Commander of the G. A. R. in Michigan. Politically
he was a Republican. He died at New Lothrop, July 24, 1922.

HENRY A. NORTON

Representative from Oakland County, 1869-70. Was born in Bristol, N. Y., Aug.
29, 1826. He did not receive a common school education. He became a resident
of Oakland County in 1830. Politically he was a Republican. He was a delegate to the Republican National Convention at Philadelphia in 1872. He
moved to Duluth in 1881, and in 1887 was State Weighmaster of Minnesota.

JOHN D. NORTON

Representative from Oakland County, 1875-6 and 1877-8. Was born in Onondaga County, N. Y., Dec. 18, 1842. He graduated at Hamlinton College, N. Y., in 1867, and removed to Michigan in 1868. Mr. Norton married and took up his residence in Pontiac in 1869. He was a director in the First National Bank of Pontiac. His occupation was dealing in pine lands and lumber. In politics a Democrat.

JOHN M. NORTON

Senator from the Fifteenth District, 1883-4. Was born in Richmond, N. Y., May 5, 1820. He settled with his father in Avon, Mich., in 1824. He had a limited education. He was a farmer; in politics first Whig, then Republican, later a Greenbacker. He held several local offices, and served four years as Deputy Sheriff. He died at Rochester, Mich., August, 1902.

PLEASANT NORTON

Representative from Cass County, 1850 and 1853-4. Was born in Grayson County, Va., in 1806. When two years of age he removed to Champaign County, O., and afterwards to Logan County in the same state. He moved into Jefferson, Cass County, Mich., in 1832, and resided there until his death in 1877. By occupation he was a farmer, in politics a Democrat. He was for nine years Supervisor of Jefferson, and four years Town Treasurer. He was a man of native ability and force and character, and left a large property, the result of persistent industry.

WILLIAM A. NORTON

Representative from Clinton County, 1907-8. Was born at Farmington, Oakland County, Mich., Oct. 21, 1853. He received his early education in the district schools and later attended Hillsdale College and the Michigan Agricultural College. He was admitted to the bar in 1878, held the office of Circuit Court Commissioner, was twice elected Prosecuting Attorney of Charlevoix County, and served two terms as Prosecuting Attorney of Clinton County. Married. A resident of St. Johns in 1907, where he was engaged in the practice of his profession. Deceased.

JOHN NORVELL

Delegate from the First District to the Constitutional Convention of 1835; United States Senator, 1835-41; member of the Board of Regents of the University of Michigan, 1837-9; and Representative from Wayne County, 1842. Was born in Garrard County, near Danville, Ky., Dec. 21, 1789. He was the son of Lipsocomb Norvell, a Virginian, who served as an officer in the War of the Revolution, and lived to enjoy a pension until he was over ninety years old. The son, on the advice by letter of Thomas Jefferson to learn a trade, went to Baltimore and learned the trade of a printer. He at the same time studied law, was admitted to the bar, and became a journalist and politician. He was a friend and correspondent of President Madison, gave him warm support on the

stump and in his paper, especially his war measures. At the close of the war
in 1816, Mr. Norvell became the Democratic editor of·a paper in Philadelphia,
and resided there sixteen years. He was in Battle of Blandensburg, 1814, and
in the Patriot War. In May, 1832, he came to Detroit, Mich., having been appointed Postmaster of that city by Andrew Jackson. In the Constitutional Convention of 1835, he was chairman of eight committees, and a member of several
others. His work in that Convention was of great value to the welfare of the
State. He and Lucius Lyon were elected as the United States Senators, and
went to Washington before the admission of Michigan to the Union, and he, with
his colleague, managed well in securing the mineral wealth and territory of a
large portion of the Upper Peninsula, to compensate for the loss of a small strip
of land on the southern boundary. After the expiration of his term as Senator
in 1842, he resumed the practice of law in Detroit. In 1845 he was appointed
U. S. District Attorney of Michigan, which he held until 1849. He supported the
administration in the prosecution of the Mexican War, and sent three sons.to
serve in the field. He died Apr. 11, 1850, at Detroit.

DAVID M. NOTTINGHAM

Representative from the First District of Ingham County, 1903-4 and 1905-6.
Was born Jan. 5, 1855, in Marion, Ind., of French and English parents. He
lived on a farm until sixteen years of age. He taught school, attended college,
and worked at the harness trade until he attained the age of twenty-three. He
graduated from Hahnemann Medical College, Chicago, Ill, in 1881, and practiced
three years in Bronson, Branch County, Mich. In 1884 he commenced the
practice of medicine in Lansing. He was a member of the Common Council of
Lansing for two years, City Health Officer, and a member of the Board of Education. In politics a Republican.

MOSES R. NOWLAND

Representative from Wayne County, 1865-6. Was a native of New York, born
in 1828, and came to Michigan in 1831, with his parents, who settled in the
township of Huron, where he lived. He was a Democrat in politics. He combined the profession of lawyer and farmer, and served his township for many
years as Treasurer, Clerk and Supervisor.

BETHUEL NOYES

Representative from Wayne County, 1848 and 1850. Was born in Chenango
County, N. Y., Nov. 12, 1813. He came to Michigan in 1833. He was a lawyer
by profession, and a Democrat in politics. He died at Plymouth, Oct. 30, 1873.

HORACE A. NOYES

Delegate from Wayne County to the First Convention of Assent, 1836; and
Representative from Wayne County, 1835 and 1836. Was born in Preston,

N. Y., Feb. 20, 1810. He received a fair education, became a teacher, studied law, and was admitted to the practice in 1833. He came to Michigan the same year, and began practice at Plymouth, where he remained until 1840. He then removed to Marshall. In 1844 he was elected Judge of Probate of Calhoun County, and held the position for twelve years. In 1857 he resumed law practice and was regarded as an able counsel. In politics he was a Democrat. He died Apr. 20, 1877.

MICHAEL J. NOYES

Representative from Washtenaw County, 1873-4. Was born in Washington, Mich., May 23, 1838. He finished his education at Romeo Academy. In 1859 he went to Washington Territory, traveled extensively in Oregon and California, and passed over the gold fields of Montana and Idaho previous to their discovery. He afterwards spent six years in the silver mines of Nevada, and was interested in the silver mines of that country. In 1861-2 he served on the staff of Brigadier General Welty, with the rank of Major, in the Indian campaigns. In 1859 he made a trip to California, over the plains, with an ox team, and again in 1866 by overland stage. In politics he was a Republican. In 1867 he removed to Washtenaw County, and settled in Chelsea. He was engaged in the banking business in that village from 1868 to 1871.

MARSHALL A. OAKLEY

Representative from the First District of Bay County, 1913-14 and 1915-16. Was born in Ulster County, N. Y., July 10, 1878. He was married in 1901 to Miss Anna Mae MacNeil, of Bay City. He engaged in newspaper work for a number of years, and during this time he was actively identified with the labor movement in Michigan, having held the highest offices in Bay City central labor organizations. During the Spanish-American War he enlisted in Co. E, 35th Mich. Vol. Infantry, and was a member of the Spanish War Veterans and the National League of Veterans and Sons, a member of the Knights of Pythias, Loyal Home Fraternity, Loyal Americans and other fraternal societies and labor organizations. In politics a Republican.

WILLIAM RICHARD OATES

Representative from the First District of Houghton County, 1909-10. Was born at Cornwall, England, in 1878, of English descent. He was educated in the schools of England, and a graduate of the law department of the University of Michigan. He came to Houghton County with his parents when he was fourteen years of age. In 1899 he was graduated from the law department of the University of Michigan, and engaged in the practice of law at Calumet, Mich. He was appointed Attorney for Laurium six terms and was twice elected Circuit Court Commissioner of Houghton County on the Republican ticket. A director of the First National Bank of Laurium and a director of the Laurium Park Association.

NELSON M. O'BEIRNE

Representative from Ionia County, 1923—. Was born in Berlin Township, Inoia County, November 30, 1869, of Scotch and Irish ancestry. He is married and has two sons. Mr. O'Beirne has been a farmer practically all his life; has been master of the local grange five years; is a member of the board of managers of the Farmers' Mutual Fire Insurance Co., of Ionia County, and a member of the board of managers of the Alto Creamery Association. He is a Republican and has served several terms in various township offices and twenty-one consecutive years as member of the school board. He was elected to the Legislature November 7, 1922.

WILLIAM J. OBERDORFFER

Representative from Menominee County, 1897-8 and 1899-1900; Delegate to the Constitutional Convention of 1907-8; and member of the State Board of Agriculture, 1905-12. Was born in Germany, Mar. 18, 1855, where he acquired his education; came to America in 1871, locating at Masonville, Delta County, Mich., where he was engaged in lumbering for two years; went to Escanaba and entered the employ of the C. & N. W. Railway Company, which occupation he followed three years. In 1876 he went to Stephenson, Menominee County, and located on a farm. In religion a Methodist Episcopal. In politics a Republican. He was Supervisor seven years; was a member of the Board of Education five years; member of the Republican County Committee for six years.

MORGAN O'BRIEN

Delegate to the Constitutional Convention of 1850, from Washtenaw County. Was born at New Castle, County Limerick, Ireland, Oct. 4, 1814. He came to Washtenaw County about 1835. He had a very fine farm and home. He died June 1, 1876.

PATRICK O'BRIEN

Representative, 1915—, from the Iron District, comprising the counties of Baraga, Iron, Keweenaw and Ontonagon. Was born in western Pennsylvania, Mar. 9, 1858. In 1871 he came to Michigan with his parents, locating at Brighton, Livingston County, where he attended high school and worked on a farm during the summer. In the fall of 1876 he entered the office of the Brighton *Citizen* to learn the printing trade, and has continued in that business ever since, working on different papers in Michigan and Wisconsin. In 1887 he purchased the Iron River-Stambaugh *Reporter*, and is still editor and publisher of the same. He was postmaster under President Harrison for four years, has been President and Trustee of the village of Iron River, a member of the Board of Education, member of Board of Directors of Chamber of Commerce; is president of executive committee of the Iron County Agricultural Society, secretary of the Republican committe, and a member of the board of directors of the U. P. Development Bureau. He is married and has two daughters.

JEREMIAH O'CALLAHAN

Representative from Wayne County, 1853-4. Was a native of Ireland, born in 1823. Very little is known of him except that he was a grocer and trader, was a Democrat in politics, and died in 1856.

HORACE N. O'COBOCK

Representative from Wayne County, 1875-6. Was born in Cayuga County, N. Y., Feb. 17, 1832. He received his education in the schools of Auburn, N. Y., and came to Wyandotte, Mich., in 1860. He was an Alderman and Mayor of Wyandotte. By occupation he was a mechanic, in politics a Republican.

PHILIP O'CONNELL

Representative from Sanilac County, 1923——. Was born at Cársonville, in 1872, of American parents. Mr. O'Connell is a farmer and has lived in Michigan for fifty years. He is a Republican and was elected to the Legislature November 7, 1922.

ARTHUR U. ODELL

Representative from the First District of Allegan County, 1911-12, 1913-14 and 1923——. Was born in Trowbridge Township, Allegan County, June 9, 1868, of American parentage. He was educated in the district schools, Allegan high school and Hope College, of Holland Michigan. In 1892 he was married to Ethel O'Brien and they have two children. At the age of eighteen he began teaching school and continued for six years after which he engaged in farming and stock raising. For several years he has been a director of the Allegan and Ottawa Insurance Co. and is now its vice-president. He served ten years as a school officer and ten years as Supervisor of his twonship, being at present chairman of the board. Mr. Odell is a Republican.

JAMES O'DELL

Delegate from the Twelfth District to the Constitutional Convention of 1835; Delegate from Cass County to the First Convention of Assent, 1836; and Representative from Cass County, 1835 and 1836 and 1838. Was born in Virginia, July 20, 1779. At the age of twenty-one he removed to Ohio, and in 1831 came to Michigan, settling near Vandalia, Cass County, 1832. He was by occupation a farmer and miller. He died Aug. 23, 1845.

SAMUEL O'DELL

Representative from Oceana County, 1909-10 and 1911-12; Senator from the Twenty-sixth District, 1913-14 and 1915-16; and State Treasurer, 1917-19. Was born at Shelby, Mich., Aug. 30, 1881, of English parents. He acquired his education in the schools of Detroit and the University of Michigan. He has always resided in Michigan, and has been engaged in business at Shelby since 1902. In politics he is a Republican. He was Supervisor of Shelby Township two terms. He was elected State Treasurer at the election held Nov. 7, 1916, and re-elected in November, 1918. He resigned May 21, 1919, to become a member of the Michigan Public Utilities Commission.

THOMAS O'DELL

Representative from Cass County, 1873-4. Was born in Porter, Mich., June 30, 1831. He received a common school education, and held from time to time responsible town offices. He was a farmer by occupation.

LEWIS O'DETT

Representative from the Third District of St. Clair County, 1897-8. Was born in Northumberland County, Canada, Apr. 29, 1843. At eleven years of age he came to Michigan with his parents and located on a farm in Burtchville Township, where he acquired a common school education. He remained on the farm until enlisting in the government employ as messenger boy in the Quartermaster's Department, continuing in the service until the close of the war. On July 18, 1871, he married Miss Ellen Bingham and settled on the farm in the township of Kenockee. In politics a Republican. He was School Director eleven years; School Inspector two years; and Township Clerk seven years.

JAMES O'DONNELL

Member of Congress, 1885-7 to 1891-3. Was born in Norwalk, Conn., Mar. 25, 1840. He removed with his parents to Michigan in 1848, and resided in Jackson after 1849. He did not have early educational advantages, but made up this deficiency by study after working hours. He commenced to learn the printer's trade in 1856. At the breaking out of the war he entered the First Michigan Infantry as a private, and served his time, participating in the Battle of Bull Run. In 1863-4-5-6 he was elected Recorder of the city of Jackson as a Republican, though it was a strong Democratic city. In 1872 he was chosen Presidential Elector, and was designated by the State Electoral College to take the vote of Michigan to Washington. He served as secretary of the State Electoral College. In 1876 he was elected Mayor of Jackson, being the only Republican successful at the election. He was re-elected in 1877. His administration was marked by thoroughness, economy and prompt meeting of the obligations of the municipality. In 1878 he was appointed by Governor Croswell as a member of his staff, with the rank of Colonel and Aide-de-camp. He became editor and proprietor of the Jackson *Daily Citizen* in 1864; also engaged in the manufacture of paper and banking. He was elected to the 49th, 50th, and 51st, and re-elected to the 52nd Congress. He died at Jackson, Mar. 17, 1915.

CORNELIUS O'FLYNN

Representative from Wayne County, 1857-8. Was born in 1810, at Tralee, County Kerry, Ireland, and came to America about 1828. He was admitted to the bar in Detroit in 1834. He was a classical scholar, a man of comprehensive views of things, and a Democrat. He was City Attorney of Detroit in 1842, Judge of Probate two terms, 1844-52, and Postmaster at Detroit during a portion of Buchanan's term. As Judge of Probate he gave a system of practice to the State through the blank forms that he prepared. He died in Detroit in 1869.

ROBERT Y. OGG

Representative from the First District of Wayne County, 1887-8, 1909-10 and 1911-12; and Senator, 1913-14 and 1915-16, from the Fourth District of Wayne County, comprising the eighth, tenth, twelfth and fourteenth wards of the city of Detroit. Was born in the town of Dundas, Ont., July 22, 1860, of Scotch parentage. His education was acquired in the common schools and the composing room and editorial room of the daily newspaper was his alma mater. He began his business career as a newsboy and learned the printer's trade. He was subsequently newspaper writer, public official and business man, occupying offices in the Majestic building, Detroit, as manufacturers' representative for paving materials. He was married to Miss Susie M. McCarthy, in 1888, and lived in Detroit since boyhood. In politics active in Republican, Labor and Masonic circles. In 1886 he was elected to the House of Representatives, being the youngest member of that body. Twenty-two years later, in 1908, he was elected to the House of Representatives and was re-elected in 1910. In 1912 he was elected to the State Senate, and re-elected Nov. 3, 1914.

JAMES O'GRADY

Representative from Marquette and other counties, 1865-6. Was born Dec. 18, 1822, in Shelburne, Vt., was educated there, was admitted to the bar in 1848, and in 1849 went to California. He was Register of Probate in San Francisco, and subsequently Register and Recorder of the city and county. From 1852 to 1864 he resided on his farm in Shelburne, Vt. In 1864 he came to Marquette, and engaged in law practice. In 1866 he removed to Houghton, and in 1869 was elected Judge of the 12th circuit, and held that position until his death, Dec. 24, 1878. His judicial decisions were rarely reversed. In politics he was a Democrat.

GEORGE A. O'KEEFE

Representative from Wayne County, 1843. Was a typical Irishman, born in Cork in 1792. He was a graduate of Trinity College, Dublin, and was educated for the bar. He came to New York in 1816, spent three years in the study of American law and practice in the office of Judge Brady, and in 1820 came to Detroit, his future home. In politics he was a Democrat. He was Judge of Probate, 1837-40, and was an Alderman. He was a finished lawyer and profound jurist. He was an Irish gentleman in the truest and fullest sense, learned, cultured, brilliant, and witty. In stature, he was tall and massive, with large blue eyes, large head, and curly hair. He died June 16, 1853.

RICHARD D. O'KEEFE

Representative from the Second District of Sanilac County, 1885-6, 1887-8 and 1889-90. Was born at Tilsonburgh, Oxford County, Ont., Mar. 19, 1855. He removed to Sanilac County, Mich., February, 1868, where he remained on his father's farm a number of years. He taught school several terms, was elected Superintendent of Schools for Delaware, Sanilac County; was in the service of mercantile and mill men for a time, and was engaged for a number of years as station agent and telegraph operator by the P. H. & N. W. R'y Co. at Minden City. In 1885 he opened a law, loan, real estate, insurance and collector's office at Minden City. In 1887 he removed to Carsonville, transferring his business to that point and locating on his farm, one-half mile east of that village. He was Clerk of the village of Minden. In politics a Republican.

MARTIN OLDS

Representative from Branch County, 1843. Was born in Bolton, Mass., resided in New York and Ohio, and settled as a farmer in Batavia, Mich., in 1838, and was the first Supervisor and held the office seven years, also other local offices. He was Judge of Probate eight years, and president of the company that started the first paper in Branch County. He removed to Oregon in 1851, where he was Postmaster, Probate Judge, and Delegate to the Constitutional Convention. He died in 1873.

CHARLES OLIN

Representative from Calhoun County, 1841. Was born at Coventry, R. I., Mar. 4, 1802. He removed from his native state to Bedford, Calhoun County, in 1833, and was one of the earliest settlers. He was the first Supervisor in 1836, and was Associate County Judge in 1839-40. He was a farmer, and politically a Democrat. He died July 4, 1860.

JOHN F. OLIVER

Representative from Kalamazoo County, 1879-80 and 1881-2. Was born in Springfield, N. Y., Oct. 2, 1820, and removed with his parents to Niagara County, in 1826, and in 1843, to Portage, Mich. He received a common school education. He was a farmer by occupation. He held the offices of School Inspector, Town Clerk, Supervisor for five years, and Justice of the Peace for several terms. In politics he was a Republican.

CLIFFORD GEORGE OLMSTEAD

Representative from Midland County, 1915-16 to 1921-2. Was born in Midland, May 20, 1879, his father being one of the pioneers of that county. He attended Midland High School and graduated with the class of 1896. He attended Alma College one year and the Michigan Agricultural College one year, leaving the latter to engage in the general mercantile business in which he is still interested. He was married in 1903 to Ethel M. Stumm, of Elkhart, Ind. He served the city of Midland as Alderman for eight years; was Superintendent of the Poor for four years and Under Sheriff two years. He was active in war work in 1917-18, being a member of the County War Board and secretary of the Midland County Chapter of the Red Cross. In politics a Republican.

CHARLES M. O'MALLEY

Representative from Mackinac County, 1846, 1847 and 1849. Was born in Dorada, County Mayo, Ireland, and came to this country in 1834, and to Michigan in 1835. He held several offices in Mackinac County. While a member of the Legislature he was responsible for the law changing the Indian names of five counties to Irish names. He was speaker *pro tem.* He was educated for a priest, but became a merchant in Mackinac. In politics a Democrat.

CHRISTIAN A. OPPENBORN

Representative from Alpena County, 1911-12. Was born in Alpena County, Mich., Jan. 31, 1873, of German parentage. He was educated in the public schools, supplemented by courses at the Alpena Business College, and Ohio Northern University. He was a graduate of the Detroit College of Law and was admitted to the bar June 17, 1907. He was Treasurer of Alpena County four years and also served as Circuit Court Commissioner. Married. He served in the Spanish-American War as a member of the 33rd Mich. Vol. Infantry. In politics a Republican.

PLACIDUS ORD

Representative from Chippewa County, 1846. His home was Sault Ste. Marie. (Further data not obtainable).

BERNARD O'REILLY

Senator from the Third District, 1887-8. Was born in Westmeath County, Ireland, May 20, 1832. By occupation he was a ship carpenter and caulker. He came with his parents to Kingston, Canada, in 1847, and to Oswego, N. Y., in 1848. He received a limited education in the public schools. In 1859 he shipped on a vessel and followed the lakes until 1852, when he entered a shipyard and continued to work at his trade. He was Alderman of the twelfth ward of Detroit. Politically he was a Democrat.

HORACE MANN OREN

Attorney General, 1899-1901 and 1901-3. Was born in Oakland, Clinton County, O., Feb. 3, 1859. His father, Captain Charles Oren, having been killed in the siege of Petersburg, himself and mother moved to Indianapolis in 1868. Mr. Oren graduated from the Indianapolis High School in 1877, and from the Michigan University (classical course) in 1881, and law in 1883; came to Sault Ste.

Marie in 1882; was editor of the Soo *News* for three years; began the practice
of law in 1883; held the office of Circuit Court Commissioner one term; served
as Prosecuting Attorney two terms, and was Village Clerk and Attorney for
several terms. He was elected on the Republican ticket for Attorney General.

CALEB N. ORMSBY

Representative from Washtenaw County, 1839. His postoffice address was Ann
Arbor. (Further data not obtainable).

IRA G. ORMSBEE

Representative from the Second District of Genesee County, 1909-10. Was born
in Washington County, Vt., May 23, 1844, of English and Scotch parentage.
He came to Flint, Mich., with his parents in April, 1852, and at the age of
seventeen enlisted in the late T. B. Stockton's Regiment, 16th Infantry, and was
twice wounded during his term of service. Married. In politics a Republican.

WILLIAM B. ORMSBEE

Representative from the Second District of Genesee County, 1915-16, 1917-18
and 1923—. Was born in Maple Grove, Saginaw County, in 1875. He was educated in the Flint High School and Normal. For ten years he was employed in
the factory of W. A. Paterson & Co., and for eight years was department foreman in the Durant-Dort Carriage Co.'s plant. At present he conducts a sporting
goods store in the city of Flint. Mr. Ormsbee is a Republican and served in the
Legislatures of 1915-16 and 1917-18, and was again elected November 7, 1922.

GEORGE ORTH

Representative from the Iosco District, comprising the counties of Alcona, Arenac
and Iosco, 1891-2. Was born in Bavaria on the Rhine, Aug. 17, 1844, and came
to this country when five years of age with his parents. Mr. Orth was raised
on a farm in Wayne County. At the age of thirteen years he went to work
on the shoemaker's bench at Forestville, Huron County, and remained there
until about 1870, just before which time he was married, when he removed to
Au Sable. He owned shoe stores in Au Sable and Oscoda and the opera house
block and a shoe store at St. Ignace. He served as Supervisor three terms,
Township and Village Treasurer, Poor Superintendent several terms, was on the
first Village Council and elected to the same position several times; was also
Village Marshal, and Deputy Sheriff. As a Democrat Mr. Orth was elected to the
House of 1891-2.

CHASE SALMON OSBORN

Member of the Board of Regents of the University of Michigan, 1908-11; and
Governor of Michigan, 1911-13. Was born in a log house in the woods of Huntington County, Ind., on Jan. 22, 1860, of English, Irish and French descent.

His father and mother were both regular physicians. He was educated in the schools of Lafayette, Ind., and at Purdue University. Mr. Osborn was engaged in newspaper work at Lafayette, Chicago and Milwaukee until 1883. He was married to Miss Lillian G. Jones, of Milwaukee, May 7, 1881. In 1883, he purchased the Florence, Wis., *Mining News*, sold it in 1887, and purchased the Sault Ste. Marie *News*. In 1902 Mr. Osborn, with Walter J. Hunsaker, purchased the Saginaw *Courier-Herald*. He discovered the Moose Mountain iron range in Canada in 1903. Mr. Osborn has traveled in every State in the Union, and in all countries of Europe, North and South America, in most countries of Asia and Africa, Australia, New Zealand, China, Japan, Philippines, Siberia and Sandwich Islands, etc. He is the author of "The Andean Land," a two volume work on South America. He has held the offices of State Game and Fish Warden, State Railroad Commissioner and Postmaster of Sault Ste. Marie. He is a member of many fraternal orders and scientific societies, has always been a student and is a member of the Presbyterian Church. In politics he is a Republican. He was appointed a member of the Board of Regents of the University, July 3, 1908, in place of Peter White, deceased; was nominated at the primaries Sept. 6, 1910, for the office of Governor and was elected Nov. 8, 1910.

DONALD C. OSBORN

Senator, 1921—, from the Sixth District, comprising the counties of Kalamazoo and St. Joseph. Was born in Franklin, Pa., Mar. 26, 1879, and is of Scotch-English descent. He was educated in Kalamazoo public schools, Berkeley School, N. Y., and University of Michigan, graduating from the latter institution in 1904. He is engaged in the practice of law. He served as assistant steward of Michigan State Hospital, 1905-10; was Delegate from the Third Congressional District to the 1920 Republican National Convention, and at present Republican County Chairman. During the late war he served as appeal agent for Kalamazoo County.

FRANK A. OSBORN

Representative from the Second District of Kalamazoo County, 1901-2 and 1903-4. Was born in Pavilion Township, Kalamazoo County, Dec. 21, 1852. He obtained his education in the common schools, one year at the Kalamazoo High School and one term in the Baptist College at that place. He taught school four years, afterwards settling on a farm. Married. He held the offices of Township Clerk, Superintendent of Schools and Supervisor. In politics a staunch Republican.

GEORGE W. OSBORN

Representative from St. Joseph County, 1891-2. Was born in Middlefield, Otsego County, N. Y., Aug. 30, 1827, and came to Michigan with his parents in 1838, settling in Florence, St. Joseph County, and four years later removed to Park, where he lived until his marriage to Miss Ann Eliza Van Ness; after his marriage he returned again and assisted his father on the farm until 1853; from that time until 1863 he farmed in Mendon and Nottawa, and also engaged in machine work in Goshen, Ind. After a short sojourn in the latter place he returned to Parkville, where he followed the trade of a shoemaker until April,

1876, when he again returned to Mendon and leased the farm of Jacob Van Ness. He was elected Supervisor of Park in 1866 and retained the office until he removed from the township ten years later, and also held the offices of Clerk and Justice. In politics a Democrat.

HENRY ALFRED OSBORN

Representative from Chippewa County, 1921—. Was born Feb. 6, 1858, in Simcoe County, Ont., of English parentage. He was educated in the Ontario public schools. He came to Chippewa County in 1879, engaging in farming, and has always been active in developing the county as a farming community. He has been associated with the Chippewa County Agricultural Society since its organization, having been its president a number of years and vice president or a director nearly continuously. He was County Road Commissioner of Chippewa County and originated the building of stone-macadam roads in that county. Mr. Osborn is married. He and his family are affiliated with the Congregational Church. He is a Shriner, Knight Templar, member of I. O. O. F., K. of P., B. P. O. E., and other societies, being past chancellor of the Knights of Pythias. He is also a past master of Pine Grove Grange and past master of Pomona Grange of Chippewa County. In politics he is a Republican.

JOHN M. OSBORN

Representative from Hillsdale County, 1869-70 and 1871-2; and Senator from the Ninth District, 1875-6. Was born in Monroe County, N. Y., Mar. 9, 1829. He received a good education in the district and select schools of that state, and removed to Michigan in 1840, locating at Hudson. In 1847 he purchased a farm in Hillsdale County, upon which he continued to reside. He engaged in various occupations; teaching, mercantile, produce and lumber operations, and in banking. He was head of the banking firm of Osborn, Perkins & Co., of Hudson. He held several township offices. In politics he was a Republican.

WILLIAM H. OSBORN

Representative from Lenawee County, 1865-6 and 1867-8. Was born in Ovid, N. Y., Oct. 29, 1814. He received an academical education, and taught several winters. In 1839 he settled on a farm in Macon, Lenawee County, Mich. He held many town offices. In politics he was a Republican.

CHARLES Y. OSBURN

Representative from Shiawassee County, 1871-2. Was born in Meadville, Pa., in 1842; moved to Owosso, Mich., in 1857. He enlisted in the 5th Mich. Cavalry in 1862; was discharged therefrom on account of wounds in 1864. He removed to Marquette in 1873, and was Collector of Customs, District of Superior, from 1877 to 1885. He was a Republican in politics, and still lived at Marquette in 1887.

LEANDER D. OSBURN

Representative from Cass County, 1867-8. Was born Dec. 27, 1825, in Wayne County, Ind., and in 1835 removed with his father to Calvin, Mich. He was educated by his mother. At the age of twenty-one he became a teacher, afterwards read medicine with Dr. Bonine, attended Rush Medical College in 1851 and 1852, and commenced practice at Vandalia, Mich., in 1853. He became Justice in 1856 and held the position many years; was also Supervisor.

REUBEN H. OSBURN

Senator from the Thirty-second District, 1877-8. Was born in Bloomfield, O., June 27, 1823. He was educated in common schools, supplemented by academical instruction. He studied medicine and graduated from the Western Reserve College, Cleveland, O., in 1849. He moved to the Upper Peninsula in 1852, where he resided. He held various township offices. In 1887 he was the oldest practicing physician in the Upper Peninsula. In politics he was a Republican.

GILBERT R. OSMUN

Secretary of State, 1887-9 and 1889-91. Was born in Newark, N. J., Oct. 8, 1845. He was left fatherless at the age of seven years, and then earned his own living. In early boyhood he did "chores" on farms and in shops for his board and clothes, and got his schooling as best he could, his longest continuous term at school being one year at the Chester, N. Y., Academy, where he did the janitor work to pay his bills and buy books. He enlisted in the 69th N. Y. Volunteers, one of the regiments of the famous Irish brigade. After much hard service he was severely wounded at Petersburg, Va., Mar. 25, 1865, and was honorably discharged July 5, 1865, coming home on crutches. He then worked at his trade of tinsmithing until the following year, when he enlisted in the 43d U. S. Infantry; did garrison duty in his regiment at Fort Wayne and Fort Gratiot, Mich., for about two years, and was again discharged for disability arising from his old wounds. He engaged in various occupations in Port Huron, and eventually became city editor of the Port Huron *Times*. Later he went to East Saginaw, where he was city editor of the Saginaw *Republican*, and thence to Detroit, where for ten years he was State editor of the Detroit *Evening News*. Governor Alger selected him as Private Secretary, which place he filled until he assumed the duties of Secretary of State.

WILLIAM E. OSMUN

Delegate in the Constitutional Convention of 1907-8, from the Twenty-third District, Muskegon County. Was born in Cayuga, N. Y., in 1850, of German-American parents. He acquired his education at the Ithaca Academy and two years at Cornell University. He came to Michigan in 1880, and published newspapers at Shelby and Montague. He was admitted to the State Federal Courts in 1886, and enjoyed a lucrative practice. He served as President of the Village of Montague for five terms and president of the School Board three years. He served as Postmaster seven years, also as a member of the Republican State Central Committee, and a member of the Commission of Inquiry on Michigan Tax Lands and Forestry.

RUSSELL COWLES OSTRANDER

Justice of the Supreme Court, 1905-19. Was born at Ypsilanti, Mich., Sept 1, 1851, and removed with his parents to Lansing in April, 1858, where he resided. Pure Dutch on his father's side, on his mother's he was a descendant of John Cowles, one of the first settlers of Farmington, Conn., and member of the General Court of that colony. He was educated in the ward and high schools of Lansing, teacher of a country school as early as 1868, and received a practical and thorough commerical education. He entered the law department of the University of Michigan in 1874, receiving his degree in 1876, in which year he was admitted to the bar. In 1876 and again in 1878 he was elected Circuit Court Commissioner, and in 1880 Prosecuting Attorney of Ingham County. He was City Attorney of Lansing in 1895-6, and Mayor of the city in 1896-7. From its organization in 1895 to Dec. 31, 1904, he was a member of the State Board of Law Examiners. He was nominated by the Republicans in convention at Saginew, Sept. 8, 1904, for Justice of the Supreme Court, and was elected Nov. 8, 1904, for the term of seven years and re-elected Apr. 4, 1911. He died at Lansing, Sept. 12, 1919.

ASA H. OTIS

Member of the First Constitutional Convention of 1835; and Representative from Wayne County, 1850. Was a native of the State of New York, and a farmer by occupation. He was a County Auditor of Wayne County, in 1845, and Supervisor of Greenfield, 1847-52, and again in 1854. He died in 1855. He was Democratic in politics.

LAUREN FORD OTIS

Representative from the First District of Allegan County, 1895-6 and 1897-8. Was born in DeWitt, Onondaga County, N. Y., Sept. 10, 1842. When eleven years of age, he moved with his parents to Aurora, Ill., where he attended the public schools and the Clark Seminary. In 1860 he began clerking with the dry goods firm of Hawley & Otis, which occupation he followed ten years; then he became one of the members. He continued in said firm until 1885; sold out and moved to Casco Township, Allegan County, Mich. In politics a Republican. He was Treasurer of the city of Aurora and Supervisor of his Township from 1890-3.

DANIEL B. OVIATT

Representative from Antrim County, 1903-4 and 1905-6. Was born at Wellsville, N. Y., in 1847, of Scotch and Irish parents. He was educated in the common schools and Battle Creek College. Married. While living in New York he was elected to the office of Township Assessor several terms. For a time he followed the profession of Minister of the Gospel. For several years he was editor and publisher of the Alden *Wave*. Mr. Oviatt was Supervisor of Helena Township, Antrim County, Mich., for five years and Justice of the Peace seven years. In politics a Republican.

GEORGE OVIATT

Representative from Lake and Wexford counties, 1885-6 and 1887-8. Was born at Newton Falls, O., Mar. 12, 1849. He removed to Michigan in 1860, and settled in Lake County in 1865. Mr. Oviatt was a real estate dealer and publisher of a newspaper, and had been Sheriff of Lake County two terms. Politically he was a Republican. He died Apr. 12, 1888.

JOHN OWEN

Member of the Board of Regents of the University of Michigan, 1841-8; State Treasurer, 1861-7. Was born in Toronto, Canada, Mar. 20, 1809. He removed with his mother to Detroit in 1818, and received a limited education. He then became a clerk in a drug store of Dr. Chapin, subsequently a partner, the house finally becoming the wholesale drug house of John Owen & Co., the precursor of the house of T. H. Hinchman & Sons. But the connection of Mr. Owen with the financial and shipping interests of Detroit, and with philanthropic enterprises, left a permanent impress. He was an Alderman several times; was a member of the Board of Water Commissioners, 1865-79; was appointed Regent of the University in 1841 in the place of Francis J. Higginson, was re-appointed in 1844 and served until 1848; president of the Fire Department, 1841-3; and trustee of the Detroit Medical College. In 1845 he became president of the Michigan Insurance bank and held it for twenty years, until it was merged in a national bank. It was the only bank in Michigan which did not suspend in the panic of 1857, and his financial ability placed him at the head of the finances, which he managed with great ability during the war. He was president of the Detroit Dry Dock Co., and the Merchants' Navigation Company. He was a member of the Methodist Episcopal Church, and identified with its progress in Michigan. He died at Detroit, Mar. 31, 1892.

JOHN G. OWEN

Senator from the Sixth District, 1861-2. Was born at Woodchurch, England, Mar. 28, 1824. He came to this country in 1842, and to Michigan in 1843. He was at Armada one year, two years a clerk in Detroit, in 1846 settled at Clarkston as a merchant, and also became a farmer in 1854. In 1860 he owned and operated the flouring mills at Waterford in connection with a store. After 1865 he became a leading merchant at East Saginaw, and after 1872 was extensively engaged in lumbering. In politics he was first a Whig, then a Republican.

TUBAL C. OWEN

Representative from St. Clair County, 1870. Was born at Caledonia Springs, N. Y., Mar. 24, 1819. He came to Newport (now Marine City), Mich., in 1845, resided there until 1852, then on a farm in China until 1859, then at St. Clair up to 1871, when he removed to Detroit. He was Clerk of St. Clair County from 1857 to 1863; Mayor of St. Clair, 1864; Supervisor four years; Clerk of Draft Commission, and war census taker for St. Clair County. First he was a Whig, then a Republican, and by profession a lawyer. He was elected Representative in place of Nathan S. Boynton, resigned.

ALBERT PACK

Representative from Sanilac County, 1865-6. Was born in Chittenango, N. Y., Nov. 10, 1842. He came to Lexington, Mich., in 1849, and moved to Alpena in 1870. He was Mayor of Alpena in 1872. For many years he engaged in lumbering with great success. He was a Republican in politics.

WILLIAM F. PACK

Representative from St. Joseph County, 1899-1900. Was born in the Raisin Valley, between Adrian and Tecumseh, Mich., July 4, 1861, and received his early education in that vicinity, subsequently attending the Michigan Agricultural College. His father was a Baptist minister, and the subject of this sketch an only son. Upon reaching manhood he engaged in mercantile business, became prominent as a Democratic campaign manager in St. Joseph County, and was Postmaster of Centerville, during President Cleveland's last term. At the opening of the Spanish-American War, Mr. Pack enlisted in the 33d Regiment of Mich. Vol., went to Cuba as a Second Lieutenant, was in active service before Santiago, and received a scratch in the shoulder from a Mauser bullet while in front of Aquadores, July 1, 1898.

FRANKLIN S. PACKARD

Representative from St. Joseph County, 1875-6. Was born in Cattaraugus County, N. Y., Feb. 10, 1838. He received an ordinary common school education, removed to Michigan in 1840, and settled at Sturgis. His occupation was that of a lumber dealer. In politics he was a Democrat.

WILLIAM PACKARD

Representative from Allegan County, 1865-6 and 1867-8. Was born in Plainfield, Mass., July 23, 1808. He received a common school education. In early life he was a farmer. He removed from the State of New York to Chatham, O., in 1836, where he cleared a farm and remained until 1859, when he removed to Allegan County, Mich., and in 1870 to Covert, Van Buren County. He occupied all prominent offices of his township while living in Ohio. In politics he was a Republican. In Michigan he was for many years engaged extensively in lumbering, owning thousands of acres of timber, and operating four saw mills.

WM. O. PACKARD

Senator from the Forty-second District, 1877-8. Was born Sept 14, 1832, in Rensselaer County, N. Y. In 1836 he removed with his father's family to Chatham, O., where he received a common school education. In 1859 he moved to Ganges, Mich., where he subsequently held the office of Postmaster for several years. In 1870 he moved to Deerfield (Covert postoffice), Van Buren County, Mich. In the eighties he was engaged in lumbering, farming, manufacturing, merchandising and real estate transactions. In politics he was a Republican.

HENRY PACKER

Representative from Hillsdale County, 1845. Was born in Colchester, Conn., Nov. 1, 1800. He received an academical education and taught school several years; then moved to western New York and engaged in getting out staves; then for five years was selling books in the southern States. In 1835 he settled at Jonesville, Mich., and became a farmer. He was four years Judge of Probate, Highway Commissioner, Justice of the Peace and Supervisor. He was a Democrat until 1856, then a Republican until 1872, then a Democrat. He died at Jonesville, Nov. 9, 1881.

ALFRED PADDOCK

Senator from the Eleventh District, 1853-4. Was born in Litchfield, N. Y., January 30, 1805. By occupation he was a merchant and farmer, in politics a Whig. He settled in Concord, Mich., about 1844, and resided there until his death, Mar. 29, 1870. He commenced business life as a merchant, was afterwards a farmer and miller.

ROBERT W. PADDOCK

Representative from Charlevoix County, 1903-4. Was born in Lake County, Ill., Mar. 13, 1861. His early boyhood was spent working on the farm and attending the common schools of Illinois. He attended the Wauconda Academy two years and then entered the Valparaiso Normal School, Ind., from which he graduated in 1879. After graduation he taught school for several terms. He was married in 1885 to Miss Mary F. Nicholls, settled in Ohio, where for two years was factory superintendent, and for twelve years an officer at the Boys Industrial School at Lancaster. He came to Michigan in 1899 and purchased a large tract of stump land and engaged in live stock raising. In politics a Republican.

CHARLES J. PAILTHORP

Representative from Charlevoix County, 1879-80. Was born Dec. 25, 1848, in Mt. Morris, Mich. He received a common school education, and graduated from the law department of the University of Michigan in 1875. He then removed to Petoskey and commenced the practice of law. He was Prosecuting Attorney, also United States Commissioner for the Western District of Michigan. In politics a Democrat.

RODNEY C. PAINE

Senator from the Nineteenth District, 1855-6. Was born in New Milford, Conn., in 1806. When young he removed with his parents to Auburn, N. Y. He left home at seventeen, passed several years in the State of New York, and came from Albany to Michigan in 1836. He settled at St. Joseph and took charge of the Farmers' and Mechanics' Bank. He removed to Niles in 1842, and was there engaged in private banking until his death in 1882. He was County Treasurer of Berrien County from 1836 to 1838; President of the village of Niles in 1855; Mayor in 1873, and Trustee of the union school from 1854 to 1874. He was actively interested in every work that promised to benefit the growth of Niles.

AMBROSE E. PALMER

Senator, 1901-2, from the Twenty-seventh District, comprising the counties of Antrim, Benzie, Charlevoix, Grand Traverse, Kalkaska, Leelanau and Wexford. Was born in Pleasantville, Westchester County, N. Y., Aug. 5, 1849. His early education was received in the rural schools of that county, graduating later from Wesleyan Academy at Wilbraham, Mass. He entered college at Middletown, Conn., but owing to lack of means was unable to complete the course, and came to Michigan in 1869, taking charge of a lumber plant at Torch Lake until 1875, when he engaged in the mercantile business at Kalkaska until 1885, after which time he successfully conducted the dairy farm where in 1901 he resided. Married. He held the offices of Supervisor and County Road Commissioner. In politics a Republican.

CHARLES H. PALMER

Member of the Board of Regents of the University of Michigan, 1852-9. Was born at Lenox, N. Y., in 1814; graduated from Union College in 1837; was principal of Fredonia and Geneseo Academies; in 1847 became principal of Romeo, Mich. Academy, and conducted it successfully many years. Through his exertions as Regent of the University the services of Dr. Tappan were secured. From 1853 until his death, Apr. 9, 1887, he was a resident of Pontiac. He was largely interested in mines in the Upper Peninsula, also in building canals and railroads in that part of the State. He opened the Pewabic Mine. He was a trustee of the Michigan Military Academy.

CHARLES S. PALMER

Representative from Saginaw County, 1846. His postoffice address was Saginaw. (Further data not obtainable).

GEORGE PERRY PALMER

Representative from the First District of Wayne County, 1913-14 and 1915-16. Was born at Detroit, Mich., July 13, 1868, of American and English parents. He was educated in the Detroit High School, the Cass Public School and the University of Minnesota. He was Assistant City Attorney of Detroit during the incumbency of Frank A. Rasch, Assistant Corporation Counsel under Hon. John J. Speed, a former member of the Michigan Legislature and later Judge of Wayne Circuit Court and Corporation Counsel. He was also Assistant Corporation Counsel under Hon. Charles Flowers, a member of the 1913 and 1915 Legislatures. Married. In politics a Republican.

JOHN R. PALMER

Representative from Calhoun County, 1853-4. Was born in the State of New York, June 27, 1809. He came to Michigan in 1844. He was a farmer and a Democrat. He died May 1, 1877.

LEWIS G. PALMER

Senator, 1887-8 and 1889-90, from the Twenty-third District, comprising Mecosta and Montcalm counties. Was born in Herkimer County, N. Y., Sept. 17, 1852, and in 1857 removed with his parents to Michigan. When he was thirteen years old he enlisted as a drummer boy and served nearly three years, receiving his discharge at Jackson, Mich., in 1865. His education was obtained in the public schools of Detroit and the State Agricultural College at Lansing. He removed with his parents to Big Rapids in 1869, where he resided. He began his active life as a teacher, was afterwards elected to the office of County Superintendent of Schools for Mecosta County, which position he held until the law providing for such officials was repealed. He next studied law with Judge Fuller of Big Rapids, was admitted to the bar in 1877, was elected to the office of Prosecuting Attorney in 1878, in which capacity he served the people of his county three terms. For several years he was county agent of the State Board of Corrections and Charities and a member of the Board of Education of Big Rapids. In politics a Republican.

MILTON R. PALMER

Representative from the First District of Wayne County, 1921—. Was born at Grand Rapids, Mich., Jan. 25, 1878, of Scotch and American parents. He received his education in the public schools and West Side Business College of Chicago and studied accountancy in the Institute of Technology but never practiced as a certified public accountant. He left school at the age of sixteen and worked on a stock farm in Indiana; learned bookkeeping and also the soap-making trade. He followed different occupations until 1899 when he came to Detroit as a soapmaker. In 1900 he entered the newspaper business with the Detroit *Journal*. He has also been with the Cleveland *News*, Detroit *Times*, Detroit *Saturday Night* and editor of the *Detroiter*. For a time he was office manager of Wolverine Motor Supply Co., and also publicity secretary of the city of Detroit. He is now connected with Wm. N. Alber Co., advertising counsel, and is editor of the Oakland *Sales News*. Mr Palmer is married. He is a member of Corinthian Lodge, F. & A. M., an officer of King Cyrus Chapter, R. A. M., past master of Monroe Council R. & S. M., Fellowcraft Athletic Club, Meadowbrook Country Club, Adcraft Club and Detroit Board of Commerce. He has been active for a number of years in advocating good roads and also in furthering the Great Lakes-St. Lawrence Waterway Project. In politics he is a Republican.

OSCAR PALMER

Representative from Crawford and other counties, 1883-4; and member of the State Board of Agriculture, 1889-91. Was born at Westfield, N. Y., Nov. 8, 1841. He moved to Hudson, Mich., with his parents in 1843, received an academical education and graduated at Georgetown Medical College, D. C. He was in the service as soldier, hospital steward, and assistant surgeon nearly three and a half years. Then he was in business several years at Jonesville, Mich., also edited the *Independent*, but in 1881 removed to Grayling, engaged in farming and manufacturing, and publishing the Crawford *Avalanche*. Politically he was a Republican. He was a member of the State Board of Agriculture from 1889 to Jan. 23, 1891, when he resigned.

SAMUEL H. PALMER

Representative from Jackson County, 1848. Was born at Poughkeepsie, N. Y., in 1801. He was by trade a carriage maker, and in politics a Democrat. He came to Michigan in 1835 and moved to Jackson in 1841. Deceased.

THOMAS WITHERELL PALMER

Senator from the Second District, 1879-80; and United States Senator, 1883-9. Was born in Detroit, Jan. 25, 1830; educated in the public schools at Thompson's Academy, at Palmer, now St. Clair, Mich., and at the Michigan University. His occupation was manufacturer and farmer. In politics he was a Republican. He served on the Board of Estimates of Detroit, and as State Senator in 1879-80; elected to the United States Senate upon the eighty-first joint ballot of the Legislature, to succeed Hon. Thomas W. Ferry, Republican, and took his seat Dec. 3, 1883; served until Mar. 3, 1889. He was appointed United States Minister to Spain in 1889 by President Harrison, and two years later resigned; elected president of the World's Columbian Exposition and served throughout the entire exposition. He died June 1, 1913, at Detroit.

WALTER H. PALMER

Representative from Osceola and other counties, 1877-8 and 1879-80. Was born Aug. 30, 1845, in Oakland County, Michigan. He was a graduate of the State Normal School, and of the law department of Michigan University. He held the offices of Circuit Court Commissioner, Justice, Superintendent of Schools, and Supervisor. By profession he was a lawyer and in practice at Reed City. In politics he was a Republican.

HEMAN PALMERLEE

Representative from Kent County, 1881-2. Was born at Grandville, Washington County, N. Y., Dec. 3, 1820, and came to Michigan in 1832, settling in Bruce, Macomb County. During six years of his early manhood he lived in Rochester, Oakland County, and was engaged in mercantile business. He then, in 1850, removed to Walker, Kent County, where he followed farming for about twenty-two years. After that time he was employed as an accountant and collection agent. His education, beyond that of the common schools of the new State, was obtained in the Romeo Academy. Politically he was a Republican.

AMAZIAH B. PARDEE

Representative from Ionia County, 1887-8. Was born in 1834, in Jackson County, Michigan. By occupation he was a farmer; by political persuasion, a Fusionist, on which ticket he was elected Representative.

PETER E. PARK

Senator, 1891-2, from the Third District, comprising a portion of Wayne County. Was born in Milford, Oakland County, Mich., Mar. 15, 1859. He attended school and worked on a farm until sixteen years of age; after attending the New Hudson Union School two years, he taught school five years in Wayne and Oakland counties. He tended toll gate for the Detroit and Saline plank road nights for two years and studied law during the day. In 1884 he went into the real estate and collection business and studied law during spare time; and was admitted to the bar in 1886, and practiced law. He was elected to the Senate of 1891-2 on the Democratic ticket.

BURTON PARKER

Representative from Monroe County in 1883-4. Was born in Dundee, Mich., Apr. 24, 1844. He served a few months in the Mich. Mechanics and Engineers, being discharged from ill health. He was a Justice of the Peace in 1867, and graduated from the law department of the University in 1870. He was Circuit Court Commissioner, Mayor of Monroe, and President of the School Board. Politically he was a Republican.

JAMES H. PARKER

Representative from Lenawee County, 1855-6. Was born in Masonville, N. Y., Sept. 2, 1803. He received a common school education, became a teacher, then for ten years a carpenter. He settled in 1833, on a farm at Romeo, Mich. He was a Supervisor six years, and six terms a Justice. He and his wife were long conductors on the "underground railroad." He died at Adrian, February, 1887.

JOHN PARKER

Senator from the Twentieth District, 1859-60. Was born in Cavendish, Vt., Feb. 7, 1813. By occupation he was a farmer; a Democrat until 1854, then a Republican. He settled in Portage, Kalamazoo County, in 1832, where he was Supervisor several years; was also United States Marshal. He died Nov. 20, 1880.

LEONARD B. PARKER

Senator from the Twenty-fifth District, 1863-4. Was born at Moses, N. Y., July 19, 1818. He received a common school and academical education. He taught school, then studied medicine, graduating at Castleton, Vt., in 1842. He practiced at Cambridge, Vt., but in 1845 settled at Newport, now Marine City, and built up a large practice. He filled several local positions.

LEROY PARKER

Representative from Genesee County, 1874-5. Was born Dec. 15, 1844, at Flint, Mich. He graduated at Hamilton College, N. Y., in 1865, and attended the law department of the Michigan University in 1865-6. He studied law and was admitted to the bar in 1867, and continued practice in Flint. He was elected Representative in 1847, to fill a vacancy caused by the death of Levi Walker. In politics he was a Republican. He was a member of the State Board of Health.

SAMPSON PARKER

Representative from Washtenaw County, 1867-8. Was born in Otsego County, N. Y., Nov. 22, 1818. He was reared on a farm and came West with his parents, who settled in Lima, Mich., in 1833. He served as Justice several times. He cultivated a large farm. In politics he was a Democrat.

WARREN PARKER

Representative from Macomb County, 1879-80 and 1881-2. Was born in Greig, N. Y., Nov. 15, 1829. His father removed to Michigan in 1833, and settled in Chesterfield, Macomb County. He obtained most of his education in the primary schools. By occupation he was a farmer. The public trusts he held were township only: Justice, Superintendent of Schools and Supervisor. Politically he was a Democrat. Deceased.

WARREN J. PARKER

Representative from the First District of Lenawee County, 1905-6 and 1907-8. Was born at Clarence, Erie County, N. Y., Dec. 18, 1844, of English parents. He received his education in the district schools of Clarence, N. Y. Mr. Parker was married to Adell E. Stowell, Dec. 20, 1865. At the age of seventeen he enlisted in the 100th Regiment, N. Y. Vol. Infantry, served two years and eleven months, and was mustered out in September, 1865. He moved to Lenawee County, Mich., Feb. 1, 1867, and settled in Tecumseh, working on a farm until July 1868, when he purchased a farm of seventy-two acres in Woodstock Township. He followed farming as an occupation. In politics he was a Republican. He held the offices of Township Clerk, Justice of the Peace, Supervisor and Register of Deeds of Lenawee County. He was a Mason, member of Brooklyn Chapter, R. A. M., Adrian Commandery K. T., and Eastern Star. He died at Woodstock, June 29, 1920.

JONATHAN G. PARKHURST

Representative from Van Buren County, 1885-6. Was born in Hastings, N. Y., in 1828. Coming to Detroit he entered upon the study of the law, and was admitted to the bar in 1858. With the exception of five years spent in Kansas (1870 to 1875), where he served as District Judge, he continuously engaged in the practice of his profession in this State. He was a resident of Decatur in 1887, and in addition to law business was extensively interested in fruit growing and stock raising. In politics he was a Republican.

NATHAN C. PARKHURST

Representative from Oakland County, 1849 and 1853-4. Was born in Darien, N. Y. After the age of ten he was a resident of Ohio, and later came to Michigan. By occupation he was a farmer, in politics a Democrat.

CHARLES P. PARKILL

Representative from Shiawassee County, 1857-8. Was born in Niagara County, N. Y. He came to Michigan at the age of nineteen, and to Owosso in 1841. He was a printer by trade and worked a year on the Owosso *Argus*. He was afterwards a teacher, but finally studied medicine and graduated from the Willoughby Medical College, Ohio, in 1846. After practicing at Bennington. Mich., twenty years, he removed to Owosso and opened a drug store. He was crippled when twelve years old. He died at Owosso, Nov. 28, 1893.

THOMAS H. PARKINSON

Representative from the Third District of St. Clair County, 1895-6. Was born in London, Canada, June 17, 1848; he came to Michigan in 1857; settled on a farm in Emmet Township, St. Clair County, acquired a common school education, and remained on the farm until 1893, when he removed to Yale. His occupation was that of a farmer. In politics a Republican.

BYRON F. PARKS

Representative from St. Clair County, 1883-4. Was born in Otsego County, N. Y., Aug. 24, 1829. He received a common school education and worked on a farm until 1862, then became a Lieutenant of Infantry, and after expiration of service was engaged in recruiting, and later in farming and the sale of agricultural implements. He was Deputy Sheriff, Justice, and held other town and county positions. Politically he was a Democrat.

JOHN HUNTER PARKS

Representative, 1911-12, from the Iron District, comprising the counties of Baraga, Iron, Keweenaw and Ontonagon. Was born in Bradford County, Pa., June 4, 1844, of Scotch parentage. He was educated in the public schools. In April, 1876, he was married to Eva A. Jewett, and two years later removed from Wisconsin to Michigan. He enlisted in September, 1862, and served in the Civil War, being a member of Co. A, 5th Wis. Infantry. Mr. Parks was the first President of Crystal Falls and also was its first Mayor. Mr. Parks followed the occupation of farming, lumbering and merchant. In politics a Republican.

ABNER C. PARMALEE

Representative from Barry County, 1844. Was born in Benson, Vt., Jan. 3, 1806. He settled in Hastings, Mich., in 1837, and built the second log house. He was six years Register of Deeds and four years Deputy County Treasurer.

He was one of six Whig members of the House, the Senators being all Democrats. In 1849 he went overland to California. He was also a clerk at Washington, D. C. In politics he was a Republican. He died at Marshall, Feb. 9,
1889.

LINUS S. PARMALEE

Representative from Hillsdale County, 1867-8. Was born Aug. 20, 1815, at
Spofford, N. Y., removed to Cattaraugus County, N. Y., in 1823, and in 1840
to Wisconsin. In 1856 he came to Reading, Hillsdale County. He was a clergyman forty years, and in thirty years officiated at 501 weddings and 1,351
funerals. He was a trustee of Hillsdale College fifteen years. He was Postmaster of Reading some ten years, under Johnson and Grant. He was also
Justice of the Peace. At first he was a Whig, but a Republican after 1854.

ANDREW PARSONS

Senator from the Sixth District, 1847-8; member of the Board of Regents of the
University of Michigan, 1852-3; Lieutenant Governor, 1853; Acting Governor,
1853-4; and Representative from Shiawassee County, 1855. Was born in
Hoosick, N. Y., July 22, 1817. He traced his ancestry back to Walter Parsons,
born in Ireland in 1290. Governor Parsons came to Michigan in 1835, at the
age of seventeen, and taught school a few months at Ann Arbor, then was a
clerk at Prairie Creek in Ionia County. He settled in Shiawassee County in
1836, and was soon elected Register of Deeds, which he filled by re-election for
six years. In 1848 he was Prosecuting Attorney; in 1851 was elected Regent
of the University, but resigned when he became Governor; and in 1852 was
elected Lieutenant Governor by the Democrats. By the appointment of Governor
McClelland to the position of Secretary of the Interior, March 4, 1853, he became Governor. In 1854 he was elected a Representative to the Legislature,
and retired from the executive chair to serve in the session of 1855, dying three
months after the close of the session. He was a man of spotless character, a
fluent and persuasive speaker; as a politician, candid, frank and free from
bitterness, and as an executive officer, firm, constant and reliable. Politically
he was a Democrat. He died at Corunna, Michigan, June 6, 1855.

FAYETTE PARSONS

Representative from St. Joseph County, 1867-8 and 1873-4. Was born in
Benson, Vt., Aug. 12, 1812, and received an academical education. He came to
Burr Oak, Michigan, in 1857. By occupation he was a physician, in politics a
Republican. In 1862 he was appointed an examining surgeon for St. Joseph
County, a position he held many years.

JONATHAN PARSONS

Representative from Kalamazoo County, 1877-8 to 1881-2. Was born in West
Springfield, Mass., Oct. 7, 1820. He settled at Marshall, Mich., in 1835, removed to Kalamazoo in 1844. By occupation he was a merchant, in politics a

Republican. He was a Trustee of Kalamazoo several times, for many years Trustee and Treasurer of the Michigan Female Seminary, also president of the Kalamazoo Paper Company and a Bank Director. He died at Kalamazoo, Aug. 17, 1892.

LUKE H. PARSONS

Member of the Board of Regents of the University of Michigan, 1858-62. Was born in western New York, Feb. 12, 1812, was liberally educated, and was admitted to the bar at Ann Arbor, Mich., about 1835. He removed to Corunna about 1839, and became a law partner of his brother, Governor Andrew Parsons. He held the positions of Register of Deeds, Judge of Probate, Prosecuting Attorney, and Regent of the University, serving in the last office until his death, Feb. 19, 1862.

ORRIN PARSONS

Representative from Washtenaw County, 1846. Was born in Sandisfield, Mass., in 1794, and settled on a farm in Saline, Mich., in 1826. The next year, with his brother, he built the first saw-mill in the town. He was Supervisor in 1831, and held that office eight terms. He was also a Justice and held other offices. He erected and managed a grist mill. He died in 1851.

PHILO PARSONS

Member of the State Board of Agriculture, 1861-3. Was born in Scipio, Cayuga County, New York, February 7, 1817. He married Anne Eliza Barnum, June 27, 1843, at Perry, New York. She was born at Danbury, Conn. He was educated at Gouverneur and Homer, N. Y. He was at one time a Presbyterian but later a Congregationalist, always an active worker in the church, and in politics a Republican. He was first in business at Perry, N. Y., with his father; in 1844 he moved to Detroit and took up the business of a wholesale grocer; established a private bank; for many years president of the First National Bank in Detroit; traveled in Europe; member of the Common Council; sent on first relief train to Chicago after the great fire in 1871; president of the Chamber of Commerce; president of the State Agricultural Society; trustee of Olivet College for 36 years; chairman of a committee to secure a design and have erected at the National Capital a statue of General Cass; active in securing Belle Isle Park; a large benefactor to home and foreign missions, aiding young men to the ministry, gave $60,000 to Olivet College; presented the Rau library to the State University; could not enlist in the army because of personal defects, but gave much to aid the cause, banqueting the second regiment of Michigan Volunteers. He was loyal to his church, city and State to an extraordinary degree. He died at Winchendon, Mass., January 12, 1865.

S. TITUS PARSONS

Representative from Shiawassee County, 1863-4 and 1867-8; and Delegate from Shiawassee County to the Constitutional Convention of 1867. He was a brother of Governor Andrew Parsons, came to Michigan when a young man, and studied

law with his brother at Owosso. He was admitted to the bar in 1854, and located
at Corunna, where he practiced for more than twenty years. He was Prosecuting Attorney six years. He removed to Detroit in 1877, and engaged in
practice, but died several years prior to 1887. He was a Republican in politics.

LEVI P. PARTLOW

Representative from Clinton County, 1903-4 and 1905-6. Was born in Eagle
Township, Clinton County, in 1846. He took up the occupation of a farmer
when he was eighteen years of age, which pursuit he followed. He held several
offices of trust, being elected Justice of the Peace for five consecutive terms.
He was also Postmaster for twelve years. In politics a Republican.

AZARISH S. PARTRIDGE

Representative from Genesee County, 1881-2. Was born in Saratoga County,
N. Y., Dec. 19, 1834. He was a farmer and fruit grower by occupation. In
politics he was formerly a Republican, then a Prohibitionist. He came to Flushing, Mich., about 1856. As a young man he was a teacher for several years.

BENJAMIN F. PARTRIDGE

Commissioner of the State Land Office, 1877-9; and Representative from Bay
County, 1881-2. Was born in Shelby, Mich., April 19, 1822. He received a
common school and academical education, was a teacher, was engaged a year
in the study of law, was a surveyor and civil engineer, then a lumberman until
1857. He was appointed Sheriff of Bay County, and followed surveying several
years. In 1861 he went into the army, and by regular promotion reached the
rank of Brevet Brigadier General. He was in the U. S. revenue service, 1867-71,
was Supervisor eight years and chairman of the board six years. He was a
farmer near Bay City, and in politics a Republican. He died at Bay City, Oct.
19, 1892.

GEORGE W. PARTRIDGE

Representative from the First District of Wayne County (Detroit), 1895-6.
Was born in Pittsfield, Mass., Oct. 23, 1834. He came to Michigan in 1842
locating in Detroit in 1877, where for several years he engaged in a general
insurance business. He prepared for college in the Wesleyan Methodist Seminary, of Albion, Mich., and graduated in the law department of the Columbian
University, Washington, D. C., in 1872. During the early part of the war he was
clerk in the Commissary Department in the field; afterwards for eight years a
clerk in the Quartermaster-general's office, Washington, D. C.; four years clerk
for the United States Senate committee on commerce; law clerk in the Department of the Interior; and first assistant examiner in the United States Patent
Office; was private secretary for Senator Zach. Chandler for eight years; Special
Deputy Collector of Customs, port of Detroit, 1879-83; special inspector Treasury Department and special agent of the United States Census Office; was for

several years one of the directors of the Detroit *Post and Tribune* and was Washington correspondent of the former and of western papers. In 1872 he was assistant secretary of the Union Congressional Republican Committee, Washington, D. C., and later secretary of the State Central Committee. In Detroit he was a member and president of the City Board of Estimates. In politics a Republican. He was elected to the House of Representatives of 1895-6 on the general legislative ticket of the city of Detroit.

JOHN J. PASCOE

Representative from the Second District of Marquette County, 1919-20. Was born Dec. 31, 1873, at Dover, N. J., of English parents. He was educated in the public schools. In 1919 he had been a miner or interested in mines for over thirty years. Married. In politics a Republican.

PETER PASCOE

Senator 1893-4 and 1895-6, from the Thirty-first District, counties of Alger, Dickinson, Iron and Marquette. Was born in England in 1831; attended private school; came to the United States in 1854, locating in West Virginia, from thence to Pennsylvania and in 1861 to northern Michigan, where he engaged in the mining business and as mining expert. In politics a Republican.

LEVI PATCHEN

Representative from St. Joseph County, 1848. Was born in the State of Connecticut, Jan. 5, 1804. He lived in Yates County, N. Y., from 1808 until 1843, when he settled in St. Joseph County, Mich., and was a nurseryman and farmer by occupation, and politically a Whig. He died Sept. 25, 1851.

HENRY R. PATTENGILL

Superintendent of Public Instruction, 1893-5 and 1895-7. Was born in Mount Vision, Otsego County, N. Y., Jan. 4, 1852. A few months later the family moved to Akron, Erie County, where the father, Rev. L. C. Pattengill, served as pastor of the First Baptist Church for the six years following. The family next moved to Wilson, Niagara County, where they remained seven years and then came to Michigan, locating at Litchfield, Hillsdale County. Mr. Pattengill's early education was obtained in the district and village schools, and later at the University of Michigan, where he was graduated from the literary department in 1874. The following ten years he was Superintendent of Schools in St. Louis and Ithaca, and most of this time was president of the Gratiot County Teachers' Association and a member of the Board of School Inspectors, and later of the County Board of Examiners. In 1885 he became associate editor of the *Michigan School Moderator* and one year later sole owner and proprietor.

He was author of a "Civil Government of Michigan" and a "Manual of Orthography," a set of "Michigan Historical and Geographical Cards," and several other books for teachers. From 1885 to 1889 he was assistant professor of English in the State Agricultural College. In politics he was a Republican. He died at Lansing, Nov. 26, 1918.

ORLANDO R. PATTENGILL

Representative from Wayne County, 1871-2. Was born in Stow, Vt., Feb. 24, 1828. He came to Michigan in 1845, and resided at or near Plymouth. He received a common school education, worked as a farm laborer, and from 1849 was a teacher for twelve years, in winter. By occupation he was a farmer, politically first an Abolitionist, later a Republican. He was secretary and deputy treasurer of the Farmers' Mutual Insurance Company of Wayne and Monroe Counties after 1871.

JAMES PATTERSON

Representative from Oakland County, 1851. His postoffice address was Fenton. (Further data not obtainable).

JOHN C. PATTERSON

Senator from the 8th District, 1879-80 and 1881-2. Was born in Eckford, Mich., Mar. 27, 1838. He graduated at Hillsdale College in 1864, and from the law department of the Albany, N. Y., University in 1865. He commenced practice at Marshall in 1867, was a trustee of Hillsdale College, and a lecturer there before the senior class on constitutional law. Politically he was a Republican. He died at Marshall, May 24, 1910.

JOSEPH H. PATTERSON

Delegate from the Third District to the Constitutional Convention of 1835; and Representative from Lenawee County, 1839-1843 and 1848. Was born in Ireland in 1801, came to America in 1819 and located at Lockport, N. Y. In 1828 he removed to Adrian, Mich., where he settled on a farm. He was prominent in early Michigan politics. He is said to have given the names to four Counties in the State: Antrim, Wexford, Roscommon and Clare. In politics he was a Democrat.

MICHAEL A. PATTERSON

Member of the Board of Regents of the University of Michigan, 1840-2 and 1852-8; Representative from Lenawee County, 1846; and Senator from the Third District, 1844-5. Was born in Easton, Pa., Mar. 11, 1840, and was educated there until early manhood. He studied medicine in the University of Pennsylvania, and graduated with honor at the age of nineteen. He practiced in western New York for four years, and settled in Tecumseh, Mich., where he continued in active practice until 1875. He then sought a southern climate for health. He was a Regent of the University, and held many local offices. Politically he was a Democrat. He died at Westham Locks, Va., Apr. 17, 1877.

WILLIAM H. PATTISON

Senator from the Seventh District, 1855-6 and from the Eighth District, 1857-8. His postoffice address was Saline, Washtenaw County. (Further data not obtainable).

JOHN PATTON, JR.

United States Senator, 1894-5. Was born at Curwensville, Clearfield County, Pa., Oct. 30, 1850; prepared for college at Phillips Academy, Andover, Mass.; graduated from Yale College in 1875; studied law at Columbia Law School, New York City, graduating in 1877. He moved to Grand Rapids, Mich., in 1878, and practiced law. In politics he was a Republican. Upon the death of Senator Francis B. Stockbridge, Apr. 30, 1894, he was appointed by the Governor of Michigan, to serve as Senator until the election of a successor by the Legislature in January, 1895, took his seat May 10, 1894, and served until Jan. 15, 1895.

JOHN PAUL

Senator from the Seventeenth District, 1915-16. Was born at Whithorn, Wigton-shire, Scotland, Apr. 1, 1849. He was educated in the district schools. While he was quite young, his parents located on a farm in Kent County, Mich., where he later assisted his father in the rough work of clearing the land, attending school during the winter. He engaged in farming, and in the real estate and insurance business. He served as School Trustee, Village President, Trustee, Justice of the Peace, Supervisor and County Treasurer. Married. In politics a Republican.

JIRA PAYNE

Representative from Lenawee County, 1838. His postoffice address was Clinton. (Further data not obtainable).

JAMES H. PEABODY

Representative from the First District of Oakland County, 1889-90. Was born in the town of Wilson, Niagara County, N. Y., in 1839. He was the fourth son of a family of seven boys. He moved to Conneautville, Pa., at ten years of age, educated in the academy of that town, commenced teaching school at the age of fifteen years, clerking in store summers until the war. He enlisted as a private after the first Battle of Bull Run; afterwards made 1st Lieutenant, and commanded Battery M, 1st N. Y. Artillery, in Gen. Bank's famous retreat in Shenandoah Valley, covering retreat and saving a large amount of government property. He was severely injured at the Battle of Winchester and resigned on account of physical disability from active service and went into the Quarter-master's Department at Washington. He came to Michigan in 1864 and engaged in farming in Bloomfield, or engaged in wood and coal business at Detroit, and supplying the chain of forts along the lakes with forage and fuel. He was elected on the Republican ticket to the House of 1889-90.

RUSSELL R. PEALER

Representative from St. Joseph County, 1889-90. Was born in Greenwood, Columbia County, Pa., Jan. 1, 1842; reared on a farm, educated in the common schools, the Orangeville Academy and the New Columbus Normal School; taught school; volunteered as a private soldier in the 16th Pa. Cavalry, Sept. 9, 1862; later was promoted to Sergeant Major of his regiment "for meritorious conduct as a soldier," and afterwards commissioned Second, then First Lieutenant; was wounded at Hatcher's Run, Va., Feb. 6, 1865, while in command of his battalion and leading it in a charge; took port in thirty-five battles and cavalry engagements, and was discharged with his regiment, Aug. 11, 1865. In politics a Republican. After the war, he engaged in surveying and studied law in Bloomsburg, Pa., and was admitted to the bar Sept. 3, 1867. He came to Three Rivers, Mich., Nov. 12, 1867, and engaged in the practice of his profession, and since the first year had a lucrative business. He served on school and other local boards, was twice elected Circuit Court Commissioner, was Prosecuting Attorney of his county three years, and was elected and served as Judge of the Fifteenth Judicial Circuit for six years. He was elected to the House of 1889-90 on the Republican ticket. He died at Three Rivers, Mar. 7, 1918.

PERRY DIAMOND PEARL

Representative from the Fifth District of Wayne County, 1871-2. His postoffice address was Belleville. (Further data not obtainable).

STEPHEN PEARL

Representative from Clinton County, 1867-8, and Senator from the Twenty-first District, 1869-70. Was born in Livingston County, N. Y., Nov. 19, 1817. He came to Michigan in 1838 and settled as a farmer in Ovid, Clinton County. In 1887 he lived in Greenbush, same county. He was Supervisor and County Treasurer ten years. Formerly he was a Republican, later Independent in politics.

RICHARD PEARSON

Representative from the Second District of Sanilac County, 1895-6, 1897-8 and 1899-1900. Was born in Whitby, Ont., Oct. 6, 1853. In December, 1860, he came with his parents to Sanilac County, Mich., where he spent his early days in helping to clear up a farm, and attending district school; worked in the lumber woods and saw-mills seven years; married in 1876, and two years later moved to a farm in Moore Township, Sanilac County, where he made his home. In politics a Republican. He held the offices of Justice of the Peace, Highway Commissioner, Township Treasurer, and a member of the Republican Legislative Committee for four years; was president of the Farmers' Institute of Sanilac County and succeeded in organizing six institutes for the winter of 1896-7.

WILLIAM J. PEARSON

Representative from Charlevoix County, 1909-10 and 1911-12; and Senator from the Twenty-ninth District, 1923——. Was born in London, Canada, May 10, 1860. He came to Charlevoix County when he was twenty-four years ald and taught school for three years. He has always been interested in farming and lumbering and has potato warehouses at Boyne Falls. Mr. Pearson is married and has three daughters and one son. He served four years as Sheriff and four years as Register of Deeds of Charlevoix County. He was Representative from Charlevoix County during the sessions of 1909-10 and 1911-12.

WILLIAM H. PEASE

Representative from Jackson County, 1845. Was born in Seneca County, N. Y., June 7, 1804. He came to Michigan in 1829, and settled on a farm in Grass Lake. He served on first grand jury in Jackson County, 1833. He died Nov. 13, 1866.

EDWARD W. PECK

Delegate from Oakland County to the First Convention of Assent, 1836. Was born at West Bloomfield, N. Y., Mar. 19, 1807. He received a common school education and was a teacher. He settled in Troy, Mich., in 1831, and was a merchant there for 20 years. He resided at Pontiac in 1887. He held many offices, including County Clerk, Postmaster, etc. He was a Republican. He died about 1911.

GEORGE W. PECK

Representative from Livingston County, 1846 and 1847; and Member of Congress, 1855-7. Was born in New York City, June 4, 1818. He received an academical education, studied law, came to Michigan in 1839, was admitted to the bar in 1842, and commenced practice at Brighton. He removed to Lansing in 1847, and was the first Postmaster. He was Speaker of the House in 1847. He was proprietor of the *State Journal* and State Printer from 1852 to 1855. In 1864 he went into practice at East Saginaw. He removed to St. Louis, Mo., in 1875, and was attorney of St. Louis & Iron Mountain Railroad. Politically he was a Democrat.

WILLIAM PECKHAM

Representative from the Second District of Jackson County, 1913-14. Was born in Parma Township, Jackson County, June 9, 1851, and was educated in the district schools and Jackson High School. Married. Occupation farming. He served as Justice of the Peace, School Director twenty-one years, and eight years on Board of Review. In politics a Democrat.

ARCHIBALD J. PEEK

Representative from the First District of Jackson County, 1897-8; and Senator, 1905-6 and 1907-8, from the Tenth District, comprising the counties of Jackson and Washtenaw. Was born in Onondaga County, N. Y., June 8, 1854, of Scotch descent. He acquired his education in the Jackson High School and after being graduated moved with his parents on a farm. He remained with them until married to Libby Morrill. He then moved to a farm of his own and continued active farming until elected Sheriff of Jackson County, which office he held for two terms. He was elected to the Legislature of 1897-8, after which he engaged in the hack and omnibus business in Jackson city.

GEORGE W. PEER

Representative from the First District of Genesee County, 1895-6. Was born in Penfield, Monroe County, N. Y., Mar. 15, 1832. He attended district school and in 1852 went to California, where he spent three years in the mines, returning to New York in 1855. The following year he came to Michigan, locating in Mundy Township, Genesee County, and engaged in farming. In politics he was a Republican. He held township offices for twenty years, that of Supervisor for several years.

EDGAR PEIRCE

Representative from Mecosta County, 1883-4. Was born May 6, 1841, in Erie County, Pa.; was educated in common schools and an academy; followed milling until 1862; enlisted in the Fourteenth Pennsylvania Cavalry, and served through the war, and rose to the rank of Lieutenant. In 1871 he settled in Mecosta County and engaged in making shingles. He was four years County Treasurer. In politics a Republican.

JAMES P. PENDILL

Representative from Marquette County, 1863-4. Was born near Batavia, N. Y., in 1812. He was a resident of Niles, Mich., as early as 1837, and was often seen there driving his four-in-hand, in broadcloth suit and white gloves. He was engaged at the Sault in mercantile business from 1845-1855, when he engaged in the same business at Marquette. In 1867 he became a resident of Negaunee, and was Mayor in 1872-3. He returned to Marquette and was Mayor from 1879 to 1882, and many years Supervisor and Chairman of the Board. He long served as a School Trustee. He died March 9, 1885.

EDWARD W. PENDLETON

Senator from the Tenth District, 1879-80. Was born at Broadalbin, N. Y., December 13, 1825. He received a common school education. In 1844 he removed to Orleans County, N. Y., where he engaged in farming until 1849, when he went to California. In 1851 he returned to Orleans County, and in 1852 settled at Sturgis, Mich. He was engaged in mercantile, manufacturing and agricultural pursuits. He held many offices of trust, and was Justice for seven years. In politics he was a National.

OLIN PENGRA

Representative from Huron County, 1883-4. Was born in Seneca County, N. Y., Oct. 19, 1847. He received such education as the common schools afforded. He was in the army during the last year of the war as a member of the 98th Pennsylvania Regiment. He removed to Michigan in 1867. He taught school for ten years in the counties of Tuscola and Huron. He was admitted to the bar in January, 1878; held many township offices. In politics he was a Republican.

ORRIN G. PENNELL

Senator from the Fourteenth District, 1885-6. Was born in Cortland County, N. Y., in 1827. After receiving a thorough academical education he engaged in teaching. Relinquishing this pursuit he purchased a farm. Deciding to go West, he sold his farm and bought one in Washtenaw County, Mich., to which he removed in 1861, remaining there until 1869, when he removed to DeWitt. He was elected Supervisor of DeWitt in 1883 and 1884. He was U. S. Marshal for the eastern district of Michigan in 1887. He died at DeWitt in 1900.

HARVEY A. PENNEY

Representative from the First District of Saginaw County, 1915-16; and Senator, 1917—, from the Twenty-second District, comprising the County of Saginaw. Was born of English parents, Apr. 26, 1866, in the house adjoining his present residence. He attended the public schools of Saginaw, and the University of Michigan, receiving his LL. B. degree in 1889. In 1890 he took a post-graduate course at the State University and received the first diploma given in the course conferring the LL. M. degree. He held the office of Alderman for more than six years, was a member of the Board of Assessment and Review, and in 1912 was appointed local white slave officer by the United States Government for the city of Saginaw, which position he resigned in 1914. He is a member of the F. & A. M., I. O. O. F., K. of P., B. P. O. E., and other fraternal societies and social clubs. Mr. Penney is married. In politics he is a Republican.

EBENEZER J. PENNIMAN

Member of Congress, 1851-3. Was born at Lansingburg, N. Y. At the age of thirteen he was apprenticed to the art of printing at Keene, N. H.; went to New York at the age of eighteen and engaged in mercantile pursuits; removed to Plymouth, Mich., in 1835, and engaged in business. He was elected a member of Congress as a Whig and Free Soil Coalitionist. He still resided at Plymouth in 1887.

HENRY F. PENNINGTON

Senator from the Thirteenth District, 1883-4. Was born in Seneca County, Ohio, Sept. 9, 1842. In 1852 he removed with his parents to Eaton County, Mich. He received an academical education, and became a farmer. He studied law and graduated from the law department of the University in 1868, and engaged in practice at Charlotte. In politics he was a Democrat. He died at Chicago, Ill., Feb. 4, 1921.

HENRY PENNOYER

Representative from Ottawa County, 1849; and Senator from the Thirty-first District, 1859-60. Was born in Norwalk, Conn., Feb. 9, 1809. He received a common school education, and removed in 1819 to Cayuga County, N. Y., where he worked on a farm. From 1834 to 1836 he lived in Chicago, Ill., when he removed to Muskegon, Mich., and was elected the first Sheriff of Ottawa County, of which Muskegon County then formed a part. In 1838 he was appointed Postmaster of Muskegon, and held the office until 1843. He removed to Grand Haven in 1843, where he kept a hotel until 1856. He then became a farmer in Crockery Township. He was always a Democrat. He was Justice, Supervisor, County Treasurer, and Deputy Collector at Grand Haven. He was a political leader, and among the foremost in the promotion of every enterprise, agricultural, moral, social and educational. He died at Nunica, Ottawa County, Apr. 25, 1886.

JOHN B. PERHAM

Representative from Ottawa County, 1881-2 and 1883-4. Was born in Mayfield, N. Y. He came to Spring Lake, Mich., in 1860, and for several years was principal of the public schools, was for many years a member of the Board of Education, also Supervisor. By occupation he was a merchant, in politics a Republican.

EDWIN Z. PERKINS

Representative from Cheboygan and other counties, 1887-8. Was born in June, 1849, in Oxford County, Ontario. His occupation was attorney at law. He was a graduate of the University of Michigan, class of 1878. Mr. Perkins held the offices of Circuit Court Commissioner, Judge of Probate two terms, and County Treasurer, all in Cheboygan County. In politics he was a Republican.

JABEZ PERKINS

Representative from Shiawassee County, 1859-60. Was born at Defiance, O., Oct. 26, 1820. He received an academical education at Delaware, studied medicine, and graduated at Cleveland, in 1849. He practiced medicine at Springville, Mich., for ten years, but at Owosso after 1860. He took charge of a hospital at Nashville in 1862, became a surgeon of Kentucky volunteers, medical director of the 2d army corps, and then medical director of the Cavalry corps, army of the Cumberland. In politics he was first a Whig, then a Republican.

JOHN PERKINS

Representative from Menominee County, 1891-2. Was born in a small mining town in Devonshire, England, Mar. 31, 1844; came to America in 1865, just after the close of the war, and made the copper regions of Michigan his home. He worked in the copper mines for three years, after which he became a contractor, taking contracts from mining companies to mine certain portions of mines; and was a contractor for Hon. Edward Breitung, then had charge of one part of the mine. In 1873 he became mining captain of the Saginaw mine, which position he held until 1879, when he removed to the Menominee Range and took the position of mining superintendent of the Perkins Mine, which he held until the Saginaw Mining Company released its claim on the said Perkins mine, in the fall of 1886, when he became proprietor of the mine and continued mining ore from the property. He was elected to the House of 1891-2 on the Republican ticket.

JOHN J. PERKINS

Representative from Barry County, 1901-2 and 1903-4. Was born in Franklin Township, Portage County, O., Dec. 14, 1827. He attended the district school winters and worked on his father's farm summers, until he attained the age of seventeen years, when he entered the academy to finish his education. He was married at the age of twenty, and in 1856 he moved to Michigan, and settled on the farm. In politics he was a Republican. He was elected Treasurer three times and held the office of Highway Commissioner for eighteen years and the office of Supervisor for ten years.

SANFORD S. PERKINS

Representative from the Third District of Saginaw County, 1893-4. Was born in Erie County, Pa., in 1830. In 1837 he came with his parents to Michigan. He spent five years at Owosso, Shiawassee County, then moved to Saginaw City. Here, after his school days, he engaged in the manufacture of carriages. Eight years later he quit this business to construct a street railway connecting Saginaw with East Saginaw. This line he managed for thirteen years then moved to his farm in Saginaw Township, two miles from the city. In politics a Democrat. He held most of the local township offices, member and chairman of County Board of Supervisors, also Alderman of Saginaw City.

JOHN J. PERREN

Senator from the First District of Wayne, 1899-1900. Was born at Buffalo, N. Y., Apr. 21, 1848, but became a resident of Detroit by the removal of his parents a year after his birth. He acquired his education in the schools of that city, and after leaving school he went to work in a hat, cap and fur store, remaining there until 1877, when he was appointed chief clerk in the office of the Receiver of Taxes. In 1885 he was appointed a member of the Board of City Assessors by Mayor S. B. Grummond for a term of three years, at the close of which he was appointed for a second full term by Mayor John Pridgeon, Jr., serving altogether six years on the Board of Assessors. In 1891 he engaged in insurance and real estate.

HENRY M. PERRIN

Senator from the Twenty-second District, 1865-6. Was born at Berlin, Vt., July 23, 1829. He was educated at Dartmouth College, graduating in 1853. He removed to Michigan in 1855, residing two years in Detroit, when he settled

in St. Johns, still his home. He was admitted to the bar of Clinton County in
1858. He was Judge of Probate from 1861 to 1865. He successfully followed
his profession, and was also a dealer in real estate. He indulged in farming as
a diversion.

PORTER K. PERRIN

Senator from the Sixteenth District, 1877-8. Was born Sept. 13, 1833, in Berlin,
Vt. He received a common school and academical education and was a graduate
of the Law University of Albany, N. Y., in 1856-7. He removed from Cincinnati,
Ohio, to Michigan in 1860. He held the positions of First Lieutenant, Company
I, and Captain of First Company Sharpshooters, Twenty-seventh Michigan Infantry, and was commissioned Major of the Second Michigan Infantry. He was
also Judge of Probate for Clinton County from 1869 to 1872 inclusive; United
States Commissioner for about six and a half years, and held some minor positions. By profession he was an attorney; in politics a Republican.

PAUL PERRIZO

Representative from Menominee County, 1913-14. Was born at Fond du lac,
Wis., Jan. 26, 1865, and received his education in the public schools. He lived on
a farm until twelve years of age, after which he worked in saw mills nine years,
then engaged in lumbering, general store business and farming. He served
three years as village President of Daggett and was Postmaster two terms.
He served as chairman of the Democratic County Committee. Mr. Perrizo was
married to Mary J. Selma, of Marinette, Wis., Aug 20, 1895. In politics a Democrat.

AARON PERRY

Representative from Oakland County, 1873-4. Was born in Oakland, Mich.,
Nov. 11, 1848, and graduated from the University of Michigan in 1870. He
was an attorney and practiced at Pontiac. He was the third oldest member
of the Oakland County Bar Association and father of Stuart H. Perry, one of
the leading editors of the State. In politics he was a Democrat. He died Feb.
12, 1920.

CHARLES W. PERRY

Representative from Manistee County, 1895-6 and 1897-8. Was born in Ludlow,
Windsor County, Vt., Jan. 9, 1845; removed with his parents to Waukesha,
Wis., in 1854; attended district school, and one term in the city schools of
Waukesha; after his father's death, he in 1861 went to work in a country
store; Aug. 27, 1862, he enlisted in Co. F, 1st Wis. Cavalry, was promoted
successively to Corporal, First Sergeant and First Lieutenant; served through
the war, and mustered out with his regiment, July 18, 1865. Following the
war he spent three years in the book and stationery business in New York City,
then came to Michigan; married in 1872, located at Pierpont, Manistee County,
where he operated a saw mill, grist mill and general store; also engaged in wood

and shipping business. In politics he was a Republican. He held the offices of Justice of the Peace, School Director and Supervisor; was a candidate for Representative to the Legislature of 1893-4, and was defeated by James W. Dempsey.

EDWIN PERRY

Representative from the Western District of Branch County, 1857-8 and 1859-60. Was born in Franklin County, N. Y., July 9, 1810. He removed to Michigan in 1837. He then removed to Wisconsin, where he lived until 1841. He returned to Jackson County and lived at Parma and Concord until 1851, when he removed to Union City. He was Sergeant-at-Arms in the State Senate of 1855; Postmaster of Union City from 1861-1870; and was Justice of the Peace for thirty-two years.

GIDEON D. PERRY

Representative from Lenawee County, 1857-8; and Senator from the Tenth District, 1859-60. Was born in Palmyra, N. Y., Oct. 25, 1811. He was brought up to farming, left home at nineteen, became a scholar and teacher until 1833, when he commenced preaching, and was admitted to the Genesee conference of the Methodist Episcopal Church. He preached for eleven years, when from poor health he abandoned it, came to Michigan in 1843, and settled on a farm in Franklin, Lenawee County. He was Supervisor of the Town; Chairman of the Board of Supervisors. He preached more or less every year.

JOHN M. PERRY

Representative from Osceola County, 1907-8, 1909-10 and 1911-12. Was born in Orleans County, N. Y., May 12, 1864, of English descent. He came to Michigan with his parents in the spring of 1870, when his father located on a homestead in Burdell Township, Osceola County. His education was received in the district schools and the Valparaiso Normal School, Valparaiso, Ind. Mr. Perry was married in 1889, to Miss Allie A. Bickhart. He was a clerk, school teacher, merchant and banker, and cashier of the bank at Tustin. A member of the I. O. O. F., K. O. T. M., M. W. A., I. O. F., and the Modern Brotherhood. In politics a Republican.

ROLLIN HARLOW PERSON

Justice of the Supreme Court, 1915-16. Was born in Livingston County, Oct. 15, 1850. He was reared on the old family homestead and his father supervised his early education. When nineteen years of age he secured a teacher's certificate and taught school for a time. In 1872 he began the study of law with Dennis Shields and in 1872-3 was a student in the law department of the University of Michigan. In 1873 he married Ida May Madden and moved to Republic City, Nebr. He returned to Michigan and began the practice of law in Howell, in 1875. He served as Recorder of Howell in 1876 and 1877; Circuit Court Commissioner, 1877-8 and 1891-4; and Judge of Thirtieth Judicial Circuit, 1893-9. He resumed the practice of law in Lansing. He was appointed Justice of the Supreme Court July 16, 1915, to succeed Aaron V. McAlvay, deceased, and held that office until Dec. 31, 1916.

SEYMOUR H. PERSON

Representative from the First District of Ingham County, 1915-16, 1917-18 and 1919-20. Was born in Howell Township, Livingston County, Mich., Feb. 2, 1879, of American parents. He lived on a farm until he was nine years of age, when his father removed to Howell. He received his early education in the district school and the Howell High School. Later he worked four years in the Postoffice at Howell, after which he entered the University of Michigan, where he received his degree of B. L. in 1901. He then removed to Lansing, where he later formed a partnership with the Hon. Patrick H. Kelley, under the firm name of Kelley & Person. Later the firm was dissolved and Mr. Person continued law practice under his own name. Married. In politics a Republican. He was elected to the Legislature in 1914 and 1916, and re-elected Nov. 5, 1918, while he was serving in France with the American Y. M. C. A. Owing to his absence in France at the opening of the 1919 session he was not placed on any of the House committees. He returned, however, in time for the final adjournment, and served in the extra session, which convened June 3, 1919.

ALONZO E. PERSONS

Representative from Alpena County, 1861-2. Was born at Smithville, N. Y., Apr. 25, 1818. He received a common school education, became a sailor, and in 1840 was master of a vessel. He continued in that business until 1849, when he removed to Bay City and engaged in the fishing business. He removed to Alpena in 1859, and was Town Clerk. From 1861 to 1874 he was keeper of the Thunder Bay Island light. He built the first steam tug for fishing. He was master and part owner of the steamer Golden Eagle. He was Justice and Coroner. In politics he was first a Whig, after 1854 a Republican.

ALBERT EDWARD PETERMANN

Representative from the First District of Houghton County, 1913-14, 1915-16 and 1917-18. Was born at Calumet, Mich., Mar. 3, 1877, of German parentage. He was educated in the Buffalo, N. Y., High School and Cornell University, graduating from the literary course of the latter in 1900. He was admitted to the bar in 1901. He entered the law office of A. W. Kerr at Calumet where he remained until 1911. A member of the law firm of Rees, Robinson and Petermann. Married. In politics a Republican.

GEORGE PETERS

Representative from Monroe County, 1861-2; and Senator from the Seventh District, 1867-8. Was born in Delaware County, N. Y., Sept. 22, 1822, and came to Michigan in 1831. He was a farmer and a Republican. He resided in Petersburg in 1887. He was Postmaster sixteen years, and Supervisor nineteen years.

WILLIAM PETERS

Representative from the Second District of Marquette County, 1897-8. Was born in Cornwall, England, Nov. 29, 1864. When only eight years of age he started out in life for himself and found employment in the tin mines of his native country and attending a parish night school for a short time. He came to America in 1886, locating at Ishpeming, Marquette County, where he immediately procured work in the iron mines of that place, following said occupation for some time; then went to Old Mexico, New Mexico, Utah and California, where he was engaged in mining; returned to Ishpeming and followed the occupation of mining until Aug. 12, 1891, when he received serious injury in a mining accident. In 1893 he was appointed to a clerkship in the Auditor General's office; commenced the study of law and was admitted to practice before the Ingham County bar Oct. 29, 1894. In politics a Republican.

FRANK W. PETERSON

Representative from the Third District of Kent County, 1917-18. Was born in Courtland Township, Kent County, on the farm on which he later lived, May 26, 1877, of American parents. He attended district school until seventeen years of age when he entered the Ferris Institute at Big Rapids, from which institution he graduated in 1899. Later he took the civil service examination and was appointed to a position in the U. S. Pension Bureau at Washington, D. C., remaining there five years, when he was detailed for field service, at which he was employed for eight years. In 1914 he engaged in farming. He graduated from the Columbian (now George Washington) University and was admitted to the bar in the District of Columbia and Michigan. He was Supervisor of his township in 1915 and 1916. Married. In politics a Democrat.

JENS G. PETERSON

Representative from Wayne County, 1861-2. Was a native of Germany, born in 1821. He was a retail grocer, and subsequently, in 1854, a co-partner in the Cabinetmakers' Association, a manufacturing firm in Detroit. In politics he was a Republican. He was register of the U. S. land office in Detroit, 1861-3, and probably died in the last named year.

CHARLES HENRY PETROWSKY

Representative from the First District of Wayne County (Detroit), 1897-8. Was born in Danzig, Germany, Aug. 22, 1873; attended public and parochial schools until fourteen years of age; then he entered the Dwight Lumber Company as machine hand. After a short time he engaged in the Brass Rolling Mills of Detroit, which occupation he followed until he started to clerk in a grocery store, which occupation he followed for some time, finally drifting into the saloon and restaurant business at 476 Dix avenue. In politics a Republican. He was Deputy Sheriff for two years, and elected Representative to the House of 1897-8 on the general legislative ticket of Detroit.

ALVIN D. PETTIT

Representative from the Third District of Houghton County, 1903-4 and 1905-6. Was born in Emerson Township, Gratiot County, Dec. 6, 1856. He was educated in the district schools and the public schools of Ithaca village. He was left an orphan at the age of ten, and the next five years of his life were spent in working upon farms in summer and attending school in winter. At the age of fifteen he entered a printing office, and with the exception of four years as Post-master, 1891-5, at Ithaca, followed the printing business. In politics a Repub-lican, and prominent in the party both in Gratiot and Houghton counties, having been chairman of the Republican County Committee of the former county, also a member of the County Committee of the latter county.

TIMOTHY H. PETTIT

Representative from Clinton and Gratiot counties, 1855-6. Was a native of New York State, came to Tecumseh, Mich., in 1835, and in 1837 settled on a farm in Essex, Clinton County, where he remained until 1854, then went into business at DeWitt. He was Justice, Postmaster and Town Treasurer. He died in 1860.

WILLIAM H. H. PETTIT

Representative from Hillsdale County, 1887-8. Was born in Columbian County, Ohio, in 1840, and was a resident of Michigan after 1854. Mr. Pettit served three years as a private in Company C, 1st Mich. Infantry. He served eleven years as Supervisor of Ransom Township. He was elected Representative on the Republican ticket.

EDWIN PHELPS

Member of the State Board of Agriculture, 1891-5. Was born in Pittsfield, Mass., Apr. 7, 1828. He was the son of Elnathan Phelps, of Pittsfield, Mass., and Clarissa (Colt) Phelps, of Richmond, Mass. He married Mary Irish of Oakland County, Mich., June 16, 1858, who died in July 1870; (2) Delia Kimball, Nov. 12, 1874, Pontiac, Mich. His ancestors lived in Connecticut, and were religious, energetic and ambitious. When five years old Edwin went to Michigan with his father where they were pioneers. He attended the common school in a log house, later went to an academy, taught by R. C. Kedzie, later a professor at the Agricultural College in Rochester, Oakland County, Mich. At the age of 21 he went overland to California for gold, coming back in two years with $7,000, with which he bought his father's farm, called Maple Place. He made it the show place of that region. He was the first man in the State to import Hereford cattle; he also imported Holstein cattle, built a silo and in other respects was a thorough up-to-date farmer. He was a Universalist and a Democrat; was economical, generous, industrious. He was for the last ten years of his life crippled with rheumatism. He was Justice of the Peace for twenty years; prominent in political circles; a member of the executive com-mittee of the State Agricultural Society; appointed a member of the State Board of Agriculture by Governor Winans in 1891 and resigned January 1895. He died May 22, 1904, at Pontiac, Mich.

FITCH PHELPS

Representative from Mecosta and other counties, 1877-8 and 1879-80; and Senator from the Twenty-seventh District, 1883-4 and 1885-6. Was born at Guilford, N. Y., June 30, 1831. He received an academical education and was a merchant. In 1862 went to California, and was provost marshal of San Mateo County in 1863. In 1868 he located at Colfax, Mich., built a mill, engaged in lumbering, also in farming, later moved to Big Rapids. In politics he was a Republican. He died at Big Rapids, Jan. 22, 1890.

JOHN W. PHELPS

Representative from Ingham County, 1859-60. Was born in Seneca County, N. Y., June 14, 1819. He came to Michigan with his father in 1829, and settled at Plymouth. He studied medicine and engaged in practice at Mason in 1841. He was also, during the latter portion of his life, a hardware merchant. He was for several terms a Justice. He died Aug. 31, 1864.

WILLIAM PHELPS

Representative from Wayne County, 1861-2. Was born in Scipio, Cayuga County, N. Y., Nov. 19, 1816. He received an academical education, and went into business at Detroit in 1835, which he continued until his death, July 24, 1879, being the head of the firm of Phelps, Brace & Co. In 1862-3 he was an "Allotment Commissioner" for Michigan, and became a Paymaster in 1863, and in 1865 was made Lieutenant Colonel. He was on the military staff of Gov. Crapo, and was Post Commander and Adjutant General of the G. A. R. for Michigan. He was a leading Mason and Odd Fellow, politically a Republican, in religion a Methodist, and an ordained preacher. He was a member of "Under the Oaks" convention.

NATHAN S. PHILBRICK

Representative from Oakland County, 1841. Was born in Maine, June 12, 1789. He was a farmer and hotel keeper, and a Democrat. He settled in Farmington, Mich., in 1826. He was commissioned a Justice by Gov. Mason in 1834, and held that office several terms. He died in 1854.

CHARLES CURTISS PHILLIPS

Representative from the First District of Van Buren County, 1897-8 and 1899-1900. Was born in Kalamazoo, Mich., June 8, 1845. His early education was acquired in the district schools of Kalamazoo County, supplemented by one year at Olivet College and two years at Hillsdale College. On Jan. 2, 1864, he enlisted in Co. H, 25th Mich. Infantry, and served in it and in the 28th Michigan for two and one-half years. In 1875 he engaged in newspaper work at Bangor, which occupation he followed until 1888; also published a paper at Hartford four years, then returned to Bangor and engaged in mercantile business. In politics a Republican. He served as Township and County Superintendent of Schools; and was Postmaster at Bangor seven years.

DELOS PHILLIPS

Senator from the Nineteenth District, 1869-70. Was born in Hamburg, N. Y., Oct. 24, 1839. He came to Ypsilanti in 1845, graduated at the public schools, taught two years, and was a student in the University from 1859 to 1862. He enlisted in 1862 as a private in the 17th Mich. Infantry, and was promoted through all the grades to Captain in 1863. In 1864 he was taken prisoner at Spottsylvania Court House, but escaped from the cars at night and after 300 miles' travel, reported for duty. He became Lieut. Colonel of the 28th Mich. Infantry, but resigned before the close of the war, and graduated from the University in 1865. He was Presidential Elector in 1876 and messenger to carry the vote to Washington. He was for six years a member of the Board of Supervisors. His life was that of a manufacturer and business man. In politics he was a Republican. He died at Kalamazoo, Feb. 23, 1887.

GEORGE W. PHILLIPS

Member of the State Board of Agriculture, 1871-83. Was born in Livingston County, N. Y., July 17, 1829. He came with his father to Armada, Mich., in 1831, who settled upon a farm. The son was raised a farmer. He was a charter member of the County Agricultural Society, many times its president, and almost continuously an officer. For twelve years he was a member of the State Board of Agriculture; an officer of the State Agricultural Society twenty-two years, and its president in 1880 and 1881. He was a Republican in politics. He died at Armada, May 5, 1902.

JOHN I. PHILLIPS

Representative from Genesee County, 1871. Was born in Canada, Sept. 3, 1823. He removed to Monroe County, N. Y., with his parents the next year, where he lived until 1844, when he settled in Vienna, Mich. He held several town offices, and was engaged in several kinds of business until Aug. 13, 1861, when he enlisted as Sergeant of Company "G," 8th Mich. Infantry. He served with the regiment in South Carolina and was promoted to 2d Lieutenant Jan. 1, 1863. He resigned on account of ill health, Dec. 15, 1863, and returned to his home. He died before the close of his Legislative term, and was succeeded by Frederick Walker. In politics he was a Republican.

MILLARD F. PHILLIPS

Representative from the County of Cass, 1897-8. Was born in Allen County, Ind., Mar. 4, 1857. At the age of two years he came to Michigan with his parents, and seven years later moved to a farm. He attended the Detroit public schools; was married in 1878 to Miss Olive O. Jessup. His principal occupation was that of a farmer; also one of the board of directors of the Farmers' Mutual Fire Insurance Company of Cass, Van Buren and Berrien counties. In politics a Republican. He held the various township offices from School Inspector to Supervisor. He was elected to the House of 1897-8 on the Democratic People's Union Silver ticket.

NATHANIEL G. PHILLIPS

Representative from Shiawassee County, 1865-6. Was born at Preston, Conn., Nov. 20, 1825. He attended an academy at Norwalk, O., for three years, and came to Shiawassee County with his widowed mother and settled on a farm in 1840. From 1851 to 1853 he was in California. His farm formed the location of the village of Bancroft. He died at Bancroft, June 6, 1888.

PITTS PHILLIPS

Representative from Oakland County, 1837. Was born in the State of New York, Apr. 24, 1792. He lived in Stafford and Sempronius, N. Y., and married Mary Daniels at the latter place. He settled in Southfield, Mich., in 1830. He was Supervisor in 1836, and held the office of Justice both in New York and Michigan. By occupation he was a farmer and cooper, in politics first a Whig, then an Abolitionist. He died April 10, 1842.

RALPH WILLIAM PHILLIPS

Senator 1921-2, from the Twenty-fourth District, comprising Bay and Midland counties. Was born in Williams Township, Bay County, Sept. 18, 1892, of English and French descent. He received his education in the public and high schools of Bay City, McLachlan Business University and Battle Creek Business College. After finishing school he was elected County Auditor, and soon after moving to Bay City accepted a position with the Bay City *Tribune*. Later he was with the Peoples Commercial Bank and at present is a member of the Phillips-Oviatt Co., dealers in and distributors of automobiles. Mr. Phillips is married and has one son. In politics he is a Republican.

EDWIN R. PHINNEY

Representative from Saginaw County, 1883-4. Was born at Bangor, Me., Aug. 3, 1846. When young he lived in New York city and Pennsylvania, removing to Richmond, O., in 1855. He came to Michigan in 1872, engaged in the manufacture of boat oars at Carson City, removed the business to East Saginaw in 1876, also engaged in the manufacture of lumber, shingles and salt. In politics he was a Republican.

PETER PICOTT

Representative from Monroe County, 1837. Was elected to fill the vacancy caused by the death of Lemuel Colbath but did not take his seat. (Further data not obtainable).

ANSEL B. PIERCE

Representative from Wayne County, 1887-8. Was born at Canton, N. Y., in 1836. He, at the age of fifteen years, entered the St. Lawrence Academy, remaining there four years and teaching three terms in the meantime. At the age of twenty-one he came West and settled in Redford, Wayne County, where he resided, teaching school during the winter and working on his farm in the summer. Mr. Pierce held the offices of Supervisor, Town Clerk, School Inspector and Justice of the Peace. He was president of the Redford Agricultural Society from its organization, and was a practical and thorough agriculturist. In politics he was a Democrat.

CHARLES SUMNER PIERCE

Senator from the Twenty-eighth District, 1893-4. Was born in Redford Township, Wayne County, Mich., June 12, 1858. He attended district school and worked on his father's farm until 20 years of age, when he entered the State Normal School, graduating from the Latin and German course in 1882. He was principal of the Au Sable schools the following two years, during which time he purchased the *Au Sable and Oscoda News*, changing its name to *The Saturday Night*, and later to *The Press*. Two years later he began the study of law in the office of the Hon. O. E. M. Cutcheon and in 1885 entered the law department of the Michigan University, from which he graduated in 1887. He immediately began practice at Oscoda. In politics a Republican. He held the office of Attorney of Oscoda village for three years, and Commissioner of Schools of Iosco County for two years.

DARIUS PIERCE

Representative from Washtenaw County, 1846 and 1847. Was born Sept. 2, 1801, at Farmington, N. Y. He came to Michigan in 1832, and was a farmer of the town of Lima. He was Justice of the Peace four years, County Commissioner, and ten years a Supervisor. Looking to the future of the State, he voted to remove the capital from Detroit to Lansing, although Ann Arbor was a contestant. Deceased.

JOHN D. PIERCE

State Superintendent of Public Instruction from 1836-41; Representative from Calhoun County in 1847 and 1848; and Delegate from Calhoun County, to the Constitutional Convention of 1850. Was born at Chesterfield, N. H., Feb. 18, 1797. From the age of two to twenty he lived with an uncle at Worcester, Mass., having only eight weeks' schooling. He then went to work and earned one hundred dollars, his grandfather gave the same amount, and in 1817 he walked fourteen miles to take his first lesson of Rev. Enoch Pond, who fitted him for college. He graduated at Brown University in 1822; was principal of Wrentham Academy in 1823; the same year entered Princeton Theological Seminary; in 1824 was licensed to preach as a Congregational minister, and became pastor of a church at Oneida, N. Y. He came as a home missionary to Marshall, Mich., in 1831, and held the first religious meetings in Jackson, Calhoun and Eaton counties. Gov. Mason appointed him the first Superintendent of Public Instruction, and he proved to be the right man in the right place, and his plans were adopted by the Legislature of 1837 without a dissenting vote. A full sketch of his labors can be readily found. He died at Medford, Mass., Apr. 6, 1882.

JOSEPH B. PIERCE

Representative from Jackson County, 1850. Was born in St. Johnsbury, Vt., July 20, 1812. His parents removed to western New York in 1814. He came to Grass Lake, Mich., in 1837, but removed to Leoni in 1839, where he kept a hotel. Later he removed to Jackson and was Justice for eight years. He had a genial, happy disposition, was a great humorist, and delighted in entertaining friends with stories and anecdotes. He died July 17, 1862.

NATHAN PIERCE

Representative from Washtenaw County, 1839 to 1841, and from Calhoun County, 1850 and 1851; Delegate from Calhoun County to the Constitutional Convention of 1850; and Senator from the Fourteenth District, 1853-4, and from the Thirteenth District, 1857-8. Was born in Cheshire, Mass., Sept. 27, 1790. In 1795 he removed with his parents to Ontario County, N. Y., where he was brought up on a farm, and received a common school and academical education. He served in the war of 1812. in 1832 he located thirty eight acre tracts in Calhoun, St. Joseph and Washtenaw counties, and settled on a farm in Sylvan, Washtenaw County, removing twelve years after to Marengo, Calhoun County, where he remained through life. He took his seat in the House of Representatives, Feb. 7, 1839, as successor to Calvin Smith, deceased. He was a Whig until 1854, then a Republican. He was a man of gigantic stature, strong will, noted for his integrity, and one of the ablest of the farmer pioneers.

ONESIMUS O. PIERCE

Representative from Wayne County, 1873-4. Was born in Potsdam, N. Y., Aug. 16, 1809. He was educated at the Potsdam Academy. In 1833 he emigrated to Michigan, and settled in Redford, Wayne County, where he still resided in 1887. He held various township offices. By occupation he was a farmer.

PETER R. L. PIERCE

Senator from the Twenty-ninth District, 1869-70. Was born in Geneseo, N. Y., May 25, 1823. As a boy, he attended common schools, but in 1836 came to Detroit, there attending night schools and reading law. In 1840 he removed to Grand Rapids and kept a book store, reading law with Judge Martin. From 1843 to 1850 he was in mercantile business at Cincinnati, Ohio, and wrote a history of the Sons of Temperance, which had a circulation of 100,000 copies, and also wrote for several papers. From 1850 to 1857 he was a merchant at Grand Rapids. In 1854 he was City Clerk; Mayor in 1873-5-6; several terms Clerk of Kent County, and Postmaster of Grand Rapids from 1877 until his death, about 1880. In politics he was a Republican. He was a man of wit and humor, kind and genial. Few men had warmer friends, or better deserved them.

BENJAMIN PIERSON

Representative from Wayne County, 1871-2. Was born Oct. 4, 1802, near Cayuga Lake, N. Y. When young he moved with his parents to Victor, N. Y. He worked on a farm until fifteen years of age, then at carding wool and dressing cloth until 1826, when he came to Michigan and purchased land at Plymouth. He returned to New York and remained until 1836. He then settled on a farm in Livonia, Wayne County. He was Justice, and held various town offices. In politics he was a Democrat. Deceased.

RICHARD PIERSON

Representative from the Second District of Sanilac County, 1895-6. Was born in Whitley, Ont., Oct. 6, 1853. In December, 1860, he came with his parents to Sanilac County, Mich., where he spent his early days in helping to clear up a farm, and attending district school; worked in the lumber woods and saw mills seven years; married in 1876, and two years later moved to a farm in Moore Township, Sanilac County. In politics a Republican. He held the office of Justice of the Peace, Highway Commissioner, Township Treasurer, and a member of the Republican Legislative Committee.

WILLIAM S. PIERSON

Senator, 1901-2, from the Thirteenth District, comprising the counties of Livingston and Genesee. Was born in Genesee County, Nov. 29, 1872. His early education was acquired in the country and city schools, supplemented by a course at the University of Michigan, from which he graduated in 1896 from the law department. He practiced his profession until he enlisted in the Spanish-American war, in the 33d Mich. Vol., after which he returned to Flint and resumed his practice. Single. In politics a strong Republican.

ELIJAH H. PILCHER

Member of the Board of Regents of the University of Michigan, 1846-52. Was born in Athens County, Ohio, June 2, 1810. He was a student at the Athens University, and was ordained a Methodist minister in 1829. From 1830 until his death, he was a resident of Michigan, preaching at Detroit, Ann Arbor, Jackson, Kalamazoo, Baattle Creek, and other places. He was ten years secretary of the Conference, and for nearly twenty-five years a presiding elder. He was one of the founders of Albion College. He received several degrees, including D. D., and was admitted to the bar in 1846. He was appointed Regent of the University, Mar. 16, 1846, re-appointed in 1850, serving until Jan. 1, 1852. He was the author of "Protestantism in Michigan." He toured Europe, 1868-69. He died Apr. 7, 1889, at home of his son in Brooklyn, N. Y.

HAZEN S. PINGREE

Governor of Michigan, 1897-9 and 1899-1901. Was born at Denmark, Me., Aug. 30, 1840, the fourth child of Jasper and Adaline (Bryant) Pingree. The son resided with his parents until fourteen years of age, when he went to Soco, Me., and secured employment in a cotton factory. In 1860, he went to Hopkinton,

Mass., and secured employment in a shoe factory. Here he learned the trade of cutter, at which he worked until Aug. 1, 1862, when he enlisted as a private in Co. F, 1st Mass. Regiment of Heavy Artillery, for the unexpired three years' term of the regiment. When the regiment was mustered out at the end of the term, he re-enlisted on the battlefield for three years more, or during the war. On May 25, 1864, Mr. Pingree, with a number of his comrades, while guarding a wagon train en route to Port Royal, was captured by a squad of Mosby's men. After the capture, he was confined for nearly five months at Andersonville Stockade, Salisbury, N. C., and Millen, Ga. At the latter place in November, 1864, he was exchanged, rejoined his regiment in front of Petersburg. He was mustered out of service in August, 1865, and shortly after went to Detroit, Mich. Here for a time, he was employed in a boot and shoe factory. Deciding to embark in business for himself, in December, 1866, with C. H. Smith, he purchased a small boot and shoe factory. The first year they employed but eight persons, and the value of their porduction reached only $20,000. Intreasing business compelled their removal to larger quarters, and in time they secured and maintained their position as the most extensive boot and shoe manufacturers in the West. From the beginning of this enterprise, Mr. Pingree had the general supervision of the entire establishment. His success was the result of hard work and good management. He married Frances A. Gilbert, of Mount Clemens, Feb. 28, 1872. He was elected Mayor of Detroit in 1889 and at once introduced needed reforms. On Aug 7, 1896, he was nominated for Governor of Michigan on the Republican ticket, and was elected Nov. 3, 1896. On Sept. 21, 1898, he was again nominated for Governor of Michigan on the Republican ticket, and was elected on Nov 8, 1898. He died in 1901.

DAVID D. PIPER

Representative from Lenawee County, 1861-2 and 1863-4. His postoffice address was Clinton. (Further data not obtainable).

WASHINGTON PITCHER

Representative from St. Joseph County, 1835. Was born in Norwich, Conn., Dec. 28, 1816, and received a fair education. He removed to Parma, N. Y., in 1831, was two years a clerk at Rochester, N. Y., and came to White Pigeon, Mich., in 1836. In 1844 he removed to Constantine. He was a merchant, and the late Gov. Bagley was for one year his clerk, when a boy. In 1858 he removed to Illinois, residing at Franklin Grove, then Wall Lake, Kansas, where he resided in 1887. In politics he was a Democrat.

ZINA PITCHER

Member of the Board of Regents of the University of Michigan, 1837-52. Was born in Washington County, N. Y., Apr. 12, 1797. He received an academical education, and graduated as a physician in 1822. He served as an army surgeon until 1836, then became a resident of Detroit. The medical department of the University was essentially his work. He was Mayor of Detroit in 1840-1-2, and

the Whig candidate for governor in 1843. He was physician of St. Mary's
hospital from 1848 to 1867; surgeon of the Marine Hospital under Buchanan;
trustee of the Kalamazoo Asylum; a member of many scientific and medical
societies, and one of the ablest and most widely known physicians in Michigan.
He died at Detroit, Apr. 5, 1872.

CLARENCE G. PITKIN

Representative from Muskegon County, 1921—. Was born at Ypsilanti, Mich.,
Nov. 2, 1868, of Scotch and French descent. He received his education in
Brighton public schools and Ypsilanti Seminary. He entered the drug store of
his brother, Geo. L. Pitkin, of Brighton, Mich., as a student in pharmacy, in 1883,
and passed the Michigan Board of Pharmacy examination in 1887, and soon
after located at Whitehall, Mich., and established the firm of C. G. Pitkin's & Co.,
continuing in the business until Jan. 1, 1920, when he retired from the firm.
Mr. Pitkin was married in 1891 to Anna M. Knudsen of Montague, Mich. Mr.
Pitkin is now secretary and general manager of White River Power & Light Co.
He has served as Trustee of the village of Whitehall, Township Treasurer,
Secretary of Whitehall Lodge, No. 310, F. & A. M. In politics he is a Republican.

FREDERICK PITT

Representative from Ionia County, 1883-4. Was born in London, England,
June 10, 1824, and came to Ionia County, Mich., in 1850. When young worked
at engraving, making of pianos, was later a carpenter, and then a farmer. He
was several terms a Supervisor, and held other offices. In politics he was a
Republican.

CHARLES M. PITTS

Representative from Monroe County, 1865-6.. Was a farmer and for a number
of terms Supervisor in Monroe County. He was a man of considerable influence
in the town where he resided. He died several years prior to 1887.

LESTER B. PLACE

Representative from St. Joseph County, 1915-16. Was born in Delaware County,
O., Feb. 14, 1842. Occupation an iron moulder, having worked at that trade
for over forty years; for twenty years being superintendent of the Sheffield Car
Co., of Three Rivers. He was a veteran of the Civil War, having served in the
136th O. Infantry. For eight years he was Postmaster of Three Rivers. In
politics a Republican.

WILLIAM DALLAS PLACE

Representative from the First District of Ionia County, 1893-4 and 1895-6.
Was born Sept. 25, 1847, on the farm one mile east of the city of Ionia. He
attended school in the village of Ionia, and at the Agricultural College, graduating from the latter in 1868; taught school eight years, and then gave his
attention to his farm. In politics a Republican. He held the offices of Township Clerk, Supervisor and County Clerk.

EDGAR ALLAN PLANCK

Senator, 1915-16 and 1917-18, from the Seventh District, comprising the counties of Berrien and Cass. Was born at LaGrange, Ind., Sept. 27, 1868, of German-American parentage. He was educated in the public schools of Indiana and Michigan, and at Valparaiso University and the University of Illinois. In early life he taught school, studied medicine and graduated from the College of Physicians and Surgeons, of Chicago, in 1894. In that year he located at Union, Cass County, Mich., for the practice of medicine. He was married in 1892 to Grace E. Hartman. A member of various fraternal and beneficiary orders, including the various branches of the Masonic fraternity, Knights of the Maccabees, Loyal Americans and the Order of Gleaners. In politics a Republican.

FREDERICK A. PLATT

Member of the State Board of Education, 1899-1901. Was born in Utica, Macomb County, Oct. 19, 1856. He received his education in the University of Michigan, graduating in the literary course in 1875. He was a teacher and superintendent of the School for the Deaf at Flint for seven years. In 1883, he engaged in the mercantile business. He held the office of City Treasurer for two terms, and that of member of the Board of Education for nine years. On Nov. 8, 1898, he was elected on the Republican ticket as a member of the State Board of Education. He resigned and was succeeded by Lincoln Avery who was appointed Apr. 10, 1901.

ZEPHANIAH PLATT

Attorney General of Michigan, 1841-3. Was born at Poughkeepsie, N. Y., Feb. 22, 1797. He graduated at Hamilton College, studied law, practiced in western New York and New York City, and settled at Kalamazoo in 1837. In 1839 he removed to Detroit. In 1850 he resumed practice in New York City, and was commissioner to adjust claims of the United States on the Pacific coast. He was then appointed United States Judge for the second district of South Carolina. He acquired distinction in that position, and died at Aiken, S. C., Apr. 19, 1872.

EMERY M. PLIMPTON

Representative from Berrien County, 1869-70. Was born in Canton, O., June 1, 1826. His father was a pioneer Methodist minister in Ohio and preached for fifty-five years. The son received a good education and commenced teaching when eighteen, and taught in several states for nine years. He was a Whig until 1854, later a Republican. He came to this State in 1849, was in railroad business two years, and taught school at Niles from 1851 to 1853. He was admitted to the bar in 1853, and was Justice and Prosecuting Attorney. He went into the service as Captain in 4th Mich. Cavalry, but resigned in 1863, from ill health. He was Deputy Provost Marshal in 1863-5, Circuit Court Commissioner 1871-2, and held other offices. He died Mar. 26, 1888.

BENJAMIN FRANKLIN PLUMLEY

Representative from Huron County, 1913-14. Was born at Park Hill, Ont., Mar. 21, 1881, of Welsh parentage. He came to Michigan with his parents in 1887. The first nineteen years of his life were spent on a farm. He then spent one year as a sailor on the Great Lakes and then taught school—six years in the district schools and six years as Superintendent at Kinde and Port Hope. He received his education in the district schools, Bad Axe High School and Ferris Institute. He was married to Mabel S. Walker in 1905. He was elected a member of the Board of Examiners of Huron County in 1908 and re-elected in 1910. He also served two terms as vice president of the Huron County Teachers' Association. In politics a National Progressive.

ENOS A. POMROY

Representative from Hillsdale County, 1881-2. Was born in Bristol, N. Y., Mar. 16, 1832. He came with his father to Allen, Mich., in 1844, and removed to Litchfield in 1851. He was six times a Supervisor. He was a farmer; in politics a Republican.

ALFRED POND

Representative from Genesee County, 1847. Was born in Camden, N. Y., Feb. 10, 1806. By occupation he was a farmer, in politics a Democrat. He settled in Clayton, Genesee County, in 1839, and lived there until 1880, but after that time was a resident of Flushing. He helped change the Capitol, while as land agent, employed by Henry Seymour. He died at Flushing, July 29, 1887.

ELIHU B. POND

Senator from the Seventh District, 1859-60. Was born in Wilmington, N. Y., July 15, 1826. He lived in Ohio from 1832 to 1835, when his father settled at Branch, then the County seat of Branch County, removing to Coldwater in 1843. He learned the trade of printer, and worked as a young man at various points. He was in 1847, a student at Albion College. From 1848 to 1854 he owned and edited the Coldwater *Sentinel;* then removed to Ann Arbor and was editor and proprietor of the *Michigan Argus* until 1879. He was County Clerk, Alderman, member and president of the School Board, Warden of the State Prison, etc. He was president of the State Press Association in 1868-9. In politics he was a Democrat. He was a Justice at Ann Arbor. He died in 1898.

JARED POND

Representative from Branch County, 1839. Was born at Poultney, Vt., Sept. 26, 1790. He served in the war of 1812. He was a surveyor and iron manufacturer at Wilmington, N. Y., and after a few years' residence in Ohio became a resident of Branch County, Mich., in 1835, and was a surveyor. He was Register of Deeds from 1843 to 1847. Later he removed to Ann Arbor. He was father of E. B. and Ashley Pond. He died at Ann Arbor, Apr. 12, 1856.

ORRIN POPPLETON

Representative from Oakland County, 1853-4. Was born in Richmond, N. Y., Apr. 22, 1817, and came to Troy, Michigan., with his parents in 1825. He received a common school education and was a teacher in 1834-5 and 1839-40. In 1837-8 he attended Grandville, O., Academy, and then was a clerk in the postoffice at Pontiac. From 1840 he was a successful merchant at Birmingham, Mich., and was Postmaster from 1853 to 1861. He was also a farmer. He was a member of the Democratic Congressional Committee sixteen years. In politics he was a Democrat. He was a valuable member of the State Pioneer Society. He died at Birmingham, Mar. 18, 1892.

WILLIAM POPPLETON

Representative from Oakland County, 1843. Was of revolutionary ancestry, and was born at Poultney, Vt., in 1795, but removed to Richmond, N. Y., at the age of seventeen. He purchased a farm in Troy, Mich., in 1823, and settled upon it with his family in 1825, coming in a "covered wagon," the journey taking 32 days. The small farm increased in size until in 1845 he owned 1,200 acres. In 1856 he removed to a place near the village of Birmingham, where he died in 1869.

AUGUSTUS S. PORTER

United States Senator, 1839-45. Was born in Canandaigua, N. Y., Jan. 18, 1798. He was of a distinguished family, his father, Augustus Porter, subsequently removing to Niagara Falls, where he became the first proprietor of a property which he occupied. The son graduated from Union College in 1818, studied law, and was admitted to practice. After locating in Detroit he acquired a leading position at the bar, and was identified with the social, political and educational history of the city, serving as Recorder in 1834 and Mayor in 1838. The election of Senator for the term for which he was chosen should have been made at the Legislative session of 1839, but the two houses, both Democratic, failed to agree, and allowed the election to go by default. The Whig party carried the State and the Legislature in 1839, and at the session of 1840 elected Mr. Porter to the Senate for the term commencing March 4, 1839. He returned to Niagara Falls in 1848, after the death of his father. He died there, Sept, 18, 1872.

GEORGE BYRON PORTER

Governor of the Territory of Michigan, 1831-4. Was born in Morristown, Pa., February 9, 1791. He was of revolutionary ancestry and served in the Legislature of Pa. He was very active in the Black Hawk War, worked for good roads and schools, and was one of the first to aid in the incorporation of railroads. He was a lawyer by profession, and prior to his coming to Michigan had been United States Marshal of the Eastern District of Pennsylvania. He removed with his family to Michigan, bought a farm in Springwells, and began the construction of a fine residence. He was a man of executive ability and popular. He died at Detroit, July 6, 1834.

GEORGE FORD PORTER

Senator, 1891-2, from the Twenty-first District, comprising the counties of Muskegon and Ottawa. Was born in Hamilton, Madison County, N. Y., Aug. 28, 1832, and came to Michigan with his parents at the age of fifteen years, settling in Walker Township, Kent County, and remaining there until 1861, during which time he spent five years attending school at Grand Rapids. At the age of 29 he removed to Chester, Ottawa County, where from the dense forest, by perseverance and hard labor, he carved out for himself a beautiful home. He served as County Treasurer in 1868, as Justice of the Peace for four years and Supervisor for 17 years. In politics a staunch Democrat.

IRA PORTER

Representative from St. Clair County, 1841. His postoffice address was Port Huron. (Further data not obtainable).

JAMES B. PORTER

Secretary of State, 1861-7. Was born at Marcellus, N. Y., in Sept. 1824. He came to Michigan in 1833, and removed to Allegan in 1840, and lived there until 1865, then removed to Lansing in 1866. He was County Clerk and Register of Deeds of Allegan County from 1851 to 1861. His occupation was real estate and insurance; politics, Republican. He died in Lansing, Mar. 7, 1897.

JOHN PORTER

Representative from Kent County, 1863-4. Was born in Tompkins County, N. Y., in 1819. He came to Michigan in 1838, in 1845 settled in Montcalm County, and on the organization of that county was elected County Treasurer, holding the position four years. By occupation he was a farmer, in politics a Republican. He removed to Kent County in 1855 and resided at Wyoming in that County in 1887.

JOHN FREDENRICH PORTER

Member of the Board of Regents of the University of Michigan, 1837-8. Was born at Albany, New York, Mar. 17, 1806, of German parentage. He came to Michigan in 1835, and settled at St. Joseph, where he developed a large commission and shipping business. About 1845 he removed to Niles. He was State Commissioner of Internal Improvements in 1846 and represented the State in the disposal of the Michigan Central Railroad. From 1853 to the time of his death he was the New York City agent of the Michigan Southern Railroad. He was appointed Regent of the University June 2, 1837, in place of Thomas Fitzgerald resigned, but after a brief term of service he in turn laid down the office. He died in Brooklyn, N. Y., Nov. 16, 1866.

LEWIS PORTER

Representative from Kent County, 1857-8; and Senator from the Twenty-ninth District, 1859-60. Was born in the State of New York, Nov. 4, 1823. He came to Michigan in 1838. He was engaged in the clothing trade at Grand Rapids, and was an active Republican in politics. Among other positions he was Assistant Postmaster at Washington, D. C., and the first Clerk of the U. S. District Court of Western Michigan. He died Jan. 10, 1882.

MICAH PORTER

Representative from Washtenaw County, 1844. Was born in Weymouth, Mass., Aug. 2, 1793, his ancestors having settled there in 1635. He learned the trade of mason at Rome, N. Y., working at it summers and teaching winters. During the war of 1812 he was a leading supporter of Madison. He built a parliament house at Little York, near Toronto, Canada. He then resided at Rochester, N. Y., until 1832, when he became a farmer at Sharon, Mich., and was many years a Justice there and Supervisor. He died July 7, 1870.

FLOYD L. POST

Delegate in the Constitutional Convention of 1907-8, from the Twenty-fourth District. Was born at Belvidere, N. Y., in 1857. He came to Michigan in 1868, and was engaged in lumbering, milling and mercantile business. Later he engaged in the practice of law. In politics he was a Republican. He held the office of President of Clare Village, Township Clerk, Supervisor and Treasurer of Midland County.

SAMUEL POST

Representative from Washtenaw County, 1871-2. Was born at Ypsilanti, Mich., Nov. 9, 1834. He received a common school education, and became a clerk at the age of twelve. At the age of nineteen he became a dry goods and clothing merchant, and continued it successfully for seventeen years. In 1873 he was appointed U. S. pension agent at Detroit, and held that position nearly thirteen years, until removed by President Cleveland. In politics he was a Republican. He was in business at Detroit in 1887. He died at Miami, Florida, Dec. 10, 1921; buried at Ypsilanti, Mich.

ALLEN POTTER

Representative from Kalamazoo County, 1857-8; and member of Congress, 1875-7. Was born in Saratoga County, N. Y., Oct. 2, 1818; removed to Michigan in 1838, and located at Kalamazoo in 1845; engaged in manufacturing, mercantile pursuits and banking; was elected President of the village in 1859, 1863, 1870 and 1872, and president of the Board of Education in 1870 and 1871. He was elected president of the Kalamazoo & South Haven Railroad Company in 1870, and was very efficient in securing the building of that road. In 1874, as the candidate of the Democrats and Liberals, he was elected Representative to Congress. He died May 8, 1885.

CALVIN B. POTTER

Representative from Berrien County, 1875-6. Was born July 15, 1837, at Brownville, N. Y. He removed to Michigan in 1838. He was a lawyer by profession, in politics a Democrat.

EDWARD K. POTTER

Representative, 1899-90, from the Alpena District, comprising the counties of Alpena, Montmorency and Otsego. Was born at Marlborough, Canada East, Mar. 19, 1840. He served as Supervisor, member of the School Board and Postmaster at Alpena from 1861 to 1863. He was elected on the Republican ticket to the House of 1889-90.

FORDYCE H. POTTER

Representative from Shiawassee County, 1883-4 and 1885-6. Was born in Wayne County, N. Y., Apr. 8, 1833. He received a common school education, and became a carpenter. In 1856 he removed to Bancroft, Shiawassee County, Mich., and was a contractor and builder. He held many local offices. He was elected as a Fusionist.

GEORGE N. POTTER

Senator from the Eleventh District, 1887-8. Was born at Ira, N. Y., Oct. 16, 1827. He came with his parents to Saline, Mich., in 1830, his father building the first frame house in that village. They removed to Eaton County in 1844. The son received a common school education, became a farmer, and was the founder of the village of Potterville; was one of thirteen that effected the organization of the Peninsula Railroad, now a part of the Grand Trunk, and was a director; was engaged in manufacturing and lumbering. In politics he was a Republican. He was a Recruiting Officer and Deputy Provost Marshal during the Civil War. He died at Potterville, Nov. 1, 1902.

WILLIAM W. POTTER

Senator, 1899-1900, from the Fifteenth District, comprising Barry and Eaton counties. Was born at Maple Grove, Mich., Aug. 1, 1869. He spent his boyhood upon his father's farm, attended the district school, and taught school in 1889 and 1890, subsequently entering the Nashville High School, graduating in June, 1891, and entered the summer school at the State Normal in the same year. He was Principal of the Harrison Public Schools from September, 1891, to June, 1894; was admitted to the bar, and entered the University of Michigan the same year, graduating in 1895, and commencing the practice of law at Hastings. In November, 1895, he entered the firm of Barrell & Potter, but became a member of the firm of Colgrove & Potter in August, 1896. He is a Republican in politics. At present he is a member of the Michigan Public Utilities Commission.

ANTHONY POUCHER

Representative from Washtenaw County, 1838. Was born Nov. 24, 1801, at Claverack, N. Y. He emigrated to Michigan in 1833, and settled on a farm in Bridgewater, Washtenaw County. He died Oct. 7, 1870. As a Democrat he was a Representative in 1838.

GARDNER POWELL

Representative from St. Joseph County, 1903-4. Was born in the Township of Porter, Cass County, Mich., Feb. 9, 1844. His parents were pioneers, having moved from New York to this State in 1836. He moved from Cass County to St. Joseph County in 1890, and resided in the village of Constantine since 1899. He taught school and engaged in farming. In politics a Democrat. He was elected to several township offices in Constantine Township.

HERBERT ERNEST POWELL

Representative from Ionia County, 1901-2 and 1903-4; Delegate from the Eighteenth District in the Constitutional Convention of 1907-8; and Senator, 1913-14 and 1915-16, from the Eighteenth District, comprising the counties of Ionia and Montcalm. Was born in Ronald Township, Ionia County, Mich., Apr. 27, 1866, of American descent. He received his schooling in the district schools and the Ionia High School. In 1887 he assumed the management of his father's farm, and gave special attention to raising stock and the breeding of Shropshire sheep. He was married in 1888 to A. May Waterbury. In 1915 he was a stockholder and second vice president of the National Bank of Ionia, president of the Ionia Hardware Company, and in many ways identified with the commercial interests of the county. In politics a Republican.

MILO POWELL

Representative from St. Joseph County, 1848. Was born in Berkshire County, Mass., Oct. 3, 1809. He came to Michigan in 1835. He was Supervisor in Cass County, and Justice both in Cass and St. Joseph counties. In politics he was a Democrat. He was engaged in banking for years, but retired from business, and resided at Constantine in 1887.

NATHAN POWER

Representative from Oakland County, 1855-6. Was born in Farmington, N. Y., Apr. 19, 1801. He settled in Farmington, Oakland County, in 1826. He taught the first school in 1826. He was a man of extensive reading, extraordinary memory, and well informed in regard to affairs of the State and Nation. In politics he was a Free Soil Republican; by occupation a farmer; in religion, a Friend. He died in 1874.

PLINY POWER

Representative from Oakland County, 1844; and from Wayne County, 1855-6. Was born in Vermont, in 1798. He became a physician, practiced for a time

in Tioga County, Pa., and removed to Oakland County about 1840. He subsequently removed to Detroit and was county physician there in 1852. He was
originally a Democrat, but became a Republican in 1854. He was active in the
temperance cause, sometimes lecturing on that subject. He died in Detroit in
1861.

ROBERT D. POWER

Representative from Livingston County, 1844 and 1845. Was one of the
earliest settlers of Brighton. The erection and opening of a public house by
him in 1836, was the first step taken to give that place the character of a village. He was Sheriff from 1839 to 1843, and was also Moderator and Director
of the public schools. He was a man of much force of character, intuitive
shrewdness and exerted a strong influence in politics. Deceased.

JAMES POWERS

Representative from the Second District of Kalamazoo County, 1897-8. Was
born in Detroit, Hamtramck Township, Wayne County, Mich., May 17, 1843.
He acquired his education in the district schools, and select school at Climax,
also attending the union schools at Galesburg and Battle Creek, attending school
winters and working on his father's farm summers, until 1863; he taught school
during the winter of 1863-4. On Aug. 31, 1864, he enlisted for one year as
private in Co. D, 12th Regiment, Mich. Vet. Vol. Infantry; he joined the regiment early in September, 1864, at Duvalls Bluff, Ark. He was discharged Sept.
9, 1865. In 1866 he moved on the farm in Colfax Township and has devoted
his attention to farming. Married. In politics a Greenbacker; formerly a
Republican. He was elected Highway Commissioner and Township Clerk on
the Republican ticket. He was elected to the House of 1897-8 on the Democratic
People's Union Silver ticket.

PERRY F. POWERS

Member of the State Board of Education, 1888-1901; Auditor General, 1901-3
and 1903-5. Was born in Jackson, Jackson County, O., Sept. 5, 1858. He received such early school education as his home town afforded and on account of
the death of his father, who was killed in the war, was at an early age compelled
to provide for himself, commencing work at the age of twelve in the coal mines
of Jackson County. He continued his studies at night and during spare moments
in the day time; learned the printer's trade at Jackson, O., and in 1879 went
to Davenport, Ia., where he worked as printer and reporter four years. He then
engaged in editing and publishing Republican newspapers, locating first at
Cambridge, Henry County, Ill., where, with Geo. C. Smithe, he published the
Cambridge *Chronical* two years; thence to Ypsilanti, Mich., in partnership with
the same gentleman, as editor and publisher of the *Ypsilantian*. In 1887 he sold
out his interest in the *Ypsilantian* and removed to Cadillac, where he engaged
as proprietor and editor of the Cadillac *News and Express*. In politics a Republican. He held several honorary positions, such as president of the Michigan
Press Association in 1890; president of the Republican Press Association 1892-3;
was president of the Michigan Republican State League, 1897; was elected member of the State Board of Education for the term of 1888-94; and re-elected for
the term of 1895-1901, six years of the time serving as president of the board.

RANDALL D. POWERS

Representative from Branch County, 1905-6 and 1907-8. Was born in the village of Bronson, Branch County, Mich., Nov. 25, 1859, of English descent. Was educated in the village schools and Hillsdale College. At the age of seventeen he began clerking in his father's store, and after thirteen years became proprietor. He married and was prominent in social and business affairs of his locality; an active member of several secret orders, including I. O. O. F., A. O. U. W., F & A. M., and Knights Templar. He held the offices of Village Clerk, Treasurer, Trustee, and a member of the School Board. In politics a lifelong Republican.

WILLIAM POWERS

Representative from St. Clair County, 1885-6 and 1887-8. Was born in Tipperary County, Ireland, in 1842. He was a resident of Michigan since 1859. Mr. Powers was a farmer, held the office of Township Treasurer six years, the office of Supervisor eight years. In politics he was a Democrat.

WILLIAM H. POWERS

Representative from Kent County, 1879-80. Was born in Troy, N. Y., Apr. 7, 1841. He received a common school education at Grand Rapids, Mich., to which place he removed in 1847. He was a member of the firm of Powers & Walker, manufacturers of undertakers' goods, also of the firm of Wm. T. Powers & Son, manufacturers of lumber, lath and shingles. He held the office of City Clerk, Alderman, and a member of the Board of Fire Commissioners of Grand Rapids. In politics he was a National. Deceased.

ABNER PRATT

Senator from the Fourth District, 1844-5; and Representative from Calhoun County, 1863-4; and Justice of the Supreme Court, 1850-2. Was born in Springfield, N. Y., May 22, 1801. He was brought up on a farm, had limited educational advantages, read law, and commenced practice, first at Rush, afterwards at Rochester, N. Y., where he remained until 1839, when he resigned the office of District Attorney, and removed to Marshall, Mich. In 1858 he went to Honolulu as U. S. Consul, where he remained several years. He was Circuit Judge from 1852-1857, when he resigned. He was always a Democrat, and a prominent Mason. He was an able, fearless Judge, and a man of great ability. He died at Marshall, Mar. 27, 1863.

DANIEL L. PRATT

Delegate from Hillsdale County to the Constitutional Convention of 1867. Was born in Plainfield, Mass., June 24, 1820. In 1830 he removed with the family to Geauga County, Ohio. Having studied law, he was admitted to the bar in 1844. In 1845 he commenced the practice of law at Hillsdale, where he resided. He was elected Prosecuting Attorney for Hillsdale County in 1856, and reelected in 1860; was twelve years a member of the board of trustees of the

Michigan Asylum for the Insane; was elected Circuit Judge of the first circuit in 1869; was re-elected in 1875, no nomination having been made against him. He was a trustee of Hillsdale College from its organization in 1853, and contributed liberally of time, money and counsel to its support. He was a Whig until the organization of the Republican party, with which party he then acted. He resided on a farm, just outside of Hillsdale, which he cleared and improved himself. Deceased.

FOSTER PRATT

Representative from Kalamazoo County, 1859-60. Was born at Mt. Morris, N. Y., Jan. 9, 1823. His ancestors landed in Plymouth in 1622. He received an academical education, at seventeen engaged in teaching, and was principal of an Academy at Angelica, N. Y., and from 1844 to 1847 of one at Moorfield, Va. He graduated as a physician in 1849, from the University of Pennsylvania, and practiced his profession at Romney, Va., until 1856, when he removed to Kalamazoo, resuming his practice. He aided in procuring appropriations for the Asylum at Kalamazoo, of which he was trustee. He was a Democrat in politics. He was surgeon of the 13th Michigan Infantry from 1861 to 1865; president of Kalamazoo village in 1871; chairman of Democratic State Committee 1872 to 1876; Postmaster of Kalamazoo, 1866-7.

FRANK STERLING PRATT

Delegate in the Constitutional Convention of 1907-8 from the Twenty-fourth District, Bay County. Was born in Scio, Allegany County, N. Y., Oct 1, 1854, of English descent. Mr. Pratt graduated from the Bay City High School, and commenced the study of law in the office of Geo. P. Cobb, at Bay City, in 1874, being admitted to practice June 19, 1877. In December, 1885, he was married to Eleanor Louise Gaines, daughter of John and Mary Gaines. He was elected to the Constitutional Convention by a large majority. He was a candidate for Circuit Court Commissioner in 1877 and candidate Circuit Judge, Eighteenth Judicial Circuit, April, 1893.

GILBERT E. PRATT

Representative from Clinton and Gratiot Counties, 1861-2. His postoffice address was Ithaca. (Further data not obtainable).

WILLIAM A. PRATT

Representative from Oakland County, 1843 to 1845. Was born in Vermont. By occupation he was a millwright. He came to Franklin, Mich., at an early day. There he built several mills, and in 1838 built a flouring mill, of which he and Winthrop Worthing were proprietors. He was Supervisor of the town of Southfield in 1842-3, and Justice of the Peace. He was speaker *pro tem.* of the House in 1845. He removed later to Sault Ste. Marie, where he made money in land transactions, and finally removed to Detroit. Politically he was a Democrat. Deceased.

ERNEST GEORGE PRAY

Representative from Eaton County, 1913-14 and 1915-16. Was born in Windsor Township, Eaton County, Mich., Oct. 4, 1874, on the farm where, thirty-six years before, his father, Esek Pray, was born, the latter being the first white child born in that township and the third in Eaton County. He acquired his education in the country schools and at Olivet College. With the exception of four years at Charlotte he resided upon the same farm. He was married Oct. 4, 1893, to Ernestine Gowdy. In politics a Republican. He served as County Clerk two terms, he having resigned Nov. 2, 1912, to become a candidate for Representative.

ESEK PRAY

Delegate from Washtenaw County to the Second Convention of Assent, 1836; and Representative from Washtenaw County, 1838. Was born in East Killingly, Conn., Nov. 29, 1790; in 1814 removed to Angelica, N. Y. In May, 1825, he came to Michigan, and became a farmer in the town of Superior. He kept a Tavern many years at Dixboro. Gov. Cass appointed him Justice, which position he held for twenty-four years. He was a Democrat. He died July 5, 1856.

GEORGE PRAY

Representative from Ionia County, 1879-80. Was born Aug. 27, 1825, in Angelica, N. Y. He received an academical education, graduated from the University of Michigan in 1845, and from the medical department of Western Reserve College in 1849. He removed to Michigan and settled in Superior, Washtenaw County. He commenced the practice of medicine in Salem in 1849. In 1856 he removed to Ronald, Ionia County, and invested his means in lands. From 1863 to 1867 he resided at Ann Arbor, practicing his profession, but at the expiration of that time returned to Ronald. He was a Supervisor, and chairman of the Board of Supervisors for many years. In politics he was a Republican.

GEORGE A. PRESCOTT

Senator from the Twenty-eighth District, 1895-6 and 1897-8; and Secretary of State, 1905-7 and 1907-9. Was born in Reynoldsville, Pa., Mar. 1, 1862. He attended the common schools of his native State until sixteen years of age; came to Michigan, attended the Bay City High School two years, business college of Detroit three months, completing his education with one year's course in the Colgate Academy, Hamilton, N. Y., 1880-1. In the fall of 1881 he moved to Tawas City and was connected with the firm of C. H. Prescott & Sons, lumber manufacturers and general merchants. In politics a Republican. He held the offices of Village President, Village Trustee and member of the School Board; represented his district in the State Senate of 1895-6 and 1897-8. He was the unanimous choice for the office of Secretary of State of the Republican State Convention held at Detroit, June 30, 1904, and was elected for the term of 1905-7 and re-elected Nov. 6, 1906.

ALMON E. PRESTON

Representative from Calhoun County, 1875-6. Was born July 15, 1832, in Orleans County, N. Y. He removed to Battle Creek, Mich., in 1844. He was educated in common schools, and was by occupation a mechanic. He held the position of Second Lieutenant in 1861 in the Michigan Engineer Corps, and was Captain of Co. "L" of the Regiment of Merrill's Horse, serving in the western department until 1864. He was three terms a Supervisor in Battle Creek, and also a member of the Board of Education. In politics he was a Republican.

JOHN L. PRESTON

Representative from the First District of Lapeer County, 1889-90; and Senator 1895-6 and 1897-8, from the Twenty-first District, counties of Lapeer and Tuscola. Was born in Eastford, Conn., Apr. 15, 1853, and came with his parents to Armada, Macomb County, Mich., in 1855. He attended the public schools at Armada and the Ypsilanti Union School, worked as clerk and bookkeeper in his father's general store; taught district school and for some time followed the business of buying and selling live stock. In 1875 he located at Columbiaville, Lapeer County, where he engaged in the mercantile and insurance business. He was Postmaster at Columbiaville from 1880 to 1885, chairman of the Lapeer County Republican Committee and a member of the Republican State Central Committee. Deceased.

LOOMIS K. PRESTON

Representative from the First District of Berrien County, 1923—. Was born in Michigan, July 22, 1882, of English and Irish parentage. His education was acquired in the St. Joseph High School and the University of Michigan, graduating from the law course in the class of '08. He has been engaged in lumbering and farming, but for the past ten years has been a practicing attorney. He is a member of the Masonic Lodge and of the Elks. He is a Republican and was elected to the Legislature November 7, 1922.

OTIS PRESTON

Representative from St. Joseph County, 1842. His postoffice address was White Pigeon. (Further data not obtainable).

S. HORACE PRESTON

Representative from Ingham County, 1887-8. Was born in Oneida, Mich., Oct. 25, 1837. He was educated in common schools and at Olivet College. In 1865 he settled on a farm in the town of Lansing. He was a farmer, was a Supervisor seven years, and two years chairman of the Board. In politics he was a Democrat. He was prominent in the work of the Farmers' Insurance Co. He spent his winters in the South and died at Chattanooga, Tenn., on his way home to Lansing, Jan. 1916.

WALLACE W. PRESTON

Representative from Isabella County, 1889-90. Was born in the town of Alexander, Genesee County, N. Y., Oct. 9, 1837. He was a farmer by occupation. He held various township offices: Township Treasurer, Supervisor and County Treasurer. In politics he was a Republican.

FRANCIS J. PREVOST

Representative from Clinton and Shiawassee counties, 1843; and Delegate from Shiawassee County to the Constitutional Convention of 1850. He came from New York to Michigan before 1830. After living some years in Washtenaw County he organized a company, known as the Byron Company, and bought lands on which the village of Byron is located. He moved there in 1836, and was the principal man for many years. He was first Postmaster. Soon after 1850 he removed to California, where he died previous to 1887.

JACOB PRICE

Representative from Oakland County, 1850. His postoffice address was Brandon. (Further data not obtainable).

LYMAN B. PRICE

Representative from Macomb County, 1847; and Senator from the Fifth District, 1871-2. Was born at Rush, N. Y., Nov. 22, 1811, and came with his father to Shelby, Mich., in 1827, where the village of Utica now stands. His grandfather, Jacob Price, built the first grist mill and saw mill in that part of the county, in 1828. The son became a farmer, but was a merchant after 1852. He was Sergeant-at-Arms of the Senate in 1837, and Sheriff of Macomb County in 1840. He resided at Lakeville, Oakland County, and was Senator from that County in 1871-2.

DELIVERANCE S. PRIEST

Representative from the Second District of Macomb County, 1871-2 and 1873-4. Was born in Arlington, Vt., Aug. 7, 1814. His education was obtained in the common schools. He settled as a farmer in Ray, Macomb County, Mich., in 1838. In politics he was a Republican. He died Feb. 4, 1888.

CLARENCE W. PRINDLE

Representative from Kent County, 1877-8 and 1881-2. Was born in Rutland, Mich., Dec. 20, 1849, and was two years a student at Albion College. He studied medicine and graduated from Hahnemann Medical College of Chicago in 1871. He was in practice at Grand Rapids in 1887, also a member of the drug firm of Prindle Brothers. In politics he was a Republican. He died in Grand Rapids, about 1898.

FRANK L. PRINDLE

Senator, 1891-2, from the Twenty-fourth District, comprising the counties of Gratiot, Isabella, Midland, Clare and Gladwin. Was born at Chester, Eaton County, in 1852, where he spent his boyhood days on his father's farm and at district school. He attended the high school at Charlotte and afterwards entered Albion College in the classical course, being a member of the class of '72. He left college in 1870, taught school for two years and was admitted to the bar in 1874 at Charlotte, where he practiced several years. He removed to Gladwin, Gladwin Co., in 1882, where he devoted himself to his profession. He twice held the office of Prosecuting Attorney of that county and was the first President of the village of Gladwin, to which office he was re-elected.

EUGENE PRINGLE

Representative from Jackson County, 1861-2; and Senator from the Tenth District, 1867-8; and Delegate from Jackson County to the Constitutional Convention of 1867. Was born in Richfield, N. Y., Dec. 1, 1826, and received an academical education. He studied law, was admitted in 1849, and commenced practice at Jackson, Mich., in 1850. He was Circuit Court Commissioner, Prosecuting Attorney, City Recorder, Mayor, military secretary under Gov. Blair, register in bankruptcy, State Insurance Commissioner, 1885-7, and Democratic candidate for Lieutenant Governor in 1882. He was also active in the building of railroads. In politics he was a Whig until 1854, a Republican until 1872, then a Democrat.

BENJAMIN D. PRITCHARD

Commissioner of the State Land Office, 1867-71; and State Treasurer, 1879-83. Was born in Nelson, Ohio, and educated at Western Reserve College. He came to Michigan in 1856, graduated from the law department of the University in 1860, and commenced practice at Allegan. He went into the war as Captain in the Fourth Mich. Cavalry, and was promoted to the rank of Brevet Brigadier General, and a part of his war record was the capture of Jefferson Davis. In politics he was a Republican. He was president of the National Bank at Allegan in 1887. Deceased.

KINTZING PRITCHETTE

Secretary of State, 1835-8. Came to Michigan under the favor of Governor George B. Porter, about the year 1831. He was a favorite with Gov. Porter, also with Gov. Mason, by whom he was appointed Secretary of State. He was a gentleman, neat and exact in dress, above medium height, straight, clean shaven, and a pair or spectacles added to the dignity of his port. Richard R. Elliott, of Detroit, in a note, says of him: "I remember his personal appearance, which was certainly distinguished, and his peculiar name struck my childish imagination." He was a lawyer and an educated man, was appointed to the office of Bank Commissioner in 1838, and returned east after the close of Gov. Mason's administration. His nativity is unknown, but understood to have been Pennsylvania or New Jersey.

WILLIAM PROBERT

Representative from Manistee County, 1879-80 and 1889-90. Was born in Gloucestershire, England, Mar. 24, 1835. He came to this country in August, 1850, and settled in Jefferson County, N. Y., and engaged to work on a farm. In 1852 he began a seafaring life on the chain of lakes and on the ocean between Europe and America, and also followed a coasting trade. In 1855 he bought a small farm in Jefferson County, Wis., still following sailing as an occupation. Mr. Probert enlisted in 1861 in the 1st Wis. Infantry for ninety days, participating in the engagements at Falling Waters, Martinsburg and Harper's Ferry, and was mustered out of service at the expiration of enlistment. He removed in 1861 to what is now the township of Pleasanton. He served as Supervisor, Highway Commissioner, Justice of the Peace, and held other offices in the township; was elected on the Democratic ticket to the House in 1879-80 and was re-elected to that of 1889-90.

HALLEY H. PROSSER

Representative from the First District of Genesee County, 1905-6 and 1907-8. Was born in Lansing, Ingham County, Mich., Mar. 13, 1870, of English parentage. He received his education in the public schools at Lansing and South Lyon, and in 1889 he passed the examination of the State Board of Pharmacy, and engaged in the drug business for eight years. He entered the produce business in 1897 with J. E. Ottaway & Co., of Flushing. Mr. Prosser was married Jan. 6, 1897. In politics a Republican.

ABRAM CLIFFORD PRUTZMAN

Member of the State Board of Agriculture, 1862-73; and senator from the Fourteenth District, 1869-70 and 1871-2, and from the Eleventh District, 1873-4. Was born in Columbia County, Penn., March 6, 1813, and when a lad moved to Danville, Penn. He married Mary L. Phillips, July 14, 1836. She was born in Dauphin County, Penn., Nov. 5, 1816. Mr. Prutzman was educated in the common school. In religion he was a Presbyterian, in politics a Whig, later a Republican. When he was fourteen he was indentured by his parents as an apprentice to Colb & Donaldson to learn to become a merchant and remained four years. He then went to Pottsville, Schuylkill County, Penn., where he followed the same business until the fall of 1834, when he formed a co-partnership with his brother-in-law, Edward S. Moore, and removed to St. Joseph County, Mich., sending their goods around the lakes to the mouth of the St. Joseph River. He went into business in Prairie Ronde, Kalamazoo County, where they remained two years, then removing to Three Rivers and a year later leased the flouring mills of Smith & Bowman, purchasing the same in 1840, and continuing until 1859, when they dissolved partnership, Mr. Prutzman becoming a merchant until 1867 when he retired. He was elected member of the State Board of Agriculture to fill a vacancy on the resignation of Mr. Yerkes. He died Jan. 2, 1899, at Minneapolis, Minn., age over 85 years.

NICHOLAS W. PULLEN

Representative from Wayne County, 1845. Was born in Ontario County, N. Y., in 1803. He came to Michigan in 1831, first settling near Royal Oak, but subsequently removing to Romulus, where he resided for twelve years, serving much of the time as Supervisor and Justice. He was by occupation a farmer, and politically a Democrat. Failing health induced his removal to Detroit in 1847, and from thence he removed to Birmingham, where he died in 1863.

HENRY H. PULVER

Senator from the Twentieth District, 1885-6. Was born Sept. 12, 1843, in Yates County, N. Y. He came to Michigan in 1844, served in the 8th Mich. Infantry four years, studied law, was admitted in 1859, and went into practice at Laingsburg. In politics he was first a Republican, later a Greenbacker.

WILLIAM PURCELL

Delegate from Wayne County to the Constitutional Convention of 1867; and Representative from Wayne County, 1869-70. Was a native of Ireland, born in 1818. Mr. Purcell was engaged in the foundry business, and was a man of character, conscientious in the discharge of his duties. He served his ward four consecutive terms, from 1861 to 1868, as Alderman, was Controller of the city June, 1870, to March, 1871, and was a member of the board of public works from 1876 to 1879. He was a Democrat politically. He died in 1880.

ROBERT PURDY

Representative from Washtenaw, 1837 and 1843; and Delegate from the Fourth District to the Constitutional Convention of 1835. His Postoffice address was Summit. (Further data not obtainable).

WILLIAM H. PUTHUFF

Member of the Legislative Council from Michilimackinac, 1824-5. (Further data not obtainable).

UZZIEL PUTNAM, JR.

Representative from Cass County, 1869-70; and Senator from the Fifteenth District, 1871-2. Was born in Pokagon, Mich., Aug. 12, 1826. He was the first white child born in Cass County, and was the son of Uzziel Putnam, a pioneer farmer. He received a good education, and graduated from the State University in 1853. He read law with E. C. & C. I. Walker of Detroit, and was admitted to the bar in 1855, but practiced only a short time. He held the offices of School Inspector, Justice, and Circuit Court Commissioner. He was president of the Cass County Pioneer Society, and took great interest in all matters of pioneer history. In 1874 he was appointed a member of the State Board of Charities, and held that position until his death, Feb. 10, 1879.

CHARLES G. PUTNEY

Senator, 1911-12, from the Twentieth District, comprising the counties of Huron and Sanilac. Was born at Lisbon, St. Lawrence County, N. Y., Dec. 4, 1866, and was educated in the district schools, and at the Fenton Normal and State Normal College. He spent the first twelve years of his life on the farm and attending school. He later taught district school three years and was Superintendent of Schools at Port Sanilac and Sandusky for nine years. In 1901 he was elected Commissioner of Schools and resigned in 1910. He took an active part in school work and served as president of the State Reading Circle Board. He was married in 1894 to Jessie A. Moore. Mrs. Putney died in 1904. In politics he was an active Republican, and served four years as county chairman. He was a Mason and a member of the Methodist Episcopal Church and an enthusiastic Sunday School worker. He died at his home in Oklahoma City, Mar. 29, 1922.

ELMORE PUTNEY

Representative from the First District of Sanilac County, 1897-8. Was born in Lisbon, St. Lawrence County, N. Y., Jan. 12, 1839. He acquired a common school education and spent his boyhood days on his father's farm. At the age of sixteen, he came to Michigan where he followed farming and lumbering until December, 1860, when he returned to Lisbon, N. Y., and engaged in farming. In 1862 he enlisted in Co. B, 106th N. Y. Vol. Infantry, where he served until June 22, 1865; he was married Dec. 25, 1865; came to Michigan in March, 1867, and purchased a farm in Speaker Township, Sanilac County. In politics he was a Republican. He was Supervisor and held several local offices of public trust.

DANIEL QUACKENBOSS

Representative from Lenawee County, 1848, 1850 and 1853-4. Came to Michigan from New York State. At the expiration of his term he left Tecumseh and was reported as dead before 1888; place and time unknown.

AUGUST QUINTEL

Representative from the Second District of Bay County, 1915-16 and 1917-18. Was born in Germany in 1857, and came to this country when nineteen years of age. In 1878 he located in Williams Township, Bay County, where he purchased a farm, working four seasons in a saw mill to help pay for the farm. He attended school at night in order to obtain the needed rudiments of an English education. He successfully served his township as Justice of the Peace, Treasurer, School Director and Supervisor. Married. In politics a Republican.

JOHN RAIRDEN

Senator from the First District, 1887-8. Was born in Ireland, June 24, 1831. He came when young to Canada, moved to Toledo, O., and from there to Detroit in 1843. He attended public and private schools, and learned the trade of chair painting and furniture finishing. He continued his studies, and acquired the German, French and other languages. He opened a night school in 1856 and continued it for several years. He was a teacher in the German-American Seminary in 1864; from 1865 to 1867 was a letter carrier; then taught in private and public schools, and after 1874 was principal of a private school. He was elected as a Labor-Republican.

STILLMAN RALPH

Representative from Hillsdale County, 1837 and 1855-6. Was born at Reading, Vt., Nov. 7, 1803. He received a common school education, and taught school several terms. He commenced the study of medicine in 1827, graduating at Waterville, Maine, in 1830. The same year he commenced practice at Canandaigua, N. Y. In 1835 he removed to Moscow Plains, Hillsdale County, which was his home at the time of his death. He resided in Jonesville from 1840 to 1847. He was first a Whig but became a Republican in 1854. He died at Lansing, Feb. 18, 1855.

NORTON R. RAMSDELL

Representative from Washtenaw County, 1844. Was a native of New York and removed to Ann Arbor in 1835. Before coming to Michigan he had been a licensed exhorter in the Methodist Episcopal Church, but studied law, was admitted to the bar, and came West to practice. He was regarded by his colleagues as a good lawyer, and one who excelled as an advocate. In politics he was a Democrat. Deceased.

THOMAS J. RAMSDELL

Representative from Manistee and other counties, 1861-2. Was born in Plymouth, Mich., July 29, 1833. He worked on his father's farm summers, attending school winters until eighteen years of age, when he became a student at Plymouth Seminary, then at the State Normal School. He read law in Lansing, and graduated at the National Law School at Poughkeepsie, N. Y., in 1858. He was admitted to the bar in New York, returned to Lansing and opened a law office. In the winter of 1859-60 he removed to Manistee and engaged in practice. In 1867 he formed a law partnership with E. E. Benedict. In politics he was a Republican. He died at Manistee, Apr. 22, 1917.

EDWIN B. RAMSEY

Representative from the First District of Ingham County, 1921-2. Was born Dec. 2, 1876, in Putnam County, O., of Scotch parentage. His education was acquired in the high school at Leipsic, O. He engaged in general contracting and is at present in the business of farming. Mr. Ramsey is married. In politics he is a Republican. He served the city of Lansing as Alderman for ten years.

CALEB D. RANDALL

Senator from the Thirteenth District, 1871-2. Was born in Conquest, N. Y., in 1831, and was a descendant of Wm. Randall, who settled in Scituate, Mass., in 1635. He removed with his father's family to Bronson, Mich., in 1835. He graduated at the Albany Law School in 1855. He settled at Coldwater in 1857 and practiced law until 1871. It is largely through his efforts that the State School for Dependent Children was established at Coldwater. He was a delegate to the Republican National Convention of 1880. He was president of the Southern Michigan National Bank of Coldwater from its organization in 1872, and for many years was one of the State Board of Control of the public school at Coldwater. In politics he was a Republican.

EDMOND S. RANDALL

Representative from Oceana County, 1899-1900, 1901-2 and 1903-4. Was born at Morristown, St. Lawrence County, N. Y., Oct. 16, 1845. He moved with his parents to Kent County, Mich., in May, 1851, locating on a farm in Cannon Township, and residing there until Nov. 19, 1861, obtaining his education in the schools of Kent County and the high school of Otisco, Ionia County. On the date last mentioned he enlisted in Co. C, 13th Mich. Vol. Infantry, serving in the army of the Cumberland and Tennessee during the Civil War, until February, 1864, when he re-enlisted, following Sherman from Chattanooga to Savannah and thence to Washington; returned from Washington to Louisville, Ky., where he was mustered out, and returned to Jackson, Mich., being discharged July 5, 1865. He was married Dec. 24, 1867, and in February, 1879, moved with his family to Lawrence County, Tenn., where he engaged in farming and lumbering until September, 1884, when he came back to Michigan, locating in Grant Township, Oceana County. He was Supervisor of Grant Township for eleven years, chairman of the Board of Supervisors of Oceana County two years and was elected Justice of the Peace, in 1896.

HARVEY RANDALL

Representative from Calhoun County, 1867-8. Was born in Sweden, N. Y., June 10, 1819. By occupation he was an insurance agent, politically a Republican. He settled at Tekonsha, Mich., in 1841. He was Justice of the Peace fifteen years, Supervisor three years, enrolling officer during the rebellion, clerk of the Baptist church over thirty years, and held other offices. He died Apr. 1, 1887.

JAMES ANDRUS RANDALL

Representative from the First District of Wayne County, 1889-90. Was born in Detroit, Dec. 15, 1848. Early in his boyhood he evinced an aptitude for business matters, and while yet in his teens began the study of law in the office of Larned & Hebden. After he had been complimented by Gov. Brownlow with a commission as Major of the 6th Tenn. Vol. Infantry, when he was but 16 years of age, he turned his attention to completing his school and legal education. He was admitted to the bar in February, 1869, and at once began practicing. He ran for Circuit Court Commissioner in 1874, was elected, and his administration endorsed by two re-elections. In 1882 he was defeated for the Circuit Court Judge nomination. He was chosen a member of the Board of Estimates for Detroit in 1887, and was a conspicuous figure in cutting down heavy park appropriations. The same year Mr. Randall was an almost unanimously supported candidate for the nomination as Circuit Judge, but was defeated in the convention. He turned his attention to real estate, newspaper, and other business ventures. In politics he was a Democrat.

DANIEL D. RANKIN

Representative from Oceana County, 1921. Was born at Appin, Ont., Feb. 6, 1862, of Scotch parents. He was educated in the public schools of Marquette. He came to Oceana County in 1879, engaging in the charcoal manufacturing business, being engaged in general farming in 1921. Mr. Rankin was married and had a family of five children. He was a member of the Masonic and Odd Fellow orders. He served four terms as Township Treasurer and twelve years as Good Roads Commissioner. He was elected to the Legislature Nov. 2, 1920. He died at Ann Arbor, Sept. 28, 1921.

FRANCIS H. RANKIN

Representative for Genesee County, 1861-2 and 1863-4; and Senator from the Nineteenth District, 1877-8. Was born in Cheymore, Ireland, Oct. 29, 1818, and was educated at private schools and Belfast Academy. He came to Pontiac, Mich., in 1848, worked two years as a printer, and in 1850 established the *Wolverine Citizen*, later the Flint *Citizen*, at Flint, and continued to publish and edit it at least until 1887. He was State Prison Inspector, 1865-9; Clerk and Recorder of Flint, 1871-7; and was postmaster of Flint eight years. He was one of the commissioners appointed in 1867 to examine into the condition of the prison and reformatory institutions of the State and report, which resulted in establishing the State Board of Charities. In politics he was a Republican. He died in August, 1904.

HENRY C. RANKIN

Representative from the Second District of Washtenaw County, 1911-12. Was born in Reading, Pa., Dec. 1, 1843. The Rankins moved to Michigan in 1856, settling on a farm in Jackson County. During the Civil War, Mr. Rankin served three years in the Ninth Mich. Infantry and one year in the Fifth U. S. Veteran Volunteers. During Grant's administrations he was an active figure in Jackson County politics, although he persistently declined office. In 1876 he graduated from the Ypsilanti State Normal and later took the full classical course in Olivet College, receiving his degrees from that institution. He was Superintendent of Schools at Cassopolis, Leslie, Buchanan and Lapeer. For more than twenty years his services as an educator were in demand. He was successful in soliciting college endowments and in later years taught in the Cleary Business College at Ypsilanti. Married. In politics he was a Republican. He died at Ypsilanti, July 7, 1915.

LEMUEL S. RANNEY

Representative from Hillsdale County, 1875-6. Was born in Ashfield, Mass., Jan. 17, 1831. He removed to Phelps, N. Y., in 1833, received a common school education, and in 1843 emigrated to Allen, Mich. In 1852 he crossed the plains to California, and again in 1859, and in all spent ten years in various States and Territories on the Pacific coast. He was Supervisor, and was by occupation a farmer. In politics he was a Republican.

PEYTON RANNEY

Representative from the First District of Kalamazoo County, 1883-4; and Senator, 1889-90, from the Eighth District, comprising the counties of Kalamazoo and St. Joseph. Was born at Westminster, Vt., Nov. 28, 1826. Mr. Ranney was a Vermont farmer previous to coming to Michigan. He was a successful grain trade, and the balance of the time he was an active business man in various lines of trade. He served as City Alderman, Village President and Mayor, two terms each.

EPAPHRODITUS RANSOM

Justice of the Supreme Court, 1836-47; Governor of Michigan, 1848-50; member of the Board of Regents of the University of Michigan, 1850-2; and Representative from Kalamazoo County, 1853-4. Was born at Shelburne Falls, Hampshire County, Mass., February, 1797. He accompanied his parents while still a young lad to Townshend, Windham County, Vermont, where he was raised to manhood, working upon the rugged hillsides of the Old Fletcher farm during the winters. With such preparation as he was able to make at the common district schools, he entered the Chester Academy in Windsor County, Vt., then one of the most prominent literary institutions in New England. Graduating from the Academy after four years' attendance, he entered the law office of Judge Taft, at Townshend, where he commenced the study of law. After two years study with Judge Taft he entered the law school at Northampton, Mass., from which he graduated with distinction in 1823. After graduating from the law school Mr. Ransom returned to Windham County, where he had a successful law practice for some years, meanwhile, although belonging to the minority party in politics, being returned several sessions as a member of the popular branch of the Legislature of Vermont. In 1834, he emigrated to Michigan, then just beginning to attract considerable attention at the East. He reached the town of Bronson, now Kalamazoo, in October of the last mentioned year. He at once entered upon the practice of his profession, afterwards associating with himself the late Hon. Charles E. Stuart. The firm enjoyed a large and lucrative business until the admission of the State into the Union in 1836, when he was appointed by Governor Mason Judge of the 2d Judicial Circuit, and associated Justice of the Supreme Court, being the first to receive a judicial commission under the constitution of the new State. In 1843 Judge Ransom was promoted to the chief justiceship by Governor Barry, and continued in that position until elected Governor by a majority vote of every county in the State in 1847. He occupied the gubernatorial position but one term. He was appointed Regent of the University Jan. 8, 1850, for two years, in place of Edwin M. Cust resigned. In 1857, after serious reverses in fortune, he emigrated to Kansas, having been appointed receiver of the Osage land office in that territory by President Buchanan. He died at Fort Scott, Kansas, on Nov. 9, 1859, in the 63d year of his age, and his remains were subsequently brought to Kalamazoo, where they are buried in the Mountain Home Cemetery at that place.

FLETCHER RANSOM

Representative from Kalamazoo County, 1845 and 1846. Was born in Vermont in 1800. By profession he was a physician. He came to Kalamazoo, Mich., in 1836. He was elected as a Whig to the Legislature, but later was a Democrat. He died June 3, 1867.

JAMES W. RANSOM

Representative from Kent County, 1875-6. Was born at Liberty, N. Y., May 20, 1829. He was educated at the Wilson Collegiate Institute, N. Y., adopting the profession of the law. He removed to Michigan in 1853, taking up his residence in Grand Rapids, of which place he was City Attorney. He moved to Portland, Oregon, and died there about 1913.

WILLIAM E. RASMUSSEN

Representative from Montcalm County, 1921—. Was born Aug. 5, 1881, at Gowen, Mich., of Danish and Norwegian parentage. He received his education in the district schools and the Ferris Institute at Big Rapids. He is engaged in farming and also operates a grain elevator. He served his county two terms as Sheriff and as member of the Board of Education, and during the World War was Federal Appeal Agent. Mr. Rasmussen is married and has two daughters and one son. In politics he is a Republican.

JOHN C. RAUCHHOLZ

Representative from the Second District of Saginaw County, 1921—. Was born in Germany, June 10, 1865, of German parentage. He was educated in the public schools of Saginaw, Mich. He is engaged in farming. He has been Supervisor of the Township of Richland, Saginaw County, for the past twenty-six years, and served as chairman of the Board of Supervisors for six years; he has also served as Highway Commissioner. Mr. Rauchholz is married and has three children. He is a member of the Masonic order, I. O. O. F., B. P. O. E., and Gleaners. In politics he is a Republican.

RICHARD RAUDABAUGH

Representative from the First District of Ingham County, 1911-12. Was born at Celina, O., Feb. 19, 1866, of German parentage. He was educated in the public schools and at Ohio State University, Cincinnati. He was married Oct. 15, 1891, to Sue E. Fanger. He has engaged in the practice of law. He has served as Alderman from the fourth ward, Lansing. In politics he is a Democrat.

ROBERT H. RAYBURN

Representative from Alpena County, 1913-14. Was born in St. Clair County, Oct. 31, 1866, of Scotch and Irish parentage, and received his education in the Alpena High School. Married. He engaged in the manufacturing business, being president and manager of the Island Mill Lumber Company, operating a saw mill, and president of the Michigan Veneer Company, operating an excelsior mill and also a mill for the manufacture of veneers and built-up panels. In politics a Democrat.

HENRY RAYMOND

Representative from Bay County, 1859-60. Was born at Woodstock, Vt., Aug. 29, 1804, his ancestors coming to Massachusetts in 1654. He received a common school education. He came to Detroit in 1829, and resided there until 1850, when he removed to Bay City and engaged in the manufacture of lumber. From 1862 until the close of the war he was a commissioner on the Provost Marshal Board of the 6th district. In 1868 he was appointed Assessor of that district and served four years. From 1872 to 1884 he was a resident of southern California. He was a resident of Detroit, in 1887. He was a Whig until 1854, then a Republican.

HIRAM RAYMOND

Representative from Lenawee County, 1863-4. Was born in Cohocton, N. Y., Jan. 4, 1819. His father settled on a farm in Raisin, Lenawee County, in 1833, where the son commenced the life of a pioneer. He was Supervisor of Raisin two years. In 1868 he removed to Tecumseh, and engaged in the manufacture of agricultural implements. He was Justice in Tecumseh four years.

MAHLON H. RAYMOND .

Representative from Jackson County, 1879-80. Was born in Sharon, Mich., June 19, 1836. He received a good education. In 1859 he graduated from the Medical department of the University of Michigan. He removed to Grass Lake and commenced the practice of his profession. In 1862 he was commissioned assistant surgeon of the Twenty-sixth Regiment Michigan Volunteers, and in 1863 was promoted to surgeon. He was a member of the School Board for twelve years, and was chosen president of the village. In politics he was a Republican.

SELAH H. RAYMOND

Representative from Lenawee County, 1891-2 and 1893-4. Was born in the Township of Rollin, Lenawee County, Aug. 31, 1840. His parents were both natives of New York, and came to Lenawee County in 1837, where they settled upon the farm owned and occupied by the subject of this sketch, who was the first son of a family of four children. At the age of 16 he was bereft of his father and from that time has fought the battle of life aided only by his wife, whom he married in 1861, she being Miss Martha A. Pawson, of Franklin Township. In politics a Republican. He held the offices of Commissioner of Highways, Township Clerk, and Supervisor of the Township in which he was born.

EBENEZER RAYNALE

Delegate from the Fifth District to the Constitutional Convention of 1835; Senator from the Fifth District, 1835-7; and Delegate from Oakland County to the Constitutional Convention of 1850. Was born in Hartland, Vt., Oct. 21, 1804. He studied medicine, and received the degree of M. D., in 1826, and settled in Franklin, Mich., in 1828, and became a successful and distinguished practitioner. He was also Postmaster. He married Eliza Cassidy in 1830. He was Postmaster of Franklin under Jackson. He was the last surviving member of the first State Senate. In politics he was a Democrat. He aided in organizing the first State Medical Society of Michigan. He settled at Birmingham in 1839, where he resided until his death, Mar. 24, 1881.

EDWARD G. READ

Representative from the Second District of Kalamazoo County, 1919—. Has, always lived in Kalamazoo County, having been born in Richland Township, Sept. 3, 1864, of American parents. He was educated in the rural schools, Kalamazoo College, and Parsons' Business College of Kalamazoo. At the age of fourteen years, his father having died five years previous, he assumed the responsibility of the farm upon which he now resides. He is one of the largest feeders of sheep and lambs in the State, and has won many prizes at the Chicago International Expositions. He is also interested in many of the financial and manufacturing institutions of the county, being director of the Kalamazoo City Savings Bank, the Monarch Paper Company, and the General Casualty and Surety Company of Detroit. His uncle, the Hon. Gilbert E. Read, was Representative from Kalamazoo County during the Civil War, from 1861 to 1865, serving as Speaker of the House during the latter session. He was also State Senator in 1877. Mr. Read is married, and has three children, two boys and one girl. In politics he is a Republican.

GILBERT E. READ

Representative in 1861-2 to 1865-6; and Senator from the Eleventh District, 1877-8. Was born in Ludlow, Vt., May 6, 1822. His father, Rev. Peter Read, was the first Congregational minister in that town, and its first Representative in the Legislature. He received a limited education, commenced teaching at the age of eighteen, and followed it for seven years in winter. In 1842 he came to Richland, Mich. He was a prosperous farmer, and was also engaged in the manufacture and sale of lumber. He was first a Whig, a Republican after 1854. As a Legislator he served on many important committees, and was the Speaker of the House in 1865. He served several years as Supervisor, and for three years was chairman of the County Board. He was a member of the Presbyterian church, and for many years superintendent of its Sabbath school. He died at Richland, Mar. 16, 1898.

J. HERBERT READ

Representative from Manistee County, 1899-1900 to 1905-6. Was born in the Township of Potter, Yates County, N. Y., Jan. 24, 1858, and resided there until

March, 1884, when he came to Mansitee County. Mr. Read was educated in the district school of Yates County with the exception of two terms spent in the union school at Rushville. He was married in 1885. He held the offices of Township Clerk and Supervisor and was chairman of the Board of Supervisors. In politics a Republican.

THOMAS READ

Representative from Oceana County, 1915-16, 1917-18 and 1919-20; and Lieutenant Governor, 1921—. Was born at Rochester, N. Y., May 28, 1881, and is of English and Scotch descent. He came to Michigan in 1889 and was educated in the public schools, the Ferris Institute of Big Rapids, and the University of Michigan, graduating from the law department of the latter institution in 1913. For the last eight years he has been practicing law at Shelby. Mr. Read is married. In politics he is a Republican. He has served as Township Clerk, and in the Legislatures of 1915-16, 1917-18 and 1919-20 and at the opening of the 1919 session he was elected Speaker of the House. He was elected to the office of Lieutenant Governor at the general election, Nov. 2, 1920, and re-elected Nov. 7, 1922.

GEORGE H. READER

Representative from Mason County, 1887-8. Was born at Lyme-Regis, England, Nov. 4, 1853. He came with his parents to the State of New York in 1854, and with a high school education settled in Mason County, Mich., in 1874, taught school, worked in a factory, then in a store, and after 1882 was a manufacturer of wooden bowls at Scottville. In politics a Republican.

FRANCIS W. REDFERN

Representative from the County of Clinton, 1893-4 and 1895-6. Was born in Toronto, Canada, July 20, 1842; came to Michigan in 1853, and attended the district and Marshall High School; taught school six years and then engaged in farming. In the early part of the war, he served in the United States Navy, and later as Sergeant in Co. C, 1st Mich. Cavalry. For a number of years he was connected with the Michigan State Grange, and an active member and commander of the G. A. R. In politics a Republican.

ALEXANDER H. REDFIELD

Senator from the Fourth District, 1848-9, and from the First District, 1857-8; and member of the Board of Regents of the University of Michigan, 1844-52. Was born in Manchester, N. Y., Oct. 5, 1805. He was well educated, spending three years in Hamilton College, and his fourth year in Union College. He read law with Gen. James Lawrence of Onondaga County, N. Y. He was admitted to the Supreme Court of New York in 1830, removed to Cass County, Michigan, in 1831, and engaged in the practice of law. He and Mr. Sherman were the only lawyers present at the first court held in 1832 by Judges Sibley and Woodbridge, under an oak tree near the public square in Cassopolis. He was interested with Sherman in the site of Cassopolis. He was the first Postmaster in 1837. He did not sit in the extra session of the Legislature in 1858. In politics he was a Democrat. He died at Cassopolis, Nov. 24, 1869.

GEORGE REDFIELD

Representative from Cass and Van Buren counties, 1841; Senator from the Fourth District, 1848-9, and from the First District, 1857-8; State Treasurer, 1845-6; Secretary of State, 1850; and Delegate from Cass County to the Constitutional Convention of 1850. Was born at Duffield, Conn., Oct. 6, 1796. He received a common school education and one term in an Academy, and at the age of twenty-five had a fine farm under good cultivation at Clifton Springs, N. Y. In 1822 he leased his farm and spent four years teaching in Georgia. In 1826 he returned to his farm, and in 1834 purchased eight hundred acres of land in Cass County, Michigan, removing there in 1835. He owned at various times ten thousand acres of land, cultivating himself eight hundred. In 1844 he was Presidential Elector. He held no office after 1850. In politics he was a Democrat. He died in the winter of 1887-8.

HEMAN J. REDFIELD

Senator from the Fifth District, 1875-6 and 1877-8. Was born in Leroy, N. Y., Feb. 25, 1823. He graduated at Canandaigua Academy in 1836. His education was further continued under his father, who was a teacher and a fine classical scholar. He removed to Cass County in 1850 and came to Monroe in 1858. His occupation was farming, and at the same time he was largely engaged in real estate transactions. He was president of the Monroe Board of Education several years, and for four years was Mayor of Monroe. He was a Democrat in politics. He died in Monroe, Sept. 6, 1883.

CHARLES P. REED

Representative from Muskegon County, 1883-4. Was born in Ingham County, Mich., July 26, 1844, where he resided until 1861, and served during the war. He moved from Lyons to Berlin in 1866, and from there to Ravenna, Muskegon County, in 1873, where he resided, engaged in milling and lumbering. He held the offices of Town Clerk and Supervisor. In politics he was a Republican.

CLARENCE J. REED

Representative from the Second District of Jackson County, 1915-16 and 1917-18. Was born in Fairfield, Lenawee County, Mich., May 8, 1867, of Scotch and Dutch parentage. He was educated in the Spring Arbor Seminary, from which he graduated in 1884. He engaged in general farming and stock raising. He served five years as Supervisor of Spring Arbor Township and in 1913 was elected chairman of the board. In December, 1914, he was elected first vice-president of the Michigan State Association of Farmers' Clubs and at present president of the Jackson County Farmers' Club. Mr. Reed was married in 1885 to Miss Frankie M. Crouch. In politics a Republican.

GEORGE W. REED

Representative from Mecosta County, 1899-1900. Was born in Howell, Livingston County, Mich., July 8, 1846. He attended the public schools at Howell.

At the outbreak of the Civil War he (at the age of fifteen) enlisted in Co. I, 16th Mich. Vol. Infantry, and served as a private; after the close of the war he went to Mecosta County, Mich., and located on a homestead; shortly afterward he engaged in general merchandise. He was also connected with farming, dairying, creamery and other general business. In politics he was a Republican; was Supervisor of his township several terms. He died at Stanwood, Mich., July 17, 1922.

LUCIEN REED

Representative from Ingham County, 1865-6. Was born in Moriah, N. Y., Nov. 22, 1824. By profession he was a lawyer; politically, first a Republican, then a Prohibitionist. He was Clerk of Ingham County in 1861-2. He engaged in practice at Mason in 1887.

MARSHALL REED

Representative from Lenawee County, 1875-6. Was born in Richmond, N. Y., Aug. 21, 1833. He received a common school education, removed to Michigan in 1855, and settled in Rome, Lenawee County. He held the offices of School Inspector and Justice. His occupation was that of farmer. In politics he was a Republican.

RASSELAS REED

Representative from Shiawassee County, 1877-8 and 1879-80. Was born Oct. 8, 1826, at Dryden, N. Y. He removed to Michigan in 1836, and settled in Vernon, in which township he resided in 1887. He received a common school education. He was Supervisor of Vernon five terms, and held minor township offices. His occupation was farming. In politics he was a Republican.

WILLIAM A. REED

Representative from the Second District of Jackson County, 1899-1900 and 1901-2. Was born at Mt. Morris, Livingston County, N. Y., Mar. 11, 1850, and in the same year his parents removed to Hanover Township, Jackson County. He was educated in the district schools of Hanover and pursued the usual avocation of a farmer's son. In 1872, when but twenty years of age, he purchased thirty acres of land, paying $100 down. Within twenty-six years he had paid for the original farm and owned 240 acres in three separate farms, with residences and buildings on each, and all connected by telephones. He was one of the most extensive dealers in sheep in south-central Michigan, and was for two years president of the National Merino Sheep Register Society. In 1895 he was elected Township Supervisor on the Republican ticket in a Democratic town; re-elected in 1896 and 1897 and declined a fourth term in 1898; president of the Hanover Township Pioneer Association and for three years president of the West Liberty Farmers' Club.

HENRY L. REEVES

Representative from the Second District of Monroe County, 1859-60. His post-office address was Roseville. (Further data not obtainable).

LAWRENCE T. REMER

Representative from St. Clair County, 1873-4 and 1875-6. Was born in Benton, N. Y., May 22, 1810. He received an academical education at Ovid, N. Y. In 1843 he emigrated to Michigan, and settled in the township of China, afterward changed to East China. He was Supervisor of the town many years. His occupation was that of a farmer. In politics he was a Republican. Deceased.

GEORGE B. REMICK

Representative from Wayne County, 1881-2. Was born Aug. 4, 1846, in Lincoln, Maine. He removed with his father's family to this State in 1853, and was a resident of Detroit. He graduated in the classical department of the State University in 1866, and in the law department in 1868. He however was in the active practice of his profession only after 1876. He was also interested in lumbering operations, having inherited some valuable pine lands from his father, Royal C. Remick, who died in the spring of 1878. In politics he was a Republican.

JOHN RENO

Representative from Detroit, 1853-4. Was a native of the French province of Lorraine, born in 1807, and became a resident of Detroit in 1832. He was by trade a tailor, but became a retail grocer in Detroit many years ago, continuing in the business until his death, Dec. 8, 1880. He filled at various times the local offices of City Assessor, Collector, and member of the Board of Education. He was a Democrat in politics.

THEODORE RENTZ

Representative from Wayne County, 1887-8; and Senator from the Second District of Wayne, 1889-90. Was born in the Republic of Switzerland in 1837, and came to Detroit in 1850, attended the public school, and was subsequently employed as clerk. He then commenced business for himself and continued it with exception of two years—1860-2. In 1882 he was elected to the Upper House, or Board of Councilman, of the city of Detroit, in 1883 President and Acting Mayor of the city of Detroit, term of office expiring second Tuesday in January, 1887. He engaged in general merchandise trade. In politics he was a Democrat. He was a delegate to the National Convention at Chicago, when Cleveland was nominated for the Presidency.

GEORGE RENWICK

Member of the Legislative Council from Washtenaw County, 1832-3 and 1834-5; and Representative from Washtenaw County, 1839 to 1841 and 1847. Was born in England, Oct. 31, 1789, and came to America with his father's family in

1802. They settled in Gorham, N. Y. He attended school in Canandaigua, and taught winters. He learned the trade of carpenter, which with farming he followed through the early part of his life. He was in service during the War of 1812-15. In 1817 he moved to Greece, N. Y., and in 1828 came to Michigan and located land in Salem, Washtenaw County. He was the first Supervisor and Justice, which offices he held several years. He was an old line Whig in politics. He died in June, 1863.

JOHN RENWICK

Representative from Washtenaw County, 1850 and 1853. Was born in Gorham, N. Y., May 2, 1803. He moved with his father's family in 1817, to Greece, Monroe County, N. Y. He attended school at Rochester, N. Y., and taught school winters. In 1824 he married Eliza Pratt, and in 1827 emigrated to Michigan, locating land in Salem, Washtenaw County. In 1833 he was elected the first Supervisor, and held that office and that of Town Clerk for several years. He was Captain of the First Militia Company organized in the town. He was in politics a Whig. He died Sept. 24, 1866.

ALBERT H. REUTTER

Representative from the First District of Wayne County, 1919-20 and 1921-2. Was born at Detroit, Oct. 27, 1877, of German-English parentage, and has always resided in that city. He was educated in the public schools of Detroit, and after leaving school secured employment as clerk with the Newcomb-Endicott Company of that city. Later he acted as traveling salesman for the same concern. He severed his relations with this firm to engage in the real estate business, in which he is now engaged. He served the city two years as estimator on the Board of Estimates. He is not married. In politics he is a Republican.

EDGAR REXFORD

Member of the State Board of Education, 1875-87. Was elected Nov. 3, 1874, for a six-year term, and re-elected Nov. 2, 1880, for another six-year term. (Further data not obtainable).

ROSWELL B. REXFORD

Senator from the Eleventh District, 1855-6. His Postoffice address was Napoleon, Jackson County. (Further data not obtainable).

ASA REYNOLDS

Representative from Oakland County, 1855. Was born in Greenville, Schenectady County, N. Y., Nov. 25, 1810. He removed with his parents to Avon, N. Y., in 1817, remained on his father's farm until 1834, and taught eschool in Monroe County, N. Y. In 1836 he removed to Rose, Mich., and became a farmer. He was Supervisor ten years and Justice of the Peace sixteen years. In politics he was a Democrat. He died at Fenton, Sept. 9, 1888.

EDWIN W. REYNOLDS

Representative from Cass County, 1859-60. Was born in Shoreham, Vt., in November, 1820. He was left an orphan at the age of seven, but with self denial fitted himself for college, and graduated from the Western Reserve College at Hudson, O., in 1846. He studied law at Akron, and practiced four years at Medina, O. He was first a Whig, but became a Republican. He was for many years Supervisor of Mason. His health failing he removed to Mason, Cass County, Michigan, residing there until his death, Oct. 15, 1863.

HENRY GRAHAM REYNOLDS

Member of the State Board of Agriculture, 1879-85. Was born July 4, 1851, at Buffalo, N. Y. He married Frances Arbuthnot Llewellyn of Louisville, Ky., at Mexico, Missouri, Sept. 24, 1874. Mr. Reynolds was educated in a grammar school and the high school of Chicago, and was graduated from the Michigan Agricultural College in 1870 with the degree of B. S.; M. S. in 1873, M. H. in 1893, spent one year (1872) in Fresenius Laboratory, Wiesbaden, Germany. He was an earnest Christian; violently opposed to the further protection of our adult industries, also of any further pauperization of what began as the G. A. R., but which he considered largely a Base Army of Leeches. In 1871 he was bore-man of the Horticultural department; 1872-1884, fruit grower at Old Mission, Mich.; June 1885-June 1893, secretary of the State Board of Agriculture; 1894-1911, retired on account of ill health. At one time he was Supervisor of his township; member of the Board of School Examiners; city Councilman. The details of his office were so well in hand that at any moment the Board could know from his statement just what money was at their disposal. He was a good business manager. He drafted the bill which passed, placing the entire management of the remaining college lands in the hands of the State Board of Agriculture. He was still living in 1915.

RICHARD B. REYNOLDS

Representative, 1903-4, from Leelanau District, comprising the counties of Benzie and Leelanau. Was born at North Kingston, R. I., Dec. 25, 1849. His ancestors came from England. He received his education in the district schools and Providence Conference Seminary, East Greenwich, R. I. When eighteen years of age he moved to Benzie County, Mich., with his parents. Mr. Reynolds married twice but was a widower. He engaged in general merchandise and farming. In politics a Republican. He held the office of County Clerk three terms.

RUSH W. REYNOLDS

Representative from Hillsdale County, 1909-10 and 1911-12. Was born Aug. 22, 1858, on a farm near Tiffin, Seneca County, O. He came to Michigan with his parents in 1867, and received his education in the village schools of Waldron and at Hillsdale College. In 1881 he was married to Miss Florence M. Fay, of Hillsdale. He resided on his fine, well improved farm just south of the village of Waldron. In politics a Republican. He held the office of Deputy Sheriff; a member of the Council of the village of Waldron.

JOHN A. RICE

Representative from Lenawee County,. 1846. Was born in Cambridge, N. Y., Nov. 29, 1806. He settled on a farm in Tekonsha, Calhoun County, in 1836, where he lived until 1842, then removed to Adrian, where, with the exception of two years, he was connected with the Michigan Southern Railroad as ticket agent, or general baggage agent, during life. He died Nov. 6, 1871.

JUSTIN RICE

Senator from the Fourth District, 1840-1. Was born in West Brookfield, Mass., in 1798. He was a physician by profession. He came to Detroit in 1825, and practiced medicine for nine years, when he engaged in the manufacture of lumber at Port Huron, St. Clair, and Detroit, and was a pioneer in the lumber business. He was Indian agent at Mackinac in 1842-3-4. He was an active member and elder of the First Presbyterian church at Detroit. Politically he was first a Whig, then a Republican. He died at Detroit in 1854.

NELSON C. RICE

Representative from the First District of Berrien County, 1907-8 and 1909-10. Was born at Phelps, N. Y., July 7, 1848. He received his education in the public schools at Fond du Lac, Wis. Married. He was a successful business man and was engaged in the grocery and crockery business. He held the offices of Alderman, City Treasurer, member of the Board of Education, and Mayor of St. Joseph City. In politics a Republican.

THOMAS J. RICE

Representative from Washtenaw County, 1842 and 1843. His postoffice address was Scio. (Further data not obtainable).

WAYNE REMINGTON RICE

Representative from Newaygo County, 1913-14, 1915-16 and 1917-18. Was born on a farm in Plainfield Township, Kent County, Mich., July 26, 1885, of Irish and American parentage. He was educated in the Grand Rapids High School and graduated from the law department of the University of Michigan in 1908. He then located at White Cloud, Newaygo County, where he engaged in the practice of law. During the year 1910 he served as Circuit Court Commissioner. In politics a Republican. He was elected to the Legislatures of 1913-14 and 1915-16, and re-elected Nov. 7, 1916. At the opening of the 1915 session he was elected speaker *pro tem.* of the House and was the unanimous choice for speaker at the 1917 session.

WILLIAM E. RICE

Representative, 1895-6, from the Cheboygan District, composed of the counties of Cheboygan, Emmet, Presque Isle and Manitou. Was born in Orleans County, N. Y., Nov. 28, 1852. In 1836 he came to Michigan with his parents and settled near Lansing. Here he attended school at Mason and the State Normal, and at the age of eighteen engaged in teaching, in which occupation he continued for about ten years; studied law; was admitted to the bar and located at Rogers City where he engaged in the practice of his profession. In politics a Republican. He held the offices of Prosecuting Attorney and Circuit Court Commissioner.

ARTHUR LAWRENCE RICH

Representative from Newaygo County, 1901-2. Was born near Bridgeton, Mich., June 8, 1873, and obtained his education in the district schools, supplemented by a course in the Bryant and Stratton Business College in Chicago, Ill., after which he returned to Michigan and taught school four years. In 1890 he settled on the farm. Unmarried. A member of the Patrons of Husbandry and helped to organize the Grangers' Mutual Insurance Company. In politics a strong Republican.

CHARLES RICH, JR.

Member of the State Board of Agriculture, 1861-7. Was born July 30, 1802, son of Charles Rich, Sr., and Molly (Watts) R. He married Elizabeth Treadway, March 18, 1827. From the time he was married he was a successful tenant farmer for ten years, when he sold out and moved to Conneautville, Pa., where he engaged in keeping store for ten years (1847) when his property was gone. He moved to Lapeer, Mich., with the purpose of going onto a farm in the woods; while waiting for the log house he lost both his children by typhoid fever, he and his wife both recovering. In 1848 they moved into the primitive log house. In 1856 he was elected County Clerk and Register of Deeds and moved to Lapeer where he lived until his death in 1872. While living in Lapeer he held the office of Judge of Probate. He took great interest in the college. The timber from the last farm was cut off at a profit and left him in comfortable circumstances.

HAMPTON RICH

Senator from the Twenty-eighth District, 1867-8 and 1869-70. Was born in Sharon, Vt., Dec. 1, 1815. He removed with his father, first to St. Lawrence County, N. Y., then to Prescott, Canada. He received a common school and academical education and at the age of nineteen had entire charge of a store at Kemptville, Canada. He settled at Ionia, Mich., in 1837. He was three years a Clerk; in mercantile business from 1846 to 1875; was Town Clerk in 1838, also Justice; County Clerk two terms; was director and president of the Ionia & Lansing Railroad Company, and active in building the line, and secured the railroad shops at Ionia; superintended the erection of the high school building; and was active in securing the location of the House of Correction, of which he was a trustee. In politics he was a Republican. He was vice-president Michigan Pioneer and Historical Society. Deceased.

IRVING B. RICH

Representative from the First District of Jackson County, 1895-6. Was born in Spencerport, N. Y., in 1852; came to Lenawee County, Mich., in 1861, attended the common schools, and later learned the printer's trade, which was his life occupation. In 1868 he commenced his trade in the office of the *Clinton Republican*, at St. Johns. Two years later he went to Jackson and commenced work as an apprentice in the *Citizen* job room, in which office he remained, having had charge of the job and press room since 1878. In politics a Republican. He served as Alderman of his ward, and president of the Common Council of the city of Jackson.

JOHN T. RICH

Representative from Lapeer County, 1873-4 to 1879-80; Senator from the Twentieth District, 1881; member of Congress, 1881-3; Governor of Michigan, 1893-5 and 1895-7; and State Treasurer, 1908. Was born in Conneautville, Pa., Apr. 23, 1841. He came to Michigan in 1848 with his parents, locating at Elba, where he made his home. His early education was obtained at the district school, the old academy at Clarkston, and the public schools of Lapeer. His occupation was that of a farmer. In politics he was a Republican, and for a number of years was identified with State and National politics. He was Representative in the State Legislature from 1873 to 1880 inclusive, and elected to the Senate of 1881-2; Mar. 11, 1881, he was nominated to the United States House of Representatives from the Seventh District, to succeed Mr. Conger, who had been promoted to the Senate; he resigned his seat in the Senate to accept this position, to which he was elected. He was strongly supported for Governor in 1880; was Commissioner of Railroads under Governor Luce; was nominated for Governor for the term of 1893-5, and elected; was re-elected for the term of 1895-7. He was appointed State Treasurer Jan. 23, 1908, to succeed Frank P. Glazier.

GABRIEL RICHARD

Territorial Delegate to Congress, 1823-5. Was born at Saintes, France, Oct. 15, 1764, and was a descendant on his mother's side of Bishop Bossuet. He received a thorough classical and theological education, and in 1791 became a priest of the order of Sulpitians, a society devoted to the education of young men for the sanctuary. He came to Baltimore in 1792, and accepted the charge of the Catholics in Illinois, where he remained six years, coming to Detroit in 1798 as permanent pastor. He at once interested himself zealously in the causes of religion and education, and commanded the highest respect of both Catholics and Protestants. In 1804 he opened a school for the education of young men, and an academy for ladies in 1805, with four teachers. He brought the first printing press overland from Baltimore, and in August, 1809, issued the first newspaper west of the Alleghany mountains. The same year he published the first prayer book. Up to 1812 this was the only printing establishment in the Northwest. He had the first organ in Michigan and composed music. In 1812 he was taken prisoner and confined at Sandwich, where by his eloquency and influence he saved many prisoners from horrors of Indian torture. In 1823 he was elected delegate to Congress, over Gen. John R. Williams and Maj. John Biddle, and received a large support from the Protestant population. Through his exertions grants were obtained for the Fort Gratiot, Pontiac, Grand River, and Chicago roads. He was defeated as a candidate in 1825. During the progress of the cholera in 1832 he stood at his post giving consolation to the sick and dying, until he fell a victim to the disease, Sept. 13, 1832.

GEORGE D. RICHARDS

Representative from Cheboygan County, 1903-4. Was born in Yarmouth, Elgin County, Ont., Dec. 7, 1855. He removed to Michigan in January, 1864, with his parents, locating at North Branch, Lapeer County. His early education was acquired in the schools of Ontario and northern Lapeer County. He worked on farms, in the lumber woods, drove the Flint and Thunder Bay Rivers until January, 1880. He located in March, 1880, at the junction of the Sturgeon rivers, Cheboygan County. Here he established the postoffice of Wolverine, and appointed postmaster in January, 1881, holding the office six years. He was married July 11, 1881, to Miss Susie Casler of North Branch. He took up a government homestead in June, 1880, residing there summers and at Wolverine winters. For an income, he built new roads, bridges, looked lands, scaled logs, lumbered for self and others, was trespass agent of the J. L. & S. R. R. Co. several years; at the same time, and since, doing a general real estate, land-looking and timber estimating business. He was elected County Road Commissioner of Cheboygan County two terms; a member of the Wolverine School Board twelve years, and Director of its graded schools eight years; was a W. of W., a K. of P. In politics a Republican. He was nominated for Representative by the Republicans, and elected Nov. 4, 1902.

JAMES A. RICHARDS

Representative from the First District of Calhoun County, 1923—. Was born in Ontario, Canada, October 31, 1862, of English parents. Coming to Michigan with his parents, when two years of age, he lived and worked on a farm until 1890 when he removed to the state of Washington where he looked after the farming interests of George Vanderbilt for five years. After ranching for a few years he returned to Michigan and followed farming until 1910. Removing to Albion, he has since been engaged in looking after the interests of non-residents and the administration of estates. Mr. Richards is married and has two daughters. He is a Republican and has served on the Board of Supervisors. He was elected to the Legislature November 7, 1922.

WILLIAM P. RICHARDS

Representative from Hillsdale County, 1859-60. Was born in the State of Vermont, in 1815. He came to Michigan in 1837, and settled in Hillsdale County. By occupation he was a farmer and lawyer, in politics a Republican. In 1860 he removed to Morenci, and engaged in mercantile business. He moved to Toledo, Ohio, in 1867, and died in 1882.

CHARLES W. RICHARDSON

Representative from the First District of Marquette County, 1913-14 and 1923—. Was born in Simcoe County, Ont., Canada, Sept. 17, 1872, of English and Scotch parentage. He received his education in the public schools. He came to Michigan in 1889 and entered the employ of the South Shore & Atlantic Railway in 1892 as a locomotive fireman. He was promoted to engineer in 1900. Mr. Richardson was married in 1905 to Miss Jennie Sandie, of Lucknow, Canada; a member of division 94, B. of L. E., Marquette Lodge No. 101 A. F. & A. M., Marquette Chapter No. 43, R. A. M., Lake Superior Commandery No. 3, K. T., and Ahmed Temple A. A. O. N. M. S. In politics he is a Republican.

DAVID M. RICHARDSON

Senator from the Second District, 1873-4. Was born Jan. 31, 1826, in Concord, N. Y. He received his education at the Springville Seminary, N. Y. In 1856 he emigrated to Michigan and settled in Detroit. He was a member of the Board of Education in Detroit for two years. He was extensively engaged in the manufacture of matches.

GEORGE F. RICHARDSON

Representative from Ottawa County, 1887-8 and 1891-2; and member of Congress, 1893-5. Was born at Jamestown, Ottawa County, Mich., July 1, 1850; received his education in the common schools; elected Township Clerk eight years in succession; elected to the Michigan Legislature in 1884, and again in 1890. The Democrats controlled the organization of the House, and he was elected speaker *pro tempore*. He was elected to the Fifty-third Congress by the Democrats and Populists. He died March 1, 1923.

GEORGE W. RICHARDSON

Representative from the Second District of Monroe, 1895-6. Was born in Niagara County, N. Y., in 1856. When eight years old he went to live with an older brother, and five years later began life for himself. Taking Horace Greeley's advice, he went to Iowa, and after one year's work on a farm, he engaged to do chores for his board and lodging, and attended the public school at Webster City; this he continued for two years, and went to a ranch near Omaha, Nebr., where by his labor he acquired means to attend the Omaha High School, from which he graduated in 1875. Returning to his old home in New York, he entered a doctor's office and began the study of medicine, later attending a medical school at Cleveland, and the University of Buffalo, and graduated from the latter in the spring of 1878; came to Michigan and engaged in the practice of his profession; located at first near Milan, then moved to East Milan, and in August, 1880, removed to Dundee. In 1890 he visited the Pacific Coast, spending four months in the State of Washington. A 32d degree Mason, and a member of the Mystic Shrine. In politics a Republican.

JOHN H. RICHARDSON

Senator from the Thirtieth District, 1883-4. Was born at Randolph, Vt., Jan. 24, 1814. He removed to Ipswich, Mass., in 1832, and for seven years was overseer for a Boston firm, in the manufacture of cotton goods; then for eight years was at Palmer, Mass., as overseer of the first cambric cotton mill in this country. In 1847 he settled at Tuscola, Mich., and engaged in lumbering and farming. In 1861 he enlisted, and was a Captain in the 7th Mich. Infantry; was promoted to Major in March, 1862, and made Lieutenant Colonel in Feb., 1863. He saw much hard service and resigned from ill health. In 1864, as commissioner, he took the soldiers' vote in Alabama. He was Supervisor fifteen years, and Justice eighteen years. In politics he was an Independent.

ORIGEN D. RICHARDSON

Delegate from Oakland County to the First Convention of Assent, 1836; Representative from Oakland County, 1835, 1836 and 1841; and Lieutenant Governor, 1842-6. Was born in the State of Vermont in 1795. He studied law and was admitted to practice in Vermont. He came to Pontiac, Mich., in 1826, and entered upon practice. He was Prosecuting Attorney of Oakland County in 1832. He continued in practice in Pontiac until 1854, when he removed to Omaha, Nebr. He was a member of the first and second sessions of the Legislature of that State, and took a prominent part in framing the laws now on the statute books. In politics he was a Democrat. He was one of the three commissioners to codify the laws of Nebraska.

PASCHAL RICHARDSON

Representative from Tuscola County, 1853-4 and 1859-60. Was born in Randolph, Vt., Dec. 29, 1808. He came to Michigan in 1842. In politics he was a Democrat and by occupation a tanner. He was also engaged in lumbering. He was also Postmaster, and served in other town offices during his residence in Michigan for thirty-five years. He died in Tuscola, Tuscola County, Apr. 6, 1878.

CHARLES H. RICHMOND

Delegate from Washtenaw County to the Constitutional Convention of 1867; and Senator from the Fourth District, 1883-4. Was born in Aurora, N. Y., Mar. 6, 1821. He received an academical education, and from 1837 to 1839 was bookkeeper and teller in a bank at Grand Rapids, Mich., when he returned to Aurora from ill health. He was fifteen years engaged as a farmer and merchant, then chief clerk of the Superintendent and Indian Agent of Michigan in 1848-9. In 1858 he removed to Ann Arbor, then engaged in banking in New York City, and in 1861 organized and was the first cashier of the First National Bank at Ann Arbor, and afterwards vice president. He was a Delegate to the Democratic National Convention at Cincinnati. In politics he was a Democrat.

CHARLES L. RICHMOND

Representative from Saginaw County, 1845. Was born in Woodstown, N. J., Feb. 6, 1800. He came to Michigan in 1836. He was a merchant at Saginaw City, and in politics first a Whig, then a Republican. He married Amanda M. Sibley, of Canandaigua, N. Y., in 1828. He died in Saginaw City, Sept. 6, 1857.

WILLIAM A. RICHMOND

Delegate from Ottawa and other counties to the First Convention of Assent, 1836; and Senator from the Fifth District, 1844-5. Was born at Aurora, N. Y., Jan. 28, 1808. He was brought up on a farm, educated at Cayuga Academy, was for two years a Clerk in Geneseo, and in 1828 visited Michigan. He was two years clerk in a New York Silk House, and two years in business for himself. In 1836 he settled at Grand Rapids, and with Charles H. Carroll, Lucius Lyon and John Almy purchased the "Kent plat." In 1838 he was appointed receiver of the Ionia land district; in 1845 became Superintendent of Indian affairs under President Polk; and in 1851 was the Democratic candidate for Lieutenant Governor. He was twice Brigadier General of the State Militia, and for several years was Director of the Michigan Southern Railroad. In politics he was a Democrat, in religion an Episcopalian. He was a man of clear intellect and sound judgment. He died at Grand Rapids in 1870.

IRA RIDER

Representative from Washtenaw County, 1853-4. Was a native of the State of New York, born in 1797. He came to Michigan in 1831, and settled in Salem, where he died Aug. 17, 1868. He was a farmer by occupation, and a Democrat in politics.

JOHN MICHAEL RIEGEL

Representative from the Second District of Bay County, 1901-2. Was born in Bavaria, Germany, Dec. 9, 1852. After a course of seven years in the elementary school he studied one year at college in Germany. He came to Michigan in 1881 and engaged in general merchandise business. In politics a strong Republican. He held the office of County Treasurer for two terms, 1894-8. Married.

ALMOND B. RIFORD

Representative from Berrien County, 1869-70 and 1871-2. Was born in Orange County, Vt., Jan. 31, 1839. He removed when young to Middlebury, Ind., was in Hillsdale College four years, and graduated from the law school at Ann Arbor in 1865. He located at Benton Harbor, where he was successful in law practice. In politics he was a Republican. He was Postmaster at Benton Harbor for nearly eight years, until his death, July 10, 1884.

HENRY H. RILEY

Senator from the Fourth District, 1850-1, and 1862. Was born at Great Barrington, Mass., Sept. 1, 1813. He received a common school education, and commenced to learn the trade of a printer at the age of seventeen. In 1837 he became the editor and publisher of the *Seneca Observer* at Waterloo, N. Y., where he remained five years, and studied law. He came to Kalamazoo in 1842, and after six months was admitted to the bar, and began practice at Constantine, always his home. He was four years Prosecuting Attorney. In 1873 he was one of the commissioners appointed to revise the State Constitution. In later years he was a trustee of the Insane Asylum at Traverse City. For many years he was a contributor to the old *Knickerbocker Magazine*, and the "Puddleford papers" first appeared in that monthly, giving him a national reputation. It was published in book form by Derby & Jackson, and republisted by Lee & Shepard, of Boston. These papers were striking and humorous pictures of pioneer life in Michigan. In politics he was a Democrat. In the Senate he succeeded Joseph R. Williams who died in 1862. He died at Constantine, St. Joseph County, Feb. 8, 1888.

CLAUDE N. RIOPELLE

Representative from Wayne County, 1869-70. A descendant of a well known French family, of Detroit, his grandfather having come to this country with the forces of Lafayette during the Revolution. He was born in Detroit in 1845, was educated and graduated at Notre Dame University, at South Bend, Ind., studied law, and was admitted to practice in 1866. He was the first scion of French stock admitted to the bar in Detroit, and was the youngest Representative during his term. He was still in active law practice in Detroit in 1887. His politics were Democratic.

HYACINTHE F. RIOPELLE

Representative from Wayne County, 1883-4. Was born in Wayne County, Mich., Aug. 8, 1836, and was a member of a pioneer French family. He received a common school and commercial college education, and became a teacher. He was Justice after 1863, Supervisor after 1867, and held other local offices. He was a farmer, and a Democrat.

OSCAR A. RIOPELLE

Senator from the Fifth District, 1921—. Was born at Wyandotte, Mich., Aug. 23, 1880, of French parents. He received his education in the public schools of Detroit and attended night classes at the law departments of the Detroit College of Law and the University of Detroit, while employed as cashier of the Board of Water Commissioners. In 1915 he received his degree at the University of Detroit, since which time he has been engaged in the practice of law. Mr. Riopelle was married in 1903 to Mae L. Churchell, of Romeo, Mich., and has a family of nine children. He served as School Inspector of Springwells Township, Treasurer of the village of Delray, Justice of the Peace and Alderman, city of Detroit, and was elected to the Senate Nov. 2, 1920, on the Republican ticket, and re-elected Nov. 7, 1922.

THOMAS C. RIPLEY

Representative from Saginaw County, 1873-4. Was born in the town of Easton, N. Y., Jan. 2, 1807. He received his education in a common school and commenced the study of law. He completed his studies with the late Judge Hurlburt of the State Supreme Court, and afterwards entered into partnership with him. He was a Representative in Congress from the Troy District in 1846-7, to fill a vacancy. In 1854 he removed to Michigan and settled in Saginaw, where he resided in 1887. His occupation was that of a farmer.

ORANGE RISDON

Representative from Washtenaw County, 1838. Was born at Rupert, Vt., Dec. 28, 1786. When young he removed to Saratoga County, N. Y., studied surveying, surveyed 100,000 acres of land in Genesee and Alleghany counties in 1807, and in 1809 helped lay out the cities of Lockport, Brockport and Buffalo, N. Y. He settled at Saline, Mich., in 1824. He laid out the State road from Detroit to Pontiac in 1825, was chief surveyor of the military road from Detroit to Chicago, and from that time until 1856, in the employ of the Government, surveyed 75 townships in Michigan, and resurveyed 45. He was Postmaster of Saline ten years and Justice twelve years. At the time of his death he was the oldest living Knight Templar in the United States, having taken that degree in 1815. He officiated at the laying of the corner stone of the old Capitol at Detroit in 1823, and was present at the laying of the corner stone of the new capitol in 1873. In politics he was a Democrat. He died Nov. 28, 1876.

ELIJAH WALDO RISING

Member of the State Board of Agriculture, 1883-9. Son of Sylvester Rising, was born Oct. 8, 1822, in Franklin County, N. Y. In 1843 he married Mary Ann Drake of Onondaga County, N. Y. Mr. Rising's education was limited. In 1848 he and his wife moved to Richfield, Genesee County, Mich. In 1871 they moved to Davison in the same county, where he planned the village of that name. For a number of years he was awarded the first prize on his farm as the best in the county. He was a member of the executive committee of the State Agricultural Society; president of the County Agricultural Society, first President of the village; Postmaster, appointed by President Cleveland during his first term; served as a member of the State Board of Agriculture, 1883-9, by appointment of Governor Begole. He belonged to the Methodist Episcopal Church. In politics he was a Democrat. He died at Davison, Apr. 30, 1893.

OEL RIX

Representative from St. Clair County, 1843 and 1844; and Senator from the First District, 1846-7. Was born at Royalton, Vt., Aug. 1, 1804. He came to Romeo in 1835, and was five years a merchant there; then went to Memphis, and built and used a saw mill and grist mill. He afterwards returned to Romeo, thence back to Memphis. In politics he was a Democrat. He built the first house in the village of Memphis. He died Sept. 8, 1880.

RICHARD B. ROBBINS

Representative from Lenawee County, 1875-6 and 1877-8; and Senator from the Sixth District, 1879-80. Was born at Kingwood, N. J., Apr. 27, 1831. He was admitted to the bar of Lenawee County in 1859. In 1862 he received a commission as Second Lieutenant, and raised a company for the Fourth Mich. Cavalry. He was gradually promoted and finally was Brevetted Lieutenant Colonel, U. S. Volunteers, Mar. 13, 1865, "for gallant and meritorious services." He was mustered out July 20, 1865. He served three terms as Justice in Adrian, and one term as Mayor. He was chairman of the Republican County Committee for four years. In politics he was a Republican. He served several years as consul in Canada.

ALTON T. ROBERTS

Senator, 1915-16 and 1917-18, from the Thirty-first District, comprising the counties of Alger, Dickinson, Gogebic, Iron and Marquette. Was born in Stockton, Me., Mar. 9, 1880. He was educated in Phillips Exeter Academy and Harvard College. He removed to Michigan and engaged in the real estate and publishing business. In politics a Republican.

CHRISTOPHER T. ROBERTS

Representative, 1893-4, from the District composed of the counties of Dickinson, Baraga and Iron. Was born in Cornwall, England, in 1851. In 1872 he came to Michigan locating in the mining regions of the Upper Peninsula, where he engaged in the mining interests. He located at Crystal Falls, engaged as mining expert. In politics a Republican. He held the office of Supervisor of Crystal Falls ten years.

ELIJAH J. ROBERTS

Delegate from Chippewa County to the Constitutional Convention of 1850; Representative from Keweenaw County, 1850; and Senator from the Sixth District, 1851. Was a native of New York, and in 1850 gave his age as 52. He was by profession a lawyer, and was in earlier life in professional practice at Detroit. He was Master of Chancery in 1839; Justice in 1835-6; publisher of the *Craftsman* in 1838; merged it in the *Morning Post and Craftsman* in 1839 and 1840; School Inspector, 1842; and Adjutant General of Michigan, 1842 to 1844. He went to the Upper Peninsula in 1847. He died Apr. 26, 1851.

JOHN ROBERTS

Senator from the Twenty-first District, 1857-8. Was born in Warwick, Bucks County, Pa., Mar. 17, 1812. He came to Jonesville in 1840, and located at Hastings in 1845. By profession he was a physician and surgeon, in politics, first Whig, then a Republican. He was Postmaster of Hastings from 1847 to 1851, and again from 1869 to 1876. He was appointed examining surgeon of Barry County at the close of the war, and held it until his death, Dec. 18, 1886.

ALEXANDER ROBERTSON

Representative from Cass County, 1873-4. Was born Mar. 3, 1826, in Argyle, N. Y. In 1835 he removed to Spafford, N. Y. He received a high school education. In 1854 he removed to Michigan, and settled in Pokagon, Cass County, where he still resided in 1887. He served in several offices of trust in his town and county. By occupation he was a farmer.

ANDREW S. ROBERTSON

Delegate from Macomb County to the Constitutional Convention of 1850; and Senator from the Fourth District, 1863. Was born in Brumley, England, Aug. 12, 1822, and was educated at the University of Glasgow. He came with his parents to this country in 1836, who settled at White Lake, Mich. The son became a teacher in Oakland and Macomb counties, studied law, and was admitted in 1846, and commenced practice at Mt. Clemens. He died while Senator in 1863, and a fitting eulogy was delivered by Gov. Croswell, then a Senator, Dec. 20, 1864. In politics he was a Democrat.

ARCHIBALD ROBERTSON

Representative from the First District of Saginaw County, 1915-16 and 1923—. Was born in New York city, April 7, 1850, of American-Scotch parentage. He established the Robertson Valley Laundry in Saginaw forty-three years ago, and has since continued in the business. Prior to that time he was engaged in the life insurance business. Mr. Robertson is a Republican and has held the office of Supervisor for seventeen years.

GEORGE ROBERTSON

Representative from Calhoun County, 1879-80 and 1881-2. Was born in Dryden, N. Y., March 20, 1826. He came to Albion, Mich., with his parents in 1837, and was educated in public schools and Albion Seminary. After 1850 he was a farmer at South Albion. He was a Democrat until 1872, then a Republican. He died at Albion, Mar. 3, 1889.

JOHN M. ROBERTSON

Representative from the Second District of St. Clair County, 1895-6. Was born of Scotch parentage, in Algonac, May 26, 1846. He attended the public schools of Algonac, and at seventeen years of age enlisted in Co. I, 1st Mich. Engineers and Mechanics, serving until the close of the war, participating in the campaign from Chattanooga to Atlanta, and in Sherman's march to the sea; was at the surrender of Johnston's army at Raleigh, and in the grand review of Sherman's army at Washington, May 24, 1865. After the war he sailed on the lakes until 1872; married and settled in Algonac, where he engaged in conveyancing, insurance, and as a pension attorney. A member of the G. A. R., Maccabees and a Mason. In politics a Republican. He held the offices of Supervisor and Justice of the Peace for a number of years, and for ten years Deputy Collector of Customs.

LESLIE B. ROBERTSON

Delegate in the Constitutional Convention of 1907-8, from the Fifth District, Lenawee County. Was born in Ogden Township, Lenawee County, in 1871. He received his education in the West Blissfield schools, graduating from the high school in 1888, and from the law department of the University of Michigan in 1891. He was engaged in the active practice of the law in Adrian until 1901, when he became connected with the Page Woven Wire Fence Company. He was married in 1899 to Bertha H. Page, of Adrian.

ALFRED T. ROBINSON

Representative from the First District of Saginaw County, 1919-20 and 1921-2. Was born in Vassar, Mich., Sept. 22, 1864, of English parentage. He was educated in the public schools of Vassar and at the University of Chicago. He worked in various railroad offices fifteen years, and for the past ten years has been engaged in the real estate and insurance business in Saginaw. Mr. Robinson is married and has one son and two daughters. In politics he is a Republican.

CARL A. ROBINSON

Representative from the First District of Calhoun County, 1917-18. Was born in LaGrange, Ill., June 20, 1886. His early education was obtained in the public schools, and his legal education was secured under a preceptor in a Chicago law office. He was admitted to the Illinois bar in 1913, and the Michigan bar in 1914. He was married Sept. 29, 1914, to Catherine Van Court, of Memphis, Tenn. A member of the Masonic and Woodman lodges. In politics a Democrat.

ELISHA S. ROBINSON

Delegate from Jackson County to the Constitutional Convention of 1850. Was born in Saratoga County, N. Y., Mar. 2, 1801. He received a limited education and learned the trade of a tanner, which he followed, combined with harness and shoe making, for years. He settled as a farmer in Waterloo, Mich., 1843. He was a Supervisor for seventeen years, Justice twelve years, and held other offices. In politics he was a Democrat.

GEORGE J. ROBINSON

Representative from Alpena and other counties, 1883-4. Was born in Detroit, Mich., Feb. 3, 1838, and was educated in the public schools. He was engaged in mechanical, commercial and speculative pursuits; and was a commissary clerk during Sherman's march to the sea. He was a Republican until 1876, then a Democrat.

GEORGE P. ROBINSON

Representative from Branch County, 1875-6. Was born June 7, 1827, at Swanton, Vt. He received a common school education and removed to Noble, Mich., in 1863. He held the office of Supervisor. By occupation he was a farmer; in politics a Republican.

HIRAM WHITE ROBINSON

Representative from the Third District of Saginaw County, 1889-90 and 1891-2. Was born at Ithaca, N. Y., in 1837. Mr. Robinson graduated from Hamilton College in 1859. His occupation was that of a dealer in real estate and farming. He was elected on the Democratic ticket to the House of 1889-90, and re-elected to that of 1891-2.

JAMES L. ROBINSON

Representative from Cass County, 1899-1900 and 1901-2. Was born in Howard Township, Cass County, Jan. 28, 1848, and was educated in the public schools of Howard and Jefferson Townships. At the age of nineteen he removed to Jefferson Township and thence to Calvin Township at the age of twenty-four. While farming was his principal occupation he was a trusted adviser for a large number of people in the county as guardian for minors and administrator for numerous estates. At the time of his election to the House of 1899-1900 he was serving in that capacity for eight estates. Politically he was a Republican, and a persistent worker for the entire ticket, serving many terms as a member of the Republican County Committee.

JAMES W. ROBINSON

Representative from Montcalm County, 1887-8. Was born near Port Huron, Mich., Sept. 11, 1854. He attended public schools, and at the age of twenty-one was Clerk of Jonesfield, Saginaw County. He was Supervisor, and Superintendent of schools, and later became a merchant and shingle manufacturer at Vestaburg, and was Supervisor there four terms. In politics he was a Fusionist.

LOTE C. ROBINSON

Representative from the First District of Calhoun County, 1903-4. Was born in the Township of Battle Creek, Nov. 15, 1857. He received his education in the district schools of the county. When ten years of age his parents moved on a farm in Eckford Township. He was married Dec. 15, 1880. In politics a Republican. He was chairman of the Republican County Committee for two years and was re-elected in September. He held the offices of Clerk and Treasurer of his township.

ORRIN W. ROBINSON

Representative from Houghton County, 1895-6; Senator from the Thirty-second District, 1897-8; and Lieutenant Governor, 1899-1901 and 1901-3. Was born in Claremont, N. H., Aug. 12, 1834, where he acquired a district school education. At the age of nineteen years he moved to Ontonagon, Mich., where he remained two years and then started for Green Bay, Wis., making an overland trip with snow shoes, while the provisions and blankets were carried by dog-train. He camped in the woods nights, taking about two weeks to make his trip. From Green Bay he went to Kossuth County, Ia. In May, 1862, he returned to Hancock, Houghton County, Mich., where he engaged as receiving and shipping clerk for the Quincy mine, which occupation he followed twelve years. In 1873 he organized the Sturgeon River Lumber Company, and built mills at Hancock, which were removed to Chassel in the fall of 1887. In politics a Republican. He was Deputy Collector of Customs, and Superintendent of the Poor for Houghton County; was Delegate to the National Convention in 1892.

RIX ROBINSON

Senator from the Fifth District, 1846 and from the Seventh District, 1847 to 1849; and Delegate from Kent and Ottawa counties to the Constitutional Convention of 1850. Was born in Richmond, Berkshire County, Mass., Aug 28, 1792, and moved to Cayuga; studied law and was admitted to the bar in 1811; evaded draft of 1812. He was protege of Astor. He became an Indian trader in the Grand River Valley in 1821, and was the first white settler in Kent County. He established several trading posts, the central one at Ada, where he died. When lands were opened for settlement he became a farmer. In 1887 a monument was erected to his memory in Ada. He was Supervisor; Associate Judge; and commissioner of Internal Improvements in 1846. In politics he was a Democrat. He married an Indian woman who died leaving him a son, Rev. John Robinson. Afterward he married a chief's daughter and refused nomination for Governor by request of the Indian wife. He died in 1873.

ROBERT ROBINSON

Representative from the Second District of Muskegon County, 1887-8 and 1889-90. Was born in Scotland, May 7, 1830. In April, 1849, he immigrated to the United States and was employed in Stack & Patterson's shipyard in Williamsburg, N. Y., and in June of that year removed to Oakland County, Mich., where he worked on a farm until November of that year. He then removed to Saginaw County and entered the employ of James Fraser in the lumber business, continuing there until 1852. Subsequently he went to Muskegon and was employed as a sawyer and log scaler until 1857. His occupation from 1857 to 1889 was farming. He held the offices of Supervisor, chairman of the Board twelve years, Township Clerk, Treasurer, School Inspector and Justice of the Peace. In politics a Republican.

SOLON E. ROBINSON

Representative from Calhoun County, 1873-4. Was born in Clarendon, N. Y., Aug. 17, 1820. He received a common school education. In 1842 he emigrated to Tekonsha, Calhoun County. In 1854 he removed to Battle Creek, and in 1867 to Eckford, where he resided in 1887. He was honored with several official positions in his town and county. His occupation was that of a farmer.

WALTER ROBINSON

Representative from Lenawee County, 1867-8. Was born in Macedon, N. Y., Dec. 17, 1818. He worked on the farm until fourteen years of age, then was clerk in a store for four years, and clerk in the Erie canal collector's office for five years. He came to Adrian in 1846, was engaged in livery and staging for eight years, and then was a merchant for four years. After that time he engaged in farming. He was Deputy Provost Marshal during the war, and for one year Deputy Revenue Collector. Politically he was a Republican.

WALTER CLARENCE ROBINSON

Representative from the First District of Wayne County, 1903-4 and 1905-6. Was born at Uxbridge, Ont., Nov. 21, 1871, of Scotch and English parents. He was educated in the Saginaw common and high schools and Detroit College of Law, receiving the degree of LL. B., from the latter in June, 1893. He carried papers for two years while in high school, later spent five years in newspaper work, and was admitted to the bar in 1892. He studied law as a member of the Cooley Law Club, out which grew the Detroit College of Law, and began the practice in 1892, in the city of Detroit. Married. In politics a Republican.

ANDREW ROBISON

Representative from Washtenaw County, 1859-60. Was born in Phelps, N. Y., Nov. 18, 1800. He was apprenticed to the tanner's trade at Palmyra, N. Y. In 1822 he was married to Gertrude Hoag. He came to Michigan in 1841 and purchased a farm in Sharon, Washtenaw County. He filled various offices of public trust; for several years Justice and Supervisor; and was appointed in 1864 one of the receivers of soldiers' votes in the south. He was a man of pronounced views on all leading subjects. In politics he was a Democrat until 1854. He assisted in the formation of the Republican party, of which he remained a member to the close of his life. He died Jan. 27, 1879.

JOHN J. ROBISON

Senator from the Eighth District, 1863-4; and Representative from Washtenaw County, 1879-80. Was born in Phelps, N. Y., Aug. 13, 1824. He received a common school education, removing to Michigan in 1843, settling in Sharon. His occupation was that of a farmer. He was County Clerk in 1868, and again in 1870; delegate to the Democratic National Convention in 1872; Supervisor several terms. He was twice nominated for Congress in the Second District. In politics he was a Democrat. He was County Clerk of Washtenaw County in 1887.

JOHN ROBSON

Senator, 1901-2, from the Fourteenth District, comprising the counties of Ingham and Shiawassee. Was born in Canada, Aug. 25, 1833. He came to Michigan with his parents in 1837, and located in Farmington, where he studied in the district schools until seventeen years of age, when he entered mercantile life as clerk in a general store. He settled in Lansing in 1854 and continued the mercantile business. He was married. In politics he was a Republican. He held the offices of Alderman and Mayor of the city of Lansing. He died at Lansing, July 14, 1916.

HEWLETT C. ROCKWELL

Representative from the First District of Berrien County, 1891-2. Was born at Tarrytown-on-the-Hudson, N. Y., July 9, 1843. His boyhood days were spent in this historic locality. He attended for several years the Tarrytown Academy. He served for some time in the war in the 25th N. Y. Infantry, and was one of the charter members of George H. Thomas Post No. 14, G. A. R., of this State. He graduated at the Pennsylvania College of Dental Surgery in 1865, and practiced dentistry in St. Joseph and Benton Harbor after 1870. In politics a Democrat, though not a partisan.

KLEBER P. ROCKWELL

Delegate in the Constitutional Convention of 1907-8, from the Twelfth District, comprising the counties of Oakland and Macomb. Was born at Bloomfield, Oakland County, Mich., Nov. 8, 1868, descendant of William Rockwell, who came to this country from England, May 30, 1630. He was reared to young manhood upon his father's farm. His education was obtained in the public schools, supplemented by a college course. He followed the occupation of school teaching until 1892, when he took up the study of law, being admitted to the bar Jan. 8, 1895, and in active practice in Oakland and adjoining counties, maintaining his office with Congressman S. W. Smith of Pontiac. Mr. Rockwell was married to Miss Maud A. King, Sept. 10, 1896. Politically a Republican. He was elected Prosecuting Attorney of Oakland County, in November, 1898, and re-elected November, 1900, and November, 1902. In the Constitutional Convention he was a member of the Judiciary committee and the committee upon public service corporations.

CHANDLER H. ROCKWOOD

Representative from Genesee County, 1867-8. Was born in York, N. Y., May 17, 1825. He received an academical education, worked on a farm, and for two years at making fanning mills. He settled in Flint in 1848, and engaged in the manufacture of fanning mills. He purchased a farm, and after 1856 lived in the town of Genesee. He was Supervisor thirteen years; was Assistant Assessor of Internal Revenue for Genesee, Shiawassee and Clinton counties from 1871 to 1873; deputy collector for eighteen months; and County Treasurer from 1880 to 1885. In politics he was a Republican.

LINCOLN RODGERS

Representative from Muskegon County, 1901-2 and 1903-4. Was born in Muskegon, June 2, 1866, and obtained his education in the schools of his native city. He was a successful manufacturer of lumber and iron in Wisconsin and Michigan for many years. In politics a Republican.

FRANK FOSTER ROGERS

State Highway Commissioner, 1913—. Was born in Raisin Township, Lenawee County, Mich., Aug 30, 1858, acquiring his early education in the rural schools of Lenawee County. He later attended the Raisin Valley Seminary and in the fall of 1879 entered the Michigan Agricultural College, from which he graduated in 1883, receiving the degree of B. S. and later the degree of C. E. After graduation, Mr. Rogers located at Marlette, Sanilac County, where he followed the profession of surveying and civil engineering until 1890, when he removed to Port Huron and continued the same work. He was married at Marlette to Ada A. Lee, daughter of the late Rev. S. P. Lee. He resided at Port Huron until 1905, when he removed to Lansing, having been appointed Deputy State Highway Commissioner when the department was first organized, July 1, 1905. He served as City Engineer of Port Huron for four terms,—1891 to 1899. He served as Deputy State Highway Commissioner under Commissioner Horatio S. Earle and Townsend A. Ely, succeeding the latter to the present office, having been elected Apr. 7, 1913. He was re-elected Apr. 2, 1917, and was elected for a third term Apr. 4, 1921.

JEREMIAH M. ROGERS

Representative from Barry County, 1887-8 and 1889-90. Was born in Hector, Tompkins County, N. Y., Mar. 17, 1832. He came to Michigan with his parents in 1836, settling at Carlton, Barry County. He engaged in farming and stock buying principally, and in addition, buying grain and farm products and selling agricultural implements at Hastings. He was a Republican member of the House of 1887-8, and was re-elected on the same ticket to the House of 1889-90.

LEVI ROGERS

Representative from Washtenaw County, 1841. His postoffice address was Fredonia. (Further data not obtainable).

TOM F. ROGERS

Representative from Muskegon County, 1915-16. Was born at Ravenna, Mich., Oct. 29, 1852, of Irish and Scotch parents. He was educated in the public schools and the Michigan Agricultural College. After leaving college he taught school for four years and read law one year in the law firm of Smith, Nims, Hoyt & Erwin, in Muskegon. He later engaged in the drug business at Ravenna. In the spring of 1878 he removed to Lakeview and established the Lakeview *Enterprise* which he conducted for ten years. He returned to Ravenna in 1888 and established the Ravenna *Times*. Married. In politics a Republican.

JOHN J. ROGNER

Representative from the First District of Tuscola County, 1893-4 and 1895-6. Was born in Germany in 1838; at the age of thirteen years he came to America with his parents, locating on a farm in Saginaw County, Mich., where he worked with his father and attended night schools. In 1861 he removed to Tuscola County, locating on a farm in Denmark Township. In politics a Republican.

JAMES W. ROMEYN

Representative from Wayne County, 1869-70; and Senator from the First District, 1871-2 and 1883-4. Was born in Detroit in 1839. He graduated at Columbia College, N. Y., in 1858, studied law, and was admitted to practice in 1860. He was senior aid of the staff of General commanding the 1st division, 9th Army Corps, with a commission in the 4th Mich. Infantry. He also held in this State the rank of Major and Colonel. In politics he was a Democrat. He was Consul in Chili in 1887.

HORACE D. ROOD

Representative from Lapeer County, 1871-2. Was born in Barre, Vt., Dec. 13, 1819. He settled as a farmer in Lapeer County, Michigan, in 1836. He was Treasurer of the Township of Lapeer as far back as 1842, was Supervisor of Lapeer and of Mayfield, Road Commissioner, and a Superintendent of the County Poor for twenty years. In politics he was a Democrat.

ADAM L. ROOF

Representative from Ionia and other counties, 1845; and Senator from the Seventh District, 1849-50. Was born at Canajoharie, N. Y., Feb. 22, 1810. He graduated at Hamilton College, in 1832, was admitted to the bar in 1836, and settled in practice at Lyons, Mich., in 1836. He held the offices of Register of Deeds, Prosecuting Attorney, and Judge of Probate. In 1859 he retired from practice and devoted himself to farming. He was the first lawyer in Ionia County. In politics he was a Democrat. Education, temperance, morality and religion received his support, and he was a strong man in the early days of the Grand River Valley. He died Jan. 26, 1885.

ALBERT K. ROOF

Representative from Ionia County, 1871-2; and Senator from the Nineteenth District, 1887-8. Was born in Lyons, Mich., Apr. 6, 1841. By profession he was an attorney at law. He was a graduate of the law department of the State University at Ann Arbor. He held the office of Township Treasurer, Justice, Register of Deeds, was chairman of the Board of Supervisors in 1878 and 1886. He was elected Senator on the Fusion ticket.

JOHN ROOST

Representative from Ottawa County, 1871-2; and Senator from the Twenty-third District, 1883-4. Was born Oct. 9, 1823, in Harderwyk, Netherlands. He emigrated to this country in 1847, locating in Ottawa County, then a part of Kent. He followed his trade as a wagon-maker. He removed to Holland in 1854, and was Supervisor in 1858-59-60. The "Holland Colony" in 1859 appointed Mr. Roost financial agent to negotiate a loan of $30,000 to open a harbor, connecting Black River and Lake Michigan, which he accomplished in the East, Gerrit Smith being the first one to invest in the bonds. Soon after he secured 11,000 acres of swamp land from the State for the same purpose. In 1860 he established "De Grondwet," a Holland Republican paper, which had great influence in politics. In 1861 he became Postmaster but was removed by Pres. Johnson, and in 1862 U. S. Enrolling Officer and Assistant Assessor. He was a Republican until 1876, then a Democrat. He died May 31, 1885, at Holland, Mich.

AMOS ROOT

Representative from Jackson County, 1853-4. Was born at Fort Ann, N. Y., Apr. 8, 1816. With a common school education, at the age of sixteen, he became a clerk at Mohawk, N. Y., where he remained six years. He came to Michigan in 1838, and commenced business at Michigan Center. In 1841 he removed to Jackson. For sixteen years he was a merchant, when he sold out and operated in lands and city property. He also did much hard work to make Jackson a prominent railroad center. He was efficient in building the branch of the Michigan Southern from Jackson to Adrian. He was also one of the main supporters of the Grand River Valley Road, from Jackson to Grand Rapids, and was president of the company for many years. He was for many years a trustee of the village, Alderman of the city of Jackson; Mayor in 1860; Postmaster from 1861 to 1865, member and president of the Board of Public Works, and nine years Inspector of the State Prison. He was first a Whig, from 1848 to 1854 a Free Soiler, then a Republican.

LYMAN C. ROOT

Representative from the First District of Allegan County, 1915-16 and 1917-18. Was born in Lorain County, O., Sept. 29, 1852, of Yankee parentage. He was educated in the district schools of Allegan County. He engaged in farming. Married. In politics a Republican.

ROLAND ROOT

Representative from Branch County, 1850 and 1851. Was born in Onondaga County, N. Y., Dec. 25, 1813. He received a district school education, taught school, and at the age of eighteen became clerk in a store at Norwalk, O. His employer, Judge Baker, sent him to examine property he had purchased in Branch County. He reported favorably, and was entrusted with $1,600 worth of goods and opened a store in 1835 at Coldwater. He was for a long time the leading merchant of Branch County. He also built and operated a large flouring mill. In 1861 he enlisted in the celebrated Loomis Battery, and became First Lieutenant in October, 1861, but was obliged to resign from ill health in 1862. He married Harriet Chapin in 1837, and his wife and eight children survived him. He died Aug. 11, 1885.

ROSWELL ROOT

Representative from Wayne County, 1841. Was born in New Hampshire in 1780, and settled in the Township of Plymouth, in 1825, locating land upon which he lived until his death in 1873. He was Justice from 1826 to 1842, and Postmaster of Borodino postoffice 1826 to 1860, when the office was discontinued. He was also Supervisor for several terms. He was Whig and Republican in politics.

WILLIAM W. ROOT

Representative from Ingham County, 1881-2. Was born in Cato, N. Y., June 28, 1837. He received a common school and academical education. He studied medicine, graduated as physician from the Michigan University in 1862, became Assistant Surgeon of the 75th N. Y. Volunteers, afterwards Surgeon, served until the close of the war, and was Executive Officer of the 18th Army Corps Hospital during Sheridan's campaign in the Shenandoah Valley. Afterwards he attended and received a degree at Bellevue Hospital College. He settled in practice at Mason, Mich., in 1866, and held several terms as Supervisor, served many years on the Board of Education, and was four years president of the County Agricultural Society. In politics he was a Republican, then a Prohibitionist.

ASA D. RORK

Representative from Barry County, 1877-8. Was born Feb. 29, 1832, at Sheridan, N. Y. His parents removing to Wisconsin in 1841, he resided in that State until 1843, in which year they came to Rutland, Mich., where he continued to reside. He received a common school education, taught school several terms, and entered the State Normal School in 1854, but on account of the death of his father left school to take charge of his business. He held various county and township offices, including that of Supervisor for five terms, County Surveyor four years, and County Treasurer four years. His occupation was farming, in politics a Republican.

ALLEN S. ROSE

Representative, 1893-4 and 1895-6, from the Iosco District, composed of the counties of Alcona, Iosco, Ogemaw and Roscommon. Was born in Sullivan County, N. Y., Sept. 6, 1842; attended the common schools, and exchanged his collegiate course for service in the Civil War, being engaged as private and non-commissioned officer in the 128th and 56th New York Infantry, and Lieutenant of 103d U. S. C. Troops. He came to Michigan, locating in Ogemaw County, then unorganized. His postoffice address, Rose City, was named in his honor, as was the township of Rose, in which he resided, in honor of his father. He engaged in real estate, mercantile and lumber business. In politics a Republican. He held the offices of Postmaster, Justice of the Peace, Supervisor, Register of Deeds, County Treasurer, and County Agent for the State Board of Corrections and Charities.

DAVID G. ROSE

Senator from the Fourth District, 1881-2. Was born in Sharon, Conn., Jan. 24, 1826. His parents removed to Sharon in 1833, where he still resided in 1887. He received a common school education. He held several township offices— School Inspector, Justice of the Peace, and Supervisor. In politics he was a Democrat.

ELIAS O. ROSE

Representative from Mecosta and other counties, 1873-4. Was born at Independence, O., Oct. 13, 1838, and was educated at Hillsdale College. He studied law and was admitted in 1859. He lived at Steuben, Ind., two years, then enlisted in the 44th Indiana, became a Lieutenant, in 1862 was wounded and resigned. He removed to Big Rapids in 1863; was Prosecuting Attorney four years, and was a Supervisor and chairman of the Board four years. He started the Big Rapids *Independent* in 1870, afterwards the *Magnet*. In politics he was a Republican.

HARRY C. ROSE

Representative from Gratiot County, 1915-16 and 1917-18. Was born in Watertown, Clinton County, Mich., June 30, 1872, of German and French parentage. He was educated in the district school and the high school at Ashley. He conducted a mercantile business for many years. He held the offices of Supervisor, Township Treasurer and Village Treasurer. Married. In politics a Republican.

WILLIAM H. ROSE

Representative from Clinton County, 1881-2 and 1883-4; and Commissioner of State Land Office, 1905-7 and 1907-9. Was born at Bath, Clinton County, Mich., July 25, 1844. He received his education in the public schools and under private instruction, and at the age of eighteen enlisted in the 15th Regiment Mich. Infantry. At the age of twenty-two he was united in marriage to Miss Hattie Gardner of Steuben County, N. Y., and immediately commenced active business as an agriculturists in connection with lumbering and real estate transactions. He was a member of Charles E. Gibson Post, G. A. R., Eastern Star and of the Lansing Commandery of Knights Templar. He held various township offices, County Treasurer, and represented his district as Representative in the Legislature of 1881-2 and 1883-4. He was placed in nomination for Land Commissioner at the Republican Convention held at Detroit, and was elected for the term of 1905-7 and re-elected Nov. 6, 1906. He died at Bath, Nov. 21, 1913.

WILLIAM O. ROSE

Representative from Macomb County, 1845. His postoffice address was Roseville. (Further data not obtainable).

WILLIAM A. ROSENKRANS

Senator, 1911-12 and 1913-14, from the Fourteenth District, comprising the counties of Ingham and Shiawassee. Was born at Flint, Mich., Mar. 25, 1864, of American parents. His education was acquired in the Pinckney, Byron and Corunna high schools, graduating from the latter in 1884. He immediately secured a clerkship in the then First National Bank, now the Old Corunna State Bank, and remained with the institution having served as its cashier since 1894; also connected with other financial institutions, being vice-president of the State

Savings Bank of Owosso, Mich., and the Bank of New Lothrop, Mich. He was married in 1891 to Hattie E. Harper, daughter of Judge A. A. Harper. He was Mayor of the city of Corunna for four successive terms, member of the Board of Education of Corunna for fifteen years and in 1897 was appointed by Governor Warner a member of the Board of Control of the Industrial School for Boys, which position he resigned upon election to the Senate. A member of the Masonic fraternity and the Order of Elks. In politics a Republican.

GILES ROSS

Representative from Livingston County, 1871-2 and 1877-8. Was born in Dover, N. Y., Mar. 23, 1816. His education was acquired in district schools. In 1826 he removed to Cayuga County, N. Y., where in 1846 he was Justice. He was appointed collector of canal tolls at Montezuma, N. Y., for two terms. In 1862 he removed to Hartland, Mich. In 1863 he was elected Supervisor. He was a farmer by occupation. In politics he was a Democrat.

HENRY T. ROSS

Representative from Livingston County, 1915-16, 1917-18 and 1919-20; and Senator, 1921—, from the Thirteenth District, comprising the counties of Genesee and Livingston. Was born Nov. 5, 1883, and has always lived in Brighton Township, Livingston County, Mich. He was educated in the district schools of that township and the Michigan Agricultural College. After graduation from the college, he returned to the farm which he has since operated. He is married. He was Supervisor of his township for four years and was chairman of the Board when elected to the Legislature in 1914. He has always been a Republican.

JOHN D. ROSS

Representative from the Delta and Menominee District, 1879-80. Was born in Lancaster, Ontario, Canada, Feb. 16, 1844. He received a common school education and followed the mercantile business previous to coming to this country. He came to Michigan in the spring of 1867 and engaged in the lumber trade which he followed. He was elected Supervisor of the Township of Ford River in 1874, which office he held for many years and served as Chairman of the Board of Supervisors of Delta County. In politics he was a Republican.

JOHN D. ROSS

Representative from Berrien County, 1855-6. Came from Indiana in 1834, and settled on the present site of Buchanan, Mich., where he resided until his death in 1888. He was for many years a merchant, and in 1864 became a banker. He was President of the village of Buchanan in 1859, 1861-2-3, and 1879, also a member of the common council, and was a prominent citizen. In politics he was a Democrat. He was the first Postmaster from 1848 to 1852.

JOHN Q. ROSS

Lieutenant Governor, 1911-13 and 1913-15. Was born on a farm near Jamestown, O., June 28, 1873, and received a common school education. He studied law with Jones and Clark at Muskegon, was admitted to the bar July 9, 1894, and engaged in the active practice of law. For a number of years he was a director of the Muskegon Chamber of Commerce and was its president in 1909. He was the first president of the Western Michigan Development Company. Mr. Ross was married June 12, 1900, to Katherine B. Schwedler. He was the nominee of the Republican party for Lieutenant Governor at the primary election, Sept. 6, 1910, and was elected Nov. 8, 1910; was renominated at the primary election, Aug. 27, 1912, and elected Nov. 5, 1912. He died at Muskegon, May 12, 1922.

FRANK G. ROUNSVILLE

Representative from Livingston County, 1887-8. Was born in Unadilla, Livingston County, Feb. 18, 1848. Was a resident of Michigan all his life, except during the years from 1854 to 1862. By occupation he was a farmer and grain dealer. Mr. Rounsville filled the offices of Clerk three years, Trustee two years of the village of Fowlerville, President four years, and Supervisor of Township two years. In politics he was a Republican.

HENRY ROUTHIER

Representative from the Second District of Marquette County, 1889-90. Was born at Montpelier, Vt., Mar. 2, 1850. His parents were French Canadians, and when he was five years of age they removed to Canada, where his father engaged in farming. The subject of this sketch attended St. Mary's College, completing the full course in French and English, and when thirteen years of age entered a mercantile house, serving as a clerk three years, thence emigrating to the United States, where he learned a mechanic's trade. He served as a member of the Common Council of the city of Ishpeming three years, having been elected in 1888 for a second term and meeting no opposition. In politics a Republican.

JOHN C. ROWDEN

Representative from the Second District of Bay County, 1891-2. Was born in Devonshire, England, Feb. 9, 1844; at 11 years of age he came with his parents to this country and settled temporarily in Troy, Oakland County; two years after they located in North Williams, Bay County, then a wilderness, with no improved roads nearer than twelve miles. He acquired a fair education chiefly by his own persistent will outside of the school room, he never having had the privilege of attending school over three years' time all told. In August, 1862, he enlisted as a private in Co. F, 23d Reg. Mich. Infantry Vols., and was with that organization until the close of the war and in all its engagements with the enemy. He was wounded at Allatoona, Ga., May 28, 1864, in left hip, and at Franklin was grazed by a bullet on the head, causing a depression of the skull bone. He was discharged July 28, 1865, as Orderly Sergeant. After returning home he located on the same farm on which he resided in 1891, having subdued it from a heavy wilderness to a well cultivated farm. He was elected to the House of 1891-2 on the Industrial and Democratic tickets.

FLOYD W. ROWE

Representative from Hillsdale County, 1921—. Was born in Steuben County, Ind., June 8, 1861, of English parents. He came to Michigan at the age of eight years, his education being acquired in the district schools. He was engaged in farming and general merchandising. In 1904 he established a private bank at Camden, Mich., later organizing the Montgomery State Bank. He was for ten years president of the Tri-State Live Stock Shippers' Association and is a member of the Executive Committee of the National Live Stock Shippers' League. Mr. Rowe is married. In politics he is a Republican.

FREDERICK C. ROWE

Senator from the Fifth District, 1919-20. Was born June 16, 1872, on a farm near Belleville, Wayne County, Mich., of English parents. He was educated in the district schools. Leaving the farm at the age of nineteen years, he secured a position as locomotive fireman on the Michigan Central Railroad at Detroit. After serving in that capacity for ten years, he was promoted to engineer. He served the Brotherhood of Engineers in various capacities, and in 1908 was elected chairman of the board of adjustment for the Michigan Central engineers. Married. In politics a Republican.

GEORGE EDWIN ROWE

Delegate in the Constitutional Convention of 1907-8 from the Seventh District, Kent County. Was born in Fowlerville, N. Y., in 1864, of English descent. He received his education in the Grand Rapids schools, Little Rock University and the Chicago University. In 1892 he married Eckka M. Robinson. Mr. Rowe entered the ministry in 1891. He was a horticulturist for many years and editor of the *Fruit Belt*.

SQUIRE W. ROWE

Representative from Oakland County, 1865-6. Was born at Camillus, N. Y., June 1, 1815. He settled as a farmer in Highland, Mich., in 1835, locating twenty-five miles from a grist mill or postoffice. He was many years Supervisor, and raised a company for the 13th Michigan, but ill health prevented active service. He died Nov. 19, 1866, during his official term.

DAVID H. ROWLAND

Representative from Wayne County, 1843 and 1844. Born in Newton, Fairfield County, Conn., May 10, 1798. He came to Michigan in the fall of 1833; was by occupation a merchant, and in politics a Democrat. He was for a time a teacher, also a local Methodist Episcopal minister, and a man of strict integrity. He died June 11, 1860.

THOMAS ROWLAND

Secretary of State, 1840-2. Was a native of Ohio, and served as a Major of Infantry under General Hull in 1813-14. He was Secretary of the Territory; United States Marshal for the Detroit district; Postmaster of Detroit under President Harrison, 1843 to 1845; and Secretary of State under Governor Woodbridge. He was a man of culture and highly esteemed. A paper of his on "Hull's Campaign," read before the Detroit Lyceum in 1819, has been quoted with commendation. He was secretary of the corporation of Detroit from 1815 to 1820, and his private seal was made the seal of the corporation; was Clerk of the County Court from 1815 to 1820; United States Pension Agent, 1824 to 1831; Probate Judge of Wayne County, 1833-4; editor of the Detroit *Journal* from 1832 to 1834; vice president of the Michigan Historical Society, and held many other positions. He was a leading citizen of the Territory and State for more than half a century. He died in Detroit in 1848.

WILLIAM A. ROWLEY

Representative from the First District of Macomb County, 1895-6 and 1897. Was born in Shelby Township, Macomb County, Nov. 8, 1843; attended the district schools, working on the farm summers. August, 1861, he enlisted in Co. B, 5th Mich. Infantry, and served until the close of the war; returned to Shelby and engaged in farming. In the spring of 1876 he removed to Clinton Township, where he continued in the occupation of farming. In politics he was a Republican. He was Treasurer of the Township of Shelby, and Supervisor of his home township; was elected Representative to the House of 1895-6, and re-elected to that of 1897-8. Mr. Rowley died July 19, 1897.

HARVEY B. ROWLSON

Representative from Hillsdale County, 1869-70. Was born at Duanesburg, N. Y., July 15, 1825. He received a common school education, and in 1843 spent several months in the printing office of the Adrian *News*, which in 1844 was removed to Hillsdale, and became the Hillsdale *Gazette*. In 1846, with S. D. Clark, started the Hillsdale *Whig-Standard*, and in 1851 became sole proprietor, and was editor and proprietor, the paper later being the Hillsdale *Standard*. He was eight years County Treasurer, was Collector of Internal Revenue for first district in 1869 to 1873, and of third district, 1873 to 1883, and 1885 was appointed member of the Board of Control of the State Reform School for six years. Politically he was a Whig until 1864, then a Republican.

GEORGE F. ROXBURGH

Representative from Osceola County, 1923—. Was born in Perth County, Ontario, June 24, 1864, of Scotch, Dutch and English ancestry. When eight years of age he removed with his parents to Michigan and they located in Lake County. In 1877 the family removed to Reed City where he attended public school. Later he attended the Ferris Institute at Big Rapids and the Valparaiso (Indiana) University. For a time he taught in the rural schools, afterwards

holding the Superintendency of Schools of Tustin, Marion and Evart. He served
on the Board of County School Examiners for five years and was Commissioner
of Schools of Osceola County for fifteen years, resigning to accept the Secretary-
ship of the teachers' retirement fund board at Lansing, which position he held
two years. During the time he was commissioner he taught three summer
terms at the Central Normal School and was also a member of the teachers'
reading circle board. Mr. Roxburgh is a Republican.

JOHN V. RUEHLE

Representative from Wayne County, 1844. Was born at Langensteinbach,
Baden, Germany, Sept. 4, 1812. He attended school until 14, then learned the
trade of a baker. He emigrated with his parents to Detroit in 1832. He was
Captain of the Scott Guards of Detroit from 1841 to 1846; Alderman of the 6th
ward, Detroit, in 1840 and 1841; Water Commissioner 1859 to 1861; Greenback nominee for Congress in 1876; Boulevard Commissioner of Hamtramck in
1880. In 1847 Michigan furnished a regiment of volunteers for the War with
Mexico, which went out under Colonel Stockton. A. S. Williams was Lieut.
Col.; J. V. Ruehle, Major; and J. E. Pittman, Adjutant. The regiment was
mustered out in 1848, having seen little service before the close of the war. In
1861 he became Lieut. Colonel of the 16th Mich. Infantry, but after eight
months' service resigned and was honorably discharged. In politics he was a
Democrat.

THEODORE CHRISTIAN RUFF

Representative from the Second District of St. Clair County, 1913-14. Was born
at St. Clair, Mich., June 21, 1871, of German parentage. He was educated in
the public and parochial schools. He served as Alderman and Mayor. Married.
He engaged in farming and dairy business. In politics a Democrat.

GEORGE W. RULISON

Representative from the Second District of Houghton County, 1897-8, 1899-1900
and 1901-2. Was born in Watertown, Jefferson County, N. Y., Mar. 7, 1834.
He was born on a farm where he lived until he was seventeen years of age. He
acquired his early education in the district school, supplemented by a normal
and academic course. After completing his course he took Horace Greeley's
advice and came West, locating in Wisconsin in 1855. Spending two years in
Wisconsin and Minnesota he went to Kansas in 1859 and remained there one
year, then he went to Colorado and engaged in gold mining, where, meeting with
very poor success, he returned to Wisconsin and taught school for two years.
In 1866 he moved to Houghton County, Mich., where he engaged in various
occupations, spending most of his time in teaching and clerking for a lumber
and mill yard firm. In politics he was a Republican. He held the offices of
Supervisor, School Inspector, Justice of the Peace, County Clerk and Village
Trustee.

JAMES FULTON RUMER

Senator, 1905-6, from the Thirteenth District, comprising the counties of Genesee and Livingston. Was born of American parentage, in Logan County, O., Dec. 12, 1852. He was educated in the common schools and Huntsville College, of Ohio; taught school for a number of years, attended the Rush Medical College, and was graduated from the Kentucky School of Medicine, Louisville, Class of 1889. In politics a Republican. He held the offices of President of Davison village, president of the School Board twelve years, and president of the Genesee County Medical Society.

JOHN G. RUMMELL

Representative from Saginaw County, 1883-4. Was born in Bavaria, Germany, Apr. 13, 1843, and came to this country with his parents in 1851, when they settled in Frankenmuth, Mich. He received a common school education, and resided there, except two years in Illinois, working at his trade as carpenter. He engaged in farming for many years. He held the office of Justice seven years, and the office of School Inspector three terms, and was secretary of the German Relief Society for ten years. In politics he was a Democrat.

HENRY RUMSEY

Member of the Legislative Council from Washtenaw County, 1828-9; and Senator from the Fourth District, 1835-7. His address was Ann Arbor. (Further data not obtainable).

MARSHALL E. RUMSEY

Representative from the Second District of Ingham County, 1885-6 and 1887-8. Was born in Bethany, N. Y., Jan. 17, 1840. He received his education at the Academy in Bethany Center, and at the high school in Geneseo, Livingston County, N. Y.; worked at farming during the summers and taught school winters, from 1857 to 1862. In 1862 he removed to Illinois, doing business in Chicago most of the time until 1867, when he came to Leslie, Mich., where he engaged in farming, lumbering, real estate business, and banking; was for several years a member of the Village Council and twelve years member of the School Board; was elected president of the First National Bank of Leslie, in Aug., 1883. In politics he was a Republican.

HIRAM D. RUNYAN

Representative from Macomb County, 1871-2. Was born in New Jersey, Oct. 10, 1827. He came with his father to Michigan in 1834, and settled on a farm near Utica, but soon removed to Utica; engaged in brick making. On the death of his wife his children were placed among strangers, and the subject of this sketch went to live with a farmer in Disco, with whom he remained until he was twenty-three. He followed farming as an occupation. He held several positions of trust.

PHILIP E. RUNYAN

Representative from St. Joseph County, 1844. Was born in the State of New Jersey, July 14, 1799. By occupation he was a farmer, in politics a Democrat. He removed from the State of New York to White Pigeon, in 1835. He was Supervisor and Town Clerk of White Pigeon. He died June 24, 1845.

LUCIUS E. RUSS

Representative from the Second District of Hillsdale County, 1889-90. Was born in York, Livingston County, N. Y., Dec. 14, 1827, and was raised on a farm in West Bloomfield, Ontario County, N. Y., where he received a good common school education. His father, Deacon Elisha Russ, was born at Woodstock, Vt., Nov. 13, 1792, and was a volunteer in the war of 1812. Mr. Russ married Miss Kate Burrows, of Bridgeport, Conn., on June 7, 1850, and on Feb. 5, 1852, sailed from New York to California. On May 9, 1854, he became a resident of Hillsdale County, where he engaged in farming and saw milling. He settled in the village of North Adams, in November, 1867, where for nearly five terms he was a Justice. He served also as Village Assessor and Village Attorney. In politics a Republican.

FREDERICK J. RUSSELL

Delegate to the Constitutional Convention of 1907-8 from the Twenty-sixth District, Oceana, Lake, Mason and Manistee counties. Was born at Orion, Oakland County, Oct. 7, 1841, and spent his boyhood days on his father's farm which was located on the present site of the city of Greenville. He attended the district school and as soon as possible began teaching, earning enough to enable him to take a course at the State Normal School at Ypsilanti. In the spring of 1860 he located in Oceana County, at that time a wilderness. He responded to the call for volunteers at the beginning of the Civil War and enlisted in the 21st Mich. Infantry. Later he was transferred to the 26th. On account of ill health he was not mustered into service. He was married to Miss Nell C. Gurney. He was elected and held the office of Circuit Court Commissioner for two terms, and later was Probate Judge for nine years. Interested in stock raising, agriculture and horticulture, he marketed as high as ten thousand bushels of fruit in a single season. His cattle and sheep interests were extensive. As a lumberman he assisted in the organization of the Hart Cedar & Lumber Company, and held valuable timber interests in Michigan and the West; also engaged in the banking business. Early in life he joined the Masonic Order.

HENRY C. RUSSELL

Senator from the Twenty-fifth District, 1881-2. Was born in Plainfield, Mich., in 1842. He received a common school education, resided in Grand Rapids several years, became a merchant in 1864 at Cedar Springs, and afterwards a druggist. He was also extensively engaged in lumbering in Lake County, and in banking and farming. He was Supervisor, Town Treasurer and President of the village.

HUNTLEY RUSSELL

Senator from the Seventeenth District, 1905-6 and 1907-8; and Commissioner of the State Land Office, 1909-11 and 1911-13. Was born at New Britain, Conn., in 1858, of Scotch descent. He acquired his education in the public, English and classical schools of Waterbury, Conn., completing his education at Trinity College, Hartford, in 1884. He married Clara C. Comstock, daughter of Congressman C. C. Comstock. He was a civil engineer on the N. Y. & N. E. Railroad, and after coming to Michigan gave his attention to farming. A director of the Commercial Savings Bank, Grand Rapids, and of the West Michigan State Fair Association; a member of the Maccabees, M. W. A., I. O. O. F., B. P. O. E., and York Lodge F. & A. M. He represented the Seventeenth Senatorial District in the State Senate for the years 1905-6 and 1907-8. At the Republican State Convention, held at Detroit, Sept. 29, 1908, he was placed in nomination for Commissioner of the State Land Office and was elected Nov. 3, 1908. He was renominated at the State Convention held at Detroit, Oct. 6, 1910, and elected Nov. 8, 1910.

JAMES RUSSELL

Representative from Monroe County, 1841. His postoffice address was Summerfield. (Further data not obtainable).

JAMES I. RUSSELL

Representative from Monroe County, 1848. Was a farmer and a Democrat. He held many offices of trust in the Town of Summerfield, Monroe County.

JOSIAH RUSSELL

Senator from the Twenty-fifth District, 1853-4. Was born in Neary, Maine, Apr. 25, 1804. He settled in Oakland County, Michigan., in 1835, removed to Ionia County in 1842, and in 1845 to Greenville, where he was elected County Judge, and opened the first Court of Record in Montcalm County. He became a resident of Oceana County in 1859, and was Probate Judge, County Surveyor, and several times Supervisor. He died at Hart, Mich., Apr. 25, 1874.

ORLANDO D. RUSSELL

Representative from St. Joseph County, 1911-12. Was born in Nottawa Township, St. Joseph County, Mich., Mar. 15, 1840, of English parents. He acquired his education in the Sturgis schools and at the Michigan Agricultural College. He was married in 1864 to Miss Louisa Schoch, of New Berlin, Union County, Pa. His early life was spent in farming. He located at Sturgis, where he served as Councilman two terms and Supervisor eight terms. He later engaged in buying farm produce. In politics he was a Republican.

FRANK J. RYLAND

Representative from the First District of Sanilac County, 1891-2. Was born in Rutland County, Vt., Mar. 24, 1838. When 18 years of age he came to Michigan and engaged in farming. He served as Clerk, Treasurer, Justice of the Peace and Supervisor of Elk Township, Sanilac County, serving eight years as Supervisor. He was Census Enumerator for his township in 1890. He was a staunch supporter of the Republican party from its organization.

CHARLES RYND

Member of the Board of Regents of the University of Michigan, 1872-80. Was born in Donegal County, Ireland, Dec. 28, 1836, son of Charles and Anna (Coulter) Rynd. In his fifteenth year he came to Canada alone and settled at St. Mary's. Here he worked on a farm for a time, and was then engaged in teaching for about five years. Meanwhile he studied medicine under the instruction of Dr. Daniel Wilson, of St. Mary's, and later entered the University of Michigan, where he was graduated Doctor of Medicine in 1859. He began practice at Adrian, Mich., the same year, and continued to reside there. He served on the Common Council for four years and also on the Board of Education. In April, 1871, he was elected Regent of the University and served the full term of eight years from January 1, following. He took an active part in politics and was a Delegate to the National Republican Convention at Cincinnati, in 1876. He was a fluent speaker and a ready writer. He was married three times; in 1859, to Elizabeth Hughes, of Ann Arbor, by whom he had two children, Charles and Eva; August, 1866, to Sarah Thomas, of Chatham, Ontario, by whom he had five children, Fred, Lena, Fannie, Anna, and Burke; and in 1879, to Jessie Reid, of Adrian, by whom he had one son, Paul. He died suddenly at Adrian, Aug. 20, 1884.

FRANCIS C. ST. AUBIN

Representative from the Second District of Wayne County, 1855-6. Was of French descent, and a native of Hamtramck, born in 1831. After the annexation he represented his ward at different times as Alderman in the Common Council of Detroit. He was a carpenter and builder by occupation, a Democrat in politics, and died Feb. 15, 1872.

EUGENE G. ST. CLAIR

Representative from the Second District of Marquette County, 1891-2. Was born in Strongsville, Cuyahoga County, O., Apr. 15, 1847, and came to Michigan with his father, J. J. St. Clair, M. D., and settled in Marquette when there were but about 500 inhabitants there. He was educated at the common school at Marquette until he was 15 years old, when his father died, in April, 1861, when the family moved to Albion, N. Y., where he remained until 1866, clerking in a grocery store. After that time he resided in Marquette County, engaged in mining business in all capacities. He served as Township Treasurer of Ely Township from 1868 to 1873. He was elected to the House of 1891-2 on the Republican ticket.

WILLIAM M. ST. CLAIR

Representative from St. Clair County, 1849. Was born in Bedford County, Pennsylvania, Mar. 15, 1809, and moved to Ohio with his parents in 1814. He became there a merchant. He came to Michigan in 1839, and resided at Algonac, St. Clair County, when elected as a Whig Representative to the Legislature of 1849.

JOHN B. ST. JOHN

Representative from Macomb County, 1848. Was born in Rensselaer County, N. Y., Nov. 17, 1804. He came to Michigan in 1830, and settled on a farm three miles west of Utica, which he had purchased in 1827, and where he resided in 1848. In politics he was a Democrat.

MARDEN SABIN

Senator from the Eighth District, 1891-2, and from the Sixth, 1893-4. Was born at Orland, Ind., Jan. 2, 1840. He was raised on a farm just outside the village and prepared for college while attending school winters at the Orland seminary. In the fall of 1859 he entered the literary department of the University of Michigan, where he remained three years and had successfully passed the examination admitting him to the senior class. He went to his Indiana home as usual to work during vacation, when the call came for 300,000 more troops for the struggling Union army and he enlisted as a private in Co. B, 100th Ind. Infantry Volunteers, Aug. 15, 1862. During these three years of service he was promoted to 5th Sergeant of his company, to Captain of his company. He had served as Adjutant of his regiment on staff duty, as member and Judge Advocate on courts martial and had commanded his company while around Atlanta, on the march to the sea and until the muster out in June, 1865. Capt. Sabin then completed a course of study of medicine at Ann Arbor and Cleveland, from which latter college he graduated Feb. 27, 1867. He settled in the practice of medicine at Centerville, Mich., in July, 1867. He was chairman of the School Board and President of the village several successive terms. He died at the home of his son at Battle Creek, Apr. 10, 1917.

DAVID SACKETT

Representative from Wayne County, 1850. Was born in Steuben County, N. Y., in 1817. He came to Michigan in 1831, settling in Redford, where he died July 2, 1880. He was Supervisor, 1852-56, County Auditor, 1857-60, and County Drain Commissioner in 1866. He also held the office of Justice and other local positions. He was a farmer by occupation and a Democrat in politics.

GEORGE W. SACKRIDER

Representative from Saginaw County, 1877-8. Was born near Grass Lake, Mich., Sept. 8, 1842, and received a liberal education at the district and union school of that township. In 1867 he removed to Mason, and engaged in the furniture and lumber trade, and held the offices of Township Clerk and Under-Sheriff. He removed to Oakley, Saginaw County, September, 1871, and engaged in lumbering, farming and general merchandising. He held the office of Supervisor of Brady. In politics he was a Democrat. In 1891 he removed to Owosso, elected Sheriff; moved to Roscommon, was Supervisor several terms. He died at Owosso, Dec. 19, 1919.

***

ABIRAM D. SALISBURY

Representative, 1889-90, from the Midland District, comprising the counties of Clare, Gladwin and Midland. Was born in Jefferson County, N. Y., June 17, 1841. When he was two years old his parents moved to Oakland County, Mich., and from there three years later to Genesee County, locating in what was then the Township of Flint but was subsequently named Burton. He received his early education in the district school at home and the union school at Flint. In 1862 he entered the medical department of the University of Michigan, graduating therefrom with honors in 1865. He at once began the practice of medicine in Genesee County; then he spent the years 1869 and 1870 in Kansas and Nebraska, following his profession successfully, and in 1871 he returned to Michigan and established himself as a druggist, physician and surgeon in Midland. He was Moderator on the School Board of Midland City, County Physician and Mayor of the town twice, and resigned his position as Superintendent of Poor of this county after his election as Representative in the Legislature of 1889-90.

***

IGNATIUS JAMES SALLIOTTE

Delegate in the Constitutional Convention of 1907-8, from the Fourth District, Wayne County. Was born in Ecorse, in 1877, of Irish, French and English descent. He received his education at the Ecorse public schools, Detroit College, where he received the degree of A. B. in 1896, and the Detroit College of Law, graduating therefrom with degree of LL. B., in 1899. In 1905 he was married to Miss Grace Stinson, of Jackson, Mich. He engaged in the practice of law in Detroit, and was Village Attorney of Ecorse.

***

NATHAN SALYER

Representative from Washtenaw County, 1849. Was born in Hopewell, N. J., Mar. 15, 1804. In 1832 he removed to Romulus, N. Y., and was there engaged in various pursuits, among them farming and carriage making. He also held various public offices. He married in 1837, and in 1839 removed to Northfield, Mich., where he engaged in farming. He was Supervisor in 1846 and 1847. In politics he was a Whig.

***

CUMMINGS SANBORN

Representative from St. Clair County, 1842. Was born at North Haverhill, N. H., Jan. 15, 1799. In politics he was a Democrat, in business a lumberman. He came to Michigan as early as 1835, and was a prominent business man. He was Postmaster of Port Huron in 1846. He died Sept. 17, 1852.

JAMES L. SANBORN

Representative from Alpena County, 1907-8 and 1909-10. Was born at Sanborn, Niagara County, N. Y., Mar. 17, 1856, of English and Irish descent, his father being the Hon. Lee R. Sanborn. He received his education in the common schools of Niagara County and the high school of Lima, N. Y. He came to Ossineke, Alpena County, Mich., in the spring of 1873, and engaged in the lumber business, which occupation he followed twenty years. Then gave his attention to real estate and farming, materially aiding in the development of agricultural interests in Northern Michigan. Mr. Sanborn was married to Loretta R. Roberts in 1878. He was President of the county fair, and held the offices of Township Clerk, Treasurer, Supervisor and chairman of the Board of Supervisors. In politics a Republican.

JAMES W. SANBORN

Representative from Lapeer County, 1840 and 1846, and from St. Clair County, 1855-6; and Commissioner of the State Land Office, 1859-61. Was born at Falmouth, Me., in Apr. 1813. He was the son of a physician, one of eleven children. He was in early life a sailor and often crossed the Atlantic. He left the sea at the age of twenty-one, and came to Port Huron in 1835, in company with Abner Coburn, since Governor of Maine; Charles Merrill, late of Detroit; and Joseph L. Kelsey. Together they located 25,000 acres of land in St. Clair and Sanilac counties, and Mr. Sanborn, at the age of twenty-two was left in charge of the purchase. In 1836 he established himself at Metamora, Lapeer County. In 1847 he engaged in the dry goods and lumber business at Port Huron, with Alvah Sweetzer, the partnership being dissolved by the death of the latter in 1864. He had large lumber interests on the Muskegon and its tributaries, the Au Sable, Thunder Bay River, Pine River, on the Cheboygan, and in the Upper Peninsula. He also owned real estate and personal property in Port Huron and Fort Gratiot. He was first a Whig, and was one of the founders of the Republican Party at Jackson, in 1854. He died at Port Huron, April 1872.

WILLIAM SANBORN

Senator from the Twenty-fourth District, 1867-8. Was born in Belgrade, Me., Nov. 2, 1834. By occupation he was a lumberman, in politics a Republican. He was Deputy Commissioner of the State Land Office from 1859 to 1861. He was commissioned Major of the 22d Mich. Infantry, Aug. 8, 1862; Lieutenant Colonel, Jan. 5, 1863; wounded in action at Chickamauga, Tenn., Sept. 20, 1863. He was discharged for disability, June 7, 1864. He was made Brevet Colonel U. S. Volunteers, Mar. 13, 1865, "for conspicuous gallantry at the battle of Chickamauga, Tenn."; and Brevet Brigadier General U. S. Volunteers, Mar. 13, 1865, "for conspicuous gallantry and meritorious services during the war." His residence was at Port Huron for many years. He died at San Diego, Calif., June 23, 1876.

GARRY E. SANDERS

Representative from the Second District of Ingham County, 1909-10. Was born Oct. 4, 1865, near St. Joe, DeKalb County, Ind., of Swiss and English descent.

His education was acquired in the district schools of Indiana and Michigan, and Mason High School, graduating in June, 1886. In April, 1877, he came with his parents to Michigan and they resided in Alaiedon Township until after Mr. Sanders was admitted to the bar in the spring of 1891. For nearly two years he practiced law in Owosso and Eaton Rapids, after which he removed to Mason, Nov. 29, 1892, where he practiced law until Apr. 22, 1897. He then went to Nevada, where he practiced law until 1898. At the beginning of the Spanish-American War, Mr. Sanders organized a company of infantry and was commissioned its Captain by the Governor of Nevada. He was mustered out Sept. 29, 1898, returned to Mason and resumed the practice of law until Feb. 1, 1902, when he moved onto his farm in Vevay Township. In politics a Republican.

RODOLPHUS SANDERSON

Representative from Calhoun County, 1865-6 and 1873-4. Was born in Milton, Chittenden County, Vt., May 30, 1818. He was brought up on a farm and received a common school education. He was first a clerk then a merchant in Milton, Vt., and served two terms in 1849 and 1850 in the Vermont Legislature. On coming to Michigan he purchased a farm in Newton, Calhoun County, where he resided twenty-one years, afterwards moving to Battle Creek. He was Supervisor of Newton for nine years, also Alderman of Battle Creek. At first he was a Whig, after 1854 a Republican.

ASA T. SANDERSON

Representative from the Second District of Saginaw County, 1901-2 and 1903-4. Was born in the Township of Fenner, Madison County N. Y., May 2, 1854. In 1857 he came to Michigan with his parents and located on a farm near St Charles. His education was obtained in the common schools of Saginaw County. At the age of twenty-two he learned the carpenter's trade and conducted lumbering operations and bought out the hardware store of B. J. Downing. He read law two winters, but, failing health compelled him to return to the farm, where he engaged extensively in stock raising and farming. He held all the township offices except that of Clerk. Married. In politics a strong Republican.

GEORGE P. SANFORD

Representative from Ingham County, 1869-70. Was born at Byron, N. Y., July 6, 1835, and came with his parents to Saline, Mich., in 1837. He worked at farming, learned the trade of a carpenter, and taught school. He graduated at the Normal in 1856, and from the University in 1861. The same year he entered the service as Captain in the 1st Mich. Infantry, resigning from ill health in 1862. In 1864 he became Paymaster, with rank of Major. He resigned in 1866 and was brevetted Lieutenant Colonel. Then he resided at Lansing. He was a Republican until 1872, then a Democrat. He owned and edited the Lansing *Journal* from 1872 to 1883; four years member of Board of Education and one year president; Democratic candidate for Regent in 1879, and for Auditor General in 1884; Postmaster, member Democratic State Committee, president of State Press Association, and of the Alumni of the State University.

WILLIAM C. SANSON

Representative from Tuscola County, 1921—. Was born in 1865, in La Crosse County, Wis., of Scotch parents, and came with his parents to Tuscola County, Mich., the same year. He acquired his education in the district schools and at the Michigan Agricultural College, graduating therefrom with the class of 1887. He engaged in teaching school for six years, and was connected one year with the staff of the Industrial School for Boys of Illinois. He engaged in the farming and timber business in Virginia for five years, after which time he and his family returned to his parents' farm in Tuscola County, where he still resides. Has always been closely affiliated with the Republican party, and has held a number of township offices, and in 1917, was elected to the office of County Treasurer.

JOHN R. SANTO

Representative from Grand Traverse County, 1913-14. Was born at London, Ont., June 29, 1865, of English parents, and received his education in the district and city schools. In May, 1892, he was married at Grand Rapids and in 1894 removed to Traverse City. He served as Mayor of Traverse City. He engaged in the fire insurance business. Fraternally a 32d degree Mason, member of K. of P. and past exalted ruler of B. P. O. E. Secretary and treasurer of the Traverse City Refrigerator Company. Politically a Democrat.

EDWARD L. SARGENT

Representative from Emmet County, 1921—. Was born in Orange County, Vt., Apr. 3, 1873, of English and Scotch parents. He received his education in the public school at Saranac, graduating in 1889, and also attended the Ferris Institute at Big Rapids. He was employed for fourteen years as a drug clerk, now being engaged in the retail drug business located at Levering, Mich. Mr. Sargent is married. In politics he is a Republican.

SAMUEL SATTERLEE

Member of the Legislative Council from the Third District (Oakland County), 1834-5. (Further data not obtainable.)

HARRY SAUNDERS

Representative from Wayne County, 1839 and 1844. Was born at Whitehall, N. Y., in 1802. He removed to Michigan with his family in 1832. He filled the office of Supervisor for several terms, and was County Auditor, 1849-52. He was a prominent officer of Militia in New York before coming to Michigan, and in Michigan began with a Captaincy, and was advanced by promotions to the rank of Brigadier General. He was a farmer by occupation, a Democrat in politics.

HIRAM A. SAVAGE

Representative from the First District of Saginaw County (Saginaw city), 1897-8. Was born in Albee Township, Saginaw County, Mich., Aug. 28, 1864. His education was acquired in the district schools and spent his boyhood days on his father's farm. He was married in 1886 and went to Lansing where he entered the employ of James M. Turner, remaining with him until the fall of 1888, when he returned to Saginaw and entered the employ of the Michigan Central R. R. as truck man in the warehouse, being promoted from the warehouse to the office where he secured the position of settlement clerk, then as line and joint abstract clerk, thence billing clerk, then car service clerk, and later as car recorder. In politics a Republican.

WILLIAM SAVIDGE

Senator, 1897-8, from the Twenty-third District, composed of the counties of Muskegon and Ottawa. Was born at Spring Lake, Mich., Sept. 30, 1863. His early education was acquired at Spring Lake and in the Grand Rapids High Schools, and later he entered the University of Michigan, where he graduated with the class of 1884, with degree of A. B. In 1886 he entered the law department of Harvard University, where he remained for two years. On his return from school he became interested in the lumber business, and became vice-president of the Cutler & Savidge Lumber Company. In politics he was a Republican. He died May 9, 1916.

ANDREW J. SAWYER

Representative from Washtenaw County, 1877-8, 1879-80 and 1897-8. Was born in Caroline, N. Y., Nov. 18, 1834. He received an academical education, and engaged in teaching from the age of eighteen to twenty-five. He removed to Michigan in 1857; was admitted to the bar in 1860, and devoted himself exclusively to the practice of his profession. He held various township offices. In politics he was a Republican.

EUGENE F. SAWYER

Delegate in the Constitutional Convention of 1907-8, from the Twenty-seventh District, Wexford County. Was born in Grand Rapids, in 1848, a descendant of English and French Huguenots. Until Mr. Sawyer was twenty-one years of age he lived on a farm near Grand Rapids. He was a graduate of the Grand Rapids High School and of the law department of the University of Michigan. In 1875 he married Miss Kate M. Sipley. In 1873 he removed to Cadillac, where he had a large practice in all the courts of that part of the State.

FRANKLIN SAWYER, JR.

State Superintendent of Public Instruction, 1841-3. A graduate of Harvard University, came to Michigan about 1830, and studied law with Gen. Charles Larned. He was for a short time a law partner of Hon. Jacob H. Howard. He practiced but a few years. He was an editor of the Detroit *Courier*, and afterwards an editor and one of the proprietors of the Detroit *Daily Advertiser*. He was one of the founders of the Detroit Young Men's Society, and its first president. He had literary taste and was a brilliant, forcible writer, and withal a man of public spirit. He was appointed by Gov. Gordon Superintendent of Public Instruction. He gave his whole energy to the work, with important results to education. Soon after leaving office he went to New Orleans and was there several years Superintendent of Public Instruction. He finally went back to his old home in Massachusetts, and died prior to 1887.

JACOB C. SAWYER

Delegate from Lenawee County to the Constitutional Convention of 1867; and Representative from Lenawee County, 1877-8. Was born Dec. 26, 1822, in Manchester, N. Y.; removed to Ashtabula County, Ohio; was admitted to practice law in that state in 1848; removed to Lenawee County, this State, in 1853, and engaged in farming in the township of Medina; was a graduate of the law department of the University of Michigan in the class of 1861.

MEREDITH P. SAWYER

Representative from Menominee County, 1919-20. Was born at Menominee, Mich., July 3, 1890, of American parents. He was educated in the public schools of that city, graduating from the high school in 1907. He entered the law department of the University of Michigan and received his degree in 1911, after which time he practiced law in Menominee. Married. A Mason and also a member of the Knights of Pythias. He was active in war work in 1917 and 1918. He was elected to the Legislature Nov. 5, 1918, and was one of two Democrats to serve in the 1919 Legislature.

WALTER HULME SAWYER

Member of the Board of Regents of the University of Michigan, 1906—. Was born in Lyme Township, Huron County, O., Aug. 10, 1861. He received his high school training in the Grass Lake, Jackson County, High School, after which he entered the medical department of the Universtiy of Michigan, graduating from that institution in 1884. He has been practicing medicine and surgery in Hillsdale since that time. He has been a member of the School Board since 1890 and a trustee of Hillsdale College since 1896. He was a member of the Republican State Central Committee from 1894 to 1898, and served on the State Board of Registration in Medicine from 1901 to 1906. He was president of the Michigan State Medical Society in 1913. He is Michigan member of the legislative council of the American Medical Association, fellow of the American College of Surgeons, member of the State Committee of National Defense, and a member of the state executive committee of the Volunteer Medical Service Corps. He was active in war work and acted as contract surgeon for the United States Army for a short time in 1918. Dr. Sawyer was married to Harriet Belle Mitchell, of Hillsdale, Mich., in 1888, and has one son. He was elected a member of the Board of Regents of the University in April, 1905 and 1913 and was again re-elected Apr. 4, 1921.

WILLIS F. SAWYER

Senator, 1893-4, from the Thirty-second District, composed of the counties of Houghton, Baraga, Keweenaw, Gogebic, Ontonagon and Isle Royale. Was born in Kent, O., Sept. 21, 1858. He graduated from the Kent High School in 1874; worked at the cabinet makers trade four years and engaged in the mercantile business. In politics a Republican. He held the offices of Supervisor and Village President.

ARTHUR WILMONT SAXTON

Representative from the Second District of Jackson County, 1895-6. Was born in Broome County, N. Y., Apr. 7, 1849; received a common school education, engaged in the mercantile business for ten years; entered the medical college of Cleveland, O., graduating in 1879; came to Michigan, engaged in the practice of medicine, locating at first in Ypsilanti, where he remained one year, then moved to Jackson, from which place he removed to Henrietta, in 1885. In politics he was a Republican. Deceased.

IRA T. SAYRE

Senator, 1899-1900, from the Thirteenth District, comprising the counties of Livingston and Genesee. Was born in Hector, Schuyler County, N. Y., Mar. 6, 1858, came to Michigan in 1864, and resided in Genesee County. He was educated at the public schools of Flushing, at the Agricultural College, and at the University of Michigan. He engaged in the practice of law and in farming.

GEORGE W. SCHAEFFER

Representative from St. Joseph County, 1913-14. Was born in White Pigeon Township, Aug. 31, 1864, of English and German descent. He was educated in the district schools and the Sturgis High School. He was Supervisor, also served as Township Treasurer and as School Director. Married. He followed the occupation of farming. In politics a Democrat.

WILLIAM H. SCHANTZ

Representative from Barry County, 1905-6, 1907-8 and 1909-10. Was born at Canal Fulton, Stark County, O., Oct 7, 1850, of German parentage. He acquired his education in the schools of Canal Fulton, O., and Woodland Township, Barry County, Mich., and taught school for four years. He came to Barry County with his father when fourteen years old, and remained on the farm for about six years when he started out for himself. Mr. Schantz had considerable business experience; was employed one year in a railroad office, six and one-half years in the Lumberman's National Bank of Muskegon, and engaged in mercantile pursuits for eight years. After a few more years of office work and traveling salesman, he returned to the farm where he gave special attention to raising pure bred sheep and swine. He served as Superintendent of the sheep department of the International Live Stock Show at Chicago for several years. Married. A member of the Methodist Church, a Mason, State Recorder of the Court of Honor, and member of Star Grange No. 860, of Barry County, and four years was secretary of the Barry County Agricultural Society. In politics a Republican.

PETER SCHARS

Representative from Macomb County, 1865-6 and 1867-8. Was born in Germany, Oct. 24, 1812. His occupation was that of a farmer. He came to Michigan in 1853 and resided at New Baltimore, Macomb County. In politics he was a Republican.

CASPER F. SCHATTLER

Representative from Macomb County, 1875-6. Was born in Germany in 1838, and received an academical education. He removed to Michigan in 1848, and settled in Wayne County. He held the office of Justice, and other positions of trust. By occupation he was a farmer, in politics a Democrat.

B. F. SCHELLBERG

Representative from the First District of Wayne County, 1893-4. Was born in Holstein, Germany, in 1843. He landed at Quebec, Canada, July 25, 1859, and came to the United States in January, 1862, settling in the State of Vermont. He served in the war as private in the 10th Vermont Vols. In 1864 he was married at Montpelier, Vt., to an American girl and the next year came to Michigan, locating at Detroit, where he lived until 1873, when he moved to Alabama. While there he served as Postmaster at Germania for three years, and United States Deputy Sheriff for a short time. In 1880 he returned to Detroit where he engaged in the real estate business. He was awarded his seat in the House of 1893-4 by contest, over Wm. W. Griffin, Democrat.

BARTH W. SCHERMERHORN

Representative from Cass County, 1857-8. Was born in Schenectady, N. Y., Dec. 7, 1823. He came to Michigan in 1851, lived at Niles one year, removed to Cass County. He followed at first the occupation of a farmer, and held many official positions. He was Alderman of his native town, twelve years Supervisor, Justice sixteen years, two years President of Dowagiac and Sheriff of Cass County. In politics he was a Democrat.

HENRY L. SCHMIDT

Representative from the First District of Kent County, 1917-18. Was born in Grand Rapids, Mar. 18, 1891, of German and Austrian parentage. He was educated in the Grand Rapids schools. He was employed in Chicago for four years when he returned and established a merchant tailoring business. In politics a Democrat.

HENRY M. SCHMIDT

Representative from the First District of Saginaw County, 1899-1900. Was born at Saginaw (west side), Jan. 9, 1866. Was educated in the parochial and public schools of Saginaw, and began business life at an early age. In 1884, when but eighteen years old, he engaged in handling meats, continuing in that business seven years, when, upon the death of his father in 1891, he succeeded him in the real estate business, and became a member of the real estate firm of Schmidt & Deindorfer, Saginaw. Somewhat interested in farming, he owned several farms, and a forty acre "truck" garden, all in operation; also secretary of the Hemmeter Cigar Company, of Detroit, and president of the Crescent Cheese and Butter Manufacturing Company of Saginaw. Politically a Democrat. He served his constituents of the twelfth ward two terms in the City Council, holding the position of chairman of the finance and auditing committee in that body four years. He was elected to the House of 1899-1900. The seat was contested in the House, an investigating committee appointed, and after a recount of the votes the committee reported in favor of Mr. Schmidt. Their report was adopted by the House.

JOHN SCHMIDT

Representative from Osceola County, 1913-14, 1915-16 and 1917-18. Was born in Richmond Township, Osceola County, Mich., Mar. 11, 1865, of German descent. He was educated in the district schools and the Reed City High School. At the age of twenty-seven he was married to Miss Mathilde C. Blank. In 1902 he was elected Supervisor and held this office for six consecutive years, being chairman of the board in 1906. He was also treasurer of the School Board for nineteen years and secretary of Richmond Grange for a number of years. He lived on the farm and besides being interested in real estate made a specialty of shorthorn cattle. In politics a Republican.

HENRY R. SCHOOLCRAFT

Member of the Board of Regents of the University of Michigan, 1837-41. Was born in Albany, N. Y., Mar. 28, 1793, and was educated at Middlebury College. In 1817 he visited the West and published "A view of the lead mines of Missouri." In 1820 he was geologist of the exploring expedition, under Gen. Cass, to Lake Superior and the head of the Mississippi, and published a report in 1821, and the next year made a second tour and published his travels in the Mississippi Valley. In 1822 he was appointed Indian Agent for the Northwest; from 1828 to 1832 was a member of the Michigan Territorial Council; in 1822 founded the Michigan Historical Society at Detroit; and in 1831 the Algic Society. In 1832 he discovered the source of the Mississippi; in 1834 made an Indian Treaty that secured 16,000,000 acres. In 1841 he removed to New York city and published valuable works for the State of New York, and for the general government, his various works numbering thirty-one. He was also a fine poet. He died at Washington, Dec. 10, 1864.

JAMES L. SCHOOLCRAFT

Representative from Chippewa County, 1843 and 1844. His postoffice address was Fort Brady. (Further data not obtainable).

ANTHONY B. SCHUMAKER

Senator, 1901-2, from the Fifteenth District, comprising the counties of Eaton and Barry. Was born in Hambach, Prussia, June 1, 1847, where his early education was obtained. In 1854 he emigrated with his parents to America, locating in Coldwater, Mich., where he attended school and later went to school in Elmira, N. Y. At seventeen he entered the drug and grocery business in Coldwater, where he remained eight years, when he went to Grand Ledge and formed the drug and grocery business of Schumaker and Tinkham, later assuming entire control of the business. In politics a strong Republican. Single. He held the position of Alderman and City Treasurer. One of the incorporators of the Grand Ledge Sewer Pipe Company and the Grand Ledge Canning Company.

JOHN E. SCHWARZ

Delegate from Wayne County to the Second Convention of Assent, 1836; Representative from Wayne County, 1845; and Senator from the First District, 1847-8. Was born in Vienna, Austria, in 1799. He received a finished scientific education, part of which was military. His first years in America were spent in Philadelphia. He came to Michigan in 1828, having business connections with John Jacob Astor in the northwestern fur trade, which took him to the distributing points for that trade, and familiarized him with the language and customs of the Indians. He held the office of Adjutant General of Territorial Militia in 1831, and the same office under the State government, 1836-9, and 1844 to 1855. In 1852 he purchased a considerable tract of land and platted what is now the village of Schwarzburg, in Wayne County, where he built a family residence, which continued the home of the family until the death of Mrs. Schwarz, in 1879. During his later years, Gen. Schwarz lived the life of retired farmer until his death in February, 1858. He was buried at Detroit with marked civic and military honors. In politics he was a Democrat.

ARTHUR W. SCIDMORE

Representative from St. Joseph County, 1905-6 and 1907-8. Was born on a farm in Jackson, Mich., Oct. 7, 1867, of American parents. When old enough he became a farm hand, and by carefully saving his money he accumulated enough to attend the Grass Lake High School from which he graduated in 1887. While in high school he was employed as postoffice clerk two years and clerk in a general store for two years more. After finishing high school he attended the University of Michigan and graduated from the medical department in 1890. He immediately located in Three Rivers where he earned an enviable reputation for professional skill and ability. He served in the City Council, on the School Board, and as Mayor of Three Rivers. In politics a Republican.

ANDREW J. SCOTT

Representative from the First District of Saginaw County, 1901-2 and 1903-4. Was born in Canada, Dec. 1, 1840. At the age of thirteen he came to Michigan and engaged in the lumbering business. Married. He held the office of Alderman. In politics he was a Republican.

FRANK DOUGLAS SCOTT

Senator from the Twenty-ninth District, 1911-12 and 1913-14; and member of Congress, 1915—. Was born at Alpena, Mich., Aug. 25, 1878. His education was acquired in the Alpena High School. In 1901 he graduated from the law department of the University of Michigan, and has since practiced law. He has served as Circuit Court Commissioner, Prosecuting Attorney and City Attorney. Mr. Scott is married and has always resided in Michigan. He is a past master of the F. and A. M., and member of the Odd Fellows and Elks. In politics a Republican. He was a member of the State Senate during the sessions of 1911-12 and 1913-14. He was elected to the 64th, 65th, 66th and 67th Congresses, and was re-elected to the 68th Congress Nov. 7, 1922.

GEORGE G. SCOTT

Representative from Wayne County, 1905-6 and 1907-8; and Senator from the Fifth District of Wayne County, 1909-10 to 1917-18. Was born at Detroit, Mich., Sept. 16, 1874, of Scotch descent. He was the son of Rev. John P. Scott, deceased, former pastor of the Second Avenue Presbyterian Church of Detroit. He received his education in the National Normal University of Lebanon, O., graduating from the scientific and business departments and later graduating from the law department of the University of Michigan. A member of the bar of Ohio as well as of Michigan and engaged in the practice of law with offices at 713 Ford building, Detroit. He was married to Miss Hattie A., daughter of Otto and Johanna Krause, June 5, 1907. In politics a Republican.

JOHN SCOTT

Representative from Wayne County, 1842. Was born in Peterboro, N. H., in 1798, and came to Detroit in 1829. He was a mason and builder, and built the old city hall and market in Detroit in 1834. He subsequently became a wholesale grocer. He held at various times the local offices of City Assessor, City Marshal, and Alderman. He was a Democrat in politics. He died in 1846.

SAMUEL M. SCOTT

Representative from Clinton County, 1846, 1848 and 1850. Was born at Stoddard, N. H., June 29, 1814. He was a resident of Keene, N. Y., from 1815 to 1838, then coming to Michigan. He settled in the town of Essex, Clinton County, in 1841, and died in 1850. He held the offices of Sheriff, County Clerk, and Register of Deeds. He was also in early life a teacher, both in New York and this State.

WINFIELD SCOTT

Representative from Wayne County, 1873-4. Was born Sept. 22, 1819, in the town of Ovid, N. Y. He was educated at the Ovid Academy. In 1842 he emigrated to Michigan and settled in Fairfield, Lenawee County. In 1845 he removed to the village of Plymouth, where he resided in 1887. He was Supervisor, and held other responsible offices. By occupation he was a farmer.

JAMES EDMUND SCRIPPS

Senator from the Third District, 1903-4. Was born in London, England, Mar. 19, 1835. He came to this country in 1844, was brought up on a farm in Illinois and received a common school education. He became a reporter for the Chicago *Tribune* in 1857, settled in Detroit in 1859 and managed the Detroit *Tribune* until 1873 when he founded the *Evening News*. Mr. Scripps was married in 1862 to Harriet J. Messinger. He was active in the establishment of the Detroit Museum of Art in 1844, and served as Park Commissioner and member of Detroit Public Library Commission. He received the Republican nomination for the Senate in October, 1902, and was endorsed by the Democrats of the districts. Deceased.

WILLIAM P. SCULLEN

Senator from the First District of Wayne County, 1903-4. Was born in Detroit, Mich., Dec. 12, 1873, of Irish ancestors. He was educated in Detroit College and Detroit College of Law. A lawyer in Detroit. In politics a Democrat.

CHARLES B. SCULLY

Senator, 1917-18 and 1919-20, from the Twenty-first District, comprising the counties of Lapeer and Tuscola. Was born on a farm in Almont Township, June 17, 1878, of American parents. He was educated in the district school and the Almont High School, later studying privately with special training from the Michigan Agricultural College. Mr. Scully is married. He has always been active in social and fraternal affairs; is a member of several Masonic bodies, the Gleaners and the Grange, and president of the Michigan State Association of Farmers' Clubs. He was secretary for three years of the Michigan Berkshire Association, and vice-president of the American Leicester Sheep Breeders' Register Association. He is also well known as a lecturer on agricultural subjects, and is recognized as a pioneer in the good roads movement in Lapeer County. He is affiliated with the Lapeer County Farmers' Mutual Fire Insurance Association and with several other insurance companies. In politics he is a Republican. After holding various township offices he was elected to the Senate in 1916.

JAMES SCULLY

Representative from the First District of Ionia County, 1897-8 and 1899-1900. Was born in Oceola Township, Livingston County, Mich., June 13, 1862; attended district school, supplemented by a course in the Howell High School and Fenton Normal School. His boyhood days were spent on his father's farm, attending school winters and working on the farm summers. In 1888 he commenced the study of law, and was admitted to practice at Ionia May 17, 1890, and engaged in the practice of his profession with J. B. Chaddock as partner. In politics he was a Democrat. He was Attorney for the city of Ionia; elected Representative to the House of 1897-8, and re-elected to the House of 1899-1900. He died at Ionia, Sept. 13, 1913.

GEORGE SEDGWICK

Representative from Washtenaw County, 1850. Was born in Great Barrington, Mass., and came to Ann Arbor, as a lawyer, about 1835. He was Judge of Probate of Washtenaw County from 1840 to 1844. He was a brainy lawyer, active and industrious, and as a man stood high in the estimation of his fellow citizens. He was the head of the law firm of Sedgwick, Gott & Walker. He went to Chicago early in the sixties and became a leading lawyer there. He was a Whig in politics. He died in Chicago.

ELIJAH B. SEELEY

Representative from Hillsdale County, 1839. Was born in 1795, came from Warren, N. Y., in 1835, and settled on a farm in Pittsford, Hillsdale County. He was frequently called upon to fill town offices. He was the first Supervisor in 1836, 1837 and 1838, and also held it in 1840 and 1849. He was founder of the "First Presbyterian Church of Bean Creek," afterwards the "Congregational Church of Hudson," and an elder or deacon for forty years. He died Apr. 10, 1876.

HARVEY SEELEY

Representative from Oakland County, 1843. His postoffice address was Pontiac. (Further data not obtainable).

JESSE SEELEY

Representative from Oakland County, 1847. His postoffice address was White Lake. (Further data not obtainable).

MARVIN L. SEELEY

Representative from the Second District of Genesee County, 1891-2. Was born in Flint, Apr. 15, 1840. His father's family moved on a farm when he was a boy, where he worked and attended school winters; taught school one winter, and finished his school days at the union school in Flint; entered upon the study of law in the office of the late Lieut. Gov. Wm. M. Fenton, in Flint, and after being admitted to practice at the bar of the different courts in the State, he took a one year's course in the law school at the Michigan University. He practiced law in his native city and later went to farming. He served as Supervisor and Justice, and was elected to the House of 1891-2 on the P. of I. and Democratic tickets.

THADDEUS D. SEELEY

Representative from the First District of Oakland County, 1901-2 and 1903-4; and Senator, 1905-6 and 1907-8, from the Twelfth District, comprising the counties of Oakland and Macomb. Was born at Pontiac, Mich., Aug. 26, 1867. He received his education in the common schools of Pontiac, and with the exception of five years in Bay City was a resident of Oakland County. Mr. Seeley was married to Eva Palmer of Pontiac in 1888. He engaged in stock farming, and carried on a general live stock business as shipper and dealer. In politics a Republican. He held various township offices, and was elected to the Legislatures of 1901-2 and 1903-4, was nominated by acclamation, and elected to the Senate of 1905-6 and re-elected Nov. 6, 1906.

L. McKNIGHT SELLERS

Representative from Kent County, 1883-4 and 1885-6. Was born in Franklin County, Pa., July 2, 1849. He received an academical education, learned the trade of a printer, and settled at Cedar Springs in 1869, and founded and owned the Cedar Springs *Clipper.* He was speaker *pro tem.* in 1885. In politics he was a Republican.

ALONZO SESSIONS

Representative from Ionia County, 1857-8 to 1863-4; and Lieutenant Governor, 1877-81. Was born in Marcellus, Onondaga County, N. Y., Aug. 4, 1810. He received a fair education, and became at first a teacher, then a clerk for two years in Bennington, Genesee County. In 1833 he came to Michigan, most of the way on foot, locating land in Ionia County. He clerked at a store in Ohio one year, and afterwards taught school at Dayton, O., until 1835. He settled on a farm in Berlin (then Cass), Ionia County, which always remained his home. He built the second log cabin in the town, and the first bridge across the streams between Saranac and Ionia. In 1837 he married Celia, daughter of Samuel Dexter, the pioneer of Ionia County. He was the first Supervisor in 1883 of Cass (Berlin) and the chairman of the Board of Supervisors. He was Supervisor eighteen times, and often chairman of the Board. He was also Justice several years, and Sheriff of Ionia County in 1841 and 1842. He was Assessor of Internal Revenue for the fourth district for four years. In 1872 he was a Presidential Elector. He helped organize a National Bank in Ionia, and was a director and president from 1866. His farm comprised eight hundred acres, and was well cared for and valuable. He had a family of thirteen children. In politics he was a Republican. He died July 3, 1886, at Berlin, Ionia County.

WILLIAM SESSIONS

Representative from Ionia County, 1873-4. Was born in Marcellus, N. Y., May 2, 1821. He received a common school education. In 1837 he removed to Michigan and settled in North Plains, Ionia County. In 1871 he removed to Ionia, where he resided in 1887. He held several positions of trust in his township. By occupation he was a farmer.

JULIAN M. SEWARD

Representative from Berrien County, 1869-70. Was born in Alexander, N. Y., in 1829. His father settled in Bertrand, Mich., in 1836. The son in early life worked at the clearing of land, farming, and cooperage, and had small oppertunities for an education. He remained at home until 1854, afterwards married, and was Postmaster of Bertrand for several years. He was Sheriff of Berrien County from 1865 to 1869; twice Assistant Sergeant-at-Arms of the Senate; and when Sheriff was Deputy U. S. Marshal of western Michigan. In 1886 he was engaged in the grocery trade at Jackson. He was a Republican in politics.

JARED SEXTON

Representative from Wayne County, 1851. His postoffice address was Dearbornville. (Further data not obtainable).

JARED A. SEXTON

Representative from Wayne County, 1867-8. Was born in Dearborn, Mich., Sept. 29, 1838. His primary school education was supplemented by a term at the Normal School at Ypsilanti. His business was that of a farmer, merchant, and banker. He held many local offices, and was Sheriff of Wayne County in 1875-6. His residence in 1887 was Dearborn. His politics were Democratic.

ELISHA G. SEYMOUR

Representative from Chippewa County, 1847. Was born in Camillus, N. Y., May 25, 1817. By profession he was a lawyer. He settled at Detroit in 1840, where he was socially very popular. Later he went to Sault Ste. Marie. He died June 18, 1850.

HENRY SEYMOUR

Representative from Kent County, 1865-6, and Senator from the Twenty-ninth District, 1867-8. Was born at Camillus, N. Y., Dec. 16, 1821. He came to Grand Rapids in 1842, where he resided until his death, June 7, 1877. He was engaged in wool buying. In politics he was a Republican. He was a prominent officer in the Congregational Church and Sabbath school at Grand Rapids.

HENRY W. SEYMOUR

Senator from the Thirty-first District, 1883-4, and from the Thirtieth District, 1887-8; and member of Congress, 1887-9. Was born July 21, 1834, in Brockport, N. Y. He graduated at Williams College in 1855, studied law, attending the Albany law school, and was admitted to the bar in 1856. He settled at Sault Ste. Marie in 1873, where he built a saw mill and cleared a farm. He was a prominent officer of the National Bank, and president of the St. Mary's Falls Water Power Company. In February, 1887, he was nominated and elected to Congress to fill vacancy caused by the death of Hon. Seth C. Moffatt. In politics he was a Republican.

JAMES SEYMOUR

Representative from Genesee County, 1853-4, and Senator from the Twenty-fourth District, 1857-8. Was born in Litchfield, Conn., Apr. 20, 1791. From 1829 to 1846 he was a resident of Rochester, N. Y., and was a merchant and banker. In 1836 he bought part of the land where North Lansing now stands, and also the site of Flushing, Genesee County. He removed to Flushing in 1846. He did not sit in the extra session of the Legislature in 1858. He was active in securing the location of the Capital at Lansing, and in promoting its growth and improvement. The Seymour house at North Lansing, the first hotel in the city, was built by him. He was a polished gentleman of culture and refined manners. Politically he was a Republican. He died at Flushing, Dec. 30, 1864.

GEORGE T. SHAFFER

Commissioner of the State Land Office, 1891-3. Was born near Springfield, Clark County, O., Oct. 9, 1822, and came with his parents to Calvin Township, Cass County, in the spring of 1832. In 1843 he went to Edwardsburg and attended a select school for two years. He then became a teacher in winter, a farmer in summer. In 1850 he went to California where he worked first at gold mining; then engaged in the grocery business; next conducted a hotel, and afterwards established a ranch in the Sacramento Valley. In 1858 he returned to Michigan, purchasing a farm of 320 acres in Calvin Township, upon which he resided. He enlisted in Co. A, 19th Mich. Infantry, and became 1st Lieutenant of the Co., and was five times promoted for gallant and meritorious service. His regiment was retained in the service one year and three months after Lee and Johnston surrendered, during which Gen. Shaffer held several important positions. He was elected Commissioner of the Land Office for 1891-3 on the Democratic ticket. Deceased.

CHARLES SHALER

Secretary of the Territory of Michigan, 1835. Was a native of Pennsylvania. August 29, 1835, he was appointed by President Jackson, Secretary of Michigan Territory, to supersede Stevens T. Mason, but the appointment was declined. Sept. 8, 1835, John S. Horner received the appointment to this position.

EDWARD SHANAHAN

Representative from Cass County, 1861-2. Was born in Sussex County, Delaware, in 1806, and lived in that State until 1832, when he came to Michigan, settling at Beardsley Prairie, Cass County, where he lived until 1855, when he removed to Jefferson, same county. By occupation he was a farmer on a large scale.

HULBERT B. SHANK

Representative from Ingham County, 1861-2. Was born in Springport, N. Y., May 31, 1820. He became a teacher at the age of eighteen. He graduated as a physician from Geneva Medical College in 1846, practiced two years in New York, then settled at Lansing, Mich. As a physician and surgeon he enjoyed a large and successful practice. He was a Whig until 1854, then a Republican. He was a Delegate to the Republican National Convention of 1856. He was surgeon of the 8th Mich. Infantry until compelled to retire from ill health, and then became examining surgeon for the Third District until the close of the war. He was several years a member of the Board of Control of the State Reform School; many years a member, and president of the Lansing Board of Education; president of State Medical Society; and Delegate to the National Medical Society. He died at Lansing, Apr. 23, 1889.

GEORGE W. SHARP

Senator, 1891-2, from the Thirteenth District, comprising the counties of Alger, Delta, Schoolcraft, Luce, Chippewa, Mackinac and Emmet. Was born in Mt. Gilead, Morrow County, O., on Mar. 14, 1859. He was educated in the public schools of his native State, having graduated from the high school of Elyria, O., in 1878. In the fall of 1880 he entered the law department of Michigan University and graduated from there in 1882. The next six years he spent in the South, and was, during one year, lecturer on commercial law in the Fort Worth, Texas, Business College. In the summer of 1888 he went to Newberry, Mich. He was one of the promoters of the Burrell Chemical Company, doing business in that town. In politics a Democrat.

JAMES EVERETTE SHARP

Representative from Newaygo County, 1911-12. Was born at Morgan, Ashtabula County, O., Feb. 17, 1849, of Holland parentage. He was educated in the district schools. Feb. 2, 1865, just fifteen days before he was sixteen years of age, he enlisted in the 196th regiment O. V. I. He was one of five brothers, all of whom served in the War of the Rebellion. He engaged in farming. He held the offices of Township Clerk, Justice of the Peace and was Supervisor of Ashland Township thirteen successive years; also served as Sheriff of Newaygo County for one term. He was elected to the Legislature from Newaygo County on the straight Democrat ticket, having been elected Nov. 8, 1910.

JOHN C. SHARP

Senator from the Sixth District, 1887-8. Was born in Scott, N. Y., July 18, 1843, where he resided until May, 1863. He received his education at Cortland Academy, Homer, New York, and at the Normal School at Albany. In 1863 he removed with his parents to Brooklyn, Jackson County, Mich., where he remained upon his father's farm for four years, spending the winters in teaching school. In the spring of 1867 he commenced the study of law in city of Jackson, was admitted to the bar in 1869, and practiced his profession in that city until 1884, after which time he extensively engaged in farming and stock raising. He was City Attorney of Jackson in 1877, Supervisor of census of the southern district of Michigan in 1880, and Prosecuting Attorney for Jackson County for 1881-2. In politics he was a Republican.

ALBERT E. SHARPE

Representative, 1901-2, from Iosco District, comprising the counties of Iosco, Alcona, Roscommon and Ogemaw; and Delegate to the Constitutional Convention of 1907-8, from the Thirtieth District. Was born in Trenton, Ont., May 30, 1860, where he received his education in the common schools, supplemented by a course in Albert College at Belleville, Ont., after which he taught school three years. He came to Michigan in 1881 and located in West Branch, where he was principal of schools for five years and a member of the Board of School Examiners. He also held the offices of County Commissioner and Superintendent of the Poor. In 1884 he purchased the West Branch *Times*, which he successfully conducted for five years. In 1889 he removed to East Tawas and in 1894 was elected Prosecuting Attorney of Iosco County and re-elected again in 1896 and 1898. Married. In politics a staunch Republican.

NELSON SHARPE

Justice of the Supreme Court, 1918——. Was born in Northumberland County, Ont., Canada, on Aug. 25, 1858. He was educated in the public schools and at Albert College, Belleville. He served as Prosecuting Attorney of Ogemaw County for two terms, and as Circuit Judge of the Thirty-fourth Judicial Circuit from 1893 to 1918, when he was appointed to fill the vacancy on the Supreme Bench caused by the death of Russell C. Ostrander. At the general election in November, 1920, he was elected to fill the unexpired term.

PETER SHARPE

Representative from Lenawee County, 1859-60. Was born at Willsborough, N. Y., May 14, 1812. His father removed to the Genesee Valley, and later to Franklin County, Ohio, and the son became a traveling minister in 1832, by admission to the Ohio conference of the M. E. Church, then including nearly all the territory of Michigan. After twenty-one years' service as a minister, he settled at Ridgeway, Mich., as a retail dealer in drugs and groceries. He was a Whig until 1854, then a Republican. He was thirty years Postmaster, also a Justice. He still lived at Ridgeway in 1887.

DERWIN W. SHARTS

Representative from Shiawassee County, 1877-8 and 1879-80. Was born in Oxford, N. Y., Aug. 31, 1830. He graduated from Madison University, Hamilton, N. Y., in 1854, and from the Auburn Theological Seminary in 1857. Soon after the close of the war, having spent a portion of the last year at the front, he moved into Ohio, thence in 1871, to Shiawassee County. He was a Presbyterian clergyman; was ordained by the Catskill presbytery in 1857, and preached in the State of New York, in Cleveland, Ohio, and several years for the Congregationalist Church in Owosso. Having pursued the ministry for seventeen years, he retired from the work for rest and recuperation. In politics he was a Republican.

GILBERT SHATTUCK

Delegate from the Fourth District to the Constitutional Convention of 1835; and Representative from Washtenaw County, 1837. Was a resident of Ypsilanti. He was one of the stockholders of the "Huron River Bank," a "wild cat" bank, started in 1838, which after career of 18 months went down. No other information has been obtained of him.

WILLARD SHATTUCK

Representative from Saginaw County, 1879-80. Was born in Saginaw, Mich., Sept. 21, 1845. He received a good education and graduated from Goldsmith's Bryant & Stratton Commercial College of Detroit. He held several township offices, was Justice, and County Superintendent of the Poor for several years. In politics he was a Democrat.

BRACKLEY SHAW

Representative from Lenawee County, 1869-70; and Senator from the Sixth District, 1881-2 and 1883-4. Was born in Plainfield, Mass., May 21, 1818, and removed with his parents to Ira, N. Y., in 1825, and in 1835 to Dover, Mich. He was educated in common schools, and was a farmer. He held various political positions, and was a prominent agriculturist. Politically he was a Republican. Deceased.

EDWIN O. SHAW

Senator, 1895-6, from the Twenty-fifth District, composed of the counties of Isabella, Mecosta, Newaygo and Osceola; Delegate to the Constitutional Convention of 1907-8 from the Twenty-fifth District. Was born in Edwardsburg, Cass County, Mich., July 21, 1846; attended the district and village schools, working on the farm summers; learned the printer's trade and in 1867 established the *Montcalm Herald* at Stanton; sold out and Jan. 1, 1869, assumed control of the *Newaygo Republican.* In politics a Republican. He held the office of Supervisor of his township and chairman of the County Board of Supervisors; President of the village of Newaygo and Justice of the Peace; was admitted to the bar in January, 1892; served his party as member of State Central Committee and chairman and secretary of County Committee and chairman of the Ninth District Committee in the last campaign.

HENRY A. SHAW

Representative from Eaton County, 1857-8, 1859-60 and 1873-4. Was born in Benson, Vt., June 21, 1818. He received an academical education, studied law in Ravenna, O., and was admitted to the bar in 1839. In 1842 he removed to Eaton Rapids, Mich. He was twelve years Judge of Probate for Eaton County, and was several times President of the village of Eaton Rapids. He was a leading member of the bar in Eaton County. In 1859 he was speaker of the House, and was a recognized leader of the Republican party. In 1861 he went into the army as Major of the 2d Mich. Cavalry, and served two years. He was for some years a director of the Grand River Valley Railroad. For many years he was a Republican, but later acted with the Greenback party. He died at Eaton Rapids, Jan. 29, 1891.

JAMES SHAW

Representative from Cass County, 1845 and 1847. Was born in Berlin, N. Y., Feb. 28, 1813. He married in 1839, and in 1840 settled on a farm in Howard, Michigan, where he resided in 1887. He was Supervisor in 1844 and 1846. By occupation he was a farmer, in politics a Democrat.

JOHN SHEA

Representative from the First District of Wayne County, 1903-4. Was born in London, England, June 4, 1855, and was educated in the English and American schools. At the age of thirteen he came to New York and served as apprentice to trade of plastering. At the age of twenty-one he returned to England and remained for four years. He was married in Brighton, England, and returned to America in 1880, taking up his residence in Detroit. Besides working at his trade he filled the position of inspector of building construction for the Board of Education of Detroit and for nearly four years acted as business agent for the Building Trades Council of Detroit. In politics a Republican. He was elected on the general legislative ticket of Detroit to the Legislature of 1903-4.

JAMES SHEARER

Member of the Board of Regents of the University of Michigan, 1880-8. Was born at Albany, N. Y., May 12, 1823, received a common school education, and when young became a clerk. In 1838 came to Detroit, and served as an apprentice six years to a builder, studying architecture, etc., under competent instructors. He then attended an Academy at Albany, N. Y., went South, and in 1846 supervised the buliding of the State Capitol at Montgomery, Ala. In 1848 he went into business at Detroit, as an architect and builder, and continued in that business until 1863, and was twice an Alderman. He removed to Bay City in 1865, where he was largely interested in manufactures. He was president of the First National Bank; president of the Board of Water Works; from 1871 to 1878 one of the three commissioners for the building of the Capitol at Lansing. In politics he was a Republican. He died at Bay City, Oct. 14, 1896.

JONATHAN SHEARER

Senator from the First District, 1842 to 1844; Representative from Wayne County, 1851; and Delegate from Wayne County to the Constitutional Convention of 1867. Was a native of Coleraine, Mass., born Aug. 23, 1796. His early education was academical, with a partial study of medicine, law, and business. He settled in Plymouth, Wayne County, in 1836, and was a leading citizen of the county, serving many terms as Supervisor, and as County Commissioner, 1838 to 1841. He was a leading agriculturist, an efficient member of the State Pioneer Society, and its president in 1876. He was politically a Democrat, but favored the Greenback Party in his later years. He died Sept. 26, 1881.

FRANCIS W. SHEARMAN

State Superintendent of Public Instruction, 1849-55. Was born at Vernon, N. Y., June 20, 1817. He graduated from Hamilton College at the age of nineteen. He was employed by Hon. H. R. Schoolcraft to assist him in negotiating treaties with the Indians and in that capacity first came to Michigan. He settled at Marshall in 1837, and soon found employment as editor of the *Michigan Journal of Education*, the official organ of the State Department of Public Instruction. In 1840 he became chief editor of the *Democratic Expounder*, published at Marshall, and that paper soon took a leading position as a Democratic organ. He was Associate Judge of Calhoun County in 1843-44. He was appointed Superintendent of Public Instruction by Governor Ransom, Mar. 28, 1849, and held the office under that appointment until 1851. He was elected to that office twice, and held it continuously until Jan. 1, 1855, and made an able public officer. His report for 1852 attracted great attention, was widely distributed, and often quoted by educators. He returned to Marshall, became editor of the Marshall *Expounder*, which he held through life. He was also an acting magistrate for sixteen years. As a writer he was forcible, polished, independent, and aggressive. He died at Marshall, Mich., Dec. 7, 1874.

CARLOS DOUGLAS SHELDEN

Representative from the Second District of Houghton County, 1893-4; Senator from the Thirty-second District, 1895-6; and member of Congress, 1897-9, 1899-1901 and 1901-3. Was born at Walworth, Walworth County, Wis., June 10, 1840; seven years later moved with his parents to Houghton County, Lake Superior District, Mich.; educated in the Union School, Ypsilanti, Mich., and returned to his home in the fall of 1861; served through the War of the Rebellion as Captain in the 23d Mich. Infantry. At the close of the war he returned to Houghton and entered mercantile life with his father. In politics a Republican. He was selected to represent his district in the lower branch of the Michigan Legislature in 1892, and promoted to the State Senate in 1894; elected to the Fifty-fifth Congress and re-elected to the Fifty-sixth and Fifty-seventh Congresses.

CHARLES P. SHELDON

Representative from Van Buren County, 1853-4. Was born in Watertown, N. Y., in 1817. By occupation he was a farmer, in politics a Democrat. He moved to Hartford, Mich., in 1841, and was Supervisor and Justice for most of the time for ten years. In 1854 he moved to Cedar County, Iowa. He held various offices there, and was a member of the Iowa Legislature in 1868. He died at Tipton, Ia., about 1879.

CLARENCE LEANDER SHELDON

Representative from the First District of Bay County, 1903-4. Was born at Lenox, Macomb County, Mich., in 1849. He was educated in the common schools. He worked at surveying railroad lines and constructing railroads in 1869 and 1870, and from 1870 to 1893 was in the lumber business in the counties of Lapeer and Roscommon. A manufacturer of sash, doors and a general planing mill business. Married. In politics a Democrat. He was elected Alderman of the eleventh ward, a strong Republican precinct.

HORACE J. SHELDON

Delegate from Lenawee County to the Constitutional Convention of 1867. Was born in Kinderhook, N. Y., Oct. 23, 1812. At the age of eleven he was sent to learn the tanners' and curriers' trade, which he followed for many years. He prospected Michigan in 1833, and opened a boot and shoe shop at Blissfield in 1836. After a few months he went to Grand Haven and established a tannery. After four years he returned to Blissfield, purchased a farm, opened another boot and shoe shop, and made that place his home. He was Justice some thirty years. In politics he was a Republican.

JAMES SHELDON

Representative from Calhoun County, 1844. Was born in Seneca County, N. Y., Apr. 4, 1800. He moved to Michigan in 1833, selecting and locating lands in Calhoun County. He settled at Albion in 1835 on lands which he owned and occupied up to 1860. He held the positions of State Prison Inspector, Justice, School Director, and other minor offices. He was also President of Albion College. His business was that of farmer and general merchandise, politically he was a Democrat. He died Nov. 9, 1866.

NEWTON SHELDON

Representative from Washtenaw County, 1842 and 1869-70. Was born at Brutus, N. Y., July 9, 1810. He received a common school education. He settled on a farm in Lodi, Mich., in 1832, where he remained until 1871. He was a Democrat, and held some public trust nearly all his life. He was Supervisor, Town Clerk, Justice and Treasurer, and for many years secretary of the Washtenaw County Agricultural Society. For nine years, from 1871 to 1880, he was secretary of the Washtenaw County Mutual Insurance Company. He died at Ann Arbor, Jan. 12, 1883.

ORSON SHELDON

Representative from Macomb County, 1838. His postoffice address was Utica. (Further data not obtainable).

SUEL ANDREWS SHELDON

Senator, 1899-1900 and 1905-6, from the Twenty-third District, comprising the counties of Muskegon and Ottawa. Was born in Husterford Township, Dodge County, Wis., Dec. 6, 1850. He removed at an early age with his parents to Ottawa County, Mich., and for three years his father, Eli Sheldon, worked in the lumber woods along Grand River. He then settled on the farm in Wright Township. The early life of Mr. Sheldon was that of the typical pioneer youth, and his only schooling was such as could be obtained in the short winter terms of the district school, supplemented by home study, and while yet in his teens became a teacher in the district schools of the county. He was married, Nov.

13, 1879, to Eleanor Gear. As a business man he had an active and varied career. From a county pedagogue he became western manager for Austin, Tomlinson & Webster Mfg. Co., of Jackson, holding this position for five years. Subsequently he became advertising manager for the Grand Rapids *Evening Press*, was for a time connected with the *Michigan Tradesman*, and afterwards acted as business manager of the *Workman, Practical Farmer* and the *Fruit Grower*. In politics a Republican. He held the offices of Supervisor, School Director and President of the Ottawa and West Kent Agricultural Society.

TIMOTHY F. SHELDON

Representative from Wayne County, 1839. Was born in New York, July 31, 1797. He came to Michigan in 1826 and settled in Canton, Wayne County, where he continued to reside until his death, Sept. 15, 1869. He was prominent during the thirty years of his residence there, and was honored with the more responsible local offices. He was a Democrat until the time of the Civil War, when he became a Republican.

ALANSON SHELEY

Senator from the Second District, 1867-8 and 1871-2. Was born at Albany, N. Y., Aug. 14, 1809. His early life was spent on his grandfather's farm in Jefferson County, N. Y., and attending common schools. As a boy he took a timber raft down the St. Lawrence River to Quebec, and at 16 was apprenticed three years to learn the trade of a mason, and became a foreman on the Rideau Canal, Canada. He came to Detroit in 1831, and in 1832 built a stone lighthouse on Thunder Bay, Lake Huron, the oldest now standing. He was a builder and contractor at Detroit several years, and later was interested in lumbering for the Black River Steam Mill Company. In 1859 he became a partner with J. S. Farrand in the drug trade. He was an active Whig in politics, but helped organize the Republican party in 1854. He was an Alderman five years. He was a leading Presbyterian, and acted as Superintendent of a Sunday school for many years. He was always a strong temperance man. He possessed great strength, and many stories are told of his prowess in his younger days. He died before 1894.

MARTIN G. SHELLHOUSE

Representative from St. Joseph County, 1837. His postoffice address was Colon. (Further data not obtainable).

FRANCIS MARION SHEPARD

Representative from Shiawassee County, 1897-8. Was born in Niagara County, N. Y., Oct. 14, 1840. The following year he came to Owosso, Shiawassee County, Mich., with his parents, in a lumber wagon. His early education was acquired in the district schools, supplemented by one term at the Michigan Agricultural College, in 1865; taught school a number of years, after which he engaged in farming and stock raising, and later gave particular attention to the raising of Galloway cattle and Shropshire sheep. In politics he was a Republican. He was Supervisor and Township Clerk; filled the offices of his township except that of Treasurer.

JAMES M. SHEPARD

Senator from the Twelfth District, 1879-80. Was born in North Brookfield, Mass., Nov. 24, 1842, but soon afterwards removed to Boston. He received a classical education at Wesleyan University, Conn., and studied medicine and dental surgery in Boston. During the war he served in the medical department of the U. S. Navy. In 1868 he located at Cassopolis, Mich., where he engaged in publishing the *Vigilant*. In politics he was a Republican. For several years he was private secretary of Senator Palmer.

LUMAN SHEPARD

Representative from Eaton County, 1883-4. Was born June 17, 1819, at Skaneateles, N. Y. He attended school until twenty-one years of age. He married in 1841, and the following year began farming upon land of his own, continuing until 1855, when he sold out and removed to Chelsea, Mich., and engaged in farming one mile south of that village. Disposing of his farm he removed to Olivet, Eaton County, in 1872. In politics he was a Republican.

FRANK SHEPHERD

Representative, 1897-8 and 1899-1900, from Cheboygan District, comprising the counties of Cheboygan, Emmet, and Presque Isle. Was born in Dover Township, Lenawee County, Mich., Jan. 28, 1853; attended school at Adrian, the State Normal at Ypsilanti, and Oberlin College, O.; taught school five years, and was employed as clerk in a store for a short time; studied law in the office of Stay & Underwood at Adrian, Mich.; was admitted to the bar in 1879, and engaged in the practice of his profession. In politics a Republican. He was Prosecuting Attorney in 1880-2; was appointed Judge of Probate in 1886 and elected to the same office in 1888; was a member of the board of control of the Upper Peninsula Prison in 1890-1; grand patriarch of the Order of Odd Fellows of Michigan, and one of the representatives from this State to the sovereign grand lodge of that order.

THOMAS SHEPHERD

Representative from Allegan County, 1867-8. Was born in Arygle, N. Y., May 19, 1821, and came to Martin, Allegan County, in 1844, where he resided. By occupation he was a farmer. He was a Republican until 1834, when he joined the Prohibition party. For five years he was Supervisor, and for twenty years Justice. He was also the Prohibition nominee for that office.

ABNER SHERMAN

Representative from Houghton and Ontonagon counties, 1853-4 to 1857-8 and 1863-4. His postoffice address was Ontonagon. (Further data not obtainable).

ALBERT A. SHERMAN

Representative from Branch County, 1913-14. Was born in Wayne County, N. Y., July 2, 1841, and was educated in the country schools. The first eight years of his life were spent in Wayne County, N. Y. He then accompanied his parents to Noble County, Ind., and in 1871 came to Coldwater, Mich., where he embarked in the building contracting business. He was married in 1862 to Miss Julia Helman. After her death he married Miss Mary Holland. He was a Mason, a member of Jacobs Commandery number ten, a member of Coldwater lodge I. O. O. F., number 31, and a member of B. P. O. E., Coldwater lodge number 1023. He served as Alderman of Coldwater and was Mayor. In politics a Democrat.

ALONZO J. SHERMAN

Representative from Tuscola County, 1913-14. Was born in Canada on May 8, 1857. His education was acquired in the district schools. In 1859 the family removed to Michigan and located on a farm in Watertown Township, Tuscola County. Mr. Sherman was married Dec. 25, 1880, to Hannah L. Summers. He served as Township Highway Commissioner, Supervisor, and member of the School Board; was a director of the Tuscola County Mutual Fire Insurance Company. In politics a Republican.

BENJAMIN SHERMAN

Representative from St. Joseph County, 1835 and 1836. Was born in Connecticut in 1792. He settled in Genesee County, N. Y., and came to Nottawa Prairie, Mich., in 1825. Before coming to Michigan he was a contractor on the Erie Canal. In politics he was a Democrat. He was Register of the U. S. Land Office at Ionia under the administration of Van Buren and also of Pierce. He died in 1872.

CYRUS SHERMAN

Representative from the County of Clinton, 1889-90. Was born in Onondaga County, N. Y., Sept. 30, 1841, at the age of thirteen he went with his parents to Wisconsin, where he earned his own living working on a farm. In the spring of 1860 he entered Hillsdale College, paying his own way by extra work. In December, 1861, he left college to join the army, enlisting in Co. C, 11th Mich. Vol. Infantry. He was taken prisoner and confined for a time in the famous Libby prison, but at once joined his regiment when he was exchanged. He was mustered out with the rank of Orderly Sergeant in 1864. He removed in December, 1865, to Ovid Township and settled upon a new farm. He served his township as Highway Commissioner, Treasurer and Supervisor; was Post Commander of the G. A. R. at Ovid, and vice-president of the Michigan Association of ex-prisoners of war. He was elected to the House of 1889-90 on the Republican ticket.

ROGER SHERMAN

Representative from Shiawassee County, 1893-4. Was born in Conway, Livingston County, Mich., Jan. 16, 1843. He acquired his education at the district school and at twenty took a course in the commercial college at Poughkeepsie, N. Y. He began life a farmer, and followed the occupation twenty years, when he engaged in the mercantile business, which, in connection with private banking was his occupation at Bancroft. In politics he was a Republican. He held the office of Supervisor.

ALONZO SHERWOOD

Representative from Berrien County, 1879-80. Was born in Lima, O., Apr. 22, 1832. His parents removed to Michigan the following January, settling in Berrien County. His occupation was farming. He held the offices of Justice, Supervisor, and School Director. In politics he was a Republican.

ELEAZER SHERWOOD

Representative, 1895-6, from the Chippewa District, composed of the counties of Chippewa, Luce and Mackinac. Was born in Halton County, Canada, of English parents, in 1843; attended the common schools; remained on the farm until twenty-four years of age, when he engaged in the wholesale and retail of groceries and liquors; married in 1869; continued in the mercantile business until 1882, when he removed to St. Ignace, where he engaged in the hotel business. In 1888 he built the hotel known as the Sherwood. In politics he was a Republican. He held the office of Alderman, and Mayor of his city.

GEORGE SHERWOOD

Representative from Cass County, 1851. Was born in Amenia, N. Y., Apr. 2, 1819. He moved to Cass County, Mich., in 1833, and engaged in mercantile business with his brother at Edwardsburg. He was Town Clerk of Ontwa, County Clerk, 1844 to 1850. He removed to Elkhart, Ind., in 1852, where he was a merchant until 1862, and was County Treasurer of Elkhart County. In 1865 he removed to Chicago, where he was in business as a general commission merchant, and dealer in coal and wood.

HARVEY C. SHERWOOD

Senator from the Eleventh District, 1885-6. Was born at Jamesville, N. Y., Feb. 9, 1835. He received a thorough academical and scientific education, with reference to making farming his vocation; he graduated in 1853. In 1870 Mr. Sherwood and his family came to Michigan, and settled in Watervliet, Berrien County, on an unimproved tract of land called Lake View farm, containing 400 acres, and classed among the finest fruit and grain farms of western Michigan. Mr. Sherwood devoted his whole energies to farming and was enthusiastic in its pursuit. He was the Democratic candidate for Congress in 1886, but was defeated.

THOMAS RUSSELL SHERWOOD

Justice of the Supreme Court, 1882-9. Was born at Pleasant Valley, Ulster County, N. Y., Mar. 28, 1827. His parents removed to Monroe County, N. Y., when he was four years old. He remained at home, working upon the farm in summer, and attending school winters, until he was fourteen years of age, when he commenced his academic education at Macedon Center Academy, and concluded it at Canandaigua Academy in 1847. After teaching several terms, he commenced his legal studies with Gen. Ira Bellows, of Pittsford, N. Y., where he remained one year, and then entered the office of Jerrad and George Wilson, at Canandaigua, where he continued his clerkship until admitted to the bar in June, 1851, at Rochester, N. Y. He practiced his first year at Port Jervis, in that State, and removed to Kalamazoo in 1852, where he devoted himself exclusively to the practice of his profession. He was formerly a Democrat in politics, but later was a National. He served as City Attorney in Kalamazoo, twice nominated Prosecuting Attorney, once for Judge of Probate, and in 1875 refused to become a candidate for Circuit Judge in his district. He was nominated upon a Union ticket for Justice of the Supreme Court, to succeed Judge Marston, who had resigned, and was elected.

SETH K. SHETTERLY

Representative from Macomb County, 1867-8 and 1877-8. Was born in Union County, Pa., Oct 15, 1820. He came to Utica, Mich., with his parents in 1833, where he still resided in 1887. By profession he was an attorney, in politics a Democrat. He was a Justice after 1854, and was for ten years a Circuit Court Commissioner.

FRANCIS J. SHIELDS

Senator, 1909-10, from the Thirteenth District, comprising the counties of Genesee and Livingston. Was born at Howell, Mich., in 1874, of Irish-American descent. His education was acquired in the Howell High School and the University of Michigan, graduating from the literary and law departments. Mr. Shields practiced law. In politics a Republican.

JOSEPH A. SHIELDS

Representative from the Second District of Houghton County, 1915-16. Was born in Woodstock, Canada, Nov. 28, 1859, of Scotch and English parentage. Most of his years were spent in railroad work, and for many years was a locomotive engineer. Mr. Shields was married in 1891 to Miss Avrina Davey. Fraternally he was a member of the F. & A. M., the Chapter and Knights Templar. In politics he was a Republican. He died Nov. 2, 1922.

CHARLES SHIER

Representative from Washtenaw County, 1855-6, 1865-6 and 1869-70. Was born in the State of New York, Jan. 30, 1805. He was for over twenty years a resident of Paterson, N. J., where he was engaged in the manufacture of cotton goods. He came to Ypsilanti in 1845, engaged in farming, and resided near there thirty-eight years, until his death, Jan. 29, 1883. In politics he was first a Whig, a Republican from 1854. He was a member and class leader in the Methodist Episcopal Church for many years.

JOHN W. SHISLER

Representative from the Second District of Kent County, 1897-8 and 1899-1900. Was born (of German parents, whose ancestors emigrated from Germany in October, 1690, and located in Lancaster County, Pa.), on the Niagara frontier, Fort Erie, Ont., Aug. 19, 1840. He received his education in the district school, supplemented by one year at Alfred University, N. Y., and one year at Ft. Edward Institute, Washington County, N. Y.; taught school five years and spent several years in mercantile business. He was married July 2, 1863, to Miss Phiannah E. Bovenmoyer, of Amherst, Erie County, N. Y., and engaged in farming until 1869, when he moved to Michigan; he became a resident of Caledonia Township. He proved himself a successful and energetic farmer and a capable business man. In politics he was a Republican. He was treasurer of the Citizens' Mutual Fire Insurance Company of Kent, Allegan and Ottawa counties, and one of its directors; School Director in his district; was one of the promoters of the Caledonia Union Fair Association and president seven years; also held several official positions in his township.

DEWITT SHOEMAKER

Representative from the First District of Kent County, 1853-4. His postoffice address was Grand Rapids. (Further data not obtainable).

JOSEPH P. SHOEMAKER

Senator from the Twenty-fourth District, 1879-80. Was born Aug. 30, 1820, at Mohawk, N. Y. He received a common school education. In 1837 he removed to Joliet, Ill. In 1840 he removed to Sandusky, O., and remained one year, helping in locating railroads. In 1842 engaged in merchandise and buying grain at Republic, O., and in 1852 went to Covington, Ky., and engaged in manufacturing iron, having charge of a rolling mill. In 1855 he came to Jackson, this State, and engaged in farming. He was Postmaster at Jackson two years, and in 1861 removed to Montcalm County and engaged in farming and lumbering. He was vice-president of the Michigan Pioneer Society. He was elected Justice in 1866. In politics he was a National. He died at Amsden, Montcalm County, Mar. 22, 1903.

MICHAEL SHOEMAKER

Senator from the Second District, 1848 to 1851, and from the Seventh District, 1877-8, 1883-4 and 1885-6. Was born at German Flats, N. Y., Apr. 6, 1818. He attended school until fourteen, then was a clerk at Albany. At the age of seventeen he located at Joliet, Ill., was seven years a partner in the mercantile business, and filled contracts in building the Illinois and Michigan canal. In 1852 he purchased the mills at Michigan Center, which he owned for 28 years. He resided at Jackson and owned large farms near that city. He held many offices, including Inspector of State Prison; Collector of Customs at Detroit; president of the State and County agricultural societies; several terms Grand High Priest of Royal Arch Masons; and chairman of the Democratic State Committee. In January, 1862, he was appointed Colonel of the 13th Mich. Infantry, took part in many engagements, with honor to himself and his command, and was for a short time an inmate of Libby Prison. He was long an active member of the State Pioneer Society, and served as president. He died at Jackson, Nov. 10, 1895.

ABRAM N. SHOOK

Representative from Montcalm County, 1903-4 and 1905-6. Was born at Pierson, Montcalm County, Mich., in 1869, of English parentage. He was educated in the Coral schools, supplemented by a course at Kalamazoo. Married. He was associated with his father in the general mercantile business at Coral, Mich. In politics a Republican; Secretary of the Republican County Committee.

DAVID SHOOK

Representative from Macomb County, 1851. Was born in Milan, N. Y., Dec. 27, 1804. He located at Mt. Clemens, Mich., in 1836. He was a government contractor and civil engineer, a Democrat in politics up to 1861, then a Republican, and a prominent politician in Macomb County. While a resident of the State of New York he was a Lieutenant in the State militia. In 1864 he emigrated to Central City, Colo., where he died Aug. 2, 1865.

JACOB SHOOK

Representative from Macomb County, 1847. Was born in Dutchess County, N. Y., Nov. 28, 1779. In 1841 he settled on a farm one mile from Mt. Clemens, where he resided until his death, Apr. 11, 1862. He was a prominent Democratic politician, and a leading business man in the State of New York, owning and controlling an ashery, woolen factory and general store. He was a captain of N. Y. Militia.

PHILIP P. SHORTS

Representative from Mason County, 1885-6. Was born at Newburg, Ontario, Canada, Aug. 4, 1845. He came to Michigan in 1873, and continuously engaged in the practice of his profession, which was that of a physician. His residence was in Ludington, of which city he was Alderman for two terms. He died Feb. 16, 1890.

JOHN D. SHULL

Representative from the First District of Lenawee County, 1891-2. Was born in Huntington County, Ind., Oct. 25, 1844. After the death of his father, eleven months later, his mother with three small children returned to her former home in Franklin County, Pa. The subject of this sketch here acquired such education as he could in a country school, and a three years' course in the Chambersburg Academy. He learned the "art preservative" in the office of the Franklin *Repository*. He participated in the Civil War as a private in Co. G.

8th Pa. Cavalry, and was severely wounded in the Battle of Salio's Creek, Va., Apr. 6, 1865. He was engaged in the drug trade for two years at Frederick, Md., six years at Topeka, Kan., and nine years at Lansing, Mich. He was married to Mary C. Adams in 1873, daughter of Hon. P. R. Adams, of Tecumseh, Mich., to which place he moved in September, 1883, after which time his principal occupation was farming. He served one term as Alderman in the city of Lansing and two terms as Supervisor of Tecumseh Township.

FREDERICK SHURTZ

Representative from St. Joseph County, 1839 and 1844; and Senator from the Sixteenth District, 1857-8. His postoffice address was White Pigeon. (Further data not obtainable).

SOLOMON SIBLEY

Auditor of Public Accounts, 1814-17; Territorial Delegate to Congress, 1820-3; and Justice of the Supreme Court, 1824-37. Was born in Sutton, Mass., Oct. 7, 1769. He studied law and removed to Ohio in 1795, establishing himself first at Marietta, and then at Cincinnati, in the practice of his profession. He removed to Detroit in 1797, and in 1799 was elected a delegate from Wayne County to the Territorial Legislature of the Northwest Territory. In 1815, he was appointed by President Madison, United States District Attorney of Michigan, which position he held until 1824, when he was appointed one of the United States Judges of the Territory, holding it until 1837, when he resigned. He was interested in a company which erected the first saw and flouring mills in Pontiac. He was a Democrat in politics. As a lawyer, Judge and citizen he was universally respected. He died at Detroit, Apr. 4, 1846. He left three sons, all of whom became prominent as public men. One was Henry H. Sibley, first Governor of Minnesota, and a General in the Civil War.

AARON SICKLES

Representative from Clinton County, 1869-70. Was born at Palmyra, Wayne County, N. Y., Oct. 2, 1817. He came with his parents' family to Plymouth, Mich., in 1836. In 1838 the son moved to Howell, and began life as a farmer, which he followed until 1856, when he removed to Elsie, resuming his calling as a farmer. He filled various positions of public trust. In politics he was a Republican. He engaged in mercantile pursuits, first at Walton, Grand Traverse County, and then at Elmira, Otsego County.

WILLIAM N. SIGGINS

Representative from the First District of Wayne County, 1903-4. Was born at Rochester, N. Y., July 1, 1846, of Scotch-Irish descent. He was educated in the public schools of Detroit, where he moved with his parents when an infant. His father died leaving a family of four children for him to support. When the Civil War broke out he ran away from school and enlisted as musician in Co. G,

9th Mich. Infantry. He was taken prisoner and was exchanged and transferred
to the 11th U. S. Infantry and served three years and three months. A widower.
A member of the orders of I. O. O. F., A. O. U. W. and the G. A. R. In politics
a Republican. He was elected to the Legislature of 1903-4 on the general
legislative ticket of Detroit.

JOHN M. B. SILL

Member of the Board of Regents of the University of Michigan, 1867-9. Was
born at Black Rock, Nov. 24, 1831. His parents died when he was eleven, and
he came to Jonesville, Mich., where he attended school. He was a graduate of
the State Normal School in 1854. He became a teacher in the school, and wrote
an English grammar, published in New York. He was president of the Michigan State Teachers' Association in 1861. In August, 1863, he became Superintendent of the Detroit schools, but resigned in 1863, and for ten years was
principal of the Detroit Female Seminary. In 1875 he became again Superintendent of the Detroit schools, which position he held for many years. He was
president of the State Normal School, and everywhere recognized as an able
educator. He was appointed Regent of the University to fill a vacancy caused
by the death of Henry C. Knight. In 1894 President Cleveland appointed him
Minister to Korea, serving until 1897, when he returned to the United States.

ABIEL SILVER

Delegate from Cass County to the Second Convention of Assent, 1836; and Commissioner of the State Land Office, 1846-50. Was born in Hopkinton, N. H., in
1797. He moved to St. Lawrence County, N. Y., first teaching, and afterwards
becoming a merchant. In 1831 he came to Cass County, Mich., and opened a
store with his brothers at Edwardsburg, and a branch the next year at Cassopolis.
He was a man of ability and culture, and had great influence among the early
pioneers. He was an Associate Judge in Cass County. Under his administration
the seat of government was laid out at Lansing, and the various state lands
there were cut up into lots and placed in market.

JAMES W. SIMMONS

Member of the State Board of Education, 1896-8. Was born in Farmington,
Oakland County, Mich., Aug. 6, 1849. His father, William W. Simmons, lived
at Farmington, Grand Ledge, Salem and Porter, Mich., where he died July, 1896.
The subject of this sketch was a farmer's boy and learned by experience all the
details of a farmer's life; his early education was acquired in the public schools,
supplemented by a course at Hillsdale College, from which he graduated in
June, 1874, and the same year took charge of the graded schools at Lawrence,
where he remained for five years. Constantly in school teaching and superintending; he was at Otsego, four years; Dowagiac, six years; and Owosso, eight
years; was author of a published work on Qualitative Chemical Analysis;
prominent worker in the Michigan State Teachers' Association and the State
Superintendents' Association, as well as in the State Teachers' Institutes held
in various parts of the State; Secretary of the Michigan Pupils' Reading Circle;
and member of the Shiawassee County Board of School Examiners; also a direc-

tor in the Shiawassee Building and Loan Association, and a director in the Citizens' Savings Bank at Owosso; and connected with other prominent business enterprises and a member of the Owosso Business Men's Association. On the resignation of Hon. David A. Hammond as member of the State Board of Education in August, 1896, Governor Rich appointed him to fill the vacancy, and he was elected to that office to succeed himself for the term of 1897-8. He resigned May 13, 1898.

CHARLES C. SIMONS

Senator from the Second District of Wayne County, 1903-4; and Delegate to the Constitutional Convention of 1907-8, from the Second District, Wayne County. Was born in 1876, the son of David W. Simons, former president of the Detroit Lighting Commission. He received his education in the Detroit schools and the University of Michigan, graduating from the department of literature, science and arts with degree of B. L. in 1898 and from the law department with the degree of LL. B. in 1900. In 1906 he was married to Miss Lillian Bernstein, of Chicago. Lawyer by profession. A Republican in politics.

JAMES B. SIMONSON

Representative from Oakland County, 1857-8. Was born at Roxbury, N. Y., Jan. 8, 1805, and received a common school education. He was a merchant at Roxbury from 1825 to 1835, then in trade at Royal Oak, Mich., for six years, at Birmingham two years, and at Springfield for sixteen years. He removed to Holly in 1860, was in trade until 1866, then organized and became president of the First National Bank of Holly. He was for five years Supervisor of Springfield. Politically he was a Republican. Deceased.

EMERY H. SIMPSON

Representative from Van Buren County, 1873-4, and 1887-8. Was born in Carlton, N. Y., Jan. 17, 1828. By occupation he was a farmer; in politics a Republican. He held the office of Supervisor and Township Clerk.

NATHAN F. SIMPSON

Representative from Van Buren County, 1905-6 and 1907-8. Was born at Carlton, Orleans County, N. Y., Oct. 12, 1862, and while an infant moved to Michigan with his parents, spending his early life on the old homestead in Hartford, Van Buren County. He was educated in the rural schools, supplemented by a short term at the Brockport State Normal of New York. He followed teaching for a few years, and was married to Harriet Duncombe, of Keeler, Mich., Apr. 13, 1886, and settled on the plains of western Nebraska. He assisted in organizing Box Butte County, Nebr., and was elected County Superintendent of Public Instruction. He returned to Michigan in 1888 and located on a farm near his former home in Van Buren County. Mr. Simpson was Captain of the 35th Mich.

Vol. Infantry, commanding Co. G, in the Spanish-American War, and was later Captain and Quartermaster of the 45th U. S. Volunteers, serving nearly two years in the Philippines; was detailed Chief Quartermaster, Third District, Department of South Luzon, on Gen. Bell's staff during an active campaign. He was mustered out of the service in June, 1901, and returned to his home to engage in fruit culture and general farming. In politics a Republican.

DANIEL D. SINCLAIR

Senator from the Third District, 1848. Was born at Broadalbin, N. Y., Apr. 16, 1805. While young he was a clerk at Albany, then learned the trade of a tailor, and was in the clothing trade in western New York. He settled in Adrian, Mich., in 1835. He was in the clothing trade for several years. He was Justice; County Treasurer six years; Brigadier General of State militia; superintendent of the Michigan Southern Railroad from 1850 to 1858; Supervisor for eighteen years, and a School Trustee.

CHARLES ALBERT SINK

Representative from the First District of Washtenaw County, 1919-20; and Senator, 1921-2, from the Twelfth District, comprising Oakland and Washtenaw counties. Was born in the township of Western, Oneida County, N. Y., July 4, 1879. While a child he removed with his parents to North Chili, where he attended district school. Later he attended the high school at Churchville where he graduated in 1898. In 1900 he entered the University of Michigan and graduated in 1904. Since that time he has been secretary and business manager of the University School of Music and under his management practically all of the world's greatest musical artists and organizations have been brought to Michigan. He is also a director of the Farmers and Mechanics Bank and of the Ann Arbor Chamber of Commerce. In 1905 he married Mabelle Robbins of Waterford, and they have two children, Pauline and Charles Albert, Junior. Mr. Sink has served on the Ann Arbor City Council six years, and on the Board of Education for nine years. He has also served as president of the Michigan Association of School Board Members and Superintendents, and for three years was secretary of the Michigan League of Municipalities. During the war he was a member of the War Board and served on several other patriotic committees. He is a member of the following fraternal and social orders: Masons, Acacia and Sinfonia College fraternities, the Ann Arbor Club, the Barton Hills Country Club and the Rotary Club. In politics he is a Republican.

RUFUS F. SKEELS

Representative from Oceana County, 1913-14. Was born on a farm in Oceana County, Mich., Sept. 15, 1873, and received his education in the district schools and Muskegon Business College. In 1894 he graduated from the law department of the University of Michigan and went into the law office of F. W. Cook, of Muskegon. He remained there for a year when he was obliged to go onto a farm on account of his health. Mr. Skeels was married on June 26, 1895, to Bertha Millen, also of Oceana County. Upon his election as Prosecuting Attorney in November, 1896, he removed to Hart. In politics he was a Republican. He died Feb. 13, 1914, at Hart, Mich.

ELIAS M. SKINNER

Delegate from Washtenaw County to the Constitutional Convention of 1850; member of the State Board of Education, 1850-51. Was born at Woodstock, Conn., Oct. 28, 1798. After an academical education he entered Brown University and graduated in 1820. He studied law with Governor Stoddard, spent a few years teaching, came to Ypsilanti in 1826, and commenced the practice of his profession. He took an active part in favor of temperance and Sabbath School instruction. He served several years as Prosecuting Attorney, and was elected Judge of Probate in 1845. He was appointed member of the State Board of Education Apr. 19, 1850, and served until the close of the session of the Legislature of 1851. He died Aug. 6, 1859.

GEORGE N. SKINNER

Member of the State Board of Education, 1850-1. Was appointed Mar. 29, 1850, for a three year term. He died during the term of office.

DAVID G. SLAFTER

Representative from Tuscola County, 1863-4. Was born in Norwich, Vt., Jan. 1, 1817. In 1849 he removed to Tuscola, Mich. With the exception of one year he held the office of Justice after 1852. He was Judge of Probate of Tuscola County four years, and was Enrolling Officer and Deputy Provost Marshal from 1863 to the close of the war. His principal business was real estate and lumbering. At first he was a Whig, then a Republican. He was vice president of the national bank at Vassar in 1887.

THOMAS J. SLAYTON

Representative from Kent County, 1867-8 and 1869-70. Was born in Middlesex, N. Y., Jan. 9, 1837. In 1847 he removed with his parents to Grattan, Mich. He graduated at Hillsdale College in 1862, and from the University law school in 1864. He was for a short time at Vicksburg, Miss., in the Freedmen's bureau service, but commenced law practice at Lowell, Mich., in the fall of 1864. He retired to a farm in Grattan in 1874. In politics he was a Republican. He died July 15, 1875.

ALBERT E. SLEEPER

Senator from the Twentieth District, 1901-2 and 1903-4; State Treasurer, 1909-13; and Governor of Michigan, 1917-21. Was born at Bradford, Vt., Dec. 31, 1862. He was educated at the Bradford Academy and came to Lexigton, Mich., in the fall of 1884. For several years he engaged in mercantile pursuits and as a traveling salesman but has been actively engaged in the banking and real estate business for over twenty years. Mr. Sleeper was married July 30, 1901, to Mary C. Moore of Lexington. He is president of the First National Bank of Yale, State Savings Bank of Bad Axe, Commercial State Bank of Marlette, Citizens Bank of Ubly, The Clark & McCaren wholesale grocery company of Bad Axe and is also interested in several other prosperous business concerns. He was Trustee and President of Lexington village several terms and president of the Library Board. He represented the Twentieth Senatorial District, known as the Thumb district, in the Legislatures of 1901-2 and 1903-4. Mr. Sleeper is a lifelong Republican and has been a member of the State Central Committee. He was the unanimous choice of the State Convention, held at Detroit, Sept. 29, for State Treasurer and was elected Nov. 3, 1908. He was renominated at the State Convention held at Detroit, Oct. 6, 1910, and was elected Nov. 8, 1910. Mr. Sleeper is a member of the Episcopal Church, a 33rd degree Mason, a member of Bay City Consistory, El Elf Khurafeh Temple, A. A. O. M. S. of Saginaw, the Blue Lodge F. & A. M. of Lexington, Lebanon Chapter R. A. M. of Bad Axe, Bad Axe Commandery No. 52 Knights Templar, the I. O. O. F. of Marlette and Bad Axe lodge Knights of Pythias. He was nominated for Governor at the August primary of 1916 and elected in November. He was re-elected Nov. 5, 1918.

CHARLES R. SLIGH

Senator from the Sixteenth District, 1923—. Was born in Grand Rapids, of Scotch-Irish parentage. He acquired his education in the public schools in Grand Rapids; spent four years working at the bench and four years as hardware clerk; after which he engaged in the furniture business. He organized the Sligh Furniture Company which has been his chief interest, he being its president. In addition to this he is officer or director of various banking and business enterprises in Grand Rapids and has extensive irrigation and timber interests in the West. Mr. Sligh is married and has four daughters and one son. Previous to the world war he attended the Plattsburg training camp, and later organized the Business Men's Battalion of Grand Rapids. He served on the aircraft production board with a commission as major. He is a Roosevelt progressive Republican; was appointed by Governor Osborn as a member of the Workmen's Compensation Commission and was elected a member of the commission which drafted the present charter of Grand Rapids. He has also served on the Board of Education. He was elected to the senate November 7, 1922.

DANIEL D. SLOAN

Representative from Washtenaw County, 1850. Was born in Herkimer County, N. Y., Nov. 28, 1799. By occupation he was a millwright, in politics first a Whig, then a Republican. He came to Michigan in 1844, built the first large mill at Grand Rapids, also one at Ann Arbor, and one at Dover Mills, which he operated until his death, Jan. 29, 1861. He was several times Supervisor and Assessor of the town of Dexter, and was a man of sterling worth and integrity.

ALBERT B. SLOCUM

Representative from Hillsdale County, 1865-6. Was born in Macedon, N. Y., Mar. 19, 1818. He removed to Michigan in 1842 and settled in Wheatland, Hillsdale County. He was a Supervisor, and president of the Hillsdale County Agricultural Society. He was a Democrat in early life, became a Republican in 1854. By occupation he was a farmer. He died May 14, 1883.

ELLIOTT T. SLOCUM

Senator from the Third District, 1869-70. Was born at Trenton, Mich., in 1839. He graduated at Union College in 1862, and was a resident of Detroit, and after 1886 a Park commissioner. In politics he was a Republican. His time was given to the management of a large estate inherited from his father. He was a member of the Michigan Pioneer and Historical Society. He died at Detroit, Nov. 20, 1915.

WILLIS M. SLOSSON

Representative, 1889-90, from the Osceola District, comprising the counties of Osceola and Missaukee. Was born in Newark Valley, Tioga County, N. Y., May 25, 1849. He was a dealer in real estate. He held various offices, viz.: Village Trustee, Village President and Supervisor, each two terms. In politics he was a Republican.

ALEXANDER SLY

Representative, 1915-16, from the Schoolcraft district, comprising the counties of Alger, Luce, Mackinac and Schoolcraft. Was born in Worth Township, Sanilac County, Mich., in 1863, of German and English parents. He was educated in the district schools. He removed to Mackinac County in 1884, being one of the first settlers of Newton Township. He served Newton Township nine years as Supervisor and was chairman of the board two years. Married. In politics a Republican.

HERBERT SMALLEY

Representative from the First District of Wayne County, 1893-4; and Senator, 1895-6, from the Fourth District, comprising the twelfth, fourteenth and sixteenth wards of the city of Detroit, the city of Wyandotte and certain townships of Wayne County. Was born in Oakland County, Mich., July 13, 1864; was educated in the public schools of Fenton and Ann Arbor; located at Detroit, where he engaged in the lumber business, also interested in real estate dealing. In politics a Republican. He was a member of Board of Estimates of the city of Detroit in 1891; a member of the House of Representatives in the Legislature of 1893-4; and the youngest member in the Senate of 1895-6.

JAMES F. SMILEY

Representative from the First District of Calhoun County, 1895-6. Was born in Elba, Genesee County, N. Y., June 2, 1835; attended district school until seventeen years of age; two years at graded school; one term at Alexander Seminary, N. Y., and in 1854 finished his course in Cary Collegiate Institute at Oakfield, N. Y., taught school during winters from 1853-9; entered the medical department of the Michigan University, graduating in 1862 and engaged in the practice of medicine, thirteen years in Ingham County, Mich., and for the past twenty years at Marshall; also served as a contract surgeon in the U. S. Army during the war. In politics a Republican. He held the offices of Supervisor, Township Treasurer, and Alderman of his city.

ABNER C. SMITH

Senator from the First District, 1845-6. Was born in Vermont, Feb. 14, 1814. He was a lawyer and a Democrat. He came to Michigan in 1839, and was a Postmaster, Judge of the county court and Judge of Probate. He edited the *Macomb County Gazette* some years, and published the *Ancient Landmark*, a Masonic magazine. He died at Litchfield, Minn., Sept. 20, 1880.

ABRAM SMITH

Representative from St. Clair County, 1863-4. Was born in Clay, Mich., Sept. 8, 1819. He received a common school education, worked four years in a saw mill, and then sailed a vessel between Algonac and Sandusky. In 1844 he engaged in lumber business which he continued for many years. He owned a large farm and valuable timber lands. He held various offices, including Supervisor, President of the village of Algonac, and Moderator of the School Board for more than twenty years.

ALVAH G. SMITH

Senator, 1899-1900, from the 29th Senatorial District, comprising the counties of Gladwin, Oscoda, Alcona, Ogemaw, Iosco, Crawford, Missaukee, Roscommon and Clare. Was born in Sunfield Township, Eaton County, Mich., Mar. 14, 1862. He was a son of Edward O. Smith who with two others were the first three settlers of Sunfield Township. He removed with his parents to Lyons Township, Ionia County, in 1864. His early life was spent on a farm. He attended district school until fourteen years old, then entered Portland High School, and after his graduation taught school winters and managed a farm summers for eight years. He graduated in the class of 1882, C. L. S. C., and received the degree of L. B. from the University of Michigan in 1890, but was admitted to the bar in 1889. Mr. Smith began practicing law at Stanton but removed to Lake City, Missaukee County, in 1891. He was married May 21, 1884, to Miss Ada M. Willett, of Leavenworth, Kan. In politics a Republican. He held the offices of Circuit Court Commissioner, and Prosecuting Attorney of Missaukee County. He was also interested in agriculture, having himself purchased and cleared a farm.

AMOS SMITH

Senator from the Fifteenth District, 1869-70. Was born at Springfield, Pa., Aug. 7, 1829, where he received an academical education, and also graduated from a business college at Pittsburgh. He taught school in Cass County, Mich., in 1848, then in Yazoo County, Miss. He settled in Vandalia, Mich., in 1852, taught school several years, owned and managed a farm, and gave much time to locating lines and corners in Cass County. Several years he was secretary of the Cass County Farmers' Institute; Supervisor several terms; County Surveyor eighteen years; and held many other offices. In politics he was a Republican.

ANDREW J. SMITH

Attorney General of Michigan, 1875-7. Was born near Chillicothe, O., Sept. 2, 1818. He removed with his parents to Indiana in 1825, and to the present site of Valparaiso in 1835. After 1840 he was a resident of Cass County, Mich. He was several years a clerk, then studied law and was admitted to the bar in 1857. He was Prosecuting Attorney twelve years, and held other local offices. In 1878 he was appointed Judge of the Second Circuit to fill vacancy, and was elected to that office in 1881, without opposition, serving until the close of 1887. In politics he was a Republican. Resided at Cassopolis in 1887.

AURA SMITH

Representative from Branch County, 1863-4. Was born in the State of New York. He came to Michigan in 1844 and settled on a farm in the township of Girard. He was Supervisor from 1850 to 1855. In 1864 he removed to Missouri, and was still living in that State in 1887. He was a farmer by occupation, and in the latter years of his residence in Michigan, a dealer in stock.

AVERY ALMON SMITH

Representative from the First District of Hillsdale County, 1891-2 and 1893-4. Was born near Fremont, Steuben County, Ind., July 25, 1842, and at the age of five years moved to Cambria Township, Hillsdale County, with his parents, where he lived on the farm with them, receiving his education as many other Michigan sons at the district school; and at the breaking out of the rebellion in 1861 he enlisted in the 10th Michigan Infantry, which command served in the Western Department, under Pope, Hallock, Rosecrans, Grant and Sherman; was in active service nearly three years; received a commission in the spring of 1862; later promoted and commanded company over two years; resigned in fall of 1864, came home, married, and moved on a farm. In politics he was a Republican. He held the offices of Township Treasurer and Supervisor, each two terms.

C. CLIFFORD SMITH

Representative from Wayne County, 1867-8. Was born in New Hampshire in 1828. He graduated as a physician from Portsmouth Medical College (N. H.) in 1852, and the same year came to Michigan, locating at Redford, where he resided. He was a surgeon in the Civil War, and a member of the jury commission for Wayne County in 1884. In politics he was a Democrat.

CALVIN SMITH

Representative from Washtenaw County, 1839. Died before the Legislature convened and was succeeded by Nathan Pierce. (Further data not obtainable.)

CARMIE R. SMITH

Representative from the Second District of Berrien County, 1898. He was elected to fill the vacancy caused by the resignation of Edwin H. Williams, in 1898.

CHARLES SMITH

Representative from the First District of Houghton County, 1895-6 and 1897-8; and Senator, 1899-1900 to 1909-10, from the Thirty-second District, comprising the counties of Baraga, Houghton, Keweenaw and Ontonagon. Was born in the township of Livonia, Wayne County, Mich., Dec. 24, 1839, and remained on the farm until 1857. He attended the union school at Ypsilanti until 1862, with the exception of three months' service as a private in Co. H, 1st Reg. Mich. Infantry. In 1863 he located in Houghton County; was in the employ of copper smelting companies; vice-president of the First National Bank of Lake Linden and director of the Northern Michigan Building & Loan Association of Hancock. In politics he was a Republican. He served twenty consecutive terms as Supervisor of his township. He died Oct. 24, 1915, at Lake Linden.

CHARLES H. SMITH

Senator, 1895-6, from the Tenth District, comprising Jackson and Washtenaw counties. Was born Feb. 7, 1857, on a farm in the town of Leoni, in Jackson County. His father was killed in the great battle in the wilderness on May 5, 1864, leaving him an orphan at the age of seven years. He acquired his education in the district schools of the township, and in the high school at the village of Grass Lake. He followed the profession of teaching for four years, when he entered upon the study of law with Gibson & Parkinson, attorneys in Jackson. He was admitted to practice in 1880 and pursued his profession in the city of Jackson. He was married to Miss Nettie E. Wing in 1882. In politics a Republican. In 1894 he was selected chairman of the Republican County Committee for Jackson County, and directed the most effective and successful canvass ever made in that county. He was nominated to succeed Senator Watts, deceased, and was elected at the April election, 1895.

CHARLES WALLACE SMITH

Representative from Lapeer County, 1911-12, 1913-14, and 1915-16. Was born in Lapeer County Apr. 22, 1864, and was educated in the Lapeer City schools. He was a building contractor for twenty years, and for eight years treasurer and secretary of the Lapeer Gas-Electric Company. He was Supervisor for the first district of Lapeer city, serving one year as chairman of the board. He served as president of the Water Board and secretary-treasurer of the Park Board of Lapeer. In politics a Republican.

DAVIS SMITH

Representative from Lenawee County, 1839. Was born in Dutchess County, N. Y., in 1808. By occupation he was a farmer, in politics a Democrat. He came to Tecumseh, Mich., in 1830. He held several public offices, and took part in the Black Hawk and Toledo Wars. He bore the title of General. He died Mar. 26, 1868.

ELBERT V. SMITH

Senator, 1915-16 and 1917-18, from the Fifteenth District, comprising the counties of Barry, Clinton and Eaton. Was born in Castleton Township, Barry County, Mich., Oct. 26, 1864, of American parents. His early education was acquired in the district schools. He engaged in farming, buying grain and in the insurance business. He served ten years as Supervisor and was Assessor six years. Married. In politics a Republican.

EZEKIEL C. SMITH

Representative from Cass County, 1850. Was born in Erie County, N. Y., June 6, 1811. He settled in 1835 on a farm in Pokagon, Cass County, and lived there. He held the office of Supervisor nine years, and was a Justice for thirty-six years. In politics he was a Democrat.

F. HART SMITH

Representative from the Second District of Hillsdale County, 1891-2. Was born in the township of Danbury, Fairfield County, Conn., Dec. 14, 1834. His father came to Michigan in 1838, purchased the northeast quarter of section 25, township of Somerset, Hillsdale County, erected a small frame house in the forest and was joined by his wife and children, three boys and one girl, in June of 1839. F. Hart Smith devoted his life to farming. In 1863 he was married to Mary Selina Burr. In the spring of 1865 he purchased the southeast quarter of section 24, Somerset. He was elected a member of the executive board of the State Agricultural Society in 1885 and was re-elected in 1887 and 1889. In politics a Republican.

FRANK SMITH

Senator, 1891-2, from the First District, comprising a part of Wayne County. Was born in the city of Detroit, July 25, 1848, and engaged in the real estate business. His former occupation was that of a florist and vegetable gardener. In 1885 he was elected Alderman of the fifteenth ward in Detroit, on the Democratic ticket and was continued in the same position until Jan. 1, 1891. As a Democrat he was elected to the Senate of 1891-2.

FRANK A. SMITH

Representative, 1915, from the Wexford district, comprising the counties of Lake and Wexford. Was born at Lynchburg, O., Jan. 8, 1874. In 1884 he removed with his parents to Blackford County, Ind., and attended the public schools at Hartford City. He removed to Michigan in 1902, and engaged in farming and shipping of farm produce. He is a member of the Grange, I. O. O. F., F. & A. M., and Maccabees. He is married and has two daughters. In politics he is a Republican.

FRANK L. SMITH

Representative from Jackson County, 1871-2. Was born at Stafford Springs, Conn., July 8, 1830. In 1842 he removed with his parents to Armada, Mich. As a young man he worked in the railroad shops at Adrian, came to Jackson in 1855, and was manager of the American, afterwards the Marion house, then clerk of the Hibbard house until 1864. He was Quartermaster of the 29th Mich. until that regiment consolidated with the 28th, then took charge of the Tremont house, 1865-8. He had charge of the Hurd house from 1869 until the fall of 1886. He served as Alderman and Supervisor. He died Dec. 5, 1886.

GAD SMITH

Senator, 1901-2, from the Thirty-first District, comprising the counties of Alger, Dickinson, Iron and Marquette. Was born in Norwalk, Conn., Dec. 26, 1845, where his education was acquired in the public schools. He enlisted as private in Co. G, 19th Conn. Vol. Infantry, early in 1862 and served until the close of the year 1865, when he was mustered out as Captain of Co. D, 2d Conn. Heavy Artillery, and returned to Connecticut and engaged in mercantile pursuits. In 1866 he was elected to the Legislature of Connecticut. In June, 1873, he located at Negaunee, Mich., engaged with the Iron Cliffs Company as accountant. He removed to Marquette in 1876, and held the office of County Clerk, Register of Deeds, and Deputy Collector of Customs, district of Superior, and was admitted to the bar of Marquette County in 1881. He was married. In politics he was a Republican.

GEORGE A. SMITH

Representative from Hillsdale County, 1863-4; and Senator from the Twelfth District, 1867-8, and from the Ninth District, 1885-6. Was born in Danbury, Conn., Mar. 8, 1825, and settled at an early day as a farmer in Somerset, Mich. He was also a merchant. He was a member of the board of control of the Reform School from 1879 to 1884, when he resigned. He was also a Supervisor. In politics he was a Republican. He died at Somerset, Jan. 29, 1893.

GEORGE M. SMITH

Representative from Muskegon County, 1877-8. Was born Mar. 16, 1841, at Springfield Centre, N. Y. He was educated at Alfred University, N. Y., and removed to Michigan in 1867. He was President of the village of Whitehall, and a member of the lumbering firm of J. Alley & Co. At the age of nineteen he engaged with the Atlantic & Great Western railroad at Salamanca, N. Y., as telegraph operator, from which position he was subsequently promoted to that of Superintendent of telegraph and train dispatcher, and afterward to a similar position on the Blossburg, Corning & Tioga railroad at Corning. In politics he was a Republican. He died several years prior to 1887.

HENRY SMITH

Representative from Monroe County, 1838 and 1845. Was a native of the State of New York, and graduated at the United States Military Academy in 1815. He was made a Lieutenant and served in the army until 1836, when he resigned. From 1836 to 1840 he was a civil engineer, superintending harbor improvements on Lake Erie, and resided at Monroe. He was Major General of Michigan militia from 1841 to 1846; Mayor of Monroe in 1846. In 1847 he was re-appointed to the army with the rank of Major. He died while on duty in the Mexican War, at Vera Cruz, July 24, 1847.

HENRY C. SMITH

Representative from Kent County, 1849 and 1853-4. Was born at Scituate, R. I., Jan. 9, 1804. He worked on a farm until of age and enjoyed fair opportunities for an education. He was a mason by trade and worked at it until 1836, when he came to Michigan. He was engaged both in merchandising and lumbering, and finally became a farmer in Plainfield, Kent County. He held various town and county offices. He died at Grand Rapids, Jan. 27, 1886.

HENRY CASSORTE SMITH

Member of Congress, 1899-1901 and 1901-3. Was born at Canandaigua, Ontario County, N. Y., June 2, 1854, and received his early education in the common schools of New York and Michigan. His parents were educated people, but his father met with financial losses during the panic of 1857, removed to Michigan in 1860, located on a farm in Palmyra Township, Lenawee County, and followed farming until his death. The subject of this sketch, being thrown upon his own resources at an early age, "worked out" and obtained the means for a college course, taught school winters, and graduated from Adrian College in June, 1878. After his graduation he went into the political campaign of 1878 as a speaker under the direction of Zachariah Chandler. He subsequently read law in the office of Geddes & Miller, of Adrian; was admitted to the bar Sept. 25, 1880; appointed City Attorney a month later and Assistant Prosecuting Attorney Jan. 1, 1881, in which position he served two years. Dec. 10, 1883, he formed a partnership with Judge Watts. Mr. Smith was the complainant and of counsel with Attorney General Maynard in the celebrated case against the L. S. & M. S. railway, which reached the U. S. Supreme Court, to compel that corporation to sell Mr. Smith and wife a 1,000 mile ticket at two cents a mile. He was elected to the 56th Congress of the United States, and re-elected to the 57th Congress.

HIRAM SMITH

Representative from Calhoun County, 1848. Was born in Westchester County, N. Y., May 24, 1804. By occupation he was a merchant and miller, in politics a Democrat. He came to Homer, Mich., in 1837, and was a prominent business man and leading Democrat for many years. He was a good neighbor and of a social nature. He was Moderator of School Board, took great interest in schools, and often presided at public meetings. He died May 4, 1874.

HIRAM H. SMITH

Representative from Ingham County, 1843. Was born at Malone, N. Y., Dec.
9, 1809. When young he was a resident of Brandon, Vt. He received an
academical education; was five years a clerk at Castleton, Vt.; from 1830 to
1835 a merchant at Granville, N. Y.; in 1836 became a farmer in Ingham
County, Mich.; was County Treasurer in 1838, and County Clerk in 1841; a
merchant at Mason; removed to Lansing in 1847, built the first flour mill,
and carried on the milling and mercantile business in 1851-2 and was engaged
in building the plank road from Lansing to Howell; was the first Mayor of
Lansing in 1859; was vice president and managing director of the J., L. & S.
R. R.; removed to Jackson in 1864, and from 1868 to 1870 superintended
the building of the D., L. & N., and the Detroit & Bay City railroads. He had
large property interests, and was president of the Ingham County Savings
Bank. He was a Democrat until 1856, then a Republican. He was vice president of the Michigan Pioneer Society. He died at Jackson, May 14, 1898.

JAMES L. SMITH

Representative from Sanilac County, 1851. Was born in Kilconquhar, Scotland, May 11, 1813. He came to Tecumseh, Mich., in 1838, then to Sanilac
County, in 1840. His business varied; in politics a Republican. He removed
to Toledo in 1853, and to Minneapolis in 1882, where he resided in 1887.

JEREMIAH R. SMITH

Representative from Genesee County, 1838 and 1842. Was born in Lyme,
Conn., June 19, 1795. He came to Michigan in 1828. He was a blacksmith
by trade, and carried on the business at Avon, N. Y., before coming to Michigan. Settling in Genesee County he became a farmer. He was Associate
County Judge of Genesee County, Justice for twenty years, and Supervisor for
several years of Grand Blanc. He died Mar. 23, 1868.

JOB SMITH

Representative from Wayne County, 1837. His postoffice address was Van
Buren. (Further data not obtainable.)

JOHN M. C. SMITH

Delegate from the Fifteenth District to the Constitutional Convention of 1907-
8; and member of Congress, 1911-23. Was born in Ireland in 1853, and removed to Michigan from Ohio in 1867, locating in Eaton County. He received his education in the Potterville and Charlotte high schools and the
University of Michigan. He lived on a farm until he was eighteen years of
age, after which he worked as a mason for ten years. Later he engaged in the

practice of law, manufacturing and banking. He was married in 1887 to Miss Lena Parkhurst and has two children, a son and a daughter. In politics a Republican. He was elected to Congress in November, 1910, and has served in each succeeding Congress. Because of the death of William H. Frankhauser, of Hillsdale, which occurred on May 9, 1921, a special election was held in the Third Congressional District on June 28, 1921, to fill vacancy occasioned thereby, and Mr. Smith was elected to fill out the unexpired term of Mr. Frankhauser. He was re-elected Nov. 7, 1922 and died March 30, 1923.

JOHN S. SMITH

Senator from the Thirtieth District, 1853-4. Was born Mar. 26, 1822, at Dighton, Mass. His father removed to Ontario, N. Y., where the son studied medicine, and graduated from Cleveland Medical College in 1844; practiced medicine in Ontario County, N. Y., for two years; removed to Armada, Mich., in 1847, and was engaged in medical practice until 1860. In 1858 he commenced the study of law, graduated from the law department at Ann Arbor, and went into practice. In 1863 he entered the army as Quartermaster and served one year. He then engaged in farming and dealing in hops, buying large quantities and sending to distant markets. As a Democrat he was Senator. He died Sept. 19, 1868.

JOHN W. SMITH

Representative from the First District of St. Clair County, 1919-20 and Senator, 1921—, from the Eleventh District, comprising the counties of Macomb and St. Clair. Was born Mar. 24, 1871, at Middlesex, Ont., of German-Irish descent. He came to Michigan in 1875, locating on a farm near Minden City, which said farm he still owns, and where he resided until five years ago when he removed to Port Huron. He received his education in the district school of Minden Township. Mr. Smith is married and has two daughters. He is interested in banks of the Thumb District and at present is giving much of his time to the John W. Smith Agency, bonds, insurance and real estate. During the World War Mr. Smith was chairman of Draft Board, Port Huron. In politics he is a Republican. He has been active in politics, serving as Supervisor, Highway Commissioner during 1919-20 and County Drain Commissioner.

JOHN WILLIAM SMITH

Senator from the Second District, 1921-2. Was born at Detroit, Mich., Apr. 12, 1883, of American parents. He was educated in the public schools and the Detroit College of Law. He has served as Deputy U. S. Marshal, Deputy Commissioner of Labor, Deputy Sheriff and Deputy County Clerk of Wayne County, and is at present postmaster of Detroit. Mr. Smith served in the Spanish-American War in the 32nd Mich. Vol. Infantry, and Philippine insurrection, with 38th U. S. Infantry. He is married. In politics he is a Republican.

JOSEPH SMITH

Representative from Cass County, 1835 and 1836; and Delegate from Cass County to the Second Convention of Assent, 1836. Was born in Botetourt County, Va., Apr. 11, 1809. He removed with his parents to Ohio, in 1812, and settled in Calvin, Mich., in 1831. He bought a mill property and ran it until 1835, when he sold out and bought one thousand acres of land in Jefferson, Cass County. In 1847 he engaged with partners in the mercantile business, after three years carrying it on alone. In 1855 he removed to Cassopolis and continued his business. In politics he is a Democrat. He died Apr. 18, 1880.

LEGRAND J. SMITH

Representative from Lenawee County, 1873-4. Was born in Bethel, Conn., Jan. 8, 1837. He received a common school education. In 1839 he settled in Somerset, Hillsdale County. In 1859 he removed to Woodstock, Lenawee County, where he still resided in 1887. In business he was a merchant.

LUTHER SMITH

Representative from Gratiot and other counties, 1865-6 and 1867-8. His post-office address was St. Louis. (Further data not obtainable.)

MILTON H. SMITH

Representative from Monroe County, 1917-18. Was born in Carroll County, Md., Oct. 18, 1854. His education was secured in the district schools of Pennsylvania and Michigan, and one year at the State Normal School of Ypsilanti. He came to Michigan with his parents in 1871, and located on a farm in Erie Township, Monroe County, and in 1876, they removed to the township of Ida, where he helped clear the farm and erect the buildings, and taught school during the winter season. He served his township as Supervisor and School Inspector. In politics a Democrat.

MORGAN L. SMITH

Representative from Oakland County, 1855-6. Was born at Charlton, N. Y., Aug. 30, 1810. He learned the trade of hatter and carried on that business at Eaton, N. Y. He removed to Milford, Mich., in 1837, where he was Justice eighteen years, and Postmaster four years. He was Associate Judge of Oakland County four years. He removed to Branch County and farmed it ten years. In politics he was a Republican. He died in Chicago, Oct. 12, 1866.

NATHAN D. SMITH

Representative from St. Clair County, 1861-2. Was born in the State of New York in 1803. He came to Michigan in 1833. His business was miscellaneous; politically a Republican. He resided at Algonac, Mich., in 1887.

NEWEL SMITH

Representative from Gratiot County, 1913-14 and 1915-16. Was born in Trumbull County, O., May 1, 1852, of German parentage and acquired his education in the district schools. At the age of ten years he removed to Gratiot County, Mich. He studied law at home and in 1889 was admitted to the bar and in 1897 and 1898 held the office of Prosecuting Attorney. He held the offices of Supervisor and Justice of the Peace; was also City Attorney of St. Louis, and Alderman for several terms. Married. In politics a Republican.

NEWMAN SMITH

Representative from the First District of Wayne County, 1919-20. Was born Sept. 4, 1873, on a farm in Bunker Hill Township, Ingham County, Mich., of Irish parents. He received his early education in the district schools of that township. Later he attended school at the Ferris Institute, Michigan Agricultural College, State Normal School at Mt. Pleasant, and the Detroit College of Law, receiving a degree from the latter institution in 1912. He practiced law in Detroit since that time. Married. In politics a Republican.

OLIVER S. SMITH

Representative from the Second District of Shiawassee County, 1889-90. Was born in Cuyahoga County, O., in 1839. His profession that of attorney. During the war he served in the 1st and the 4th Mich. Infantry and the 123d U. S. C. T. He served as Supervisor of Locke Township, Ingham County, three terms, also Supervisor at large of the city of Owosso three times. In politics he was a Republican.

OSMUND H. SMITH

Delegate to the Constitutional Convention of 1907-8 from the Twenty-eighth District, Alcona County. Was born in Hillsdale County in 1853. He received his education in the district schools and the academy at Medina, Mich., and one year at Morenci High School, and one year in Oberlin, O., Business College. He taught district school in Lenawee and Hillsdale counties, spending his spare time in studies and finally entered and graduated from the law department of the University of Michigan in 1885, going directly from there to Harrisville, where he practiced law. His father died in the Civil War, when he was eleven years old, his mother dying two years previous. He lived with relatives until he was fourteen years of age and then went to live with the family of Edwin Brotherton in Medina Township, Lenawee County, where he stayed until he was twenty-one years of age. Married. He held the office of Prosecuting Attorney in Alcona County for a number of years.

ROBERT B. SMITH

Representative from Ionia County, 1867-8 and 1869-70. Was born at Fairfield, N. Y., April. 21, 1834; was educated as a physician and graduated from the University of New York in 1854; practiced four years at Fairfield, then became surgeon on an ocean vessel; in 1863 settled at Ionia, Mich., purchased a mill and engaged in the manufacture of flour; was President of the village, and for years a director of the Detroit, Lansing & Northern railroad. In politics he was a Republican. He resided in Chicago in 1887.

SAMUEL J. SMITH

Representative from Cheboygan County, 1915-16 and 1917-18. Was born in County Grey, Ont., Jan. 16, 1859. He was educated in the Bruce County, Ont., Newaygo County, Michigan, schools. In 1871 he removed from Ontario to Newaygo County, Mich., where he attended school and lumbered with his father until 1881. He then removed to Antrim County where he secured a position as stationary engineer with the Elk Rapids Iron Company. In 1886 he received marine papers to run an engine on the Great Lakes which occupation he continued until 1893, when he removed to Mackinaw City and embarked in the hotel business. He was married in 1892. He served one term as County Treasurer, twenty-one years as Supervisor of Mackinaw Township, seven years as President of Mackinaw City and fourteen years as School Director. A member of the Masonic fraternity, having received all the degrees except the 33d. In politics a Republican.

SAMUEL L. SMITH

Representative from St. Clair County, 1859-60. Was born at Algonac, Mich., in 1830. For many years he was a leading merchant at Houghton, Mich. He always resided in Michigan, and was a resident of Lansing in 1887. He was a Democrat in politics, and was their candidate for Commissioner of the State Land Office in 1862, and was the Democratic nominee for Congress in the 6th District in 1864. He moved to Detroit where he died May 7, 1917.

SAMUEL WILLIAM SMITH

Senator from the Fifteenth District, 1885-6; and member of Congress, 1897-9 to 1913-15. Was born in the township of Independence, Oakland County, Mich., Aug. 23, 1852. His education was acquired in the Clarkston and Detroit public schools. He taught school six years. He commenced the study of law in 1876 and was admitted to practice in 1877. He was graduated from the law department of the University of Michigan in the class of '78, after which time he engaged in the practice of his profession at Pontiac until he became a member of Congress. Mr. Smith was married to Miss Alida E. DeLand in 1880. He was elected Prosecuting Attorney of Oakland County in 1880 and re-elected in 1882; was a member of the State Senate of 1884; was elected to the 55th, 56th, 57th, 58th, 59th, 61st and 62nd Congresses, and was re-elected Nov. 5, 1912.

SHELDON OGDEN SMITH

Representative from the First District of Wayne County, 1905-6. Was born at Detroit, Mich., Jan. 5, 1872. He received his education in the public high school of Detroit. Upon leaving school he entered the office of his father, the late Mortimer L. Smith, where he acquired the architect's profession. After the death of his father he continued the business in partnership with his brother and later succeeded to the business of the old firm. Single. In politics an active Republican.

SIDNEY T. SMITH

Representative from Jackson County, 1857-8. Was born in Chenango County, N. Y., Oct. 27, 1809. He received an academical education, taught school two winters, and engaged in mercantile business at Pulaski, N. Y. He also with others built a vessel to transport grain from Chicago to Oswego. In 1836 they bought a schooner and went into the lumber trade on Lake Michigan. In 1839 he settled on a farm in Grass Lake, Mich., opened a store and bought and sold produce on a large scale. He sold out in 1855 and retired to his farm. He was for a long time secretary of the Farmers' Insurance Company, and acquired a competence. In politics he was a Republican. He died Apr. 25, 1878.

THADDEUS G. SMITH

Representative from Genesee County, 1863-4; Delegate from Genesee County to the Constitutional Convention of 1867; and Senator from the Twenty-third District, 1869-70. Was born at Cato, N. Y., Apr. 12, 1828. Receiving an academical education, he studied law and was admitted at Albany in 1852. He practiced his profession in Troy and New York City until 1861, when he removed to Fentonville, Mich., where he practiced law until 1877. He was a commissioner under Gov. Blair to take the votes of the soldiers in the field. In 1876 he was elected Probate Judge, and removed to Flint. He was a Republican in politics.

WALKER O. SMITH

Representative from Mecosta County, 1891-2 and 1893-4. Was born in Cortland, N. Y., in 1833. In 1838 he moved with his father's family to eastern Pennsylvania; while there he attended district school in the winter, working on the farm during the summer seasons. In 1853 he was one of a company to establish a select school at Brookland, Pa., with Chas. Allen, now of the State Normal of Wisconsin, as principal. Afterwards he visited extensively in the West and on returning in 1861 was married to Miss Sara A. Kern, of East Springwater, N. Y. He came to Michigan in 1869 and settled on a farm near Crapo. In politics he was a Republican. He held the offices of School Inspector, Justice of the Peace and Supervisor.

WILLIAM ALDEN SMITH

Member of Congress, 1895-7 to 1905-7; United States Senator, 1907-19. Was born at Dowagiac, Mich., May 12, 1859. He received a common school education and removed with his parents to Grand Rapids in 1872. Mr. Smith was appointed a page in the Michigan House of Representatives in 1879; studied law, and was admitted to the bar in 1883. He was a member of the Republican State Central Committee in 1888, 1890 and 1892. In June, 1901, he was honored with the degree of Master of Arts by Dartmouth College. He was elected to the 54th, 55th, 56th, 57th, 58th and 59th Congresses, and reelected to the 60th Congress Nov. 4, 1906. He was elected United States Senator for the full term Jan. 15, 1907, and elected United States Senator to fill the unexpired term of the late Senator Russell A. Alger, Feb. 5, 1907, and immediately resigned his seat in the House of Representatives, entering upon his duties as United States Senator, Feb. 11, 1907. He was nominated at the primary election Aug. 27, 1912, and elected by the Legislature Jan. 15, 1913, for a term beginning Mar. 4, 1913.

WILLIAM H. SMITH

Representative from Jackson County, 1875-6. Was born Apr. 15, 1832, at Gorham, N. Y. He received an academical education, removed to Michigan in 1854 and settled in Grass Lake, Jackson County. He was Supervisor of Grass Lake. By occupation he was a farmer.

WILLIAM M. SMITH

Senator, 1913-14, from the Fifteenth Senatorial District, comprising the counties of Barry, Clinton and Eaton. Was born in Bath Township, Clinton County, Mich., on Apr. 27, 1870, of Irish parentage. His parents, James M. and Hannah Smith, were born and married in Ireland, coming to America during the Civil War. They resided for a time in the State of New York, and afterwards came to Bath Township, where James M. Smith engaged in farming. Both his parents died within one year, when Mr. Smith was fifteen years of age. At seventeen he began teaching in the district schools of Clinton County, his last work as a public school teacher being as principal of the schools of the village of DeWitt. In the meantime he had studied privately and in summer schools, and at the Michigan Agricultural College and University of Michigan, and had been granted a State teacher's life certificate by the State Board of Education, and had also been admitted to the bar. During 1895 and 1896 he taught in the village of DeWitt, and also practiced law; in the fall of 1896 he was elected County Clerk of Clinton County, serving two terms; in the fall of 1900 he was elected Prosecuting Attorney of Clinton County, serving three terms. He has also been City Attorney of St. Johns. Mr. Smith was a Republican Presidential Elector in 1904, and a delegate to the Republican National Convention of 1912. He served from 1906 to 1910 as a member of the Republican State Central Committee from the Eighth Congressional District. He is a member of all the Masonic bodies, the Elks, Knights of Pythias, Grange, and other fraternal societies. In politics he is a Republican.

WILLIAM T. SMITH

Representative from St. Joseph County, 1865-6. Was born in Scott, N. Y., June 26, 1829. He received an academical education and became a teacher. He was in the recruiting service for two years. He came to Centreville, Mich., in 1862, taught several years, and was admitted to the bar in 1866. He was for two terms Superintendent of Schools in Kalamazoo County. He was a Justice in 1887 and engaged in furnishing school supplies. Politically he was a free trader.

WILLIAM WALLACE SMITH

Senator, 1917-18 and 1919-20, from the Twenty-seventh District, comprising the counties of Antrim, Benzie, Grand Traverse, Kalkaska, Leelanau, Missaukee and Wexford. Was born at Constantia, N. Y., Aug. 22, 1849, of American parentage. He received his education in the common schools of Traverse City. He engaged in the mercantile and milling business. He served as Mayor of Traverse City, as Alderman, on the Water Commission and as Charter Commissioner. Married. In politics a Republican.

JOSEPH W. SNELL

Representative from Huron County, 1869-70. His postoffice address was Ora Labor. (Further data not obtainable).

LAWRENCE W. SNELL

Representative from the Second District of Wayne County, 1905-6 and 1907-8; and Senator from the First District of Wayne County, 1909-10 and 1911-12. Was born in Hamtramck, Wayne County, May 28, 1870, of German descent. He was educated in the common schools, supplemented by a course in the Detroit Business University. He was married in November, 1900, to Estelle M. Chamberlin, of Berlin, Green Lake County, Wis. Early in his career he was a dealer in real estate, but in later years has engaged in the dairy business and owned and operated the Log Cabin Creamery of Detroit; also a member of the firm of Snell & Seeley which firm handled all vaccine cattle for Parke, Davis & Co. Mr. Snell served as Village Trustee, as well as Justice of the Peace, and member of the Michigan State Agricultural Society; a Mason, a member of Palestine Lodge, Michigan Sovereign Consistory and Moslem Temple Mystic Shrine, Detroit, and belongs to Greenfield tent of the Maccabees. In politics an active Republican.

WILLIAM SNELL

Representative from Oakland County, 1843 and 1844. Was born in the State of Rhode Island in 1796. By occupation he was a farmer, in politics a Democrat. He settled as a farmer in Oakland, Oakland County, in 1828. He died July 28, 1870.

HORACE G. SNOVER

Member of Congress, 1895-7 and 1897-9. Was born at Romeo, Macomb County, Mich., Sept. 21, 1847; received his early education in the public schools of Romeo and in the Dickenson Institute, located there; graduated from the literary department of the University of Michigan, in the classical course in 1869, and from the law department in 1871; admitted to the bar in 1871. He was engaged in the practice of his profession, except for two years, during which he was principal of the public schools of Port Austin, Mich., to which place he moved in the fall of 1874. In politics a Republican. He served as Probate Judge of Huron County from Jan. 1, 1881, to Jan. 1, 1885; was elected to the 54th Congress, and re-elected to the 55th Congress.

BYRON A. SNOW

Representative from Saginaw County, 1887-8. Was born in Jackson County, Aug. 21, 1850. By profession he was a lawyer, by persuasion a Democrat. Mr. Snow held the office of Supervisor.

ERNEST ALBERT SNOW

Delegate to the Constitutional Convention of 1907-8 from the Twenty-second District, Saginaw County. Was born at Hanover, in 1875, of American descent. He was educated in the public schools of Saginaw, graduating from the high school in 1893, and graduating from the University of Michigan in 1896. He was married to Miss Jennie J. Frazee in 1900. After leaving the University, Mr. Snow went into partnership with his father, Eugene A. Snow, at Saginaw, and entered in the active practice of law, under the firm name of Snow & Snow. He was Chairman of the Saginaw County Democratic Committee. He served as Judge of the Recorder's Court at Saginaw.

FIELDER S. SNOW

Representative from Lenawee County, 1843; and Senator from the Third District, 1849-50, and from the Tenth District, 1853-4. Was born in Ashford, Conn., May 17, 1814. He became a clerk at the age of fifteen, and settled in Clinton, Mich., in 1837. He was a merchant and miller, in politics a Democrat. He was a leader in public enterprises, and was administrator of many estates. For twenty-five years he was a Justice. Deceased.

MILO A. SNOW

Representative from the Second District of Kalamazoo County, 1915-16. Was born in Oshtemo Township, in the same county, Jan. 12, 1858. After leaving the district school he attended the Plainwell High School three years, the Kalamazoo Business College two years, and one year at Parsons' Business College in Kalamazoo. He was married May 23, 1888, to Kate Boyles of Richland. He lived on a farm, owning five hundred acres on Gull Prairie, adjoining the village of Richland, and was also president of the Farmers' State Savings Bank in Richland. He served as Supervisor, one year as chairman of the Board. In politics a Republican.

WILLIAM T. SNOW

Representative from Oakland County, 1850. Came from the State of New York, and settled on a farm in Addison, Oakland County, in 1835. He was a clergyman, an excellent man, and was highly esteemed by the Indians, many of whom became Christians under his preaching. He was Town Clerk in 1838-9, and Supervisor from 1847 to 1854.

STEPHEN F. SNYDER

Representative from Calhoun County, 1883-4 and 1885-6. Was born in Cayuga County, N. Y., Dec. 27, 1829, and received a common school education. He settled as a farmer at Homer, Mich., in 1866. He was a Supervisor several years, and was County Register of Deeds six years. In politics he was a Republican.

DANIEL E. SOPER

Secretary of State, 1891. Was born at Saratoga Springs, N. Y., June 3, 1843. His father died in January, 1844, and for a time the widow took in washing to support herself and little ones. When Daniel was six years old his mother moved to Oneida County and placed him in the care of a farmer. In 1854 his mother brought her little family to Michigan and located in Lenawee County. Here Daniel obtained employment in a woolen factory, where he worked 12 hours per day and attended a night school. When the war broke out he immediately announced a determination to enlist in the 1st Mich. Vol. Infantry, but yielded to the pleadings of his mother and returned to his work. He subsequently enlisted in the Fourth Regiment, but being under age, was prevented from going to the front by his mother forbidding the recruiting officer to swear him in. He then went to Hillsdale to commence life for himself. He worked in a dye-house and embarked in trade as a newsboy and when he had amassed sufficient capital started a news stand and prospered. In 1865 he sold out his business, married Mary A. Howell, a daughter of Wm. T. Howell, a pioneer of the State and a prominent politician of Hillsdale County, and engaged in the drug business at Newaygo. Later he engaged in the real estate and insurance business there. He was on the Democratic electoral ticket in 1884 and was appointed Postmaster at Newaygo by President Cleveland. He served as member of the School Board and as Alderman. He was elected Secretary of State in November, 1890, and resigned Dec. 19, 1891. Deceased.

JULIUS MASON SOPER

Representative from the First District of Eaton County, 1899-1900. Was born on a farm in Onondaga County, N. Y., Feb. 24, 1858, and came to Eaton County, Mich., with his parents in December, 1865, who located and settled upon the farm where the subject of this sketch spent nearly his entire life. He was educated in the country schools, and farming was his sole occupation. In politics a Republican.

MILO SOULE

Delegate from Calhoun County to the Constitutional Convention of 1850. Was born in Madison County, N. Y., July 3, 1804. He had fair schooling, and from 1820 to 1830 taught winters, working on his father's farm summers. He married in 1830 and was a farmer in Murray, N. Y., for five years. In 1835 he came to Michigan and bought a farm in Marengo, Calhoun County, which he cultivated until 1869. He was a Justice for thirty-six years; County Treasurer six years; Supervisor four years; and Town Clerk several years. In politics he was a Democrat.

LOWELL SOURS

Representative from Grand Traverse County, 1915-16 and 1917-18. Was born at Battle Creek, Mich., May 11, 1852, of German-American parentage. His education was acquired in the Elk Lake district school. He removed from Battle Creek to Grand Traverse County in August, 1855. He was married in 1880 to Emma J. Sherman of Whitewater Township. A member of the Grange, he held most of the offices in the local and county granges. In politics a Republican.

HARRY C. SOUTHWORTH

Representative from Houghton County, 1889-90. Was born Feb. 26, 1857, in Stoughton, Mass. He graduated from the Massachusetts Institute of Technology, in the year 1877, and removed to Houghton County, Mich., in September of the same year, where, with the exception of six months spent in Marquette County, from April to October in 1885, at which time he had charge of the Rogers gold mine, he practiced his profession in its various branches. In politics a Republican.

FREDERICK F. SOVEREIGN

Senator, 1901-2 and 1903-4, from the Seventh District, comprising the counties of Berrien and Cass. Was born in Bristol, Elkhart County, Ind., Aug. 27, 1846. He removed to Valparaiso, Ind., in 1862, and entered Valparaiso Male and Female College, where he remained until 1864, when he enlisted as private in Co. C, 131st Indiana, and was discharged as Orderly Sergeant of Co. B, 151st Indiana, Sept. 20, 1865. He re-entered Valparaiso College, from which he graduated in 1866, and began the study of medicine in Rush Medical College of Chicago, Illinois, graduating from that institution in February, 1869. He came to Michigan in 1874, where he successfully practiced his profession in Three Oaks, and held various township offices, being School Director and School Inspector of Three Oaks Township. In politics he was a strong Republican.

CHARLES SPAFFORD

Representative from Lenawee County, 1838. Was a merchant and miller at Tecumseh, and a Whig in politics. Deceased.

ERASTUS SPALDING

Representative from Oakland County, 1867-8. Was born in Tompkins County, N. Y., July 1, 1818. He grew to manhood in that State, studied medicine, removed to Michigan in 1845, settled in Oakland County, and followed his profession there for twenty-four years. He was a Whig, but in 1854 became a Republican. He removed to Grand Rapids in 1879, and engaged in medical practice. He voted the National Greenback Union ticket in 1887.

LEVI SPARKS

Senator from the Twelfth District, 1873-4. Was born Oct. 3, 1823, in Centre, Ind. He emigrated to Michigan in 1828, and settled in Niles Township, Berrien County, where he resided in 1887. He was educated in common schools. In 1864 he was appointed by Governor Blair to go to Arkansas and receive the vote of the Twelfth Michigan Infantry. He held various offices of trust in his township. By occupation he was a farmer, politically a Democrat.

JOHN SPARLING

Representative from Huron County, 1893-4. Was born in Tipperary County, Ireland, Feb. 8, 1841. He came to America with his parents in 1851, locating on a farm in Canada. Here he attended school winters, working on the farm during the summer months. He also learned the carpenter's trade. In occupation a farmer and veterinary surgeon, having begun the study of his profession at eighteen years of age. He came to Michigan and located on the farm in Bingham Township, and devoted his attention exclusively to stock and stock raising. He organized the first agricultural society in his township and was its president for three years. In politics he was a Democrat.

GEORGE SPAULDING

Member of Congress, 1895-7 and 1897-9. Was born in Scotland, in 1837. He came to Buffalo, N. Y., with his parents in 1843, and ten years later to a farm in Monroe County, Mich. His early education was principally received in the public schools of Buffalo before coming to Michigan. At his home in Monroe County he worked on a farm. During the winter of 1860-1 he taught school, and at the outbreak of the Civil War he enlisted as private in the United States Service, was promoted to Lieutenant Colonel. He was mustered out of service Oct. 24, 1865, and returned to Monroe; appointed Postmaster in 1866. In 1871 he was appointed by President Grant special agent Treasury Department, ordered to Brownsville, Texas, to report on commerce at that point, between Mexico and the United States. In 1876 he was Mayor of Monroe city; admitted to the bar in 1878 and engaged in the practice of law. In 1877 he was made cashier of First National Bank at Monroe, which position he held until 1893, when he was elected its president. In politics he was a Republican. He was elected to the 54th Congress and re-elected to the 55th. He died at Monroe Sept. 13, 1915.

OLIVER LYMAN SPAULDING

Member of the Board of Regents of the University of Michigan, 1858-64; Secretary of State, 1867-71; and member of Congress, 1881-3. Was born at Jaffrey, N. H., Aug. 2, 1833, son of Lyman and Susan (Marshall) Spaulding. He was graduated Bachelor of Arts from Oberlin College in 1855. He began his active work as a teacher, giving his leisure time to the study of the law. He was admitted to the Bar in 1858 and began his practice at St. Johns, Mich. At the November election of that year he was chosen Regent of the University in place of the Rev. John Van Vleck, who was elected to the office but who had resigned in October after a brief term of service. He filled out the term, retiring Jan. 1, 1864. In 1862 he enlisted as Captain in the 23d Mich. Infantry, and passed through all the grades to the rank of Colonel. In 1865 he was in command of the Second Brigade of the Second Division of the Twenty-third Army Corps and was brevetted Brigadier General. In 1875 he was appointed special agent of the United States Treasury Department, in which office he continued until he was nominated for Representative to Congress in 1880. In 1885 he again filled the position of special agent for the Treasury. In 1883 he served as chairman of a commission sent by the government to the Sandwich Islands, to investigate alleged violations of the Hawaiian Reciprocity Treaty. From 1890 to 1893 he was Assistant Secretary of the Treasury of the United States, and was again appointed to the same position in 1897. He married the daughter of John Swegles, former Auditor General of Michigan, and they had five children. Deceased.

PHINEAS S. SPAULDING

Representative from Eaton County, 1867-8. His postoffice address was Elmira. (Further data not obtainable).

CAMERON C. SPEER

Representative from the Second District of Saginaw County, 1905-6, 1907-8 and 1909-10. Was born in Union Township, Muskingum County, O., July 5, 1849, of American parents. His father, Robert Speer, was the first white child born in Union Township, O., in 1807. He received his education in the district schools of Union Township and Muskingum College, O. He came to Michigan in 1874, labored in a lumber mill in Genesee County for ten years, then moved to Maple Grove, Saginaw County, in 1884, where he engaged in farming. He was a member of the School Board for fifteen consecutive years, Supervisor of his township, and a member of the Republican County Committee. In politics he was a Republican. He died at Saginaw Apr. 3, 1919.

JOHN J. SPEED

Representative from Wayne County, 1873-4. Was born in Ithaca, N. Y., Jan. 14, 1839. In 1848 he came to Detroit; graduated at the State University; studied law in Detroit; was admitted to the bar in 1861; practiced his profession in Detroit; was appointed one of the two additional Judges of the 3d Circuit in 1881, and was elected Judge in 1882. His term expired in 1887. In politics he was a Republican. He died in Detroit.

THOMAS R. SPENCE

Representative from Wayne County, 1867-8. Was a native of Scotland, born in 1825. He was a druggist and physician, but went to Cincinnati, O., soon after the close of his legislative term, to engage in the tobacco business.

ASA SPENCER

Representative from Ionia County, 1863-4. Was born in Herkimer County N. Y., in 1807. He settled at Ionia, Mich., in 1845, where he kept hotel two years, when he moved to Smyrna, Ionia County, went into mercantile business, continuing his residence until his death in 1876. He held various town offices and was a Justice. In politics he was a Republican.

EDWARD R. SPENCER

Representative from Cass County, 1889-90 and 1891-2. Was born in that county Mar. 28, 1842. His parents were both natives of New York and came to Cass County in 1837, and settled upon the farm which he later owned. He was the first son of a family of five children. He attended high school in Niles and Dowagiac, leaving school to enlist in Co. A, 19th Mich. Infantry, Aug. 9, 1762; was captured at Thompson's Station, Tenn., Mar. 5, 1863. After starvation and exposure and confinement in Libby Prison was paroled from that place, reaching Annapolis, Md., so broken in health that he did not rejoin his regiment in over a year. He was with Sherman in his "March to the Sea," and through the Carolinas and Virginia to Washington, where he was mustered out with his regiment, June 10, 1865. He immediately returned home and attended one term of school at Decatur, Mich. On the 17th of December, 1866, he was married to Miss Frances E. Rich of Decatur and engaged in farming. The death of his wife Dec. 21, 1888, nine days before the assembling of the Legislature, to which he had just been elected, caused his removal from the farm to Dowagiac, where he resided. In politics he was a Republican.

GROVE SPENCER

Representative from Washtenaw County, 1840, 1841, 1848 and 1850. Was born at West Stockbridge, Mass., Aug. 3, 1806. He came to Ypsilanti, Mich., in 1826. By profession he was a lawyer, but health failing, he removed in 1844 to his farm near Ypsilanti, which he managed successfully until his death Aug. 29, 1854. He was for years a director of the State Agricultural Society; was twice a candidate for member of the State Board of Education; was President and Recorder of Ypsilanti and deeply interested in locating the Normal School. In politics he was a Whig.

HORACE C. SPENCER

Senator from the Nineteenth District, 1885-6. Was born at Cortland, N. Y., July 27, 1832. He removed when young to Springville, N. Y. Was educated at an academy, clerked for years, was then a merchant until 1866, when he settled at Flint, Mich., in the hardware trade. He bought a stock farm in 1876, and devoted himself to farming, and especially interested in raising fine horses. Politically he was a Republican.

JAMES W. SPENCER

Representative from Tuscola County, 1887-8. Was born in Dutchess County, N. Y., Oct. 8, 1827, and was a resident of Pennsylvania from 1849 to 1861, when he settled in Indian Fields, Mich. He was Supervisor nine terms, twice chairman of the Board, Town Treasurer, Village President, County Register two terms, and held other offices. For nine years he was a merchant, then a farmer and real estate dealer.

MICHAEL SPENCER

Representative from Calhoun County, 1841. Was born at East Hartford, Conn., Nov. 5, 1804. He came to Calhoun County, Mich., in 1831, and located on a farm in Emmett, on which he resided until his death Oct. 10, 1854. In religion he was a Baptist, in politics a Democrat.

NEWTON C. SPENCER

Representative from Menominee County, 1901-2. Was born in Ashland, O., June 16, 1866, and received his early education in the high school of Champaign, Ill., from which school he graduated and entered the University of Illinois where he studied mechanical engineering for two years, after which he entered upon newspaper work in New York until 1889 when he enlisted in the Seventeenth Infantry and was engaged in the campaign against the Sioux Indians in South Dakota in 1890-1. He was discharged from service in 1892 and taught school until 1893, when he entered the University of Michigan, from which he graduated with the degree of LL.B. in 1896. He was a successful lawyer. In politics a Republican.

PAUL S. SPRAGUE

Representative from the Second District of Shiawassee County, 1863-4. His postoffice address was Nebraska. (Further data not obtainable).

ROGER SPRAGUE

Member of the Territorial Council, 1824 and 1832. Was born at Lebanon, Conn., in 1769. He settled first at Bloomfield, N. Y., and was for seven years Sheriff of Ontario County, which then included nearly all of western New York, and was a member of the Assembly in 1816-17. In 1821 he settled at Avon, Mich. He died in July, 1848.

ROLLIN SPRAGUE

Representative from Oakland County, 1840. Was born in East Bloomfield, N. J., in 1806. By occupation he was a merchant, politically a Republican. He came to Michigan about 1830. He died in August, 1872.

WILLIAM SPRAGUE

Member of Congress, 1849-51. Was born in the State of Rhode Island; removed to Michigan and settled at Kalamazoo. He was a Free Soiler in politics. He died at Kalamazoo soon after the close of his term as Congressman.

WILLIAM B. SPRAGUE

Representative from Branch County, 1846. Was born in the State of New York, Feb. 28, 1797. He graduated as a physician at Fairfield Medical College. He practiced in New York until 1835, then settled in practice at Coldwater, Mich. He gave up medical practice in the fifties. In 1836 he formed a partnership and built a saw mill and flouring mill, the largest roller mill in the county. He was the first Town Clerk of Coldwater in 1836; in 1837 was elected Associate Judge of the County Court; in 1842 was elected Judge of Probate, which he held until 1845. At the age of ninety-one he was in good health, had good sight, enjoyed books and society, and was often seen on the streets. He married in 1831 a daughter of Rev. Francis Smith. In religion he was a Methodist.

WILL J. SPROAT

Representative from the First District of Kent County, 1913-14. Was born of Irish-American parentage near Ashland, O., Jan. 4, 1848. In October, 1851, his parents, Robert and Sarah J. Sproat, came to Michigan and settled in the woods of Dorr Township, Allegan County. His youth was spent in helping to clear the farm. At the age of ten years he began attending the district school and at the age of seventeen began teaching in a neighboring district. He attended the high school at Grand Rapids one term and taught winter terms of district schools until twenty-seven years of age. In Dorr Township he held the offices of Justice of the Peace, Township Clerk and Supervisor. On June 16, 1875, he was married to Gertrude L. Moore, of Byron Township, Kent County. In 1879 he moved to Grand Rapids and a year later entered the newspaper business as a canvasser and collector and was connected with the papers of that city, as circulator, business manager, reporter and editor. In politics a Democrat.

CONSIDER A. STACY

Member of the State Board of Education, 1851-4. Was appointed Apr. 2, 1851, for a three year term. (Further data not obtainable).

HENRY H. STAFFORD

Representative from Marquette County, 1877-8. Was born in Boston, Mass., Jan. 6, 1833. He received an academical education. He came to Michigan in 1855, and took up his residence in Marquette in 1856. He held numerous public offices. He was receiver of the United States Land Offices at Marquette five years, the first Mayor of Marquette, Town Treasurer, member of the School Board, etc. By occupation he was a druggist, in politics a Republican.

OLIVER O. STANCHFIELD

Representative from Mason and Lake counties, 1877-8 and 1879-80. Was born in Washington County, Me., Aug. 16, 1836. He was educated in the academies of his native county, and studied law in the office of Hon. F. A. Pike, in Calais, Me. In 1857 he came West and located at Cedar Rapids, Ia., and was admitted to practice by the Linn County District Court, of Iowa, in 1860. In 1861 he was appointed Sheriff and was subsequently re-elected twice to the .same position. In 1871 he was a member of the Iowa Legislature from Linn County, and was appointed one of the trustees of the Iowa State Agricultural College, which office he held until his removal to Michigan in 1874. In politics he was a Republican.

JOSEPH GARDNER STANDART

Representative from the First District of Wayne County, 1907-8. Was born at Detroit, Mich., Nov. 27, 1879, of Dutch and English descent. He attended the public schools of Detroit, St. Paul's School, Concord, N. H., and graduated from the law department of the University of Michigan in 1903 with the degree of LL. B. After graduation he actively engaged in the practice of law at Detroit, being a member of the firm Moore, Standart & Drake. Unmarried. In politics a Republican.

JOHN H. STANDISH

Senator from the Thirty-first District, 1867-8 and 1869-70. Was born in Benson, Vt., Feb. 10, 1816, and was direct descendant of Captain Miles Standish, of Puritan fame. Receiving a common school education, at the age of fifteen he taught school in Orleans County, N. Y., and in Ohio, and the next year was a clerk in Chicago. From thence he traveled through Iowa, and down the Mississippi, and at the age of seventeen was in the Texan service, where he rose to the rank of Lieutenant. He spent a year in Louisiana, came North, and taught school in Mt. Carmel, Ill., where he married Hester A. Courter. He became a lecturer on psychology, and traveled extensively. He was admitted to the Illinois bar, and in 1839 settled at Middleville, Mich. In 1852 he became a resident of Newaygo. He was Register of Deeds, County Clerk and Prosecuting Attorney of Newaygo County. In 1863 he became Captain of Co. "A," 10th Mich. Cavalry, and rose in service to the rank of Lieutenant Colonel. In 1869 he was appointed U. S. District Attorney for western Michigan, and held that position eight years. For some years was engaged in practice at Muskegon, but in 1881 returned to Newaygo. In politics he was a Republican.

ABIEL S. STANNARD

Representative from Ionia County, 1867-8 and 1869-70. Was born in Newport, N. H., Dec. 28, 1823. He was a farmer by occupation, politically a Republican. He came to Michigan with his father in 1837, who located a farm in Boston, Ionia County. They were among the first pioneers of that section of the State. Mr. Stannard served several terms Supervisor of Boston.

WILLIAM LINUS STANNARD

Representative, 1905-6 and 1907-8, from Iron District, comprising the counties of Baraga, Iron, Keweenaw and Ontonagon. Was born in Rockland, Ontonagon County, Mich., Mar. 1, 1871, of American and German parentage. He received his education in the Rockland High School. Mr. Stannard clerked in his father's store for three years. At the age of twenty-one he was employed as shipping clerk in a wholesale hardware concern at Marquette for one year and left there and engaged in the general merchandise business in partnership with his brother at Wakefield. The brothers carried on this business for six years at Wakefield, and moved to Greenland in 1899. He was married to Martha Chynoweth, Feb. 14, 1894. A 32d degree Mason, member of the Shrine and Knights of Pythias. In politics a Republican. He was treasurer of the County Committee of Ontonagon County, and was chairman of the Board of Superintendents of the Poor for Ontonagon County and resigned after receiving the nomination for Representative.

ERASTUS H. STANTON

Senator from the Twenty-fourth District, 1881-2. Was born in Durham, N. Y., Nov. 13, 1816, and received an academical education. He was of Welsh descent. His mother was a Quaker and, persecuted under Charles II, fled from the country. He was four years a clerk, then became a merchant at Greenville, N. Y., and was also engaged in farming, banking and lumbering. He settled at Ionia, Mich., in 1867. He was a Supervisor six years, and President of the village and Mayor of the city of Ionia. In politics he was a Republican. He died May 8, 1880, at Ionia.

HIRAM E. STAPLES

Representative from Muskegon County, 1885-6. Was born in the State of New York, June 1, 1836. He was a resident of this State, with the exception of the time he served in the war as member of the 5th Wis. Vol. Infantry, having engaged in business as a lumberman, residing at Whitehall, where he held the office of president of the Common Council for six years. He also served as a Supervisor. In politics he was a Republican. He died at Whitehall, Nov. 21, 1915.

GEORGE P. STARK

Representative from Kent County, 1885-6; and Senator from the Twentieth District, 1887-8. Was born at Stow, O., Aug. 19, 1832, and received a common school education, with a term or two at Hiram College. He learned the trade of cooper, followed it until 1853, when he became a farmer. He was for one year, 1866, in the drug trade at Palestine, Ill., then was a farmer until 1871, when he removed from Hudson, O., to Cascade, Mich., where he became a merchant and farmer. In politics he was a Fusionist.

LEWIS F. STARKEY

Senator from the Fifth District, 1843-4. Was born in the State of New Hampshire, in 1801. He studied medicine at Norwich, N. Y., and at Philadelphia. He practiced as a physician and surgeon in a Philadelphia hospital, in Otsego County and Binghamton, N. Y. He came with his family to Detroit in 1836, and settled at Kalamazoo in 1837, where he practiced his profession until his death in 1848. By appointment of the Governor he was one year a visitor to the State University.

GEORGE A. STARKWEATHER

Representative from Wayne County, 1859-60. Was born in Plymouth, Mich., Feb. 26, 1826, of New England parentage. He was the second white child born in the township, as his mother was the first white woman to settle there. His early education was such as the time and the locality afforded, and his pursuits were farming and mercantile. He was president of the First National Bank of Plymouth, and held various local offices. He was originally a Whig, and subsequently a Republican in politics.

BENTON R. STEARNS

Representative from Berrien County, 1879-80. Was born in Delaware County, O., Dec. 12, 1842. He received a common school education, and removed to Berrien County, Mich., in 1848. In 1861 he enlisted in Co. E, 12th regiment, Mich. Vols., receiving commissions as Second and First Lieutenant in same regiment, serving four years and a half. His occupation was that of a druggist, which he engaged in at Galien, Mich. He filled the offices of Township Treasurer five years, and Supervisor. In politics he was a Republican.

JUSTUS SMITH STEARNS

Secretary of State, 1899-1901. Was born in the township of Pomfret, Chautauqua County, State of New York, April 10, 1845. His father, Heman S. Stearns, was a farmer and lumberman. His education was received at the district school of that township. In the year 1861 his father removed to Erie, Pa., and was engaged in lumbering for ten years, when he went to Toledo, O., continuing in the lumbering business there until 1876. Soon after, Justus S. located at Ludington, Mich., and served as clerk in the Catherine L. Cameron store until 1882, when he began the manufacture of lumber, in a small way, in Lake Township, Lake County, Mich. He had mills at Stearns, Lake County, Mich.; Ludington, Mich.; Lac du Flambeau, Wis., and Odanah, Wis. The largest manufacturer of lumber residing in the State of Michigan, having manufactured, during 1898, 125,000,000 feet. He served as School Director at Ludington, and Presidential Elector from the Ninth Congressional District in 1892.

WESLEY J. STEARNS

Representative from Montcalm County, 1917-18 and 1919-20. Was born in Iowa, May 20, 1868, of English parents. His education was secured in the public schools of Sheridan, Mich. He was a meat dealer for fourteen years, and then devoted his time to farming. He held the offices of Village Trustee, Village Clerk, Assessor, Supervisor, Township and County Treasurer. Married. In politics a Republican.

GEORGE A. STEEL

Senator from the Nineteenth District, 1893-4; and State Treasurer, 1897-9 and 1899-1901. Was born in St. Johns, Mich., June 19, 1862. He acquired his early education in the public schools of that place. In July, 1878, he went to Sauk Rapids, Minn., to take a position as bookkeeper and paymaster for James McIntire & Co., bridge constructors, later discharging similar duties for the same firm at St. Paul, Minn. In 1879 he went to Nevada, being paymaster on the Nevada Central railway during its construction; the following year he became general paymaster and purchasing agent of the Oregon Construction Company in the construction of about four hundred miles of railroad in Oregon, Washington and Idaho, later combining those duties with that of secretary of the corporation, having full charge of the finances of the company. In 1885 he returned to Michigan and became interested in banking, mercantile and manufacturing institutions, and also in real estate. He became vice president of the St. Johns National Bank, at St. Johns, Mich., upon its organization in 1885. On Jan. 28, 1885, he was married to Miss Cora Stout, of St. Johns. He organized and became president of the Ithaca Savings Bank at Ithaca, Mich., in 1893. In January, 1895, he formed a partnership with F. A. Smith, of Detroit, under the firm name of Steel, Smith & Co., for the purpose of carrying on the business of buying and selling municipal bonds and commercial paper. He was a member of the Republican State Central Committee for 1892-3; was elected to the Senate from the Nineteenth District for the term of 1893-4; elected State Treasurer on the Republican ticket for the term of 1897-9, and was re-elected to the office of State Treasurer for 1899-1901.

AMOS E. STEELE

Representative from Ingham and Livingston counties, 1840. Was born in Queensbury, N. Y., June 28, 1806. He settled in Onondaga, Mich., in 1836, and was elected Associated Judge of Ingham County in 1838; took the county census in 1840; removed to Mason in 1844, and was elected Judge of Probate in 1848; and was Justice twenty-seven years, and filled many local offices. In politics he was a Republican after 1854. He died Mar. 15, 1878.

GEORGE E. STEELE

Representative from Antrim and other counties, 1877-8. Was born in West Andover, O., Oct. 28, 1842. He removed to Kingsville, O., in 1845, and in 1861 to Benzonia, Mich. He received an academical education. In 1864 he removed to Homestead; attended the State Agricultural College; was County Surveyor of Grand Traverse County, then including Benzie, and Supervisor; removed to Elk Rapids, Antrim County, in 1872, after which time he was County Surveyor of Antrim County, and Supervisor of Elk Rapids, and largely engaged in examinations of lands, estimates, civil engineering and surveying, and in a small way in farming. In politics he was Republican, later a Prohibitionist.

JOSEPH HALL STEERE

Justice of the Supreme Court, 1911—. Was born at Addison, Lenawee County, May 19, 1852. He was educated at the Raisin Valley Seminary, Adrian High School and University of Michigan, graduating from the latter institution in

the classical course, with the degree of A. B., and in 1892 received the degree
of LL.D. Subsequently he studied law for two years in the office of Geddes
and Miller, of Adrian, and was admitted to the bar upon examination. He
taught school for some time before engaging in the practice of law. He served
as Circuit Judge of the Eleventh Judicial District for a number of years. Mr.
Steere was appointed to the Supreme Bench, Aug. 30, 1911, to fill the vacancy
caused by the death of Frank A. Hooker, and at the general election held on
Nov. 5, 1912, was elected to fill the unexpired term. At the election held on
Apr. 7, 1913, he was elected for the full term, and was again re-elected Apr.
4, 1921.

WILLIAM M. STEPHENS

Representative from Ingham County, 1875-6. Was born in Chittenden County, Vt., in 1825, where he resided until 1832, when his father's family removed to Niagara County, N. Y. In 1835 the family removed to Michigan
and settled in Stockbridge, Ingham County, where he resided, with the exception of four years spent in California. He received a common school education, and was a farmer by occupation. In politics he was a Democrat.

ROBERT STEPHENSON

Representative from Delta and Menominee counties, 1881-2. Was born in
New Brunswick in 1836. He removed to Delta County in 1846, and to Menominee County in 1849. He received a common school education; engaged
principally in lumbering, in which he was largely interested in 1887; was
Superintendent of the Ludington, Wells & Van Schoick Lumber Co., in which
he was a large stockholder. He was also closely identified with several other
important business enterprises in that section of the country. In politics he
was a Republican.

SAMUEL M. STEPHENSON

Representative from Delta and Menominee counties, 1877-8; Senator from the
Thirty-first District, 1879-80 and 1885-6; and member of Congress, 1889-91 to
1895-7. Was born in New Brunswick, in 1831. He received a common school
education. In 1846 he located in Delta County, Mich., where he engaged in
lumbering. In 1858 he removed to Menominee and built the second sawmill
on the river, and largely interested in real estate, lumbering and general mercantile business, and farming, and an officer in the Kirby Carpenter Co., of
Menominee, and the Stephenson Banking Co., of Marinette, Wis. In politics
he was a Republican. He was chairman of the Board of Supervisors of
Menominee County for several years, Representative in the Legislature in
1877-8, and in the Senate of 1879-80 and 1885-6. He was a delegate to the
National Republican Convention of 1888, and elected a member of the 51st,
52nd, 53rd and 54th Congresses.

LEWIS THOMAS STERLING

Representative from Dickinson County, 1909-10. Was born in Gouverneur,
St. Lawrence County, N. Y., of Scotch parentage. He acquired his early educa-
tion in the schools and academy of that place, later attending Olivet College,
Mich., one year, and completed his education at Washington University, St.

Louis, Mo. After leaving the University he engaged in commercial pursuits at Rochester and New York City, and some years later returned to Gouverneur and opened an insurance, real estate and loan office. In 1891, Mr. Sterling came to Iron Mountain to accept the position as manager of the insurance department of the First National Bank. At the time of the formation of the U. S. Steel Corporation, he was engaged as an insurance expert to make rates for their insurance department. He conducted his insurance and real estate business, and was secretary and treasurer of the Iron Mountain Electric Light and Power Company. In politics a Republican.

EZRA STETSON

Representative from Kalamazoo County, 1851. Was born in Otsego County, N. Y., in 1811. He settled as a physician at Galesburg, Mich., in 1837, and was in practice there for twenty years. He was a graduate of Fairfield Medical College, N. Y. He was Supervisor of Comstock, and a public spirited, active and influential citizen. In 1857 he removed to Bureau County, Ill., where he became a farmer and stock raiser, giving much attention to the Percheron breed of horses, and was among the first to bring them to this country. He acquired a fortune.

AMOS STEVENS

Delegate from Wayne County to the Constitutional Convention of 1835; and Representative from Wayne County, 1849. Was born in Sangerfield, N. Y., May 31, 1801. He removed to Steuben County in 1806, and to Canton, Mich., in 1831, where he died in 1876. He filled many local offices. He was a farmer by occupation, a Democrat in politics, and a Presbyterian in religion.

APPLETON STEVENS

Representative from Bay County, 1861-2. Was born at Moodus, Conn., Aug. 17, 1818. He settled at Portsmouth, Bay County, in 1856, and was the first Supervisor of that town. He died Aug. 29, 1878.

FITZ H. STEVENS

Senator from the Twentieth District, 1853-4. Was born in Tyngsboro, Mass., May 27, 1817. He came to Michigan in 1837, and resided in Berrien and Van Buren counties nearly the entire period from that date until his death, which occurred at St. Joseph, Sept. 7, 1870. In politics he was a Democrat. He was Register of Deeds in Van Buren County from 1840 to 1842; also Postmaster of St. Joseph. He was active in raising troops for the 12th Mich. Infantry, and went out as the chosen Quartermaster of the regiment, but did not finally receive his commission.

HESTOR L. STEVENS

Member of Congress, 1853-4. Was born at Lima, N. Y., October 1803; received and academical education; studied law, and was admitted to the bar, and commenced practice in Rochester, N. Y., where he was also connected with the press. He attained eminence as an attorney, removed to Michigan in 1845, and locating at Pontiac engaged in practice. He was Prosecuting Attorney of Oakland County in 1847 and 1848. He was elected Representative to Congress in 1852, as a Democrat. In 1854 he was defeated as a candidate for re-nomination. Soon after the expiration of his term he removed to Washington, where he practiced before the court of claims. He was an able lawyer, and a man of high social position. He died in Georgetown, D. C., May 7, 1864.

HORACE STEVENS

Representative from Oakland County, 1845. Was born in Sharon, Conn., Aug. 29, 1799. He came to Michigan in 1835, was in business as mill owner and speculator, in politics a Democrat. He was a prominent local politician, and a man of wealth and position. He was one of the commissioners that located the State Prison, and was also a Judge. He was prominent in securing the Clinton and Kalamazoo Canal. He gave the casting vote in the Congressional Convention which nominated Kinsley S. Bingham to Congress the first term. He died in March, 1849.

J. FRANK STEVENS

Representative, 1913-14, and 1915-16, from the Missaukee District, comprising the counties of Kalkaska and Missaukee. Was born at Ames, Story County, Ia., Sept. 24, 1872, of English parentage. He was educated in the Ames schools and the Capital City Commercial College. In 1881 he removed from Iowa to Parma, Mich., and attended school there at the time Senator Townsend was principal. In 1883 he returned to Iowa and resided on a farm continuously with the exception of the time spent at school. In 1903 he removed to Missaukee County, Mich., and resided on his ranch at Star City. He was principal of the Star City schools in 1908-10. He was Postmaster at that place during the years 1910 and 1911, and was secretary of the Missaukee County Farmers' Institute Association. Married. In politics a Republican.

JOHN H. D. STEVENS

Senator, 1891-2, from the Thirty-second District, comprising the counties of Baraga, Gogebic, Houghton, Iron, Isle Royal, Keweenaw and Ontonagon. Was born in Rockland, Ontonagon County, Feb. 22, 1858; removed to Houghton when ten years of age, and attended the public schools until twelve years old, after which he engaged in the Quincy copper mine at Hancock, being the first boy employed in any underground capacity. He did general work, both underground and on the surface; also worked in silver mines in Canada, and was one of the hundreds of Northern Michigan men who were induced to visit the Black Hills during the gold and silver fever in 1879. He again returned to the copper mines in 1881 and moved to the Gogebic iron range in 1884, and built the first residence there; was one of the first men to commence exploratory work at the Ashland & Norris Iron mines, for which he received the paltry sum of $1.50 per day. He was prominently identified with the labor interests of Northern Michigan. In 1887, after the creation of Gogebic County, he was elected to the office of Judge of Probate, and was re-elected in 1888. He was elected Grand State President of the order of the Sons of St. George in July, 1890.

JOHN J. STEVENS

Representative from Monroe County, 1867-8. Was born in Cleveland, O., Oct. 17, 1823. By occupation he was a builder, in politics a Republican. He came to Monroe, Mich., in 1834. He served as Alderman and Supervisor. He was Captain of Co. K, 18th Mich. Infantry, from June 18, 1862, until the regiment was mustered out in June, 1865. He died Apr. 4, 1888, at Monroe.

STEPHEN R. STEVENS

Representative from Montcalm County, 1877-8 and 1879-80. Was born near Geneva, N. Y., Dec. 19, 1826. He received an education at Hobart College, Geneva. He was engaged in teaching for a number of years. He removed to Michigan in 1863, and became a citizen of Greenville in 1866. He filled various offices of trust. By occupation he was a merchant, in politics a Republican.

WILLIAM C. STEVENS

Auditor General, 1883-7. Was born at Plymouth, Mich., Nov. 14, 1837, and from 1846 to 1861 resided at Whitmore Lake. He entered the service as a Lieutenant in the 3d Mich. Cavalry in 1861, was discharged in 1862 for disability, but in the fall of that year became a Captain in the 9th Mich. Cavalry, and was promoted to Major, serving until the close of the war. He studied law and graduated from the University law class of 1868, went into practice at East Tawas, served as Prosecuting Attorney, and ten years County Treasurer. In politics he was a Republican. He died at his home in Detroit, Aug. 20, 1921.

WILLIAM N. STEVENS

Representative from Washtenaw County, 1861-2. Was born at Elizabeth, N. J., Apr. 29, 1813. He learned the trade of a carpenter and worked at it for several years. He moved from New York City to Plymouth, Mich., in 1834, and from there to Whitmore Lake in 1847. He was engaged in mercantile business from 1847 to 1872. He was County Clerk in 1872. In 1882 he removed to Ann Arbor.

JOHN STEVENSON

Representative from the First District of Wayne County, 1909-10, 1915-16, 1917-18 and 1921—. Was born in Ayrshire, Scotland, Apr. 22, 1854. He was educated in the public schools and business university. He came to Detroit in 1870 and was in the steamboat business for fifty years, at the foot of Randolph Street, Detroit. Mr. Stevenson is married. In politics he is a Republican.

ALBERT E. STEWART

Representative from the First District of Wayne County (Detroit), 1897-8 and 1899-1900. Was born in the Township of Clay, St. Clair County, Mich., Sept. 23, 1847. He attended district school winters and worked on his father's farm until he was seventeen years of age, when he enlisted in Co. K, 22d Mich. Infantry Vol., where he remained until the regiment disbanded, July 11, 1865. On his return home he engaged as clerk in a store until 1867, when he began sailing, becomingg master in 1876, and in 1879 he purchased an interest in a vessel, and then engaged in the vessel business, being vice president and general manager of the Stewart Transportation Company. In politics a Republican. He was elected to the House of 1897-8 on the general legislative ticket of Detroit, and re-elected to the House of 1899-1900.

EARL RUTHVEN STEWART

Representative from the First District of Kent County, 1909-10 and 1911-12. Was born at Byron, Kent County, Mich., Oct. 5, 1872, of Scotch-German descent. He was educated in the district schools, high school, and University of Michigan, graduating in 1900 from the latter. He was married; was a member of the Michigan National Guard after 1891, missing one year from his college course on account of the service of the Michigan National Guard in the Spanish-American War. After his graduation from the University he practiced law at Grand Rapids, Mich. In politics he was a Republican. He died May 1, 1923.

EDWIN STEWART

Representative from St. Joseph County, 1861-2 to 1865-6. Was born at Cambria, N. Y., Aug. 28, 1819. He came to Michigan in 1837. In 1839 he taught school in Pine Lake, Oakland County. He attended the branch of the State University at Kalamazoo, graduated as a physician at Rush Medical College, Chicago, in 1850, and after that time was a practicing physician. He resided at Mendon. He was a Representative as a Republican. He was Postmaster at Mendon during President Arthur's administration.

HUGH A. STEWART

Senator, 1917-18, from the Thirteenth District, comprising the counties of Genesee and Livingston. Was born in Lapeer County, Mich., Aug. 4, 1882, of Scotch parentage. He was educated in the high school of Fostoria, Mich., and graduated from the Detroit College of Medicine in 1906. He practiced in North Branch, Lapeer County, one year and at Alba, Antrim County, one year, removing to Flint in the spring of 1909. He was married Oct. 23, 1907, to Anna M. Vandecar, of North Branch. In politics a Republican.

HUGH P. STEWART

Delegate to the Constitutional Convention of 1907-8, from the Sixth District, St. Joseph County. Was born in 1856 of Scotch descent. He was educated in the common schools supplemented by private teaching. He was admitted to the bar in 1878, and practiced law in Centerville, also practiced law in Battle Creek as a member of the law firm of Stewart & Sabin. Married. He served as Prosecuting Attorney of St. Joseph County.

JAMES STEWART

Representative from Wayne County, 1869-70. Was born near Glasgow, Scotland, in 1830. His early occupations were machine work and railroading. He came to the United States in 1851. After a year spent in Penn Yan, N. Y., he removed to Michigan, settling in Van Buren, Wayne County, where he engaged in lumbering. In 1887 he was still in the same business in the village of Belleville, although for several years he had carried on a flouring mill at New Boston. In politics he was a Democrat. He was honored with various offices, and in 1887 was a Justice.

ELI L. STILLSON

Representative from Calhoun County, 1845. Was born in Scipio, N. Y., May 20, 1804. When young he removed with his father to Rochester, N. Y., and was in the mercantile business in early life. In 1836 he came to Battle Creek, Mich., and devoted himself to the profession of law. He held the offices of Master of Chancery, and Justice. His court was regarded as a model in point of dignity, precision and practice. He died Nov. 11, 1862.

JOSEPH W. STINCHCOMB

Representative from Barry County, 1877-8. Was born in Perry County, O., July 2, 1828. He removed to Seneca County, O., in 1830. He received a common school education. In 1860 he removed to Michigan and settled in Sunfield, Eaton County, removed again to Woodland, Barry County, where he resided in 1887. He held the offices of School Inspector, Highway Commissioner, and Justice. In politics he was a Republican.

FRANCIS B. STOCKBRIDGE

Representative from the First District of Allegan County, 1869-70 and Senator from the Seventeenth District, 1871-2; United States Senator, 1887-94. Was born at Bath, Me., Apr. 9, 1826; received a common school education. He was a clerk in a wholesale house in Boston from 1843 to 1847, when he went to Chicago and opened a lumber yard, being interested in saw mills in Michigan. He moved to Allegan County, Mich., in 1851, taking charge of his mills. In politics he was a Republican. He was elected to the Legislature in 1869, and to the Senate in 1871; elected to the United States Senate to succeed Omar D. Conger, and took his seat Mar. 4, 1887; re-elected in 1893, serving until his death, Apr. 30, 1894.

DAVID STOCKDALE

Representative from the Second District of Allegan County, 1905-6 and 1907-8. Was born at Wainfleet Lincolnshire, England, July 26, 1838. The family emigrated from England to America in 1854, and settled on a farm in Branch County, Mich., where the parents resided until their death. He attended school at Croft, England, until twelve years of age, when he was obliged to begin work as a blacksmith's apprentice. In the year 1858 he opened and carried on a blacksmith's shop at Wayland, Allegan County, until 1865, when he purchased a farm and devoted his time to agriculture. While on the farm he commenced the study of law, was admitted to the bar and began practice in the year 1884. He held the offices of Justice of the Peace, Supervisor, President of Wayland Village, president of Allegan Village, Judge of Probate of Allegan County. Extensively engaged in agriculture and senior member of the firm of David Stockdale & Son, attorneys. In politics he was an ardent Republican. He was a member of the Republican State Central Committee for two years, and chairman of the Republican County Committee for ten years.

DORA HALL STOCKMAN

Member of the State Board of Agriculture, 1920——. Was born in a log cabin at Marilla, Manistee County, Mich., Aug. 4, 1872, of American parents. She received her education in the public schools of Benzonia, Benzie County, Benzonia College, and Hillsdale College. She taught school three years, the last one at Hillsdale College, and has a teacher's life certificate given her by the State Board of Education. She was married in 1889 to F. M. Stockman, who was operating a farm near Benzonia. In 1903 they bought the "Grand River View Farm," a short distance northwest of Lansing, and have succeeded in building up what was at that time a "worn out" place. Mrs. Stockman is well known throughout the State as a lecturer on agricultural subjects, having been one of the State Grange speakers for the past ten years. In 1914 she was elected lecturer of the Michigan State Grange, which office she still holds. In addition to the rearing of three children, all boys, Mrs. Stockman has found time, outside of her other numerous duties, to do considerable literary work and has three books to her credit. In recognition of her work along agricultural lines she was nominated on the Republican ticket as candidate for the office of member of the State Board of Agriculture and was elected Apr. 7, 1919.

JOHN STOCKTON

Member of the Legislative Council from Macomb County, 1824-5 to 1830-1, and 1834-5; Senator from the Fifth District, 1835-6; and Representative from Macomb County, 1840, 1841 and 1850. Was born in Lancaster, Pa., Dec. 24, 1798, and when young removed with his parents to Chillicothe, O., became a clerk, and served in the War of 1812, and was in command of Fort Malden when peace was declared. In 1815 he was the private secretary of Gov. Cass, and in 1816 became a Detroit merchant. He removed to Mt. Clemens, and was Postmaster there three years, also County Clerk and Register of Macomb County. He was a Justice of the Peace from 1819 to 1874. He was speaker *pro tem.* in 1850. In 1824 he was Government Superintendent of the Lake Superior copper mines. He raised the 8th Mich. Cavalry in 1862, and escorted it to the field, two of his sons being Captains in the regiment. He died Nov. 26, 1878.

CYRUS MOSES STOCKWELL

Member of the Board of Regents of the University of Michigan, 1865-72. Was born at Colesville, N. Y., June 20, 1823. He was educated at Oxford, N. Y., and began life as a school teacher. He subsequently studied medicine and received the degree of Doctor of Medicine from the Berkshire Medical College, Pittsfield, Mass., in 1850. In 1852 he emigrated to Michigan and settled in Port Huron, where he practised his profession until 1895, retiring then on account of advancing years. He passed through all the rugged experiences of the pioneer physician. At the outbreak of the Civil War he entered the army as Surgeon of the 27th Mich. Infantry, but resigned in November, 1863. After the close of hostilities he rendered service for a time as Assistant Surgeon at Fort Gratiot. In 1866 he was instrumental in founding the Michigan State Medical Society and became President of the Northeastern District Medical Society, and was prominently identified with the professional interests of the State. He was appointed Regent of the University early in 1865 to fill the vacancy caused by the death of Alvah Sweetzer nearly a year before, and served until the end of the term, Jan. 1, 1872. He was twice married. He died at Port Huron, Dec. 9, 1899.

MARTIN P. STOCKWELL

Delegate from Lenawee County to the Constitutional Convention of 1867. Was born in Cato, N. Y., and located a farm in Dover, Lenawee County, in 1837. He held the offices of Justice and Supervisor, and for eight years was County Superintendent of the Poor. Politically he was a Republican.

CAMERON C. STODDARD

Representative from Tuscola County, 1861-2. Was born in Essex County, N. Y., in February, 1830. By occupation he was a farmer, in politics a Republican. He came to Michigan from western New York in 1858. He enlisted as a private in Co. A, 29th Mich. Infantry, in 1864, and returned home in September, 1865, with a commission as First Lieutenant. He was Supervisor several terms, and Clerk of Tuscola County from 1872 to 1876. He died Jan. 24, 1876.

CLAUDE M. STODDARD

Senator, 1919-20, from the Thirteenth District, comprising the counties of Genesee and Livingston. Was born in Richfield Township, Genesee County, Mich., June 6, 1875, of English parentage. He was educated in the public schools of Flint and the Flint Normal School. After teaching school three years he was engaged for nineteen years in the general merchandise business. Interested in farming and operated the farm on which he lived. Married. In politics a Republican.

JESSE STODDARD

Representative from Hillsdale County, 1849. Was born in Litchfield, Conn., July 3, 1792. He married in 1814, removed to Genesee County, N. Y., in 1816, and from there to Hillsdale County in 1836. By occupation he was a farmer.

WILLIAM STODDARD

Representative from Hillsdale County, 1857-8; and Senator from the Twelfth District, 1871-2, and from the Ninth District, 1873. Was born Aug. 31, 1821, in Sheldon, N. Y., received a common school education, came to Michigan in 1836, and settled as a farmer in Litchfield, Hillsdale County. He was a Republican in politics. He died in 1873, and was succeeded in the Senate by John P. Cook.

HENRY L. STOFLET

Representative from the Fourth District of Wayne County, 1889-90. Was born in Seneca County, N. Y., in 1842. During the Civil War he served in the 4th Mich. Infantry. In politics he was a Republican.

ALBERT STOLL

Senator, 1889-90, from the Second District, composed of the first, second, third, fifth and seventh wards of Detroit. Was born at Detroit, Mich., Aug. 10, 1852. His education was received at the public schools and the German-American Seminary of that city. He began business life as a manufacturer of cigars in his native city, and continued until 1875, when he engaged in insurance and real estate. From 1881 to 1885 he was Assistant City Clerk; from 1886 to 1888, inclusive, was County Auditor; was a member of the Soldiers' Relief Commission from 1889 to 1891, inclusive, and Receiver of Taxes from July 1, 1892, to June 30, 1898; then in the business of real estate and insurance.

OTTO STOLL

Representative from the First District of Wayne County (Detroit), 1895-6. Was born in Detroit, Sept. 14, 1862; educated in the Detroit public schools and German-American Seminary; a son of Julius Stoll, who was one of the leading German citizens of Detroit. At the age of sixteen years he began the manufacturing jeweler's trade. In politics a Republican. He was elected Representative to the House of 1895-6 on the general legislative ticket of the city of Detroit.

ALVAH GARDNER STONE

Representative from the Second District of Lenawee County, 1901-2, 1903-4 and 1905-6. Was born in Charleton, Worcester County, Mass., Mar. 2, 1853, of Revolutionary stock, his great grandfather being one of the famous minute men and Captain in the Revolutionary army. His early education was obtained in Massachusetts, supplemented by a common school course at Medina, Mich. Married, and a farmer since 1870. In politics a Republican.

CHARLES W. STONE

Representative from Newaygo County, 1883-4. Was born in the County of Warren, N. Y., June 2, 1833, and received his education in the common schools. He came to Michigan in 1854 and settled in Newaygo County. He was a farmer and breeder of shorthorn cattle, and had lumber interests. He was nine times elected Supervisor of his township, and twice elected County Treasurer. He was a National in politics.

CLEMENT W. STONE

Representative from Roscommon and other counties, 1877-8. Was born May 30, 1840, in Gloucester, Mass. In 1843 he removed to Michigan and located in Kalamazoo. He received an academical education. In 1861 he enlisted as Commissary Sergeant in the 6th Regiment, Mich. Vol., and was promoted to the Captaincy of Co. D, of that regiment. At the close of the war he held the position of Inspector General of the district of south Alabama and west Florida. In 1866, in connection with his brother, he purchased the Kalamazoo weekly *Telegraph*, and afterwards established the daily *Telegraph*. In 1872 he located at Houghton Lake. In 1874 he was elected Supervisor of Roscommon Township, at that time being attached to Midland County. In 1875 he was elected County Treasurer of Roscommon County. He was engaged in farming and real estate. In politics he was a Republican. Deceased.

EDWARD L. STONE

Representative from the First District of Saginaw County, 1891-2. Was born in Wayne County, Mich., Jan. 9, 1853, and during his boyhood days was a resident of Commerce and Pontiac, Oakland County, removing to Saginaw in 1860. He graduated from the high school in Saginaw in 1870, and entered the University that fall in Latin and scientific course. During 1871 he studied law with Gaylord & Hanchett at Saginaw, and entered the law school in the fall of 1871, graduating with the class of 1873; was admitted to the bar at Saginaw in 1874, and removed to St. Paul, Minn., in 1875, returning to Saginaw in 1881. He filled the office of Deputy County Clerk from 1882 to 1886, and Justice from then until 1890. He was defeated for Circuit Court Commissioner in 1886 and Judge of Probate in 1888. He engaged in the practice of law at Saginaw. He was elected to the House of 1891-2 on the Republican ticket. He vacated his seat by removal from the district before the session of 1892.

GEORGE W. STONE

Auditor General, 1891-3. Was born in Newbern, N. C., Aug. 27, 1849. His father was a sea captain in the West India and coasting trade. When two years old his father moved to Brooklyn, N. Y., where he resided for six years, when reverses in his father's family threw him into the Children's Aid Society, and he, with thirty-one other little ones were given away to the charitable people of Michigan. He found a good home on a farm at Albion, and remained there until Dec. 12, 1862, when he enlisted in Co. D, 1st Mich. Sharpshooters, and served with his company and regiment until Aug. 11, 1864. From 1865 to 1869 he attended the common schools and Albion College. In 1869, he and C. J. Comstock, succeeded W. G. Powers, of Albion, in the dry goods business. In the fall of 1870 the firm moved to Petersburg, Va., but, being so soon after the war, the new enterprise did not meet with success. In 1872 Mr. Stone came to New York and bought a canal boat and outfit all on credit, and when he came to balance his books at the close of navigation he found himself financially ahead, after being driver, steersman and captain on his boat. In 1873 he embarked in the grocery trade at Lapeer, Mich. In 1881 he was elected City Clerk of Lapeer. In February, 1882, his friends, regardless of politics, indorsed him for a clerkship in the Auditor General's office at Lansing, which position he held until 1885. In that year, he, in partnership with Dr. Rush J. Shank and Geo. E. Lawrence, loaded five cars with merchandise, teams and stock, and was among the first to move into and develop McIntosh County, Dakota. In 1887 Mr. Stone returned to Clare County, Mich., and embarked in the lumber and milling business. He was elected Clerk of Clare County in 1888. In 1884 and 1885 he was Adjutant General of the Department of Michigan G. A. R., in 1887 aid-de-camp on the staff of Commander-in-Chief Fairchild, and in 1889 Junior Vice Commander of the Department of Michigan G. A. R., and in 1890 delegate to the National Encampment at Boston. He received the Democratic nomination for Auditor General and was elected.

HIRAM STONE

Representative from Monroe County, 1844, 1845 and 1848. Was a lawyer in fine practice at Monroe. He died while on his way to California.

HIRAM H. STONE

Representative from Wayne County, 1848. His postoffice address was Dearbornville. (Further data not obtainable).

JOHN W. STONE

Member of Congress, 1877-9 and 1879-81; and Justice of the Supreme Court, 1910——. Was born at Wadsworth, Medina County, O., July 18, 1838, of American parentage. He is a widower, Mrs. Stone having died in January, 1902. He was educated in the public schools and academy at Spencer, O. In April, 1856, he came to Michigan and settled in Allegan County. He was elected County Clerk of Allegan County in 1860 and re-elected in 1862. He was admitted to the bar in January, 1862, and in 1864 was elected Prosecuting Attorney of Allegan County and twice re-elected. In April, 1873, he was elected Circuit Judge of the Twentieth Judicial Circuit, comprising the counties of Allegan and Ottawa. In November, 1874, he resigned the office and removed to Grand Rapids and resumed the practice of law. In 1876 he was elected a member of Congress to represent the Fifth Congressional District, composed of Kent, Allegan, Ottawa, Muskegon and Ionia counties, and was re-elected in 1878. In 1882 he was appointed United States Attorney for the western district of Michigan. He removed to Houghton in May, 1887, and practiced law there until April, 1890, when he was elected Circuit Judge of the Twenty-Fifth Judicial Circuit, composed of Marquette, Delta, Menominee, Dickinson and Iron counties. He held this office until Dec. 31, 1909. He was elected Justice of the Supreme Court, April 5, 1909, for the term beginning Jan. 1, 1910; re-elected Apr. 2, 1917, for the term ending Dec. 31, 1925.

RALPH STONE

Member of the Board of Regents of the University of Michigan, 1924——. Was born November 20, 1868, in Wilmington, Delaware, of American parentage. He received his early education in the public schools of that place and later entered Swarthmore College in Pennsylvania, where he graduated in 1889 as Bachelor of Arts. He then took up the study of law under Hon. Anthony Higgins, U. S. Senator from Delaware. After one year Mr. Stone came West and entered the law department of the University of Michigan, which graduated him in 1892 as LL. B. During his career he has rendered valuable service in many responsible positions, and is at present president of the Detroit Trust Co. Mr. Stone is married. At the biennial election, April 2, 1923, he was elected a member of the Board of Regents of the University.

LEWIS A. STONEMAN

Representative from the First District of Wayne County (Detroit), 1897-8. Was born in Indianapolis, Ind., Sept. 7, 1868. He graduated from the Indianapolis High School and University of Michigan law school, class of 1894. After completing his studies he located in Detroit, where he engaged in the practice of his profession. In politics a Republican. He was elected to the House of the Legislature of 1897-8 on the general legislative ticket of the city of Detroit.

WILBUR F. STOREY

Delegate from Jackson County to the Constitutional Convention of 1850. Was born in Vermont in 1820. He was a publisher. With R. S. Cheney he commenced the publication of the Jackson *Patriot*, a Democrat paper, in 1848. He was later connected with the publication of the Chicago *Times*. He was a member of the Board of Internal Improvements.

WALES F. STORRS

Representative from Ottawa County, 1867-8; and Senator from the Thirtieth District, 1871-2. Was born at Westport, N. Y., Jan. 19, 1816. He received the education of common schools, moved with his parents to Portage County, O., in 1834, worked on a farm until 1836, and then taught school for several years. In 1859 he removed to Grand Haven, Mich., and engaged in lumbering. He was a Whig until 1854, then a Republican.

WILLIAM L. STOUGHTON

Attorney General, 1867-9; Delegate from St. Joseph County to the Constitutional Convention of 1867; and Member of Congress, 1869-73. Was born in Bangor, N. Y., Mar. 20, 1827. He received an academical education, studied law, and was admitted to the bar in 1851. He was Prosecuting Attorney of St. Joseph County, 1855-9, and for some time U. S. District Attorney for Michigan. He resigned, became Lieutenant Colonel of the 11th Mich. Infantry, became Colonel Apr. 1, 1862, lost a leg in battle, was made Brigadier General, and at the close of the war Major General, "for gallantry in the field." He practiced law several years at Grand Rapids, then resumed practice at his old home in Sturgis, where he died June 6, 1888.

BYRON GRAY STOUT

Representative from Oakland County, 1855-6 and 1857-8; Senator from the Fifth District, 1861-2; and member of Congress, 1891-3. Was born in Richmond, Ontario County, N. Y., in 1829, and came to Michigan with his parents in 1831, and settled in Oakland County. He was graduated from the literary department of the Michigan University in 1851; and three years later was elected to the State Legislature, and re-elected in 1856, when he was chosen speaker. In 1861 he held a seat in the State Senate and was chosen president *pro tem.* In 1862, against his earnest protest, he received the nomination of the "Union" party of that year for Governor, but was defeated by Hon. Austin Blair. In 1868 and 1870 he was nominated by the Democrats for Congress, but his competitor, Hon. O. D. Conger, was successful. In 1883 he was the candidate of the Union Party for the United States Senate against Hon. Thomas W. Ferry. For many years Mr. Stout divided his time between his books and his farm. In 1890 he was elected to the 52nd Congress. He died June 19, 1896.

DAVID B. STOUT

Representative from Allegan, Barry and Eaton counties, 1838. Settled at Allegan, Mich., in 1836. In politics he was a Whig. He removed to New Jersey in the forties, was a Free Soiler in 1848, became a preacher, and died in that state.

STEPHEN S. STOUT

Representative from the First District of Allegan County, 1889-90. Was born in New York in 1829. By occupation a farmer and physician. He served during the war in the 24th Michigan Infantry. He held the offices of Supervisor of Cheshire Township, County Agent of the State Board of Corrections and Charities, and Township Clerk. In politics he was a Republican.

ISAAC STOW

Representative from Livingston County, 1875-6. Was born in Weybridge, Vt., Dec. 10, 1830. In 1836 he came with his parents to the western part of Livingston County. He had the advantage of a good high school for some months. He filled nearly every position in the gift of his township, and with the exception of three years held the office of Supervisor between 1865 and 1887. He was engaged in agriculture. In politics he was a Democrat.

ALEXANDER H. STOWELL

Senator from the Second District, 1853-4. Was born in Vermont in 1808. He came to Michigan at an early day, and was a bookbinder by trade. He identified himself with the business of Detroit, and became a trader in a general way, especially in real estate. He was Alderman, 1850-3, and served as Assessor and City Marshal at various times. He was a Democrat in politics. Deceased.

HENRY E. STRAIGHT

Representative from Branch County, 1909-10 and 1911-12; and Senator, 1913-14 and 1915-16, from the Ninth District, comprising the counties of Branch and Calhoun. Was born on a farm in Coldwater Township, Branch County, Mich., Dec. 26, 1864, of American descent. His education was acquired in the district schools, the Business College, Valparaiso, Ind., and the State Normal College at Ypsilant. He followed farming and school teaching for two years and held several township offices. Early in life he identified himself with grange and farmers' institute work, holding the office of worthy lecturer of Branch County Pomona, and for four years held the office of secretary and treasurer of the Branch County Farmers' Institute Society. He was committee clerk in the Senate in 1900; a member of Coldwater lodges B. P. O. E. and I. O. O. F. and was for six years a member of Co. A, 2nd Regiment, M. N. G. In 1899 he married Sarah B. Depue. He engaged in the clothing and gents' furnishing business in Coldwater. In politics a Republican. He served two terms as County Clerk of Branch County.

JAMES J. STRANG

Representative from Newaygo and other counties, 1853-4 and 1855-6. Was born at Scipio, N. Y., Mar. 21, 1813, and was the son of a farmer. He received a common school education, followed by a short term at Fredonia Academy. When young he became a conspicuous debater in the rural clubs, and had a morbid desire for distinction. At the age of twelve he joined the Baptist Church, and was for some time an active member. He was restlessly active, taught school, delivered temperance addresses, worked on his father's and other farms, and at the age of twenty-one commenced the study of law. He was admitted to the bar in 1836, and soon after married Mary Perce. He practiced law at Mayville and Ellington, N. Y., and was Postmaster at Ellington. In 1843 he emigrated to Burlington, Wis., and formed a law partnership with C. P. Barnes. In 1844 he visited Nauvoo, Ill., the Mormon headquarters, was speedily converted and baptized into that faith. He was authorized by Joseph Smith, as an elder and minister, to establish a Mormon colony in Wisconsin. Strang founded his colony at Voree, (Now Spring Prairie) Wis., and published the Voree *Herald*. The colony grew. In May, 1847, he explored the Beaver Islands, and made it his headquarters. St. James was named from him, and in 1850 the colony elected him king. He then published the *Northern Islander*, and the saints became the owners of homesteads. In 1849 his first wife left him, and he had another wife in 1851, a second in 1852, and two others in 1855. In July, 1856, he was murdered on Beaver Island, and was buried at Spring Prairie, Wis. He was elected Representative as a Democrat. He was a man of ability, and aside from polygamy, of upright character, scholarly life and studious habits, and a good writer and speaker.

WILLIAM P. STRAUCH

Representative from Shiawassee County, 1921—. Was born in Shiawassee Township, Shiawassee County, Mich., July 6, 1870, of German descent. He was educated in the district schools of Shiawassee County. Mr. Strauch is a farmer and has also contracted and built state roads. He is a 32nd degree Mason, and member of the B. P. O. E. He is married and has one son and one daughter. In politics he is a Republican.

SAMUEL STREET

Representative from Berrien County, 1850. Was a native of North Carolina. He located a farm in Bertrand, Berrien County, in 1835, and built a double log house, where he lived until his death in 1861. He was Supervisor of Bertrand.

RANDOLPH STRICKLAND

Senator from the Twenty-second District, 1861-2; and member of Congress, 1869-71. Was born at Dansville, N. Y., Feb. 4, 1823. His grandfather was a Revolutionary soldier. His education was obtained under great difficulties, mostly at night by the light of burning pine knots. From sixteen to twenty-one he was employed in a saw mill, working sixteen hours a day. In 1844 he taught school in Ingham County, Mich. For five years he was engaged in studying and working, and was admitted to the bar in 1849. After a short time spent in practice at Detroit, he was elected Prosecuting Attorney of Clinton County, and held that position for eight years. He first resided at Dewitt, after that at St. Johns. He was a delegate to the Republican National Convention of 1856; and Provost Marshal, 1863-5. He was a Republican in politics. He died at Battle Creek, May 5, 1881.

DANIEL STRIKER

Secretary of State, 1871-5. Was born in Rose, N. Y., Apr. 9, 1835, and came with his parents to Concord, Mich., the same year. In 1851 they moved to Baltimore, Barry County. He became a clerk at Hastings from 1855 to 1858. He was Clerk of Barry County six years; Deputy County Clerk three years; Supervisor and chairman of the County Board; was admitted to the bar in 1870; was engaged in the drug and hardware trade, and a national bank director. He was chairman of the Albion College endowment fund committee, and devoted his time to that and to banking. In politics he was a Republican. He was also a member of the Michigan Pioneer and Historical Society. He died at Hastings, Apr. 12, 1898.

GILBERT STRIKER

Representative from Barry County, 1873-4. Was born in Washington, N. Y., Oct. 13, 1811. In 1818 his parents removed to Wayne County, N. Y. He received a common school education. In 1835 he removed to Michigan and settled in Concord, Jackson County. In 1852 he removed to Baltimore, Barry County. He served in several responsible positions in his township. He was a farmer by occupation, and a Republican in politics.

OLIVER P. STROBRIDGE

Representative from Lapeer County, 1850. Was born in Claremont, N. H., June 1, 1818. By profession he was a physician. He came to Michigan in 1840, and lived at Farmington until 1845, when he removed to Almont, and practiced his profession until 1873. Then he went to California for his health and did not return to Almont until a short time before his death, Feb. 1, 1880.

EDWARD B. STROM

Representative from the First District of Kent County, 1921-2. Was born in the county of Kent, Jan. 14, 1887, of Swedish and Irish descent. He was educated in the public school of Central Lake, and also studied law, being admitted to practice in 1912. He is engaged in the electrical jobbing business and the Taylor-Strom Letter Co. Mr. Strom enlisted in the M. N. G. in 1911 and during the European War was Major, 126th Infantry, 32nd Division, A. E. F., engaging in the battles of Alsace Trenches, Aisne-Marne, Oise-Aisne and Meuse-Argonne. He was first Commander of Carl A. Johnson Post No. 2, American Legion. He is married and has two children, a boy and a girl.

JOHN STRONG

Representative from Wayne County, 1835 and 1836. Was a native of England, born 1799. He came to Michigan in 1822, was a farmer by occupation, and died Mar. 25, 1881. His son (of the same name) since held seats both in the House and Senate, from Wayne and Monroe counties.

JOHN STRONG

Representative from Wayne County, 1861-2; and from Monroe County, 1879-80; Senator from the Fifth District, 1881-2 and 1883-4; and Lieutenant Governor, 1891-3. Was born in Greenfield, Wayne County, Apr. 7, 1831. He received a common school education and followed farming in his native township until 1863, when he removed to South Rockwood, Monroe County, and engaged in milling, in manufacturing staves, heading and lumber, in mercantile trade, and in farming and raising shorthorn stock. In politics he was a Democrat. He was twice elected to the House of Representatives, from the Second District of Wayne County in 1861-2 and from the Second District of Monroe County, in 1879-80; was elected to the Senate from Monroe County in 1880 and re-elected in 1882; and was the regular Democratic candidate for Lieutenant Governor in the campaign of 1890 and was elected for the years 1891-3. He died at South Rockwood, Apr. 2, 1913.

MYRON STRONG

Representative from Cass and Van Buren counties, 1841. Was born and brought up in Rochester, N. Y. He removed to Cass County, Mich., in 1835, and settled on a farm near Edwardsburg. In 1838 he was elected an Associate Judge of the county. He sold his farm in 1847 and returned to Rochester, N. Y., where he lived until the close of the late war, when he removed to Florida, and died there about 1872.

SYLVESTER A. STRONG

Representative from the Second District of Jackson County, 1879-80 and 1893-4. Was born Sept. 10, 1833, in St. Lawrence County, N. Y.; removed to Michigan in 1834, and became a resident of Jackson County in 1840. He received a common school education, and chose a farmer's life. He held many offices, including Treasurer, Highway Commissioner, and Justice. In politics he was a Democrat until the organization of the Greenback Party which he gave his support; also endorses principles of the Prohibition Party; member of the House of 1879-80, elected on the Greenback ticket; and was re-elected to the House of 1893-4 on the People's Party and Democrat tickets.

ALONZO J. STROUD

Representative from Charlevoix County, 1905-6 and 1907-8. Was born in Parma, Cuyahoga County, O., May 6, 1843, of American parentage. He spent his boyhood days on his father's farm, and acquired his education in the public schools of Middleburg, O. Early in the Civil War he enlisted in the 14th O. Vol. Infantry, but was discharged for disability. He was in the quartermaster's department of the army of the Cumberland nine months, later enlisting in the 188th O. Vol. Infantry and remained until the close of the war. He was married to Cecelia A. Norton in 1866, and came to Horton Bay, Mich., and engaged in the lumber business. He was a member of several secret orders, and was grand master of the I. O. O. F., 1900-1. He held the offices of Supervisor, Sheriff, and Judge of Probate of Charlevoix County. In politics he was a Republican.

JOHN STRUBLE

Representative from Cass County, 1875-6. Was born in Union County, Pa., Feb. 9, 1823, removed to Michigan in 1846, and settled at Three Rivers, St. Joseph County. He received a common school education, and held the offices of Supervisor and Justice. His occupation was farming. In politics he was a Democrat.

CHARLES E. STUART

Representative from Kalamazoo County, 1842; member of Congress, 1847-9 and 1851-3; and United States Senator, 1853-9. Was born at Canaan Corners, Columbia County, N. Y., Nov. 25, 1810. His father soon removed to Waterloo, N. Y., where he received the education of common and grammar schools. At the age of nineteen he commenced the study of law, and was admitted to the bar of Seneca County. In 1835 he settled at Kalamazoo, Mich., and began his distinguished career as a lawyer and politician. With great intellectual endowments, keen perception and courage, he attained high position at the bar, and in the political arena. In the Senate he was presiding officer. On account of ill health, he retired from practice and public life. He was a delegate at large from Michigan to the Democratic National Convention in 1860, and was the leader of the Douglas delegates. He was also a delegate at large to the Democratic National Convention in 1868, and was a delegate to the Union Convention at Philadelphia in 1866. For the last seventeen years of his life he was an invalid, but never lost his interest in public affairs. He raised the 13th Mich. Infantry in 1862. He died at Kalamazoo, May 19, 1887.

DAVID STUART

Member of Congress, 1853-5. Was born at Brooklyn, N. Y., Mar. 12, 1816; moved to Michigan and located at Detroit. He was elected a Representative from Michigan to the Thirty-third Congress as a Democrat. He died at Detroit, Sept. 19, 1868.

PATRICK STUART

Representative from Wayne County, 1887-8. Was born at Tulnagingay, Fermanagh County, Ireland, Mar. 17, 1820. His father was a mechanic, and died leaving a widow and four children, of which Patrick was next to the youngest. In a few years their means were exhausted, and when the subject of this sketch was but seven years old he was compelled to help make his own living. Afterwards he traveled through Ireland, Scotland and England, and finally, in 1843, sailed for America, where he learned the brass molder's trade, married and settled in Detroit, where he resided, working at his trade until 1884, when he was made sewer inspector. In politics he was a Democrat.

ROBERT STUART

State Treasurer, 1840-1. Was born at Callander, Perthshire, Scotland, in 1785. He received a fair education, and at the request of his uncle, David Stuart, then an agent of the Northwest Company, he came to Montreal, Canada, when twenty-two years of age. There he made himself master of the French language, and subsequently entered the office of the Attorney General of the province. He, with his uncle, John Jacob Astor, and others, in 1810 became partners in a scheme for establishing trading posts on the Pacific coast and its rivers. In September, 1810, the Stuarts with a crew of fifty-one sailed for the mouth of the Columbia River, where they founded Astoria, and established several trading posts on the Columbia and its tributaries. The War of 1812 compelled them to sell out to the Northwest Fur Co., and Mr. Stuart with a party of six traveled overland from Astoria to New York. In 1817 he removed to the island of Mackinac as the general agent of the American Fur Company, which he successfully managed until 1835, when the business was closed out and he removed to Detroit, investing largely in real estate. He became a director in the old bank of Michigan, and was appointed State Treasurer in 1840, which position he held nearly one year. He was a ruling elder in the Presbyterian Church. In all religious matters his place was in the front rank. He died Oct. 29, 1848.

HENRY STUMPENHUSEN

Representative from the Second District of Washtenaw County, 1899-1900 and 1901-2. Was born in Ypsilanti, Washtenaw County, Mich., Aug. 15, 1843, of German-Irish parentage. At the age of three years he removed with his parents to a farm in Ypsilanti Township. He received his education in the district and union schools of Ypsilanti and taught school for two years. At the age of twenty-nine he married Florence C. Dansingburg of Augusta, in the same county. He held many positions of trust; several times a candidate for township office but owing to the strong Republican sentiment existing in his township was never elected.

DAVID STURGIS

Delegate from Clinton County to the Constitutional Convention of 1850; and Senator from the Seventh District, 1851. Was born in Brant County, Ont., Mar. 10, 1810. By occupation he was a merchant; in politics a Democrat. He came to Detroit in 1837 and engaged in peddling for the wholesale house of Beecher & Abbott, making his trips by the way of Pontiac and DeWitt to Grand Rapids, which gave him an opportunity to find a place to settle. He commenced mercantile business at Portland, then removed to DeWitt in 1840, and remained there merchandizing and milling until the founding of St. Johns, in which he took an active part with Auditor General Swegles and others in 1853-4. He was Associate Judge in 1842; Supervisor of DeWitt in 1850 and 1853; and trustee of the Union School at St. Johns. Fond of pioneer life, he took pride in the advancement of the State, and was a great favorite of the Indians, speaking their language fluently. He died in February, 1864.

FRANK P. SULLIVAN

Representative, 1893-4, from the district composed of the counties of Chippewa, Luce and Mackinac. Was born Mar. 7, 1864, on a farm near Petersborough, Madison County, N. Y. He acquired his education at the Evans Academy and the State Normal School of New York. He came to Michigan in 1885 and studied law, was admitted to the bar and in 1887 began practice at Sault Ste. Marie. June 7, 1890, he was married to Miss Minnie W. Hall, of Saginaw, Mich. He was appointed City Attorney of Sault Ste. Marie Sept. 1, 1890, and reappointed in 1891. In politics a Democrat.

JAMES SULLIVAN

Delegate from Cass County to the Constitutional Convention of 1850; and Senator from the Eighteenth District, 1855-6. Was born in Exeter, N. H., Dec. 6, 1811, and was of illustrious ancestry, his grandfather being General Sullivan of the Revolution, who was Governor of New Hampshire from 1786 to 1789, and Representative in Congress. His father, George Sullivan, was an eminent lawyer, and was Attorney General of New Hampshire, and Representative in Congress. James Sullivan graduated from Dartmouth College at the age of eighteen, studied and practiced law at Concord, N. H., in 1837 came to Niles, Mich., soon after removing to Edwardsburg, and thence to Cassopolis. He was a practitioner at the bar of Cass County from 1838 to 1878, and was an able lawyer. He was Prosecuting Attorney from 1852 to 1854. In 1853 he removed to Dowagiac, where he resided until his death in August, 1878.

JACOB SUMMERS

Representative from Macomb County, 1835 and 1836; and Senator from the Fifth District, 1837-8, from the Fourth District, 1839-40, and from the First District, 1849-50. Was born in the State of New Jersey, Jan. 7, 1787. He was by occupation a farmer, in politics a Democrat. His father became a Judge of

Records in Philadelphia. The son settled in Shelby, Macomb County, in 1831. He was Supervisor in 1836 and Associate Judge of Macomb County. He was a man of strong mind, but uneducated, indolent and eccentric. But as a Legislator he had great influence, and often defeated the strongest men of the State in legislation. He was familiarly known as "Uncle Jake." He died July 25, 1863.

JOHN D. SUMNER

Representative from the First District of Kalamazoo County, 1893-4. Was born in Westville, Franklin County, N. Y., Aug. 24, 1842. He came with his parents to Michigan the next year, locating in Kalamazoo County. His early education was received at the public schools at Kalamazoo, and by working upon the farm and teaching he was enabled to attend the "Prairie Seminary" at Richland. In 1861 he was prepared to enter the Michigan University, but instead, at the outbreak of the war, enlisted in Co. I, 2nd Mich. Infantry. His parents prevented his going to the field, and shortly afterwards he enlisted in the 7th Mich. Infantry with like results.. He was successful in his third attempt and went to the front Sept. 7, 1861, as 1st Sergeant of Co. F, 8th Mich. Infantry. He was promoted to 2d and 1st Lieutenant, Adjutant, and Captain of his regiment, in which last capacity he served at the Battle of the Wilderness, Dec. 5, 1864. He was promoted to Lieutenant Colonel, and was mustered out June 30, 1865. He was severely wounded at James Island, S. C., June, 1862, and at the Battle of Weldon railroad. At the close of the war he returned to his home in Kalamazoo. In politics he was a Republican. He held the offices of Treasurer and Clerk of the village (now city) of Kalamazoo, and Supervisor of the 2d ward of the city and Sheriff of the County.

JOHN J. SUMNER

Representative from Monroe County, 1871-2; and Senator from the Fifth District, 1873-4. Was born Apr. 17, 1832, in Sodus, N. Y., and received the education of common schools. In 1847 he emigrated with his parents to Bedford, Monroe County, where he resided in 1887. He was Postmaster at Lambertville twenty-two years; Justice eight years; Supervisor five years. His occupation was that of general merchant and farmer. He was a Republican until 1884, then a Prohibitionist.

JABEZ G. SUTHERLAND

Delegate from Saginaw County to the Constitutional Convention of 1850 and 1867; Representative from Saginaw County, 1853-4; and Member of Congress, 1871-3. Was born in Onondaga County, N. Y., Oct. 6, 1825; removed with his father to Genesee County in 1836. He studied law and was admitted in 1848. In 1849 he began practice in Saginaw City, and became Prosecuting Attorney of the county. After that he devoted himself to his practice with signal success. In 1858 he was the Democratic candidate for Attorney General. In 1863 he was elected Circuit Judge of the Tenth Circuit, and was re-elected in 1869 without opposition. He acquired distinction as a Judge. In 1870 he was elected to the Forty-seventh Congress as a Democrat. He was practicing law with success at Salt Lake City in 1887.

JAMES B. SUTHERLAND

Representative from Berrien County, 1855-6. Was born in North Castle, N. Y. He became a clerk in the dry goods with T. Peck, on Cedar Street, New York City. He went to Missouri in 1840, and in 1841 engaged in mercantile and lumber business at St. Joseph, Mich., had a lumber yard at Chicago, and was in the trade for twenty years. He was a member of the Legislature as a temperance Democrat, spoke and voted for the Maine law and free railroads. He married the daughter of J. B. Lame in 1853; was an independent Democrat up to 1884, then a Prohibitionist. He was a deacon in the Congregational Church at St. Joseph.

JUSTIN L. SUTHERLAND

Delegate in the Constitutional Convention of 1907-8 from the Eighteenth District, Ionia County. Was born on a farm near Grand Ledge, Mich, in 1873. Mr. Sutherland attended district school until fifteen years of age, afterwards graduating from the public schools of Grand Ledge. Teaching school and working during vacations on a farm and in a store, then occupied his time for a while, and this was followed by a course at the Michigan Agricultural College. In 1896 Mr. Sutherland entered the law department of the University of Michigan and graduated in 1899, immediately taking up the practice of law. In 1905 he was married to Miss Marion L. Newton, a resident of his native town.

WILLIAM SUTHERLAND

Representative from the Third District of Bay County, 1899-1900. Was born at Kawkawlin, Bay County, Mar. 8, 1863, and educated in the schools of Kawkawlin and Bay City. Occupation, a farmer.

DANIEL B. SUTTON

Representative from the First District of Washtenaw County, 1913-14. Was born in Northfield Township, Washtenaw County, June 12, 1872, of American parents, receiving his education in the district schools and the Ann Arbor High School. He was married Apr. 25, 1906, to Miss Bessie Meade. Occupation, farmer and dealer in live stock. He was for four years Sheriff of Washtenaw County. His grandfather and father both served in the Legislature,—the former in 1875 and the latter in 1885. In politics, a Democrat.

EDWIN SUTTON

Representative from Cass County, 1857-8. Was born in Ulster County, N. Y., Apr. 1, 1821. He settled in Mason Township, Cass County, Mich., in 1846. He was a farmer and district school teacher, and Town Clerk and School Inspector. He was a Democrat until 1854, then a Republican. He died June 12, 1862.

ELI RANSOM SUTTON

Member of the Board of Regents of the University of Michigan, 1900-2. Was born at Greeley, Kan., Aug. 25, 1868, son of Ottawa and Elizabeth Permelia (Poplin) Sutton. After a preparatory training in the public schools he entered the Kansas State Normal School and was graduated from that institution in 1888. He then became a student of the University of Michigan, taking the degree of Bachelor of Laws in 1891 and the degrees of Bachelor of Science and Master of Laws in 1892. Immediately after leaving the University he took up the practice of law in Detroit, where he held in succession the offices of Assistant City Counselor, Assistant City Attorney, and Assistant Corporation Counsel. Upon the accession of Mr. Pingree to the Governorship in 1897 he was appointed Colonel on the Governor's staff. He was elected Regent of the University in April, 1899, and took his seat the following January, but resigned the office on leaving the State in June, 1902. He was married July 1, 1896, to Grace Louise Williams, of Sodus, N. Y.

GEORGE SUTTON

Representative from Washtenaw County, 1875-6. Was born in Oxford, Warren County, N. J., Feb. 17, 1810. He came with his father to Michigan in 1830, and settled upon a farm of five hundred acres in Northfield, always having been a farmer. He received his education in the common schools. He held office in his township from its organization to 1887, having filled the positions of Supervisor, Justice of the Peace, and other offices. In politics he was a Democrat. He died at Northfield, Washtenaw County, May 18, 1890.

NATHÁN E. SUTTON

Representative from Washtenaw County, 1885-6. Was born in Northfield, Jan. 17, 1842, upon the farm purchased in 1824 of the United States, by his father's family, who were the first settlers in the township. Here he still resided in 1887, and followed the occupation of a farmer and dealer in live stock. In early life Mr. Sutton received a good education, passing through the common schools and graduating at the Ann Arbor Commercial College in 1861. He filled the office of Supervisor for two terms, and was elected Representative as a Democrat..

WILLIAM C. SUTTON

Senator from the Third District, 1873-4. Was born Dec. 3, 1811, in Warwick, N. Y. He was educated in the common schools. In 1857 he emigrated to Michigan and settled in Battle Creek. In 1865 he removed to the town of Dearborn, Wayne County. He served in several responsible offices in the town where he resided, and before leaving New York held various public offices. His occupation was a miscellaneous character.

JAMES H. SWEENEY

Representative from Lenawee County, 1846. Was a physician. He came from the State of New York about 1835, and lived many years at the village of Morenci. Deceased.

EDWIN F. SWEET

Member of Congress, 1911-13. Was born at Dansville, N. Y., Nov. 21, 1847, and
was educated at Yale. He graduated from the law department of the University of Michigan and practiced law from 1874 to 1904. He was married.
As a member of the Grand Rapids Board of Education he led the fight against
the bribery methods employed by book companies and aided in eliminating
politics from educational matters and making the Board of Education and
Library Commission elective by the city at large. While Mayor he started a
non-partisan movement in Grand Rapids outlining a practical plan for local
elections which has been endorsed by the voters of Grand Rapids. He inaugurated flood protection measures for Grand Rapids, better hospital location
and system, the fight which resulted in taking away the charter from the private
corporation competing with the city in the water business. He was nominated
for Congressman at the primaries Sept. 6, 1910, and elected Nov. 8, 1910.

JOHN B. SWEETLAND

Representative from Cass County, 1875-6. Was born July 4, 1834, in Tompkins County, N. Y., and removed to Michigan in July, 1861. He was educated
at the district schools and New York Central College, and was a graduate of
the medical department of the University of Buffalo. He enlisted as a private
in the 4th Mich. Cavalry, serving thirteen months, when he received an appointment upon the medical staff in the regular army. In politics he was a
Republican.

ALVAH SWEETZER

Member of the Board of Regents of the University of Michigan, 1864. Was
born at Gray, Me., Feb. 9, 1801, son of John and Jane (Rideout) Sweetzer.
He was of Dutch ancestry. He was given a good academical education, and
spent some time in teaching. He then entered upon a business career in Portland, Me., from which place he removed to Michigan. He was married while
in Portland, to Mary Jane Sanborn, daughter of Dr. William Sanborn, of Falmouth, Me. In 1845 he became co-partner with his brother-in-law, James W.
Sanborn, the firm doing an extensive business in lumbering, merchandise, and
real estate, with headquarters, after 1847, at Port Huron. He was a man of
scholarly tastes and a zealous advocate of public education. He served for a
time on the Port Huron School Board. He was elected Regent of the University in 1863 and drew the long term of eight years; but he lived to attend
only a single meeting of the Board. He died at Port Huron, Feb. 7, 1864.

JAMES A. SWEEZEY

Representative from Barry County, 1863-4 and 1867-8; member of the Board
of Regents of the University of Michigan, 1864-72. Was born at Brook Haven,
Long Island, N. Y., Sept. 19, 1828. He was a lawyer by profession; a Republican in politics. He came to Michigan in 1834, and lived with his parents at
Napoleon, Jackson County, until June, 1851, when he settled in Hastings, and

was admitted to the bar at Grand Rapids in 1853. He was Prosecuting Attorney of Barry County for six years. He was twice elected and for two years
filled the trust of grand chancellor of the order of Knights of Pythias of Michigan. He died at Hastings, Feb. 13, 1898.

JOHN SWEGLES

Auditor General, 1851-5. Was born in Hector, N. Y., Apr. 10, 1819. He commenced the study of medicine at the age of eighteen, and abandoned it to become purser's clerk on the brig Porpoise of the Atlantic coast survey. In 1840
he removed to Jonesville, Mich. He was clerk of Hillsdale County from 1845
to 1849. In 1853 he selected for a company of which he was a member the
site of the present village of St. Johns, the land purchased comprising 920 acres.
He built a saw mill and stave house the next year, and employed men to clear
the land. The village was named St. Johns, as a mark of honor to him. He
died many years prior to 1887.

ALDEN B. SWIFT

Representative from the Second District of Eaton County, 1889-90 and 1891-2.
Was born in the township of Bellevue, Eaton County, Mich., Jan. 3, 1855. His
ancestors were pioneers of the county, his grandfather and father having moved
from New York State and settled in Bellevue Township in March, 1839. When
but six years of age Mr. Smith removed with his parents to the adjoining township of Kalamo and settled upon the farm which he later owned. His educational advantages consisted, in addition to the district school, of a term at
Olivet College, and a year at the Michigan Agricultural College. He taught
school several winters and worked upon his father's farm summers until, at
the age of twenty-one, he began farming for himself. In 1880 he was married
to Miss Hattie A. Babcock, daughter of one of Kalamo's early pioneers. Politically, a Republican. He held the offices of Superintendent of Schools and
School Inspector for his township.

GEORGE W. SWIFT

Representative from Wayne County, 1867-8 and 1869-70. Was born in Palmyra,
N. Y., May 21, 1817. In 1825 he came with his father, Rev. Marcus Swift, to
Michigan, the family settling on a farm in Nankin, Wayne County, where he
remained until twenty years of age, receiving his education largely at home.
In 1837 he went to New York and enjoyed for four years good educational advantages. As a speaker he early distinguished himself in debate, especially
upon the subjects of temperance and anti-slavery, and delivered many public
addresses. He removed to Lansing with his family and was State Librarian
from 1857 to 1859. In 1859 he had charge of the State fund for the relief of
destitute settlers in Gratiot, Montcalm, Isabella and adjoining counties, and
purchased over 120 tons of provisions and supplies, which were loaned, notes
being taken in over 2,000 cases. For this work he received the thanks of the
State officers. In politics he was a Republican. He was sergeant-at-arms of the
House in 1865. In 1869 he was appointed Consul at Windsor, which he held for
four years. He died at Northville, Mich., Apr. 28, 1885.

JOHN M. SWIFT

Representative from Wayne County, 1865-6. Was born in Nankin, Mich., Feb. 11, 1832, and was the youngest son of Rev. Marcus Swift. His early life was that of a farmer's son, and his education was largely obtained at home, with one year at common schools and a short academical course. He commenced the study of medicine in 1851, and graduated in 1854, at the eclectic medical institute of Cincinnati. He attained distinction as a physician, and was elected a member of various medical societies both in this country and in England. Rush College, Chicago, Ill., conferred a degree on him in 1864. He was also a fine tenor singer, took great interest in music, and through him largely, Northville had a wide reputation as a musical town. In politics he was a Republican, in religion a Presbyterian. He was one of the commission who located the House of Correction at Ionia in 1876.

ORSON SWIFT

Representative from Barry County, 1885-6. Was born in Huntington, Vt., Aug. 3, 1838. He came to Michigan in 1862, and located in Leroy, Calhoun County. Five years later he removed to Maple Grove, Barry County. He engaged in the business of farming. He held the office of Supervisor of his township six years. In politics he was a Fusionist.

WILLIAM F. SWIFT

Senator from the Thirty-first District, comprising Mackinac, Chippewa, Schoolcraft, Delta, Menominee, Marquette and Baraga counties, 1881-2. Was born in the town of Sharon, Litchfield County, Conn., July 10, 1848. He removed to Ishpeming, Mich., in 1873. He was the Republican candidate for Senator in 1880.

ALBERT P. SWINEFORD

Representative from Marquette and other counties, 1871-2. Was born in Ashland, O., Sept. 14, 1836. He was a printer by trade, in politics a Democrat. He came to Michigan in 1867, and published the *Mining and Manufacturing News*, the first paper at Negaunee. He started the *Mining Journal*, at Marquette, in 1868. Prior to coming to Michigan he had published the *Star*, at Alberta Lea, Minn.; *Banner*, at La Crescent, Minn.; started the first daily at La Crosse, Wis., published the *Daily Enquirer* at Milwaukee in 1860, and the *Democratic Press* at Fond du Lac, in 1864-6. Then he was in the oil business in Canada, then an express messenger, thence to Lake Superior. He was a commissioner to the New Orleans exposition. He was appointed early in the administration of President Cleveland, Governor of Alaska, and filled that position in 1887, residing at Sitka.

CHARLES D. SYMONDS

Representative from Menominee County, 1911-12 and 1915-16. Was born at Beloit, Wis., July 30, 1873, and was educated at the Ferris Institute, Big Rapids, afterwards taking a law course at the University of Michigan, Ann Arbor. He taught school for six years and after 1904 practiced law. He was married July 3, 1900, to Roxanna Anderson, of Big Rapids. In politics, a Republican.

ALEXANDER TACLES

Representative from Macomb County, 1835, 1836 and 1839. Came to Michigan in 1822, and settled at Romeo. He was a farmer by occupation, politically a Democrat. He died Apr. 12, 1855.

MOSES TAGGART

Attorney General, 1885-9. Was born at Wilson, N. Y., Feb. 27, 1843. He was by profession an attorney at law. Mr. Taggart's early life was spent on a farm. He prepared for college at Wilson Collegiate Institute. He was graduated in the class of 1867, from the law department of the University of Michigan, and was admitted to the bar at Buffalo, N. Y., December, 1867. He was elected Attorney General on the Republican ticket.

HORACE S. TARBELL

State Superintendent of Public Instruction, 1877-8. Was born at Chelsea, Mass., Aug. 19, 1838. He graduated at Wesleyan University, Middletown, Conn., in 1859. For three years was professor of natural sciences in Belleville Seminary, Canada; from 1862 to 1865 was principal of Farmerville County grammar school; in 1865 principal of Central Academy, McGrawville, N. Y.; from 1866 to 1871 principal of schools in Detroit, and in 1869 organized the evening school in Detroit House of Correction; and was superintendent of the East Saginaw schools from 1870 to 1877. Elected Superintendent of Public Instruction in 1876, he served from Jan. 1, 1877, until Aug. 31, 1878, when he resigned to accept the position of Superintendent of Schools at Indianapolis, Ind.

TIMOTHY E. TARSNEY

Member of Congress, 1885-7 and 1887-9. Was born at Ransom, Mich., Feb. 4, 1849; was educated at the common schools; served seven years as a marine engineer, meantime reading law; entered the law department of Michigan University in 1870, and graduated in the class of 1872; was a Justice in 1873-4; was City Attorney in 1875-8, when he resigned, serving as ex-officio member of the Board of Supervisors at the same time; was elected to the Forty-ninth, and re-elected to the Fiftieth Congress as a Fusionist.

WILLIAM ALDRICH TATEUM

Representative from the First District of Kent County, 1893-4. Was born in Worcester County, Mass., in 1859. He had the advantages of a thorough education, graduating from the Wesleyan University, Middletown, Conn., and taking a special course at the Boston University Law School, Boston, Mass. He was a lawyer by profession, having been a member of the Massachusetts bar before he came to Grand Rapids, Mich. In 1887 he was married to Miss Mary Adele Morris, of Grand Rapids. In politics a Republican. In 1891 he was elected a member of the Board of Aldermen of the city of Grand Rapids, and in 1892 was elected to the present Legislature from the city of Grand Rapids by a vote of 8,764 on the general legislative ticket of the city of Grand Rapids. He was chosen as the nominee for speaker of the present House in the Republican caucus, and was elected to that position.

LEO TAUBE

Representative from the First District of Wayne County, 1917-18. Was born in Stettin, Germany, Sept. 6, 1861, of German parents. His education was secured in the public and high schools of Germany and Chicago, Ill. He engaged in the meat business until 1912, when he retired from active business; was president of the Auto Bow Co., Detroit; vice-president American Brewing Co., Detroit; past master Schiller Lodge, F. & A. M. No. 263; director of Harmonie Society and member of Concordia and Arbeiter societies. He was married Feb. 21, 1884, to Augusta Marie Younke, of Detroit. In politics a Republican.

CHARLES COFFIN TAYLOR

Member of the Board of Regents of the University of Michigan, 1846-50. Was born at Rowley, Mass., Feb. 16, 1805. He was graduated Bachelor of Arts from Bowdoin College in 1833. He studied theology and was ordained to the Episcopal ministry in 1838. He removed to Michigan, and during the years 1844-50 and 1852-3, was rector of St. Andrew's Church in Ann Arbor. He was president of St. Mark's College, in Grand Rapids, in 1850-1. Afterwards he became rector of St. Luke's Church in Kalamazoo, where he died Feb. 1, 1855. Mar. 16, 1846, he was appointed Regent of the University and served the full term of four years.

CHARLES H. TAYLOR

Representative from Kent and Ottawa counties, 1847 and 1848; and Secretary of State, 1851-3. Was born at Cooperstown, N. Y., Nov. 20, 1813. He was educated at an academy, and settled in Grand Rapids, Mich., in 1837. He was Clerk of Kent County for eight years. He was one of five commissioners who selected sites for the insane asylum at Kalamazoo, and the deaf and dumb asylum at Flint. He was the first Secretary of State elected under the Constitution of 1850. From 1847 to 1855 he edited the Grand Rapids *Enquirer*. Later he was chief editor and part proprietor of the Detroit *Free Press*, but ill health compelled him to retire. In politics he was a Democrat. He was in business at Grand Rapids in 1887.

DANIEL W. TAYLOR

Representative from Lapeer County, 1845. Was born in the State of New York, Oct. 5, 1804. By occupation he was a farmer and carriage maker; politically a

Democrat. He was one of the earliest pioneers in Lapeer County. He was Postmaster seven years, and Justice of the Peace several terms. He was a prominent Mason. He died Oct. 10, 1860.

EDWARD BANCROFT TAYLOR

Representative from the First District of St. Clair County, 1895-6. Was born in Milwaukee, Wis., Aug. 13, 1841; received his education at Milwaukee Academy, and in 1861 was working on the Philadelphia *Ledger*, when at the outbreak of the war he enlisted in the 71st Penn. Vol. Infantry, and at the Battle of Ball's Bluff was wounded twice, losing a hand. In 1869 he settled in Port Huron. For nine years he was engaged as railroad superintendent, after which time he was engaged in the manufacture of doors, sash, etc. In politics he was a Republican. He held the office of Alderman of his city.

GEORGE E. TAYLOR

Senator from the Nineteenth District, 1883-4. Was born in Oakland County, Mich., Mar. 21, 1838. He received a common school and academical education. He commenced teaching at the age of seventeen, and continued in that occupation until twenty-eight years of age. He delivered an address at the laying of the corner stone of Albion College. He held the office of School Inspector six years, Supervisor eight years, Register of Deeds six years, and was one of the Aldermen of the city of Flint for three years. In politics he was a Republican.

HENRY W. TAYLOR

Representative from Calhoun County, 1847. Was born in Deerfield, Mass., Feb. 2, 1796. By occupation he was a lawyer; politically Whig and Republican. He graduated at Yale College in 1816, and received the degree of LL.D. from that institution in 1849. He went to Ontario County, N. Y., in 1816, studied law and practiced until 1840, when he removed to Marshall, Mich., to practice his profession. He took high rank as a lawyer, and was learned and eloquent. He returned to Canandaigua, N. Y., in 1848, was a member of the Legislature of that State four years, and Judge of the county and Supreme Court. He was appointed Judge of the Court of Appeals in 1850. He was made a corporate member of the A. B. C. F. M. in 1846. He died at Canandaigua, N. Y., Dec. 17. 1888.

LORISON J. TAYLOR

Representative from Shiawassee County, 1874-6; and Senator from the Seventeenth District, 1877-8. Was born at North Raisinville, Mich., June 30, 1842. He fitted for and entered the University at Ann Arbor, but in 1861 enlisted in the 2nd Mich. Infantry, serving until November, 1863, when he was discharged from wounds received at Fort Saunders. He re-enlisted in 1865, and became a Captain in the 11th Mich. Infantry, serving until September of that year. He succeeded Benjamin Walker, deceased, in the House in 1874. Resided at Laingsburg in 1887, and was a farmer.

ROBERT L. TAYLOR

Senator, 1889-90 and 1891-2, from the Sixteenth District, comprising the counties of Lapeer and Sanilac. Was born at Almont, Lapeer County, Nov. 3, 1839, of Scotch parentage. His father at the time was owner of a quarter section of wild land, which he had purchased a few years before, and which he was engaged in clearing up. As a consequence the son was brought up on the farm, working at home as soon as he was able to be of any use and attending school in the winter time, thus becoming well acquainted with all the hardships of those early times. At 18 years of age he lost his father by accidental drowning, and so was charged with the oversight of the farm, being the oldest of the seven brothers of the family. Having a taste for books he succeeded in preparing himself for entering the University of Michigan, and was admitted to that institution at the age of 22. After pursuing his studies there in the classical course for three years, he severed his connection with the University to take advantage of an opening presented for engaging in the mercantile business at Almont, near his old home. After engaging in this business very successfully for three years, he sold out and began the study of law, passing one year in the law department of the University and was admitted to the bar in 1869 at Lapeer. Then engaging in the practice of law at Almont, he built up a prosperous business which he pursued until the fall of 1872, when he was elected Register of Deeds. He removed to the County seat, Lapeer city, to perform the duties of the office, and being re-elected he filled the office for four years. After the expiration of the four years as Register of Deeds he devoted his time to practice of law, and in 1880 was elected Prosecuting Attorney of the county, and served two years in that capacity. Feeling a return of the old taste for country life he declined a renomination and gave more time to the home and rural affairs connected with his place in the suburbs of the city of Lapeer. He was married in 1866 to Miss Margaret I. Birrell.

THOMAS CHALMERS TAYLOR

Representative from the Second District of Lapeer County, 1889-90. Was born at Almont, Lapeer County, Mich., Apr. 19, 1843, upon the farm. He entered Michigan University in 1865, in literary department, graduating in 1869; in charge of schools at Leslie, Mich., 1869-70; Superintendent of Schools at Hastings, Mich., and studied law, 1870-1; admitted to the bar at Hastings, November, 1871, and practiced there until December, 1872, then removed to Almont, where he succeeded his brother, Robert L. Taylor, in the practice of his profession. He was Township Superintendent of Schools, 1875-82; Township Treasurer, 1881-2, 1885-6; Director School Board, 1876-81 and after 1883; Village Attorney 1874-80, and after 1883 farming and stock raising as well as practicing law. He was married in 1872 to Hannah C. Fowler, of Aurelius, Ingham County.

THADDEUS BLAKE TAYLOR

Representative from the Third District of Kent County, 1911-12 and 1913-14. Was born at Middleville, Mich., July 4, 1887, of American parents. He was educated in the Middleville public school, Grand Rapids High School, Ferris Institute and graduated in June, 1909, from the law department of the University of Michigan. He was married July 10, 1907, to Miss Hazel Hendrick, daughter of Mr. and Mrs. H. E. Hendrick, of Middleville, Mich. Mr. Taylor was admitted to the bar July 9, 1909, and practiced law at Cedar Springs. In politics a Democrat.

WALTER R. TAYLOR

Delegate to the Constitutional Convention of 1907-8 from the Ninth District; and Senator, 1909-10, 1911-12 and 1915-16 from the Sixth District, comprising the counties of Kalamazoo and St. Joseph. Was born in Kent County, Mich. In 1890 he was admitted to the bar, and engaged in the legal profession. He held the office of Mayor of Kalamazoo; was a member of the Constitutional Convention in 1907-8. In politics a Republican. He died at Rochester, Minn., Oct. 4, 1920.

WILLIAM H. TAYLOR

Representative from the Third District of Kent County, 1861-2. His postoffice address was Sparta. (Further data not obtainable).

WILLIAM H. TAYLOR

Representative from Saginaw County, 1865-6 and 1867-8. Was a native of the State of New York, born Feb. 9, 1816. He was a resident of Michigan in 1837-8, but returned to New York, kept hotel two years, then for two years was in business at Harrisburg, Pa. Then he sold patents until 1846, then moved to Ontario, Canada, engaged in lumbering and ran grist and woolen mills. He made his home in Saginaw, Mich., in 1856, was a lumberman until 1865, then kept the Taylor house until 1870. He removed to St. Louis, Mich., built the Eastman house and kept it until 1874. Deceased.

JAMES B. TAZIMAN

Representative from Livingston County, 1899-1900. Was born in Tompkins County, N. Y., Sept. 18, 1852, and came to Michigan when two years of age. He was educated in the common schools and at Howell High School; made farming his chief work in Michigan, but taught district schools eighteen winters. He held the offices of Township Superintendent of Schools, member of the Board of School Examiners and Township Supervisor.

GEORGE W. TEEPLE

Senator, 1897-8, from the Thirteenth District, comprising the counties of Livingston and Genesee. Was born in Steuben County, N. Y., Aug. 13, 1848, came to Michigan with his parents in the spring of 1859, and located on a farm in Hamburg Township, Livingston County. In the spring of 1860 he moved to Pinckney, where he acquired his early education and in 1865 he attended the

Ann Arbor High School; on his return from school, he worked at the tinner's trade for two years, and on Mar. 1, 1867, he commenced clerking for W. S. Mann and remained in that capacity until Mr. Mann's death in 1877, when he became business manager for the W. S. Mann estate up to Apr. 29, 1884, when he established the Pinckney Exchange Bank. On Mar. 2, 1887, his bank building was destroyed by fire, but he immediately commenced the erection of a brick two-story building which was completed Oct. 1, 1887. Mr. Teeple's principal occupation after 1884 that of a banker. In politics he was a Republican. He held various public offices of trust and honor.

HENRY M. TEFT

Representative from the Second District of Jackson County, 1897-8. Was born on a farm in the township of Spring Arbor, Jackson County, Mich., Aug. 23, 1842. He acquired a district school education but under very adverse circumstances, working on the farm summers and attending school winters, supplemented by a course at a seminary. At the outbreak of the Civil War, in 1861, he enlisted in the 1st Mich. Infantry Vols. and served three years and three months. On his return home in 1865 he engaged in farming, which occupation he followed. In politics he was a Democrat. He was Justice of the Peace; was candidate for Commissioner of Highways, and Supervisor; and elected to the House of 1897-8 on the Democratic People's Union Silver ticket.

CONRAD TEN EYCK

Delegate from the First District to the Constitutional Convention in 1835; Senator from the First District, 1835 to 1837; and Representative from Wayne County, 1846. Was of Dutch extraction, born in Albany, N. Y., July 17, 1782. He came to Detroit in 1801. His early occupation was that of a merchant, to which he added farming by the purchase of a farm in Dearborn, which was his family residence during the gretaer part of his life, although his own time was largely spent in Detroit. Mr. Ten Eyck's first record is as one of the protestants against the brutal expulsion order of the British General Proctor in 1813. He was County Treasurer from 1817 to 1825. He resigned as Senator Feb. 24, 1837, to accept the appointment of U. S. Marshal under President Van Buren, which office he held until 1841. He was a Democrat of undoubted orthodoxy, was a man of energy and purpose, of decided character, and by reason of these traits of marked influence during his active life. He died Aug. 21, 1847.

PETER TERNES

Representative from Wayne County, 1869-70. Was born in Germany in 1831, and came to America with his parents during his minority. His occupation was that of a farmer in Greenfield for many years, during which time he held various local offices, including that of Supervisor for six years. He resigned as Representative during extra session, 1870. He removed to Detroit in 1870, and was more or less in the service of the city, being assistant receiver of taxes in 1887. His politics were Democratic.

HENRY D. TERRY

Representative from Macomb County, 1848. Was born in Hartford, Conn., in 1814. By profession he was a lawyer, politically first Whig, then Republican. He came to Michigan in 1842, and located at Mt. Clemens, where he practiced his profession until 1855, when he removed to Detroit and practiced law there until 1861. June 15, 1861, he was commissioned Colonel of the 5th Mich. Infantry, and took the field in September. The regiment took part in many battles, and made the first successful bayonet charge at Williamsburg, taking the enemy's works, and leaving sixty-three rebel dead in the enemy's rifle pits, all killed by the bayonet. Generals McClelland, Kearney and Barry all wrote highly complimentary letters in praise of the regiment. Colonel Terry was wounded in this action. He was made a Brigadier General July 18, 1862, and continued in service until Feb. 7, 1865, when he resigned. While a resident of Detroit he was Prosecuting Attorney of Wayne County. He located at Washington, D. C., and practiced law until his death, June 29, 1869.

FRANK E. THATCHER

Representative from the Second District of Muskogon County, 1891-2. Was born on a farm near Coudersport, Potter County, Pa., Jan. 1, 1859, and moved with his parents to Ravenna, Muskegon County, in 1866. He lived on the farm with his parents until the age of twenty-one when he removed to Kansas. Not being favorably impressed with the grasshopper State he removed to Ottawa, Ill., and the next year returned to Michigan and engaged in the business of house and sign painting in summer and in the winter teaching school and occasionally clerking in the drug store. His education was obtained in the district schools of Ravenna and a commercial course at the Valparaiso, Ind., Normal School. He was married in 1885 to Miss Sadie Bennett of Muskegon, and engaged in the business of a druggist at Ravenna. He held the offices of School Inspector, Supervisor of his township, being chairman of the Board of Supervisors when elected to the Legislature. In politics Mr. Thatcher was a Greenbacker during the life of that party; was elected as a Democrat to the House of 1891-2.

GEORGE W. THAYER

Representative from Genesee County, 1863-4 and 1865-6. Was born in Heath, Mass., Dec. 19, 1809. He came to Michigan in 1849, and was a resident of Flint. He was a Republican in politics.

NAHUM P. THAYER

Representative from Wayne County, 1837. Was born at St. Thomas, Ont., July 31, 1802. He came to Greenfield, Mich., in 1820, and located a farm still occupied by his descendants. He built the first three miles of the Chicago turnpike, now Michigan avenue, Detroit. He held various local offices, and was a Colonel of the State militia. In politics he was a Democrat. He died on his farm near Detroit, Oct. 26, 1851.

SIMEON M. THAYER

Rpresentative from Sanilac County, 1871-2. Was born Jan. 17, 1841, in Haldimand County, Ontario, Canada. He came with his parents to Michigan in 1852, and settled in Sanilac County. In the spring of 1872 he removed to the northwestern country, where he was a Sheriff in 1885-6. In politics he was a Republican, in business a real estate dealer.

CHARLES N. THEW

Delegate in the Constitutional Convention of 1907-8 from the Eighth District. Was born in Allegan in 1867, of American descent. He was a graduate from Hope College at Holland, taking the classical course. Later he became a practicing attorney at Allegan, Mich., and served as Prosecuting Attorney two terms. Married.

CHARLES HOWARD THOMAS

Delegate to the Constitutional Convention of 1907-8 from the Fifteenth District, Barry County. Was born in the township of Yankee Springs, Barry County, in 1870, of English descent, his mother's ancestors coming over in the Mayflower. When he was one and one-half years old his parents moved to Osborn County, Kan., where they resided fourteen years. He then returned to Michigan. He was a graduate of the University of Michigan, taking the degree of LL.B. in 1892. In 1893 he married Miss Effie A. Snyder, of Hastings. He served as Prosecuting Attorney of Barry County for two terms; also Great Lieutenant Commander of the Knights of the Modern Maccabees.

GEORGE THOMAS

Senator from the Fifth District, 1851, and from the Twentieth District, 1869-70; and Representative from Barry County, 1859-60 and 1863-4. Was born in Cayuga County, N. Y., Dec. 23, 1812. He emigrated to Michigan in 1837, and settled on a farm in Ross, Kalamazoo County. He served several times as Supervisor. He became a resident of Barry County in 1855. In politics he was a Whig until 1854, then a Republican and in the eighties a Greenbacker.

HENRY F. THOMAS

Representative from Allegan County, 1873-4; Senator from the Fourteenth District, 1875-6; and member of Congress, 1893-5 and 1895-7. Was born in Jackson County, Mich., Dec. 17, 1843; he was in Albion College from 1859 until the outbreak of the Civil War when he enlisted in Co. D, 7th Mich. Cavalry as private, promoted 1st Sergeant and 2d Lieutenant. He participated in the Battle of Gettysburg, and accompanied Gen. Kilpatrick in his raid on Richmond; served under Sheridan in his raid on Lee's rear at the Wilderness; was with Sheridan during his Shenandoah Valley campaign, and took part at the siege of Petersburg. At the close of the war he accompanied his regiment to the West, and served in the Indian campaign during the summer of 1865 in Colorado and Dakota territories. He returned to Michigan, took a course at the University, graduating in 1868; later he received the degree of M. A. at Albion College. Located in the city of Allegan and engaged in the practice of medicine. In politics he was a Republican.

JOHN THOMAS

Representative from Oakland County, 1846. Was born in Allegheny, Pa., in 1802. When young he removed with his parents to Penn Yan, N. Y., and from there to Farmington, Mich., in 1835. He was a partner of Daniel S. Lee in a large mercantile business, which he continued after his partner removed. In company with Charles P. Bush and Daniel S. Lee, he purchased in 1847 a tract of land in Lansing, just south of the school section on which the capitol was located, now a part of the city. They opened a store on the east side of the Grand River, and sold goods six years. They also built the Benton, later Everett house. The first postoffice was in their store. He returned to Farmington in 1852, and died Mar. 18, 1863.

LEONARD R. THOMAS

Representative from Huron County, 1903-4, 1905-6 and 1907-8. Was born at Ontario. Married. Occupation a farmer. He was educated in the common schools. He served as Township Clerk, Supervisor and County Treasurer. In politics a Republican.

WALTER JOSEPH THOMAS

Representative from St. Joseph County, 1923—. Was born at Schoolcraft, Feb. 11, 1868, of American parentage. He graduated from the Schoolcraft schools and attended the Baptist college at Kalamazoo, afterward teaching for two years. For twenty years he conducted a grain elevator business at Schoolcraft, adding to it the flour milling business at Constantine. At present he is retired from business and devotes time to farming and public affairs. He is married and has a family of two sons and one daughter. He is a member of the Congregational church and fraternally is a member of the M. W. A. and the K. of P. lodges and is a 32nd degree Mason. Mr. Thomas is a life-long Republic and has served as township treasurer and an officer of the school board of Schoolcraft, also as village president of Constantine and supervisor of Constantine township. He was elected to the legislature November 7, 1922.

WILLIAM THOMAS

Representative from Van Buren County, 1875-6. Was born in Washington County, N. Y., Mar. 20, 1815. He became a resident of Michigan in 1843. He was a farmer by occupation, in politics a Liberal. He was Supervisor of Hartford seven years, Town Clerk and Treasurer eight years, Justice four years. He served as Representative in the place of G. B. Yeckley, deceased. He was active in securing $15,000 from the town to aid in building a railroad connection. He resided at Hartford in 1887.

ZIMRI D. THOMAS

Representative from Hillsdale County, 1865-6. Was born at Rowe, Mass., Sept. 16, 1809, and removed to central New York in 1820. He was for six years Postmaster at Hamburg, N. Y. He came to Michigan in 1835, and was three years Supervisor of Allen; was Coroner, and a Justice for many years. He resided at Hillsdale in 1887. He was a Republican in politics.

ALBERT THOMPSON

Senator from the Thirteenth District, 1875-6. Was born in Waterbury, Vt., Apr. 28, 1831. He educated at Oberlin College; graduated from the medical department of the University of Michigan. He removed to Michigan in 1860, and enlisted in the 3d Mich. Cavalry when it was organized in 1861; was made hospital steward; afterwards promoted to Lieutenant, next as assistant surgeon, and finally surgeon, and was mustered out with his regiment in 1866. He held the office of Supervisor of South Haven for two terms. He was practicing physician. In politics he was a Republican.

ALMON A. THOMPSON

Representative from Eaton County, 1869-70. Was born in Richmond, Vt., Mar. 26, 1829, and removed to Avon, O., in 1840. He graduated from Oberlin College in 1854, and from the medical department of the Michigan University in 1856. He was Assistant Surgeon of the 12th Mich. Infantry and afterwards of the 11th Cavalry. He practiced as a physician at Vermontville. From 1870 to 1878 he was Consul at Goderich, Canada. He vacated his seat as Representative before extra session of 1870 and was succeeded by Albertus L. Green. He was in practice at Flint in 1887 and was physician to the deaf and dumb institute, and a member of the local pension board. In politics he was a Republican.

CHARLES C. THOMPSON

Representative from Muskegon County, 1873-4. Was born in Beekmantown, N. Y., June 4, 1831. He received a common school education. In 1857 he removed to Michigan and settled in Whitehall, Muskegon County. He was president of the Common Council, Trustee of the village, and held other responsible offices. By occupation he was a lumberman.

CHARLES D. THOMPSON

Delegate to the Constitutional Convention of 1907-8 from the Twentieth District, Huron County. Was born in Huron County in 1873, of Scottish descent on his mother's side and a descendant of John Thompson, one of the first who arrived at Plymouth Colony in 1722. He was a student in the literary department and a graduate of the law department of the University of Michigan with the class of 1896, and practiced law after graduation.

GEORGE W. THOMPSON

Representative from Kent County, 1883-4. Was born Mar. 3, 1844, in the township of Florida (now Jefferson), Hillsdale County. He was educated at Oberlin College. He was admitted to the bar in 1869, at Hillsdale. He resided in Grand Rapids after 1874.

HENRY W. THOMPSON

Representative from Delta and Iron counties, 1887-8. Was born in Brooklyn, July 14, 1847; removed with his parents to Tyrone. He was educated in the common schools. In 1864 he enlisted as a private in the 10th Mich. Infantry, and served until the close of the war. At the age of twenty-four he became a minister and preached in Ingham, Shiawassee, Baraga and Delta counties. In politics he was a Republican.

JAMES HERBERT THOMPSON

Member of the State Board of Education, 1901. Was born in Flushing, Genesee County, Apr. 6, 1866. He received his education in primary and high schools at Reed City, supplemented by a course at the Ypsilanti State Normal, from which he graduated in 1890. He was Superintendent of Evart Schools for five years, from which he resigned to enter mercantile business, but never lost his identity with educational work. He was Superintendent of the Northern Michigan School Masters' Club; member of County Board of School Examiners, and secretary and member of Evart School Board, conducted successfully many county institutes under the State Board, and was essentially a school man; also a prominent Mason, and belonged to several secret societies. He was elected a member of the State Board of Education. He resigned and was succeeded by Patrick H. Kelley who was appointed Apr. 10, 1901.

JEREMIAH D. THOMPSON

Delegate from Lenawee County to the Second Convention of Assent, 1836; and Representative from Lenawee County, 1838 and 1853-4. Was born in Dutchess County, N. Y., in 1790. He settled on a farm in Madison, Lenawee County, in 1834. He was several years Supervisor, and Justice many years. He died at Hudson, Feb. 16, 1873.

ROBERT THOMPSON

Representative from Macomb County, 1859-60. Came to Macomb County when a boy and taught school some years in Mt. Clemens, and then sold goods several years. He removed to New Batlimore, and was bookkeeper for Hiron Hathaway several years; then was in the employ of F. B. Merrill, then removed to Marine City. Later he was elected County Treasurer of St. Clair County, and died while holding that office. He was first a Whig, then a Republican.

ROBERT R. THOMPSON

Representative from Clinton and Shiawassee Counties, 1845. Moved into Washtenaw County at an early day. He settled on a farm in Caledonia, Shiawassee County, in 1837. He was connected with A. McArthur in a saw-mill, and also engaged in commercial ventures in Corunna. He afterwards sold out and removed to Saginaw, where he died several years prior to 1887.

STACY C. THOMPSON

Representative from Manistee County, 1907-8. Was born in Clearfield County, Pa., Jan. 18, 1856. He came to Michigan in 1869 and to Manistee in 1870. He received his education in the public schools of Manistee, learned the printer's trade and for nearly twenty years followed that line of business, and occupied the various positions of printer, editor and publisher. In 1892 he sold out his printing and publishing interests, after which time he engaged in the real estate business. In politics a Democrat.

WILLIAM G. THOMPSON

Senator, 1895-6 and 1897-8, from the Second District, composed of the first, second, third, fifth and seventh wards of Detroit. Was born in Lancaster, Pa., 1840; was a student in Amherst College when the war broke out; enlisted in a Pennsylvania three months' regiment, served his term, joined the Lancer Cavalry Regiment at Detroit, serving until disbanded; obtained a commission as Second Lieutenant, 6th N. J. Vol.; was detailed as aide-de-camp on staff of General Mott, promoted to First Lieutenant at Chancellorsville, where he was severely wounded; served until his regiment was mustered out. On his return from the war he studied law in Columbia College, N. Y., one year, came to Detroit in 1866, continued his studies in law office, and later engaged in practice. Subsequently he engaged in real estate dealing. In politics he was a Republican. He served as member of Board of Estimates, president of Common Council, and two terms, 1880-4, as Mayor of the city of Detroit; was elected to the Senate of 1895-6, and re-elected to that of 1897-8. He died at Yonkers, N. Y., July 20, 1904.

EDWARD H. THOMSON

Senator from the Sixth District, 1848-9; and Representative from Genesee County, 1859-60. Was born at Kendall, England, June 15, 1810, and came with his parents, to Boston, Mass. He received an academical education. He studied law with Millard Fillmore, and commenced practice at Buffalo, N. Y., in 1832. He located at Atlas, in 1837, afterwards in Lapeer County; was appointed Prosecuting Attorney. He removed to Flint in 1838, and became one of the firm of Barton & Thomson. He was Prosecuting Attorney of Genesee County, 1845-6; Commissioner of Emigration under Gov. Ransom, a portion of the time residing in Germany. U. S. Deputy Commissioner to the London Exposition in 1851; president of the State Military Board, during the war; Mayor and member of School Board at Flint; and the Democratic nominee for Lieutenant Governor in 1880. His Shakesperian library was purchased after his death by James McMillan for the Michigan University. He died Feb. 2, 1886.

JAMES B. THOMSON

Representative from the Second District of Berrien County, 1893-4. Was born Aug. 19, 1853, and lived on the farm in Niles Township. His early education was received at the rural district school and his life's occupation that of a farmer. He was a single man. In politics he was a Democrat. He served as Supervisor of his township.

JOHN S. THOMSON

Representative from Sanilac County, 1877-8 and 1879-80. Was born at Manchester, England, Aug. 28, 1833. He was educated at the Scotch sessional school at that place, and emigrated to Michigan in 1850. He was a merchant and salt manufacturer. In politics he was a Republican.

JUSTUS THORINGTON

Representative from Midland County, 1903-4. Was born in New York State in 1849, of Scotch and Irish ancestors. He was educated in the common schools. He engaged in lumbering, manufacturing of lumber and shingles and farming. He held the offices of Supervisor and Sheriff. He was married. In politics he was a Democrat.

CALVIN J. THORPE

Representative from Branch County, 1879-80. Was born Sept. 14, 1834, in Warrensville, O. In 1838 he removed to Volinia, Cass County. In 1859 he graduated from the Michigan Normal School. In 1862 he became principal of the graded schools at Union City. He was also principal at Eaton Rapids, Paw Paw, Sturgis, and Manchester. In 1875 he bought a controlling interest in the Coldwater *Reporter*, which he sold in 1876, and became connected with *Truth for the People*, in Detroit. In 1877 he removed to Sherwood, Branch County, and became a druggist. In politics he was a National.

GEORGE B. THROOP

Representative from Wayne County, 1847. Was a native of New York, and came to Detroit as a bank officer during the flush times of 1836-8. He had previously been a member of the New York Legislature. He was a brother of Enos B. Throop, once Governor of New York. He was a member of the Detroit bar. He was a Democrat politically. He died Feb. 23, 1854.

JEFFERSON G. THURBER

Representative from Monroe County, 1851; and Senator from the Third District, 1844-5 and 1846-7. Was born in 1807, and settled at Monroe, Mich., in 1833. In politics he was a Democrat. He was a lawyer by profession, and earnestly devoted to the practice. He held the offices of Prosecuting Attorney and Judge of Probate of Monroe County, and was a Presidential Elector in 1849. He filled all positions with honor to himself and the State. He died at Monroe, May 6, 1857.

JOHN S. TIBBITTS

Representative from Wayne County, 1861-2. Was born in Arcadia, N. Y., Dec. 21, 1821. He came to Plymouth, Mich., with his father's family in 1825, the first white settlers in that town. He was educated at common schools, taught at the age of sixteen, and winters thereafter for twenty-five years. He was elected Supervisor at the age of twenty-one, and was subsequently Supervisor, School Inspector, Postmaster, etc. He was some time Superintendent of the Agricultural College farm; three years auditor of Wayne County, and one year horticulturist at the Colorado Agricultural College. He published the "Free Guide," for the benefit of officials. In politics he was a Republican. He resided at Santa Rita, Calif., in 1887.

ALEXANDER F. TIFFANY

Delegate from the Third District to the Constitutional Convention of 1835; Delegate from Lenawee County to the Constitutional Convention of 1850; and Representative from Lenawee County, 1855-6. Was born in Niagara, Canada, Oct. 16, 1796. His father, Sylvester Tiffany, a native of Massachusetts and one of four brothers who graduated at Dartmouth College, published a paper at Canandaigua, N. Y., and the son learned the art of printing. Afterwards he studied law with John C. Spencer, Chief Justice of New York. He commenced practice at Palmyra, N. Y. About 1823 he was appointed first Judge of the county court of Wayne County, N. Y., and held the place until compelled to resign from ill health. In 1832 he settled at Palmyra, Mich., was Territorial Associate Judge in 1833-4; County Judge, 1846-50. In 1834 he was appointed Prosecuting Attorney of Lenawee County; in 1836 was elected Judge of Probate, and held that office eight years. He was the author of "Tiffany's Justice Guide" and "Tiffany's Criminal Law." He was a man of small stature, a lawyer of learning and ability, with a candor and sincerity that carried weight with court and jury. With poor health he worked incessantly. He died at Palmyra, Jan. 14, 1868.

HARLOW A. TIFFANY

Representative from Mecosta County, 1905-6 and 1907-8. Was born in Hancock County, O., Apr. 23, 1843, of American parentage. He received his education in the common schools. He came to Michigan with his parents in 1855 and settled on a farm in Alamo Township, Kalamazoo County. In 1865, Mr. Tiffany removed to Millbrook Township, Mecosta County, and cleared up a farm where he resided for six years. He then moved into the village of Millbrook, engaged in mercantile trade for four years, was proprietor of the hotel for three years, disposed of his hotel property and followed contracting and building for five years. He moved to Chippewa Lake in 1883, engaged in the hotel business for a period of nine years, after which time he gave his attention to agriculture. He held every office in the gift of a township and was chairman of the Board of Supervisors. In politics he was a Republican.

JUNIUS TILDEN

Representative from Monroe County, 1849. He traced his ancestry to the Mayflower and the Revolution. He served two terms in the Massachusetts Legislature. He lived in that State until 1838, when he removed to Dundee, Mich. By profession he was a lawyer, in politics Independent. He was Prosecuting Attorney in Monroe where his death occurred Mar. 1, 1861.

PHILO TILLSON

Representative from Macomb County, 1844. Was born in Winfield, N. Y., in 1810. By profession he was a physician, in politics a Democrat. He came to Mt. Clemens, Mich., in 1833, where he practiced medicine ten years, then removed to Romeo, where he continued practice until his death, June 25, 1882.

JEFFERSON K. TINDALL

Representative from Oakland County, 1887-8. Was born in Sussex County, N. Y., Nov. 25, 1829; and came with his parents to Oakland County in 1833. He received a good education, served as clerk in a store, then a partner, selling out in 1861, and became a farmer. He served through the war in the 8th Mich. Cavalry. He was eight years Supervisor of the town of Rose, and six years secretary of the Monitor Insurance Company. In politics he was a Republican.

ALEXANDER TINHAM

Representative from Wayne County, 1863 and 1883-4. Was born in Middlesex County, England, in 1819. He came to Monroe, Mich., in 1829, in 1830 removed to Detroit, and was a brick maker by occupation. In politics he was a Democrat.

JACOB N. TINKLEPAUGH

Representative, 1889-90 and 1891-2, from the Grand Traverse District, composed of Grand Traverse and Kalkaska counties. Was born near Sodus Point, N. Y., Nov. 13, 1850. He received such educational advantages as a district school afforded, and at an early age from necessity rather than choice, became a sailor on the lakes, and following that calling for a number of seasons. In 1873, he embraced an opportunity to learn the printer's trade. He came to Michigan in 1878, and in May of that year was one of the founders of the Kalkaska *Leader*, and was editor and business manager of same. He was an earnest advocate of everything that tended to increase the material prosperity of Kalkaska County and the Grand Traverse region, and the first to represent said county in the State Legislature. Though a life-long Republican, and active in politics, his aspirations were confined to township, village, and school district offices. He was married in December, 1880, to Miss Alma M. Wooden.

RUFUS TINNEY

Representative from Oakland County, 1841. Settled in Highland, Mich., in 1833, coming from Wheatland, Monroe County, N. Y. He was a farmer, and resided where he first located until his death in 1858. He was the first Supervisor of the town in 1835, and filled that office for six terms.

ALBION B. TITUS

Representative from the First District of Kalamazoo County, 1921—. Was born at Hartford, Mich., Sept. 16, 1886. At the age of five years he removed with his parents to Paw Paw, Mich. He graduated from the Paw Paw High School in 1904 and spent the next three years studying law under the tutelage of his father, Lincoln H. Titus. He graduated from the law department of the University of Michigan in 1909 and practiced law in Kalamazoo from that time until 1916. Mr. Titus was elected Circuit Court Commissioner in 1915 and judge of the municipal court for the city of Kalamazoo in 1916. On leaving the bench he again engaged in the practice of law with his father, and is at the present time a member of the firm of Titus & Titus. He is a member of Kalamazoo Lodge No. 87, F. & A. M., R. A. M., No. 13; B. P. O. E., No. 50; and L. O. O. M., No. 88. Mr. Titus is married. In politics he is a Republican.

WILLIAM TOAN

Senator, 1889-90 and 1891-2, from the Nineteenth District, comprising the counties of Clinton and Ionia. Was born in Vernon, Oneida County, N. Y., June 1, 1832. His occupation was that of a farmer. He was sheriff of Ionia County four years, Jan. 1, 1881 to 1885.

BRACEY TOBEY

Representative from St. Joseph County, 1871-2. Was born in Saratoga County, N. Y., Mar. 26, 1802. He settled with his family in Burr Oak, Mich., in 1855, but removed to Sturgis in 1861. He had the confidence of the people, and in New York and Michigan held office of some kind for half a century. He was an Associate District Judge in New York. In politics he was a Democrat, a Republican after 1861. He was Justice for many years, also director in the national bank at Sturgis. He died in April, 1886.

ALBERT M. TODD

Member of Congress, 1897-9. Was born at the family farm home near Nottawa,

St. Joseph County, Mich., June 3, 1850. His early life was spent on the farm, where he attended the district school until about 15 years of age, after which he attended the Sturgis High School, from which he graduated. He studied some time at the Northwestern University. He was elected to the 55th Congress by a union of the Democratic, Union Silver, People's, and National parties.

ANDREW F. TOEPEL

Representative from the First District of Wayne County, 1917-18 and 1919-20. Was born at Detroit, May 5, 1866, of German parents. He was educated in the German Lutheran School. He worked in a jewelry store in Detroit for six years, and then removed to Chicago, where he remained for twelve years, after which he returned to Detroit and engaged in the jewelry business. He served two terms as president of the local club of retail dealers and two terms as president of the Michigan State Retail Jewelers' Association. Married. In politics a Republican.

ALEXANDER TOLL

Representative from Mackinac County, 1853-4, 1861-2 and 1863-4. His post-office address was Mackinac. (Further data not obtainable).

ISAAC D. TOLL

Representative from St. Joseph County, 1846; and Senator from the Fourth District, 1847. Was born at Schenectady, N. Y., Dec. 1, 1818, on the family homestead of two centuries. Both of his great-grandfathers were killed by the French and Indians in 1748. His grandfather served in the Revolution, and his father in the War of 1812. Mr. Toll was educated in the Academy at Ovid, N. Y., settled with his father at Centerville, Mich., in 1834, and engaged with him in manufacturing and real estate. He was thirteen years Supervisor of Fawn River, where his father built flouring and saw mills. He held military offices by regular promotions, from Lieutenant Colonel to Major General of State militia. In the Mexican War, he was Captain of Co. E, 15th U. S. Infantry, and distinguished himself at Contreras and Churubusco. He was Chief of division in Pension office in 1853-4; examiner of patents, 1854 to 1861; and commandant of the interior guard in 1861. He settled at Petoskey in 1880, and was President of the village in 1881-2. His wife was the daughter of Judge Charles Moran, of Detroit. In politics he was a Democrat. He was Postmaster at Petoskey. He was very prominent in pioneer circles and died at Petoskey, Mar. 27, 1908.

JAMES B. TOMPKINS

Delegate from Branch County to the Second Convention of Assent, 1836; and Representative from Branch County, 1855. Came from Schoharie County, N. Y.; settled in Girard, the first white settler in that township. He surveyed the ground upon which the city of Coldwater now stands. He was the first Supervisor of his township in 1834, serving many years. He was also a Justice. He died about 1878.

WILLIAM M. TOMPKINS

Representative from Eaton County, 1867-8. Was born in New Rochelle, N. Y., Mar. 6, 1820. He came to Michigan in 1844, went into the mercantile business at Eaton Rapids in 1845, was successful, and retired to go into the banking business in 1858. He died in 1868.

JOHN S. TOOKER

Senator from the Sixteenth District, 1879-80 and 1881-2. Was born in Tyrone, N. Y., July 7, 1836. He removed to Ann Arbor, Mich., with his parents in 1838, thence to Woodhull in 1840, and to Lansing in 1847. He received a common school education, purchased a foundry at North Lansing at the age of eighteen and manufactured farming implements for fourteen years. He served one year in the 6th Mich. Cavalry, but was discharged from ill health; was in both the drug and boot and shoe trade. He was three times Mayor of Lansing. He was Secretary of Montana under Arthur, and was in business at Helena, Mont., in 1887. In politics he was a Republican.

JOSEPH W. TORREY

Member of the Fifth Legislative Council from Wayne County, 1832-4. Was a native of Connecticut and a lawyer by profession. He was at one time a law partner with Col. Chas. Larned, and stood high at the bar. He was Judge of Probate, 1829-33, and Recorder of Detroit in 1829. He returned to Connecticut, and died there in 1844. Politically he was an administration or Jackson man, during his residence in Detroit.

LOUIS E. TOSSY

Delegate to the Constitutional Convention of 1907-8 from the First District, Wayne County. Was born in Detroit in 1849, of French descent. He received his education in the public schools and through private study. He was a carpenter by trade and pursued that occupation until 1897. In 1870 he married Miss Eleanor St. Amour. Interested all his life in the labor question, he served two terms as president of the Detroit Federation of Labor, two terms as president of the State Federation of Labor and two terms as vice-president of the United Brotherhood of Carpenters and Joiners of America. He served several years as Alderman of the ninth ward.

WILLIAM D. TOTTEN

Representative, 1901-2, from Antrim District, comprising the counties of Antrim, Charlevoix, and Kalkaska. Was born near New London, Oneida County, N. Y., Oct. 17, 1858. He removed with his parents to Michigan in 1865, remaining in this State until 1872 when he returned to New York State. His early education was obtained in the district schools. He was a canal driver on the Erie Canal for five years, when he returned to Michigan, locating on a farm in Kalkaska County. He taught school four years, during which time he studied law and was admitted to the bar in 1880 and became a practicing lawyer. In 1886 he was elected Prosecuting Attorney and was re-elected in 1888. He was admitted to practice before the Supreme Court of the United States Mar. 3, 1897. Married. In politics a staunch Republican.

OSMOND TOWER

Senator from the Thirtieth District, 1859-60. Was born in Cummington, Mass., Feb. 16, 1811. He received a common school and academical education. He settled in Ionia in 1835. He built the first school house in the Grand River Valley; was engaged in building until 1844; then for twenty years manufactured fanning mills; for seven years partner in dry goods house of J. S. Cooper & Co.; in real estate; in the foundry and hardware trade; director of the Ionia & Lansing railroad, and its first treasurer; director and president of the Ionia & Stanton railroad; Clerk of Ionia County, and several times Supervisor; U. S. Marshal of western Michigan from 1863 to 1866; member of the Board of Education, and its president. He was a Whig until 1854, then a Republican. He died Aug. 4, 1886.

CALVIN JAY TOWN

Representative from the Second District of Jackson County, 1919. Was born at Liberty Township, Jackson County, Mich., June 29, 1875. At the age of eight years he removed with his parents to Tompkins Township, Jackson County, where he received his education in the public schools. After teaching school two years, he purchased a farm in Tompkins Township on which he now resides. Mr. Town is married and has six children, three boys and three girls. He is a member of the I. O. O. F., the Grange, the Gleaners, and the Modern Woodmen. In politics he is a Republican. He served his township as Treasurer, Clerk and Supervisor, and was chairman of the County Board of Supervisors during 1918.

OKA TOWN

Delegate from Allegan County, to the Constitutional Convention of 1850; and Representative from Allegan County, 1851. Was born in Stoddard, N. H., July 2, 1806. By occupation he was a farmer, in politics a Democrat. He came to Michigan in 1831, and resided in Allegan County after 1834. He received two commissions from Governor Mason when Michigan was a Territory, one as Justice of the Peace in 1834 and one as Judge of Probate in 1835. He was Probate Judge in 1869. He died at Allegan, Mar. 24, 1895.

WILLIAM B. TOWN

Representative from Lenawee County, 1885-6. Was born in Norwich, Ont., July 23, 1830. He became a resident of Michigan when eight years old; received a thorough education, and entered upon the study of medicine, receiving his diploma as a physician and surgeon. He continuously engaged in the practice of that profession, residing at Rollin. In 1854 he was appointed Postmaster at Geneva, the office near his residence, a position which he held for seventeen years. Politically he was a Democrat.

AMOS C. TOWNE

Representative from Barry County, 1875-6. Was born in Bakersfield, Vt., Apr. 10, 1818. From 1843 up to 1848 he resided in the southern states. In 1850 he engaged in farming in DeKalb County, Ill. In 1854 he purchased a farm in Prairieville, Barry County. He held the office of Justice and was Supervisor for several consecutive terms. For thirty-five years he was identified with the insurance business and conveyancer. In politics he was a Republican.

CASSIUS B. TOWNER

Representative from the Second District of Kent County, 1905-6 and 1907-8. Was born at Byron Centre, Kent County, Mich., Sept. 6, 1859, of American parents. Acquired his education in the district schools, supplemented by one term each in the Mendon High School and at Grand Rapids High School. With his father he formed a partnership and engaged in the lumbering business, in 1880, and continued this business in connection with a general store, which stock was added in 1895. Married. In politics a Republican.

CHARLES ELROY TOWNSEND

Member of Congress, 1903-5 to 1909-11; and United States Senator, 1911-22. Was born at Concord, Mich., Aug. 15, 1856, of New England parentage. He received his education in the Concord and Jackson high schools and the University of Michigan. He worked on a farm until twenty years of age, when he became principal of schools at Parma, Mich., which work he pursued seven years. Mr. Townsend is married, and has always resided in Michigan. He was admitted to the bar at Jackson in 1895 where he has since practiced his profession. He held the office of Register of Deeds ten years and was elected to the 58th, 59th, 60th, and 61st Congresses. At the primaries Sept. 6, 1910, he was nominated United States Senator to succeed Julius Caesar Burrows whose term expired Mar. 4, 1911, and was elected by the Legislature Jan. 17, 1911, for the term ending Mar. 4, 1917. At the primary election held on Aug. 29, 1916, he was renominated and at the election held on Nov. 7, 1916, was re-elected for the term ending Mar. 4, 1923.

EMORY TOWNSEND

Senator from the Twenty-second District, Saginaw County, 1895-6. Was born on a farm in the township of Superior, Washtenaw County, Mich., Oct. 18, 1859; attended district school, Ann Arbor High School, and in 1881-2 the law department of the University. The two years following he traveled in the western and southern states, and in 1885 was married and located at Saginaw, where he engaged in the practice of law. In politics a Republican.

GEORGE H. TOWNSEND

Representative from the First District of Jackson County, 1921-2. Was born in the village of Akron, Erie County, N. Y., Aug. 16, 1865, of American parentage. He came to Michigan in 1869. He received his education in the public schools, and entered Olivet College from which he graduated in 1888. He then taught in high school at Alpena for three years when he entered the College of Physicians and Surgeons of Chicago and received the degree of M. D. from Louisville Medical College in 1894. He practiced in Jackson County until 1908, when he was elected County Clerk and served four years and has served as Deputy County Clerk for six years, retiring Jan. 1, 1921. Mr. Townsend is married and has three sons. In politics he is a Republican. He was chairman of the Republican County Committee of Jackson County from 1914 to 1920.

URIEL TOWNSEND

Representative from Lapeer County, 1875-6. Was born Dec. 4, 1830, in Hunter, N. Y. He received a common school education. In 1834 he emigrated to Michigan, and settled in Bruce, Macomb County. In 1859 he removed to Almont. He was Supervisor. By occupation he was a farmer, in politics a Republican.

WILLIS T. TOWNSEND

Delegate to the Constitutional Convention of 1907-8 from the Twenty-ninth District, Otsego County. Was born in Jackson County, in 1858, of English descent. He attended the district schools in Branch County, and then taught district school and attended high school fall and winter terms as long as his earnings from teaching lasted. He taught school eleven winters and seven summers. He graduated from the Hillsdale Commercial College in 1882 and from the law department of the University of Michigan in 1891. He commenced the practice of law at Gaylord, Otsego County, in the same year. He married Miss Fannie A. Beem, of Reading, Mich. He served as Village Assessor and Village Attorney of Gaylord and was Prosecuting Attorney of Otsego County for six years.

FLAGGET H. TRABBIC

Representative from Monroe County, 1907-8. Was born in Erie, Monroe County, Mich., Feb. 11, 1866, of Italian, French and English ancestors. His early education was acquired in the district schools of his native village followed by a two years' course at St. Mary's Institute, Dayton, O. In 1885 on retiring from school, he took up the management of his father's farm consisting of several hundred acres and followed the occupation of a farmer. He was elected Supervisor for the years 1893 to 1896, was chairman of the Board of Supervisors in 1896, and was again elected in 1906. In politics a Democrat.

JARVIS C. TRAIN

Representative from Kent County, 1883-4. Was born in Tunbridge, Vt., July 8,

1834. He came with his parents to Boston, Mich., in 1840. He lived in White-side County, Ill., ten years as a farmer, then settled at Lowell, Mich., and en-gaged in buying and selling farm products. He served in the Legislature as a Fusionist.

SENECA CHAMBERLAIN TRAVER

Senator from the Fourth District of Wayne County, 1905-6 and 1907-8. Was born in Newton, Ia., May 17, 1867, of English and Dutch descent. He received his education in the high schools of Seneca Falls, N. Y., and at the Waterloo Academy, Waterloo, N. Y. Before coming to Michigan he was for three years engaged in teaching in the public schools of the State of New York. A lawyer by profession, having been admitted to the bar in the city of Detroit, in 1893. Unmarried. In politics a Republican.

WILLIAM R. TRAVER

Representative from Hillsdale County, 1853-4. Was born in Rensselaer County, N. Y., Oct. 26, 1818. By occupation he was a harness maker; in politics a Re-publican. He came to Litchfield, Mich., in 1844. He held offices of trust.

SEYMOUR B. TREADWELL

Commissioner of the State Land Office, 1855-9. (Further data not obtainable).

LOREN L. TREAT

Senator from the Fifth District, 1865-6. Was admitted to the Oakland County bar Nov. 20, 1844, and located at Canandaigua, now Orion, where he had a good practice. He was an effective lawyer before a jury. Later he removed to Ox-ford, and followed farming. He was the first Justice of the Peace and several times Supervisor.

ARTHUR ROLLIN TRIPP

Representative from the First District of Oakland County, 1891-2 and 1893-4. Was born at Hunter's Creek, Lapeer County, Nov. 15, 1850. At the age of eleven years he moved with his father's family to Commerce, Oakland County, and settled upon a farm. While here he worked upon the farm in the summer and attended district school winters until the fall of 1868 when he entered the Pontiac High School, at which place and the University of Michigan he con-tinued his studies until 1876. He then studied law with Judge Michael E. Croffot, and after his admission to the bar he engaged in the practice of his profession at Pontiac. In 1883 he was married to Miss Alicia F. Dandison of Pontiac. In politics a Democrat. He held the offices of School Inspector, Circuit Court Commissioner (two terms), and Prosecuting Attorney (two terms).

BURRELL TRIPP

Senator, 1915-16 and 1917-18, from the Eighth District, comprising the counties of Allegan and Van Buren. Was born at Bangor, Mich., May 19, 1862, of Scotch and French Huguenot ancestry. He was educated in the Bangor High School from which he graduated in 1879. On June 9, 1883, he was married to Anna W. Jennings, of Lawrence, Mich. He engaged in the mercantile business. In politics a Republican.

CHARLES TRIPP

Senator from the Sixth District, 1855-6. Was born in Epsom, N. H., Dec. 2, 1812. He came to Ann Arbor in 1843 and engaged in the foundry business. He resided there until his death Jan. 16, 1878. He was Railroad Commissioner under Gov. Bingham. He was always interested in public affairs, was a man of strong conviction. In politics he was a Republican.

CHARLES C. TROWBRIDGE

Members of the Board of Regents of the University of Michigan, 1839-42. Was born in Albany, N. Y., Dec. 29, 1800. He came to Detroit in 1819. He was the first secretary of the Board of Regents, filled positions at Green Bay and Detroit as Indian agent and interpreter; was cashier or president of the Bank of Michigan from 1825 to 1843; except three years; president of the Michigan State Bank from 1844 to 1853; then became secretary and afterwards for many years president of the Oakland & Ottawa Railroad Co., and afterwards the Detroit & Milwaukee. He held many local positions, and was the Whig candidate for Governor in 1837. He was an Alderman, and Mayor of Detroit in 1834. He was a perfect type of the old school gentleman, and on his eighty-second birthday was given a public banquet at the Russell House, by the most distinguished men of the city and State. He died at Detroit, Apr. 3, 1883.

ROWLAND E. TROWBRIDGE

Senator from the Fifth District, 1857-8 and 1859-60; and member of Congress, 1861-3 and 1865-7. Was born at Horseheads, N. Y., June 18, 1821, and was brought the same year to Troy, Oakland County, Mich., by his father, S. V. R. Trowbridge, who settled in that town upon a farm. The son graduated from Kenyon College, O., in 1841. Unable to follow his chosen profession of the law, from failure of eyesight, he became a farmer, and settled in Barry County in 1848, and cleared up a farm. In 1849 he was Supervisor of the town of Thorndale. In 1851 he exchanged his farm for one in Bloomfield, Oakland County, settled upon it, having married that year Miss Mary E. Satterlee. He worked the farm until 1860, then exchanged for milling property, and removed to Birmingham. He was Supervisor of Bloomfield in 1855. In 1873 he took charge of the Chandler farm near Lansing, where he was successful. In 1880 he was appointed Commissioner of Indian affairs by President Hayes, and died while holding that office, Apr. 20, 1881. He was president of the Central Michigan

Agricultural Society, and was recognized throughout the State as a leading agriculturist, and an honest, incorruptible man. In politics he was first a Whig, a Republican after 1854.

STEPHEN V. R. TROWBRIDGE

Member of the Legislative Council from Oakland County, 1828; and Senator from the Third District, 1839-41, and from the Sixth District, 1842. Was born at Albany, N. Y., July 4, 1794. He was married to Elizabeth Conkling at Horseheads, N. Y., in 1815, and came to Michigan in the fall of 1821. He settled for life on a farm, purchased of government, in Troy, Oakland County. He was the first Supervisor of Troy in 1827, and held that position in 1828, and four terms afterwards. His home was headquarters for early emigrants coming to Troy. His services for the town and State were of a high order, and he identified himself with every project calculated to benefit society. The family of eleven children imitated his example. Among them were Charles A., a New York merchant; Rowland E., long in Congress; William P., professor in Yale College; General Luther S., of Detroit; and Guy M., of Pontiac. One of the daughters was the wife of Rev. Mr. Goodell, long a distinguished missionary in Turkey. He helped organize the Presbyterian Church in Troy, and was an elder. He was always a staunch friend of temperance, and an active Christian. In politics he was a Whig and Republican. He died Mar. 1, 1859.

STEPHEN V. R. TROWBRIDGE

Attorney General, 1889-91. Was born Jan. 1, 1855, upon a farm in Oakland County, Mich. He was educated entirely under the Michigan educational system, his early education being begun in the common district schools of his native county. He afterwards attended the public school in the village of Birmingham, Oakland County, where he strengthened and broadened the foundation, before well started, for a good education. He entered the University of Michigan with the class of 1876 in the literary department, and practically completed the literary course, although he was prevented from graduating with his class by a severe attack of sickness in his senior year. He was elected orator of his class in senior year, then regarded a high honor; In 1879 he entered the office of Hon. Allen B. Morse of Ionia, Mich., and began the study of law. In June, 1881, he was admitted to the bar and began the active practice of his profession with the firm known as Morse, Wilson & Trowbridge, at Ionia. In politics his sympathies steadily leaned toward the Republican party. His ancestors were Whigs or Republicans, Samuel Satterlee, his maternal grandfather, being a member of the first convention of assent to the first Constitution of Michigan, and both the latter and Stephen V. R. Trowbridge, the grandfather of the subject of this sketch, being members of the Third Legislative Council which convened in 1828. He was elected Attorney General in 1888; resigned Mar. 25, 1889.

AARON D. TRUESDELL

Representative from Washtenaw County, 1847 and 1851-2. His postoffice address was Bridgewater. (Further data not obtainable).

WALTER F. TRUETTNER

Senator from the Thirty-first District, comprising the counties of Alger, Dickinson, Gogebic, Iron and Marquette, 1923—. Was born at Dundas, Wis., July 24, 1881, but has been a resident of Bessemer since 1888. His education was acquired in the Bessemer High School and Oberlin College, Ohio. In 1899 he entered the employ of the First National Bank of Bessemer as clerk and bookkeeper and has won steady promotion until at present he is vice-president. Mr. Truettner is a member of all Masonic orders. Always actively interested in Republican politics, he served several terms as alderman, fifteen years on the board of education and eight years on the board of supervisors, three years of which he was chairman. He was elected to the Senate November 7, 1922.

CHARLES WALTER TUBBS

Representative from the Second District of Washtenaw County, 1909-10. Was born in Scio Township, Washtenaw County, Mich., July 14, 1872, of American parentage. He acquired his education in the Ann Arbor High School, graduating with the class of 1891. After his graduation he returned to the farm and followed the occupation of farming. He was married to Cora V. Orcutt, Aug. 25, 1897. In politics a Republican.

TRUE PAOLI TUCKER

Representative from St. Clair County, 1839 and 1840. His postoffice address was St. Clair. (Further data not obtainable).

CHARLES TUFTS

Representative from Mason County, 1911-12, 1913-14 and 1915-16; and Senator 1917-18, 1919-20 and 1921-2, from the Twenty-sixth District, comprising the counties of Lake, Manistee, Mason, Newaygo and Oceana. Was born in Canada in 1856, of Scotch and English parentage. He was educated in the public schools. In 1878 he entered the life-saving service and served as surfman at Ludington, Mich. In 1884 he was appointed keeper; and in 1893 he and his crew were sent in charge of the life-saving station at the World's fair, Chicago, to give exhibition drills. In 1895 he had a similar charge at the Cotton States fair, Atlanta, Ga. He left the service in 1897 on account of ill health and moved on to a farm. Five years later he was elected Sheriff and served two terms. Mr. Tufts is married and has two children. In politics he is a Republican.

MYRON TUPPER

Representative from Ionia County, 1865-6. Was born in Monroe County, N. Y., May 19, 1816. He was a clergyman and farmer, politically a Republican. He came to Michigan in 1838. He was ordained a Free Will Baptist minister in 1848. Held the positions of Postmaster and Supervisor. He died Mar. 4, 1879.

WILLIAM S. TURCK

Representative from Gratiot County, 1877-8 and 1879-80. Was born in Port Hope, Ont., in 1839. He received a common school education. He came to Michigan in 1860, and entered the service in the 26th Mich. Infantry in 1862, and was mustered out with the regiment in 1865 as Captain of Co. D. He was Treasurer of Gratiot County for six years, Supervisor four years, and president and treasurer of the Farmers' Mutual Fire Insurance Company of Gratiot and Isabella counties. He was a farmer by occupation, and a Republican in politics. He died at Alma, Sept. 19, 1902.

EDWARD AUGUSTUS TURNBULL

Delegate to the Constitutional Convention of 1907-8 from the Fifteenth District, Eaton County. Was born in England in 1856, of English descent. He was educated in a private school in England, and after leaving school spent three years in London in an importing tea house. He then went to South Africa and spent some time there. He came to America in 1879. He engaged in the manufacturing business at Grand Ledge. Married.

JAMES D. TURNBULL

Representative from the Alpena District, 1879-80 and 1881-2; and Senator from the Twenty-ninth District, 1893-4. Was born in Harvey, New Brunswick, Feb. 5, 1813. He came to Michigan in 1858, locating at Chelsea. In 1862 he enlisted in the 20th Mich. Infantry and remained through the war, being promoted to Lieutenant. After the war he attended the State Normal School and at the close of his course, he engaged in teaching at Memphis, which he continued three years, and after a private study of law was admitted to the bar in 1871. The next year he located at Alpena and began the practice of his profession. He was a Democrat in politics. He was defeated for Circuit Judge of the Twenty-sixth Circuit, and for the Legislature of 1888. He held the office of Comptroller of the city of Alpena.

GEORGE B. TURNER

Representative from Cass County, 1848 and 1849. Was born in Franklin County, N. Y., in 1822. His parents, named Brunt, left him an orphan at the age of three years, and being adopted by Sterling A. Turner, a Virginian, he took his name. In 1835, at the age of thirteen, he became a clerk in an auction and commission store in Detroit. In a few months he went to Cassopolis, and until 1840 was occupied as pupil, teacher and clerk. He studied law with A. H. Redfield and was admitted to the bar in 1844. In 1850 he abandoned practice from ill health and became a farmer. He was a delegate to the Democratic National Convention of 1876. As a Democrat he was the candidate of his party for Probate Judge, also for Senator, and in 1856 ran on the defeated ticket for Secretary of State. He was editorially connected with the *Cass County Advocate*, the first paper published in that county.

JAMES TURNER

Senator from the Twenty-first District, 1867-8. Was born at Cazenovia, N. Y., Apr. 1, 1820, and was a descendant of Humphrey Turner, who settled at Plymouth, Ct., in 1628. With a fair education, self obtained, he came to Leoni, Mich., in 1840, and acted as clerk in a store. In 1841 he removed to Mason, engaging in mercantile business until 1847, when he came to Lansing, erecting the first frame house, helped to start first female college at Lansing, and for twenty years was superintendent of the M. E. Sunday School, continuing the mercantile business, and engaged in the construction of the Lansing and Howell plank road, of which he was treasurer. In 1860 he became Deputy State Treasurer, which he held for six years. In 1864 he became Treasurer and Land Commissioner of the Jackson, Lansing & Saginaw Railroad, holding it until his death. He was also director and treasurer of the Lansing & Ionia railroad, was agent for non-resident Michigan land holders, and loaned money largely for the New Lebanon Shakers. In 1867 he had been a member of the Lansing Board of Education for nine years. He was a Republican in politics, a Methodist in religion. He died Oct. 10, 1869.

JAMES MUNROE TURNER

Representative from Ingham County, 1877-8. Was born in Lansing, Mich., Apr. 23, 1850. He received a common school education, and afterwards spent two years at Oneida Conference Seminary, Cazenovia, N. Y. In 1868 he was elected paymaster and assistant treasurer of the Ionia & Lansing Railroad. In 1869 he was elected treasurer of the same company, being the successor of his father. In 1871 he organized the real estate and loan agency of Turner, Smith & Co., of Lansing, which dissolved by the retirement of D. S. Smith. On the organization of the Chicago & Northeastern Railroad Company, in the year 1874, he was elected president. He was the youngest member of the Legislature of 1877. He was extensively engaged in manufacturing, mining and real estate, and resided at Lansing. He had a large farm well stocked with horses, cattle and sheep. He was Mayor of Lansing, 1889 and 1895, candidate for Governor in 1888 and member of the board for School for the Blind. He died at Lansing, July 7, 1896.

JEROME E. TURNER

Representative from Muskegon County, 1905-6 and 1907-8. Was born at Howell, Livingston County, Mich., Dec. 29, 1858, of Scotch and Irish descendants. He acquired his education in the common and high schools of Owosso and Corunna. He first assumed the duties of a drug clerk, bank clerk for two years, later clerked in the law office of Maybury & Conely at Detroit, Mich. He remained with this firm until admitted to the bar, Dec. 22, 1881. He moved to Muskegon in 1890 and entered into partnership with his brother, Willard J. Turner, under the title of Turner & Turner. He held the offices of City Attorney of Owosso for three years and Attorney for the city of Muskegon Heights. He married Mrs. Belle Hovey, of Muskegon, Aug. 29, 1900. In politics a Republican.

JEROME W. TURNER

Senator from the Twenty-second District, 1869-70. Was born at Sheldon, Vt., Jan. 25, 1836. By occupation he was a lawyer, in politics, formerly a Republican, then a Democrat. He came to Michigan with his father, Judge Josiah Turner, in 1839, who settled in Howell, and afterwards moved to Owosso. He graduated from the University in 1857. He studied law, and actively engaged in his profession at Owosso. As a Republican he was Senator, and at that time wrote a series of humorous articles, that attracted great attention, and were published in the Detroit *Tribune*. As a Democrat he was Mayor of Owosso in 1879; delegate to the Democratic National Convention at Cincinnati in 1880; also to the convention at Chicago in 1844. He was Adjutant of the 30th Mich. Infantry, and was the Democratic candidate for member of the State Board of Education in 1886. He wrote short poems of great merit. Deceased.

JESSE F. TURNER

Senator from the Fourth District, 1844-5. Was born in Albany, N. Y., in 1810. He came to DeWitt, Mich., in 1838, and engaged in mercantile business. Afterwards he studied law with Joab Baker. He was County Commissioner of Clinton County in 1841; Register of Deeds; Supervisor of DeWitt, and County Judge in 1846. In politics he was a Democrat. He went to California in 1851, and was Collector of the Port of Sacramento under President Pierce. He was Circuit Judge of the Sacramento judicial circuit for twelve years. He died at Oakland, Calif., in 1880.

JOHN W. TURNER

Representative from Clinton and other counties, 1851. Was born in Oneida County, N. Y., Feb. 23, 1800. He was several years a clerk. He resided at Oswego, N. Y., from 1819 to 1846, and a part of the time was Deputy Collector at Oswego. He settled at DeWitt, Mich., in 1848, and engaged in milling and mercantile business. He was five years a Supervisor, and was Sheriff in 1858-9. He removed to Vermillion, Dakota, was for eleven years a member of the Territorial Council and from 1869 to 1873 was Superintendent of Public Instruction in Dakota. While in Michigan he was a Democrat. He died at Turner, Dakota, Apr. 11, 1883.

JOHN W. TURNER

Representative from Lenawee County, 1847 and 1849. Was born in Putney, Vt., in 1818. By profession he was a lawyer. He came to Hudson, Mich., in 1841, later removed to Coldwater. He was a Democrat until 1854, then a Republican. He was the first Republican nominee for Lieutenant Governor, but declined in favor of Coe. As a public speaker and legal advocate he always stood high in southern Michigan. He published a volume of poems of considerable merit.

JOSIAH TURNER

Justice of the Supreme Court, 1857; and Delegate from Shiawassee County to the Constitutional Convention of 1867. Was born in New Haven, Vt., Sept. 1,

1811. He received his education at St. Albans and Middlebury, studied law, and was admitted to the bar of Vermont in 1833. After a short practice in that State, he came to Michigan and settled at Howell. In 1842 he was elected County Clerk by the Democrats, and served six years, also holding the positions of Justice, Township Clerk, and Master in Chancery. On the adoption of the County court system he was elected Judge of Livingston County, and held the position until 1850, when the office was abolished. In 1856 he was elected Probate Judge on the Republican ticket. In 1857 he was appointed by Gov. Bingham to a vacancy on the Supreme Court bench, and the same year was elected Judge of the seventh judicial circuit for six years, and received three successive re-elections, the fourth time being elected without opposition, serving from 1857 to 1881. In 1860 he removed from Howell to Owosso, and was Mayor of that city in 1864-5. After he retired from the bench he was U. S. Consul at Amherstburg, Canada. He was a charter member of the Michigan Pioneer and Historical Society. He died at Owosso, Apr. 7, 1907.

MILO H. TURNER

Representative from Clinton and Shiawassee counties, 1842. Was born at Albany, N. Y., in 1812. He came to Michigan in 1837, and was the pioneer merchant of DeWitt, Clinton County. He was elected Register of Deeds in 1839. In politics he was a Whig. He removed to California in 1851, and was living at Oakland in 1887.

REUBEN D. TURNER

Representative from Mackinac County, 1840. His postoffice address was Mackinac. (Further data not obtainable).

STANLEY W. TURNER

Representative from Ingham County, 1877-8; and from the Ogemaw district, 1889-90; and Auditor General, 1893-5 and 1895-7. Was born at North Fairfield, O., July 15, 1843; came with his parents to Reading, Hillsdale County, Mich., in 1851; attended public school and began a course at Hillsdale College which was interrupted by the outbreak of the Civil War. He enlisted as a private in the 18th Regiment, was commissioned as Second Lieutenant before leaving the State; resigned and a little later enlisted as private in the First Mich. Sharpshooters; was speedily promoted through the various offices and ultimately obtained a Captaincy. At the mine explosion in front of Petersburg, Va., he was captured and confined in both Danville and Libby prisons. After the war he returned to Michigan, locating at Mason, Ingham County, where he studied law with the Hon. H. L. Henderson. In 1866 he was elected Clerk of Ingham County and re-elected in 1868; was a member of the House of Representatives of 1877-8; was chairman of the Republican County Committee of Ingham County, for eight years. In 1877 he removed to Roscommon County, where he engaged in the practice of law and dealing in pine lands. He was again elected a member of the House of Representatives from the Ogemaw District for the session of 1889-90. He was elected Auditor General for the term of 1893-5, and re-elected for the term of 1895-7.

JAMES TURRILL

Representative from Lapeer County, 1849. Was born in Shoreham, Addison County, Vt., Sept. 24, 1797. At the age of twenty-one he engaged in the mercantile business. In 1836 he came to Michigan and bought lands near Lapeer. In 1842 he moved from Vermont to this State, locating in Lapeer, following the mercantile business and interested in banking. He was the first Mayor of Lapeer and held many local offices. His eldest son, a Captain in the Civil War, was killed at Antietam. He died July 31, 1876.

ARTHUR J. TUTTLE

Senator, 1907-8 and 1909-10, from the Fourteenth District, comprising the counties of Ingham and Shiawassee. Was born in Leslie Township, Ingham County, Mich., Nov. 8, 1868. He was graduated from the Leslie High School in 1888, from the literary department of the University of Michigan in 1892 and from the law department of the University of Michigan in 1895. He practiced law at Leslie after leaving the University. In the fall of 1898 he was elected Prosecuting Attorney of Ingham County and in January, 1899, opened a law office in the city of Lansing. He was re-elected in the fall of 1900. Many important criminal cases were tried by him during his term of office, including the so-called military fraud and State cases. He was elected President of the village of Leslie in 1905; was President of the People's Bank of Leslie, interested in farming and various business enterprises but devoting nearly all of his time to his legal business. He maintained law offices at both Leslie and Lansing. In politics a Republican. He was married Mar. 11, 1903, to Jessie B. Steward.

WARREN TUTTLE

Delegate from Wayne County to the Second Convention of Assent, 1836; and Representative from Wayne County, 1849. Was born in Poultney, Vt., Dec. 24, 1804. He came to Michigan in 1826, and located a farm in Livonia. As a pioneer he made the wilderness to bud and blossom as the rose, and died Sept. 17, 1849, on the farm that he had made. He served his town as Justice for many years, and the County as Superintendent of the Poor, 1847-9. His politics were Democratic.

RODNEY K. TWADELL

Representative from Branch County, 1877-8 and 1879-80. Was born in Marion, Wayne County, N. Y., Nov. 7, 1827. He received a common school education, and removed to Quincy, Mich., in April, 1851. He was a farmer by occupation; in politics a Republican.

ROYAL T. TWOMBLY

Senator from the Nineteenth District, 1853-4. Was born at Portland, Me., in 1813. He settled in Niles, Mich., in 1837. In business he was a merchant; politically a Democrat. He was for several years a trustee of the union school at Niles, was Mayor of Niles in 1877, and a candidate for Presidential Elector on the Douglas ticket in 1860. He died Oct. 14, 1885.

COLUMBUS V. TYLER

Senator, 1877-8, 1879-80 and 1889, from the Twenty-fifth District, which embraced the counties of Bay and Arenac. Was born in Auburn, N. Y., in 1825. His father's family removed to Genesee County, Mich., in 1836, where young Tyler remained working on a new farm until 1846, when he commenced the study of medicine with his uncle, Hon. N. B. Eldridge, who was then practicing medicine and surgery. Dr. Tyler received a good common school education, but never attended any seminary or college. After completing his medical studies he settled at Flushing, Genesee County, Mich., and commenced the practice of medicine in 1850. Here he remained until 1869. He was married to Marie Antoinette Herrick. He had a large practice, and was Postmaster of Flushing from 1856 to 1860. In 1869 he moved to Bay City, where he practiced. In 1883 he was appointed a member of the State Board of Health by Governor Begole. He was also, in 1885, appointed by the President one of the Board of Medical Examiners for Pension Claimants, and was President of Bay City Board of Health. Friends supported him as candidate for Congress in 1878. He served in the Senate of 1877 and 1879, and was re-elected in November, 1888. He died at Bay City June 1, 1889.

COMFORT TYLER

Representative from St. Joseph County, 1841; Senator from the Sixteenth District, 1859-60; and Delegate from St. Joseph County to the Constitutional Convention of 1867. Was born in Marcellus, N. Y., Mar. 7, 1801; where his parents came from Connecticut in 1788. He received a common school education. He assisted his father in farming, milling and carding wool and dressing cloth until he was twenty-four. In 1834 he removed to Colon, St. Joseph County, and bought a large farm, where he resided until his death, Jan. 16, 1873. He was twenty-five years a Supervisor. He was first a Whig, a Republican from 1854.

JOHN EDWARD TYRRELL

Representative from the First District of Jackson County, 1889-90. Was born at the city of Dublin, Ireland, in 1847. He was formerly a resident of the State of New York from his fourth year, and was educated at Fordham College, N. Y. During the war he served in the 56th N. Y. Infantry, and was an active member of Edward Pomeroy Post, No. 48, at Jackson, Mich. He organized Co. H, 1st Regiment (Emmet Rifles), and commanded the company six years, and was elected Major of the 1st Regiment in March, 1888.

ISAAC J. ULLMAN

Representative from St. Joseph County, 1835-6. His postoffice address was Constantine. (Further data not obtainable).

MADISON J. ULRICH

Representative from Kent County, 1885-6. Was born in Park, Mich., Dec. 5, 1835; was reared upon a farm, and for a time followed the occupation of a

farmer, finally engaging as a tea and coffee merchant in Grand Rapids. He was
School Inspector, Collector, School Trustee, and Supervisor. He was elected
Representative on the Fusion ticket.

DANIEL K. UNDERWOOD

Representative from Lenawee County, 1840. Was born at Enfield, Mass., June
15, 1803. He prepared for college at Amherst Academy, spent two years at
Williams College, then went to Dartmouth, graduating as a physician in 1826.
He practiced two years at Yarmouth, Mass., then was a druggist at Amherst
until 1836. He settled that year at Adrian, Mich., and was in the drug trade
until 1849. With the exception of a short time in the banking business, the rest
of his life he gave to reading, study and horticulture. He made a study of fruits
and varieties best adapted to the climate, and was employed by the United States
Pomological Society to prepare a work, published by the Government. He gave
the land for the site of Adrian College, and was liberal in other directions. He
died at Adrian, May 6, 1875.

G. JOSEPH UNSOELD

Representative from the First District of Wayne County, 1909-10, 1911-12 and
1913. Was born at Ulm, Germany, Apr. 20, 1845, of German parentage.
He received his education in the public schools of Germany and night schools
of Detroit. He was married and a molder by trade. He was apprenticed to
J. B. Wilson of Detroit and traveled three and one-half years as journeyman;
was connected with the Detroit Stove Works many years, beginning as a journeyman molder, then foundry foreman, and after 1892 superintendent, retiring in
1904. In politics he was an active Republican. He died at his temporary home
at Lansing, Feb. 25, 1913.

EDWARD W. UPHAM

Representative from the Second District of Kalamazoo County, 1917-18. Was
born in Otesgo, Allegan County, June 2, 1860. His education was secured in
the Otsego and Athens high schools. After the death of his father in 1880, the
family moved to a farm in Alamo Township, Kalamazoo County, where Mr.
Upham made his home with the exception of two years on the Great Lakes as an
engineer, and two years in the West. He was married in 1889 to Miss Carrie
E. Brown of Wyoming, Kent County. He served as Justice of the Peace, Supervisor, Deputy Sheriff and member of the Board of County Canvassers. In politics a Democrat.

WILLIAM UPJOHN

Member of the Board of Regents of the University of Michigan, 1852-8. Was
born at Shaftesbury, Dorset, England, Mar. 4, 1807, son of William and Mary
(Standard) Upjohn. He received his early education at the Bluecoat School
of Shaftesbury and later was given a collegiate training. In 1828 he came to

America in company with his brother, Uriah, and pursued medical studies in New York. He then came West and entered upon the practice of his profession in Barry County, Mich., Nov. 1, 1863, he was appointed Surgeon of the 7th Mich. Cavalry, and later was promoted to be Surgeon-in-Chief of the First Brigade of the 1st Cavalry Division of the Army of the Potomac. He was with Kilpatrick in his raid on Richmond and accompanied General Sheridan in his raid up the James River. At the close of the war he returned to Hastings, Mich., and resumed the practice of his profession. He was Register of Deeds for Barry County in 1853 and 1854, and Coroner in 1880. He was married in 1842 to Affa Connett, no children of this union surviving. In 1847 he was married to Lydia Connett. In 1872 the University conferred upon him the honorary degree of Doctor of Medicine. He died at Hastings, Aug. 2, 1887.

A. I. UPSON

Senator from the Thirty-second District, 1855-6. Was for a few years a merchant at Eagle Harbor, Keweenaw County. Nothing further is known of him.

CHARLES UPSON

Senator from the Seventeenth District, 1855-6, and from the Tenth District, 1881-2; Attorney General, 1861-3; and member of Congress, 1863-5 to 1869-71. Was born at Southington, Conn., Mar. 19, 1821. He received a common school and academical education. In 1834 he began the study of law, and was one year in Yale Law School. He came to Constantine, in 1845, and the next year removed to Centreville. He taught school, and in 1847 was Deputy County Clerk; admitted to the bar in 1847. He engaged in practice at Centreville, was County Clerk two years, and two years Prosecuting Attorney of St. Joseph County. He removed to Coldwater in 1856, and from 1857 to 1861 was a Railroad Commissioner. In 1869 he was elected Judge of the fifth circuit; resigned Dec. 31, 1872. In 1871 he was one of two commissioners to examine the compilation of the laws, made that year. In 1873 he was one of eighteen commissioners to revise the State Constitution. In 1876 he declined the office of Commissioner of Indian Affairs. He was first a Whig, a Republican from 1854. He died at Coldwater, Sept. 5, 1885.

DANIEL UPTON

Representative from Jackson County, 1867-8. Was born at Fishkill, N. Y., Aug. 12, 1818, and came with his father's family in 1835 to Jackson County, Mich. Bred a farmer, he became a clerk, was a merchant at Parma, also a farmer. He was eight years clerk of Jackson County. He removed to Muskegon in 1868, and purchased a fruit farm on Lake Harbor. He was one of the firm of Upton & Webb, dealers in real estate. He held the offices of Supervisor, Town Clerk and Treasurer.

WILLIAM W. UPTON

Representative from Clinton County, 1847. Was born in Victor, N. Y., and was educated at the Lima Seminary. He was a surveyor employed on railroads and canals. He located a farm in Victor, Mich., studied law, was admitted in 1845, and practiced first at DeWitt, then at Lansing from 1847 to 1852. Then he removed to California, was in practice twelve years, was a member of the California Legislature in 1856, and District Attorney of Sacramento County in 1861 to 1863. He removed to Portland, Ore., in 1864, practiced law until 1868, was then appointed Judge of the Supreme Court to fill vacancy, and was elected to that position for six years in 1872. From 1872 to 1874 he was Chief Justice. In 1877 he was appointed second comptroller of the Treasury Department, a position he held for many years.

WILLIAM S. UTLEY

Representative from Newaygo County, 1865-6; and Delegate from Newaygo County to the Constitutional Convention of 1867. Was born in Richmond, N. Y., Nov. 6, 1827. He came with his parents to Michigan in 1828, was educated in the common schools, learned a trade at Lansing, and settled in Newaygo County in 1850. He was County Clerk 1859 to 1863. He built the first bridge across the Muskegon River, at Croton, in 1850; put up the first mail ever sent from the county; and claims to have married more couples than any other magistrate in northern Michigan. He was for thirty-two years Town Clerk of Big Prairie, also Town Treasurer. He was a Whig until 1854, a Republican until 1876, then a Greenbacker. He died at Big Prairie, July 19, 1909.

JOSEPH L. VALADE

Representative from Monroe County, 1877-8. Was born at Dover East, Ont., Mar. 28, 1822. He attended school in Detroit from 1833 to 1837, then at Dundas, Ont., until 1844. He then taught a French school at various places in the province until 1848, when he commenced to read medicine with the late Dr. Pitcher. In 1850-1 he attended medical lectures at Trinity College, Toronto, also at Ann Arbor in 1852, from which place he removed to Vienna, Monroe County, where he resided, and established for himself a respectable medical reputation.

GEORGE W. VAN AKEN

Representative from Branch County, 1873-4 and 1875-6. Was born in Clarkston, N. Y., Sept. 8, 1828. In 1835 he removed to Michigan and settled in Lenawee County, near Adrian. In 1838 he removed to Girard, Branch County. He received a common school education. He was Supervisor of his township for four years. By occupation he was a farmer.

SIMEON VAN AKIN

Senator, 1903-4 and 1905-6, from the Fifth District, comprising the counties of Lenawee and Monroe. Was born in the village of Hudson, Lenawee County, Mich., Oct. 14, 1842. His parents were among the early pioneers of Michigan and settled in the valley of the Tiffin before Michigan became a State. His education was acquired in the district school, supplemented by occasional select schools held in the village. At the age of nineteen he enlisted in Co. C, 1st Regiment U. S. Sharpshooters, Berdans, and shortly after the close of the war he married and removed to Ida Township, Monroe County, where he engaged in farming. In politics he was a Republican. He held the offices of Township Clerk, Justice of the Peace, and was a member of the Board of Supervisors.

HERBERT A. VAN ANTWERP

Representative from the Third District of Kent County, 1915-16. Was born at Sparta, Mich., Mar. 27, 1872, of American parents. He was educated in the Sparta High School and graduated from that institution in 1887. He learned the printer's trade in the office of the Sparta *Sentinel* and has worked in several of the towns of the State. From 1900 to 1906 he was employed on the Pittsburgh *Gazette-Times*, the most of this time being second assistant foreman. In 1910 he purchased the Rockford *Register*. He was married Dec. 31, 1895, to Miss Marie Deffinger of Filer City, Mich. In the spring of 1911 he was elected Clerk of Algoma Township, serving one year. On Nov. 3, 1914, he was elected to the Legislature on the Republican ticket.

SAUNDERS L. VAN CAMP

Representative from the First District of Berrien County, 1897-8 and 1899-1900. Was born at Erie County, Pa., Oct. 17, 1841. He was educated in the common school of his native town, and at the academy of East Springfield. In August, 1862, he enlisted for the Civil War in Co. A, 145th Regiment of Penn. Vol., was severely wounded at the Battle of Gettysburg, July 2, 1863, discharged from hospital in Philadelphia Nov. 22, 1864, and moved to Michigan in April, 1866, purchasing eighty acres of timber land near Benton Harbor, Berrien County, which he cleared and occupied as a farm. He was a Republican in politics. He held nearly all the township offices; was Supervisor for many years; was twice elected chairman of the Board of Supervisors, and twice elected Treasurer of Berrien County.

HENRY VANCE

Representative from the First District of Saginaw County, 1905-6. Was born in Rochester, N. Y., Nov. 13, 1833, of Irish parentage. He came with his parents to Saginaw, Mich., in 1846. His education was acquired in the common schools of New York and Michigan. He was employed in the various branches of the lumber industry until August, 1861, when he enlisted in Co. E, 2nd Mich. Cavalry, and served until Aug. 17, 1865, when he was mustered out as Captain with his regiment at Macon, Ga. For three years after the close of the war he was part owner and sailed a tug on the Saginaw River. From 1868 to 1898 he was employed as log scaler and ended his work in this line on Georgian Bay, Canada, 1898. He was unmarried. In politics he was a Republican.

FRANK H. VANDENBOOM

Senator, 1919-20 and 1921-2, from the Thirty-first District, which comprises the counties of Alger, Dickinson, Gogebic, Iron and Marquette. Was born on a farm in Marquette Township, Marquette County, Mich., Feb. 22, 1873, of Dutch and English parents. He has lived on the same farm all his life. He was educated in the district school, St. Joseph's Academy, in Marquette, and at the Ferris Institute of Big Rapids, Mich. He has been engaged in the dairy business about forty years and is at present owner of the Marquette City dairy. Mr. Vandenboom is married and has five children. In politics he is a Republican.

HENRY B. VANDERCOOK

Representative from the First District of Kent County, 1901-2 and 1903-4. Was born at Ann Arbor, Mich., Aug. 3, 1861, and received his education in the schools of Allegan. In 1876 he engaged in the monumental business and probably had the distinction of being the youngest business man in Michigan at that time, as he was not quite fifteen years of age. He successfully pursued the same business and in 1891 removed to Grand Rapids and established the Grand Rapids Monument Company. By home study and a membership in the Kent Law Club he was admitted to practice by Judge Adsit in 1895. Mr. Vandercook was a volunteer fireman for nine years. Married and a member of several societies. In politics a Republican. He was elected to the Legislature of 1901-2, and re-elected Nov. 4, 1902, on the general legislative ticket of Grand Rapids.

HARRY VANDER VEEN

Representative from the First District of Kent County, 1907-8 and 1909-10. Was born in the Netherlands, Feb. 4, 1868, of Holland parentage. In 1873 he came to Michigan with his parents. He was educated in the public schools. A contractor, being a member of the firm Kloote & Vander Veen. In politics a Republican.

JOHN VANDERWERP

Senator, 1911-12, from the Twenty-third District, comprising the counties of Muskegon and Ottawa. Was born in Fillmore Township, Allegan County, Mich., May 25, 1866, of Holland descent. He removed with his parents to Muskegon in 1872, and attended the public schools of that city, afterwards entering the law offices of Smith, Nims, Hoyt and Erwin and continuing his studies in the night school. At the age of twenty-one he was admitted to the bar and continued the practice of law with the above firm until the fall of 1896, when he was elected Judge of Probate. After serving one term he was re-elected. In September, 1901, he resigned to become a law partner with the members of the firm with which he had formerly been connected, and with Judge Clarence W. Sessions, the firm name then becoming Nims, Hoyt, Erwin, Sessions and Vanderwerp. Jan. 1, 1910, the firm of Cross, Vanderwerp, Foote and Ross was organized, the junior partner being Lieutenant Governor Ross. Mr. Vanderwerp was married Dec. 18, 1889, to Miss Agnes Vogel. In politics a Republican.

LAWRENCE VAN DUSEN

Representative from Shiawassee County, 1883-4. Was born at Fort Edward, N. Y., Aug. 27, 1826, and in 1832 removed with his parents to Ovid, N. Y. He was seven years clerk in a store, three years Superintendent of the Poor in Seneca County, and door keeper of the New York Senate in 1863-4. For four years he was Deputy Provost Marshal, also a Deputy Collector. He removed to Owosso, Mich., in 1869. He was engaged in the lumber business, and was a Justice and Deputy Sheriff. He was elected on the Fusion ticket, but in politics a Greenbacker.

ZACHARIAH VAN DUSER

Delegate from Hillsdale County to the Second Convention of Assent, 1836; and Representative from Hillsdale County, 1847. Was born in Catskill, N. Y., Nov. 26, 1803. By occupation he was a farmer and druggist, politically a Democrat. He settled in Moscow, Hillsdale County, in 1834 and in 1835 was the first Supervisor of that town. He was also Supervisor in 1841, 1845 and 1849. He died at Hillsdale, Mar. 10, 1852.

PETER VAN EVERY

Delegate from the First District to the Constitutional Convention of 1835; and Representative from Wayne County, 1835 and 1836. Was born near Hamilton, Canada, Jan. 3, 1795, coming with his parents to Michigan when an infant. He served as a private in the War of 1812, and was advanced to the position of Quartermaster of a regiment for faithful and meritorious services. After the close of the war he was commissioned by the Governor as Colonel of militia. He resided in Hamtramck on a farm of 400 acres bordering the river, on a portion of which the present Detroit water-works are located. He held at various times the offices of Supervisor and Justice of the Peace. In politics he was a Democrat up to 1837, and thereafter Whig and Republican. Besides being a farmer he was a miller and general business man, and in 1837 removed to Franklin, Oakland County, where he engaged in farming, milling and general merchandise, besides operating a distillery and ashery, giving employment to a large number of men, continuing in active business until near the close of his life, Dec. 22, 1859.

CALEB VAN HUSEN

Representative from Washtenaw County, 1844. Was born in Manchester, N. Y., Mar. 13, 1815. He lived at home until the age of thirteen, and became an apprentice to a cabinet maker. In 1836 he married Catharine Jackson, and became interested with his father in mercantile business. He settled as a merchant at Saline, Mich., in 1838, which he continued until 1853, when he removed to Detroit, was a merchant there until 1855, when he retired. He was a director in the Detroit Locomotive Works, also in the Michigan Insurance Company bank, and was president of the Detroit Fire and Marine Insurance Company from its organization until his death. Under his management the company prospered. His second wife was Emily C. Burr, whom he married in 1866.

He was long a trustee of Madison University, N. Y., was greatly interested in Kalamazoo College, and was a member of the Baptist Church from the age of fourteen. He left a large fortune to his wife and six children. He died Aug. 20, 1884.

CHRALES VAN KEUREN

Representative from Livingston County, 1905-6. Was born in the township of Oceola, Livingston County, Mich., June 4, 1878, of Holland-Dutch ancestry. In 1888 he moved with his parents to Howell. He was graduated from the Howell High School in 1896, and in the spring of that year he won the State High School oratorical championship. After traveling for one year with a Toledo stationery house, he entered the literary department of the University of Michigan, in 1897, and was graduated in 1902. In 1899 he was appointed special commissioner to the Paris Exposition by the Ohio Centennial Exposition Company. For one year after graduation he was employed as traveling advertising manager for the *Oaks*, a weekly magazine of Chicago, and the next year traveled for Rand, McNally & Co., publishers of Chicago, continuing with them until September, 1904. Unmarried, and belonged to Howell Lodge No. 38, F. & A. M.

JAMES VAN KLEECK

Representative from the Midland District, 1883-4; and Delegate to the Constitutional Convention of 1907-8 from the Twenty-fourth District. Was born Sept. 26, 1846, at Exeter, Mich. He enlisted as a private in the 17th Mich. Infantry in June, 1862. He was severely wounded at the Battle of Antietam. He graduated from the law department, Michigan University, in 1870. He removed from Monroe County and settled in Midland County in 1870, and began the practice of law at Midland City, moved to Bay City in 1884, where he engaged in the practice of his profession. He held various offices under the village government; also the office of Prosecuting Attorney of Midland County for six years. In politics he was a Republican. He was a member of the House of Representatives of 1883-4, was Commissioner of Emigration under Gov. Alger and a member of the Constitutional Convention of 1907-8.

CORNELIUS VAN LOO

Representative from Ottawa County, 1881-2 and 1883-4. Was born in the Netherlands, Aug. 7, 1838. He settled in Ottawa County with his parents in 1849. He attended the Agricultural College in 1858-9, also Albion College before and after that time. He taught school in 1860-1, enlisted in 1862 in the 21st Mich. Infantry, and served through the war, rising to the rank of First Lieutenant, and was twice wounded. After the war he was a student at Albion College for eighteen months. He was six years Register of Deeds for Ottawa County; four years Superintendent of Schools; Supervisor and chairman of Board two years. In politics he was a Republican.

AARON A. VAN ORTHWICK

Representative from Branch County, 1887-8 and 1889-90. Was born in Covert, Seneca County, N. Y., Dec. 19, 1829. He was three years old when his father died, leaving a widow with a family of four children in very limited circumstances. Mr. Van Orthwick remained at home until he was twenty-one years old, attending school in the village near which they resided. He then worked one year by the month, but not being satisfied with the prospect he came to Michigan in the spring of 1852. He worked by the month one year in Lenawee County when he removed to Branch County, and purchased wild land in Coldwater Township. With but little means he tried clearing land for about a year, when he resorted to work by the month for seven months. He then spent six months in Seneca County, O., attending school there, when he returned to Michigan and engaged in clearing his land. At the age of twenty-eight he married Miss Helen Nichols. In 1864 he sold his farm in Coldwater and purchased one in the township of Butler. He held the offices of Constable, Highway Commissioner, Township Superintendent of Schools, Coroner and Supervisor. He was elected Representative on the Republican ticket for 1887-8 and re-elected for 1889-90.

DIRK B. K. VAN RAALTE

Representative from the First District of Ottawa County, 1875-6, 1877-8 and 1909-10. Was born in Ommen, Netherlands, in 1844, of Holland descent. His education was acquired in the public schools and at Hope College. He was married. He represented the First District of Ottawa County in the Legislature during the years 1875-7. He served in the Civil War in the 25th Mich. Infantry. In politics he was a Republican. He was elected to the Legislature Nov. 3, 1908. He died Feb. 12, 1910.

JACOB J. VAN RIPER

Delegate from Cass County to the Constitutional Convention of 1867; member of the Board of Regents of the University of Michigan, 1850-6; and Attorney General, 1881-5. Was born at Haverstraw, N. Y., Mar. 8, 1838. He received an academical education, removed to Cass County, Mich., in 1837, but for many years resided at Buchanan. He attended the law department of the University, and was admitted to the bar in 1862. He held the offices of Deputy Collector and Assistant Assessor of Internal Revenue. He was the youngest Delegate in the Constitutional Convention of 1867. He was Prosecuting Attorney of Berrien County four years. In politics he was a Republican. In 1902 his residence was Niles, Mich.

ROWLAND S. VAN SCOY

Representative from Clinton County, 1871-2 and 1873-4. Was born in Kent, N. Y., Nov. 22, 1814. He received a common school education, and was a teacher several winters. In 1839 he came to Michigan and bought a farm in DeWitt, Clinton County. In 1854 he sold his farm and removed to Essex, Clinton County, where he resided on a farm of 1,200 acres. He owned several other farms, in all about 2,000 acres, a large number of village lots in Maple Rapids, and a large brick block, and carried on a banking business. He held many town offices, including Supervisor, Treasurer and Justice; was President of the village of Maple Rapids, and recruiting officer during the rebellion.

JOHN VAN VLECK

Member of the Board of Regents of the University of Michigan, 1858. Was born of Dutch ancestry at Shawangunk, Ulster County, N. Y., in 1828. He was graduated Bachelor of Arts from Rutgers College in 1852, and from the Theological Seminary of the Reformed Church in New Brunswick, N. J., in 1855. He was immediately called to the principalship of the Holland Academy (now Hope College) at Holland, Mich. He held that position until 1859, when he resigned it to take charge of an academy at Kingston, N. Y. After three years in that position his health having become impaired, he gave up teaching, and for the next two years was pastor of churches at Middleport, N. Y., and Wawarsing, N. Y. In April, 1857, he was elected Regent of the University of Michigan, and entered upon his duties the following January. He attended only a single meeting of the Board, and on Oct. 2, 1858, resigned the office. He was a teacher of superior qualifications and power, and his work at Holland, amid the privations of pioneer life, was an influence for good the lasting effects of which are felt to this day. He married a Miss Falkner. He died in Ulster County, N. Y., Mar. 15, 1865.

JAMES VAN VLEET

Representative from Genesee County, 1865-6 and 1867-8. Was born in Romulus, N. Y., July 28, 1818. He was brought up on a farm, received a common school education, married Mary Ann Cooley in 1841, and in 1844 settled on a farm in Gaines, Mich. He endured great hardship as a pioneer, but eventually his eighty-acre farm was increased to 320 acres, with fine farm bulidings. He was School Inspector twelve years; Justice sixteen years; Supervisor eighteen years; holding the latter office from 1847 to 1868, when he left it to accept that of County Treasurer, and was also Deputy Treasurer three years. In 1869 he removed to Flint, where he served as Alderman, and engaged in real estate and insurance business. He was a Democrat until 1854, then a Republican.

JACOB J. VAN ZOEREN

Representative from the First District of Kent County, 1901-2 and 1903-4. Was born in Vriesland, Mich., May 3, 1855, and lived on his father's farm until twenty-four years of age. His education was obtained in the district schools. After farming successfully two years he removed to western Kansas and engaged in stock raising and mercantile business. Returning to Michigan in 1889, he located in Grand Rapids, where he successfully engaged in the mercantile business. He was married in 1879. In politics a staunch Republican. He was elected to the Ligislature of 1901-2 and re-elected on the general legislative ticket Nov. 4, 1902.

COLEMAN C. VAUGHAN

Senator from the Fifteenth District, 1903-4 and 1911-12; and Secretary of State, 1915-17, 1917-19 and 1919-21. Was born at Machias, N. Y., Aug. 1, 1857, of American parentage. He was educated in the district school and at Ten Broeck Academy. He learned the printer's trade on the Lapeer *Clarion*, worked two years in the Detroit *Free Press* composing room and later purchased the *Clarion*. In 1889 he purchased the *Clinton Republican*, of which he is still the publisher. Mr. Vaughan is married. He is interested in the timber and lumber business in the South and West, and in the banking, building and loan and other business. He served two years as President of St. Johns, and was State Senator in 1903 and 1911. He served four years as a member of the Republican State Central Committee, was a delegate to the Republican National Convention that nominated Theodore Roosevelt for President, and has served upon three State Boards by appointment of Governors Rich, Pingree and Warner. He was elected Secretary of State Nov. 3, 1914, and re-elected for the third term Nov. 5, 1918.

JAMES C. VAUGHN

Representative from Wayne County (Van Buren Township), 1843. Was a native of the State of New York, and came to Michigan in 1832. He was a farmer by occupation, a Democrat in politics, and represented his township for a number of years on the Board of Supervisors. He died Mar. 29, 1880.

GEORGE F. VEENFLIET

Representative from Saginaw County, 1879-80. Was born in Wesel, Prussia, Apr. 2, 1813. He received an academical education, and graduated from the University of Bonn as professor of mathematics and physical sciences in 1839. In 1849 he emigrated to the United States and came to Michigan in 1849. In 1850 he removed to Blumfield, Saginaw County. He was appointed Commissioner of Immigration by Gov. Wisner during the seasons of 1859-60. In 1860 he was elected Register of Deeds for Saginaw County. In 1870 he was elected County Treasurer, which office he held for six conseutive years. In politics he was a Republican.

LEONARD D. VERDIER

Representative from the First District of Kent County, 1909-10 and 1911-12; and Senator, 1913-14 and 1915-16, from the Sixteenth District, comprising the county of Kent. Was born at Grand Rapids, Mich., Oct. 19, 1877, of Holland descent. He received his education in the Grand Rapids High School, from which he was graduated in 1895. He also graduated from the literary department of the University of Michigan in 1899, and from the law department in 1901. Since 1901 he practiced law at Grand Rapids. Married. In politics a Republican.

WALTER VICKARY

Representative from the Second District of Marquette County, 1887-8. Was born in Devonshire, England, Jan. 31, 1836. By occupation he was an engineer; in politics a Republican. He was Supervisor of the Second Ward of Ishpeming in 1885 and 1886.

STEPHEN VICKERY

Representative from Kalamazoo County, 1838, 1843, 1844, 1845 and 1848. Was born in the State of New York, removed to Ohio at the age of sixteen, taught school in that state several terms, then became a teacher at Monroe, Mich. He removed to Prairie Ronde in 1829, was the first County Clerk and Treasurer of Kalamazoo County, 1834-6, and was Register of Deeds, 1836-8. He was a prominent Whig, and once the candidate of that party for Governor. He was a practical surveyor and laid out the village of Schoolcraft, where he died Dec. 21, 1857.

JAMES VIDETO

Representative from Jackson County, 1842 to 1844; and Senator from the Fourth District, 1845-6. Was born in Hawkesbury, Upper Canada, July 27, 1804. When young his parents removed to the State of New York. At the age of eleven he went to live with an uncle at Shelburne, Vt., and remained there until he became of age. He came to Detroit in 1828, and was engaged for fifteen years in surveying government lands in Michigan, Indiana, Illinois, Wisconsin and Iowa. After 1832 his home was in Jackson County. He located land in Concord in 1833. He was several terms Supervisor of Spring Arbor. In later years he followed farming. In politics he was a Democrat. He died at Spring Arbor, July 18, 1886.

BIRD J. VINCENT

Member of Congress, 1923—. Was born in Brandon Township, Oakland County, Michigan, March 6, 1880. When fourteen years of age he removed with his parents to a farm in Midland County. His early education was obtained in district schools. In 1897 he began teaching and continued until 1900 when he entered Ferris Institute at Big Rapids. In 1905 he graduated from the law department of the University of Michigan and located in the city of Saginaw, where he has since practiced. He was married to Miss L. Maud Hinds, of Muskegon, and they have one daughter, Helen Louise, aged nine years. He held the office of Assistant Prosecuting Attorney from 1909 to 1915, was elected Prosecuting Attorney in 1914 and re-elected in 1916. In 1917 he resigned to enter the service in the World War, serving nearly two years, ten months of which time were spent overseas. He held the commission of first lieutenant. Since his return from service he has served the city of Saginaw as City Attorney. Mr. Vincent is a Republican and was elected to the sixty-eighth Congress from the eighth district, November 7, 1922.

EDWARD VINCENT

Representative from St. Clair County, 1883-4. Was born in Lower Canada, Oct. 31, 1825, and removed with his parents to Clyde, Mich., in 1836. He received a common school education, and was by occupation a farmer. He held the office of County Treasurer for four years, and served twenty-two terms as Supervisor of the town. In politics he was a Republican.

JOHN R. VINE

Representative from the Second District of Lenawee County, 1915-16 to 1921-2. Was born in Fulton County, O., Aug. 22, 1853, of German and French parents. He was educated in the common schools of Fulton County, O. In 1884 he removed to Fairfield Township, Lenawee County, Mich., where he has since been engaged in farming. He has been Supervisor for twelve successive years. Married. In politics he is a Republican.

DAVID VINTON, JR.

Representative from Grand Traverse and Manitou counties, 1883-4. Was born in Hampshire County, Mass., Sept. 16, 1828. At the age of ten years he was placed at work on a farm, and remained to the age of fourteen, when he was apprenticed to learn the tanning business at Newark, O. He remained there until 1852, removed to Steuben County, Ind., continuing in the same occupation until 1870, when he removed to Williamsburg, Grand Traverse County, and engaged in mercantile business. He was a Republican after 1860.

EMORY B. VOORHEES

Representative from Clinton County, 1885-6. Was born in Ovid, Mich., Oct. 22, 1853. He received a common school education. He was secretary of the Ovid Union Agricultural Society for eight years in succession, and was a Supervisor. He was a farmer by occupation. He was elected as a Democrat on the Fusion ticket.

ISAAC I. VOORHEIS

Delegate from the Fifth District to the Constitutional Convention of 1835; and Representative from Oakland County, 1835 and 1836 and 1848. Was born in Somerset, N. Y., in 1799. He removed to Pontiac, Mich., in 1824. In politics he was a Democrat. He was Supervisor of Pontiac in 1833-4, and held other town offices. He removed to Lapeer in 1866, where he died Aug. 2, 1886.

PETER VOORHEIS

Representative from the First District of Oakland County, 1895-6. Was born on a farm in Independence, Oakland County, Mich., May 2, 1849; attended the district school and the village school at Clarkston; married in 1870; engaged in farming, which he made his life occupation, paying particular attention to fine stock breeding, and to fruit-growing. In politics he was formerly a Democrat, but observing the steady decrease in the price of his products during the ascendancy of his party was convinced that his interests were ignored by that party, and after 1886 was an enthusiastic Republican. He held the offices of Supervisor and Drain Commissioner of his township.

SEBRING VOORHEIS

Representative from Oakland County, 1863-4. Was born in Fayette, N. Y., Jan. 7, 1815. He came to Michigan in 1836, and for three years lived near Ypsilanti. In 1839 he settled on a farm in White Lake, Oakland County, where he resided until his death, Feb. 8, 1882. In politics he was a Republican. He was Supervisor in 1843, and held that office seven times, the last in 1876. He was Town Clerk in 1851. He was an elder in the First Presbyterian Church of White Lake, of which he became a member in 1840.

HIRAM VOORHIES

Representative from Oakland County, 1851. Was born in Belvidere, N. Y., Feb. 5, 1809. He came to Orion, Mich., in 1836. By occupation he was a farmer; in politics a Democrat. He resided in Orion thirty-four years and held the positions of Supervisor, School Director and Justice. In 1870 he was elected County Treasurer, removed to Pontiac, and served two years in that office. He was a member of the Common Council of Pontiac at the time of his death. He died Dec. 24, 1878.

DEWITT VOUGHT

Representative from Gratiot County, 1897-8. Was born at Wolcott, Wayne County, N. Y., May 14, 1858. When seven years of age he came to Michigan with his parents and settled on a farm in Riley Township, Clinton County, where he acquired a district school education, supplemented by a course in a select school taught by Mrs. Bement at DeWitt, Mich., At the age of twenty he began painting; taught school winters and painted summers; after 1885 he devoted his time to house painting, decorating, oil, water colors and scene painting; moved to Gratiot County in 1877. In politics a Populist. He was School Inspector; was candidate for Presidential Elector on the Peoples' party ticket for the 11th district in 1892; also candidate for State Senator in 1894; was elected to the House of 1897-8 on the Democratic People's Union Silver ticket.

GEORGE VOWLES

Representative from Oakland County, 1869-70. Was born in Westbury, England, Nov. 10, 1818. He came to this country with his parents in 1829, who settled in Onondaga County, N. Y. In politics he was a Republican. He came to Michigan in 1835, and resided in Independence, Oakland County, until 1840, then at Milford until 1855, from that time living in the town of Lyon until his death Nov. 4, 1878.

JOHN J. VROMAN

Representative from Wayne County, 1887-8. Was born in Orleans County, N. Y., Aug. 5, 1840. By occupation he was formerly a farmer, later a merchant. He held the following offices; Township Clerk, Treasurer and Supervisor, and Superintendent of the Poor of Wayne County three years. He was elected Representative on the Democratic ticket.

PHILIP B. WACHTEL

Representative, 1889-90, 1891-2 and 1893-4, from the district composed of the counties of Cheboygan, Emmet, Presque Isle and Manitou. Was born Oct. 28, 1851, on a farm near Centerville, in Elk County, Pa. His early education was obtained in the district school, and the academy of Clearfield, Pa. He also took a commercial course at the Iron City College, Pittsburg, Pa. At the age of seventeen he engaged as telegraph operator, which occupation he followed for five years, then engaged in the hotel business at St. Mary's, Pa. Five years later he came to Michigan, locating in Petoskey, where he established the first bank in northern Michigan. He continued his connection with the bank for eight years, and then engaged as a real estate and insurance agent. He died at Petoskey Nov. 14, 1913.

CERREL B. WADE

Representative from the First District of Jackson County, 1861-2. His post-office address was Brooklyn. (Further data not obtainable).

FRED WADE

Representative from the Second District of Allegan County, 1921—. Was born at Douglas, Mich., June 29, 1862, of English parents. He received his education in the district schools and graduated from high school at Fremont, Mich., in 1879. He learned the printing trade and for twenty years has published a newspaper at Saugatuck. He served as Postmaster for twenty-five years. Mr. Wade is married. In politics he is a Republican. He has held most of the village and township offices.

SILAS A. WADE

Representative from Hillsdale County, 1857-8. Was born in the State of New Jersey, Sept. 4, 1797. By occupation he was a millwright and miller, in politics a Republican. He came to Rome, Mich., in 1835. He removed to Jefferson, Hillsdale County, in 1850, and was Supervisor in 1862. He died Feb. 19, 1869.

THEODOSIUS WADE

Representative from the Second District of Allegan County, 1901-2 and 1903-4. Was born in Ganges Township, Allegan County, Mich., Nov. 14, 1858. His education was obtained in the common schools and Douglas High School. He taught school two years, reading law in the meantime, until he entered the University of Michigan, from which he graduated in 1888. After spending some time in travel, he opened a law office in Fennville, holding continuously the office of Village Counsel. Married. An extensive fruit grower and shipper. He was formerly a Democrat, but later a Republican.

RALPH WADHAMS

Delegate from the Seventh District to the Constitutional Convention of 1835; Delegate from St. Clair County to the Second Convention of Assent, 1836; and Representative from St. Clair County, 1838. Was born in Goshen, Conn., in 1798. When young his parents removed to Leicester, N. Y. He received a good normal education, and became a clerk in a store. He landed at Detroit in 1823, and for several years was a member of the firm of Reese & Wadhams, general merchants. They occupied the first brick store built in Detroit, corner of Jefferson and Woodward avenues. Later the firm became Howard & Wadhams. He came into possession of a tract of pine on Black River, and commenced lumbering. In 1829 he located in St. Clair County, and in 1830 built the first grist mill in the county, and did an extensive business, employing many men. He was Supervisor of the town of Desmond in 1832, then comprising all the territory from Macomb to Saginaw. President Jackson appointed him Postmaster at Clyde Mills, which he resigned in 1874, after thirty-six years' service. Politically he was a Democrat. He died in April, 1877.

EDGAR S. WAGAR

Representative from the First District of Montcalm County, 1893-4 and 1895-6; and Senator from the Eighteenth District, 1897-8 and 1899-1900. Was born in Constantine, St. Joseph County, Mich., Aug. 30, 1850; was educated in the high school of that place, and in 1873 began his business career as clerk in a store at Cedar Springs. In this occupation and bookkeeping he continued until 1878, when he removed to Edmore, Montcalm County, and engaged in a general hardware business; sold out in 1887 and went into the lumbering business. In politics he was a Republican. He held various offices of public trust in his township and city.

GEORGE WAGNER

Representative from the First District of Marquette County, 1889-90, 1891-2 and 1893-4. Was born near the city of Coblentz, Rhine Prussia, Germany, Nov. 7, 1834. He came to the United States in October, 1853; settled in Marquette in June, 1854. He was an explorer and mineral expert, dealing largely in mineral and timber lands. In politics he was a Republican. He held the offices of Justice of Peace, Township Treasurer, Alderman of city of Marquette, and in 1888-90 Supervisor of the fourth ward of said city; was also Deputy United States Marshal from 1881 until relieved by the Democratic Administration. During the taking of the census of 1890 he was appointed agent to report the mortgages of Marquette County.

JOHN WAGNER

Representative from Calhoun County, 1869-70. Was born in Wurttemberg, Germany, Apr. 18, 1818. He came to Cleveland, O., in 1838, and remained there until 1845. He then removed to Leroy, Calhoun County, Mich., and bought a farm. He was Supervisor for six years. He filled other town offices. In politics he was a Republican. He died Dec. 13, 1876.

LEO PIERRE WAGNER

Representative from the First District of Saginaw County, 1917-18. Was born at Covington, Ky., Apr. 18, 1870, of German parents. He was married in 1903 to Miss Amelia B. D. Gehrls, of Saginaw. He engaged in the barber business for a number of years and was actively identified with the labor movement in Michigan; was secretary for thirteen years of the Barbers Local, secretary-treasurer of the Michigan State Journeymen Barbers Association, also secretary of the Saginaw Federation of Labor. He received a common school education. In politics a Democrat.

MATTHEW D. WAGNER

Senator, 1897-8 and 1899-1900, from the Twentieth District, composed of the counties of Huron and Sanilac. Was born in Ogdensburg, St. Lawrence County, N. Y., Dec. 26, 1856; was educated at Vassar, Mich., High School. On Aug. 22, 1877, he entered the banking house of Bostwick R. Noble, at Lexington, Mich., and remained there until December, 1880, when he, together with Mr. Noble, established the Huron County Bank at Sand Beach, Huron County, Mich., after which time he managed the said banking firm and engaged in real estate and insurance business. In politics a Republican. He held the offices of Village President, Village and Township Treasurer.

JONATHAN G. WAIT

Representative from St. Joseph County, 1851; and Senator from the Sixteenth District, 1863-4 and 1865-6, and from the Fourteenth District, 1867-8. Was born in York, N. Y., Nov. 22, 1811. He traced his ancestry back to 1075, and was a descendant of Richard Wait, who settled at Watertown, Mass., in 1637. He removed with his father to Perry, O., in 1825, and taught school when seventeen. He settled at Sturgis, Mich., in 1835. He engaged in lumbering, building, and was a drover, grain dealer, merchant and manufacturer. He built many houses and saw mills, and a cabinet and chair factory. As agent of the Michigan Southern, he made many contracts for railroad material. In 1857 he was one of the organizers of the Grand Rapids & Indiana Railroad, and was a director. He was ten years a Justice, and many years Supervisor. In 1860 he started the Sturgis *Journal*, and was its editor and publisher until 1872. He was Postmaster of Sturgis from 1872 to 1886. He married Susan S. Buck in 1832, and they had nine sons and three daughters. For many years he was a leading man in southwestern Michigan. He died at Sturgis, Oct. 24, 1873.

BENJAMIN W. WAITE

Representative from Washtenaw County, 1849; and Delegate from Washtenaw County to the Constitutional Convention of 1850. Was born in Aurelius, N. Y., Oct. 13, 1811. In 1839 he settled on a farm in Scio, Mich. He was for about twenty years Superintendent of the Poor in Washtenaw County, and for four years president of the Washtenaw County Mutual Fire Insurance Company. In politics he was a Whig. In 1868 he removed to Dexter, where he resided in 1887.

BYRON S. WAITE

Representative from Menominee County, 1889-90 and 1895-6. Was born in Pennfield, Monroe County, N. Y., Sept. 7, 1852; came to Michigan with his parents when three years of age, locating on a farm in Livingston County; attended district school, Baptist Seminary and high school at Fenton, taught school, and in 1876 entered the University of Michigan, graduating with the literary class of 1880; read law, was admitted to the bar, practiced in Ann Arbor and Dundee in 1881-2, moved to Menominee in August of the latter year, where he engaged in the practice of his profession; also interested to some extent in land, timber and mining. In politics a Republican.

DANIEL B. WAKEFIELD

Representative from Genesee County, 1838; and Senator from the Sixth District, 1842-3. Was a lawyer and farmer, and a Democrat in politics. He died at his home in Grand Blanc, Genesee County.

MARCUS WAKEMAN

Representative from Jackson County, 1846. Was born in Connecticut, Mar. 17, 1795, moved with his parents to Batavia, N. Y., in 1810. He was a soldier in the War of 1812, and fought in the battles of Chippewa and Lundy's Lane. He came to Michigan in 1837, and settled as a farmer in Jackson County. He was elected by the Democrats a Representative, and filled various township offices. He died Jan. 17, 1869.

DAVID S. WALBRIDGE

Senator from the Fifth District, 1849-50; and member of Congress, 1855-7 and 1857-9. Was born at Bennington, Vt., July 30, 1802. He received a common school education. He removed to Kalamazoo, Mich., in 1842, and was a farmer, a merchant and a miller. He was nominated and elected to Congress as a Republican. He was first a Whig, a Republican after 1854. He was chairman of the first Republican Convention held "Under the Oaks" at Jackson. He died at Kalamazoo, June 15, 1868.

HENRY E. WALBRIDGE

Delegate to the Constitutional Convention of 1907-8 from the Nineteenth District, Clinton County. Was born at Glover, Vt., in 1850, of English descent. His father was a leading lawyer of central Michigan and his mother was a descendant of General Ethan Allen, the hero of Ticonderoga. His early boyhood was spent in Saline, Mich., and when six years of age his family moved to St. Johns, where he pursued his early education in the Union School and St. Johns High School. He took the scientific course in Olivet College, and then entered upon the study of law in his father's office. The week after attaining his majority he was admitted to the bar and also to a partnership with his father, which relationship continued until his father moved to Ithaca in 1890. Mr. Walbridge then entered into partnership with Gen. O. L. Spaulding, but the firm was discontinued in 1892. In 1893 he became associated with J. H. Fedewa, with whom he continued until the latter's death in 1901. In 1896 Mr. Walbridge was married to Mrs. Jessie Smead Caldwell, of St. Johns. He held the office of Circuit Court Commissioner for six years.

CAMPBELL WALDO

Senator from the Fifth District, comprising the counties of Calhoun, Eaton, Branch and Kalamazoo counties, 1848-9. Was born in Middletown, Vt., Dec. 25, 1786, and was brought up on a farm. He became a physician, and practiced many years in Cayuga County, N. Y., and was a member of the New York Assembly, in 1825. In 1833 he became a merchant at Port Byron, N. Y. In 1837 he settled at Albion, Mich., built mills at various points, and was a leading man. He was a man of fine personal appearance, courteous and affable in his manners, a good physician, and a Christian. He died at Albion, Nov. 6, 1876.

GEORGE H. WALDO

Representative from the First District of Wayne County (Detroit), 1895-6. Was born in Prattsburgh, Steuben County, N. Y., May 10, 1844. He attended the public schools and Franklin Academy, working on the farm summers; also received training in vocal music; served during the war in the 50th Engineer Corps and 188th N. Y. Vols. After the war he returned to the farm and in the winter of 1865-6 took a course of instruction in voice culture and harmony. In the fall of 1866 he came to Michigan and engaged in teaching vocal music, and the next year located in Genesee County where he engaged in lumbering. Two years later he sold out, went to Virginia and operated a mill for eastern parties for one year, and then traveled through Ohio and Michigan, Pennsylvania and New York introducing improved domestic machinery including some inventions of his own which gained national reputation. In 1879 he settled in Detroit where he invented the Waldo combined road builder and was engaged in the manufacture and sale of the same until 1892 when he disposed of this invention and engaged in contract work and operating a water power roller flouring mill. In politics he was a Republican.

HENRY WALDRON

Representative from Hillsdale County, 1843; and member of Congress, 1855-7 to 1859-61 and 1871-3 to 1875-7. Was born at Albany, N. Y., Oct. 11, 1816. He graduated at Rutgers College, N. Y., in 1836; removed to Michigan in 1837; settled at Hillsdale in 1839; built the first warehouse on the Southern railroad; and from that date was engaged in manufacturing and banking. In early life he was a civil engineer. He was a director of the Michigan Southern Railroad; president of the Detroit, Hillsdale & Indiana Railroad; and president of the First National Bank of Hillsdale. He was Presidential Elector in 1848; a delegate to the Republican National Convention of 1868. He was a Republican in politics, a good speaker, a successful business man, and a political power, especially in southern Michigan. He died previous to 1887.

ADAM W. WALKER

Representative from Bay County, 1905-6 and 1907-8. Was born in Perth County, Ont., Sept. 9, 1874, of Scotch and Irish parents. He came with his parents to Huron County, Mich., when eleven years of age, where he lived the usual life of a farmer's boy, and received the benefits of a public school education. He moved to West Bay City when eighteen and entered the employ of the West Bay City Street Railway Company and continued with the same company as conductor. Married. In politics a Republican. He served two terms on the Board of Education, and was elected to the Legislature of 1905-6 from the Second District and re-elected from the First District Nov. 6, 1906.

ALVAH H. WALKER

Delegate from Clinton County to the Constitutional Convention of 1867. Was born in Rhode Island, Feb. 15, 1802, and removed to Chautauqua County, N. Y., with his parents in 1805, where he resided until 1855, when he removed to Detroit. For many years, at Fredonia, Chautauqua County, he was one of the trustees and treasurer of the Fredonia Academy, and was Supervisor of Pomfret. He was on the Whig electoral ticket in 1852, and in 1854 was a member of the New York Senate. In 1855 he removed to Detroit. In 1857 he became interested in village property in St. Johns, and removed there in 1861; for several years was engaged in meracntile business. He was an active Whig or Republican all his life.

ARNOLD WALKER

Representative from Ingham County, 1873-4. Was born in Gibson, Pa., in 1821. He removed to Seneca County, N. Y., in 1837, and to Ingham County, Mich., in 1844. He received a common school education, and was a practical business man. He was a director of the Jackson, Lansing & Saginaw Railroad for many years, and filled large railroad contracts. He was long president of the Leslie National Bank. In politics he was a Republican. He lived in Vevay until 1860, then became a resident of Leslie until his death, Dec. 5, 1884.

BENJAMIN WALKER

Representative from Shiawassee County, 1873. Was born in Whitingham, Vt., Mar. 7, 1814. He received a common school education. In 1847 he removed to Michigan and settled in Perry. He held the office of Justice twenty-four years; Supervisor two years, Town Clerk three years, and School Inspector. He was treasurer of the Shiawassee Mutual Insurance Company ten years. He was president of the Shiawassee Agricultural Association two years. By occupation he was a farmer. He died before extra session of 1874 and was succeeded by Lorison J. Taylor.

CHARLES IRISH WALKER

Delegate from Kent County to the Second Convention of Assent, 1836; and Representative from Kent County, 1841. Was born in Butternuts, N. Y., Apr. 25, 1814, his parents moving there from New England. He received a common and select school education. At sixteen he was a teacher, and then a clerk. At twenty-one he was a merchant at Cooperstown, N. Y., but sold out in 1836, and removed to Grand Rapids, Mich., as agent for eastern capitalists in the buying of Michigan lands. The panic of 1837 closed out land speculations, and he took an interest and became editor of the *Grand River Times*. He commenced the study of law, went to Vermont to complete his studies and was admitted to the Vermont bar at Brattleboro in 1842. He practiced in that state until 1851, and then settled at Detroit. He was Circuit Judge for about a year, but resigned, and was professor of the law school at Ann Arbor from 1859 to 1874. He was for several years president of the Board of State Charities. He always took an active interest in the early history of the Northwest, and wrote able papers on that subject. He was president of the State Pioneer and Historical Society. He was an able lawyer, politically a Democrat. He died Feb. 11, 1895, at Detroit.

CYRUS A. WALKER

Representative from the Second District of Kalamazoo County, 1909-10 and 1911-12. Was born at Cooper, Kalamazoo County, Mich., Jan. 2, 1859, of Scotch descent. He was educated in the common schools and at the Parson Business College, Kalamazoo. Sept. 26, 1883, he was married to Lydia Orell Earl. Mr. Walker was a son of the late Hon. John Walker who was a member of the Legislature from the Third District of Kalamazoo County, during the terms of 1869-70 to 1873-4. He served his township as Supervisor and was chairman of the board one year. In politics a Republican.

DeWITT C. WALKER

Representative from Macomb County, 1840, 1844 and 1846; and Senator from the Fourth District, 1841, and from the First District, 1842; Member of the Board of Regents of the University of Michigan, 1843-4; and Delegate from Macomb County to the Constitutional Convention of 1850. Was born in Vermont, in 1812. He was a graduate of Middlebury College, studied law at the Yale Law School, and was admitted to the bar in 1836. He then came to Romeo,

Mich., and continued there in law practice for twenty years. He was Prosecuting Attorney of Macomb County; was appointed a Regent of the State University in 1843 in the place of George Goodman resigned, but the following year he in turn resigned. He was four years Judge of Probate. He laid out the village of Capac in 1857, having settled there in 1857. He built a grist and saw-mill, donated land for churches, and for many years was President of the village. He died at Capac, St. Clair County, Aug. 17, 1904.

EDWARD A. WALKER

Representative from the First District of Genesee County, 1901-2 and 1903-4. Was born in Lee, Calhoun County, Mich., Oct. 20, 1860. His education was obtained in the district school, and at the age of seventeen he went to Muskegon where he worked in a mill and later engaged in the lumber trade. Mr. Walker was married in 1883 and removed to Genesee County in 1887, where he was a successful farmer, contractor and builder. In politics a strong Republican.

EDWARD C. WALKER

Member of the Board of Regents of the University of Michigan, 1864-82; and Representative from Wayne County, 1867-8. Was born July 4, 1820, at Butternuts, N. Y. He graduated from Yale College in 1842, studied law, attended law school, was admitted to the Detroit bar in 1845, and was long a partner of his brother, C. I. Walker, then of Walker & Kent, and later with his son of the firm of Walker & Walker. During the whole term as Regent he was chairman of the executive committee. In religion he was a Presbyterian. Politically he was a Whig and Republican. He died Dec. 28, 1894.

FREDERICK WALKER

Representative from Genesee County, 1872 and 1873-4. Was born in Yorkshire, England, in 1809. By occupation he was a farmer and lumberman, politically a Republican. He emigrated to New York City with his parents when two years of age. He settled on a farm in Genesee County, now part of Mt. Morris village, in 1836. He was a Justice for twenty years, for thirty-six years a member of the Methodist Episcopal Church, and twelve years Sabbath School Superintendent. He was elected Representative in 1872 vice John I. Phillips deceased. He died Jan. 20, 1879.

HENRY N. WALKER

Representative from Wayne County, 1844; Attorney General, 1845-7. Was born at Fredonia, Chautauqua County, N. Y., Nov. 30, 1811, and was educated at the Fredonia Academy. He came to Detroit in 1834 or 1835, and was admitted to practice as an attorney, and was thereafter a leading member of the bar for many years. During his life he held, among others, the following official positions: 1837, Master in Chancery; 1844, Supreme Court reporter. April, 1859, to September, 1860, Postmaster at Detroit; and 1883, State Immigration Agent. In business life he had extended relations. In 1836 he was State Agent of the Protection Insurance Company; in 1849 one of the founders and vice-president of the Detroit Savings Fund Institute; 1858 to 1863, president of the Detroit & Milwaukee Railroad Company; 1861 to 1875, proprietor and editor of the Detroit *Free Press*, and during the latter portion of this period was president of the western associated press. In 1845, while Attorney General, he was largely instrumental, in a semi-official capacity, in organizing the Michigan Central Railroad Company, which in 1846 purchased the Central railroad from the State. He was influential in securing the building of the Great Western Railway of Canada; also in voluntary enterprises, first in the temperance cause in the early days of the movement, 1835-6; as histriographer of Detroit, 1843 to 1845; and when the building of the Detroit observatory at Ann Arbor was first agitated he made a liberal contribution for the building, and also purchased the transit instrument at a cost of $3,500. In politics he was a Democrat, in religion an Episcopalian. He married Miss Emily Norvel, daughter of the Senator John Norvel, and left two sons and a daughter. He died Feb. 24, 1886.

HENRY T. WALKER

Representative from Washtenaw County, 1842 and 1845. Was born in Bristol, N. Y., Apr. 29, 1808. By profession he was a physician, in politics a Democrat. He came to Michigan in 1836, and settled in Washtenaw County in 1837. For several terms he was a Justice of the Peace. He died Oct. 2, 1871.

JAMES B. WALKER

Senator from the Thirty-first District, 1865-6. Was born at Philadelphia, Pa., July 29, 1805. He became an operative in a factory at Pittsburgh and subsequently a printer; was clerk to M. M. Noah in New York, and principal of an academy at New Durham, N. J.; studied law at Ravenna, O.; graduated at Western Reserve College, Hudson, O., in 1831; edited successively religious papers at Hudson, Cincinnati and Chicago; also engaged in the book trade; studied theology and was licensed to preach in 1841; was principal of a private orphan asylum at Mansfield, O.; lectured on the harmony of science and revealed religion at Oberlin College and Chicago Theological Seminary. He held pastorates at Mansfield, Sandusky and Chicago, and preached several months at Lansing, Mich. He was author of many theological works published from 1855 to 1870, also of poems published in "Poets and Poetry of the West." His first work, "The Philosophy of the Plan of Salvation," had a very large circulation in English, and was translated into several other languages. He was a trustee and interested in the prosperity of Benzonia College, at Benzie, Mich., and resided for some time in Benzonia. He received the degree of D. D., was the first president of Benzonia College, and gave largely to its support. He died at Wheaton, Ill.

JOHN WALKER

Representative from Kalamazoo County, 1869-70 to 1873-4. Was born in Deerfield, N. Y., May 12, 1818. He received a common school education. He settled in Kalamazoo in 1836, and removed to Cooper in 1840. In politics he was a Republican, by occupation a farmer. He died at Cooper, Kalamazoo County, Feb. 21, 1878.

LEVI WALKER

Representative from Genesee County, 1873. Was born in Granville, N. Y., Dec. 20, 1813. He received an academical education, studied law and was admitted to the New York bar in 1835. In 1847 he removed to Michigan and settled in Flint. He held several important and several minor offices in the town and county. He died before the extra session of 1874 and was succeeded by Leroy -Parker.

SAMUEL S. WALKER

Representative from Clinton County, 1875-6; and member of the Board of Regents of the University of Michigan, 1876-84. Was born at Fredonia, N. Y., June 11, 1841, and removed with his father to Detroit in 1855. He was educated at the Fredonia Academy, and subsequently at the Barstow Union School in Detroit, graduating at the University of Michigan in the class of 1861. He removed to St. Johns in 1861, and engaged in the mercantile business until 1865, when he established a banking office at St. Johns, under the firm name of S. S. Walker & Co., continuing that until September of the same year, when, with others, he organized the First National Bank of St. Johns, of which he was cashier until August, 1877. He was vice-president of the Michigan Pioneer and Historical Society. In 1890 he removed to Old Mission where he engaged in fruit culture. He was living in 1902.

SYLVESTER WALKER

Representative from Lenawee County, 1847. Was a hatter in Norwich, N. Y., in 1813. He settled in Cambridge, Mich., in 1838, opened a hotel at the junction of the Chicago and La Plaisance Bay turnpikes, erected fine buildings, where many a weary traveler found a genial place of rest. In politics he was a Democrat. He died Dec. 28, 1868. His widow was living in Cambridge in 1887, at the age of ninety.

JAMES WALKINSHAW

Representative from Calhoun County, 1877-8. Was born in the parish of Boithwick, Mid Lothian, Scotland, July 10, 1810. He was educated in the common schools. He emigrated in 1842 to Marshall, Mich., and was employed by the State Railroad authorities as warehouseman there, and also in the same capacity at Kalamazoo, until the Michigan Central Company bought the railroad. He then settled in Convis on a farm. He was Supervisor for sixteen years. In politics he was a Republican. He died Aug. 18, 1887; his eight sons bore his body to the grave.

JOHN B. WALLACE

Representative from Wayne County, 1859-60. Was born in Steuben County, N. Y., Oct. 22, 1809, and came to Michigan in 1832. By occupation he was a farmer and lumberman. He ran the first saw-mill in Wayne County propelled by water. He served many years as Postmaster at Wallaceville (to which he gave his name) and held most of the responsible local offices of his township. After a residence of more than fifty years on the farm which he located, he removed to Detroit in 1885. In politics he was a Republican.

ROBERT C. WALLACE

Representative from Newaygo County, 1903-4 and 1905-6. Was born at Toronto, Canada, Apr. 11, 1844, of Scotch and Irish ancestors. He obtained his education in the Canadian schools. He came to Michigan in 1864, and engaged in lumbering and farming. He was married, July 16, 1876. In politics he was a Republican. He held the offices of Township Treasurer, Supervisor and was chairman of the Board of Supervisors in 1896.

ROBERT N. WALLACE

Representative from Huron County, 1919-20. Was born at Bay Port, Mar. 17, 1887, of Irish and Scotch parentage. He received his education in the public schools and the Michigan Agricultural College. After leaving college he engaged in a number of business enterprises in that section of the State, and was president of the Bay Port Fish Company and of the Saginaw Bay Fish Company; also vice-president of the Bay Port Bank, secretary-treasurer of the Wallace Stone Company and president of the Wallace & Morley Company. Married. In politics a Republican.

WILLIAM H. WALLACE

Member of the State Board of Agriculture, 1903-21. Was born at Port Hope, Huron County, Mich., Sept. 12, 1862, of Scotch-Irish parentage. He was educated in the Huron County common schools and the Detroit Business College. He is president of the following firms: The Wallace Stone Company, Wallace & Morley Company, Bay Port Fish Company, and Bay Port Bank, all of Bay Port, Mich., also president of the Saginaw Bay Fish Company, of Caseville, Mich.; of the Bad Axe Grain Company, of Bad Axe, Mich.; of the Brimley State Bank, of Brimley, Mich.; of the Brimley Produce Company, of Brimley, Mich.; a director of the Second National Bank of Saginaw, Saginaw, Mich., and general manager and director of the Michigan Sugar Company, of Saginaw, Mich. He is married. He was appointed a member of the State Board of Agriculture Jan. 23, 1903; was elected in 1909; and at the election held on Apr. 5, 1915, was re-elected a member.

FRANKLIN B. WALLIN

Representative from Allegan County, 1861-2. Was born in Nelson, Pa., Mar. 25, 1832. By occupation he was a tanner; in politics a Republican. He came with his parents to Michigan in 1836, who located at McCoys Creek, Berrien County.

He learned the tanner's trade. In 1853 he removed to Saugatuck, where with his father and brother, he operated three tanneries under the firm name of C. C. Wallin & Sons, the store being in Chicago. He built a tannery in Grand Rapids in 1882.

ROBERT E. WALTER

Senator, 1911-12, 1913-14 and 1915-16, from the Twenty-seventh Senatorial District, comprising the counties of Antrim, Benzie, Grand Traverse, Kalkaska, Leelanau, Missaukee and Wexford. Was born at Litchfield, Hillsdale County, Mich., Sept. 16, 1877, of English parentage. He was educated in the Fife Lake Schools and the Traverse City High School. Married. Mr. Walter participated in the Spanish-American War, serving with Co. M, 34th Mich. Vol. Infantry. At the age of twenty-one he was elected Township Clerk and at the age of twenty-two was elected County Clerk which office he held five terms. In politics a Republican.

GEORGE W. WALTHEW

Representative from the First District of Wayne County, 1885-6. Was born at St. Thomas, Ont., May 30, 1860. His parents removed with him to Detroit in 1862. He drifted to Colorado when eighteen years of age, returned to Detroit when twenty-one and shortly afterwards became manager of the firm of A. Walthew & Sons, scenic artists of Detroit. In October, 1883, he took up the study of the law; was admitted to the bar in 1884; became the candidate of the labor party of Detroit for the Legislature; was afterwards put upon the Democratic and Greenback ticket and elected.

ANDREW WALTON

Representative from Bay County, 1875-6 and 1879-80. Was born at Batavia, N. Y., Jan. 11, 1826, but removed to Ohio when young. He received an academical education. In 1863 he removed to Bay City. His occupation was that of lumber merchant. He was a member of the Board of Education, and a Commissioner of the Bay City water-works for many years. He was one of the original proprietors of the state bank of Bay City, and one of the directors until its consolidation with the second national bank, and then was elected a director. His politics were Democratic.

JACOB WALTON

Representative from Lenawee County, 1869-70 to 1873-4. Was born in Buckingham, Pa., Feb. 10, 1818. He received a common school education. In 1834 he emigrated to Michigan and settled in Saline. In 1851 he removed to Raisin, Lenawee County, where he resided in 1887. By occupation he was a farmer; in politics a Republican.

JAY C. WALTON

Delegate to the Constitutional Convention of 1907-8 from the Thirteenth District, Livingston County. Was born in Hartland Township, Livingston County, in 1856, of English and German descent. He attended the district school until he was fourteen years of age, and then went to a commercial college, afterwards attending a dental college, graduating in 1881. He was a drug clerk for seven years and practiced dentistry for twenty-five years. He was married in 1882. He was a large owner of real estate and interested in farming, and a breeder of registered Holstein cattle. He served as Village President and President of the Municipal Electric Light and Water Commission of Howell.

JOSEPH WALTZ

Representative from Wayne County, 1879-80 and 1885-6. Was born in Detroit, May 24, 1844. He received his education in the public schools, receiving also a full commercial education. Mr. Waltz was a merchant, but dealt extensively in lumber and real estate. He filled various township offices, having been for two years Township Clerk, and for two terms Justice, also Supervisor of the township of Huron, in which he resided. Politically he was a Democrat.

ARTHUR N. WARD

Representative from Isabella County, 1919-20. Was born Jan. 1, 1862, at Bloomer Center, Montcalm County, Mich., of American parents. At the age of four years he removed with his parents to a farm in Isabella County. He attended the public schools and the Mt. Pleasant High School. He began teaching school at fifteen years of age and continued in that occupation for six years. In 1885 he entered the mercantile business at Mt. Pleasant and was engaged in that business for twenty-five years. He served as City Treasurer, as Mayor and County Treasurer. He was commissioned Captain of Co. 64, Michigan State Troops, July 11, 1917. A widower. In politics a Republican.

CHARLES A. WARD

Senator, 1899-1900, from the Tenth Senatorial District, comprising the counties of Jackson and Washtenaw. Was born at Shelby, Macomb County, Mich., Dec. 28, 1859. He received his education in the public schools of his native town and Portland, Ionia County, and graduated from the high school of the last named village. In 1879 he entered the Michigan Agricultural College, but left in 1881 to go to Colorado, where he remained some thirteen seasons, during ten of which he was engaged as a mining engineer and in charge of large mining interests. Returning to his native State, he located at Ann Arbor, entered the newspaper field, and soon became editor and publisher of the Ann Arbor *Democrat*. In politics a Democrat.

CHARLES E. WARD

Representative from Shiawassee County, 1903-4, 1905-6 and 1907-8. Was born in DuQuoin, Ill., Apr. 26, 1873, of English and French ancestors. General Ward of Revolutionary fame was one of the early ancestors of the family.　He received his education in the high schools of DuQuoin and was graduated from the law department of the University of Michigan in 1894.　After graduation from high school he secured a position as office manager of a manufacturing plant.　In 1894 he settled in Bancroft and was elected cashier of the bank, and later serving as vice-president of the Bancroft bank.　He married Miss Mary Sherman in 1895.　In politics a Republican.

EDGAR B. WARD

Representative from Shiawassee County, 1869-70.　Was born in Castleton, N. Y., Sept. 27, 1835, and removed with his parents to Washtenaw County, Mich., in 1836.　He was educated at Lodi Academy, and in 1854 taught school near Millersburg, Ky.　In the fall of 1854 he began the study of medicine at the University of Michigan, and graduated in 1858.　He went to Centreville, Ia., and engaged in medical practice.　In 1859 he returned to Owosso, Mich., to practice, and in 1862 removed to Laingsburg, where he continued the practice of his profession.　In politics he was a Republican.

GEORGE A. WARD

Representative from the Second District of Saginaw County, 1911-12 and 1915-16.　Was born in Brant Township, Saginaw County, Mich., July 12, 1860, of English parents.　He was educated in the district schools.　At the age of twenty he embarked in the general store business which he continued for twenty years.　He was Postmaster at Brant for eighteen years during this period.　He was Supervisor three years and Treasurer six years.　A member of the F. & A. M., Grange and Maccabees.　Mr. Ward was married Apr. 22, 1899, to Miss Alice Webb.　He resided on his 200-acre stock farm in Brant Township.　In politics a Republican.

LYMAN M. WARD

Representative from Berrien County, 1879-80 and 1881-2.　Was born in Cattaraugus County, N. Y., Oct. 5, 1836.　He removed to Wisconsin in 1850, and thence to Michigan in 1866.　He was educated in common and high schools.　He was a fruit grower by occupation.　In 1861 he enlisted in the three months' service and was appointed Orderly Sergeant of Co. I, first regiment Wis. Vol. Infantry.　After the expiration of that term he re-enlisted for three years, receiving a Captain's commission.　He was successively promoted to Major, Lieutenant Colonel, and Colonel of the 14th Regiment, Wis. Vol. Infantry. He was in command of a brigade for two years and received the brevet rank of Brigadier General.　In 1886 he came to Benton Harbor and was Postmaster in 1889.　He died Jan. 19, 1909.

NEWTON O. WARD

Representative from Mecosta County, 1901-2 and 1903-4; and Senator, 1909-10 and 1911-12, from the Twenty-fifth District, comprising the counties of Gratiot, Isabella and Mecosta.　Was born at Sheffield, Ont., Nov. 8, 1854.　He came to

Michigan in 1862 and received his education in the public schools. At the age of fifteen he was thrown upon his own resources by the sudden death of his father, and began teaching school, which profession he followed six years, after which he entered the hardware, implement and grain business, in which he successfully engaged. He was married in 1876. He held the offices of Township Clerk, Supervisor, Census Enumerator, Superintendent of Schools, member of Village Council, and Postmaster under President McKinley. In politics a Republican.

ROBERT E. WARD

Representative from Berrien County, 1837. Was born in Albany, N. Y. He came to the village of Berrien Springs in 1835, and was a merchant, the partner of Pitt Brown. On a petition drawn by him to the postoffice department, the village name was changed from Berrien to Berrien Springs, so named from valuable medical springs. He was a County Commissioner in 1837. He resigned as Representative before the extra session of 1837. He removed to Detroit, where he died in 1847.

ZAEL WARD

Representative from the Second District of St. Clair County, 1855-6. His post-office address was Bella River. (Further data not obtainable).

ROBERT D. WARDELL

Representative from the First District of Wayne County, 1923—. Was born in Manchester, England, January 3, 1882. His early education was acquired in Belfast, Ireland, and after coming to the United States he attended schools and colleges in Baltimore, Chicago and Detroit. He engaged for ten years as illuminating engineer with the Detroit Gas & Electric Fixture Co. In 1914 he organized the Wardell Light & Fixture Co., and operated this company successfully until 1921 when it was sold out. He developed the Wardell system of diffused lighting which is now used extensively throughout the country. Mr. Wardell is married and has one daughter. He was elected to the legislature November 7, 1922.

ROBERT WARDEN, JR.

Delegate from Livingston County to the Constitutional Convention of 1850. Was born in Scotland about 1815. He emigrated from Greenock, Scotland, in 1832, and after a brief residence in Onondaga County, N. Y., purchased with Governor Bingham a large tract of land in Green Oak, Mich., upon which they settled in 1833. Gov. Bingham had two wives, both of whom were sisters of Mr. Warden, while his wife was a sister of Governor Bingham. He was a farmer and was Supervisor of Green Oak, first in 1838, and served six times afterwards in that capacity. He was first a Democrat, a Republican after 1854. Deceased.

JOSEPH BRUFF WARE

Representative from the First District of Kent County (Grand Rapids), 1895-6. Was born in Butterville, Ind., May 8, 1860. In 1869 he came to Michigan, locating on a farm in Kalamazoo County, and in 1873 removed to Grand Rapids. He was educated at the city schools of Kalamazoo and Grand Rapids; taught school one year in Nebraska, and on returning, he in 1879-80, attended the Michigan Agricultural College; left college to engage in shingle manufacturing, and in the wholesale and retail of lumber and shingles; organized the Michigan Retail Lumber Association, and was two years its secretary; vice-president in 1891 and president in 1892 of the Builders' and Traders' Exchange. He was a member of the Board of Education, a director in the Y. M. C. A., and an official member of the M. E. Church; was elected Representative to the House of 1895-6 on the general legislative ticket of the city of Grand Rapids.

GUERNSEY P. WARING

Representative from Lenawee County, 1881-2. Was born Aug. 31, 1852, in Ridgeway, Mich. He attended school until of age; afterwards taught a few terms; and then mingled farming with mercantile business in the land of his adoption.

DWIGHT G. F. WARNER

Representative, 1909-10, 1911-12 and 1913-14, from the Leelanau District, comprising the counties of Benzie and Leelanau. Was born on a farm in Gaines Township, Orleans County, N. Y., Jan. 1, 1861, of American parentage. He was educated in the district school, Flushing High School and was graduated in 1883 from the law department of the University of Michigan. He taught school four terms, working on a farm during vacations, was an officer in the State Prison at Jackson from 1884 to 1889, and practiced law since. He was a member of the school board three years, was President of the village of Frankfort four years, Village Attorney fifteen years and Prosecuting Attorney of Benzie County twelve years. Married. In politics a Republican.

EBENEZER WARNER

Representative from Chippewa County, 1859-60 and 1861-2. His postoffice address was Sault Ste. Marie. (Further data not obtainable).

EDWARD A. WARNER

Senator from the Fourth District, 1842-3. Was born in 1812 or 1813. He is said to have been in Marshall, Mich., in 1837. He settled at Coldwater in 1838, and engaged in practice as a lawyer. He was an agreeable and intelligent young man, and had obtained a good practice at the time of his death, Feb. 1, 1844.

FRED L. WARNER

Representative from Ionia County, 1915-16 to 1921-2. Was born at Penn Yan, N. Y., Sept. 16, 1877, of English parents. He was educated in the Penn Yan

High School, the Palmer Institute of Lakemont, N. Y., and the University of Michigan, graduating from the law department of the latter in 1907. He immediately located in the city of Belding and began the practice of law. He held the office of secretary of the Board of Education for six years and has been City Attorney for several years. He is married and has two children. In politics he is a Republican.

FRED M. WARNER

Senator from the Twelfth District, 1895-6 and 1897-8; Secretary of State, 1901-3 and 1903-5; and Governor of Michigan, 1905-7, 1907-9 and 1909-11. Was born in Hickling, Nottinghamshire, England, July 21, 1865, his parents coming to this country when he was three months old. A few months later his mother died and he was adopted by Hon. P. D. Warner of Farmington. Mr. Warner graduated from the Farmington High School at the age of fourteen years, then attended the State Agricultural College for one term, after which he became a clerk in his father's store in Farmington. A few years later the mercantile business was turned over to him, and successfully conducted for twenty years. In 1889, Mr. Warner established a large cheese factory at Farmington and the success of that factory led to the establishment by him of like factories at other points in Oakland County and other parts of the State. He operated twelve cheese factories, the combined annual output being 40,000 boxes or 1,500,000 pounds of cheese, nearly all of which was sold to the trade in Michigan. He was largely interested in farming, especially dairy farming, a stockholder and director of the Farmington Exchange Bank, which he helped to establish in 1897, and also vice-president of the Detroit United Bank. Mr. Warner represented the Twelfth Senatorial District in the State Senate for the years 1895-6 and 1897-8, being the youngest member at both sessions. In politics he was an active Republican. He was a member of several secret societies among which were the Masons (Shrine degree), Knights of Pythias, Elks, Loyal Guard and Maccabees. In 1888 he was married to Miss Martha M. Davis of Farmington. In 1900 he was nominated to the office of Secretary of State and was elected for the term of 1901-3 and re-elected in 1902 for the term of 1903-5. At the Republican State Convention held at Detroit, June 30, 1904, he was nominated to the office of Governor and was elected Nov. 8. In 1906 he was renominated, being the first Governor to be nominated in Michigan under the direct voting system, and was elected Nov. 6. He was again nominated at the primaries, Sept. 1, 1908, and elected Nov. 3, being the first Governor of Michigan to receive three consecutive terms. He died in 1923.

HARVEY WARNER

Delegate from Branch County to the First Convention of Assent, 1836. Was born at Glens Falls, N. Y., Apr. 5, 1807. In 1830 he came to Michigan, soon settled at Coldwater, and built the first frame house and the first frame store and the first church in that city. He was the first Postmaster in 1832, and held the office many years. He was Justice in 1834, and held that position twenty-four years. He served in the Black Hawk War. He was Judge of Probate from 1849 to 1857, and for several years President of the village of Coldwater. He died in 1889.

JOSEPH EDWIN WARNER

Representative from the Second District of Washtenaw County, 1921—. Was born on a farm near Ypsilanti, Mich., Mar. 14, 1870, and is of English descent. His education was acquired in the rural schools and later in the Michigan State Normal College. In 1893 he was married to Lottie A. Ferguson of Almont, and they have three children. He is a dairy farmer specializing in the breeding of Jersey cattle. He has served his township as Clerk and Treasurer, and for six years served as District County Road Commissioner. Early in life he identified himself with the Grange and Farmers' Institute Society, having been president of the Washtenaw County Farmers' Institute Society for four years. He is also interested in Ypsilanti civic affairs, at present serving as director of the Board of Commerce. He is a member of Phoenix Lodge F. & A. M., Queen City Lodge, Knights of Pythias, and the Methodist Episcopal Church. In politics he is a Republican.

P. DEAN WARNER

Representative from Oakland County, 1851, 1865-6 and 1867-8; and Delegate from Oakland County to the Constitutional Convention of 1867; and Senator from the Fifth District, 1869-70. Was born in Hector, N. Y., Aug. 18, 1822. He came with his father to Farmington, Mich., in 1825. At fourteen he was a clerk in a country store, where he remained nine years. In 1845 he became a merchant at Farmington. He had a fair education. In politics he was first a Democrat, then a Republican. He was Deputy Postmaster three years; three times Town Clerk; Supervisor five terms, and fifteen years a member of the Board of Control of railroads by appointment of the Governor. He died at Farmington, Aug. 29, 1910.

SETH A. L. WARNER

Delegate from Oakland County to the First Convention of Assent, 1836. Was a native of Seneca, N. Y., and came to Farmington, Mich., in 1830. He became a leading citizen of that section and was the grandfather of Gov. Fred M. Warner.

WILLIAM WARNER

Representative from Washtenaw County, 1851. Was born in Connecticut in 1806. He settled as a farmer in Dexter, Mich., in 1826. He owned several large farms and was engaged in the lumber and hardware trade. In politics he was a Republican.

WILLIAM WARNER

Representative from Wayne County, 1863-4 and 1867-8. Was born at Pittsford, Vt., Jan. 28, 1812. He graduated at Middlebury College, and studied for the ministry, but abandoned it from health considerations. He was several years treasurer of the University of Vermont at Burlington, and subsequently connected with the Vermont Central Railroad, until he came to Detroit in 1855. He was there engaged in the lumber business until, in 1860, he became connected with the Detroit Bridge and Iron Works, of which he was president at the time of his death in July, 1868.

WILLIAM E. WARNER

Representative from Wayne County, 1853-4; Senator from the Fourth District, 1859-60, and from the Third District, 1863-4; and Delegate from Wayne County to the Constitutional Convention of 1867. Was born in 1820 in New York, and came to Michigan in 1837. His early occupations were those of teacher and clerk in Rawsonville. He was a Justice in 1845, and held the office of Supervisor for many years. He was Register of Deeds, 1865-9. He is listed as a lawyer, though combining the qualities of farmer, politician and general business man in about equal degree. He was a Democrat. He died at Belleville, Sept. 6, 1879.

ASA K. WARREN

Representative from Eaton County, 1873-4; and Senator from the Sixteenth District, 1875-6. Was born in Eden, N. Y., Jan. 29, 1830. He was a graduate of Oberlin College, of the class of '53. He was also a graduate of the medical department of the University, of the class of '56. He became a resident of Michigan in 1859, and settled in Olivet. He was a member of the Common Council of the town from its organization. He still continued in the practice of his profession in 1887. In politics he was a Republican.

ROBERT L. WARREN

Representative from Van Buren County, 1883-4. Was born in Bennington, Mich., Jan. 2, 1842. He removed to Flint when a boy, residing there until 1869. He entered Michigan University in 1860, leaving there to enter the military service in the Civil War, serving until the close of the Vicksburg campaign, when he was discharged by reason of disability. He entered the law department of Michigan University in 1864, and graduated in 1866, began the practice of law, continuing about one year, then assuming the duties of local editor on the *Wolverine Citizen*. Subsequently he removed to Bay City, taking control of the *Journal* of that city, which he converted into a daily, and conducted it until sold to Hon. James Birney. He also published Saginaw *Daily Enterprise*. He removed to Van Buren County in 1875, and published the Lawrence *Advertiser*, and was editor and publisher of the Decatur *Republican*. He was the editor and publisher of the Albion *Recorder*, in 1887. About 1904 he bought the Ann Arbor *Times* and sold this in 1909. He was very prominent in Masonic circles. He died at Ann Arbor Aug. 16, 1916.

SAMUEL N. WARREN

Representative from Genesee County, 1848. Was born in Orwell, Vt., Sept. 15, 1813. He attended district school and Shoreham Academy; taught school in Benson, Vt., in 1829; came to Michigan in 1833, and taught school; at the age of twenty-two was a Justice and Supervisor, holding the latter office most of the time for forty years; was Postmaster at Fentonville; director of schools in Flint for ten years; for many years chairman of the congressional committee in the sixth district; and Collector of Internal Revenue for that district under

Lincoln. He married Anne R. West in 1834, and celebrated his golden wedding at Albion, where he resided in 1887. He was a Whig until 1854, then a Republican.

STEPHEN H. WARREN

Senator from Montcalm and other counties, 1857-8. Was born in Esopus, N. Y., in 1806. Left an orphan at the age of seven, he went to live with his brother, at Harkimer, N. Y., where he remained until 1843, when he settled in Eureka, Montcalm County, as a farmer. In politics he was a Democrat until 1854, then a Republican. He held the office of Justice. He died Apr. 29, 1878.

NORMAN B. WASHBURN

Representative from Lenawee County, 1887-8. Was born in Adrian, Mich., Aug. 13, 1849. He received a common school education, and at the age of seventeen learned telegraphy, but in the following year became an iron molder, which occupation, with the trade of bricklayer, he followed. He was a charter member and commissioned officer in the Adrian Light Guard, and served from 1870 to 1876. He was elected Representative as a Labor candidate and on the Democratic ticket.

JOHN WASHER

Representative from Bay County, 1897-8 and 1903-4. Was born in England in 1855, of English descent. He was educated in the common schools of England. He came to Michigan in 1872, settled in Bay County where he resided, following the occupation of farming. Married. He served as Supervisor of Bangor Township and as chairman of the County Board of Supervisors. In politics a Republican.

I. ROY WATERBURY

Representative from the Second District of Oakland County, 1899-1900 and 1901-2; Senator from the Twelfth District, 1903-4; and member of the State Board of Agriculture, 1907-22. Was born Oct. 2, 1869, on the farm in Highland Township, Oakland County. His early education was acquired in the public schools of that community. He was married in 1892, and followed the occupation of farming. He has been president of the State Association of Farmers' Clubs. Politically a Republican. He served his township in the offices of Clerk, Treasurer and Supervisor. He was a member of the House from 1899 to 1902; was elected to the State Senate for the term of 1903-4; and was appointed a member of the State Board of Agriculture June 13, 1907; elected in April, 1909, and re-elected in 1915.

JOHN C. WATERBURY

Representative from Sanilac County, 1861-2; and Senator from the Twenty-fifth District, 1871-2; and from the Twenty-second District, 1877-8. Was born Nov. 27, 1815, at Andes, N. Y. He received a common school education, and removed to Leroy, Mich., in 1838. From 1840 to 1847 he resided at St. Clair, then removed to Lexington. He held many offices, including Justice, Judge of Probate, Assistant Assessor of Internal Revenue, and Deputy U. S. Marshal. In politics he was first a Whig, and a Republican after 1854. He for years dealt in bonds and mortgages, and did much to develop the resources of the Huron shore. He died in May, 1894, at Lexington, Mich.

ARTHUR J. WATERS

Representative from the Second District of Washtenaw County, 1905-6 and 1907-8. Was born at Manchester, Washtenaw County, Mich., Aug. 23, 1860, of English parentage. He acquired his education in the high school of Manchester and at the University of Michigan. He worked on a farm until twenty-one years of age, and taught school winters for four years, and farmed on his own account for three years. Mr. Waters decided that farm life was too strenuous and gave up the farm and engaged in law practice. Married. In politics a Republican. He served as President of Manchester village.

CHARLES H. WATERS

Representative from the First District of Saginaw County, 1907-8, 1909-10 and 1911-12. Was born in Ontario, Canada, in 1862, of Irish descent. He received his education in the district schools of Ontario and New York State. Married. Mr. Waters was engaged in railroading for about fifteen years, was a farmer fourteen years and then gave his attention to the real estate business. In politics a Republican.

CHARLES W. WATKINS

Representative from Allegan County, 1871-2 and 1873. Was born in East Salem, N. Y., Mar. 5, 1844. He received an academical education. In 1856 he removed to Leighton, Mich. He entered the 6th Mich. Cavalry as a private in 1861; was transferred to the 10th Mich. Cavalry in 1863, was commissioned Lieutenant; served as Adjutant of the regiment for a brief period, and was made a Captain by brevet for gallant and meritorious services. He followed the mercantile business in Allegan County, but removed to Grand Rapids, where he engaged in the insurance business. He resigned as Representative before extra session of 1874 and was succeeded by Wm. F. Hardin. In politics he was a Republican.

ERWIN C. WATKINS

Representative from Kent County, 1873-4 and 1875-6. Was born in Middlebury, N. Y., Jan. 15, 1839. He received a common school education. In 1844 he emigrated to Michigan and settled in Grattan, Kent County, and subsequently removed to Rockford. He studied law, and was admitted to the bar in 1861. In the same year he enlisted in a company of cavalry, and when the company was incorporated in the 1st N. Y. regiment of cavalry, he was commissioned Lieutenant, and subsequently received a commission as Captain. In 1863 he was appointed Assistant Adjutant General of the department of West Virginia, and subsequently assigned to the staff of Gen. W. H. Seward, where he served until the war ended. He held several local positions. By occupation he was a lumber merchant. He was also Warden at the House of Correction at Ionia. He was an Indian agent in the west for some years.

FRANK B. WATKINS

Representative from the Second District of Allegan County, 1909-10. Was born in Washington County, N. Y., July 4, 1848. He acquired his education in the common schools. He was married. He served in the Civil War and marched with Sherman to Savannah, Ga., from Savannah to Raleigh, N. C., and on to Washington. He engaged in the mercantile business. In politics he was a Republican.

FREEMAN C. WATKINS

Representative from Jackson County, 1861-2; and delegate from Jackson County to the Constitutional Convention of 1867. Was born in Surry, N. H., Mar. 29, 1811. He taught primary schools in New Hampshire and Michigan from 1829 to 1834. He located his farm in Napoleon in 1833, and was an early pioneer of Jackson County. He was Supervisor and Justice. He was a democrat until 1854, then a Republican. He died June 10, 1880.

LUCIUS WHITNEY WATKINS

Senator from the Tenth District, 1909-10 and 1911-12; and member of the State Board of Agriculture, 1899-1905 and 1920—. Was born Aug. 6, 1873, at Norvell, Jackson County, Mich., on the farm on which he now resides. His father, Hon. Lucius D. Watkins, was a pioneer settler and a leader in the development of general farming and live stock husbandry in Michigan. Mr. Watkins attended the district school until he was fifteen years of age, when he entered the Michigan Agricultural College, from which institution he received the degree of B. S. in 1893. He was married to Grace Edith Alley, of Dexter, Mich., in 1899, and has four children, one daughter and three sons. He is a charter member of the Michigan Academy of Science, the Michigan Ornithological Club and of the Audubon Society. He served as Deputy State Game and Fish Warden from 1896 to 1898 when he was appointed by Governor Pingree as member of the State Board of Agriculture, which office he held from 1899 to 1905. He served as State Senator in the Legislatures of 1909-10 and 1911-12, and was candidate for Governor on the National Progressive ticket in 1912. He has been a director of the West Michigan Fair, vice-president of the State Fair Association, president of the State Association of Farmers' Clubs, the Michigan Improved Livestock Breeders' Clubs, the Jackson County Farm Bureau and the Michigan Crop Improvement Association; also a director of The Peoples Bank of Manchester. He was nominated as one of the Republican candidates for the office of member of the State Board of Agriculture and was elected Apr. 7, 1919.

MILTON C. WATKINS

Representative from Kent County, 1859-60; and Senator from the Twenty-ninth District, 1863-4 and 1865-6; and Delegate from Kent County to the Constitutional Convention of 1867. Was born in Rutland, Vt., in 1806. He received a common school and academical education. After the age of eighteen he was engaged several years in teaching. In 1830 he married Susan Joy, and settled on a farm in Covington, N. Y., where he taught winters, and worked as a carpenter summers, and was also Justice and School Inspector. In 1844, he settled on a farm in Grattan, Mich., where he resided until his death, May 16, 1886. He was the first Supervisor of Grattan, and held that and the office of Justice, nearly twenty-five years. He was U. S. Assistant Assessor until the office was abolished. In politics he was a Whig until 1854, then a Republican.

ROY MILTON WATKINS

Representative from the First District of Kent County, 1915-16; and Senator, 1919-20, from the Sixteenth District, comprising the east side wards of the city of Grand Rapids. Was born at Rockford, Kent County, Mich., Oct. 17, 1874. He received his education in the Ionia and Rockford schools, graduating from the high school of the latter place in 1892. He was a clerk in the Auditor General's department in 1893 to 1897. He then studied law at the University of Michigan and graduated in June, 1899, immediately commencing the practice of law in partnership with his father in Grand Rapids. He was appointed State Examiner of Taxable Inheritances and served from 1901 to 1905, later serving as Probate Register of Kent County from 1907 to 1911. He was president of the State League of Republican Clubs and represented this State on the secretary's staff at the last three Republican National Conventions. In August, 1917, he was commissioned by the President as secretary of Local Draft Board No. 3, city of Grand Rapids, and served during the war. A 32nd degree Mason and Mystic Shriner. He was married Aug. 24, 1909. In politics a Republican.

CHARLES HENRY WATSON

President pro tem. of the Constitutional Convention of 1907-8, and Delegate from the Thirty-first District, Marquette, Dickinson, Iron and Alger counties. Was born in Binghamton, N. Y., Oct. 29, 1870, of English descent. He received his education in the public schools at Berlin, Wis., and in 1899 graduated from the University of Michigan with the degree of LL.B. Mr. Watson's parents moved to Wisconsin from New York State in 1876. In 1877 his mother died, and from that time he resided with his grandparents on a farm in Waushara County, Wis., and afterwards at Berlin, until 1888. At that time he came to the Upper Peninsula of Michigan and worked on various newspapers in the Upper Peninsula. In 1892 he married Miss Blanche Campbell. He served as City Attorney of Crystal Falls and held the office of Prosecuting Attorney of Iron County.

FRANK H. WATSON

Representative from Shiawassee County, 1887-8. Was born in Shiawassee, same County, Nov. 14, 1857. He received his education at district and union schools and worked on his father's farm summers and taught winters, until twenty-one years of age, when he entered a law office in Corunna, and was admitted to the bar in 1881. He went to Colorado, but remained only about one year, when he returned to Corunna and commenced the practice of his profession, remaining there until the spring of 1885, when he removed to Owosso. He was elected Circuit Court Commissioner. In politics he was a Republican.

GEORGE C. WATSON

Representative from the Second District of Tuscola County, 1893-4. Was born in Frankfort, Ky., Aug. 28, 1846. He left home at the age of sixteen with the 15th O. Infantry, and was with that command at Perryville, Ky. He was Second Lieutenant 8th Ky. Infantry, was detailed for staff duty and served on General Van Cleave's staff at Chickamauga. He remained in Kentucky after the war until 1879, when he moved to Chicago, Ill., and engaged in insurance. He remained here until 1890, when he moved to Alma Township, near Caro. In politics he was a Republican.

GEORGE C. WATSON

Representative from the Second District of St. Clair County, 1923—. Was born in Chicago, Illinois, April 20, 1880. His early education was acquired in the public schools of Caro, Michigan, and he is a graduate of the law department of the University of Michigan. He is married and has three children. During the session of 1915, Mr. Watson was law clerk of the Senate, and was Assistant Attorney General in 1921 and 1922. His father, George C. Watson, was Representative from Tuscola County in 1893. Mr. Watson is a Republican and was elected to the Legislature November 7, 1922.

HENRY WATSON

Representative from the Second District of Montcalm County, 1885-6, 1887-8 and 1889-90. Was born in Nottinghamshire, England, Jan. 29, 1836. By occupation he was a lumberman and farmer. He was married. He filled the offices of Justice of the Peace, Township Clerk and School Officer.

JOSEPH E. WATSON

Representative from Branch County, 1919—. Was born at Center Sandwich, N. H., July 8, 1860. His parents were descended from the early settlers of New England. He received his education in the public schools of Center Sandwich and at the Lyndon Center Seminary, Lyndon Center, Vt. He came to Michigan at the age of twenty-two years. For more than twenty years he engaged in mercantile business in Bronson, after which he entered the banking business, being president of the First State Savings Bank for nine years. He was President of the village three terms and Postmaster nearly twenty-five years. He served as Colonel four years on the staff of Governor Fred M. Warner. He is a member of the Moslem Temple, A. A. O. N. M. S., of Detroit. He was a member of the Republican State Central Committee four years.

J. CLYDE WATT

Representative from Ionia County, 1905-6 and 1907-8. Was born in the village of Saranac, Mich., Oct. 4, 1875, of American and Scotch parentage. He attended the Saranac High School, and entered the law department of the University of Michigan, being graduated with the class of 1896. In the fall of 1894, while hunting, he lost his right arm by the accidental discharge of a shot gun. He began the practice of law at Saranac in 1897. Mr. Watt was united in marriage to Miss Pearl Flint of Clarksville, Ionia County, Mar. 1, 1905. In politics a Republican. He held the office of Circuit Court Commissioner, was president and secretary of the Gridley Republican Club of Ionia County, and secretary of the Republican County Committee.

MATHEW H. WATTERS

Representative from the Second District of Marquette County, 1899-1900. Was born at Cornwall, England, July 15, 1859. His education in early life was such as he could acquire by desultory school training, but after his arrival in Michigan, in 1883, it was very effectively supplemented by observation and evening study. He was brought up a miner, and very prominent in the Upper Peninsula as a miner and prospector. In 1899 he was in the employ of the D. S. S. & A. railway at Ishpeming.

JOHN W. WATTS

Representative from the Second District of Jackson County, 1887-8, 1889-90 and 1891-2; and Senator, 1895, from the Tenth District, composed of the counties of Jackson and Washtenaw. Was born in Leoni, Jackson County, Mich., Jan. 13, 1838. He acquired a common school education and engaged in farming. In politics he was a Republican. He held several local offices of public trust; was a Representative in the Legislatures of 1887-8, 1889-90, 1891-2, and elected to the Senate of 1895-6. He died Feb. 2, 1895, and the vacancy was filled by election of Charles H. Smith.

DUNCAN WAYNE

Representative from Midland County, 1899-1900 and 1905-6. Was born in Norfolk County, Ont., Jan. 7, 1858, of Pennsylvania Dutch and English parentage. He received his education in the public schools of Ontario and Midland County, Mich. His parents came to Michigan in March, 1870, and purchased a forty-acre farm in Midland County, where Mr. Wayne later resided. He followed the occupation of a farmer. He was married to Maude C. Neff, of Lansing, Feb. 25, 1892. In politics a Republican. He served as Supervisor of his township and chairman of the Board of Supervisors.

GEORGE LEO WEADOCK

Senator, 1913-14, from the Twenty-second Senatorial District, comprising the county of Saginaw. Was born at Saginaw, Mich., Feb. 9, 1881, of Irish-American

parents. He was educated in the parochial and public schools of Saginaw, Notre
Dame University and the law department of the University of Michigan.   Mr.
Weadock was in the real estate and insurance business for some time and later
1908 practiced law.   Married.   In politics a Republican.

THOMAS A. E. WEADOCK

Member of Congress, 1891-3 and 1893-5. Was born Jan. 1, 1850, at Ballygarret,
County of Wexford, Ireland; his parents emigrated to America during his in-
fancy and settled at St. Marys, O., soon afterwards moving to a farm near St.
Marys, where they resided until their death.   He was educated in the common
schools.   On the return of his elder brother from the Army in 1865 he went
to Cincinnati, O., and began to learn the printing trade; disliking this business,
returned and attended the Union School at St. Marys for a year; taught school
in the counties of Auglaize, Shelby, and Miami for the period of five years;
entered the law department of Michigan University in 1871; read law during the
vacation at Detroit, and graduated bachelor of laws in March, 1873.   In that
year, after further study at Detroit, he was admitted to the bar, and in 1873
located at Bay City; assisted in making an abstract of title to the real estate in
Bay County; and in 1874 began the practice of law in Bay City.   In politics he
was a Democrat.   He was appointed Prosecuting Attorney of Bay County in
1877, and served until Dec. 31, 1878; Mayor of Bay City from April, 1883 to
April, 1885; member of the Board of Education of Bay City for a short time;
and was elected to the Fifty-second and Fifty-third Congresses.   He resumed
the practice of law after leaving Congress.

CHARLES W. WEATHERBY

Representative from Branch County, 1861-2. Was born in Washington County,
N. Y., Jan. 19, 1810. By occupation he was a mechanic; in politics a Republican.
He settled at Bronson, Mich., in 1836, where he held several local positions and
was a Justice.   He removed to Missouri in 1865, was a resident of Kansas City
for two years, and resided at Shelbina, Mo., in 1887.

DWIGHT WEBB

Senator from the Second District, 1848-50.   His postoffice address was Ann
Arbor.   (Further data not obtainable).

NATHAN WEBB

Senator from the Eighth District, 1861-2. Was born in Middlesex, N. Y., Jan.
25, 1808. He received a good education, mostly from private teachers, and in
1836 received his diploma as a physician, and practiced at Rushville, N. Y.   In
1846 he removed to Pittsfield, Mich., and purchased a farm.   For many years he
was Supervisor, also Justice.   He was first an anti-Mason, then a Democrat, and

from 1854 a Republican. He sent three sons to the war, and served as a surgeon for several months. His wide information, literary tastes, firm principles and ready wit, made him a man of mark and influence. He spent thirty-eight years in Pittsfield and died there Dec. 3, 1884.

ANDREW J. WEBBER

Representative from Ionia County, 1885-6 and 1887-8. Was born in Steuben County, N. Y., Jan. 3, 1831. He received a good common school education, removed to Michigan in 1852, and for four years was engaged in lumbering on the west shore, then for ten years was a farmer and merchant. He was largely interested in lumbering in Mecosta County. He was Mayor of Ionia, twice president of the County Agricultural Society, director and vice-president of the Second National Bank, and president of the Ionia Farmers' Insurance Company. In politics he was a Republican.

GEORGE W. WEBBER

Member of Congress, 1881-3. Was born in Newburg, Vt., Nov. 25, 1825. He removed to Steuben County, N. Y., in 1828; received a public school education, and worked on his parents' farm until his twentieth year, when he engaged in lumbering and mercantile business for himself. He married in 1850 and removed to northern Michigan in 1852, where he continued the lumber business until 1858. Then he became a resident of Ionia County. He was interested in farming, and in building in Ionia, where he had the management of a mercantile business. He also carried on lumbering operations in Mecosta County after 1866. He was one of the founders of the Second National Bank of Ionia, and was its president. He was also Mayor of the city two terms. He was elected Representative to Congress as a Republican. He died Jan. 15, 1900.

WILLIAM L. WEBBER

Senator from the Twenty-fifth District, 1875-6. Was born in Ogden, N. Y., July 19, 1825. He removed with his father to Hartland, Mich., in 1836. He received a common school education, taught school, studied medicine two years, then taught select school at Milford two years. He studied law and was admitted to the bar in 1851. He became a resident of East Saginaw in 1853. He practiced law until 1869. In 1857 he became the attorney of the Flint & Pere Marquette Railroad Company. He was land commissioner of the road from 1870 to 1885; a director of the road after 1864. He was president of the Tuscola & Huron Railroad; trustee and executor of the estate of Jesse Hoyt; Circuit Court Commissioner of Saginaw County, 1854-5; Prosecuting Attorney; Mayor of East Saginaw; Democratic candidate for Governor in 1876, and president of the State Agricultural Society in 1878. In politics he was a Democrat. He died at Saginaw, Oct. 15, 1902.

ALANSON J. WEBSTER

Representative from Oakland County, 1871-2. Was born in Pontiac, Mich., Aug. 21, 1827. He lived in Pontiac until 1851, then removed to White Lake, Oakland County. He was Supervisor seven years, Township Treasurer and Justice. By occupation he was a farmer, in politics a Democrat. He died in 1875.

JAMES WEBSTER

Delegate from Oakland County to the Constitutional Convention of 1850; and Representative from Oakland County, 1846. Was born in Litchfield, Conn., in 1810. He came to Michigan in 1838. He was by trade a blacksmith, but became a Methodist preacher; politically a Democrat. He removed to Fairfax, Va., in 1858.

WILLIAM W. WEDEMEYER

Member of Congress, 1911-13. Was born in Lima Township, Washtenaw County, Mich., Mar. 22, 1873, of German parents. His early life was spent on the farm and his education was acquired in the district school. He later graduated from the Ann Arbor High School and from the literary and law departments of the University of Michigan. He was admitted to the bar in 1895. In politics a Republican. He served on the Board of School Examiners and as County School Commissioner of Washtenaw County from 1895 to 1897; was Deputy Commissioner of Railroads under Governor Pingree, 1897 to 1899; American Consul, Georgetown, British Guiana, 1905, but relinquished this position on account of sickness. In 1902 he was a candidate for Representative in Congress from the Second Congressional District. He was elected to the 62nd Congress Nov. 8, 1910.

AUGUSTUS W. WEEKES

Representative from the Second District of Kent County, 1893-4 and 1895-6; and Senator, 1901-2 and 1903-4, from the Seventeenth District, comprising all the townships of Kent County and the sixth, seventh and eighth wards of the city of Grand Rapids. Was born in Keene, Ionia County, Mich., May 27, 1850. His early education was acquired in the district schools and Grand Rapids High School, and the Michigan Agricultural College. At the age of nineteen he began mercantile life as a clerk in a dry goods store, a few years thereafter becoming a partner. He continued in the business ten years, and selling his interest he went into the dry goods business for himself which he successfully conducted. On Oct. 27, 1875, he was married to Miss Henrietta Bailey. In politics he was a Republican. He held the offices of Township Treasurer, Supervisor, chairman of Board of Supervisors of Kent County one year, and President of the village of Lowell. He died at Lowell August, 1916.

EDGAR WEEKS

Member of Congress, 1899-1901 and 1901-3. Was born at Mt. Clemens, Aug. 3, 1839, and educated in the city schools. At the age of fifteen years, he began learning the printing business in his native town. At the age of seventeen he took charge of a newspaper office at New Baltimore; was subsequently employed on the *Lake Superior Journal*, published at the time at Sault Ste. Marie, and afterwards at Marquette; was afterwards employed on the Detroit *Evening Tribune* and for a short time on the *Free Press*. About 1858 he became assistant County Clerk of Macomb County, began studying law, and soon after entered the law office of Eldredge & Hubbard at Mt. Clemens, where he remained until his admission to the bar in 1861. In June, 1861, he enlisted in Co. B, 5th Mich. Vol. Infantry; was promoted and commissioned. During the winter of 1864 he resigned his commission on account of sickness and terminated his army service. Returning to Mt. Clemens, he established the Mt. Clemens *Monitor*, a leading Republican paper of Macomb County; was elected Circuit Court Commissioner in the fall of 1864, but was obliged to relinquish it because the law authorizing soldiers to vote in the field was declared unconstitutional. He was elected Prosecuting Attorney of Macomb County two terms; appointed Judge of Probate in 1875 to succeed Thomas L. Sackett, deceased, served nearly two years and retired. He then practiced his profession at his old home, Mt. Clemens. He was elected to the 56th Congress and re-elected to the 57th Congress of the United States. He died at Mt. Clemens, Dec. 17, 1904.

CHARLES A. WEIDENFELLER

Representative from Van Buren County, 1913-14; and from the First District of Kalamazoo County, 1919-20. Was born on shipboard while his parents were enroute to this country from Germany. The date was June 9, 1852. He was educated in the public schools of Newark, N. J. In 1897 he moved to Bloomingdale, Mich. He worked at the carpenter trade fifteen years and then entered the life insurance business. Married. In politics a Republican. He was elected to the Legislature of 1913-14 from Van Buren County. Later he moved to Kalamazoo, and on Nov. 5, 1918, was again elected to the Legislature.

AUGUST JOHN WEIER

Representative from the First District of Monroe County, 1897-8 and 1899-1900. Was born in the city of Monroe, Mich., Oct. 21, 1871. He acquired a practical education in the parochial and public schools of the city of Monroe, and at St. Francis' College of that city. Upon arriving at his majority he entered a manufacturing and mercantile corporation as its secretary. He early developed an aptitude for the study of social problems, and before he was a voter he was an interested auditor of political discussions and an extensive reader of political economy. In politics a Democrat.

JOSEPH WEIER

Representative from Monroe County, 1869-70. Was born in Wackernheim, Germany, Mar. 4, 1822. He came to Monroe, Mich., in 1849, where he resided in 1887. He kept a grocery store and boarding house for years with success. He was an Alderman. About 1868 he became interested in the planting of vineyards and the making of wine, his trade extending over many states. In politics he was a Democrat.

JAMES D. WEIR

Senator from the First District, 1879-80. Was born in Brooklyn, N. Y., May 20, 1832. He received his education from private teachers. In 1847 he removed to Detroit, and in 1848 apprenticed himself to the foundry business, which he followed up to 1859. He then studied law, and was admitted to the bar in 1860. He was Collector of fourth ward, School Inspector, Alderman, County Clerk, Judge of Probate, and member of the Board of Education. In politics he was a Democrat.

HENRY A. WEISS

Representative from Gratiot County, 1885-6. Was born in Champion, O., in 1843. Came to Michigan in 1873, and for some years followed the occupation of lumberman, when purchasing the land upon which he resided, in Sumner, he engaged in farming. He was a member of the 84th O. Vol. Infantry, serving his full time of enlistment, was Supervisor, and was elected Representative as a candidate on the Fusion ticket.

JOSEPH M. WEISS

Senator from the Second District, 1891-2 and 1893-4; and Representative from the First District of Wayne County, 1907-8. Was born at Detroit, Mich., May 25, 1856. He received his education in the public schools of Detroit and graduated from the high school in 1873. Married. He was admitted to the bar in 1877, and in November of that year was appointed Prosecuting Attorney for Chippewa County. He was Circuit Court Commissioner of Wayne County for two terms, 1885-9. He represented the Second District of Wayne County in the State Senate two terms, 1891-2 and 1893-4. He was at this time engaged in the practice of law at Detroit. In politics a Republican.

CHARLES A. WEISSERT

Representative from Barry County, 1915-16, 1917-18 and 1919-20. Was born in Hastings, Mich., on Aug. 22, 1878, of German and French descent. After attenting the public schools of Hastings, he entered the office of the Hastings *Banner*. In 1900 he went abroad as a newspaper correspondent, traveling 3,000 miles on a bicycle through nine European countries. The next year he entered Harvard College and completed his course in 1905. While in college he was a member of the editorial board of the *Harvard Illustrated Magazine*. After leaving college he became a member of the editorial staff of the New York *Herald*, but later resigned on account of ill health and returned to Hastings. During his residence in New York he spent considerable time traveling in the southwest, Mexico and the Canadian Northwest. Mr. Weissert is the author of several works on dramatic and historical subjects, and has written several monographs on Michigan history. He is a member of the Harvard Club in Michigan, and of Hastings Lodge, No. 52, F. & A. M. In May, 1919, he was appointed by Governor Sleeper one of ten commissioners to represent the State at the dedication on May 30, 1919, of the Michigan monument on Shiloh battlefield, Tenn. He was elected a trustee of the Michigan Historical Society in June, 1919. He is married and has two sons. Politically he is a Republican.

ADONIJAH STRONG WELCH

Member of the State Board of Agriculture, 1863-6. Was born at East Hampton, Conn., Apr. 12, 1821. He married (1) Eunice Buckingham, at Mt. Vernon, O., Apr. 12, 1851; (2) Mary B. Dudley, Feb. 3, 1868. He prepared for college at Romeo Academy; graduated in the University of Michigan, 1846, with the degree of A. B.; studied law with Lothrop and Duffield. He was principal of the Union School in Jonesville, Mich.; principal of the State Normal School, Ypsilanti, Mich., 1851-65; president of the State Teachers' Association. He went to Florida to recruit his health, and was elected United States Senator of that State in 1867. In 1868 he was elected president of Iowa Agricultural College, later called Iowa State College, and inaugurated Mar. 17, 1869. He died Mar. 13, 1889, at Pasadena, Calif., and was buried in the college cemetery at Ames, Ia.

HENRY B. WELCH

Representative from Monroe County, 1873-4. Was born in Augusta, Mich., Aug. 2, 1833. He was educated in common schools. In 1866 he removed to Monroe County, and settled in Exeter. By occupation he was a farmer. He died Oct. 18, 1886.

JOHN WELCH

Senator from the Twenty-third District, 1881-2. Was born in Augusta, Me., Sept. 5, 1825. He received a common school education, and at thirteen was apprenticed to a blacksmith. After one year he became a sailor, and followed it six years, rising to the position of Second Mate. In 1846 he went into the lumber business, and in 1863 settled at White River, Mich., where he remained until 1872, after that time resided at East Saginaw. He was a successful lumberman, and also a farmer. He was twice Mayor of East Saginaw, and held positions as Alderman and Supervisor. In politics he was a Republican.

JOHN B. WELCH

Representative from Ionia County, 1863-4 and 1865-6. Was born in the State of New York, Mar. 22, 1816. He came to Michigan in 1836. He cut the timber on the public square at Ionia. He was commandant to raise the 21st Mich. Infantry, and recruit 2,000 men for various regiments at a great sacrifice of time and money. He was a Republican while in Legislature, later a Greenbacker.

LEWIS WELCH

Senator from the Ninth District, 1857-8 and 1859-60. His postoffice address was Exeter, Monroe County. (Further data not obtainable).

WASHINGTON WELD

Representative from St. Joseph County, 1843. His postoffice address was Centerville. (Further data not obtainable).

ERASTUS J. WELKER

Representative from Branch County, 1873-4 and 1877-8. Was born in Walnut, O., Sept. 3, 1825. In 1832 he removed with his parents to Seneca County, O., they being the second family on the Seneca reservation. He was educated in common schools. In 1866 he removed to Kinderhook, Branch County. By occupation he was a blacksmith. For several years he was an officer at the Ionia House of Correction. In politics he was a Republican.

CHARLES WELLMAN

Representative from St. Clair County, 1885-6 and 1887-8. Was born in Canada, Jan. 18, 1847. He came to Michigan with his parents in 1853; engaged in various occupations, in 1887 in the milling and mercantile business at Port Huron. He was an Alderman and member of the Board of Estimates. He was elected as a Fusionist.

HOMER E. WELLMAN

Representative from Antrim County, 1913-14. Was born at Saranac, Ionia County, Mich., Mar. 10, 1881, and was educated in the Bellaire High School, McLachlan Business College, at Grand Rapids, and graduated from the law department of the University of Michigan, in 1910. Until the age of eight years he lived in Ionia County when the family removed to Montcalm County. They remained there seven years, after which they settled on a farm in Antrim County. He taught school one year and was storehouse distribution clerk for the Pere Marquette railroad one year. He afterwards entered the practice of law at Mancelona. Married. In politics a National Progressive.

FRANK C. WELLS

Representative from the Second District of Macomb County, 1899-1900. Was born at Steubenville, Jefferson County, O., Mar. 22, 1851. His early education was acquired in the public schools of that city, and in 1870 he came to Michigan and entered Michigan Agricultural College, where he remained until the summer of 1873, when failing health compelled him to cease study and return to his home in Ohio. In 1875 he returned to Michigan and engaged in farming and lumbering. In 1890 he entered the veterinary department of Detroit College of Medicine, and graduated with the degree of D. V. S. in 1893. Since then he practiced veterinary surgery at Warren, Mich. Politically a Republican.

FRANKLIN WELLS

Member of the State Board of Agriculture, 1873-1903. Was born Apr. 19, 1823, at Salem, Washington County, N. Y. He was educated in the public schools. In religion he was a Congregationalist. In politics he was a Republican. In 1837 he moved to Constantine, Mich.; 1838 to 1842, clerked in a store; 1842 to 1871, kept a general store; from 1871 to his death in 1903, took great interest in the management of his farm. He was Postmaster in 1861 for part of Presidential term; in 1895 again Postmaster. In 1873 he was appointed by Governor Bagley a member of the State Board of Agriculture and served until his death. From 1878 to 1890, he was agent for St. Joseph County for the State Board of Charities and Corrections. He served also as a member of the State Central Republican Committee. He died July 3, 1903.

FRED B. WELLS

Representative from Cass County, 1915—. Was born on a farm in Wayne Township, Cass County, Mich., Feb. 16, 1861. In April, 1866, he removed with his parents to Lagrange Township, and was educated in the district school and the Dowagiac High School. He is a member of the Masonic lodge and the Grange. Mr. Wells is married and has two children, a son and a daughter. In politics he is a Republican.

FREDERICK L. WELLS

Representative from St. Clair County, 1871-2; and Senator from the Twenty-second District, 1873-4 and 1875-6. Was born Mar. 24, 1833, in Stanford, N. Y. He received a common school education, and was instructed in the classics by a private tutor. In 1838 he emigrated to Michigan, and settled in Port Huron. He served as Mayor, City Clerk, Chief Engineer, and Alderman. By occupation he was a lumber merchant; politically a Republican.

HENRY B. WELLS

Representative from Cass County, 1867-8. Was born at Hartwick, N. Y., Feb. 4, 1829. In 1835 he removed with his father to Charleston, Mich., where he received a common school education. In 1848 be bought a farm in Wayne, Cass County. For a time he was in mercantile business in Dowagiac. In company with Z. Jarvis he built a grain elevator, and was extensively engaged in the produce business. He was Supervisor several years. In politics he was a Republican.

HENRY H. WELLS

Representative from Wayne County, 1855-6. Was born in Rochester, N. Y., Sept. 17, 1813, and came to Detroit at the age of twenty-one, where he studied law and was admitted to practice. He entered the military service as Lieutenant Colonel of the 26th Mich. Infantry, in October, 1862, was promoted to the Colonelcy of the same regiment, Mar. 30, 1864, and was brevetted Brigadier General in 1865. In April, 1868, he was appointed Provisional Governor of Virginia, holding the position until 1869. He was U. S. District Attorney for Virginia, 1869-71, and U. S. District Attorney for the District of Columbia, from September, 1875, to January, 1880. In politics he was a Republican.

HEZEKIAH G. WELLS

Delegate from the Eleventh District to the Constitutional Convention of 1835; Delegate from Kalamazoo County to the Constitutional Convention of 1850; member of the Constitutional Commission of 1873; and member of the State Board of Agriculture from 1861-83. Was born June 16, 1812, at Steubenville, O., and was educated at Kenyon College. He studied law at Kalamazoo, Mich., in 1833. From 1845 to 1849 he performed Circuit Court duties as Judge. In 1862, largely by his efforts, the 25th Mich. Infantry was mustered into service. In 1873 he was one of eighteen appointed to revise the State Constitution. In 1874 he was appointed presiding Judge of the Court of commissioner of Alabama claims, and that court distributed over $9,000,000 of the "Geneva award" to claimants. The court was re-established in 1882, and he was again its presiding officer. For many years he was an active member of the historical committee of the State Pioneer Society, and was president in 1880. He was a man of commanding form, fine personal appearance, and a recognized leader in the Republican party. First he was a Whig, a Republican after 1854. He died at Kalamazoo Apr. 4, 1885, leaving a wife, but no children.

JOHN TYLER WELLS

Representative from the Second District of Wayne County, 1889-90. Was born at Burlington, Vt., May 6, 1841. His occupation was that of farming in connection with the dairy business principally, keeping from 70 to 100 cows; was a member of Fairbanks Post, G. A. R. He served in the 17th N. Y. and was mustered out at expiration of term of enlistment. He was in every engagement in which that regiment participated. He enlisted as a private and came out of the service as such. He re-enlisted in the 77th N. Y. Cavalry, was clerk at headquarters department of the gulf, stationed at Memphis, Tenn., when the war ended. In politics he was a Republican.

MARSHALL M. WELLES

Representative from Oakland County, 1850. Was born in Genesee, N. Y., in August, 1822. His father settled at an early date on a farm in Lyon, Oakland County, where the son was reared. In 1845 he became a clerk in the office of the Auditor General. He was a Representative as a Democrat. Under Buchanan he was a Deputy U. S. Marshal. For eighteen months he was sutler of the 11th Mich. Infantry.

THOMAS M. WELLS

Representative from the First District of Marquette County, 1903-4. Was born in Connecticut in 1848, descending from New England ancestors. He was educated in Salisbury Academy, Conn. He worked on a farm, in a woolen mill and after coming West, clerked in a large store of the Iron Cliff Company at Negaunee. In 1886 he purchased the extensive mercantile department of the Iron Cliff Company and continued in the business fifteen years. He was Deputy Revenue Collector during President Harrison's administration. During the year of 1902, he was employed in work connected with the State Tax Commission. He was married in 1884. In politics he was a Republican.

WILLIAM P. WELLS

Representative from Wayne County, 1865-6. Was born at St. Albans, Vt., Feb. 15, 1831. He graduated from the University of Vermont in 1851, from Harvard Law School in 1854, was admitted to the Vermont bar in 1855, and settled in practice at Detroit in 1856. He was a partner of Judge J. V. Campbell until 1858. He was a member of the Detroit Board of Education in 1863-4; law lecturer at the University in 1874-5, and Kent professor of law from 1876 to 1886, when he resigned. In politics he was a Democrat.

GEORGE W. WELSH

Representative from the First District of Kent County, 1917—. Was born in Glasgow, Scotland, Mar. 27, 1883. He was educated in the public schools of Glasgow and Grand Rapids. He was connected with the Grand Rapids *Evening Press* from 1895 to 1906, since which time he has been publisher of a farm magazine, *The Fruit Belt*, and is manager and owner of *The United Weeklies*. He served as Alderman for two terms, and is a member of the various Masonic branches in Grand Rapids. He is married. In politics he is a Republican. At the opening of the 1923 session he was elected speaker of the House.

GEORGE T. WENDELL

Representative from Mackinac County, 1857 and 1859-60. Was born at Albany, N. Y. He was a resident of Mackinaw Island at an early day. In politics he was a Democrat. He was a merchant, and held many local positions, and was Probate Judge of Mackinac County at the time of his death, Oct. 10, 1879, then about sixty.

W. WORTH WENDELL

Representative from the Second District of Wayne County, 1891-2. Was born on a farm in Oakland County, Mich., Jan. 7, 1852. He graduated from the State Normal School and afterward had charge respectively of the Clinton and Hudson public schools of Lenawee County. He studied law with Coneley, Maybury and Lucking; graduated from the law department of the Michigan University and practiced that profession at Northville, Wayne County. In politics a Democrat.

JACOB A. T. WENDELL

Representative from Mackinac and other counties, 1855-6, 1865-6 and 1869-70. Was born in Albany, N. Y., Apr. 12, 1826. He became a resident of Mackinaw Island in 1829, and was Collector of Customs. He had a good education and was a merchant, doing much to develop the commerce of northern Michigan. He was a Democrat, and once candidate for Lieutenant Governor. He died Nov. 25, 1879.

JOHN A. WENDELL

Representative from Oakland County, 1842. Was born in Charlton, N. Y., Oct. 19, 1788. He was a soldier of the War of 1812. He settled as a farmer in Rose, Oakland County, in 1836, and in 1837 was elected the first Supervisor and was re-elected from 1838-44. He was also Town Clerk and Justice of the Peace and was Postmaster of Rose from 1837 until his death, in 1858.

PETER WENTING

Representative from Muskegon County, 1913-14. Was born at Muskegon, Mich., Jan. 4, 1887, of Holland descent. He was educated in the public schools and at the age of nineteen began to learn the carpenter trade. At twenty-four years of age he became a contractor, which occupation he followed. A member of the U. B. of C. and J. of A., local union No. 100, of Muskegon. In politics a National Progressive.

GIDEON T. WERLINE

Representative from Menominee County, 1903-4. Was born in Tioga County, Pa., in 1851, of German parents. He was educated in the common schools of Pennsylvania. He taught school for two years. He engaged in mercantile, farming and real estate business. He was married. In politics he was a Democrat. He died Nov. 16, 1920, at Morristown, Pa., where he had resided since August, 1920.

SYBRANT WESSELIUS

Senator, 1889-90, from the Twentieth District, comprising the county of Kent. Was born in the city of Grand Rapids, Mich., June 8, 1859, of Holland descent, his parents immigrating to this country from the Netherlands, in the year 1847. His education was continued in the common schools of the city of Grand Rapids until he reached the age of fifteen years, when he entered a factory for the purpose of learning the trade of trunkmaker, at which trade he continued to work for three years and until, by attending evening schools and by private instruction, he fitted himself for the position of teacher in the district schools at the age of eighteen years. By means of funds thus obtained he entered college, graduating in 1883, from Kalamazoo College, with the degree of A. B. He was a lawyer by profession, and enjoyed a large practice. On Sept. 30, 1885, he was married to Effa L. Bangs, of Hudson, Mich. In politics a Republican.

WILLIAM B. WESSON

Senator from the First District, 1873-4. Was born Mar. 20, 1820, in Hardwick, Mass. He received an academical education. He had extensive business relations, was president of the Wayne County Savings Bank; president of the trust and security and safe deposit company, of Detroit; president of the Hamtramck street railway; a director of the Detroit, Lansing & Lake Michigan Railroad, and was one of the trustees of the Detroit Medical College. His business was that of a dealer in real estate.

THOMAS J. WEST

Representative from Berrien County, 1873-4 and 1875-6. Was born in William-ston, N. Y., May 22, 1831. He received a high school education. In 1835 he removed to Michigan and settled in Charleston, Kalamazoo County. In 1864 he removed to Berrien County and settled in Bainbridge, where he still resided in 1887. By occupation he was a farmer.

CHARLES HENRY WESTCOTT

Senator from the Eleventh District, 1897-8. Was born in a log cooper shop at Leslie, Ingham County, Mich., Apr. 4, 1847. When about six weeks old he moved with his parents to Newport (now Marine City) where he acquired his education. He commenced sailing when a boy of sixteen years, beginning at the lowest round of the ladder and worked his way up until he became master of steam vessels. Under President Harrison's administration he was appointed Supervising Inspector of steam vessels for the eighth supervising district, which office he held until removed by President Cleveland. For several years he was a resident of St. Clair city. In politics a Republican. He was Treasurer of Cot-trellville, including Newport; and was elected Mayor of the city of St. Clair in 1896.

FRANK WESTCOTT

Representative from Shiawassee County, 1895-6. Was born in Flint, Genesee County, Mich., Dec. 26, 1852. With his parents he removed to Shiawassee County the next year, and in 1861 to Vernon. The common schools afforded him his early education, and in 1875 he engaged in the hardware business. In poli-tics a Republican. He was Postmaster during Harrison's administration; held the offices of Village Clerk, member of the Board of Education, and Justice of the Peace.

ANSEL W. WESTGATE

Senator from the Twenty-seventh District, 1887-8. Was born in Lenawee County, Mich., Aug. 24, 1841; he resided in Michigan twenty-three years; was educated at Hillsdale College He then went to Massachusetts, where he re-mained until 1879; then removed to Alpena and was pastor of the Congrega-tional Church in that city four years. He was a merchant and insurance agent at Cheboygan. He was School Inspector, County Examiner and Supervisor. Politically he was a Republican.

FRANK L. WESTOVER

Senator, 1901-2 and 1903-4, from the Twenty-fourth District, comprising the counties of Bay and Midland. Was born in Sheffield, Berkshire County, Mass., Dec. 17, 1853. Coming to Michigan in 1866, his education was acquired in the public schools of Bay City. He was admitted to the bar in 1879 and for four years practiced law in both State and Federal courts. In 1883 he was appointed

Postmaster of Bay City, holding the office four years. In 1894 he was elected
Clerk of Bay County and re-elected in 1896. While editor of the Bay City
Tribune he was elected to the Senate of 1901-2, and on the 4th of November,
1902, was re-elected. Later he engaged in the business of life insurance.

LUTHER WESTOVER

Representative from Bay County, 1869-70. Was born in Berkshire County,
Mass., Apr. 24, 1817, and received an academical education. In 1845 he shipped
a cargo of lumber to Connecticut, which proving profitable, he went to Canada
and engaged in lumbering. He removed to Bay City in 1865; was engaged in
lumbering until 1874; established the exchange bank, which in 1873 was
merged into the State Bank. He was active in the completion of the J., L. & S.
railroad, and was three years a director. He was a Democrat until 1861, then
a Republican.

JAMES E. WETER

Representative from the First District of Macomb County, 1899-1900 and
1901-2; and Senator from the Eleventh District, 1909-10 and 1911-12. Was
born at Palmyra, Lenawee County, Mich., Apr. 9, 1857. His parents were farmers, and his early life was spent on the farm, receiving his education at the district schools, supplemented by two years at Adrian College. After leaving
school he farmed for nine years in Lenawee County, and then engaged in the
wholesale egg business at Richmond, Macomb County, under the firm name of
Weter, Fanning & Co.; was also president of the Macomb County Savings Bank,
of Richmond, and vice-president of the Consolidated Hay-Bale Tie Company
of Richmond.

HEZEKIAH WETHERBEE

Representative from St. Joseph County, 1857-8. Was born in Washington
County, N. Y., in 1802. By occupation he was a miller and farmer, in politics
first Whig then Republican. He settled in Three Rivers in 1833, helped build
the first flouring mill in that place, worked as a miller in that mill until 1836,
when the Emery mill was built, where he worked for twelve years, and also one
winter at the Hoffman mill. In 1836 he entered land five miles from Three Rivers which afterwards became his farm home. He was for fourteen years Supervisor. He died in 1873.

WILLIAM H. WETHERBEE

Representative from the First District of Wayne County (Detroit), 1897-8.
Was born Sept. 8, 1858, at Stone Hill, Medina County, O. His education began
in the public schools of Cleveland, O.; came to Michigan with his parents when
very young, locating in Detroit, in 1870; attended private schools in Detroit
and did some work in the night schools. His father, Cyrus W. Wetherbee, a
native of New York State, who emigrated to the "Western Reserve" early in the
century, was a hardware merchant in Cleveland and left his business to go to

the front in the dark days of the Civil War. He served in the Mississippi squadron until the close of hostilities in 1865, and returned home in broken health from which he never recovered. At a very early age, therefore, young Wetherbeen was thrown upon his own resources. He had fondness for study, however, and at the age of nineteen entered the law office of Claude N. Riopelle, of Detroit, where he read law for more than a year. After spending nearly a year longer in the office of Horace E. Burt he was compelled, by adverse circumstances to seek more lucrative employment and entered into commercial pursuits, devoting the next twelve years to the coal and wood business in the employ of Lester Peacock, where he occupied a trusted and responsible position. He kept up his law studies, however, and in 1891 entered his chosen profession, afterwards taking a two years' course in the Detroit College of Law. In politics a Republican. He held the offices of Inspector of Election and Ward Committeeman; chairman of precinct; was appointed Chief Census Enumerator for Detroit in 1894; and was elected to the House of 1897-8 on the general legislative ticket of the city of Detroit.

FRED C. WETMORE

Senator, 1907-8 and 1909-10, from the Twenty-seventh District, comprising the counties of Antrim, Benzie, Grand Traverse, Kalkaska, Leelanau, Missaukee and Wexford. Was born at Rock Island, Ill., Nov. 23, 1867. His early life was spent in Illinois, Michigan, and New York. He came to Ann Arbor in 1881 and entered the high school; removed to Plymouth in 1882 and graduated from the high school in 1885; resided at Jonesville from 1886 to 1888; entered the law department of the University of Michigan in October, 1888, receiving the degree of LL.B. in 1890 and the degree of LL.M. in 1891. He began the practice of law at Cadillac, September, 1891. He was an active member of several fraternal orders, having served five years as Grand Master Workman of the A. O. U. W. and an officer of the Grand Lodge K. of P. In politics a Republican. He was appointed City Attorney of Cadillac in 1896, serving five years, and again in that capacity from 1904 to 1906; and was elected Prosecuting Attorney of Wexford County three successive terms, 1900-6.

AUGUST F. WETTLAUFER

Representative from the First District, Detroit, of Wayne County, 1889-90. Was born in Detroit, Oct. 20, 1856. His business was that of manufacturing cigars. He was elected on the Democratic ticket to the House of 1889-90.

WILLIAM WALLACE WHEATON

Representative from the First District, Detroit, of Wayne County, 1889-90. Was born at New Haven, Conn., Apr. 5, 1833. He was a mine owner, stock broker, and dealer in real estate. He was Mayor of Detroit in 1868-9, 1870-1, and was elected to the House of 1889-90 on the Democratic ticket.

A. OREN WHEELER

Senator, 1891-2 and 1895-6, from the Twenty-sixth District, counties of Lake, Manistee, Mason and Oceana. Was born in Mill River, Berkshire County, Mass.,

May 8, 1846; moved to Illinois in 1857; attended public school and at the age of thirteen years became a newsboy on Chicago, Rock Island & Pacific railroad; at the age of seventeen years was appointed baggage master, and two years later became conductor of the train, in which position he continued until 1865. Then he engaged in the hotel business for one year, and in 1866 came to Manistee, where with his brother-in-law, John Canfield, he organized the Canfield East Shore Wrecking and Tug Line; also interested in the machine shop and foundry business; was president of the Manistee Manufacturing Company which was destroyed by fire in 1889; and was first Superintendent of Harbor improvements for the Manistee River and harbor. In politics he was a Republican. He was a member of the Senate of 1891-2; a candidate for the term of 1893-4, but defeated; elected to that of 1895-6.

AMOS R. WHEELER

Representative from Oceana County, 1873-4 and 1875-6. Was born in Cavendish, Vt., Sept. 12, 1815. He received a common school education, emigrated to Kane County, Ill., in 1835, and in 1853 to Benona, Oceana County, Mich., which township he named. He was County Treasurer, and served as Supervisor five years. By occupation he was a lumberman. He died at Benona, Feb. 7, 1883.

CALVIN WHEELER

Representative from Washtenaw County, 1851. Was born in Livingston County, N. Y., Jan. 28, 1806. He settled as a farmer in Salem, Washtenaw County, in 1830. He held every town office except constable; was Postmaster at Salem several years, and station agent on the D., L. & N. R. R. for eight years. He was Captain in the Toledo War.

CHARLES P. WHEELER

Representative from St. Joseph County, 1901-2. Was born in Three Rivers, Mich., Aug. 21, 1865. His education was obtained at the Michigan Military Academy, from which he graduated to enter upon a course of study at the University of Michigan. Married. He had large farming interests. At the outbreak of the Spanish-American War he tendered his services, and went to the front as Captain of Co. K, 33d Mich. Infantry. In politics a Republican.

ELMER G. WHEELER

Representative from the First District of Genesee County, 1909-10 and 1911-12. Was born in the township of Springfield, Oakland County, Mich., Oct. 5, 1859, of German and English descent. In March, 1865, he removed with his parents to Richfield, Genesee County, Mich., and attended the Cottage School until the spring of 1875, when he started clearing out of the solid timber the farm he now owned. He was married in 1880 to Nona Alexander. In 1890 he was elected Justice of the Peace, and held that office until 1899, when he was elected Township Treasurer and served two terms. He also served as Supervisor of Richfield Township. In politics a Republican.

FRANK W. WHEELER

Member of Congress, 1889-91. Was born in Jefferson County, N. Y., Mar. 2, 1853. By occupation he was a ship builder. He was elected by the Republicans in 1888 to the 51st Congress.

GEORGE S. WHEELER

Representative from the First District of Washtenaw County, 1899-1900. Was born in the township of Leicester, Livingston County, N. Y., Apr. 22, 1830, and removed to Michigan with his parents a year later. His early education was derived largely from the common schools, although he attended Cochren's Academy at Northville, passed from there to the Ypsilanti High School, the Commercial College at Detroit, and one term in the law school of the University. At seventeen he began teaching in the public schools, and followed that occupation for the greater part of the following sixteen years. Elected County Superintendent of Schools in 1868, he served six years, after which he was a member of the County Board of School Examiners for eight years. In the winter of 1861-2 he recruited a company for the Sir Arthur Rankin's regiment of lancers, which was never mustered into the service, but on Aug. 27, 1862, he was mustered into the service of the United States as First Lieutenant of Co. D, 5th Mich. Cavalry, and went to the front in December of the same year. After the war he served as Deputy County Treasurer of Washtenaw County two years, and Supervisor of Washtenaw and Livingston counties fifteen years. He voted the Whig and Republican tickets. He died Mar. 14, 1903, at Salem, Mich.

HARRISON H. WHEELER

Senator from the Twenty-seventh District, 1871-2; and from the Twenty-fourth, 1873-4; and member of Congress, 1891-3. Was born in Lapeer County, Mich., Mar. 22, 1839. He received a common school education, and at the age of 18 years commenced teaching school winters and working upon a farm summers until the fall of 1861, when he enlisted as a private in Co. C, 10th Regiment, Mich. Vol. Infantry; in June, 1862, promoted to Second Lieutenant same company, and in April, 1863, promoted to First Lieutenant Co. E, same regiment; in April, 1865, promoted to Captain Co. F, same regiment; and wounded at Buzzard's Roost Gap, Kenesaw Mountain, and at Jonesboro, Ga., during the Atlanta campaign. In politics he was a Democrat. He was elected Clerk of Bay County, Mich., in 1866; admitted to the bar in 1863; elected State Senator for Bay and adjoining counties in 1870, and re-elected in 1872; after the session of the Legislature in 1873 moved to Ludington, Mason County, Mich., and was appointed Circuit Judge in 1874 by Governor Bagley; at the first election thereafter elected to the same office without opposition; resigned in June, 1878, and resumed practice of law at Ludington; elected to the Fifty-second Congress. He died July 29, 1896.

ISAAC P. WHEELER

Representative from Jackson County, 1875-6. Was born at Sudbury, Mass., Aug. 10, 1817. He received a common school education. In 1836 he came to

Michigan and located on a farm in Pulaski, Jackson County. He was Supervisor seven terms, Postmaster for twenty years, and held other township offices. By occupation he was a farmer.

JAMES WHEELER

Representative from Lenawee County, 1835 and 1836. Was born in Saratoga County, N. Y., Mar. 21, 1793. Later he lived in Wheeler, Steuben County, N. Y., a town named from the family. He settled in Tecumseh, Mich., in 1834, and was a Justice from 1837 to 1841. He was a farmer, in politics a Democrat. He died at Tecumseh, Feb. 20, 1854.

LYCURGUS J. WHEELER

Representative from Barry County, 1883-4. Was born in Wheeler, N. Y., Feb. 9, 1830. He came with his father to Washtenaw County, Mich., in 1835, removing to Woodland, Barry County, in 1842. He received an academical education, and taught several years. He served three years in the war, then located at Nashville as a merchant, and was still in that business in 1887. He held several local offices. Politically he was a Republican.

WILLIAM WHEELER

Representative from the Second District of St. Joseph County, 1861-2 and 1863-4. His postoffice address was Flowerfield. (Further data not obtainable).

BION WHELAN

Representative from Hillsdale County, 1913-14. Was born at Hillsdale, Mich., July 13, 1858. He was a graduate of the Hillsdale High School, the Michigan Agricultural College and the University of Michigan. He practiced medicine at Hillsdale. Mr. Whelan was married Mar. 1, 1881, to Minnie L. Allen. He was a member of the Board of Education of Hillsdale, chairman of the Republican County Committee four years and was appointed a member of the State Board of Medical Registration by Governor Pingree; a member of the various Masonic and Pythian orders of his city and served as the presiding officer of most of them. In politics a National Progressive.

JOHN JEFFERS WHELAN

Representative from Shiawassee County, 1909-10 and 1911-12. Was born at New York City, Feb. 20, 1863, of Scotch parentage. He acquired his education in the Vernon High School and studied music and literature at the University of Michigan. He came with his parents to Michigan in 1870, locating in Shiawassee County, where he resided except during the years 1888 to 1892, when, because of ill health, he went to California and Colorado. Mr. Whelan was married Jan. 27, 1892, to Nettie L. Kelley, of Byron, Mich. In 1909 he was owner and manager of a large stock farm located in Shiawassee Township. In politics a Republican.

NICHOLAS J. WHELAN

Representative from the First District of Ottawa County, 1903-4, 1905-6 and 1907-8. Was born near Montague, Mich., in 1869, of Irish-American parents. He worked in saw mills, on the boom, as section hand on the railroad, in basket factories and taught school. At twenty-one years of age he was elected Justice of the Peace in Montague, and at the age of twenty-two joined the life saving crew at Holland, Mich., and served five years. For a time he was manager of the Hotel Macatawa and Hotel Holland. He was admitted to the practice of law in 1895. He purchased an interest in the Holland City *News* and became editor of that paper. He was married in February, 1904, to Miss Jeanne Blom, of Holland, Mich. In politics a Republican.

CHARLES W. WHIPPLE

Representative from Wayne County, 1835 to 1837; and Justice of the Supreme Court, 1838-55; and Delegate from Berrien County to the Constitutional Convention of 1850. Son of Major John Whipple, of the United States army, was born in New York about 1808; was educated at West Point, subsequently studied law, and began practice in Detroit. He was principal secretary of the Constitutional Convention of 1835. He was appointed a Judge of the Supreme Court in 1838, and Chief Justice in 1848, and in 1852 was elected Judge of the Circuit in which the county of Berrien was then situated. Judge Whipple died while in office, October, 1855, after a continuous service of seventeen years on the bench. He was secretary of the Sixth Legislative Council in 1835, was County Register in 1836, a Master in Chancery, and School Inspector in Detroit. He was a Democrat in politics.

HENRY L. WHIPPLE

Auditor General, 1842. Was a son of Major John Whipple, born in Detroit in 1816. His pursuits were official in connection with the State departments at Detroit and Lansing. He was connected with the Auditor General's office after the removal of the capital to Lansing. His politics will be inferred as Democratic from his official connection. He died in Detroit in 1849.

BYRON C. WHITAKER

Representative from the First District of Washtenaw County, 1901-2 and 1903-4. Was born in Yates County, N. Y., May 30, 1835, and came to Michigan when very young. His education was obtained in the common schools and union school at Ypsilanti. He was a successful farmer forty years and was also engaged in the lumber and hardware business ten years. He was unmarried. In politics he was a Democrat. He held the offices of Supervisor, Justice of the Peace and Township Treasurer.

ALPHEUS WHITE

Delegate from the First District to the Constitutional Convention of 1835. Was a native of Ireland. He was Lieutenant of a company of which his brother was

Captain, which did gallant service in the defense of New Orleans, under Gen. Jackson. He became an architect, and in 1830 was a resident of Cincinnati. He came to Detroit in 1834, and the provision of the constitution giving suffrage to the then alien residents of the State was the result of his efforts in the convention. He had command of the artillery arm of the Michigan forces during the Toledo War. He was a Democrat, and a devout Catholic, and was the founder of Trinity Church.

ARTHUR S. WHITE

Representative from the First District of Kent County, 1891-2 and 1893-4. Was born in Ann Arbor, Mich., July 9, 1844. He acquired his early education in the public schools. He enlisted in Co. D, 1st Nebr. Infantry, April, 1861, returning to Michigan in 1865 and locating at Grand Rapids, where he engaged in the publishing business and dealing in real estate. He was a member of the Legislature of 1891-2 serving on the committees on railroads, Soldiers' Home, and liquor traffic. He was re-elected to the House of 1893-4 on the Democratic People's party tickets.

CHARLES E. WHITE

Senator, 1909-10 and 1911-12, from the Seventh District, comprising the counties of Berrien and Cass. Was born in Howard Township, Cass County, Mich., Mar. 15, 1873, and received his education in the county schools and Niles High School, from which he graduated in June, 1894. He later attended the University of Michigan, graduating from the law department in 1897. In September, 1897, he was admitted to the bar and practiced his profession at Niles, Mich. In 1898 he was elected a Justice of the Peace, served as chairman of the Republican City Committee of Niles, Mich., and chairman of the Republican County Committee of Berrien County. From 1904 to 1908 he served as Prosecuting Attorney of Berrien County. A member of the K. of P., F. & A. M., K. T., and Mystic Shrine.

DARWIN O. WHITE

Representative from Oakland County, 1869-70 and 1871-2. Was born Sept. 8, 1835. He was a farmer, a Democrat, and resided at Southfield, Oakland County. He held the local offices of Town Clerk, Treasurer, School Inspector, and Supervisor, the last several times. He died July 8, 1885.

FRANK G. WHITE

Senator from the Thirty-second District, 1871-2. Was born in Massachusetts in 1832. He came to Houghton, Mich., in 1853, and was engaged in mining until 1884. After that time he was a resident of Leadville, Col. Politically he was a Republican.

FRED J. WHITE

Representative from the First District of Wayne County, 1919-20. Was born at Ypsilanti, Washtenaw County, Mich., Aug. 17, 1881, of American parents. He received his education in the public schools and the Michigan State Normal School. He was Deputy County Drain Commissioner of Wayne County four years and housing inspector for the Board of Health of Detroit for the same length of time. He is salesman for the Federal Sign System, of Detroit. He is not married. In politics he is a Republican.

GEORGE H. WHITE

Representative from Kent County, 1863-4. Was born at Dresden, N. Y., Sept. 9, 1822. He received a common school education, and was a clerk in Indiana until 1842, when he removed to Grand Rapids. He was a clerk there two years, and was, in 1844, elected Register of Deeds, and was also partner of Amos Rathbun. He conducted a store at Rockford for five years, returned to Grand Rapids; was a Supervisor, and Mayor in 1861-2. He was a lumberman from 1863 to 1865; then engaged in the manufacture of plaster. He built, with Amos Rathbun, many stores, and was a director of the G. R. & I. railroad, and of the Continental Improvement Company. He was a Whig until 1854, then a Democrat. He died at Grand Rapids, May 28, 1902.

HARRY CLARK WHITE

Senator from the Sixteenth District, 1917-18. Was born in Grand Rapids, June 24, 1870, of English-Scotch descent. He received a common school education, supplemented by special courses in bookkeeping and music. For nearly twenty years he was church organist in various Grand Rapids churches. A practical printer, he conducted a successful business as printer, engraver and publisher. He was Alderman from the tenth ward for six terms. Married. In politics a Democrat.

JACOB W. WHITE

Representative from the Second District of Genesee County, 1889-90. Was born at Buffalo, N. Y., Aug. 25, 1835. In the Civil War he served in 1st Regiment of Engineers and Mechanics. In politics he was a Republican.

JAMES E. WHITE

Representative from Oceana County, 1881-2 and 1883-4. Was born in Kalamazoo, Mich., Apr. 8, 1839. He attended Albion College in 1857-8. He went into the army in 1861, as Lieutenant in the 13th Mich. Infantry, and became a Captain in 1863. After leaving the army was engaged in mercantile business at Wayland until 1875, when he removed to Pentwater, engaged in the hardware trade, and the manufacture of shingles. In politics he was a Republican. He died Mar. 12, 1917.

JAMES H. WHITE

Representative from St. Clair County, 1879-80 and 1881-2. Was born at Whitesboro, N. Y., Apr. 28, 1822. He received an academical education; was in business in Utica two years, the same time at Ann Arbor, Mich., and at Yonkers, N. Y. In 1849 he settled at Port Huron, and engaged in farming, insurance, banking and real estate. From 1855 to 1859 he was Sheriff, was an Alderman four years, Deputy Collector of Customs 1867 to 1876, and held other offices. Politically he was a Republican.

JONATHAN R. WHITE

Delegate from Lapeer County to the Constitutional Convention of 1850; and Representative from Lapeer County, 1855-6. Was born in South Hadley, Mass., on Sept. 10, 1806. By profession he was a lawyer; politically a Republican. He came to Michigan in 1831, and was commissioned a Colonel of State militia in 1835 by Governor Mason. He died July 12, 1881.

OLIVER K. WHITE

Representative from Oceana County, 1877-8. Was born in Peru, Clinton County, N. Y., Feb. 15, 1831, removing three months subsequently to Erie County, where he received a common school education. In 1852 he removed to Cattaraugus County, where for two years he held the positions of Township Superintendent of Schools and Justice. In 1857 he removed to Michigan and settled in Grant, where he still resided in 1887. He was Supervisor six years, and was Sheriff of Oceana County during 1875-6. He was also vice-president of the Michigan Pioneer and Historical Society. In politics he was a Republican.

ORRIN WHITE

Representative from Washtenaw County, 1842. Was born in Palmyra, N. Y., Oct. 25, 1796. He received a fair education, served in the War of 1812, and was for several years engaged in mercantile business at Palmyra. He settled as a farmer in the town of Ann Arbor, Mich., in 1824. He was a Supervisor, Judge, Justice, and Sheriff, also a member of the Constitutional Convention of 1835. He was a Colonel of militia. He died in 1864.

PETER WHITE

Representative from Chippewa and Marquette counties, 1857-8; Senator from the Thirty-second District, 1875-6; member of the Board of Regents of the University of Michigan, 1904-8. Was born at Rome, N. Y., Oct. 31, 1830, son of Peter and Harriet (Tubbs) White. His father removed to Green Bay, Wis., when the lad was very small. At fifteen the boy struck out for himself to Mackinac Island, then a busy fur-trading post. There he worked in a store, or assisted on the lake survey, until in 1849 he joined a boat expedition to the newly discovered Iron Mountains of Lake Superior; and returning from the site of the mines to the lake shore became one of the first settlers of Marquette. Here he was clerk in a general store, Postmaster, and soon a merchant on his own account. From merchandising he passed on to the study and practice of the law. He established a bank, entered into intimate relations with several important mining companies, and built up a large Fire, Life, and Marine Insurance business. In 1857 he was a member of the State House of Representatives, from the Upper Peninsula, and, in 1875, State Senator. When Marquette County was organized he became County Clerk and Register of Deeds and served also as Collector of the Port of Marquette for many years. In 1892-3 he was a member of the Board of World's Fair Managers for Michigan, and served on the Board of Judges of Awards, a member of the Mackinac Island State Park Commission; and a member of the State Board of Library Commissioners. Marquette owes to him its fine library building, with a large part of the contents; the Science Hall of its State Normal School; and the beautifying of the fine Park of Presque Isle. He was also founder of the Peter White Fellowship in American History and of the Peter White Classical Fellowship at the University. In 1900 the Regents of the University conferred upon him the honorary degree of Master of Arts. In April, 1903, he was elected Regent of the University for the full term and took his seat the following January. In 1857 he was married to Ellen S. Hewitt. Mrs. White died in June, 1905. Peter White died in 1908.

SHUBAEL F. WHITE

Senator from the Twenty-sixth District, 1883-4. Was born at Marshall, Mich., June 17, 1841. He graduated at the University of Michigan in 1864. He served in the Civil War in the 28th Mich. Infantry, and rose from a private to the rank of Captain. He was a Provost Marshal in North Carolina in 1865-6. He graduated at the Albany Law School in 1867, and engaged in law practice at Ludington. He was a Circuit Judge in 1873-4. Politically he was a Republican.

THOMAS WHITE

Representative from Washtenaw County, 1867-8. Was born in Royalton, N. Y., and his education was that of common schools. He emigrated with his parents to Novi, Mich., in 1833, who settled upon a farm. The son engaged alternately in teaching and farming. In 1852 he settled on a farm in Northfield and was successful. In 1868 removed to Ann Arbor, and became secretary and managing director of the Washtenaw Mutual Insurance Company, which he managed with great success. Politically he was a Democrat, then a Free Soiler, and eventually a Republican. He died May 10, 1868.

THOMAS W. WHITE

Representative from Kent, Ottawa and Ionia counties, 1844. Was born in Ashfield, Mass., Nov. 15, 1805. He settled in Grand Haven in 1836, and was a lumberman by occupation. He was an active business man at Grand Haven for thirty years, when he removed to Grand Rapids. In politics he was first Whig, then Republican. He died Jan. 9, 1884.

WILLIAM E. WHITE

Representative from Allegan County, 1865-6; and Delegate from Allegan County to the Constitutional Convention of 1867. Was born June 29, 1814. By occupation he was a carpenter, in politics a Whig, then a Republican. He came to Kalamazoo in 1835, lived there until 1862, when he removed to Wayland, Allegan County. He was Sheriff of Kalamazoo County from 1858 to 1862; Village Trustee, Marshal and Constable of Wayland.

HARRY H. WHITELEY

Representative from the Presque Isle District, 1915-16; and Senator from the Seventh District, 1923—. Was born in Gaylord, Mich., May 7, 1882, of English and American parents. He was educated in the Lansing High School and the Michigan Agricultural College, leaving at the end of his sophomore year. He afterwards spent two years at Washington, D. C., returning to Michigan in March, 1902. He located at Millersburg and associated with his father in the publication of the *Presque Isle County News* until December, 1913, when he consolidated it with the *Presque Isle County Advance*, at Rogers City, which in company with his brother, W. H. Whiteley, he purchased in June, 1912. He was married June 27, 1905, to Miss S. Ethel Stevens, of Clare, and they have four children. He was Postmaster of Millersburg from January, 1912, until September, 1914, resigning to make his legislative campaign. He also served as Village Assessor and member of the School Board. In 1915 he purchased an interest in the *Daily News* of Dowagiac, which paper he has since published. In politics he is a Republican.

HENRY WHITING

Member of the Board of Regents of the University of Michigan, 1859-64. Was born in Bath, N. Y., Feb. 7, 1818, attended common schools until thirteen, was a clerk four years, then attended grammar school, and became a cadet at West Point in 1836, graduating in 1840, in the same class with Sherman and Thomas. He was a Lieutenant in the army until 1846, then resigned, became a resident of St. Clair, Mich., and took charge of an academy. In 1848 he engaged in lumber business until 1851, and continued in mercantile business until 1861. He then became Colonel of the 2d Vt. Infantry, took part in the first battle of Bull Run, and in 1862 commanded the Vermont brigade, and was at Fredericksburg and in other battles, resigning in 1863, and again becoming a merchant at St. Clair. He was a Republican until 1876, then a Greenbacker. Deceased.

JUSTIN RICE WHITING

Senator from the Seventeenth District, 1883-4; and member of Congress, 1887-9 to 1893-5. Was born at Bath, Steuben County, N. Y., Feb. 18, 1847. When two years of age moved with his parents to St. Clair; received his preparatory education at the Union School, and admitted to the Michigan University in 1863, at the age of sixteen; and left college at the close of the sophomore year. He was a merchant and manufacturer. He was a Republican until 1876 when he became a Greenbacker and was among the first to favor fusion with the Democrats. He was elected Mayor of St. Clair in 1879; elected State Senator in 1882, and elected to the Fiftieth Congress by the combined votes of Democrats and Greenbackers; re-elected to the Fifty-first, Fifty-second, and Fifty-third Congresses; Democratic candidate for Governor in 1898 and defeated; Democratic candidate for Congress in 1900 and defeated; and chairman of the Democratic State Central Committee. He died at St. Clair, Mich., Jan. 31, 1903.

CHARLES RUDOLPHUS WHITMAN

Member of the Board of Regents of the University of Michigan, 1886-94. Was born at South Bend, Ind., Oct. 4, 1847, son of William Green and Laura Jane (Finch) Whitman, of Weymouth, Mass. He received a preliminary training in the common schools of his native town, and in Foster School, of Chicago. He prepared for college in the Chicago High School, the Ann Arbor High School, and the Ypsilanti Union Seminary, graduating from the latter institution in 1866. In September of that year he entered the University of Michigan, and was graduated Bachelor of Arts four years later. From 1870 to 1871 he was principal of the Ypsilanti Union Seminary. In 1871 he married Elvira C. Joslyn of Ypsilanti. In the autumn of 1871 he entered the Law Department of the University, and was graduated Bachelor of Laws in 1873. Two years later he received from the University the degree of Master of Arts. He entered upon the practice of law at Ypsilanti in 1873, in partnership with his father-in-law, Chauncey Joslyn, Esq. For several years he was secretary of the School Board of Ypsilanti. In 1876 he was elected Circuit Court Commissioner for Washtenaw County, serving two years, and by appointment becoming Injunction Master for the county. In 1882 he was elected Prosecuting Attorney, which office he filled for two terms. In 1885 he was elected Regent of the University of Michigan, and took his seat the following January, serving the full term of eight years. In 1887 he removed to Ann Arobr. In 1891 Governor Winans appointed him Railroad Commissioner for the State of Michigan, which position he held during the Governor's term of office. In 1895 he removed his law office to Detroit though continuing to reside in Ann Arbor. In 1896 he was appointed Assistant United States District Attorney at Detroit, and continued to hold hat position until something over a year after the termination of President Cleveland's second administration. In February, 1899, he removed to his old home, Chicago, where he resumed the practice of his profession.

EZRA W. WHITMORE

Representative from the Third District of Washtenaw County, 1855-6. His postoffice address was Ann Arbor. (Further data not obtainable).

CHARLES E. WHITNEY

Representative from the Second District of Muskegon County, 1897-8 and 1899-1900. Was born on a farm at Utica, Macomb County, Mich., Aug. 14, 1852. He acquired his early education in the district schools, attending school winters and working on his father's farm during the summers. Later he attended the public schools of Muskegon, studying under a brother who was Superintendent of the school at that time. He was engaged in farming and fruit raising at Utica until 1880, when he moved to Detroit and spent three years in the mercantile business. He bought a farm in Fruitport Township, Muskegon County, in 1883, and engaged in farming and fruit raising. In politics a Republican. He served his township as Treasurer, School Inspector, and member of the Board of Review; was an active member of the Muskegon County Horticultural Society, and was secretary of the Muskegon Farmers' Institute Society for the years of 1895-6.

JOSEPH HERBERT WHITNEY

Representative from the Third District of Saginaw County, 1895-6; and Senator from the Twenty-second District, comprising the county of Saginaw, 1907-8 and 1909-10. Was born at Newburg, Penobscot County, Me., Apr. 13, 1858. He removed with his parents to Saginaw County, Mich., in 1868, and settled on a farm. He attended the district schools and the high schools of Saginaw; began teaching district school at the age of seventeen years, followed this occupation thirteen winters and worked on a farm during the summer months. In 1886 he engaged in the hardware business at Merrill. Married. He was a member of the Board of Education eighteen years, President of the village several terms and Township Clerk, president of the State Bank of Merrill, director of the Bank of Hemlock and vice-president of the St. Louis Sugar Co. In politics he was a Republican. He was a member of the County Committee twenty years. He died at St. Louis, Mich., June 7, 1916.

LUTHER D. WHITNEY

Representative from Lapeer County, 1857-8. Was born at Granville, N. Y., Mar. 13, 1810. He learned the trade of a mason and also preached occasionally. He came to Michigan in 1832, and was for fourteen years a Methodist minister. He then, from a bronchial affection, retired, studied medicine, and began practice at Commerce, Mich., in 1844. In 1849 he removed to Hadley, Lapeer County, and continued practice, sometimes preaching. He was a Whig, then Free Soiler, then a Republican. In 1875 he moved to Grand Blanc, where he died Sept. 11, 1876.

NATHAN WHITNEY

Representative from Muskegon County, 1875-6. Was born in Huron County, O., Nov. 11, 1821, removed to Michigan in 1849, and settled in Sparta, Kent County. In 1854 he removed to Muskegon County. He received a common school education. He was Supervisor of Casnovia for sixteen years. In politics he was a Democrat.

THOMAS WHITNEY

Senator from the Twenty-eighth District, 1857-8. His postoffice address was East Saginaw. (Further data not obtainable).

BERNARD C. WHITTEMORE

State Treasurer, 1850-5. Was born near Rome, N. Y., in 1807. He came at an early day to Pontiac, where he was in the hardware trade. He was appointed State Treasurer Mar. 13, 1850, and elected in 1851 and served to 1855. He also served as Justice of the Peace in 1838. In politics he was a Democrat. He died Dec. 7, 1856.

GIDEON O. WHITTEMORE

Members of the Board of Regents of the University of Michigan, 1837-40; member State Board of Education, 1852-6; and Secretary of State, 1846-8. Was born at St. Albans, Vt., Aug. 12, 1800. He settled at Pontiac, Mich., in 1826, and engaged in the practice of law. He held many positions of trust, was a Justice, Associated Judge of Oakland County, and member of the Constitutional Convention of 1850. In 1854 he founded Tawas City, Iosco County, and built a large steam saw-mill, the first on Tawas Bay. He was Judge of Probate and Prosecuting Attorney of Iosco County. He was elected member State Board of Education, Nov. 2, 1852, for term of four years; resigned Mar. 28, 1856. He died June 30, 1863, and was buried at Pontiac.

GUY J. WICKSALL

Delegate to the Constitutional Convention of 1907-8 from the Eighth District, Van Buren County. Was born in Paw Paw, in 1872, of Scotch and English descent. He graduated from the Bangor High School in 1890, and from the law department of the University of Michigan in 1895. After spending several months in the law office of Edwards & Stewart, of Kalamazoo, he commenced the practice of law in South Haven, as a member of the firm of Johnson & Wicksall. In 1900 that firm was dissolved and the firm of Wicksall & Cogshall was former. In 1900 he was married to Miss Juliette L. McCarty, of Vermontville.

JOHN F. WIDOE

Representative from Oceana County, 1897-8. Was born in Danville, Knox County, O., Mar. 18, 1856. His early education was acquired in the common schools of Mt. Gilead, O.; came to Michigan in 1867 and supplemented his schooling by a course in the schools of Grand Rapids city. In 1873 he went to Hart, Mich., and entered the employ of his father as manager of a branch clothing establishment; in March, 1877, he became proprietor of said branch clothing house. He was married in 1884 to Miss Cora Eastman, of Midland, Mich. In politics a Republican. He was President of Hart village five years; was president and secretary of the Board of Education three years.

FREDERICK WIELAND

Representative from the Second District of Oakland County, 1913-14 and 1915-16. Was born in Oakland County, Mich., Dec. 24, 1860. He was a member of the bar and served the county as Prosecuting Attorney, County Clerk and School Examiner. Married. Politically a Republican.

HOWARD WIEST

Justice of the Supreme Court, 1921—. Was born in the township of Washington, Macomb County, Mich., Feb. 24, 1864, of American parentage. He was educated in the public schools, Pontiac, Mich.; learned machinist's trade; left the machine shop in 1884, and entered law office of Atkinson & Atkinson, Detroit, as office help and student. Oct. 19, 1885, he was admitted to the bar in the Wayne circuit upon examination in open court, and in practice in Detroit until April, 1890. In 1887-8 he was Circuit Court Commissioner of Wayne County, and in 1890 moved to Ingham County; in 1899 was elected Circuit Judge of the 30th Judicial Circuit and re-elected 1905, 1911 and 1917. He was married Dec. 19, 1888, and has two children. He was appointed a Justice of the Supreme Court Jan. 25, 1921, and was elected to fill the vacancy caused by the death of Justice Flavius L. Brooke, Apr. 4, 1921.

MILAN D. WIGGINS

Representative from the Second District of Van Buren County, 1889-90 and 1891-2; and Senator, 1911-12 and 1913-14, from the Eighth District, comprising the counties of Allegan and Van Buren. Was born at Independence, O., in 1846, of English parents. He was educated at Hiram and Oberlin colleges. His father died in 1850 and until 1865 he lived on a farm with his uncle. He taught school four years and was in the mercantile business until 1876. Married. He represented the Second District of Van Buren County in the State Legislatures of 1889 and 1891 and held the office of Supervisor six years. In politics he was a Republican. He died May 23, 1914.

WILLIAM H. WIGGINS

Representative from Lenawee County, 1885-6. Was born in Floy, N. Y., Apr. 12, 1839. He came to Michigan in 1861. At first he engaged in the patent medicine business, then a farmer and dealer in live stock. For eleven years he was Town Clerk. Politically he was a Democrat.

BUCKMINSTER WIGHT

Senator from the First District, 1855-6. Was a native of Worcester County, Mass., born in 1796. His education was that of common schools. He came to Detroit in 1832, engaging actively in the lumber business in 1837. He represented his ward in the council, and was a candidate for Mayor, but generally shunned office. He was a public spirited and useful citizen and amiable gentleman. In politics he was first Whig, subsequently Republican. He died Nov. 28, 1879.

STANLEY G. WIGHT

Representative from Wayne County, 1863-4. Was born in Massachusetts, Sept. 11, 1825, coming to Detroit with his father's family. His early education was academical. His active business life was passed as member of the lumber firm of B. Wight & Sons, and in the same business on his own account, 1848 to 1880. After his legislative service he declined all elective offices. He was Alderman, 1851-2, and a member of the Board of Water Commissioners 1863 to 1868. He was an old line Whig, but became a Democrat.

MARK D. WILBER

Senator from the Fourteenth District, 1873-4. Was born in Clinton, N. Y., Aug. 12, 1829. He received an academical education, and studied law in the law department of Yale College. In 1856 he was admitted to the bar. While a resident of New York he was a member of the Assembly three terms. In 1870 he settled in Allegan, Mich. During the Civil War he served in the department of the gulf, on the staff of Gen. Paine. He was vice-president of the First National Bank of Allegan, and vice-president of Wilber's Eureka Mower and Reaper Manufactory, of Poughkeepsie, N. Y. He was projector of the Poughkeepsie & Eastern railroad, a director of the same, and secretary and attorney until he came to Michigan. He was also president of the Poughkeepsie city railway. He returned to New York, and was serving as U. S. District Attorney in that State in 1887.

CHARLES A. WILBUR

Representative from Livingston County, 1855-6. Was in business a farmer and merchant and resided at Howell. He died about 1867.

ALBERT WILCOX

Representative from Lenawee County, 1841. Was born at New Marlboro, Mass., Nov. 15, 1805. His ancestors were engaged both in the French and Revolutionary wars. He was brought upon a farm, and in 1818 removed with his parents to Guilford, N. Y. He received a common school education, and became a teacher. He removed to Wheeler, N. Y., where he was a partner of his father in farming and the making of wagons, and was a Captain of the militia. In 1835 he came to Michigan and took up a farm in the town of Bridgewater. In 1836 he enlisted as carriage maker in the U. S. arsenal at Dearborn, with the rank of Orderly Sergeant. In 1839 he settled at Cambridge, Lenawee County. In politics he was a Whig and Republican. He was in the employ of the Lake Shore Railroad after 1851, in various mechanical positions. He held many local offices, including Justice and Alderman. During the rebellion he had entire charge of the water supply of 426 miles of railroad. He resided at Adrian in 1887.

ELLIOTT R. WILCOX

Representative from Oakland County, 1869-70; and Senator from the Eighteenth District, 1877-8. Was born at Rochester, Mich., Feb. 24, 1838, where his father settled in 1824. He was educated at the Rochester Academy and the University of Michigan. As a young man he held many local offices, and was a Justice. In politics he was a Democrat. He was admitted to the bar Jan. 6, 1871. He was a farmer on a large scale. He was a member several years of the Democratic State Committee. He rendered important aid in the building of the Detroit & Bay City railroad. In 1874 he built a large brick paper mill on his farm.

JAMES M. WILCOX

Representative from the Iron District, 1913-14; and Senator, 1917—, from the Thirty-second District, comprising the counties of Baraga, Houghton, Keweenaw and Ontonagon. Was born in Wales, British Isles, July 22, 1850. In 1857 the family removed to a farm in Grant County, Wis., remaining there until 1861, when they removed to Hancock, Mich. At the age of eleven he began working in the old Quincy mill. In 1868 his father was made mining captain of the Schoolcraft mine (now the Centennial Copper Company), under whose employ he worked until twenty-one years of age, at which time he secured employment as timberman for the Calumet and Hecla Mining Company, where he remained for eighteen years, later being successively employed as Superintendent of underground operations at the Wolverine, the Tower mine, Minn., the Cincinnati mine on the Mesaba range, and at the Arcadian Copper Company. In 1901 he was made superintendent and managing director of the Mass Consolidated Mining Company, where he remained for ten years. Mr. Wilcox is married. He has held the office of Supervisor of Greenland Township, Ontonagon County, and also served as chairman of the board. In politics he is a Republican.

MARCUS WILCOX

Senator, 1891-2, from the Twelfth District, comprising the counties of Ingham and Shiawassee. Was born in Pompey, Onondaga County, N. Y., Nov. 15, 1833. He worked on his father's farm until 21 years of age, and received a common school education. In 1854 he came to Michigan and worked as a farm hand until the fall of 1857 when he returned to the State of New York, where he married in 1858, and engaged in farming on his own account. In 1862 he sold his farm and returned to Michigan with his family, purchasing a farm at Corunna. He cast his first vote for the candidate of the Republican Party in 1856, and voted steadily with that party until 1884. He served twelve years as School Trustee and two years as Alderman. He was the Democratic and Industrial candidate for Senator in 1890.

MARCUS B. WILCOX

Senator from the Twenty-third District, 1857-8. Was born June 24, 1821, at Arkwright, N. Y. He received a good academical education and a pretty thorough knowledge of Latin. He removed to Pinckney, Mich., in 1852. He read law and was admitted to the bar in 1854. In politics he was a Republican. He was elected several terms Prosecuting Attorney of Livingston County. He held minor offices. He died in Cleveland, O., Sept. 8, 1868.

WILLIAM S. WILCOX

Representative from Lenawee County, 1865-6 and 1867-8; and Senator from the Ninth District, 1871-2. Was born at Riga, N. Y., Apr. 25, 1819. When young he removed with his father to Bergen, N. Y., where his father kept hotel and postoffice, and ran a stage line. He assisted him until 1836, when he became a clerk in the store of Ira Bidwell at Milan, O., and removed with him to Adrian, Mich., in 1836. From 1840 to 1855 he was a partner, then commenced business for himself, which he continued until 1855, then went into the hardware trade, and was the head of a leading banking house in Adrian for many years. He was Clerk of Adrian in 1848; State Prison Inspector from 1869 to 1881; was president of the Michigan State Insurance Company, and held many other local positions. He was Mayor of Adrian in 1865, and a Presidential Elector in 1884. In politics he was a Republican. He died at Adrian, Sept. 15, 1893.

DANIEL G. WILDER

Senator from the Twenty-seventh District, 1861-2. Was born in Chesterfield, Mass., Apr. 15, 1823. He removed from Massachusetts to New York, and came from that State to Michigan in 1848. He studied law, was admitted to the bar at Howell, and began practice at Vassar. He held town offices, such as Justice, Clerk, Supervisor, Treasurer, and School Inspector, and was County Treasurer, Judge of Probate, Prosecuting Attorney, County Clerk, and Register of Deeds. In 1872 he went into the mercantile business at Watrousville, where he resided until his death in 1885.

EDWIN A. WILDEY

Representative from Van Buren County, 1893-4 and 1895-6; and Commissioner of the State Land Office, 1901-3 and 1903-5. Was born on a farm, three miles from Paw Paw, on Jan. 5, 1848, where he resided all his life. In 1872 he was married to Miss Annie Salt. In politics a Republican. He was Supervisor of his township, and represented his district in the Legislature of 1893-5, serving as chairman of several important special committees. He was elected Commissioner of the State Land Office for the term of 1901-3, and re-elected Nov. 4, 1902.

DAVID W. WILEY

Representative from Allegan County, 1875-6. Was born at Hanover, O., June 27, 1838. He removed to Michigan in 1852, and to Douglas, Allegan County, in 1856. He served as Trustee of Douglas Village, and held other municipal positions, and was president of the Lake Shore Agricultural and Pomological Society. He received a common school education, and was a farmer and fruit grower. In politics he was a Democrat.

JEFFERSON WILEY

Representative from Wayne County, 1867-8. Was born in Boston, Mass., in 1826, and was educated at Harvard College. Coming to Detroit in 1852, he first

engaged in active business as a member of the firm of Jackson & Wiley, iron
and brass founders. A term as Inspector of the House of Correction, 1872-5,
comprised his official life except as above. He was lumber agent for the Detroit,
Lansing & Northern Railroad.

MERLIN WILEY

Representative from Chippewa County, 1915-16, 1917-18 and 1919-20; and
Attorney General, 1921-3. Was born at Shepherd, Isabella County, Mich., May
7, 1875. He was educated in the Sault Ste. Marie High School, Albion College
and the University of Michigan, graduating from the literary department of the
latter institution in 1902, and from the law department in 1904. Since that
time he has practiced law in Sault Ste. Marie, and is now the senior member
of the firm of Wiley & Green. Mr. Wiley is married and has two children, a
boy and a girl. In politics he is a Republican. He was elected Prosecuting
Attorney in 1909. He resigned the office of Attorney General in January, 1923.

ALFRED WILKERSON

Representative from Monroe County, 1859-60. Was born in Ledyard, N. Y.,
Feb. 15, 1820. He removed with his parents to Dundee, Mich., in 1836, where
he resided as a farmer. He helped organize the Republican party.

ROSS WILKINS

Justice of the Territorial Supreme Court, 1832-6; Delegate from the Third District to the Constitutional Convention of 1835; Delegate from Lenawee County
to the First Convention of Assent, 1836; Delegate from Wayne County to the
Second Convention of Assent, 1836; and member of the Board of Regents of
the University of Michigan, 1837-42. Was born at Pittsburg, Pa., in February,
1799, and was the son of John Wilkins, who served in the wars of the Revolution and of 1812, and became Quartermaster-General in the U. S. army. Judge
Wilkins graduated at Dickinson College, Pa., in 1818, studied law, and was
Prosecuting Attorney at Pittsburg in 1820. He was appointed Judge of Michigan territory by Jackson, and opened his court June 17, 1832. In 1836 became
U. S. District Judge, and held that position until December, 1869, when he resigned, never having been absent a term in thirty-two years. He was an able
judge. In politics he was a Democrat, in religion a Methodist, but died in the
Catholic faith. He died May 17, 1872.

SAMUEL M. WILKINS

Representative from the First District of Eaton County, 1879-80 and 1881-2;
and Senator, 1893-4, from the Fifteenth District, comprising the counties of
Barry and Eaton. Was born in Baughman, Wayne County, O., Aug. 16, 1836.
When thirteen years of age his parents died and he was taken in charge by his

relatives. He attended district school winters and worked on the farm summers. At the age of seventeen he attended the union school at Canal Fulton, O. He taught school the following winter and then took a two years' course at Vermillion Institute, Hayesville, O. He then went to an uncle's in Illinois, where he taught school eighteen months. In 1859, he with his brother, took a trip with an ox-team to California, where until November, 1861, he was engaged in gold mining. He returned to Ohio and continued his medical studies which he had begun before leaving. Aug. 8, 1862, he enlisted in the 102d regiment O. Infantry; at Stone River he was assigned to hospital duty as Assistant Surgeon, which position he occupied until mustered out June 6, 1865. After the war he attended medical colleges; removed to Eaton Rapids, Mich., in 1866, where he engaged in the practice of medicine and surgery. In politics he was a Republican. He held the offices of President of the Village and Mayor of the city of Eaton Rapids; was a member of the State Legislature for the term of 1879-80 and 1881-2; and was awarded his seat in the Senate of 1893-4 by that body in the contest with Milton F. Jordan, the Democrat, People's party and Prohibition candidate.

DANIEL S. WILKINSON

Representative from Lenawee County, 1849. Was born in the State of New York in 1813. He came from Albion, N. Y., to Adrian, Mich., in 1834, where he resided until his death, May 24, 1875. His business was that of loaning money. In politics he was a Democrat.

JAMES M. WILKINSON

State Treasurer, 1894-7. Was born in Novi, Oakland County, Mich., Nov. 9, 1838. His early youth was spent upon a farm and attending district school; prepared for college under the late Professor Estabrook at the Union Seminary at Ypsilanti, and entered the literary department of the University of Michigan in the fall of 1860; entered the law department in 1862, and graduated therefrom in 1864; removed to Marquette and engaged in the practice of law with Henry D. Smith, in which practice he continued until 1873, when he became interested in the banking business to such an extent that he gave up his profession and engaged in that business. He held for sixteen years the office of Receiver of Public Money at the United States Land Office at Marquette, commencing with Grant's first administration and ending with Cleveland's first administration; which covered the period of greatest activity in land sales in the Upper Peninsula, and many millions of dollars passed through his hands. He was one of the commissioners appointed by Governor Luce to select a site for and build the Upper Penisula Prison, and after its completion was a member of the Board of Control of that institution. Mar. 20, 1894, he was appointed State Treasurer to fill the vacancy caused by the removal of Joseph F. Hambitzer, and was elected to that office the following November, for the term of 1895-7.

ROBERT R. WILKINSON

Senator, 1891-2, from the Twenty-ninth District, comprising the counties of Antrim, Charlevoix, Grand Traverse, Leelanau and Manitou. Was born in Reed

Township, Seneca County, O., Dec. 28, 1834; was brought up on a farm; attended school at the Baldwin University at Berea, O., four terms, and one year at the high school at Fredericktown, O. He left school to work on his father's farm. He was married in the Spring of 1860 to Eliza Sanford. In the Spring of 1861 he was elected Treasurer of the township; the last of August of the same year enlisted as a private in Co. G, 3rd O. Cavalry, was appointed First Duty Sergeant, and soon after was promoted to Orderly Sergeant. He was discharged from the service in February, 1863, for disability caused by disease contracted in the service. In the fall of same year he moved to Jamestown, Ottawa County, Mich.; purchased 160 acres of wild land and engaged in clearing up a farm. In the spring of 1864 he was elected School Inspector of the township, and the following spring was elected Supervisor, which office he held for several years. In the fall of 1876, on account of poor health, he rented his farm and engaged in the mercantile business at Jamestown Center. In the winter of 1880 he sold his store and farm, and the following spring moved to Antrim County, and purchased a farm near Eastport. In the spring of 1881, he was elected Supervisor. In politics he was a Republican.

GEORGE WILLARD

Member of the State Board of Education, 1857-63; member of the Board of Regents of the University of Michigan, 1864-74; Representative from Calhoun County, 1867-8; Delegate from Calhoun County to the Constitutional Convention of 1867; and member of Congress, 1873-5 and 1875-7. Was born in Bolton, Vt., Mar. 20, 1824. His ancestor, Simeon Willard, settled in Concord, Mass., in 1635. He came with his father to Michigan in 1836, and graduated at Kalamazoo College in 1844. After service as a teacher he became an Episcopal minister, and was rector at Coldwater, Battle Creek and Kalamazoo. He resigned and became a professor in Kalamazoo College. In 1872 he was selected delegate to the National Republican Convention. In politics he was a Republican. He was editor and proprietor of the Battle Creek *Journal* after 1868, establishing a daily in 1872. He died at Battle Creek, Mar. 26, 1901.

ISAAC W. WILLARD

Delegate from Kalamazoo County to the Second Convention of Assent, 1836; and Delegate from Van Buren County to the Constitutional Convention of 1850. Was born in Worcester County, Mass., Dec. 1, 1803. He received a common school education, and engaged in business at Rochester, Vt. He came to Michigan in 1827, and in 1828 engaged in the mercantile business with Gov. Barry at White Pigeon, and the firm had an extensive business in several counties, there being only one other store in southwestern Michigan. From 1833 to 1840 he was a merchant at Kalamazoo, then engaged in lumbering and farming at Paw Paw, and built a flour mill and a saw mill, distillery, plank road, etc. He was a Postmaster and Supervisor, and held other offices. He was the first Clerk of the U. S. court at White Pigeon, and was timber agent under Pierce for Michigan and other states. Politically he was a Democrat. He died Apr. 8, 1879.

WM. WILLARD, JR.

Senator from the Thirty-second District, 1869-70. His postoffice address was Ontonagon. (Further data not obtainable).

A. MILAN WILLETT

Representative from Ionia County, 1881-2 and 1883-4. Was born in Oswego County, N. Y., Apr. 18, 1829. He received a common school education, learned the joiners' trade, and taught winters. He settled in Ionia County in 1854, engaged in building until 1860, then became a farmer. He served for thirteen months as Captain of Co. I, Berdan's U. S. Sharpshooters, resigning from disability. He was Supervisor several terms, and president of the agricultural society. Politically he was a Republican.

CHARLES JOSEPH WILLETT

Member of the Board of Regents of the University of Michigan, 1884-92. Was born at Essex, N. Y., June 5, 1849, son of Joseph J. and Cornelia A. (Whallow) Willett. He prepared for college at Essex Academy and the Grand Rapids (Michigan) High School, entered the University of Michigan, and was graduated Bachelor of Arts in 1871. For one year after graduation he was Superintendent of Schools at Chelsea, Mich. May 13, 1874, he was married to Harriet S. Crossman. From 1872 to 1876 he was employed in a bank at St. Louis, Mich. Meanwhile he had studied law, and on Jan. 8, 1877, he was admitted to practice law in all the courts of the State. Nov. 9, 1891, he was admitted to practice in the Supreme Court of the United States, and Oct. 16, 1893, in the Supreme Court of California. He served on the School Board of St. Louis and filled various other local offices. He was Prosecuting Attorney for Gratiot County, 1880-2. In 1883 he was elected Regent of the University and took his seat the following January, serving the full term of eight years.

JOHN WILLETT

Representative from Genesee County, 1877-8 and 1879-80. Was born in New Brunswick, N. J., in 1820. In 1822 he removed to western New York, and there received a common school education. He graduated from the Geneva Medical College in 1846, removed to Flint, Mich., and began the practice of his profession. In 1862 he received a commission as surgeon in the 8th Mich. Infantry, and remained in the service until the close of the war, returned to Flint and engaged in the drug business. He was elected Alderman in 1870. In politics he was a Republican.

ALBERT WILLIAMS

Attorney General, 1865-7. Was born at Halifax, Vt., Feb. 8, 1817, of Welsh descent. His father was a surgeon in the War of 1812. He received an academical education, and came to Michigan in 1844. He studied law at Monroe, and was admitted in 1845. He engaged in practice in Ionia. He was Prosecuting Attorney from 1847 to 1851, and acting County Clerk in 1853-4. He was a Democrat until 1854, but helped organize the Republican party, and was on the committee of resolutions and also nominations. He issued a political address which was widely circulated, and for a time edited the first Republican paper in Ionia County. He was County Treasurer from 1855 to 1859, and Prosecuting Attorney from 1861 to 1863. In 1870 he joined the Prohibition party, and was their candidate for Supreme Judge in 1872, in 1874 for Attorney General, and in 1876 for Governor. He was a Republican in 1887.

ALPHEUS S. WILLIAMS

Member of Congress, 1875-7 and 1877-8. Was born at Saybrook, Conn., Sept. 20, 1810; graduated at Yale College in 1831; was a student in the Yale Law School in 1832 and 1833; traveled in Europe from 1834 to 1836; removed to Detroit, Mich., in 1837, and commenced the practice of law; was Judge of Probate for Wayne County, 1840-4; and was proprietor and editor of the Detroit *Advertiser*, 1843 to 1848. He was Lieutenant Colonel of the 1st Mich. Infantry Vol. in the Mexican War, 1847-8; entered the union army as Brigadier General of volunteers by appointment of President Lincoln, August 1861; commanded the twelfth corps in the battles of South Mountain, Antietam and Gettysburg, and the twentieth corps in the siege of Atlanta on "Sherman's march to the sea," and in the campaign of the Carolinas, and was mustered out of the service in January, 1866. He was appointed in August, 1866, one of the commissioners to adjust the military claims of Missouri. He was minister resident to the Republic of Salvador, 1866-9. In 1874 he was elected to Congress on the Democratic and Reform tickets; was re-elected in 1876. He died at Washington, D. C., Dec. 28, 1878, before expiration of his term. The Loyal Legion of Detroit erected a statue of him.

ANTHONY WILLIAMS

Representative from Lapeer County, 1883-4. Was born in Superior, Mich., Sept. 29, 1836; removed to Dryden in 1843, and to Attica in 1851; was engaged in farming and lumbering; was several terms a Supervisor, and held other offices. Politically he was a Democrat.

ASA WILLIAMS

Representative from Washtenaw County, 1845. Was born in Norwich, Conn., in 1802. He came to Michigan in 1824, and was the owner of a large farm in Liam, Washtenaw County. He was appointed Brigadier General of State militia by Governor Cass. He died in 1869.

BUEAL M. WILLIAMS

Representative from Van Buren County, 1863-4 and 1865-6. Was born in Granville, Mass., Dec. 6, 1812. At the age of sixteen he learned the potters' trade, and continued in that business until he had saved money enough for his education, when he entered Yale College, and graduated in 1838 or 1839. Going to Ohio, he taught select school for several years, at Hudson and Shalersville; then went to Pittsburg, Pa., and taught until 1854. He then came to Lawrence, Mich., and purchased land; went to Kentucky and taught school until the war of 1861-4, when he came back to Lawrence, and took an active part in support of the union. He was Representative from Van Buren County as a Republican. He engaged in real estate and loan agency until his death, Feb. 7, 1878.

CHARLES W. WILLIAMS

Representative, 1889-90, from the Leelanau District, comprising the counties of Leelanau and Benzie. Was born at Mt. Morris, Livingston County, N. Y., Apr. 21, 1834. His parents moved to the Township of Flint, Genesee County, Mich., in 1836, where he was brought up on a farm, receiving his education in a rural district and the union school of the village of Flint. In 1857 he went West to seek his fortune, returning in 1858, satisfied with Michigan. He was married in 1859, and in 1864, settled upon a homestead in Leelanau County. He held the office of Postmaster six years, Township Clerk seven years, Justice of the Peace eight years, also School Inspector, Township Treasurer and Supervisor four years, County Treasurer two years, Judge of Probate twelve years. In politics he was a Republican after 1860. He died Aug. 24, 1913.

EDWIN R. WILLIAMS

Representative from Ionia County, 1885-6. Was born in West Bloomfield, Mich., Sept. 20, 1836, and was a farmer at Orange, and a breeder of fine stock. He held many local offices. He was elected Representative as a Fusionist.

EDWIN S. WILLIAMS

Representative from the Second District of Berrien County, 1895-6 and 1897-8. Was born in Milton Township, Cass County, Mich., Aug. 12, 1845; moved with his parents to Berrien County in 1848, and again to Cass County in 1852, where he remained until 1890, when he removed to Niles, Berrien County. His early education was very limited, being confined to a few winter months in a district school prior to 1860. At the outbreak of the war he enlisted in the 57th Regiment, Ill. Vols. and served under Grant in the Donelson and Shiloh campaign, and later under John A. Logan in the 15th corps during the Atlanta campaign. On returning from the war he engaged in farming, and later in a general produce and live stock shipping business; was for a number of years a member of the Chicago Produce Exchange, during which time he was engaged as wholesale commission merchant. Since locating at Niles he engaged in the ice, coal and wood business; also implement and carriage business. In politics a Republican. He held the office of Alderman of the city of Niles.

FITCH R. WILLIAMS

Senator from the Thirtieth District, 1877-8. Was born in Amenia, N. Y., Dec. 18, 1834. He removed to Michigan in 1845, graduated from the Michigan University in 1858, and was immediately appointed instructor in the literary department. While teaching he attended lectures in the law department. He was, for two years, a professor in Albion College, and commenced the practice of law at Albion in 1866. He removed to Elk Rapids, in 1870. He was Prosecuting Attorney of that county. He acted as Judge of Probate under appointment by the Governor. In politics he was a Republican.

GARDNER D. WILLIAMS

Representative from Saginaw County, 1835 and 1836 and 1840; Delegate from Saginaw County to the Second Convention of Assent, 1836; and Senator from the Sixth District, 1845-6. Was born at Concord, Mass., Sept. 9, 1804, and came with his father's family to Detroit in 1815, and from 1819 to 1827 resided at Silver Lake. In 1827 he engaged in the fur trade at Saginaw, as agent of the American Fur Company. He spoke the Indian tongue. He was Commissioner of Internal Improvements, County Judge and Tresaurer, and the first Mayor of Saginaw City. He died at Saginaw Dec. 10, 1858.

GEORGE WILLIAMS

Senator, 1915-16, from the Thirty-second District, comprising the counties of Baraga, Houghton, Keweenaw and Ontonagon. Was born at Oswestry, Wales, Sept. 24, 1869. In 1883 he located at Marquette, Mich., his education being acquired in the public schools of that city. At an early age he began working on the railroad and became general agent of the Copper Range Railroad. Married. In politics a Republican.

HARVEY WILLIAMS

Senator from the Twenty-first District, 1857-8. Was born in Manchester, Vt., in 1812, and settled in Chester, Mich., in 1837, and was prominently identified with the early history of Eaton County. The first political county convention met at his house. He held town offices, was twelve years County Treasurer, and a successful real estate agent. Politically he was a Republican. He died at Charlotte, Jan. 18, 1867.

HUBERT G. WILLIAMS

Representative from Marquette County and other counties, 1869-70. Did not sit in the extra session of 1870. His postoffice address was Marquette. (Further data not obtainable).

JAMES A. WILLIAMS

Representative from Branch County, 1860-70 and 1871-2. Was a native of Cayuga County, N. Y., and settled in Algansee, Mich., in 1854. He was the first resident physician of that township. For ten years he was Supervisor of his township, and County Superintendent of Schools two years.

JEREMIAH D. WILLIAMS

Representative from Washtenaw County, 1855-6. Was born in Sempronious, N. Y., May 2, 1815. He came to Michigan in 1828 with his father who settled on a farm in Webster, Washtenaw County. He received a common school education, and attended an academy at Ann Arbor for one year. In 1839 he was appointed Postmaster at Webster. He held the town positions of Supervisor, Clerk, Treasurer, Justice, and other offices. He was for ten years auditor of the Washtenaw Fire Insurance Company, and was secretary of the County Pioneer Society. He was a Whig until 1854, then a Republican. Deceased.

JOHN R. WILLIAMS

Delegate from the First District to the Constitutional Convention of 1835; and Delegate from Wayne County to the Second Convention of Assent, 1836. Was born in Detroit, Mich., May 4, 1782. He was in trade there from 1802 to 1832, except from 1812 to 1815. He was a Captain of artillery in the War of 1812, and was included in the surrender of Gen. Hull. He was one of the first trustees of the University of Michigan in 1821, and president of the Bank of Michigan in 1818. He prepared the first charter of Detroit, and was the first Mayor in 1824, also filled that position in 1825-46. He was three years president of the Board of Education; took great interest in military affairs; commanded the territorial troops during the threatened Black Hawk War, and was Senior Major General of State militia at the time of his death, Oct. 20, 1854.

JOSEPH R. WILLIAMS

Delegate from St. Joseph County to the Constitutional Convention of 1850; Senator from the Sixteenth District, 1861; and Acting Lieutenant Governor, 1861. Was born in Taunton, Mass., Nov. 14, 1808; and graduated at Harvard College in 1831. He studied law with "honest" John Davis, in Worcester, Mass., was admitted to the bar, practiced at New Bedford, Mass., and settled in Constantine, Mich., in 1839, which was his home until his death, June 15, 1861. He was president pro tem of the Senate in 1861. He died before the close of his term, and was succeeded by Henry H. Riley. He was the first president of the Michigan Agricultural College. In politics he was a Republican.

THEODORE WILLIAMS

Representative from Wayne County, 1838. Was the son of Gen. John R. Williams, and was born in Albany, N. Y., July 5, 1808. He was trained in business at Detroit. He was City Register, 1830-5, County Clerk, 1841-2, City Treasurer, 1844-5, and several times an Alderman. He was originally a Whig, but in later years a Democrat. He died Oct. 28, 1871.

THOMAS H. WILLIAMS

Representative from Jackson County, 1887-8. Was born at Kirtland, O., May 27, 1844. In 1862 he enlisted in the 103d O. Vol. Infantry, and served until the close of the war. He came to Michigan 1865, was a carpenter until 1871, then began work in the car department of the M. C. R. R. at Jackson, where he remained many years. He was an Alderman, and commander of the G. A. R. post. Politically he was a Republican.

WALTER W. WILLIAMS

Representative from the First District of Eaton County, 1887-8 and 1889-90. Was born and brought up on a farm in Lima, Washtenaw County, Mich., where his father settled in 1825, and was a member of the House of Representatives in 1845. Mr. Williams' older brother was a member also in 1869. He lived on the farm until sixteen years of age, then spent several years at Ann Arbor in school. In 1872 he married Miss Mary A. Whitaker. He then spent three years as a commercial traveler and two years "roughing it" on the Western frontier. In 1878 he settled near Eaton Rapids on a farm. Although from a family who are all Democratis he was an active Republican in politics.

WILLIAM B. WILLIAMS

Senator from the Seventeenth District, 1867-8 and 1869-70; Delegate from Allegan County to the Constitutional Convention of 1867; and member of Congress, 1873-5 and 1875-7. Was born at Pittsford, N. Y., July 28, 1826. Brought up on a farm, he received a fair education, and was a teacher. He studied law in Rochester, N. Y., and graduated from the State and national law school at Bellston Springs in 1851, and began practice at Rochester, N. Y. He settled at Allegan, Mich., in 1855. He was Judge of Probate eight years; served as Captain in the 5th Mich. Cavalry from 1872 to June, 1863, resigning from disability; was commandant of camp and organized the 28th Mich. Infantry; member of the Board of State Charities, 1871 to 1873; and Railroad Commissioner from 1877 to 1883. He was elected as Congressman in November, 1873, to fill a vacancy caused by the death of W. D. Foster. Politically he was a Republican. He died at Allegan, Mar. 4, 1905.

WILLIAM D. WILLIAMS

Representative from Ontonagon County, 1869-70. Was born at Lima, in 1835. He graduated from the University of Michigan in 1857, studied law at Detroit, was admitted to the bar in 1859, and settled in practice at Ontonagon, but later resided at Marquette. He was Prosecuting Attorney of Ontonagon County. He was elected Judge of the 12th Circuit in 1875, and was re-elected in 1881 and 1887. In politics he was a Democrat. He died Nov. 27, 1893.

ZEBULON WILLIAMS

Representative from Hillsdale County, 1848. Was born at Haverstraw, N. Y., Jan. 24, 1795. He learned the trade of a carpenter, settled at Phelps, N. Y., in 1820, worked at his trade until 1825, when he became a farmer in Clarkson, N. Y. In 1834 he came to Adrian, Mich., He remained there four years, and in 1838 settled on land in Wheatland, Hillsdale County. He was supervisor four years, Clerk and Treasurer of his town. He died Nov. 10, 1872.

GEORGE W. WILLIS

Representative from the First District of Bay County, 1901-2. Was born in St. Charles, Mich., Aug. 18, 1859. His education was obtained in the public schools and Parson's Business College in Saginaw. Graduating from the latter institution when seventeen years of age, he entered the employ of Eddy & Avery, where he remained sixteen years, after which time he was a contractor. Married. He served as Alderman and member of the Board of Education, and held the office of Deputy Game Warden. In politics a Republican.

MARK WILLIS

Representative from Sanilac County, 1901-2 and 1903-4. Was born in 1832, in Somerset England, where his early education was obtained. In 1846 he emigrated to Canada, where he remained nine years, coming to Lexington, Sanilac County, in 1855. He was married. He was a successful farmer; also engaged in the lumber business. In politics he was a strong Republican. He held the office of Highway Commissioner, and was School Director.

FRANK LESLIE WILLISON

Senator, 1917-18, from the Sixth District, comprising the counties of Kalamazoo and St. Joseph. Was born in Barry County, Mich., Aug. 18, 1861, of Scotch and Irish parentage. He was educated in the district schools and at Kalamazoo College. He lived and worked on the farm until twenty-five years of age, and later worked for nearly five years in a hardware store; then engaged in the hardware and implement business. Married. In politics a Democrat.

BARON B. WILLITS

Representative from Hillsdale ounty, 1841 and 1865-6. Was born in Independence, N. J., Jan. 1, 1812. By occupation he was a farmer, politically a Republican. He settled on a farm in Cambria, Hillsdale County, in 1835, and resided there until his death, Sept. 23, 1873.

EDWIN WILLITS

Member of the State Board of Education, 1861-73; member of the Constitutional Commission of 1873; member of Congress, 1877-9 to 1881-3. Was born at Otto,

N. Y., Apr. 24, 1830, and removed to Michigan in 1836. He graduated at the University in 1855, and located at Monroe in 1856, where he studied law with Isaac P. Christiancy, until his admission to the bar in 1857. He was Prosecuting Attorney of Monroe County; was appointed Postmaster at Monroe in 1863, by President Lincoln, and was removed by President Johnson, Oct. 15, 1866; and was editor of the Monroe *Commercial* from 1856 to 1861. In politics he was a Republican. After his retirement from Congress he resumed law practice at Monroe, but became principal of the State Normal School at Ypsilanti in 1883. In 1885 he was elected president of the State Agricultural College, and served in that position after July 1, 1885. Under his efficient management the college greatly increased in the number of students, and in popularity with the people. He died at Washington, D. C., Oct. 24, 1896, where he was acting Secretary of Agriculture.

GEORGE E. WILLITTS

Representative from the First District of Calhoun County, 1907-8. Was born at Saline, Washtenaw County, Mich., Jan. 28, 1857, where he resided until six years of age when, with his parents, he removed to Newton, Calhoun County. His education was obtained in the district schools of Calhoun County, a select school at Athens, the Union City High School and Albion College. While obtaining his education and later he devoted considerable time to teaching. In 1892 he was married to Emma L. Southworth. Mr. Willitts filled the positions of clerk, correspondence clerk and acting secretary of the State Board of Health. He founded the Marshall *News* which he edited and published eight years. In politics a Democrat. He was twice elected Supervisor of the first ward of Marshall.

WARREN J. WILLITS

Senator from the Eighth District, Kalamazoo and St. Joseph counties, 1887-8. Was born in Hillsdale County, Aug. 19, 1853. By occupation he was a manufacturer. He held the offices of Township Clerk and Trustee in village council. He was elected to the Senate on the Republican ticket.

GEORGE WILLOUGHBY

Representative from the Second District of Oakland County, 1909-10 and 1911-12. Was born in White Lake Township, Oakland County, Mich., Mar. 6, 1850, of English and French descent. He acquired his education in the district schools. His early life was spent on a farm until the age of thirty-seven, later embarking in the produce business in which he engaged. Married. He held the offices of Justice of the Peace, Township Treasurer and Supervisor; a member of the Clyde lodge, I. O. O. F. In politics a Republican.

EDWARD H. C. WILSON

Justice of the Supreme Court, 1856-7. Was selected in November, 1856, to take the place of Warner Wing who had resigned. (Further data not obtainable).

EUGENE A. WILSON

Member of the State Board of Education, 1893-8. Was born at Ridgeway, Lena-wee County, Sept. 21, 1854; attended district school at Ridgeway until nine-teen years of age; spent two years in Tecumseh High School, graduating in 1875; entered the State Normal in 1876 and graduated from the literary department in 1879. Being of limited means he supported himself while in school by teach-ing school winters and working in the harvest field during summer vacation; completing his school course he began teaching. He taught first at Mt. Pleasant and afterwards five years at Vassar. He was secretary of the County Board of School Examiners of Lenawee County in 1890-1; was Superintendent of Schools at Paw Paw two years, and Superintendent of Schools at Benton Harbor. In 1882 he was married to Miss Kittie G. Fessenden of Mount Pleasant. In politics a Republican. He was elected member of the State Board of Education in November, 1892.

FARWELL A. WILSON

Representative from Midland, Clare and Gladwin counties, 1887-8. Was born July 18, 1841, in Vienna, Mich. He received a common school education. He was first a farmer, then ran a saw-mill for five years. In 1871 he removed to Isabella County, where he bought pine land, built a saw-mill, and was inter-ested in other business. Politically he was a Democrat. He died Jan. 22, 1896, at Ann Arbor; buried in Glenwood Cemetery, Flint.

JEREMIAH C. WILSON

Representative from Oakland County, 1867-8. Settled in Rochester, Oakland County, 1857. He was a graduate of the State University, and of Castleton Medical College. In partnership with his brother he had an extensive medical practice. They were also interested in manufactures, and built and operated the Eureka mills for eight years. They were also engaged in mercantile business.

JOHN B. WILSON

Representative from Lapeer County, 1861-2 and 1883-4. Was born in Green-field, Pa., Oct. 22, 1822, and came with his parents to Detroit in 1824. In 1831 he returned to Vermont with his mother, and afterwards lived in Rochester, N. Y., and Conneautville, Pa. He settled in Arcadia, Mich., as a farmer in 1848. He removed to Lapeer in 1887, was engaged in lumbering, and built the first saw-mill in Arcadia, also did a large business in real estate and building. He was a Supervisor eleven years, Justice sixteen years, and a State Road Com-missioner. As a Legislator he was a Republican; later was a Democrat. He died at Washington, D. C., June 18, 1907.

JOSHUA WILSON

Representative from Sanilac County, 1883-4. Was born in Pickering, Canada, Jan. 9, 1827. He came with his father's family to the northern part of St. Clair

County, Mich., in 1841, of which Sanilac County was then a part. He was a farmer, politically a Republican. He held the offices of Town Clerk, School Inspector, Supervisor, Town Treasurer, and Justice.

LOUIS T. N. WILSON

Senator from the Sixteenth District, 1855-6. Was born at Milo, N. Y., Sept. 24, 1821. He came with his father to Ovid, Mich., in 1835, and learned the tailor's trade at Coldwater. He studied for the ministry and was licensed as a Methodist minister. Later he studied law and was admitted in 1843. He was an anti-slavery Whig, and made the first abolition speech ever delivered in Coldwater. In 1851 he was elected Justice, and in 1855, as a Republican he was Senator from Branch County. He was Prosecuting Attorney two terms. In 1875 he removed to Minneapolis and practiced law for two years, but returned to Coldwater in 1877, and continued his professional career until his death, Apr. 26, 1887.

PHILO WILSON

Representative from Lenawee County, 1842 and 1850. Settled in Canandaigua, Mich., about 1836, and came from the State of New York. In politics he was a Democrat. He removed to Adrian about 1870, and died there.

ROBERT S. WILSON

Senator from the Second District, 1843-4. Came from Alleghany County, N. Y., to Ann Arbor, Mich., in 1835. He was a man of ability, and as a lawyer, had great influence with the jury. He was Judge of Probate of Washtenaw County from 1836 to 1840. In 1855 he removed to Chicago, and was a Police Justice in that city for many years. He died in 1883.

THOMAS M. WILSON

Representative from Macomb County, 1861-2 and 1875-6. Was born in Shelburne, Mass., Jan. 6, 1820, and at an early age removed to Madison County, N. Y., where he received an academical education. He came to New Baltimore, Mich., in 1855, and engaged in business as a commission and forwarding merchant. He removed to Lansing in 1877, and was Clerk of the Board of State Auditors. Deceased.

WILLIAM B. WILSON

Representative from Muskegon County, 1885-6. Was born at Palmyra, N. Y., in 1829, and removed with his parents to Lenawee County, Mich., in 1837. He was with his father in business at Canandaigua, then several years clerk at Adrian, afterwards in business at Hillsdale until 1875. He became then a resident of Muskegon, and was Deputy County Treasurer, later a druggist. He was grand commander of Knights Templars of Michigan in 1880-1. He was elected Representative as a Fusionist.

JACOB M. WILTSE

Representative from Saginaw County, 1883-4. Was born in Saginaw, Nov. 13, 1839. He received a common school education. His principal occupation was that of a farmer. He held the office of Justice fifteen years, and Supervisor five years. In politics he was a Democrat.

EDWIN B. WINANS

Representative from Livingston County, 1861-2 and 1863-4; member of the Constitutional Convention of 1867; member of Congress, 1883-5 and 1885-7; and Governor of Michigan, 1891-3. Was born at Avon, N. Y., May 16, 1826, and removed with his parents to Michigan in 1834; he received a common school education, but at the age of twenty entered Albion College, where he remained two and a half years preparatory to entering the law department of the University. The discovery of gold in California induced him to leave college before finishing his course, and he started for that State, by the overland route, in March, 1850, arriving there July 20, following. He engaged in placer mining and other enterprises until 1856, when he engaged in banking in the town of Rough-and-Ready; in 1858 he closed out his California interests and returned to Michigan, settling on a farm of 400 acres in Hamburg, Livingston County. In politics he was a Democrat. He served in the Legislature as Representative in 1861-4; was a member of the Constitutional Convention of 1867; Judge of Probate from 1877 to 1881; and member of Congress in 1883-7. He was married Sept. 3, 1855, to Elizabeth Galloway, whose parents were pioneers of Livingston County. He received the Democratic nomination for Governor in 1890, and was elected. He returned to his farm in 1893 and died there July 4, 1894.

AMAZIAH WINCHELL

Representative from Ingham County, 1850. Was born in Plattsburg, N. Y., in 1810. He came to Detroit in 1833, lived in Lima until 1836, then settled in Ingham, Ingham County. There were only three houses in the county at that time. He was a farmer, in politics a Democrat. He was Sheriff of Ingham County four years, County Superintendent of Poor five years, Drain Commissioner two years, and held other offices. He was Orderly Sergeant in the Toledo War. He summoned the first jury, and opened the first court in Ingham County.

JEROME WINCHELL

Representative from Allegan County, 1877-8. Was born in Union, Ind., June 8, 1846. When young he removed to Wisconsin, and from thence to Minnesota territory. After receiving an academical education, at the age of seventeen, he engaged as teacher in public schools, which calling was abandoned a few years later for that of the printers' art. In 1870 he came from Chicago to Michigan, and established at Plainwell the *Allegan County Republic*, of which he was editor and proprietor, and actively identified with every enterprise for the improvement of the village. In politics he was a Republican.

CHARLES T. WINEGAR

Senator, 1913-14, from the Thirty-first District, comprising the counties of Alger, Dickinson, Gogebic, Iron and Marquette. Was born at Escanaba, Mich., July 28, 1878. He graduated from the Escanaba High School in 1893, and from the law department of the University of Michigan in 1904. In 1910, he was married to Alta W. Poppleton, of Detroit. He was engaged in the practice of law. In politics a National Progressive.

AUSTIN E. WING

Territorial Delegate in Congress, 1825-7, 1827-9 and 1831-3; Representative from Monroe County, 1842; and member of the Board of Regents of the University of Michigan, 1845-50. Was born in Conway, Berkshire County, Mass., Feb. 3, 1792. He graduated from Williams College in 1814 with honor. He came to Detroit in 1814, but soon settled in Monroe. He was for a number of years Sheriff of the Territory of Michigan, studied and practiced the profession of law and was also a farmer. He was United States Marshal under Polk's administration; and for many years a leading man in the affairs of the Territory and State. In politics he was a Democrat. He died Aug. 25, 1849.

GILES M. WING

Representative from Manistee County, 1881-2. Was born in Canada East, July 23, 1835, and moved to Illinois in 1844, where he lived with his parents on a farm until 1853. Then he went to Wisconsin and engaged in the lumber business. In 1867 he moved to Manistee, Mich., with his family. There he built a mill, and after that time engaged in the lumbering business. He was three times elected Supervisor. Politically he was a Republican.

MYRON WING

Representative from Barry County, 1897-8. Was born in the town of Eagle, Wyoming County, N. Y., in 1837, where he acquired a district school education, and spent his early days on his father's farm. At the age of twenty-six he came to Michigan, locating on a farm in Ross Township, Kalamazoo County, where he lived for eighteen years, then he moved to Barry Township, Barry County, locating on the farm. His life occupation was that of a farmer. In politics he was a Republican. He was Justice of the Peace of his township three terms.

WARNER WING

Representative from Monroe County, 1837; Senator from the Second District, 1838-9; and Justice of the Supreme Court, 1845-56. Was born in Marietta, O., Sept. 19, 1805, and was the son of Enoch and Mary (Oliver) Wing, an old New England family. His father removed from Conway, Mass., to Marietta, in 1796. In 1817, at the age of twelve, Judge Wing came to Detroit, and removed to Monroe in 1828. He attended law school at Northampton, Mass., and also studied law in the office of Judge Woodbridge, at Detroit. As early as 1833 he was engaged in the practice of the law in partnership with Hon. David A. Noble, at Monroe. In 1840 he became law partner with Gov. McClelland, with whom he practiced until 1845, when he became Circuit Judge, and a Judge of the Supreme Court. In 1851 he became Chief Justice, which position he held until 1856, when he resigned to act as general counsel of the Lake Shore Railroad. He was eminent as a lawyer and judge, and his able opinions are found in the State reports. In politics he was a Democrat. He became a member of the Presbyterian Church at Monroe in 1843. He died at Monroe, Mar. 10, 1876.

WASHINGTON WING

Representative from Livingston County, 1846. Was born in Sullivan, N. Y., Dec. 3, 1808. He came to Scio, Washtenaw County, in 1830, and settled with his father's family. In 1835 he settled in Iosco, Livingston County. In 1836 and 1837 he aided Godfroy in getting the Indians to Marshall, preparatory to their removal to the West, it being the remnant of a tribe numbering 150. He removed to Elgin, Ill., in 1846, and was a farmer there. He held various official positions. He was a Republican after 1856.

RICHARD WINSOR

Representative from Huron County, 1863-4 and 1865-6; Delegate from Huron County to the Constitutional Convention of 1867; and Senator from the Twenty-fifth District, 1869-70, and from the Twenty-second District, 1881-2. Was born in the county of Middlesex, Ont., in 1839. He settled in Huron County, Mich., when a young man, studied law, was admitted to the bar, and was Presocuting Attorney several terms. He resided at Port Austin in 1887, where he had a large law practice, and was also engaged in banking. In politics he was a Republican.

JAMES WINTERS

Representative from Calhoun County, 1853-4. Was born in Chenango, N. Y., Aug. 17, 1805. He came to Marengo, Calhoun County, Mich., in 1836, and from 1839 to 1842, was foreman of a large cooper shop in that town. He then removed to Athens, same county, and for several years was Supervisor, and held other town offices, and was also Postmaster. In 1861 he raised a company of one hundred men, and became Captain of Company E, 6th Mich. Infantry, but soon resigned from ill health. He afterwards drilled the officers of the 13th Mich. By trade he was a cooper; politically a Republican. He died Jan. 15, 1882.

CHAUNCEY W. WISNER

Senator, 1887-8, 1889-90 and 1891-2, from the Eighteenth District, Saginaw County. Was born Apr. 26, 1836, in Mt. Morris, Livingston County, N. Y. In politics he was a Republican prior to 1872; was a Liberal Republican delegate to the Cincinnati Convention when Horace Greeley was nominated in 1872, and a Democrat since. He practiced law in East Saginaw from 1863 to 1877, then removed to Bridgeport on a farm. He held the office of City Attorney of Flint, Prosecuting Attorney of Genesee County, Mayor of East Saginaw, and Supervisor of Bridgeport Township two terms. In 1872 he was a candidate for Congress on the Greeley ticket. He was elected to the Senate of 1887-8, 1889-90 and again re-elected to that of 1891-2. He resigned before the extra session of 1892. Deceased.

GEORGE W. WISNER

Representative from Oakland County, 1837. Was born in Cayuga County, N. Y., in 1812. He was the son of Moses Wisner, a Colonel of the War of 1812, and a brother of Gov. Wisner, of Michigan. At the age of fifteen he was apprenticed to learn the trade of printer. In 1833 at the age of twenty-one, in company with William H. Dey, he established the New York *Sun*, the first cheap daily paper in that city, of which he was editor. The work broke his health and in 1835 he settled at Pontiac, Mich., studied law, was admitted in 1837, soon acquired distinction, and in 1838 was Prosecuting Attorney of Oakland County. In 1847 he became editor of the Detroit *Advertiser*. He was a leading Whig, a fine lawyer, an eloquent speaker in a political campaign, and held a leading place in the remembrance of the pioneers of Oakland County. He died in September, 1849.

MOSES WISNER

Governor of Michigan, 1859-61. Was born at Springport, Cayuga County, N. Y., June 3, 1815. He was brought up to agricultural labor, and received only a common school education. In 1837 he came to Michigan, and purchased a farm in Lapeer County. After two years he gave up farming, removed to Pontiac, studied law with George W. Wisner and Rufus Hosmer, and was admitted to practice in 1841. He established his office at Lapeer, and became Prosecuting Attorney of that county. He soon removed to Pontiac, as one of the firm of Wisner & Hosmer, He was an anti-slavery Whig, but took little part in politics, until 1852, when he openly espoused the cause of freedom for the territories. On the organization of the Republican party in 1854, he was nominated for Attorney-General, but declined. The same year he was nominated for Congress, but was defeated by George W. Peck, the Democratic candidate. In 1856 he was on the stump for Fremont, and in 1857 he was one of the Republican candidates for United States Senator. After his term as Governor he returned to his law practice. In 1862 he raised the 22nd Mich. Infantry, largely from Oakland County, of which he took command, and went to Kentucky, in September, 1863. He was a great lawyer, an excellent Governor, a patriot, and has left his impress on the institutions of the State. In his valedictory message was embodied the principles that governed his own action in the war and that governed largely the actions of the people of the State. His eloquence was that of conviction and action, and the people believed in him. He died of typhoid fever at Lexington, Ky., Jan. 5, 1864.

ELIJAH B. WITHERBEE

Senator from the Sixth District, 1847. Was born in Hopkinton, Mass., July 19, 1804; received an academical education; became a clerk in Boston and Medford; went into business for himself until 1836; then came to Michigan, built a saw-mill in Genesee County, and engaged in the manufacture of lumber. In 1841 he removed to Flint, and was soon after appointed receiver of the land office. In 1845 he entered into the drug business. In politics he was a Whig. He died while the Legislature was in session, Feb. 20, 1847.

BENJAMIN F. H. WITHERELL

Delegate from Wayne County to the Second Convention of Assent, 1836; Senator from the First District, 1840-1; Representative from Wayne County, 1842; member of the Board of Regents of the University of Michigan, 1848-52; Delegate from Wayne County to the Constitutional Convention of 1850; and Justice of the Supreme Court, 1857. Was born at Fair Haven, Vt., Aug. 4, 1797. By reason of turbulence on the part of the Indians, preceding and following the War of 1812, the family of Judge James Witherell did not come permanently to reside in Michigan until 1817, the subject of this sketch up to that time pursuing his studies, which were classical if not collegiate. He was admitted to the bar in Detroit in 1819. He was Justice of the Peace, 1824; City Recorder, 1828; Judge of Probate, 1834-5, and Prosecuting Attorney, 1835 to 1839. In 1843 a district criminal court was organized, embracing the counties of Wayne, Oakland, Washtenaw and Jackson, and Mr. Witherell was appointed Judge, holding the position until 1848, when the court was abolished. In the fall of 1843 Judge Witherell tried one Chorr, at Ann Arbor, for the murder of a neighbor named Dunn, with whom he had had trouble. Chorr was convicted and sentenced to death, but pending a new trial, made his escape. This was the only capital sentence ever pronounced under the law of this State, the death penalty being soon after abrogated. He was Circuit Judge 1857 to 1867, acting also a portion of the time as Judge of the Recorder's Court. He held for a time the honorary position of historiographer of Detroit, was president of the State Historical Society, and of the Soldier and Sailors' Monument Association, and held high positions in the State militia, including that of Major General. He contributed to the press and to the public archives many papers of great literary and historical value. In politics he was a Democrat. He died in Detroit, June 26, 1867.

JAMES WITHERELL

Judge of the Territorial Supreme Court, 1808-28; Secretary and Acting Governor of Michigan Territory, 1828-30. Was born in Mansfield, Mass., June 16, 1759. He served through the greater part of the War of the Revolution, entering the service as a private, and rising to the rank of Adjutant in a Massachusetts regiment. He studied medicine and law, and settled in Vermont where he held

many positions of trust, including that of Judge, member of the Governor's
Council, and of the Legislature. He was elected to Congress in 1807, but resigned his seat to accept an appointment by President Jefferson, as one of the
Judges of the Supreme Court of the Territory of Michigan, coming here in 1808.
He held a local military command during the War of 1812, specially raised for
the defense of Detroit, and it is reported that on the surrender of the town by
Gen. Hull, he broke his sword to escape the mortification of relinquishing it to
an enemy. In January, 1828, after a service of twenty years, Judge Witherell
relinquished the judgeship to become secretary of the Territory. He held this
position until May, 1830, and during the first three months of 1830 was acting
Governor. He raised a family of several children. The late Judge B. F. H.
Witherell was his son, and a daughter, Mrs. Thomas Palmer, was the mother
of Senator Thos. W. Palmer. Judge Witherell died in Detroit, Jan. 9, 1838.

SOLOMON L. WITHEY

Senator from the Twenty-ninth District, 1861-2; and Delegate from Kent
County to the Constitutional Convention of 1867. Was born at St. Albans, Vt.,
Apr. 21, 1820. His father, Solomon Withey, known to early residents of Michigan as General Withey, emigrated to Grand Rapids in 1836 with his family.
Mr. Withey received a common school and academical education, and in 1839
entered the law office of Rathbone & Martin. He was admitted to the bar in
1843, and engaged in active practice for nineteen years. His career at the bar
was one that gave him the unlimited confidence of his clients, and he acquired
a competence. His cool judgment, perfect integrity and high character as a
man, and thorough knowledge of the law, made him prominent. From 1848 to
1852 he was Judge of Probate of Kent County. In 1863 he was appointed by
President Lincoln, United States District Judge for the western district of
Michigan, a position he filled with signal ability until his death, which occurred
at San Diego, Cal., Apr. 25, 1886. He married Marian L. Hinsdill, in 1846, and
left five children—four sons and one daughter. In 1869 he was tendered the
position of United States Circuit Judge for the States of Ohio, Michigan, Tennessee and Kentucky, which he declined. He was director and president of the
First National Bank of Grand Rapids for many years. He was a Republican in
politics, and a consistent member of the Congregational Church. His courts
were models of propriety and decorum.

WILLIAM H. WITHINGTON

Representative from Jackson County, 1873-4; and Senator, 1891-2, from the
Sixth District, comprising the counties of Hillsdale and Jackson. Was born
in Dorchester, Mass., Feb. 1, 1835. He attended the schools of Boston and
finished his education in Phillips Academy at Andover, after which he entered
a leather store in Boston as salesman. In 1857 he had an offer from the surviving partner of Pinney & Lamson, agricultural implement manufacturers, who
had a contract for the prison labor at Jackson, Mich., to take charge of their
matters and endeavor to straighten them out. Mr. Pinney committed suicide
and about a year thereafter the business was sold and purchased by the new

firm of Sprague, Withington & Co., which business was conducted by the Withington & Cooley Manufacturing Company. At the breaking out of the late war he was Captain of the Jackson Grays, who tendered their services to Gov. Blair and became Co. B of the 1st Mich. Infantry. On Mar. 13, 1865, he was made Brevet Brigadier General. On his return to Jackson he turned his attention once more to business. He was a Colonel in the State Militia from 1873 to 1879 and Brigadier General from that time until his resignation in 1883. In politics he was a Republican. Deceased.

ISAAC WIXOM

Representative from Oakland County, 1838 and 1839; and Senator from the Sixth District, 1842-3. Was born in Hector, N. Y., Mar. 7, 1803. He received an academical and medical education in the State of New York. He practiced medicine four years in Steuben County, settled at Farmington, Mich., in 1829, bought a farm and improved it. His practice in medicine and surgery became very extensive. In 1845 he removed to Argentine, Genesee County, and engaged in a large milling and mercantile business in connection with his practice. He was so noted as a surgeon that he was called into other states to perform difficult surgical operations. In 1861 he became surgeon of the 16th Mich. Infantry, followed it through twenty-two battles, but at the end of two years resigned from ill health and returned to practice. In 1870 he removed to Fentonville. In politics he was a Democrat. He was made a Mason when young and took the highest degree known in the United States. In June, 1845, he performed the first successful amputation of the hip joint known in the United States, and afterwards performed sixteen successful operations of that kind. Deceased.

DANIEL WIXSON

Representative from Sanilac and Huron counties, 1859-60, and from Sanilac County, 1873-4. Was born in Jersey (now Orange) Steuben County, N. Y., Feb. 1, 1822. He received a common school education, and in 1851 settled in Lexington, Mich. He held various township offices. He was a farmer by occupation; in politics a Republican.

JOSHUA WIXSON

Representative from Sanilac County, 1883. Was born in Canada, of American parentage, Jan. 9, 1827. He removed to Sanilac County in 1841. His education was self-acquired. He taught school, held offices in Worth, Sanilac County, continuously for twenty-eight years, including that of Township Clerk, Justice of the Peace, School Inspector, and Supervisor, the latter from 1876 to 1882 inclusive. His principal occupation was that of a farmer. In politics he was a Republican.

WALTER S. WIXSON

Delegate to the Constitutional Convention of 1907-8 from the Twenty-first District, Tuscola County. Was born in Lexington in 1863, of Scotch and English descent. He received his education in the public schools, the University of Michigan and the Poughkeepsie Collegiate Institute and the Michigan University law department. After graduating from the law department of the University he went into the law office of the late John Divine, who was a member of the Constitutional Convention of 1867, and of the Constitutional Commission of 1873. He then entered the employ of the American Express Co., at Milwaukee, as superintendent's clerk, where he remained for three years when he was transferred to Chicago as secretary to the general agent. He filled various positions in the express business at Chicago, as assistant cashier, traveling solicitor and special agent of the money order, telegraph transfer and order and commission departments of the American's service and the superintendent of local business covering said departments at Chicago. He resigned in 1895, and practiced law at Caro, Mich., a member of the firm of Quinn, Wilson & Quinn. Married.

GROVE H. WOLCOTT

Representative from Jackson County, 1881-2. Was born in Alabama, N. Y., Nov. 8, 1826. He removed with his parents to Hamlin, Mich., in 1837. He received an academical education, studied law, was admitted to the bar in 1862, and went into practice at Jackson. He was private secretary to Gov. Blair in 1861, and was Circuit Court Commissioner two terms. Politically he was a Democrat.

L. J. WOLCOTT

Representative from the First District of Calhoun County, 1911-12 and 1913-14. Was born in Eaton County, May 14, 1849, and was educated in the public schools, supplemented by one year at Albion College. His father, Henry B. Wolcott, was one of the pioneers, having settled in Eaton County, near Onondaga, in 1846, where he farmed until 1851. He then located near Albion and improved a farm where he spent the remainder of his life. He was married in 1871 to Flora Comstock. In 1913 he was interested in manufacturing, having given this the most of his time, although he later engaged in farming. In 1889, while Mayor of Albion, he assisted in organizing the Homestead Building & Loan Association. In 1893 he assisted in the organization of the Commercial and Savings Bank of Albion. A member of the I. O .O. F. and the K. O. T. M. M. In politics a Democrat.

THEODORE MATHEW WOLTER

Representative from the First District of Wayne County (Detroit), 1895-6. Was born in Detroit, Jan. 12, 1855; was educated in the public schools of Detroit, and at the age of sixteen years began the moulder's trade in the Detroit Stove Works. For nine years he continued in this occupation, and then engaged in the grocery business. He was vice-president and secretary of the Moulders' Union of Detroit city for twelve years. He was elected Representative to the Legislature of 1895-6 on the general legislative ticket of the city of Detroit.

ALFRED B. WOOD

Senator from the Twenty-sixth District, 1869-70 and 1871-2. Was born in Norwalk, Conn., Apr. 18, 1819, where his ancestors settled in 1648. He removed with his mother to Lyons, N. Y., in 1833, and received an academical education. From 1845 to 1851 he was engaged in the book business at Auburn and Geneva, N. Y., and then was in the same business at Ann Arbor, Mich. He then became interested in the Ann Arbor paper mills, the first in Michigan, until 1862. In 1863 he engaged in the real estate and lumber business at East Saginaw. He was an Alderman, and was president pro tem of the Senate in 1871-2. Politically he was a Republican.

ARTHUR E. WOOD

Representative from the First District of Wayne County, 1923——. Was born in Detroit, Nov. 26, 1896, of American parents, and was educated in the Detroit schools, graduating from Western High School in 1914. In 1918 he left the employ of Dodge Brothers to enlist and served until 1919 in the 105th Aero Squadron of the U. S. air service. At present he is employed as cashier with the Central States Finance Corporation. He is a Republican and was elected to the legislature Nov. 7, 1922.

ARTHUR E. WOOD

Representative from Wayne County, 1917-18; and Senator from the Third District, which comprises the central portion of Detroit, 1919——. Was born at Kalamazoo, Mich., Aug. 12, 1870, of Irish and Scotch ancestors. He removed to Detroit in 1876 and at the age of ten began earning his own living. He learned the steam boiler and structural iron trades, but after his marriage in 1903, entered the millinery business. Four years later the business was incorporated under the firm name of A. E. Wood & Company, wholesale milliners, of which concern he is president and general manager. He is also president, for the sixth consecutive year, of the Central States Finance Corporation of Detroit; president of the Grimes Improved Light Company; director of the Commercial State Savings Bank and of the Commercial Bond & Mortgage Company. Mr. Wood is a Republican and is now president, for the eighth year, of the Detroit Republican Club, of which he was one of the organizers. He was a representative in the legislative sessions of 1917-18; was elected to the Senate in 1918 and 1920 and re-elected Nov. 7, 1922.

CHAS. M. WOOD

Senator from the Eighteenth District, 1875-6. Was born at West Brookfield, Mass., Sept. 29, 1826. He received a common school education, and removed to Michigan in 1835. He resided at Pinckney in 1887. In politics he was a Republican.

EDWIN K. WOOD

Representative from Montcalm County, 1883-4. Was born in Wyoming County, N. Y., in 1840. He served from 1861 to 1863 in 17th N. Y. Infantry. He settled in Michigan in 1865; was a merchant, farmer and lumberman, and resided at Stanton in 1887. He held various local offices. In politics he was a Republican.

EMORY J. WOOD

Representative from the First District of Jackson County, 1909-10 to 1915-16. Was born at Mendon, N. Y., Nov. 12, 1839, of English parentage. His education was acquired in the common schools. He passed his early life at West Bloomfield, Ontario County, N. Y., where he was married to Malissa A. Brown, May 11, 1863. In March, 1868, he removed to Jackson County, Mich., and settled on a farm in Tompkins Township. He was elected Justice of the Peace of that township for three consecutive terms. In 1886 he removed to the city of Jackson and served as Justice of the Peace for the terms beginning in 1896 and 1904. In the years 1894-5 he also served as Supervisor of the first ward. He was elected to the Legislature of 1909-10 and re-elected for the session of 1911-12 as a Republican. In 1912 he cast his lot with the National Progressive party, and was elected to the Legislature of 1913-14. In 1914 he returned to the Republican party and was re-elected to the Legislature. He died at Jackson Jan. 13, 1919.

HENRY L. WOOD

Representative from Gratiot County, 1887-8, 1889-90 and 1899-1900. Was born in Troy Township, Wood County, O., June 17, 1848. He was educated at the common schools, Maumee Seminary, and Hillsdale Commercial College, and lived in that State until 1876, when he removed to Monroe, Mich., where he remained eighteen months and then removed to Gratiot County, following the occupation of farming and brick making. At the age of sixteen years, Mr. Wood became a member of Co. G, 189th O. V. Infantry, and served until the close of the Civil War. Politically a Republican. He served his party in the capacity of Trustee of St. Louis Union School and Supervisor of Pine River Township.

JAMES C. WOOD

Representative from Jackson County, 1875-6 and 1877-8. Was born in Decatur, N. Y., in 1813. He removed to Michigan in 1843, and settled at White Pigeon. In 1844 he removed to Jackson, where he continued to reside. He was Treasurer of Jackson County, and Mayor of the city of Jackson. By profession he was a lawyer, and also engaged in farming. He died at Tompkins, Jackson County, in 1881.

JAMES C. WOOD

Senator, 1913-14, 1915-16 and 1917-18, from the Thirtieth Senatorial District, comprising the counties of Chippewa, Delta, Luce, Mackinac, Menominee and Schoolcraft. Was born at Hastings, Mich., Mar. 31, 1872, and received his education in the Jackson public schools and at Lake Forest University. After his school life at Jackson he spent four years as clerk in the store of J. B.

Branch & Company, at Coldwater, Mich., and in 1893 entered the law department of Lake Forest University, from which he graduated in 1895. He entered the practice of law in connection with law clerkship at Chicago, Ill., later associating with George W. Hayden, at Ishpeming, Mich., in practice of law, where he remained until Mr. Hayden's death in 1902. In November, 1902, he located at Manistique. He served as City Attorney of Manistique for seven terms and was also Prosecuting Attorney of Schoolcraft County. Married. In politics a Republican.

LUCIAN E. WOOD

Representative from Cass County, 1895-6. Was born in Kalamazoo County, Mich., Oct. 5, 1852. The following year he removed with his parents to Cass County, locating first in Silver Creek Township, and later removed to Howard Township. He remained at home until twenty-two years of age, attending district school and working on the farm; also taught school a few terms. In 1874 he was married, locating on a farm in Pokagon Township. In 1881 he entered the employ of the Michigan Central Railroad Company as chief tie inspector, in which service he continued until 1894, superintending his farm at the same time. In politics he was a Republican. He died at Niles June 5, 1916.

STEPHEN R. WOOD

Representative from Chippewa County, 1841. His postoffice address was Sault Ste. Marie. (Further data not obtainable).

THOMAS WOOD

Representative from Washtenaw County, 1845. Was born at Norwich, N. Y., May 21, 1805. He came to Michigan in 1826, and located a farm in Pittsfield, Washtenaw County, where he lived until his death, Sept. 21, 1865. His farm was a fine one, and he gave much attention to horticulture.

DAVID A. WOODARD

Representative from the Second District of Monroe County, 1869-70. Was born in Phelpstown, N. Y., in 1812. He came with his parents to Michigan in 1833, who settled upon a farm in Milan, where he resided, except the last few years of his life. In 1834 he built the first flouring mill and the first saw-mill in Milan. In 1834 he was elected Justice under the territorial laws and continued to act in that capacity for thirty years. He was Supervisor of Milan for years. In politics he was a Democrat. From 1850 until his death, June 13, 1884, he devoted most of his time to the practice of law.

WILLIAM WOODBRIDGE

Secretary and Acting Governor of the Territory of Michigan, 1814-28; Territorial Delegate in Congress, 1819-20; Justice of the Territorial Supreme Court,

1828-32; Delegate from the First District to the Constitutional Convention of 1835; Senator from the First District, 1838-9; Governor of Michigan, 1840-1; and United States Senator, 1841-7. Was born in Norwich, Conn., Aug. 20, 1780, and removed to Marietta, O., with his father's family in 1791. He studied law three years at Litchfield, Conn., and was admitted to the Ohio bar in 1806. The same year he married Juliana, daughter of John Trumbull, the distinguished lawyer, judge and poet, of Connecticut. He was a member of the Ohio Assembly in 1807, and a Senator from 1809 to 1814. In 1814 he was appointed Secretary of the Territory of Michigan, and was also Collector of Customs at Detroit, and in the absence of the Governor, Superintendent of Indian agencies. In 1819 the people of the Territory were allowed a delegate in Congress, and he was selected with the concurrence of all parties, as the right to a delegate had been secured by his exertions. As a delegate he secured government aid to build the roads from Detroit to Fort Gratiot, Chicago, and through the "black swamp" to the Miami River. He also secured the settlement of the old French claims, and the expedition, under Gov. Cass, to Lake Superior and the upper valley of the Mississippi River. He refused a second term to Congress, acted as secretary until 1824, was then appointed one of the commissioners to adjust private land claims, and also engaged in law practice. In 1828 he was appointed by President Adams, Judge of the Supreme Court, and served until 1832. In 1839 he received the nomination for Governor and was elected as the Whig candidate. He served as Governor from Jan. 7, 1840, to Feb. 23, 1841, when he resigned, having been elected United States Senator, by a combination of Whigs and Democrats, over the Whig caucus nominee, Lieutenant Governor Gordon. He served six years in that office, then retired to private life. He owned the Woodbridge farm in Detroit, which has become very valuable property. In religion he was a Congregationalist. He died Oct. 20, 1861.

JAMES H. WOODBURY

Representative from Lenawee County, 1842. His postoffice address was Adrian. (Further data not obtainable).

LEMUEL WOODHOUSE

Delegate from Ingham County to the Constitutional Convention of 1867. Was born in the State of New York in 1819; became a cabinet maker and millwright, and worked near Columbus, O. He removed to Undilla, Mich., in 1840, afterwards settled at Leslie. He was eight years Treasurer of Ingham County, was in the mercantile business at Dansville, resided several years in Lansing, was a clerk in the office of the Auditor General, then ran a store and saw-mill and owned a farm at White Oak. Politically he was a Republican. He died at White Oak, Feb. 22, 1885.

ELIAS S. WOODMAN

Delegate from Oakland County to the Constitutional Convention of 1850. Was born in Rodman, N. Y., Oct. 15, 1815. He came to Michigan with his father in

1837, who settled on a farm at Novi. His education was limited. He was a farmer at Novi until 1873, then removed to Northville, where he resided in 1887. He studied law late in life and was admitted to the bar in 1870. He held many local offices. In politics he was a Democrat.

JASON WOODMAN

Senator from the Eighth District, 1903-4 and 1905-6; and Member of the State Board of Agriculture, 1912-23. Was born in Paw Paw, Van Buren County, Mich., in 1860, of New England parentage. He was educated in the public schools and the Michigan Agricultural College, from which institution he graduated in 1881. He was lecturer of the Michigan State Grange for eight years, and served as chairman of the Van Buren Republican County Committee for several years; was also a member of the State Senate during the sessions of 1903 and 1905. Mr. Woodman is married. At the election held on Apr. 3, 1911, was elected a member of the State Board of Agriculture and re-elected Apr. 2, 1917.

JONATHAN J. WOODMAN

Representative from Van Buren County, 1861-2 to 1871-2. Was born in Sutton, Vt., May 24, 1825. He received a common school education. He became a resident of Paw Paw, Mich., in 1855. He commenced teaching at the age of twenty-one, which he continued winters for several years. From 1852 to 1854 was a worker in the California gold mines. By occupation he was a farmer; politically a Democrat until 1856, then a Republican. He was one of the State Board at the Philadelphia exposition in 1876. He was master of the State Grange from 1874 to 1878, and overseer of the National Grange from 1875 to 1879. He was one of four agricultural commissioners to the Paris exposition in 1878. He was an able Legislator and an excellent presiding officer. He died at Paw Paw May 16, 1884.

ALBERT N. WOODRUFF

Representative from Berrien County, 1885-6. Was born in Bainbridge, Mich., July 22, 1850. He received an academical and collegiate education, and for three years was a teacher, then a farmer. He served as Supervisor and held other town offices. Politically he was a Republican.

ARI E. WOODRUFF

Representative from Wayne County, 1893-4, 1895-6, 1907-8, 1909-10 and 1911-12. Was born at Wyandotte, Oct. 10, 1859, of Irish parentage. He was educated in the high schools of Wyandotte. He was a farmer until 1893; was admitted to the bar in 1894, since which time he engaged in the practice of law. He was married to Ida A. Ocobock of Wyandotte in 1877. From 1897 to 1900 he held the office of Circuit Court Commissioner and was elected the first

President of Ford village, serving four terms. He also held the office of Justice of the Peace twelve years and represented his district in the Legislatures of 1893-4 and 1895-6. In politics a Republican. He was elected to the Legislatures of 1907-8 and 1909-10, and on a recount Jan. 17, 1911, succeeded Francis X. Burke.

ARI HARRISON WOODRUFF

Representative from the Fourth District of Wayne County, 1915—. Was born at Wyandotte, Mich., Nov. 1, 1888, of Irish-Dutch parentage. He was educated in the Wyandotte public schools and graduated from the Detroit College of Law in June, 1911, and has been practicing law ever since. He is a member of Washington Lodge No. 213, K. of P.; Wyandotte Lodge No. 170, F. & A. M., and E. B. Ward Lodge No. 172, I. O. O. F. He is married. In politics he is a Republican.

EDWIN W. WOODRUFF

Representative from Isabella County, 1899-1900. Was born in Sandusky County, O., Feb. 6, 1858. He attended the common schools until twelve years of age, when he moved with his father to Wood County, O., where he attended school winters and worked on his father's farm summers for four years, when he was compelled to quit school (his father having become crippled) and take charge of the farm. He married Apr. 9, 1878, and moved with his wife and three children to Ottawa County, O., in March, 1881, where his wife and one child died the same fall. He married a second time Sept. 10, 1882, and with his wife and daughter and two sons moved in 1888 to Broomfield Township, Isabella County, Mich., and moved to the farm. A Republican politically. He held the offices of Justice of the Peace, School Inspector, and Highway Commissioner; chairman and secretary of the Isabella County Republican Committee, and was a candidate for Sheriff in 1896.

HENRY WOODRUFF

Representative of the Isabella District, 1881-2 and 1883-4; and Senator from the Twenty-fourth District, comprising the counties of Gratiot, Isabella, Clare, and Midland, 1885-6. Was born in the village of Seneca Falls, Seneca County, N. Y., Feb. 13, 1813, and received his education in the common schools. In his twentieth year he came to the then Territory of Michigan and settled at Flat Rock, in Wayne County. In the year of 1855 he moved to East Saginaw, where he resided until 1871, when he moved to Clare County. Mr. Woodruff was a Whig until the organization of the Republican party, and was a delegate to Jackson, from Wayne County, at the time of the organization of that party. In 1862 he raised Co. "B," 23d Regiment Mich. Vol. Infantry, and served as Captain two years and three months. He was elected Sheriff of Saginaw County, in 1860; in 1871 Judge of Probate of Clare County. He was elected Senator as a Republican.

HENRY H. WOODRUFF

Delegate to the Constitutional Convention of 1907-8 from the Twenty-eighth District, Roscommon County. Was born at Flat Rock, Wayne County, in 1841, of English descent. He lived at Flat Rock until 1857, when his parents moved to East Saginaw. He received his education in the common schools, prepared for the University of Michigan under Claudius B. Grant, attending the union school at Ann Arbor. He, however, left for the war and never entered the University. He enlisted as a private in Co. D, 16th Mich. Infantry; was made Fourth Sergeant before leaving Detroit and promoted to Second Lieutenant, to First Lieutenant and Captain. After the war he was engaged in the lumber business until 1872. In 1866 he married Miss Caroline Ellsefer, who died in Lapeer in the year 1871. In 1877 he married Alicia H. Moiles, who died in 1907, leaving two daughters. Mr. Woodruff studied law in a law office and was admitted to the bar in 1876 and followed the practice of law. He moved to Roscommon County in 1874. He died at Roscommon June, 1916.

NEWTON R. WOODRUFF

Representative from Berrien County, 1865-6. Was born in Broome County, N. Y,. Oct. 2, 1808. In 1836 he came with his family to Michigan, and in 1837 settled in Bainbridge, Berrien County, on a farm. From 1852 to 1855 he was in California. He was a member of the Methodist Church and a patron of husbandry. He died Dec. 24, 1880.

ROY ORCHARD WOODRUFF.

Member of Congress, 1913-15 and 1921—. Was born at Eaton Rapids, Mich., Mar. 14, 1876, of Scotch-English parentage. He received his education in the public school of Eaton Rapids and the Detroit College of Medicine, graduating from the dental department in 1902, and engaging in practice of the profession in Bay City. He enlisted in the Spanish-American War as a private in Co. G, 33d Mich. Vol. Infantry, and served through the Santiago campaign. In 1911 he was elected Mayor of Bay City and served for a term of two years. In 1912 he was elected to 63d Congress as a Progressive, and was defeated for re-election in 1914. During the World War he entered the 2nd O. T. C. at Ft. Sheridan, Ill., and was graduated 1st Lieutenant of Infantry, and was assigned to the 311th Ammunition Train. He was promoted to Captain just prior to sailing for France with the 86th Division, and was made Major of Infantry while on duty in France, where he served eleven months with the A. E. F. Demobilization at Camp Dix, N. J., in August, 1919. Mr. Woodruff returned to Europe and served six months investigating conditions in England, Belgium, France, Switzerland, Germany, Austria, Czecho, Starakis and Poland. He returned to the U. S. in March, 1920, and engaged with the Union Truck Sales Co. In politics he is a Republican.

AUGUSTUS B. WOODWARD

Justice of the Territorial Supreme Court, 1805-24. Was a native of Virginia. In early life he devoted himself to literary work, and wrote and published several works. He became a lawyer, and on the third of March, 1805, was appointed by President Jefferson United States Judge for the Territory of Michigan. He, together with the two other judges, Bates and Griffin, with the Governor of the Territory, or a majority of them, possessed the legislative power of the Territory, which they exercised until 1824, when the first Legislative Council held its session at Detroit. Judge Woodward was an able lawyer, but very eccentric, and the wheels of government, with himself and colleagues often in collision, did not always run without friction. He acted as Judge until 1824. After the surrender of Detroit, in 1812, he did much to ameliorate the condition of the citizens of Detroit, who had been placed under martial law by Proctor. In August, 1824, he was appointed United States Judge for the Territory of Florida, but died about 1826. He never married.

HIEL WOODWARD

Representative from Jackson County, 1865-6 and 1867-8; and Senator from the Tenth District, 1869-70. Was born in Bridgewater, Vt., Feb. 10, 1824. His grandfather, Nehemiah, was a Baptist clergyman, and in the Revolution was an attaché of the staff of General Washington. He came to Michigan with his father in 1836, and lived at Adrian until 1845. He learned the trade of a mechanic, which he followed several years. He purchased a farm in Columbia, Jackson County. In 1858 he was elected Supervisor, and held that office ten years. In 1870 he took the census of the south part of Jackson County. In 1872 he was appointed Postmaster of Brooklyn and held it many years.

LYSANDER WOODWARD

Representative from Oakland County, 1861-2; and member of the Constitutional Commission of 1873. Was born in Columbia, Conn., Nov. 19, 1817. He removed with his parents to Chili, N. Y., in 1825. In 1838 he came to Rochester, Mich., and five years afterwards settled on a farm in Avon, same county. He was several times Supervisor and Justice. From 1866 to 1870 he was County Treasurer, and several times president of the County Agricultural Society. He was for two years president of the Detroit & Bay City Railroad Company. In politics he was a Republican.

FRED LANGDON WOODWORTH

Representative from Huron County, 1909-10 and 1911-12; and Senator, 1913-14 and 1915-16, from the Twentieth District, comprising the counties of Huron and Sanilac. Was born at Caseville, Mich., Jan. 8, 1877, of Irish-English descent. He was married in March, 1902, to Miss Gertrude Lowe. His father, Thomas B. Woodworth, a Huron County lawyer, represented Huron County in the Legislature of 1877. Mr. Woodworth graduated from the agricultural course at the State Agricultural College with the class of 1898. His occupation was that of a farmer and stock raiser in Chandler Township, Huron County. In politics a Republican.

JOHN D. WOODWORTH

Representative from Ingham County, 1863-4 to 1867-8. Was born in Pembroke, N. Y., Feb. 28, 1826. He emigrated to Jackson in 1831, and was educated in the schools of that city. He studied medicine, and graduated from Rush Medical College, Chicago, in 1853. He came to Leslie in 1849, and represented the town for fifteen years on the Board of Supervisors. He was the first President of the village of Leslie, a member of the Board of Education for twenty-five years, and Director of the Leslie schools for fifteen years. He was a Republican in politics.

THOMAS B. WOODWORTH

Representative from Huron County, 1877-8. Was born Oct. 2, 1841, in Wayne County, N. Y. He received an academical education. He removed from Auburn, N. Y., to Huron County, Mich., in 1867. He was Supervisor of the township of Caseville, 1868-76, and was County Surveyor for two years. He founded the Caseville *Advertiser* in January, 1874, and continued its editor until 1876, when it was merged in the Huron County *News*. By profession he was a lawyer; in politics a Republican.

WALTER W. WOOLNOUGH

Representative from Calhoun County, 1859-60. Was born in Suffolk County, England, in July, 1822. He came to Rochester, N. Y., with his parents in 1833, where he learned the art of printing. In 1845 he came to Battle Creek, Mich., bought the first printing material and published the *Western Citizen*, the first newspaper. In August, 1846, he began to publish the *Michigan Tribune*, which after two years was merged in the *Liberty Press*. From 1851 to 1863 he was editor and publisher of the Battle Creek *Journal*. From that date until 1871 he was not engaged in newspaper work, then edited and published the *Michigan Tribune* until 1877, when he sold out. He was a Trustee of the village of Battle Creek; an Alderman four years; nine years a member of the Board of Education, and President, and a Justice. In politics he was a Whig until 1854, a Republican until 1872, then a Democrat. He was connected with the Battle Creek *Daily Moon* in 1887.

ANANIAS WORDEN

Representative from Ionia County, 1848. His postoffice address was Montcalm. (Further data not obtainable).

ROBERT WORDEN, JR.

Representative from Hillsdale County, 1853. Was long a resident of Hillsdale County, and was County Treasurer from 1848 to 1852. He was a farmer and a Democrat. He resided near Owosso in 1887.

JABEZ B. WORTLEY

Representative from the Second District of Washtenaw County, 1895-6. Was born in Methwold, England, Apr. 20, 1847. He came to the United States when five years of age, locating at Ypsilanti, Mich., where he attended the city schools. He engaged in the clothing business at Ypsilanti as a member of the firm of C. S. Wortley & Co. In politics he was a Republican. He died at Detroit Hospital July 13, 1919.

CHAS. R. WRIGHT

Representative from Manitou County, 1861-2. His postoffice address was St. James. (Further data not obtainable).

DAVID A. WRIGHT

Representative from Oakland County, 1849; and Senator from the Fifth District, 1853-4. Was born in Granville, N. Y., June 6, 1813. In 1824 his father removed to Oneida County, and in 1843 came with his family to Michigan, and the son settled in Springfield, Oakland County. He was appointed Postmaster at Austin, and held the office twenty-five years. He was for some years Coroner of Oakland County, and was a prominent Mason. In politics he was a Democrat. He died Jan. 19, 1877.

GEORGE S. WRIGHT

Representative from the Second District of Washtenaw County, 1915-16. Was born in Essex Township, Clinton County, Mich., Mar. 17, 1875, of English parents. He was educated in the Maple Rapids High School, Ferris Institute, and graduated in 1905 from the law department of the University of Michigan. He then located in Milan where he practiced. Married. In politics a Republican.

HAMILTON M. WRIGHT

Representative from Bay County, 1883-4 and 1885-6. Was born in New Orleans, La., Oct. 26, 1852; graduated from Yale College in 1875, and from its law department in 1877. He removed to Bay City in 1878 and went into practice. He was Alderman. Politically he was a Democrat.

HENRY D. WRIGHT

Representative from Isabella County, 1901-2 and 1903-4. Was born in Grand Rapids, Mich., Oct. 15, 1857, and obtained his education in the common schools of that city. In 1882 he settled in Broomfield Township, Isabella County, and engaged in farming and lumbering. Married. He held the offices of Highway Commissioner, Township Clerk, Supervisor and Treasurer. In politics he was a strong Republican. He died Jan. 15, 1922.

HORATIO WRIGHT

Representative from Oakland County, 1867-8. Was born in Granville, N. Y., Feb. 20, 1818. In 1824 he removed, with his parents, to Oneida County, N. Y., and in 1839 located in Genesee County, N. Y. He settled at Springfield, Oakland County, in 1843, and in 1847 in Groveland, same county. By occupation he was a farmer; in politics a Democrat. He married Sarah M. Campbell in 1842. He held the office of Supervisor eight years, and was a Justice from 1852 to 1876. He was a prominent Mason.

LUTHER L. WRIGHT

Member of the State Board of Education, 1901-7; Superintendent of Public Instruction, 1907-9 to 1913. Was born at Canton, N. Y., Jan. 18, 1856, of Scotch-Irish descent. He was educated in the common schools of Wisconsin, and Ripon College, from which he was graduated with the degree of A.B. He was chosen County Commissioner of Schools of Gogebic County five successive terms without opposition; was Superintendent of the public schools of Ironwood twenty years. Mr. Wright was united in marriage to Miss Nellie Corning of Portage, Wis., in 1880. He was appointed a member of the State Board of Education in 1901 to fill the vacancy caused by the resignation of Lincoln Avery. At the Republican State Convention, held at Detroit, June, 1902, he was unanimously chosen as nominee to succeed himself and was elected that year. He was again nominated to that office by the Republican State Convention at Detroit, June, 1904, and elected for the term ending Dec. 31, 1910. At the next Republican State Convention held at Detroit in July, 1906, he was unanimously chosen candidate for Superintendent of Public Instruction and was elected Nov. 6, 1906, for the term of two years. June 18, 1908, he received the degree of Master of Arts from the University of Michigan. At the convention held at Detroit, Sept. 29, 1908, he was nominated by acclamation to succeeed himself and elected Nov. 3, 1908. The new constitution provided for another election in 1909, and at the election held on Apr. 5, 1909, he was elected for the term ending June 30, 1911. At the election held on Apr. 3, 1911, he was re-elected. At the Republican State Convention held at Lansing, Feb. 11, 1913, he was renominated and was elected Apr. 7, 1913. He resigned Nov. 15, 1913, and died at Flint Jan. 10, 1922.

ROGER I. WYKES

Delegate to the Constitutional Convention of 1907-8; and Attorney General, 1912. Was born in Grand Rapids, Mich., Sept. 6, 1875, of English parentage. After a high school and legal education in Grand Rapids schools and the University of Michigan, he was admitted to practice law in January, 1896; from then to 1904 he served as Assistant Attorney General of the State; from 1904 to 1906 he was assistant general counsel of the Grand Rapids & Indiana Railway Company; in 1907-8 a member of the Constitutional Convention and chairman of its committee on Finance and Taxation; in 1910 to 1911 a member of the Grand Rapids Charter Commission; in 1912 was a member and president of the Special Committee of Inquiry into Taxation methods in the State of Michigan provided for by the Legislature of 1912. He was appointed by the Governor as representative of the State at the International Tax Conference at Richmond, Va., in 1911, and Des Moines, Ia., in 1912. In 1912 he was appointed Attorney General of Michigan and for six months filled the unexpired term of Franz C. Kuhn; in 1915 to 1917 was general counsel for the Association of Michigan Railways; in 1918 was appointed and served ten months as Major Judge Advocate in the United States Army; is the author of "Wykes' Michigan Mechanics Liens," published in 1918; in 1911 to 1912 represented Governor Osborn as special counsel in various removals from office proceedings; from 1905 to 1920 retained by the State by each Attorney General as special counsel in railway, telegraph, telephone and express rate, tax and charter cases. At present he is engaged in the practice of law in the city of Grand Rapids, Mich.

HERMAN A. WYCKOFF

Representative from Oakland County, 1881-2. Was born in Romulus, N. Y., June 17, 1838. He came to Oakland County in 1845, with his parents, who settled near Pontiac. He received a common school education, and was a farmer and breeder of fine stock. Politically he was a Republican.

GEORGE C. WYLLIS

Representative from Hillsdale County, 1883-4. Was born at Potsdam, N. Y., Aug. 1, 1825. He settled with his father at Pulaski, Mich., in 1838. He was educated in common schools, with a few months at Michigan Central College, at Spring Arbor. He taught school winters until 1852; then settled on his farm in Moscow. He later taught eight terms, was a Justice eighteen years, and School Inspector nine years. In politics he was a Republican.

HENRY WYMAN

Representative from Lenawee County, 1845. Was born in Jefferson County, N. Y., in 1803. By profession he was a physician; in politics a Democrat. He resided at Blissfield in 1887.

EDWARD LEWIS YAPLE

Representative from the First District of Kalamazoo County, 1909-10 and 1911-12. Was born at Mendon, St. Joseph County, Mich., Feb. 7, 1874, of American parents. He received his education in the Mendon Union schools, Kalamazoo College, University of Chicago, and the Northwestern University law school, graduating from the latter in 1899. Married. In 1901 he located at Kalamazoo where he associated himself in the law business with Claude S. Carney. In politics a Republican.

GEORGE L. YAPLE

Member of Congress, 1883-5. Was born in Leonidas, Mich., Feb. 20, 1851. In 1857 he removed with his parents to Mendon, same county. He graduated in the classical course at the Northwestern University at Evanston, Ill., in 1871. He studied law and was admitted to the bar in 1872, but immediately engaged in farming, and continued in that pursuit until the spring of 1877, when he entered upon the practice of law. He was defeated as Greenback candidate for Congress in 1880. In 1882 he was elected Representative to the forty-eighth Congress on the Union ticket. In 1886 he was nominated for Governor, but was defeated by the Republican candidate. He was a fine orator on the stump, and his speech in Congress in favor of free trade was circulated throughout the country.

CHARLES YARRINGTON

Representative from Jackson County, 1881-2. Was born Apr. 28, 1839, in Napoleon, Mich. He was given the advantages of the common schools of the times. He alternated between farming and school teaching, and attended four terms at the State Normal School. When twenty-one years of age he removed to the Pacific coast, and finally located in the mining regions of Idaho. There he remained until 1866, when he returned to Norvell, with sufficient means to enter the mercantile business. He served three terms as Township Clerk; was appointed Census Enumerator for 1880, and held the office of Postmaster. In politics he was a Republican.

SAMUEL W. YAWKEY

Representative from Saginaw County, 1865-6 and 1869-70. Was born at Massillon, O., Apr. 22, 1830. He removed to East Saginaw, Mich., in 1852. He there followed the occupation of a lumber dealer. In politics he was a Republican. He was Mayor of East Saginaw in 1867 and 1869. He did not sit in extra session of the Legislature in 1870. He died at Elko, Nevada, Mar. 12, 1882.

GEORGE G. B. YECKLEY

Representative from Van Buren County, 1875. Was born in Gorham, N. Y., Feb. 13, 1831. He received a common school education and came to Ypsilanti in 1853. In 1860 he removed to Hamilton, Van Buren County. He held the office of Supervisor for seven years, also that of Justice. By occupation he was a farmer, in politics a Republican. He died Mar. 18, 1875, and was succeeded by William Thomas.

WILLIAM T. YEO

Representative, 1909-10 and 1911-12, from the Iosco District, comprising the counties of Alcona, Arenac, Iosco and Ogemaw. Was born at St. Thomas, Ontario, Canada, July 4, 1869, of English descent. He obtained his education at the Collegiate Institute, St. Thomas. He came to West Branch, Mich., in July,

1889, and was admitted to the bar October, 1893, and removed to Flint in September, 1903, where he practiced law until November, 1907, returning to West Branch. Married. In politics a Republican. He held the offices of Circuit Court Commissioner three terms, and Prosecuting Attorney one term, of Ogemaw County.

SANFORD A. YEOMANS

Delegate from Ionia County to the Constitutional Convention of 1867; and Representative from Ionia County, 1877-8 and 1879-80. Was born in German Flats, N. Y., Nov. 16, 1816. He received a common school education. In 1833 he removed to Easton, Ionia County, and held various township and county offices. He was a farmer and dealer in real estate, also a stockholder and director of the First National Bank of Ionia. In politics he was a Republican. He died at Ionia, Dec. 19, 1895.

WALTER YEOMANS

Senator, 1905-6 and 1907-8, from the Eighteenth District, comprising the counties of Ionia and Montcalm. Was born in the township of Easton, Ionia County, Mich., Feb. 13, 1848. His grandfather, Erastus Yeomans and family, were among the first settlers, locating at Ionia in May, 1833. His education was acquired in the district and high schools of Ionia County. His early years were spent on the home farm of his father, Sanford A. Yeomans, who was a member of the Constitutional Convention of 1867, and a representative in the Legislature of 1877-9. At the age of twenty-one he was married and took up the occupation of farming for himself and continued it for twenty-four years. Then he engaged in the real estate business, and served as vice-president and director of the old First National Bank of Ionia. In politics a Republican. He held various township offices, including Supervisor and chairman of the Board of Supervisors.

GEORGE YERKES

Representative from Oakland County, 1879-80. Was born in Novi, Mich., Apr. 19, 1838. He was educated in the common schools. His occupation was farming. He held the office of Justice two terms; also that of Supervisor two terms. In politics he was a Republican.

SILAS ALLEN YERKES

Member of the State Board of Agriculture, 1861. Was the son of Anthony Yerkes, born near Philadelphia, Pa., and Esther (Allen) Y., born in the State of New York. Silas was born near Manchester, Mich., Oct. 14, 1834; never married; was educated in the district school and at Hillsdale College; a Methodist and Republican. He taught school when seventeen years old with good success; served his township two or three years as Superivsor. He was named a member of the State Board of Agriculture for Lowell, Kent County, in the original act in 1861, qualified and met two or three times with the Board, but in October resigned to enter the army. He entered as Second Lieutenant of the 13th Infantry and became Captain, Feb. 26, 1863; was wounded at Chickamauga, Sept. 19, 1863; breveted Major for meritorious conduct and discharged when no longer able to serve as a soldier, May 15, 1865. He was a farmer, residing at Vergennes, Kent County, Mich. He died at home Oct. 26, 1865.

WILLIAM YERKES

Representative from Oakland County, 1837 and 1857-8. Was born in Pennsylvania, Sept. 29, 1794, and came to Michigan in 1826, settling in what is now the town of Novi, but which then embraced several other surrounding townships under the name of Farmington. He went on foot from Ovid, N. Y., to Farmington and took up land Mar., 1826, and returned in same manner, his family following later. He usually went from Novi to Detroit on foot while in the Legislature and carried his lunch of corn bread and venison. He was appointed Judge of Probate by Gen. Cass. He was a farmer by occupation, Whig and Republican in politics, and served at various times as Supervisor and Justice. He died Jan. 5, 1884.

JOHN K. YOCUM

Representative from Washtenaw County, 1851-2. Was born in Montgomery County, Pa., Mar. 27, 1819. He came with his parents to Lyndon, Mich., in 1836. For many years he worked summers and taught school winters. In 1846 he married Marie A. Johnson, and settled on a farm. He was appointed U. S. Assessor in 1863, he held the position five years, and held other offices. In politics he was a Whig and Republican. For thirty-eight years he was County or Deputy Surveyor.

CHESTER YOST

Senator from the Eighth District, 1859-60. Was born in Fayette, N. Y. He was a farmer by occupation, and a Justice in his native town. He emigrated to Michigan and settled on a farm in Washtenaw County. He then removed to Ypsilanti and became a partner of Benjamin Follett in the mercantile business. He was a Whig, then a Republican, last a Democrat. He was elected to the Senate in 1859 as a Republican, and was Justice for a number of years. He died May 24, 1874.

HENRY MELVILLE YOUMANS

Member of Congress, 1891-3; and Senator from the Twenty-second District, 1897-8. Was born in Otsego, Otsego County, N. Y., May 15, 1832. He worked on his father's farm until twenty-one years of age. He did not have early educational advantages, except what could be obtained in the common schools of the State of New York and then only attending school during the winter months, and working on the farm during the summer. He removed to East Saginaw, Mich., in 1862, and resided there up to the present time. He was superintend-

ent of the lumbering establishment of Bundy & Youmans for twelve years; then
engaged in the lumbering business with J. F. Bundy, the firm's name being
Bunday & Youmans. He was twice elected Alderman, School Inspector, president of the Board of Education and Mayor for two terms. In politics he was a
Jacksonian Democrat. He died at Saginaw July 8, 1920.

ALEXANDER VINCENT YOUNG

Representative from Mecosta County, 1911-12 and 1913-14. Was born on a
farm near Coldwater, Branch County, Mich., July 3, 1863, of Scotch and Irish
parents, and received his education in the Coldwater, Mich., and Lehigh, Ia.,
schools. At the age of fourteen, he went to Iowa where he remained five years,
returning to Big Rapids in 1882. He was married in 1889. Mrs. Young died
Dec. 23, 1905. In the shoe business for many years. Also dealer in real estate,
besides owning and operating two large farms near Big Rapids. He was for
three years owner of the Mecosta County flouring mills, but sold out in 1909.
He was a member of the Board of Education two years, Alderman four years
and Mayor of Big Rapids one year. In politics a Republican.

AMBROSE P. YOUNG

Representative from Wayne County, 1848 and 1881-2. Was born in Phelpstown,
N. Y., May 23, 1814. He followed farming until seventeen, then learned the
trade of carriage making. He settled in Romulus, Mich., in 1836, and for several years carried on blacksmithing and carriage making. He then became a
farmer. He held the offices of Town Clerk, School Inspector, Supervisor, Colonel
of militia, Associate County Judge, and vice-president of Monroe and Wayne
Mutual Fire Insurance Company. He was also a Justice for thirty-five years. In
politics he was a Democrat. He claims to have given the vote that changed the
name of the capital from Michigan to Lansing.

CARL YOUNG

Representative from Muskegon County, 1919-20. Was born in Augusta, Ill.,
Aug. 11, 1859, and was educated in the public schools of Illinois. He worked
on a farm during vacations until he was old enough to learn a trade, after which
time he followed that of carpenter. He is a member of the Carpenters' union,
and in 1906 was appointed general organizer, acting in that capacity until Jan.
1, 1916. The next year he was elected president of the State Federation of
Labor. Mr. Young has been married twice. He has held the offices of Village
Clerk, Police Justice and Justice of the Peace. In politics he is a Republican.

FRANK LANDON YOUNG

Senator from the Fourteenth District, comprising the counties of Ingham and
Shiawassee, 1923—. Was born in Esperance, N. Y., July 24, 1871, of English,

Scotch and Irish ancestry. Left an orphan at the age of twelve, he secured his schooling by working for farmers, and graduated from the high school of Coble-skill, N. Y. He removed to Michigan in 1895, locating in Lansing where he engaged in the hay and grain business, in partnership with his brother. He is at present connected with the same line of business and also with the real estate business. Mr. Young is a Republican and served two terms on the City Council and also as member and president of the Board of Police Commissioners. He is president of the Michigan Hay Association and also of the national associa-tion; president of the Boy Scout council of Lansing, and chairman of the advisory board for the order of De Molay. He was elected to the senate Nov. 7, 1922.

FRED W. YOUNG

Representative from the First District of Bay County, 1909-10. Was born at Lindsay, Ont., June 25, 1876. He acquired his education in the Toronto public schools. He was left an orphan at the age of eleven, both parents dying sud-denly, and he was thrown upon his own resources. In 1891 he removed to Bay County, Mich., and apprenticed himself in a machine shop which work he con-tinued until 1906, when he became a business representative of the International Association of Machinists. He was president of the Central Trades and Labor Council in 1906. In politics a Republican.

H. OLIN YOUNG

Representative from Marquette County, 1879-80; and member of Congress, 1903-5 to 1911-13. Was born Aug. 4, 1850, at New Albion, N. Y., of English, Scotch and Welsh descent, and received his education in the Chamberlain Insti-tute, Randolph, N. Y. By profession a lawyer. In politics he was a Republican. He held the office of Prosecuting Attorney of Marquette County from 1886 to 1896, and represented his district in the State Legislature of 1879. He was elected Representative to the 58th, 59th, 60th, and 61st Congresses and was re-elected Nov. 8, 1910. He died Aug. 4, 1917.

S. PERRY YOUNG

Representative from Montcalm County, 1883-4. Was born in Summit, Mich., Sept. 2, 1850. He received a common and high school education. He attended the law school of the University one year. He was Clerk of Montcalm County from 1875 to 1879, and extensively engaged in farming, lumbering, mercantile pursuits, and speculation. Politically a Republican.

GEORGE YOUNGLOVE

Representative from Monroe County, 1843. Was born in Berkshire County, Mass., Nov. 14, 1794. He was a blacksmith up to 1835, after that a farmer. He came to Monroe County in 1831. In politics he was a Democrat. He died Sept. 6, 1876.

HENRY JOSEPH ZACHARIAS

Representative from the First District of Saginaw County, 1907-8. Was born at Saginaw, Mich., Mar. 15, 1880. His father and mother came from Poland in 1874 and settled in Saginaw County. He attended the public and Polish schools of Saginaw and completed a course in the business college. He followed the occupation of machinist until twenty years of age, after which time he engaged in the mercantile business, being a member of the firm of Zacharias Brothers. An expert interpreter of the Polish language, and general agent for the North German Lloyd and American Steamship lines. In politics a Democrat.

ALEXANDER ZAGELMEYER

Representative from the Second District of Bay County, 1889-90. Was born at Saginaw City, Oct. 28, 1858. In politics a Republican.

ELISHA ZIMMERMAN

Representative from Oakland County, 1873-4. Was born in St. Johnsville, N. Y., Dec. 26, 1828. He received a common school education. In 1851 he removed to Michigan, and settled in Grand Blanc, Genesee County. In 1865 he removed to Pontiac. By occupation he was a merchant.

HENRY MARTIN ZIMMERMAN

Representative from the Second District of St. Clair County, 1897-8. Was born of German parents in Marine City, St. Clair County, Mich., July 7, 1867. His education was acquired in the city schools, after which he pursued a course of study in the Detroit Business University, returning in the winter of 1886-7 and entering the hardware store of his brother as bookkeeper, shortly afterwards he was instrumental in organizing and establishing the hardware firm of Zimmerman Bros., at Marine City. In 1887 he was elected City Clerk of Marine City and served two terms. Three years later he accepted a position as bookkeeper in the Marine Savings Bank, of Marine City, becoming assistant cashier. After about three years connection with that institution he resigned his position with the bank and took up the study of law, attending the law department of the University of Michigan, from which he graduated in June, 1895; then entering Yale University; pursued a graduate course of study in law, graduating in June, 1896; then returned to Marine City, and entering into partnership with one of the leading lawyers of the city began the practice of his profession. In politics a Republican. He was Clerk of Marine City two terms.

JOHN ZIMMERMAN

Representative from the First District of Wayne County, 1893-4. Was born May 22, 1850, in Boston, Mass. He came with his parents to Detroit, Mich., in 1859. He early learned the trade of cigarmaker, which occupation he pursued. In politics a Republican.